Domestic Violence at the Margins

DOMESTIC VIOLENCE AT THE MARGINS

Readings on Race, Class, Gender, and Culture

Edited by

NATALIE J. SOKOLOFF

with CHRISTINA PRATT

Foreword by Beth E. Richie

Rutgers University Press
New Brunswick, New Jersey, and London

Second paperback printing, 2006

Manufactured in the United States of America

Library of Congress Cataloging-in-Publication Data

Domestic violence at the margins : readings on race, class, gender, and culture /
edited by Natalie J. Sokoloff ; with Christina Pratt ;
foreword by Beth E. Richie.
      p. cm. Includes bibliographical references.
   ISBN 0-8135-3569-7 (hardcover : alk. paper) — ISBN 0-8135-3570-0 (pbk. :
alk. paper)
   1. Abused women—United States. 2. Wife abuse—United States.
3. Marginality, Social—United States. I. Sokoloff, Natalie J. II. Pratt,
Christina, 1951–
   HV6626.2.D663 2005   362.82′92′0973—dc22   2004018894

A British Cataloging-in-Publication record for this book is available from the
British Library.

For all the brave women at the margins,
their families, communities,
and supporters
who struggle for peace and social justice
and the right to live violence-free lives.
and
For Fred and Josh

Contents

PART II. CULTURE, RESISTANCE, AND COMMUNITY

PART III. STRUCTURAL CONTEXTS, CULTURALLY COMPETENT APPROACHES, COMMUNITY ORGANIZING, AND SOCIAL CHANGE

Acknowledgments

This book is a product of both individual and collective efforts of so many wonderful people. The initial impetus was a call for proposals by Basil Wilson, the provost of John Jay College of Criminal Justice, whose goal has been to provide an outstanding research and resource center on domestic violence at the college. Many of our students at John Jay College and the populations they serve at work are from marginalized communities—people of color, poor, immigrants, or those stigmatized because they are homeless, unemployed, previously incarcerated, and the like. If I were to teach in the area of domestic violence, then it had to represent those constituencies. Out of this concern, and to support both the struggles and the strengths of marginalized battered women and their supporters, this book was created. I hope it serves as a valuable resource in the struggle against violence against women at the margins of our society.

For several years, Provost Wilson supported this project with one course of release time for me each semester and salary for a graduate research assistant. When needed, Jacob Marini, the director of Sponsored Programs at John Jay College, found small amounts of money to support a graduate research assistant one time and another time an undergraduate library assistant. Basil and Jacob made it possible for this project to proceed on schedule. Their support, encouragement, and friendship have been unwavering. For that I am forever grateful.

Another important source of support for the graduate assistant was provided one year by the Forensic Psychology Research Institute at John Jay College and its director, Maureen O'Connor. In addition, Jim Levine, dean of the Graduate Program, has always given me his encouragement and advice. I also want to thank John Jay College President Gerald Lynch, who recently retired. He created an environment that always nurtured activist scholarship; and he had the wisdom to appoint these administrators who have provided a richness and breadth of creativity and support to the faculty and students at John Jay College, where I have worked since 1972.

At the beginning of the project, Ida Dupont, then a doctoral student in the Criminal Justice Program at the City University of New York, helped to formulate the ideas and framework of the book. She did a lot of the "leg-work" by helping to conceptualize the themes and direction of the book, scouring journals for appropriate articles, conferring with me about the importance of each article we read, and helping to write several articles, including chapter 1. I am most appreciative to Ida for all the work she did and only wish she could have remained on the project until its completion.

Christina Pratt, another doctoral student in the Criminal Justice Program at the time and an assistant professor of social work and gender studies at Dominican College of Blauvelt, was magnanimous in her support and immediately volunteered to come on board after Ida left to work on her dissertation (Ida is now assistant professor at Pace University). It was Christina's boundless energy, insightful reading of the literature, and ability to powerfully express herself in her writing that has made it a pleasure to work with her over the course of the last several years of this project. Christina never wavered in doing absolutely everything she could for this project. The book is truly a much better product because of Christina's thoughtful and powerful contributions, including her work on the introductions to both parts 1 and 3. My deepest thanks to a true domestic violence scholar and activist.

Along the way, there have been other people so important to this project. Beth E. Richie, who graciously wrote the foreword to the book, was a source of support and encouragement from the beginning. She provided me with many contacts and opened new pathways for me to explore in the early stages of work for this book. Madelaine Adelman provided insightful comments in her review of the manuscript and helped greatly in improving the introductory comments to the different chapters in the book; as a scholar in Jewish domestic violence, she also wrote the introductory statement to chapter 14 by Beverly Horsburgh. In addition to Maddie, I want to thank the people who reviewed the manuscript: in particular Andrea Smith, who ended up writing the final chapter of the book, as well as several anonymous reviewers at different publishing houses when the manuscript was in the process of being considered elsewhere. The comments of all these scholars were essential in my continually exploring new ways of thinking about some of the issues facing battered women from marginalized communities and making this a more solid contribution to the literature.

At one point in the project, Jacqueline Campbell graciously put me in touch with Kathryn Laughon, a doctoral student in nursing at Johns Hopkins University and codirector of the nursing clinic at the House of Ruth, a shelter for battered women in Baltimore. With Kathryn's exceptional help, the introduction to the second part of the book was written. Kathryn is now an assistant professor at the University of Virginia.

I also want to thank those scholar/activists who wrote original chapters for this book: Carolyn M. West; Michelle Fine, Rosemarie A. Roberts, and Lois Weis; Rhea V. Almeida and Judith Lockard; Brenda V. Smith; and Andrea Smith. In addition, my thanks to Incite!–Critical Resistance for allowing me to publish their joint statement here for the first time. There were many fine scholars whose work I could not include in this book because of length considerations. To them, my thanks for their writing and commitment and my apologies for not being able to include them in the anthology.

During the time that I was working on this book, I was simultaneously working on the third edition of *The Criminal Justice System and Women: Offenders, Prisoners, Victims, and Workers* (McGraw-Hill), which came out in the summer of 2003. My coeditor, colleague, and friend for the past twenty-five years, Barbara Raffel Price, took over almost all the administrative work for the third edition so I could work on this domestic violence book. She also came to my rescue when I needed someone to help organize the biographies for this book and did the final edit to the introductions for each part and the individual chapters of this book. My deepest appreciation to her for all her support over the years.

This work has led me to meet some of the most dedicated and courageous women (and some men) working in the field and fighting against violence against women. These women and men care with a passion about the women who have experienced so much violence in their lives. But they are also clear that the struggle to end violence against women must include active work to end violence against the men, women, and children in marginalized communities as well. Nothing less will suffice.

Ilene Kalish, now at New York University Press and who worked with me on the book for a year as its editor at another publishing house, was wise in her counsel at all times. I thank her for her good judgment and excellent skills as an editor. As well, Ilene's assistant, Salwa Jabado, was very helpful at various stages of the publishing process. I am grateful to Kristi Long, my editor at Rutgers University Press, for her continual and unswerving faith in this book. Having someone believe in your work is validation of the work itself; having someone remain loyal to the project over an extended period of time without yet being the editor, is remarkable and most gratifying, and that is precisely what Kristi did. She believed in this project from its inception. I am most appreciative to her for all her support.

The production team shepherding through a manuscript is very important, and I have been lucky to work with a superb team. My deepest appreciation to the Rutgers University Press staff: Adi Hovav, associate editor to Kristi Long, and Alison Hack, editorial coordinator through the many steps in the production process and prepress journey. A special thanks to Lisa Nowak Jerry, who smoothed out many a rough spot in the manuscript and helped it to read more smoothly.

And how many authors are so fortunate as to have beautiful and meaningful artwork on their covers. A special note of appreciation must go to the Douglas County Women's Crisis Center in Castle Rock, Colorado, and the ten women whose expression of grief, anger, and hope created the collage that is now the cover for the book.

Finally, I want to thank my partner and colleague for more than thirty years, Fred Pincus. He had to put up with me working on two books simultaneously—for a second time! His wise counsel during the many twists and turns of this project has been much needed and greatly appreciated. I thank him as always. And to my son, Josh, who turned twenty-one the week I originally turned in this manuscript, thank you for always reminding me why this work must be done—so that all young people have a chance to grow without violence, poverty, and oppression in their lives.

Foreword

BETH E. RICHIE

In the last thirty years, the social change movement organized to respond to the problem of violence against women has made a significant impact on the legislative and moral psyche of the United States. In a relatively short time, numerous victories can be claimed. A wide variety of programs have been created to respond to women who experience domestic violence: sexual assault survivors have access to a range of supportive services; a national hotline has been established to respond to women in crisis; and agencies around the country are held up as model programs that claim an impressive degree of success in securing women's safety.

The creation of intervention programs has been matched with a tremendous increase in public policy attention to the issues of violence against women. Laws designed to protect women have been created; federal and local legislation has been passed to provide resources for programs; and some high-profile national leaders have assumed an outspoken position against violence against women.

Academic and research institutions have been central in creating change by advancing new knowledge in the field. At annual academic and professional conferences on violence against women each year researchers present new data; many programs around the country engage in evaluation research to determine their impact and effectiveness; and scholarly journals that focus on violence against women provide a forum for advancing theoretical and empirical work in the field. Each year new training videos, new web sites, and new books appear.

What was once a problem hidden deeply within the private sphere is now understood to be a common social problem worthy of social, intellectual, clinical, and political attention. These gains are owing, in no small part, to the organizing of feminist activists that began in the 1970s. Linking violence against women to previous struggles for women's liberation—from slave women's resistance to the suffragette movement to the women's health movement and the sexual liberation movement—the contemporary grassroots efforts to end violence against women has made tremendous progress in influencing mainstream understanding of violence against women in a relatively short period of time. It is safe to say that many women—hundreds of thousands perhaps—are safer today than they were thirty-five years ago because of the work of the anti-violence movement.

Still, questions remain. Even though some women may be safer today, how much progress has been made to curb the epidemic of gender-based violence in those communities that are marginalized in this country? Is the experience of battering different, for example, for women who live in impoverished neighborhoods? Does rape have a different impact on a woman who is incarcerated? When a woman who is an immigrant is sexually harassed, what kind of intervention does she need?

Despite the progress in bringing mainstream attention to the issue of violence against women, we might ask how much of the work has focused on providing individual social services at the expense of addressing the structures that leave women vulnerable to abuse.

For instance, is partner abuse different for lesbians when those relationships are not even recognized by the state? How does federalism leave Native women vulnerable to abuse on reservations in this country? What is the relationship between U.S.-sponsored war in developing countries and violence against women abroad as well as in the United States?

How is state violence linked to violence in the private sphere for women in communities that experience concentrated disadvantages? What do women do if anti-violence laws are used against them or if they do not have access to legal protection because of their criminal record or their immigration status or their poverty? Dare we ask what is worse and more deserving of our attention: gang rape, rape by a police officer, the threat of rape by a foster-parent, forced sex for economic survival, having your child accused of rape because of racist stereotypes that continue to prevail in our legal system, or legitimized sexual exploitation of women because of their age, their ethnicity, their sexual identity, or their background?

Of course, there are no clear answers to these questions. And yet, by not even raising complex issues, we seriously threaten the authenticity, the legitimacy, and relevance of the anti-violence movement and the success we ascribe to it. That is, the unchallenged claims of success that tend to dominate most descriptions of the anti-violence movement in this country depend on the overly simplistic analysis that has been used to understand the very nature of violence against women in this country. The consequences for women whose lives are more complicated are unfortunate, sometimes deadly.

This edited volume urgently attempts to counter this prevailing simplistic analysis of violence against women. The book resists the tendency to make sweeping generalizations and suggests that the very nature of violence against women is different for different women. *Domestic Violence at the Margins: Readings on Race, Class, Gender, and Culture* marks an important starting point: violence against women is different for women who live in communities where disadvantage is concentrated. As a collection this volume assumes that structural arrangements seriously complicate individual options for women who are marginalized and that no one monolithic response will work to eradicate individual or systemic abuse. The book also assumes that no single voice, no central authority, and no common analysis will lead to safety for all women.

On the contrary, the individual authors whose work appears in the book provide detailed and specific arguments about the negative consequences for women when we use a simplistic analysis of violence that centers itself on the experiences of white, middle-class, U.S.-born, heterosexual women who experience abuse. These authors point to the ways that multiple forms of oppression complicate battering, rape, harassment, incest, and other forms of gender violence. In so doing, this volume becomes essential reading by offering advocates, activists, and those people concerned with eradicating violence against women a key resource to advocate serious response to women who are living in extremely complicated (and hence the most dangerous) abusive situations.

Asking hard questions and raising complicated issues may be unpopular to some. By bringing together these writings, Natalie Sokoloff has exposed the inherent biases that have influenced so much mainstream work to end violence against women. The authors do not avoid discussion of racism within organizations, the heterosexist assumptions that permeate many approaches, or the conservative and class-based strategies that have come to be accepted as model interventions. Few other volumes openly discuss difference as a feminist construct or disagreement as a key aspect of creating change at the societal level. In this volume two general assumptions are made: power is critically linked to how services are delivered, and racial and ethnic privilege and access to resources must be challenged together with men's abuse of women and children. It is rare to read such thoughtful analyses of gender violence that include ample attention to other vulnerabilities in addition to gender oppression. That the contributions are written from various feminist perspectives makes them especially important.

I suspect that this is the reason why Sokoloff was so careful to include pieces that talk about resistance, strength of communities, and creative grass-roots intervention as well as the problems many groups of women are facing in contemporary society as they attempt to be free from the various forms of abuse they experience. The collection has a decidedly empowering tone. The articles describe strength in the face of despair; they speak with confidence about survival strategies; they offer positive solutions to complex problems; and, perhaps most important, they are hopeful. I expect that readers will walk away from the book with a different understanding about violence against women as well as insights about community accountability and the need for self-critique in this movement. Few books about violence against women can make that claim. This volume is both a corrective (in the sense that it fills gaps in the literature) and a model for writing about other complex social problems that have been reduced to simple issue-oriented responses.

In the end, *Domestic Violence at the Margins: Readings on Race, Class, Gender, and Culture* is a call to action and to a different kind of work, a chorus of voices that speaks to a broad audience who want to be part of creating a different world. Readers will find information about community-specific issues, culturally appropriate responses, and a potential to expand the framework for our work to end violence against women. Beyond that, it prompts us to think in more intricate ways about the goals of our work and the truly transformative potential of it. The volume asks us to rely on new forms of organizing, to look more carefully for evidence of resistance, and to engage in social change strategies that currently exceed the scope of our work. Ultimately, in a straightforward, unapologetic manner, *Domestic Violence at the Margins: Readings on Race, Class, Gender, and Culture* calls us to be accountable to those women who are in the most serious danger and challenges us to rededicate our work in the anti-violence movement to the goals of safety and justice and the liberation of all women.

Domestic Violence at the Margins

CHAPTER 1

NATALIE J. SOKOLOFF AND IDA DUPONT

Domestic Violence

Examining the Intersections of Race, Class, and Gender—An Introduction

*D*omestic Violence at the Margins: Readings on Race, Class, Gender, and
Culture attempts to identify and make relevant the lives of women,
victims/survivors of domestic violence, from diverse racial, ethnic, socioeconomic backgrounds as well as sexual orientations and immigrant statuses.
This anthology fills a void in the domestic violence literature by addressing theory, research, services, and activism around the lives of battered
women/survivors in the United States. Moreover, this multilevel analysis is
dynamic, rather than static, a focus beyond the significance of gender inequality in the lives of battered women. Thus, the anthology studies domestic violence at the personal and structural levels as well as culturally, in academic and activist contexts, for theory and research as well as for practical
services. This anthology seeks to give voice to diverse perspectives on domestic violence, to unify themes and concerns of battered women from many
groups, and to elucidate controversies and raise questions that remain unaddressed in this emerging field.

Our choice to focus on battered *women* is consistent with a feminist perspective on domestic violence. For the purposes of this anthology, battering
includes, but is not limited to, physical, emotional, psychological, and sexual
violence and control against women; it is defined as "a purposeful course of
action buttressed by familial, institutional, social, and cultural practices"
(Jaaber, 2001, p. 2). Moreover, as Feltey (2001) argues, although woman battering occurs within individual people's lives and is experienced as a personal
event, it is "culturally produced out of intersecting relations of gender, race,
social class, and sexuality" (p. 365).

The feminist view on battering acknowledges that not only do women experience a higher rate of severe and lethal domestic violence than men (Tjaden and Thoennes, 2000) but also socially structured gender inequality is a primary reason for the high rate of violence against women in our society. Our choice to focus exclusively on women reflects both the contributions and problems of the feminist perspective. A most important contribution of feminists has been to challenge earlier sociological and psychological models of domestic violence that depicted it as either a "family problem" (Kurz, 1989) or a conflict resulting from the psychopathology of one or both parties (Karmen, 2003). The feminist explanation represented a radical departure from these theories by taking a sociopolitical perspective with gender inequality as its central organizing principle: male dominance and control in the family and society as a whole perpetuates violence against women in the family.

At the same time, we recognize the important criticisms against mainstream feminist approaches to domestic violence. Scholars, survivors, advocates and activists, and particularly women of color and lesbians, increasingly challenge the feminist view that *gender* inequality is the only or primary factor determining domestic violence. The exclusion of women of color in feminist leadership and scholarship has been identified as contributing to the shortage of race/ethnic minority theoretical perspectives in the domestic violence literature (Richie, chapter 4; Kanuha, chapter 6). Lesbian scholars, and more recently bisexual and transgendered women question whether gender inequality is the primary reason for intimate partner violence: the fact that both abuser and victim are women questions the primacy of gender inequality in explaining the dynamics of lesbian battering (Butler, 1999; Courvant and Cook-Daniels, 2000–2001; Eaton, 1994; Girshick, 2002; Ristock, 2002). And despite the long-standing tendency within the feminist movement to minimize the significance of socioeconomic class as a contributing factor to domestic violence, a substantial body of work links socioeconomic factors with violence against women in the family (Coker, chapter 22; DeKeseredy and MacLeod, 1997; McKendy, 1997; Moore, 1997; Raphael, 2003; Rennison and Planty, 2003). This anthology attempts to redress some criticisms of the mainstream feminist perspective while accepting the positive contributions of this approach by presenting works of feminist scholars, particularly feminists of color, immigrants, and lesbians, who recognize that battered women's oppression is often multiplied by their location at the intersections at particular race, ethnic, class, gender, and sexual orientation systems of oppression and discrimination.

Although much pioneering work on domestic violence approached intimate partner violence as a monolithic phenomenon that affected all women the same, this "universalizing" approach increasingly has been regarded as inadequate and inappropriate to explain the experiences or address the needs of battered women from diverse backgrounds (Richie, chapter 4; Josephson, chapter 7; Incite!, chapter 8; Russo, 2001). For these women, domestic violence is not the only or primary violence shaping family life (Bograd, chapter 2). This anthology brings such marginalized battered women's experiences to the forefront and examines their unique struggles while simultaneously trying to understand the varied ways in which male dominance operates within *all* groups.

The approach to domestic violence in this anthology walks the line between two sometimes conflicting objectives: giving voice to battered women from diverse social locations and cultural backgrounds while still focusing on the structural inequalities (that is, race, gender, and class oppression) that constrain and shape the lives of battered women, albeit in different ways. This anthology acknowledges the value of presenting the multiplicity of diverse women's lived experiences, but this approach has the potential of "annihilating group concepts like gender, race and class" (Mann, 2000) and of downplaying the significant role that racism, sexism, social class, heterosexism, and other forms of socially structured inequality and discrimination have on battered women. Our position is that the crucial task of "unsilencing" the voices of marginalized and oppressed women who are battered should not obscure the reality that "race, class, and gender . . . [are] structures of oppression that are somehow larger than the individuals who produce them" (Mann and Grimes, 2001, p. 11). As Patricia Hill Collins (1998a) argues, the treatment of cultural differences must not "erase structural power" or it will "undercut" social change of the required political activism (p. 149). For these reasons, we have chosen to privilege approaches that emphasize the structural underpinnings of abuse while not denying the existence of real differences among individual battered women from diverse backgrounds.

The theoretical perspective adopted by multicultural scholars in this anthology urges us to reject the idea that battered women are helpless and lack agency while at the same time recognizing the real obstacles battered women face when trying to free themselves from abusive relationships. In our society, we tend to understand victimization and agency as existing only in the *absence* of the other (Mahoney, 1994). As a result, it is difficult to simultaneously draw attention to and evoke sympathy for women's victimization while underscoring the strengths and resilience of battered women. Domestic violence activists and scholars attempt to address these seemingly contradictory objectives by referring to battered women not as victims, but as survivors or victim/survivors. Consistent with this perspective, Patricia Hill Collins (1998b) argues that "the status of victim can never become a way of life" (p. 928) for battered women from oppressed groups. Instead, she suggests that naming the violence is only the first step in the process of developing resistance strategies against abuse. The ultimate goal is to recognize the existence of both choice and constraint in battered women's lives at both individual and structural levels (Schneider, 2000). Therefore, throughout this anthology, battered women are referred to as "survivors" and "victim/survivors."

We also identify many new theoretical perspectives emerging from the domestic violence literature. An important contribution has been to apply the concept of "intersectionality" to explain the experiences of battered women from the margins (Crenshaw, 1994). According to this perspective, the trauma of domestic violence is amplified by further victimization outside the intimate relationship, including racism, heterosexism, and class oppression (Bograd, chapter 2). Bograd also reminds us that domestic violence does not have a singular impact on all families: "Not only do different patterns of domestic violence have different consequences for different families, intersectionality asks us to integrate into theory and practice the simple recognition that, for many families, domestic violence is not the only or primary violence shaping family life." Such structural inequalities impose additional hardships for many battered women who are seeking safety. As Incite!, a group of Women of Color Against Violence (see chapter 8), argues, battered women advocates must adopt anti-violence strategies that are mindful of the larger structures of violence that shape the lives of poor battered women of color. "That is, strategies designed to combat violence within communities (sexual/domestic violence) must be linked to strategies that combat violence directed against communities (i.e., police brutality, prisons, racism, economic exploitation, etc.)" (Incite!, chapter 8). One without the other is inadequate; for battered women on the margins of society, the two are intimately connected.

The anthology attempts to underscore the significance of structural factors in relation to domestic violence. Several studies indicate that structural issues, particularly socioeconomic factors, are significant in contributing to and perpetuating domestic violence: (1) poverty, especially extreme poverty within the African American community, has been correlated with higher rates of severe and lethal domestic violence (Hampton et al., chapter 9); (2) a majority of homeless women were once victims of domestic violence (Bassuk et al., 1998); (3) battering can significantly prevent women from keeping their jobs because of harassment by their abuser or because of the physical or mental consequences of domestic violence (Brandwein, 1999; Raphael, 2000); (4) lack of shelter space and affordable housing are significant barriers to leaving and staying out of abusive relationships (Websdale and Johnson, chapter 23; DeKeseredy and MacLeod, 1997); and (5) changes in welfare laws have serious and deleterious effects on battered women and their children caught at the intersections of race, class, gender, and heterosexist systems of power (Josephson, chapter 7; Kurz, 1998; Raphael, 2000). Chapters in this anthology directly and indirectly address the impact of structural factors—for example, poverty, racial discrimination, and gender inequality on battered women's/survivors' lives.

In this anthology scholars also make clear that battered women from different backgrounds require different interventions. For example, a fundamental concern of poor battered women is to secure safe housing (Bassuk, 1995), while many immigrant battered women require bicultural/bilingual services that understand the many structural and cultural constraints they face (Abraham, 2000, chapter 16; Dasgupta, chapter 5; Rivera, 1997), religious women (such as Jews or Muslims) may require special food and living arrangements (Horsburgh, chapter 14), and lesbian battered women of color need services that are explicitly open and accepting of lesbians (Kanuha, chapter 6; Butler, 1999). Generally speaking, services and interventions should take into account the cultural differences of clients as well as the structural conditions and particular needs that different communities have (Gondolf, 1998). Dynamic multifaceted social movements have also emerged to address the particular needs of diverse battered women (Sun-Hee Park, chapter 21; Abraham, 2000; Waldron, 1996). Thus, the anthology includes a section that looks specifically at the need for culturally competent services grounded in structural changes and social movements for battered women.

Another major contribution of the scholarly work included in this anthology is its challenge to stereotypical images of battered women in both popular culture and the mainstream domestic violence literature (Allard, chapter 13; Ammons, 1995; Harrison and Esqueda, 1999). Some groups of battered women have been characterized demeaningly, as, for example, in racist, homophobic, xenophobic (fear of foreigners) ways. Negative stereotypes of battered women can have serious consequences, which may prevent them from accessing legal and social services. For example, negative characterizations or stereotypes of black women as a whole—as overly aggressive, resilient, violent, and immune to the effects of violence—have prevented black battered women from receiving equal and sympathetic treatment in the criminal justice system, particularly by police officers, lawyers, judges, and other court personnel (Allard, chapter 13; Ammons, 1995). Stereotypical notions of women of color have also resulted in misdiagnoses of battered women by mental health practitioners (Gondolf, 1998).

The stereotype of the passive, helpless battered woman has largely been based on mainstream images of white/European (primarily middle-class) women (Ammons, 1995). Women who resist abuse or fight back have been characterized as "bad women," and race has played a major role in the cultural distinction between those defined as battered women deserving of sympathy or not (Allard, chapter 13; Stark, 1995). Likewise, we cannot generalize about all white women. The powerful stereotype that battered women are all too often said to be helpless in response to their victimization frequently transcends race, ethnicity, class, sexual orientation, and national origin differences. Contrary to common belief, battered women consistently resist abuse and challenge their partners' attempts to dominate and control them (Abraham, chapter 16; Gondolf and Fisher, 1988).

In this anthology, several controversies emerge: determining the role that culture may play in perpetuating domestic violence and talking about the relationship between the two. Feminist domestic violence literature—as well as the larger society—tended to blame *culture* for domestic violence, specifically "other," nonwhite cultures. As Dasgupta (chapter 5) argues, "Many white Americans presume that 'other' cultures, especially minority ones, are far more accepting of woman abuse than the U.S. culture. . . . American mainstream society still likes to believe that woman abuse is limited to minority ethnic communities, lower socio-economic strata, and individuals with dark skin colors. The impact of . . . public violence of imperialism, classism, and racism on battering in the private sphere of home and intimate relationships has unfortunately, received little research."

The scholars in this anthology reject simplistic analyses of the role of culture in domestic violence. Rather, they argue for addressing how different communities' cultural experiences of violence (including domestic violence) are mediated through structural forms of oppression such as racism, economic exploitation, colonialism, heterosexism, and other systems of inequality. These scholars and activists are wary of characterizing culture as a purely negative force; and yet many recognize the danger of justifying violence against women with cultural "explanations." Rhea V. Almeida (chapter 18), who is able to walk this fine line argues that "wife battering is not culture. . . . [It is a] traditional patriarchal custom that men have practiced and women have accepted for generations" (Almeida and Dolan-Delvecchio, 1999, p. 667). Sherene Razack (1998) cautions that "violence [including violence against women] in immigrant communities is viewed as a cultural attribute rather than the product of male domination that is inextricably bound up with racism" (p. 57). Sexual violence in Native communities and communities of color, she argues, must be understood as an outcome of white supremacy, patriarchy, colonialism, and economic exploitation. In this anthology, care is taken to include articles that approach domestic violence in ways that oppose sexism in all of its manifestations without denying the importance of women's cultures and their socially structured contexts. However, this approach is arguably difficult to achieve and is not always accomplished, as some articles illustrate.

Some work in this anthology critiques traditional responses to domestic violence and suggests there is an overreliance on the criminal justice system to address violence against women (Richie, chapter 4, 2000; Braithwaite and Daly, 1998; Coker, 1999) and women of color who experience the police as a negative force in their communities (Richie, chapter 4; Kanuha, chapter 6; Josephson, chapter 7; Coker, chapter 22; A. Smith, chapter 24; Rasche, 1995; Rivera, 1997). Richie argues that the over-reliance on law-enforcement to deal with social problems in poor communities of color has had several unintended negative consequences: increased use of force, mass incarceration of young men of color and police brutality (Richie, chapter 4). These conditions create tensions for poor women of color between the need for some kind of state intervention to protect them from abuse in their homes and the recognition that many of the women most in need of such protection are made more vulnerable by these very interventions. Thus, Coker (2001) elaborates three ways that state intervention can cause more intrusion in the lives of and harm to poor battered women of color by increasing the risks of (1) arrest of those very same battered women *for* domestic violence, (2) unwarranted removal by the state of children from women who have been battered, and (3) prosecution of battered women involved, even peripherally, in criminal conduct (sometimes related to their being abused). Furthermore, Coker (chapter 22) argues for state intervention to have any hope of being useful to poor minority battered women, two sets of conditions are necessary: first, significant material resources must be made available for women to better their chances of success in leaving/changing the immediate battering situation; second, battered women's organizations and coalitions must act as effective institutional reformers by monitoring police, prosecutorial and judicial responses as well as advocating for the particular needs of individual battered women from marginalized communities.

Many call for the involvement of other institutions and influential community members including institutions for economic development, religious institutions, community leaders, schools, and community-based organizations to respond to domestic violence (Almeida and Lockard, chapter 18; T. West, chapter 20; Coker, chapter 22, 1999, 2001, 2002; A. Smith, chapter 24; Almeida and Dolan-Delvecchio, 1999; Richie and Kanuha, 1993). One alternative to mainstream legal approaches to domestic violence is a form of mediation used by the Navajo which is called "peacemaking" (Coker, 1999). Coker suggests that peacemaking has many advantages over formal legal approaches to domestic violence, including its offer of tangible material and community support and assistance to women.[1] Another alternative, suggested by the North Gottingen Drop-In Centre in Halifax, Nova Scotia, is to reduce economic inequality to prevent domestic abuse. Here a group of immigrant and refugee women, many of whom where victims of woman abuse, torture, political persecution, and the violence of poverty, created an informal support group out of which came a cooperative, a catering business in which they all worked, assistance with housing needs and shared childcare, and emotional support (as reported in DeKeseredy and MacLeod, 1997, p. 169). Others emphasize the important role that religious institutions can play in addressing domestic violence (Horsburgh, chapter 14; B. Smith, chapter 19; T. West, chapter 20; Ayyub, 2000). T. West calls for black churches to take an active stand against violence perpetrated against African American women. She urges churches to engage in a continual process of self-critique that focuses on removing any messages or practices that may directly or indirectly reinforce the acceptability of woman abuse.

Another alternative response to domestic violence is the culturally competent treatment approach, the Cultural Context Model (CCM), that is used with batterers and their families at some domestic violence agencies (Almeida and Lockard, chapter 18; Almeida and Dolan-Delvecchio, 1999). This model requires abusers to take responsibility for their violence and supports the empowerment of victims and children by providing a wide range of services to the entire family under one team of therapists. The CCM links gender ideology and subordination in individual couples with experiences of racial subordination and colonization in marginalized communities, which thereby links the struggle for gender equality with the struggles for racial and economic justice—without requiring that women choose between cultural identity or group membership and their safety and autonomy.

Furthermore, Andrea Smith (chapter 24) argues that battered women, rather than being treated as "victims" or "clients" by social service agencies—even culturally competent ones—must become part of a grassroots community organizing effort in a movement for social change, the goal of which is to *end* domestic violence, not simply to react to past occurrences of domestic violence. This means that state and personal violence must be addressed simultaneously, domestic violence survivors must be seen as organizers or potential organizers in this grassroots movement, community accountability strategies that do not rely on the police or at least the police alone must ensure safety for survivors and their families, and transnational relationships must be built in the effort to end violence against all women—especially the poorest and most marginalized.

Although many of these approaches constitute promising examples of alternatives to traditional criminal justice approaches, domestic violence scholars as a whole caution that the safety of battered women and their children must remain the primary concern of policymakers. Traditionally, feminists have regarded treatment programs for batterers, mediation, and other alternative approaches with suspicion because of their potential danger to battered women. Given the disproportionately high rate of severe and lethal domestic violence among marginalized women, particularly poor black women (Websdale, chapter 10, 1999; Rennison and Welchans, 2000), agents of change should carefully evaluate and implement alternative modalities to ensure the safety of women and children.

Another controversy that emerges from some work in this anthology is the issue of appropriate speakers on behalf of "marginalized" battered women. Some scholars are redressing this problem by making women from the margins the center of their research. An example of this is Traci West's approach in her book on black battered women where she "plac[es] black women's experiences as center and norm" (1998, p. 3). This important shift in perspective raises several thorny philosophical questions: Can "outsiders" tell other women's stories? Should they? The multicultural literature is forcing more privileged women (white, higher income, heterosexual women) to question their role in studying women who are less privileged than themselves. bell hooks suggests that "even if perceived 'authorities' writing about a group to which they do not belong and/or over which they yield power, are progressive, caring, and right-on in every way, as long as their authority is constituted by either the absence of the voices of the individuals whose experiences they seek to address, or the dismissal of those voices as unimportant, the subject-object dichotomy is maintained and domination is reinforced" (hooks, 1989, p. 43).

Although bell hooks does not conclude that white or more privileged women cannot write about more disadvantaged women, she warns that "when we write about the experiences of a group to which we do not belong, we should think about the ethics of our action, considering whether or not our work will be used to reinforce and perpetuate domination" (hooks, 1989, p. 43). Many scholars in this anthology agree that they should consider how their findings may impact women who are already severely disadvantaged. Scholars need to think about how their work could be misused to create policies to further alienate and disempower some battered women. Information about domestic violence in marginalized communities should ideally be presented in such a way that their findings do not negatively either impact marginalized battered women/survivors, their children, or their partners or reinforce negative stereotypes about them. Research that is "participatory, empowering, and based in a community action model" (Kanuha, chapter 6) presents a first step. Such "culturally competent research" involves collaborative research efforts with the people who are directly affected by and living with domestic violence. By doing so, scholars can be responsive to the concerns of marginalized communities.

Despite our best efforts, there are some weaknesses in this anthology. There is a void, reflective of the entire domestic violence literature, that *simultaneously* addresses social class and race/ethnicity, although this is changing. As a result, some articles in the anthology may overemphasize the role of culture in explaining domestic violence among oppressed groups while downplaying the salience of social class. Several exceptions in the last section on alternative approaches to combating domestic violence in this anthology include Almeida and Lockard, chapter 18; Coker, chapter 22; and A. Smith, chapter 24.

We acknowledge the need for successful, culturally competent intervention programs for batterers and victim/survivors in this anthology, but we also believe that such approaches *alone* will never put an end to domestic violence. Ultimately, the root causes of this problem must be identified and addressed. As the work in this anthology reflects, we believe that structural inequalities—sexism, racism, class inequality, heterosexism—are primary sources of domestic violence. Thus, structural solutions that address aggravating and causal factors associated with domestic violence are required: more affordable public housing, additional domestic violence shelters, and adequate long-term transitional housing for women and their children (Websdale and Johnson, chapter 23; Dobash and Dobash, 1992); access to public education so that battered women without skills or job experience will become eligible for well-paying jobs (Fine and Weis, 2000); available jobs with living wages; quality, affordable child care (Fine and Weis, 2000); a flexible, humane welfare policy that can respond to battered women's needs on a case-by-case basis (Lyon, 1998); and challenges to racist, misogynistic, heterosexist, and xenophobic structures (Richie, chapter 4; Josephson, chapter 7; Coker, chapter 22; A. Smith, chapter 24).

This anthology gives voice to "marginalized" battered women, but it likewise includes a section on European-American/white battered women that focuses on white working-class and poor women. The decision to include white women in the anthology is an attempt on our part to "race" whiteness and to recognize the diversity of white women's experiences. Whites, rarely depicted as members of a racial or ethnic group, are usually defined solely by their socioeconomic status. Our inclusion of white women acknowledges the fact that they come from different social locations and that their experiences of victimization vary widely depending on their socioeconomic status, religion, sexual orientation, ethnic origins, and immigrant status. At the same time, the anthology is careful to keep women of color at the forefront of the book because history tends to treat whites as the norm, and this collection challenges that tradition.

This anthology represents a first attempt to gather what we consider to be some of the best current work that addresses race, gender, class, and culture in relation to domestic violence. The approaches to domestic violence in this anthology challenge the primacy of gender as an explanatory model of domestic violence and emphasize the need to examine how other forms of inequality and oppression intersect with sexism, give voice to battered women from a wide range of formerly excluded communities, and advocate culturally competent interventions and strategies grounded in greater structural equality. Because of the many contributions of this growing body of work, the domestic violence literature has become increasingly relevant to more and more diverse segments of our society (see Nesmith, 2001).

Given that relative newness of this domestic violence research, there are still many voids in the literature. More research needs to be done on how race and class inequality simultaneously impact different groups of battered women differently (without privileging the significance of either race or class). As well, better integration of sexuality, disability, and immigration in understanding and combating domestic violence is mandatory. Scholars must also take structural factors into account when discussing policy responses to domestic violence. As well, there must be an understanding how state interventions can have harmful as well as positive consequences for marginalized battered women. Change for battered women from diverse backgrounds must happen on multiple levels—for example, protecting individual women and children from violence in their homes while simultaneously working through larger social movements for broader social change within the larger society and the many families that make it up. Protection for battered women depends as much on social movements for structural changes and social justice as it does on culturally competent services for individual women and communities.

We hope that this anthology sparks others to probe in greater depth the causes, needs, and policies that will make all women and children safe, and in particular, women marginalized by the very structures of race, class, gender, sexual orientation, and immigrant status that so basically, and all too often in unrecognized ways, impact dramatically on their lives.

NOTE

1. Goel (2000), among others, cautions, however, that peacemaking (among Native Americans in the United States) and justice circles and principles (among First Nation people in Canada) may only *increase* the problems battered women face if it is taken outside of its historical context. Thus, she argues, peacemaking and sentencing circles can be used, but *not for domestic violence, until* Aboriginal and Native American women are given equal status in their communities *first*—something that was taken away from them under colonization.

REFERENCES

Abraham, Margaret. 2000. *Speaking the Unspeakable: Marital Violence among South Asian Immigrants in the United States.* New Brunswick, N.J.: Rutgers University Press.

Almeida, Rhea V., and Ken Dolan-Delvecchio. 1999. Addressing culture in batterers intervention: The Asian Indian community as an illustrative example. *Violence Against Women* 5(6): 667–683.

Ammons, Linda. 1995. Mules, madonnas, babies, bathwater, racial imagery, and stereotypes: The African American woman and the battered woman syndrome. *Wisconsin Law Review* 5: 1003–1080.

Andersen, Margaret, and Patricia Hill Collins. 2001. Introduction. In M. Andersen and P. Hill Collins, eds., *Race, Class, and Gender: An Anthology*. 4th ed. Belmont, Calif.: Wadsworth, 1–9.

Ayyub, Ruksana. 2000. Domestic violence in the South Asian Muslim immigrant population in the United States. *Journal of Distress and the Homeless* 9(3): 237–248.

Bassuk, Ellen. 1995. Lives in jeopardy: Women and homelessness. In Charles V. Willie, Perri Patricia Rieker, and Bernard Kramer, eds., *Mental Health, Racism, and Sexism*. Pittsburgh: University of Pittsburgh Press, 237–252.

Bassuk, Ellen, Stephanie Melnick, and Angela Browne. 1998. Responding to the needs of low-income and homeless women who are survivors of family violence. *Journal of the American Medical Women's Association* 53(2): 57–64.

Braithwaite, John, and Kathleen Daly. 1998. Masculinities, violence, and communitarian control. In Susan Miller, ed., *Crime Control and Women: Feminist Implications of Criminal Justice Policy*. Thousand Oaks, Calif.: Sage, 151–180.

Brandwein, Ruth. 1999. *Battered Women, Children, and Welfare Reform: The Ties that Bind*. Thousand Oaks, Calif.: Sage.

Butler, Lola. 1999. African American lesbian women experiencing partner abuse. In Joan McClennan and John Gunther, eds., *A Professional Guide to Understanding Gay and Lesbian Domestic Violence*. Lewiston, N.Y.: Edwin Mellen, 181–205.

Coker, Donna. 1999. Enhancing autonomy for battered women: Lessons from Navajo peacemaking. *UCLA Law Review* 47(1): 1–111.

———. 2001. Crime control and feminist law reform in domestic violence law: A critical review. *Buffalo Criminal Law Review* 4: 801–860.

———. 2002. Transformative justice: Anti-subordination processes in cases of domestic violence. In Heather Strang and John Braithwaite, eds., *Restorative Justice and Family Violence*. Cambridge, England: Cambridge University Press, 128–152.

Collins, Patricia Hill. 1998a. *Fighting Words: Black Women and the Search for Justice*. Minneapolis: University of Minnesota Press.

———. 1998b. The tie that binds: Race, gender and U.S. violence. *Ethnic and Racial Studies* 21(5): 917–938.

Courvant, Diana, and Loree Cook-Daniels. 2000–2001. Trans and intersex survivors of domestic violence: Defining terms, barriers, and responsibilities. Available through Survivor Project at: www.survivorproject.org/defbarresp.html. Retrieved 8/27/02.

Crenshaw, Kimberlé. 1994. Mapping at the margins: Intersectionality, identity politics, and violence against women of color. In M. A. Fineman and R. Mykitiuk, eds., *The Public Nature of Private Violence: The Discovery of Domestic Abuse*. New York: Routledge, 93–118.

DeKeseredy, Walter, and Linda MacLeod. 1997. *Woman Abuse: A Sociological Story*. Toronto: Harcourt Brace, Canada.

Dobash, R. P., and R. E. Dobash. 1992. *Women, Violence, and Social Change*. New York: Routledge.

Eaton, Mary. 1994. Abuse by any other name: Feminism, difference, and intralesbian violence. In M. A. Fineman and R. Mykitiuk, eds., *The Public Nature of Private Violence: The Discovery of Domestic Abuse*. New York: Routledge, 195–223.

Feltey, Kathryn. 2001. Gender violence: Rape and sexual assault. In Dana Vannoy, ed., *Gender Mosaics*. Los Angeles: Roxbury, 363–373.

Fine, Michelle, and Lois Weis. 2000. Disappearing acts: The state and violence against women in the twentieth century. *Signs: Journal of Women in Culture and Society* 25(4): 1139–1146.

Girshick, Lori. 2002. No sugar, no spice: Reflections on research on woman-to-woman sexual violence. *Violence Against Women* 8(12): 1500–1520.

Goel, Rashmi. 2000. No women at the center: The use of the Canadian sentencing circle in domestic violence cases. *Wisconsin Women's Law Journal* 15: 293–334.

Gondolf, Edward. 1998. Appreciating diversity among battered women. In Edward W. Gondolf, ed., *Assessing Woman Battering in Mental Health Services.* London: Sage, 113–131.

Gondolf, Edward, and Ellen Fisher. 1988. *Battered Women as Survivors: An Alternative to Treating Learned Helplessness.* Lexington, Mass.: Lexington.

Harrison, Lisa, and Cynthia Willis Esqueda. 1999. Myths and stereotypes of actors involved in domestic violence: Implications for domestic violence culpability attributions. *Aggression and Violent Behavior* 4(2): 129–138.

Incite! N.d. Violence against Women of Color. *Incite! Women of Color Against Violence.* Available at: www.incite-national.org/issues/violence.html. Retrieved 8/27/02.

Jaaber, Radhia A. 2001. Framing battering: Demystifying oppression. Keynote presentation at ISTSS-NY 11th Annual Conference, New York City.

Kanuha, Valli. 1996. Domestic violence, racism, and the battered women's movement in the United States. In J. L. Edleson and Z. C. Eisikovits, eds., *Future Interventions with Battered Women and their Families.* London: Sage, 34–50.

Karmen, Andrew. 2003. Women victims of crime. In Barbara Raffel Price and Natalie J. Sokoloff, eds., *The Criminal Justice System and Women: Offenders, Prisoners, Victims, and Workers.* 3d ed. New York: McGraw-Hill, 289–301.

Kurz, Demi. 1989. Social science perspectives on wife abuse. *Gender and Society* 3(4): 489–505.

———. 1998. Women, welfare, and domestic violence. *Social Justice* 25(1): 105–122.

Lyon, Eleanor. 1998. Poverty, welfare, and battered women: What does the research tell us? Available at: www.vaw.umn.edu/Vawnet/welfare.htm. Retrieved 9/17/02.

Mahoney, Martha. 1994. Victimization or oppression? Women's lives, violence, and agency. In M. A. Fineman and R. Mykitiuk, eds., *The Public Nature of Private Violence: The Discovery of Domestic Abuse.* New York: Routledge, 59–92.

Mann, Susan Archer. 2000. The scholarship of difference: A scholarship of liberation? *Sociological Inquiry* 70(4): 475–498.

Mann, Susan Archer, and Michael Grimes. 2001. Common and contested ground: Marxism and race, gender and class analysis. *Race, Gender and Class* 8(2): 3–22.

McKendy, John. 1997. The class politics of domestic violence. *Journal of Sociology and Social Welfare* 24(3): 135–155.

Moore, Angela M. 1997. Intimate violence: Does socioeconomic status matter? In Albert Cardarelli, ed., *Violence between Intimate Partners: Patterns, Causes, and Effects.* Boston: Allyn and Bacon, 90–100.

Nesmith, Caryn. 2001. Safety strategies against abuse must reflect culture. WomensENews. Available at: www.womensenews.org. Retrieved 8/3/01.

Raphael, Jody. 2000. *Saving Bernice: Battered Women, Welfare, and Poverty.* Boston: Northeastern University Press.

———. 2003. Battering through the lens of class. *Journal of Gender, Social Policy and the Law* 11(2): 367–375.

Rasche, Christine. 1995. Minority women and domestic violence: The unique dilemmas of battered women of color. In Barbara Raffel Price and Natalie J. Sokoloff, eds., *The Criminal Justice System and Women: Offenders, Victims, Workers.* 2d ed. New York: McGraw-Hill, 246–261.

Razack, Sherene. 1998. What is to be gained by looking white people in the eye? Race in sexual violence cases. *Looking White People in the Eye: Gender, Race, and Culture in Courtrooms and Classrooms.* Toronto: University of Toronto Press, 56–87.

Rennison, Callie, and Mike Planty. 2003. Non-lethal intimate partner violence: Examining race, gender, and income patterns. *Violence and Victims* 18(4): 433–444.

Rennison, Callie, and Sarah Welchans. 2000. *Intimate Partner Violence.* Washington, D.C.: U.S. Department of Justice, Bureau of Justice Statistics. NCJ-178247.

Richie, Beth E. 1996. *Compelled to Crime: The Gender Entrapment of Battered Black Women.* New York: Routledge.

Richie, Beth E., and Valli Kanuha. 1993. Battered women of color in public health care systems: Racism, sexism, and violence. In B. Bair and S. E. Cayleff, eds., *Wings of Gauze: Women of Color and the Experience of Health and Illness.* Detroit: Wayne State University Press, 288–299.

Ristock, Janice. 2002. *No More Secrets: Violence in Lesbian Relationships.* New York: Routledge.

Rivera, Jenny. 1997. Domestic violence against Latinas by Latino males: An analysis of race, national origin, and gender differentials. In A. K. Wing, ed., *Critical Race Feminism: A Reader.* New York: New York University Press, 259–266.

Russo, Ann. 2001. If not now, when? Contemporary feminist movement to end violence against women. *Taking Back Our Lives: A Call to Action for the Feminist Movement.* New York: Routledge, 3–30.

Schneider, Elizabeth. 2000. *Battered Women and Feminist Lawmaking.* New Haven: Yale University Press.

Stark, Evan. 1995. Re-presenting woman battering: From a battered woman syndrome to coercive control. *Albany Law Review* 58(4): 973–1026.

Tjaden, Patricia, and Nancy Thoennes. 2000. *Extent, Nature, and Consequences of Intimate Partner Violence: Findings from the National Violence Against Women Survey.* July. Washington, D.C.: U.S. Department of Justice. NCJ-181867.

Waldron, Charlene. 1996. Lesbians of color and the domestic violence movement. In C. Renzetti and H. Miley, eds., *Violence in Gay and Lesbian Domestic Partnerships.* New York: Harrington/Haworth, 43–52.

Websdale, Neil. 1999. *Understanding Domestic Homicide.* Boston: Northeastern University Press.

West, Traci. C. 1999. *Wounds of the Spirit: Black Women, Violence, and Resistance Ethics.* New York: New York University Press.

PART I

Frameworks and Overarching Themes

Several interconnected principles guide this anthology. Voices of women of color and other marginalized groups, either through their own work or through the work of others, provide multilayered accounts of structural and political violence as well as tragic personal experiences. P. J. Gibson's (2002) poem, "How Shall We Lighten Their Loads?" contemplates racialized class- and gender-based violence, simultaneously institutional and personal.

> If you permit yourself
> You can step through a tear in space and time
> And you will see them there
> Ashani, Cheyenne, Etta Mae, Karena, Migdalia and Yoo Ling . . .
>
> Women whose lives have ended
> Much too soon
> Much too violently.

An overarching theme of the anthology places culture at the center of analysis—both complicit and liberatory—as source and solution. Multicultural intersectional perspectives arise in part from international declarations of universal human rights to treat as problematic mainstream Eurocentric feminist discussions of violence against women and move the critique beyond the borders of patriarchy and ethnocentrism (see Volpp, chapter 3; Crooms, 1999; Narayan, 1997).

Too often, structural forces shaping cultural practices are hidden from view. Pervasive structural pressures that deny women economic and political agency include global inequalities, new articulations of patriarchy found in religious fundamentalisms or orthodoxies, and the legacies of racism and colonialism (Volpp, chapter 3).

For the last four decades feminists have challenged the private nature of violence. Some commentators insist that to use the term "domestic violence" in relation to intimate violence trivializes brutality that is multidimensional in its social structural, political, and economic foundations (Knauer, 1999; DaLuz, 1994; Crites, 2000).

To explain day-to-day realities for battered women and practitioners in the field, part 1—Frameworks and Overarching Themes—links theoretical concepts of intersectionality to the multiple sources of state oppression, institutional violence, and interpersonal violence. Activists on the front lines of antiviolence work deal regularly with the complex, multidimensional landscape of layered disadvantage—gendered, politicized, raced, and sexed—which obstructs community change, especially for women of color.

In chapter 2, Michele Bograd underscores that all women do not experience domestic violence equally or in the same ways. She applies Kimberlé Crenshaw's concept of intersectionality to theory and practice in domestic violence. Crenshaw (1998), an African American feminist lawyer, offers the valuable critique that the underlying picture of patriarchy in the United States is overly generalized, contributing to what Patricia Williams (1997) identifies as the myth of equal oppressions. In place of gender-exclusive frameworks, Ann Russo (2001) urges an analysis based on "interlocking oppressions. . . . Violence against women has multiple interconnected sources, and is not tied exclusively to an isolated system of misogyny and male dominance. Histories of conquest, immigration, and slavery account for women's differential targeting and experience of rape, torture, and murder. Misogyny, racism, classism, heterosexism, and antisemitism, among other . . . [systems of oppression], construct the differential contexts of women's lives" (p. 33).[1]

Discourse that claims that domestic violence equally affects all classes and races, all ethnic and immigrant groups, and all heterosexual and gay, lesbian, bisexual, and transgendered (LGBT) people diverts attention away from the distinctive needs of women of color from diverse backgrounds. Beth E. Richie in chapter 4 argues that women of color endure disproportionately higher unemployment, less education and consequently fewer job skills, as well as unrelenting discrimination in education, employment, and housing. These structural barriers, combined with the potency of racism in the administration of criminal justice, collude to make it harder to create needed links to people, resources, networks, and institutions for a woman to be able to escape violence (see Coker, chapter 22).

In chapter 3, Leti Volpp illustrates how the relationship between feminism and multiculturalism is constructed. She challenges us to rethink the way we consider cultural difference when we investigate issues integral to domestic violence. Volpp illustrates the tension between feminism and multiculturalism as she discusses the use of cultural defenses in legal representation. Both Leti Volpp in chapter 3 and Shamita Das Dasgupta in chapter 5 discuss the multiple contexts that differentially shape women's experiences with violence and help-seeking. In chapter 5, Dasgupta exposes race and class structures that in combination with U.S. immigration policies deter help-seeking and inhibit escape from abuse. She illustrates how immigration status, dependent on marriage to the abuser, isolates immigrant women of color.

Economic insecurity and worries about the welfare of children genuinely transcend cultural explanations of domestic violence (Josephson, chapter 7; Crenshaw, 1998). In chapter 5, Dasgupta introduces the power and control model of domestic violence. Arising from lived and practice-based experience of domestic violence survivors and advocates, this model emerges as a valuable framework for investigating the interconnections between violence and other tactics of public and private coercion and control (see also Almeida and Lockhart, chapter 18, figure 18.1).

When oppression and violence occur among communities of color, culture is often alleged to have a particularly influential explanatory power. Specific cases are conceptualized not as reflecting individual behavior; instead, entire groups are stereotyped. Communities tend to be discussed in "culturalist" language and are considered to be engaged in practices that have not changed over time (Mutua, 2001). According to Volpp (chapter 3), culture and cultural identity are forgotten in this story in constant states of becoming, neither self-contained nor impermeable. In general, behavior of devalued groups is widely perceived as more culturally determined than that of the dominant culture. The powerful are depicted as having no culture, other than the universal culture of "civilization"; in contrast, those without power are singled out and culturally endowed as a means of attributing deviance and maintaining social, economic, and political distance (Rosaldo, 1993). The collection of readings in this anthology challenges this false dichotomy. A majority of voices in the anthology asserts that "culture" is constantly negotiated and highly contested. As Beth E. Richie highlights in chapter 4, dominant cultural arguments that label groups as pathological displace attention from governmental failures. The pervasive and ubiquitous backdrop of a dominant structural race and gender paradigm tends to be erased in dominant discourse on the role of "Other" cultures and domestic violence. Within this context Dasgupta (chapter 5) contends that culture and poverty are blamed as the causes of domestic violence (see also Volpp, chapter 3).

Uma Narayan (1997) argues that attempts to link domestic violence and culture are merged with distorted representations of gender, race, sexuality, and social class that cross national borders. Narayan's scholarship compares domestic violence homicides in the United States and India. Fatal forms of violence against women from "Other" cultures have tended to be explained as "death by culture," for example, as in dowry murders in India (Narayan, 1997). Narayan's analysis connects domestic violence homicide across cultures and explains how national contexts shape the visibility of culture and influence selective and asymmetrical "understanding of Other cultures" (p. 96). Culture is invoked to explain forms of violence against immigrant women but not similarly invoked to explain forms of violence that affect mainstream Western women here in the United States.

Narayan has calculated that death by domestic violence in the United States is statistically as significant a social problem as dowry murders in India, but only the latter is used as a sign of cultural inferiority: "They burn their women there," not "We in the U.S. shoot our women here." Yet domestic violence murders in the United States are just as much a part of American culture as dowry death is a part of Indian culture.[2] In Narayan's words, when "cultural explanations" are given for fatal forms of violence in so-called Third World communities, the effect is to suggest that "Other" women suffer "death by culture." These assumptions preclude the understanding that marginalized cultures, like all cultures, undergo constant transformation and reshaping. Without doubt, mainstream cultures engage in equally horrendous behavior against women but it is not reasoned as such and thus complexities of race, class, social location, community, nationality, sexuality, and so on are negated, forgotten, or trivialized.

Illustrated throughout this anthology is evidence of the powerful courage of women from diverse cultural contexts who defy violence. Through and within their resistance, essentialized cultural identity is always contested. Parts 2 and 3 of this anthology offer several community studies of women's resistance to violence and victimhood.

Culture is constantly negotiated, as Leti Volpp explains in chapter 3. The culture we experience is shaped further by our age, gender, class, race, ethnicity, immigrant status, disability status, and sexual orientation. Our identities are always multiple, intersected, and often contradictory. Yet the manner in which culture is contested is often not recognized. This happens, in part, because cultural identity is used to explain behavior both within marginalized communities and by the dominant culture that identifies certain practices as culturally determined. Furthermore, the media plays a role in rigidifying the idea that violence against women is a product of a marginalized community's culture because the belief that "nonwhite Others" are said to engage in "primitive" and "misogynistic" cultural practices fits long-standing biases (for example, see Dasgupta, chapter 5).

Understanding cultural constructs of gender is key to any analysis of domestic violence. Crenshaw explains that narratives play an important role in the way we as a society understand experiences of oppression and discrimination.

Historically, white and middle-class feminists sometimes ignored or minimized social differences between women by focusing on a shared, "essentialized," victimization among women. Many feminists, especially in the 1970s, believed that through sharing stories, women would recognize common experiences of gender-based oppression and from that shared experience join together in a unified feminist movement. Ann Russo notes that such a notion of universal "sisterhood accomplished just the opposite because it reduced the complexities of many women's stories and it erased our historical, social, and cultural differences and divisions.... In listening for commonality, we minimize women's different histories, cultures, contexts, experiences, and perspectives" (Russo, 2001). Parts 2 and 3 of this book illustrate that women's narratives of resistance and organizing have become the groundwork for new knowledge, theories, and activism.

In discussing domestic violence, it is essential to address societal arrangements that foster oppression and violence by those with more power against those with less. Throughout the life cycle, heterosexual relationships are more dangerous for women than for men but women of color experience multiple—that is, layer upon layer—of intersectional jeopardies. Lesbians of color are at least doubly and often triply stigmatized, and they receive little legal recognition or protection (see Kanuha, chapter 6).

In looking at violence in lesbian relationships, Janice Ristock (2002) makes the point that the dominant paradigm on power and control "homogenizes experiences of relationship violence" (p. 142). Exclusionary practices are at work even within marginalized communities. It is an ongoing political struggle to resist "universalized categories of sexual identity" and respond to same-sex violence in an inclusive way (Ristock, 2002). In chapter 6, Valli Kalei Kanuha's important and now classic contribution to the literature reveals the multiple jeopardy facing lesbians of color. Kanuha confronts a pervasive feminist fear of discussing lesbian violence, and female violence generally. We want to hold women accountable for violence; moreover, we do not want to further punish women for situations of oppression. This dynamic holds true for lesbian battering and for the use and misuse of child welfare laws against women who are both battered themselves and battering their children (see Ristock, 2002; Josephson, chapter 7; Coker, chapter 22).

Gender *essentialism* refers to the ascribing of certain attributes to women. These essential attributes are considered to be shared by all women and, hence, are also seen as universal. Essentialism has been challenged by Black, Latina, Asian, Native American, lesbian, bisexual, and transgendered feminists as being exclusive and failing to recognize that women experience various forms of oppression simultaneously. Black, Latina, Asian American, Native American, and biracial/bicultural women experience complex intersections of sexism and racism. Their experiences of gender oppression cannot be disentangled from their experiences of racism because they occur simultaneously. They come to the law not just as women, but as Black women, and/or Latina women, and/or Muslim women, and/or heterosexual women, and/or LBGT women, and/or immigrant women negotiating with the dominant belief system on race, ethnicity, culture, sexuality, and/or family (Crenshaw, 1998; Razack, 1994; Koyama, 2001).

Between the cracks of gender and culture, same-sex domestic violence has been found to thrive. Intimate violence tarnishes many lesbian relationships. The National Coalition of Anti-Violence Programs (NCAVP, 1998) reports that 25 to 33 percent of same-sex couples experience violence in their relationships.[3] These numbers are consistent with estimates of abuse in heterosexual relationships. The NCAVP documented 2,574 cases of same-sex domestic violence in 1998. Women accounted for 48 percent of cases, 49 percent were men, 3 percent were transgendered M-F [male-to-female], and less that one percent transgendered F-M [female-to-male]. Such high numbers demand the attention of feminist theorists and gay, lesbian, bisexual, transgendered, and intersexed activists. As Kanuha recognizes in chapter 6, same-sex domestic violence, with the potential to disrupt existing theories of abuse, is complicated by its intersectionality with race, ethnicity, class, and culture. Fear that heterosexual violence will become "trivialized" and/or avoidance of the complicated issues inherent in same-sex violence jeopardize the safety of countless people in lesbian, gay, bisexual, transgendered, and intersexed relationships.

As Kanuha demonstrates, women in lesbian relationships experience domestic violence differently than women in heterosexual relationships, in part because of the abuser's unique potential to use homophobia to manipulate and control her partner. LBGT women find little sanctuary in feminist theories of domestic violence that are built upon the premise that domestic violence manifests male oppression of women (Knauer, 1999). The purpose of chapter 6 is to draw attention to the unique and particular obstacles lesbian battered women of color face when they attempt to reach out for legal protection. Kanuha challenges domestic violence activists to expand their theories and practices to include the reality that some women abuse women.

Having resources—for example, money, social networks, racial privilege—is highly protective, although no guarantee, against patriarchal abuse. Without skills, money, social connections, or "network embeddedness," many women are vulnerable. More than 80 percent of women on public assistance have experienced domestic violence (Raphael and Tolman, 1997). Poverty is a highly racialized and gendered problem in the United States as elsewhere (see Josephson, chapter 7). It affects Black and Latina women disproportionately more than white women. Within the social dynamics of racism, gender oppression, and homophobia, many men, and some women, have been covertly pressured to undervalue and disrespect their partners.

Multicultural and multiracial examinations of battering neither excuse or legitimate violence against women nor collude with batterers to dim the focus on violence as the primary issue. "Individual women," as James Ptacek (1999) observed in his research on battered women in court, "are assaulted by individual[s], but the ability of so many men to repeatedly assault, terrorize, and control so many women draws on in-stitutional collusion and gender inequality" (p. 9). Jock Young (1999) makes the point that conservative social policies essentialize poverty and gender-based violence as a failure of individual responsibility. Young labels this process "the vendetta against the single mother" (p. 286)—single parenthood is an identity overdetermined by race, class, and gender in the United States. This notion triggers ideas of blame, which shifts battered women , especially poor battered women of color, from a group category identified as "deserving victims" to a category of potentially "flawed, unreliable, irresponsible, exaggerat-ing, and undeserving" in the day-to-day application of laws that were originally intended to protect and support women.

In chapter 7, Jyl Josephson exposes the intrusion of the state through social welfare laws that regulate and control women's lives, especially in economically poor communities. Josephson in chapter 7 and Coker in chapter 22 illustrate how race, class, ethnicity, state coercion, paternal-ism, and unsafe policies, such as the 1996 "welfare reform" law, interact with preexisting state control of poor women and marginalized com-munities. Here, punitive policies of child removal, elimination of social provision, and a "war on drugs" construct an ideology of focused con-trol of poor women of color.

Widespread social action and fundamental social change with women's safety at the core is required in every corner of every commu-nity. The conception of justice that informs this book is the same social justice underscored by Incite!–Critical Resistance (chapter 8). This jus-tice demands respect, fairness, equity, and safety beyond the minimal-ist criteria expressed in contemporary social welfare and criminal jus-tice policies.

Social action is the central source of practice insight into domestic violence. Daily work of battered women/activists exposes violence as coercive control and articulates more clearly the impact of domestic terror on women, families, and communities.

In this anthology, we argue for the need to recognize differences and solidarities, to value local struggles and global alliances, to exam-ine intersections between the global and the local, and to accept the contradictions and differences among divergent groups and cul-tures. This requires a solidarity that both embraces and negotiates differences.

None are free until all are free. The voices in this anthology reflect the understanding that injustice against one group is connected to injustice against all. Of course, there are differences. But there are convergences as well. The goal—to end domestic violence against all women, not simply to provide programs for particular women—means making life better for individual women within the context of making life better for all women.

Christina Pratt and Natalie J. Sokoloff

NOTES

1. Russo (2001) addresses the exclusionary, limited, and sometimes dangerous politics of the mainstream feminist movement in the United States. The original radical feminist collectives "became hierarchical organizations with paid staff whose credentials were increasingly dependent upon professional degrees, and decreasingly related to first-hand knowledge of violence and grassroots activism in the community. . . . Many of these nonprofit organizations are not that different from mainstream social service agencies and increasingly they have become tied to state and national government policies and institutions" (p. 3).

2. Narayan (1997) makes clear that this issue of "dowry death" is a relatively recent phenomenon, since the 1970s, among the middle classes; it is not a part of the long-term history of Indian culture.

3. In a later publication, Ristock (2002) notes that the review of the literature reports that same-sex couple violence ranges between 17 and 58 percent.

REFERENCES

Crenshaw, Kimberlé. 1998. Intersectionality and identity politics: Learning from violence against women of color. In Mary L. Shanley and Uma Narayan, eds., *Reconstructing Political Theory: Feminist Perspectives.* University Park: Pennsylvania State University Press, 178–193.

Crites, Eric. 2000. When love hurts. *Out* (January): 88.

Crooms, Lisa. 1999. Using a multi-tiered analysis to reconceptualize gender-based violence against women as a matter of international human rights. *New England Law Review* 33(4): 881–906.

DaLuz, Carla. 1994. A legal and social comparison of heterosexual and same-sex domestic violence: Similar inadequacies in legal recognition and response. *Southern California Review of Law and Women's Studies* 4: 267–269.

Gibson, P. J. 2002. *How Shall We Lighten Their Loads?* New York: Gibson Poetry Mini Series.

Kanuer, Nancy J. 1999. Same-sex domestic violence: Claiming a domestic sphere while risking negative stereotypes. *Temple University Political and Civil Rights Law Review* 8(2): 325–350.

Karmen, Andrew. 2003. Women victims of crime. In Barbara Raffel Price and Natalie J. Sokoloff, eds., *The Criminal Justice System and Women: Offenders, Prisoners, Victims, and Workers.* 3d ed. New York: McGraw-Hill, 289–301.

Koyama, Emi. 2001. Toward a harm reduction approach in survivor advocacy. *Survivor Project Newsletter.* Available at: http://eminism.org/readings/harmreduction.html.

Mutua, Makau. 2001. Savages, victims, and saviors: The metaphor of human rights. *Harvard International Law Journal* 42: 201–245.

Narayan, Uma. 1997. Death by culture. In *Dislocating Cultures.* New York: Routledge, 81–117.

[NCAVP] National Coalition of Anti-Violence Project. 1998. *Report on Lesbian, Gay, Transgendered, and Bisexual (LGTB) Domestic Violence.* New York City Edition.

Ptacek, James. 1999. *Battered Women in the Courtroom: The Power of Judicial Responses.* Boston: Northeastern University Press.

Raphael, Jody, and Richard Tolman. 1997. *Trapped by Poverty, Trapped by Abuse.* Chicago: Taylor Institute.

Razack, Sherene. 1994. What is to be gained by looking white people in the eye? Culture, race, and gender in cases of sexual violence. *Signs* 19(4): 894–923.

Ristock, Janice. 2002. *No More Secrets: Violence in Lesbian Relationships.* New York: Routledge.

Rosaldo, Renato. 1993. *Culture and Truth: The Remaking of Social Analysis.* Boston: Beacon.

Russo, Ann. 2001. *Taking Back Our Lives: A Call to Action for the Feminist Movement.* New York: Routledge.

———. 1991. We cannot live without our lives: White women, antiracism, and feminism. In Chandra Talpade Mohanty, Ann Russo, and Lourdes Torres, eds., *Third World Women and the Politics of Feminism.* Bloomington: Indiana University Press.

Volpp, Leti. 2000. Blaming culture for bad behavior. *Yale Journal of Law and the Humanities* 12: 89–116.

———. 2001. Feminism versus multiculturalism. *Columbia Law Review* 101: 1181–1218.

Williams, Patricia J. 1997. *Seeing a Color-blind Future: The Paradox of Race.* New York: Farrar, Straus & Giroux.

Young, Jock. 1999. *The Exclusive Society: Social Exclusion, Crime and Difference in Late Modernity.* London: Sage.

CHAPTER **2**

MICHELE BOGRAD

Strengthening Domestic Violence Theories

Intersections of Race, Class, Sexual Orientation, and Gender

———————— ABSTRACT ————————

Based on the pioneering work of Kimberlé Crenshaw (1994), Michele Bograd introduces the reader to the theoretical concept of "intersectionality" to help explain the reality of battered women who simultaneously experience diverse oppressions including, but not limited to, gender violence. The traditional feminist perspective viewed gender as the primary source of women's oppression. Unlike this earlier explanatory model, Bograd underscores the fact that all women do not experience domestic violence equally or in the same way. Consequently, the inclusion of dimensions other than gender—race, class, sexual orientation, colonization, and nationality—strengthens theorizing on domestic violence.

Differences that exist among women have important consequences in terms of how they experience intimate partner violence, how others treat them, and how and whether escape and safety can be achieved. For example, some women of color do not want to involve the police when they are abused because they fear the historical and continuing maltreatment of men of color by the criminal justice system. Clearly, alternatives to the criminal justice system must be available to women of color if we hope to end domestic violence in communities of color (for examples, see Richie, chapter 4; B. Smith, chapter 19; T. West, chapter 20; and A. Smith, chapter 24).

Similarly, lesbian domestic violence can be rendered invisible when all perpetrators are referred to as male. Lesbian victims of domestic violence may consequently avoid agencies that do not explicitly promote services for lesbians.

This chapter raises some important issues. Bograd claims that the family lives of people of color, the poor, and lesbians and gays are marked by frequent disruptive intrusions by the state (see Josephson, chapter 7; Websdale, chapter 10; Coker, chapter 22). Given the fact that women from these marginalized groups may face violence in their homes, discrimination in the public domain, and brutality and insensitivity at the hands of law enforcement and other helping agencies, how can service providers address these women's multiple oppressions? How does an intersectional understanding of domestic violence allow for improved services for survivors/victims of domestic violence from different racial, ethnic, and socioeconomic backgrounds, colonial experiences, and sexual orientations?

An erasure need not take place for us to be silenced. Tokenistic objectifying voyeuristic inclusion is at least as damaging as exclusion. We are as silenced when we appear in the margins as we are when we fail to appear at all. Crenshaw, 1993, p. 116

This [chapter offers] a beginning effort to describe how . . . thinking [and practice] . . . on domestic violence can be strengthened by explicit inclusion of dimensions such as race, class, sexual orientation, and the gendered asymmetry of domestic violence.

Given the purposes of this chapter, the literature review is illustrative rather than comprehensive. The goals of this chapter are theoretical: to introduce the voices and experiences of individuals not widely represented . . . while describing omissions and their possible consequences for theory and practice. This task is simplified through the concept of intersectionality.

INTERSECTIONALITY

Through development of the concept of intersectionality, Crenshaw (1992, 1993, 1994) proposes that domestic violence is but one form of oppression and social control. We exist in social contexts created by the intersections of systems of power (for example, race, class, gender, and sexual orientation) and oppression (prejudice, class stratification, gender inequality, and heterosexist bias). In practice, social dimensions are not merely abstract descriptions as they are suffused with evaluations that have social consequences. For example, heterosexual and homosexual are formal ends of a continuum, but one end is hierarchically valued over the other. These systems are not mutually exclusive, static, or abstract. They operate independently or simultaneously, and the dynamics of each may exacerbate and compound the consequences of another.

In this framework, domestic violence is not a monolithic phenomenon. Intersectionalities color the meaning and nature of domestic violence, how it

This abridged version was originally published in *Journal of Marital and Family Therapy* 25, no. 3 (July 1999): 275–289. Reprinted by permission of the American Association for Marriage and Family Therapy; permission conveyed through Copyright Clearance Center, Inc.

is experienced by self and responded to by others, how personal and social consequences are represented, and how and whether escape and safety can be obtained. Sometimes, intersectionalities are patterned, as in the life of a poor immigrant woman of color. Sometimes the meaning of that pattern changes in different contexts, as when a light-skinned black middle-class professional is valued in his community but prejudicially treated in a court system as a batterer of color.

Most theories of domestic violence do not address such intersections. An implicit assumption of many theories and practices is that domestic violence poses a central threat to the boundaried, protected, inner space of the family. With the exception of gender inequality, other social dimensions usually are defined as stressors, rather than as key explanatory factors of the violence, and so primary attention is paid to intrapsychic, interpersonal, or intrafamilial dynamics. Almeida and coauthors (1994; chapter 18 of this volume) argue that the assumption of a boundaried, safe, domestic sphere reflects not some universal family reality but the conditions of white middle-class heterosexual families. In contrast, the family lives of people of color, poor, minority, or homosexual individuals are marked by frequent, disruptive intrusions of the state (Almeida, 1993). Here, domestic violence often occurs in the private context of a couple trying to build intimacy while experiencing racist, heterosexist, or classist discrimination, which often takes the form of actual violence in the public domain.

From this perspective, intersectionality suggests that no dimension, such as gender inequality, is privileged as an explanatory construct of domestic violence, and gender inequality itself is modified by its intersection with other systems of power and oppression. So, for example, while all men who batter exercise some form of patriarchal control, men's relationships to patriarchy differ in patterned ways depending on where they are socially located. While all women are vulnerable to battering, a battered woman may judge herself and be judged by others differently if she is white or black, poor or wealthy, a prostitute or a housewife, a citizen or an undocumented immigrant.

The Socially Structured Invisibility of Certain Victims

A basic question . . . is: who are the victims of domestic violence? Evidence of the consequences of intersectionality is immediately visible through examination of the statistics on domestic violence.

RACE AND ETHNICITY.   Although race is a standard factor examined in national surveys on domestic violence, most of the minority research is on black or Latino populations (Hampton and Gelles, 1994; Kaufman Kantor et al., 1994; Neff et al., 1995; Straus and Smith, 1990). Little is known about the experiences of battered individuals in many minority or marginalized communities (Carrillo and Tello, 1998). Current research on race can be problematic: diverse ethnic groups are often collapsed into a single category, such as Asians, or the patterns of a single group, such as Mexican Americans, are overgeneralized to all Hispanics (Campbell et al., 1997). Because of this, "[d]ata on partner violence among minority populations are so incomplete that they preclude meaningful generalizations" (Koss et al., 1994, p. 60). Research suggests that the meaning of domestic violence may differ across racial or ethnic lines, that predictors of husband violence differ among ethnic groups, and that racial differences disappear when other factors, primarily socioeconomic status, are controlled (Browne, 1995; Cervantes and Cervantes, 1993; Feldman and Ridley, 1995; Holtzworth-Munroe et al., 1997; Straus and Smith, 1990).

SOCIAL CLASS.   Research data suggest that social class is inversely related to the severity of violence, although domestic violence occurs across all classes (Holtzworth-Munroe et al., 1997). However, although class is a standard dimension of most research, "inquiries into the prevalence of violence in the lives of poor women and children remained startlingly absent" (Browne and Bassuk, 1997, p. 261), as in the lives of non-English speakers, the hospitalized or institutionalized, the disabled, the differently acculturated, rural dwellers, and the incarcerated (Browne, 1995; Gondolf, 1997; National Research Council, 1996). Browne and Bassuk found that high levels of assault and injury characterized their sample of homeless and poor-housed women (one-third of whom had been severely physically assaulted by their current or most recent partners), that lack of economic resources seriously compromised the women's ability to alter their environments, and that "across the lifespan, the majority of these young mothers had experienced only brief—if any—periods of safety" (1997, p. 275). Race, gender, violence, and class here intersect: in 1993, over one-third of all woman-headed families lived in poverty, and over half of those were Black and Hispanic (Browne and Bassuk, 1997).

GAY AND LESBIAN BATTERING.   Invisibility and lack of information also shroud gay and lesbian battering, even though conservative estimates suggest that half a million gay men are battered annually (Island and Letellier, 1991) and that the prevalence and severity of lesbian battering are comparable to that of heterosexual relationships (Coleman, 1997; Leeder, 1994; Lobel, 1986; Renzetti, 1992). There are few or no available statistics on the intersections of homosexuality, domestic violence, race, and class.

GENDER ASYMMETRY AND DOMESTIC VIOLENCE.   The invisibility of victims results not only from silence but also from assuming no differences across victims and perpetrators. Although most therapists acknowledge that, in heterosexual relationships, men have a greater capacity to injure women, controversy remains in the field about whether there is a fundamental asymmetry between men and women who are violent. However, research suggests that the sociopsychological contexts of the use of violence, its meanings, and its interactional and psychological consequences are gender specific. For example, men are more likely to use severely violent tactics, less likely to be injured, and less likely to be intimidated by their partner's violence (Cantos et al., 1994; Cascardi and Vivian, 1995; Dobash et al., 1992; Langhinrichsen-Rohling et al., 1995). While men and women alike employ violence to express anger, release tension, or force communication, women tend to use violence for self-defense, escape, and retaliation, while men employ violence for purposes of dominance, coercion, control of partner's behavior, protecting self-image, and punishment (Cascardi et al., 1992; Dobash et al., 1992; Hamberger et al., 1997; Saunders, 1988; Stets and Straus, 1990). Examining victims of husband abuse and wife abuse, Christian, O'Leary, and Vivian (1994) found that victimized wives reported more negative impact and more frequent and severe injuries than did victimized husbands, and female perpetrators experience more depression than male perpetrators (Vivian and Malone, 1996). Vivian and Langhinrichsen-Rohling (1994) suggest that highly victimized wives tend to be more unilaterally victimized than highly victimized husbands. Different patterns describe male and female batterers and their spouses (Hamberger, 1997). For example, over two-thirds of women arrested for battering their husbands were in relationships with husbands who initiated assaults more than 50 percent of the time (Hamberger and Potente, 1997). Patterns of homicide are gendered (Browne, 1994; Browne and Williams, 1993).

Research on severely violent men suggests that "[o]nly husband violence produces fear in the partner. It is largely this difference that accounts for the unique ability of husbands to use violence as a means of psychological and social control" (Jacobson et al., 1994, p. 986). In couples where the man has been quite violent, wives are verbally aggressive in reactions to husbands' violent behaviors, while husbands are violent in response to a variety of nonviolent wife behaviors; gender differences, in effect, exist in verbal arguments (Jacobson et al., 1994); and "nothing the women did predicted the onset, offset, increase, or decrease of male violence" (Jacobson, 1994, p. 100) at the interactional level (Babcock et al., 1993; Cordova et al., 1993) or over the longitudinal course of violence in the marriage (Jacobson et al., 1996).

Care must be taken not to generalize from one population to others, since the chronicity, level, frequency, and types of violence may be important distinguishing factors among couples and their dynamics. . . .

STATISTICS AND SOCIAL VALUE.   Complicated reasons explain the lack of statistics on gender asymmetries in domestic violence and on diverse ethnic, racial, and sexual orientation groups—much less on a broad range of intersections. A primary reason is whether individuals have access to and seek legal or clinical remedies in the institutions that provide the database for much family violence research. But the lack of statistics is not neutral. The invisibility of certain populations reflects more their social importance in the eyes of the dominant culture than the absence of domestic violence in their midst. The lack of statistics is also not of minor consequence. These statistics are fundamental to the distribution of funds and the creation of social policy, which in turn shape the development of mental health [and criminal justice] initiatives, the availability of services, and the possibility of safety for disenfranchised populations.

Who the "Appropriate" Victims Are and the Denial of Victimization

. . . Do our theories . . . unintentionally force those whose experiences differ from the mainstream to the margins? . . . Can we be free from socially constructed stereotypes of racial and ethnic groups, or of who batters and who is battered? The intersection of race, class, sexual orientation, and gendered violence often influences whom therapists define as "real" or "appropriate" victims, which implicitly denies the victimization of others.

Definitions [of "real" or "appropriate" victims] also inform social policy and informal practices. First, victimization can be denied by rendering it invisible or undescribed. For example, in labeling all batterers "he" and all victims "she," lesbian and gay battering disappears (Letellier, 1994), as does husband abuse. Social action strategies often focus on white, middle-class women in efforts to challenge stereotypes of poor, minority, battered women. These strategies not only draw attention to the plight of all women but can unwittingly defocus concern from poor women of color who remain unseen or defined as dehumanized Other and undeserving of services (Crenshaw, 1994). In focusing on domestic violence within the socially legitimated form of marriage, silence exists concerning evidence that the prevalence of domestic violence is higher among cohabiting or unmarried couples (Browne, 1995; Browne and Williams, 1993; Holtzworth-Munroe et al., 1997).

Victimization can also be denied when social stereotypes are employed to neutralize or obscure the presence of human suffering (Schwartz and DeKeseredy, 1993). For example, gay men are often not diagnosed as battered because men are not defined as victims, because the gay relationship is judged as neither intimate nor legitimate, or because of assumptions that homosexual domestic violence is a fight between equals (Letellier, 1994). However, preconditions for defining violence as mutual include the equal size of the combatants, equal training and socialization in the use of violence, equal propensities to use violence, and equal ability to inflict pain and to instill fear. This suggests that the sociopsychological and temporal contexts of violence must be examined carefully, as a distinction must be drawn between "bidirectional" and "mutual" violence (Vivian and Langhinrichsen-Rohling, 1994). Stereotypes also deprive battered women of care, justice, and services. Women who fight back are often judged as undeserving of protection because they violate social definitions of the helpless or passive victim (Kanuha, 1996). Less empathy is afforded battered individuals who are prostitutes, substance abusers, incarcerated, or HIV positive (Richie, 1996). Typifications of the appropriate victim are codified in social policy: in some states, domestic violence legal statutes are written in language that ensures services and protection to heterosexual persons only.

Victimization is also denied when domestic violence is defined as culturally normal for groups different from the dominant white culture. Defining domestic violence as "culturally relative" minimizes the extent of domestic violence in white families; ignores the complexity of other cultures' values concerning respectful intimate relationships and conflict resolution (Fry and

Bjorkqist, 1997); trivializes the ongoing evolution of other cultures; may confuse cultural expectations with other social, psychological, or relational factors; and diverts attention from how oppressive cultural practices may rigidify in dangerous forms in a context of discrimination by our dominant culture (Cervantes and Cervantes, 1993; R. Almeida, personal communication). In an analysis of race and family violence, Hawkins (1987) examines the finding that black men who murdered their female partners received less punishment than white men. He argues that this reflects mainstream assumptions and practices about the normality and intractability of violence among poor black families, the devalued status of black life, and the perceived dispensibility of lower-class people of color. As Crenshaw writes in a quote relevant to the lives of many disenfranchised groups, "[e]ven when the facts of our stories are believed, myths and stereotypes about black women influence whether the insult and injury we have experienced is relevant or important" (1992, p. 1470).

Real World Consequences of Intersections and Domestic Violence

While discussion of intersectionality may seem abstract, it relates to real and life-threatening consequences, as the ramifications of social location reverberate through psyche, family relations, community support, and institutional response. The trauma of domestic violence is amplified by further victimization outside of the intimate relationship, as the psychological consequences of battering may be compounded by the "microaggressions" of racism, heterosexism, and classism in and out of the reference group (Hardy and Laszloffy, 1994; Hill and Rothblum, 1996; Kliman, 1994). Efforts to seek safety in the domestic sphere often entail profound social risks beyond retaliation by the batterer. Individuals may have internalized ideologies antithetical to disclosure of violence or to help seeking, such as a Vietnamese woman taught that saving face and family unity preempt individual safety (Lee, 1997) or a gay man who believes that his physical retaliation for his abuse makes him a batterer rather than a victim (Letellier, 1994). Since Jews tend to be seen as a model minority free from domestic violence, the Jewish battered woman may be constrained by her community from going public for fear of tarnishing the Jewish image and inviting anti-Semitism. Kosher shelters are rare, and, as she grapples with domestic violence itself, she must also decide whether to honor herself as a woman deserving of safety or as a Jew, as if she is not both. Disenfranchised groups such as Palestinians in Israel (Haj-Yahia, 1996) or Catholics in protestant Northern Ireland (Cullen, 1997) may be forced to seek safety from individuals who are enemies in political contexts. As a member of several devalued identities, a dark-skinned, black, battered lesbian may fear that naming her battering will subject her partner to racist reaction from mainstream culture, confirm stereotypes of blacks as violent, expose her to skin-color biases within her social group, and alienate her from the community that provides protection from a prejudiced society (Comas-Diaz, 1994; Kanuha, 1990, 1996). Simultaneously, because of external and internalized homophobia in and out of her community, she may feel pressured to deny the abuse to protect herself from being outed, to maintain the image of a successful lesbian relationship, or to minimize significant risk because of the lack of legal protection around issues such as child custody (Almeida et al., 1994; Rasche, 1995; Robson, 1995).

Victims may sometimes employ certain intersections and social stereotypes to buy freedom. A gay man who is closeted or light-skinned individuals may be able to pass and so obtain services or privileges that would otherwise be denied them, but at the cost of defining themselves deceptively (Almeida, 1993; Almeida et al., 1994). Incarcerated, black, battered women are tutored not to mention their children in court to avoid confirming stereotypes of the welfare mother, while incarcerated, white, battered women are taught to weep about their children to capitalize on images of conventional white motherhood (Richie, 1996). In the service of safety, the conscious manipulation of images fundamentally estranges the battered individual from the truths and integrity of his or her life, a poignant repetition of dynamics often experienced with the batterer. As Crenshaw writes, "To speak, one risks the censure of one's closest allies. To remain silent renders one continually vulnerable to the kinds of abuse heaped upon people who have no voice" (1992, p. 1472).

Furthermore, when certain groups are not deemed "legitimate" victims, services may be scarce or nonexistent, and access to and the nature of available services may be strongly influenced by social location. There are few services for battered husbands, and responses to female heterosexual batterers may be insensitive to the woman's own victimization (Hamberger and Potente, 1997). Programs for gay and lesbian batterers and their victims may not be funded in some states because sodomy is still considered a crime, and public hate crimes, much less domestic violence, remain unaddressed. Many clinics do not have bilingual services, severely hindering non-English speaking women from obtaining safety. A disproportionate percentage of court-referred batterers in urban areas are men of color, but there are few racially specific programs with experienced minority staff (Gondolf, 1997; Williams, 1994; Williams and Becker, 1994). In efforts to bridge cultural gaps, minority clients are assigned to inexperienced paraprofessionals of their own culture, who themselves lack power in institutional systems.

Social service providers may respond to different kinds of victims in frankly punitive and discriminatory ways. While sometimes this is intentional, often service providers enact the prejudicial and unintended consequences of well-meaning social, legal, or clinical policy. Some battered women advocates report that judges have asked the batterer to interpret for the non-English speaking battered woman; more progressive judges have refused to proceed legally in the absence of a neutral interpreter, thus denying the women services. Battered women can lose custody of their children once it is learned that children have witnessed domestic violence, and children have been remanded to the care of the batterer, who appears to offer a more stable home than the mother does once she flees to shelter (Geffner, 1997). Some shelters do not permit adolescent boys. A battered woman must choose between not seeking safety for herself or leaving sons at home, opening herself to charges of desertion. Crenshaw (1994) describes how immigration policy unintentionally trapped battered women with their abusers when a ruling decreed that length of marriage was one of the preconditions for legal papers. After outcry from the battered women's movement, the policy was amended so that exceptions to cohabitation were made upon testimony by social service personnel. But because of cultural and linguistic barriers, women most vulnerable to abuse (such as immigrants or undocumented refugees) often lack access to services necessary for that protection.

The formal presence of legal and social services may not reflect their actual accessibility or availability, which may be a function of cultural, racial, or economic privilege. A review of 176 medical records of suicide attempts at a New Haven hospital found that one-third of all battered women attempted suicide on the same day that they visited the hospital with injuries attributable to the abuse; in contrast to nonbattered women who attempted suicide, the battered women were more often sent home and/or received no mental health referral (Stark and Flitcraft, 1995). The authors suggest that battering may be the single most important cause of female suicidality, especially among black or pregnant women, and that "the very problems caused by social inequalities based on sex, class, race, sexual orientation, or age propel women to seek help from a system that reproduces and stabilizes those inequalities" (Stark and Flitcraft, 1995, p. 58).

CONCLUDING COMMENTS

This chapter argues that domestic violence does not have a singular impact on all families. Not only do different patterns of domestic violence have different consequences for different families, [but] intersectionality [also] asks us to integrate into theory and practice the simple recognition that, for many families, domestic violence is not the only or primary violence shaping family life. Intersectionality also requires that we develop theories that go beyond single-factor descriptions of domestic violence, such as gender inequality. Intersectionalities and asymmetries are quite complex. Individuals may or may not differ on dimensions including but not limited to gender, size, class position, culture, disability, skin color, age, the use of violence, and race. These intersections shape meaning systems and concrete avenues for escape. As new theories and techniques are developed, models and practices must be anchored in descriptions of the contexts in which they were developed and the populations that they are intended to serve. Rather than assuming their universal applicability, it is crucial to ask: Who is excluded and why (Kanuha, 1996)?

. . . Criminal, psychodynamic, feminist, and interactional stances all give partial pictures of domestic violence. . . . From my perspective, one of the most critical and provocative areas for future theory development is the degree and nature of human choices in contexts of violence at the personal and social levels. Somewhat broadly speaking, two positions have typified popular ideas about responsibility and domestic violence: (1) both parties are equally responsible for the violence; and (2) the perpetrator is unilaterally responsible. Similarly, popular concepts of agency (acting for oneself) and victimization tend to assume that one capacity exists in the absence of the other (Kanuha, 1996). Again, approaches to personal choice in oppressive social contexts have tended to rest on the premise either that all individuals can create safe lives or that the disenfranchised are helpless victims in an unresponsive and unchanging hostile world. . . .

The framework of intersectionality can provide a map through this tangled context. Richie (1996) demonstrates the power of this approach through an analysis of how black and white incarcerated battered women have been differently entrapped in their lives. She examines intersectionality at the multiple and interactive levels of gender identity, family-of-origin experiences, internalized gender roles and expectations, intimate relationships, biased institutional practices, and hierarchical institutional arrangements based on race, class, and ethnicity. Her illuminating book demonstrates: (1) abuse is constituted, experienced, and addressed by intersectionalities that shape psyche, interpersonal experiences, family relationships, community location, and social value; (2) safety for individuals experiencing abuse from intimates is severely constrained, by social location and its impact on internal experience as well as on avenues of escape; (3) within a context of constraints, individuals make rational choices in efforts to optimize protection, although these choices may be compromising intrapsychically, interpersonally, and legally; (4) the actions of victims, maladaptive in some contexts, derive from resistance to domination and efforts to achieve autonomy; and (5) efforts to obtain help may be misread or punished in ways that confirm the ongoing abuse and reinforce behaviors, such as compliance and self-blame, that increase vulnerability to violence. . . .

It is incumbent upon those of us in the field who already have power and prestige to shoulder the responsibility of expanding our models, examining our practices, and giving voice to those who are silenced among us. This cannot be done without fear and discouragement: those of us who live in safe contexts experience the risks of speaking out, and we understand more clearly how in the lives of the invisible, the marginal, and the disenfranchised, every move toward safety entails risk and may intensify danger. It is sobering and distressing to realize that, although anti-domestic violence work has promoted greater safety for some individuals, many remain in a position as dangerous and vulnerable as ever (Richie, 1996). The words of the Jewish Talmud remind us, "It is not your job to finish the work, but you are not free to walk away from it."

NOTES

In great appreciation to Rhea Almeida, whose vision and courage inspire me, and to Jim Ptacek, who generously introduced me to a body of literature that expanded my way of thinking.

A portion of this paper was presented as a keynote address, "Revisiting dominant models of battering," at the annual Culture and Diversity Conference, sponsored by the Family Institute of New Jersey in 1994.

REFERENCES

Almeida, R. 1993. Unexamined assumptions and service delivery systems: Feminist theory and racial exclusions. *Journal of Feminist Family Therapy* 5: 3–23.

Almeida, R., and M. Bograd. 1991. Sponsorship: Men holding men accountable for domestic violence. In M. Bograd, ed., *Feminist Approaches for Treating Men in Family Therapy*. Binghamton, N.Y.: Haworth, 243–259.

Almeida, R., R. Woods, T. Messineo, R. Font, and C. Heer. 1994. Violence in the lives of the racially and sexually different: A public and private dilemma. In R. Almeida, ed., *Expansions of Feminist Family Theory through Diversity*. New York: Haworth Press, 99–126.

Babcock, J., J. Waltz, N. Jacobson, and J. Gottman. 1993. Power and violence: The relation between communication patterns, power discrepancies, and domestic violence. *Journal of Consulting and Clinical Psychology* 61: 40–50.

Bograd, M. 1982. Battered women, cultural myths, and clinical interventions: A feminist analysis. In New England Association for Women in Psychology, eds., *Current Feminist Issues in Psychotherapy*. New York: Haworth, 69–77.

———. 1984. Family systems approaches to wife battering: A feminist critique. *American Journal of Orthopsychiatry* 54: 558–568.

———. 1988. How battered women and abusive men account for domestic violence: Excuses, justifications or explanations? In G. Hotaling, D. Finkelhor, J. Kirkpatrick, and M. Straus, eds., *Coping with Family Violence: Research and Policy Perspectives*. Newbury Park, Calif.: Sage, 60–77.

———. 1990. Why we need gender to understand human violence. *Journal of Interpersonal Violence* 5: 132–135.

Browne, A. 1994. Violence against women by male partners: Prevalence outcomes and policy implications. *American Psychologist* 48: 1077–1087.

———. 1995. Reshaping the rhetoric: The nexus of violence, poverty, and minority status in the lives of women and children in the United States. *Georgetown Journal on Fighting Poverty* 3: 17–23.

Browne, A., and S. Bassuk. 1997. Intimate violence in the lives of homeless and poor housed women: Prevalence and patterns in an ethnically diverse sample. *American Journal of Orthopsychiatry* 67: 261–278.

Browne, A., and K. Williams. 1993. Gender, intimacy, and lethal violence: Trends from 1976 through 1987. *Gender and Society* 7: 78–98.

Campbell, D., B. Masaki, and S. Torres. 1997. "Water on the rock": Changing domestic violence perception in the African American, Asian American, and Latino communities. In E. Klein, J. Campbell, E. Soler, and M. Ghez, eds., *Ending Domestic Violence: Changing Public Perceptions/Halting the Epidemic*. Thousand Oaks, Calif.: Sage.

Cantos, A., P. Neidig, and K. O'Leary. 1994. Injuries of women and men in a treatment program for domestic violence. *Journal of Family Violence* 9: 113–124.

Carrillo, R., and J. Tello, eds. 1998. *Family Violence and Men of Color: Healing the Wounded Male Spirit*. New York: Springer.

Cascardi, M., J. Langhinrichsen, and D. Vivian. 1992. Marital aggression: Impact, injury, and health correlates for husbands and wives. *Archives of Internal Medicine* 152: 1178–1184.

Cascardi, M., and D. Vivian. 1995. Context for specific episodes of marital violence: Gender and severity of violence differences. *Journal of Family Violence* 10: 265–293.

Cervantes, N., and J. Cervantes. 1993. A multicultural perspective in the treatment of domestic violence. In M. Hansen and M. Harway, eds., *Battering and Family Therapy: A Feminist Perspective*. Newbury Park, Calif.: Sage, 156–174.

Christian, J., K. O'Leary, and D. Vivian. 1994. Depressive symptomatology in maritally discordant women and men: The role of individual and relationship variables. *Journal of Family Psychology* 8: 32–42.

Coleman, V. 1997. Lesbian battering: The relationship between personality and the perpetration of violence. In L. K. Hamberger and C. Renzetti, eds., *Domestic Partner Abuse*. New York: Springer, 77–101.

Comas-Diaz, L. 1994. LatiNegra: Mental health issues of African Latinas. In R. Almeida, ed., *Expansions of Feminist Family Theory through Diversity.* New York: Haworth, 35–74.

Cordova, J., N. Jacobson, J. Gottman, R. Rushe, and G. Cox. 1993. Negative reciprocity and communication in couples with a violent husband. *Journal of Abnormal Psychology* 102: 559–564.

Crenshaw, K. 1992. Race, gender, and sexual harassment. *Southern California Law Review* 65: 1467–1476.

———. 1993. Race, gender, and violence against women. In M. Minow, ed., *Family Matters: Readings on Family Lives and the Law.* New York: New Press, 230–232.

———. 1994. Mapping the margins: Intersectionality, identity politics, and violence against women of color. In M. Fineman and R. Mykitiuk, eds., *The Public Nature of Private Violence.* New York: Routledge, 93–118.

Cullen, K. 1997. Northern Ireland making up ground on domestic violence. *Boston Globe,* Oct. 25, A2.

Dobash, R. P., R. E. Dobash, M. Wilson, and M. Daly. 1992. The myth of sexual symmetry in marital violence. *Social Problems* 39: 71–91.

Feldman, C., and C. Ridley. 1995. The etiology and treatment of domestic violence between adult partners. *Clinical Psychology: Science and Practice* 2: 317–348.

Fry, D., and K. Bjorkqis. 1997. *Cultural Variation in Conflict Resolution: Alternatives to Violence.* Mahwah, N.J.: Lawrence Erlbaum.

Geffner, R. 1997. Family violence: Current issues, interventions, and research. In R. Geffner, S. Sorenson, and P. Lundberg-Love, eds., *Violence and Sexual Abuse at Home: Current Issues in Spousal Battering and Child Maltreatment.* New York: Haworth, 1–25.

Gondolf, E. 1997. Batterer programs: What we know and need to know. *Journal of Interpersonal Violence* 12: 83–98.

Haj-Yahia, M. 1996. Wife abuse in the Arab society in Israel: Challenges for future change. In J. Edleson and Z. Eisikovits, eds., *Future Interventions with Battered Women and Their Families.* Thousand Oaks, Calif.: Sage, 87–101.

Hamberger, K. 1997. Female offenders in domestic violence: A look at actions in their context. In R. Geffner, S. Sorenson, and P. Lundberg-Love, eds., *Violence and Sexual Abuse at Home: Current Issues in Spousal Battering and Child Maltreatment.* New York: Haworth, 117–119.

Hamberger, L. K., J. Lohr, D. Bonge, and D. Tolin. 1997. An empirical classification of motivations for domestic violence. *Violence Against Women* 3: 401–423.

Hamberger, L. K., and T. Potente. 1997. Counseling heterosexual women arrested for domestic violence: Implications for theory and practice. In L. K. Hamberger and C. Renzetti, eds., *Domestic Partner Abuse.* New York: Springer, 53–75.

Hampton, R., and R. Gelles. 1994. Violence toward Black women in a nationally representative sample of Black families. *Journal of Comparative Family Studies* 25: 105–119.

Hardy, K., and T. Laszloffy. 1994. Deconstructing race in family therapy. In R. Almeida, ed., *Expansions of Feminist Family Theory through Diversity.* New York: Haworth, 5–33.

Hawkins, D. 1987. Devalued lives and racial stereotypes: Ideological barriers to the prevention of family violence among blacks. In R. Hampton, ed., *Violence in the Black Family.* Lexington, Mass.: Lexington, 189–205.

Hill, M., and E. Rothblum, eds. 1996. *Classism and Feminist Therapy: Counting Costs.* New York: Haworth.

Holtzworth-Munroe, A., N. Smutzler, L. Bates. 1997. A brief review of the research on husband violence, part III: Sociodemographic factors, relationship factors, and differing consequences of husband and wife violence. *Aggression and Violent Behavior* 2: 285–307.

Island, D., and P. Letellier. 1991. *Men Who Beat the Men Who Love Them.* New York: Harrington Park.

Jacobson, N. 1994. Contextualism is dead: Long live contextualism. *Family Process* 33: 97–100.

Jacobson, N., J. Gottman, E. Gortner, S. Berns, and J. Shortt. 1996. Psychological factors in the longitudinal course of battering: When do the couples split up? When does the abuse decrease? *Violence and Victims* 11: 371–392.

Jacobson, N., J. Gottman, J. Waltz, R. Rushe, J. Babcock, and A. Holtzworth-Munroe. 1994. Affect, verbal content, and psychophysiology in the arguments of couples with a violent husband. *Journal of Consulting and Clinical Psychology* 62: 929–988.

Kanuha, V. 1990. Compounding the triple jeopardy: Battering in lesbian of color relationships. In L. Brown and M. Root, eds., *Diversity and Complexity in Feminist Therapy.* Binghamton, N.Y.: Harrington Park, 169–184.

———. 1996. Domestic violence, racism, and the battered women's movement in the United States. In J. Edleson and Z. Eisikovits, eds., *Future Interventions with Battered Women and Their Families.* Thousand Oaks, Calif.: Sage, 34–50.

Kaufman Kantor, G., J. Jasinski, and E. Aldarondo. 1994. Sociocultural status and incidence of marital violence in Hispanic families. *Violence and Victims* 9: 207–222.

Kliman, J. 1994. The interweaving of gender, class, and race in family therapy. In M. Mirkin, ed., *Women in Context: Toward a Feminist Reconstruction of Psychotherapy.* New York: Guilford, 25–47.

Koss, M., L. Goodman, A. Browne, L. Fitzgerald, G. Puryear Keita, and N. Russo. 1994. *No Safe Haven: Male Violence against Women at Home, at Work, and in the Community.* Washington, D.C.: American Psychological Association.

Langhinrichsen-Rohling, J., P. Neidig, and G. Thorn. 1995. Violent marriages: Gender differences in levels of current violence and past abuse. *Journal of Family Violence* 10: 159–175.

Lee, E., ed. 1997. *Working with Asian Americans: A Guide for Clinicians.* New York: Guilford.

Leeder, E. 1994. *Treating Abuse in Families: A Feminist and Community Approach.* New York: Springer.

Letellier, P. 1994. Gay and bisexual domestic violence victimization: Challenges to feminist theory and responses to violence. In L. K. Hamberger and C. Renzetti, eds., *Domestic Partner Abuse.* New York: Springer, 1–21.

Lobel, K., ed. 1986. *Naming the Violence: Speaking Out about Lesbian Battering.* Seattle: Seal.

Margolin, G., and B. Burman. 1993. Wife abuse versus marital violence: Different terminologies, explanations, and solutions. *Clinical Psychology Review* 13: 58–73.

McNair, L., and H. Neville. 1996. African American women survivors of sexual assault: The intersection of race and class. In M. Hill and E. Rothblum, eds., *Classism and Feminist Therapy: Counting Costs.* New York: Haworth, 107–118.

National Research Council. 1996. *Understanding Violence against Women.* Washington, D.C.: National Academy.

Neff, J., B. Holamon, and T. Schluter. 1995. Spousal violence among Anglos, Blacks, and Mexican Americans: The role of demographic variables, psychosocial predictors, and alcohol consumption. *Journal of Family Violence* 10: 1–21.

Rasche, C. 1995. Minority women and domestic violence: The unique dilemmas of battered women of color. In B. Raffel Price and N. J. Sokoloff, eds., *The Criminal Justice System and Women: Offenders, Victims, and Workers.* 2d ed. New York: McGraw-Hill, 246–261.

Renzetti, C. 1992. *Violent Betrayal: Partner Abuse in Lesbian Relationships.* Newbury Park, Calif.: Sage.

Richie, B. E. 1996. *Compelled to Crime: The Gender Entrapment of Battered Black Women.* New York: Routledge.

Robson, R. 1995. Violence against lesbians. In B. Raffel Price and N. J. Sokoloff, eds., *The Criminal Justice System and Women: Offenders, Victims, and Workers.* 2d ed. New York: McGraw-Hill, 312–320.

Saunders, D. 1988. Wife abuse, husband abuse, or mutual combat? A feminist perspective on the empirical findings. In K. Yllo and M. Bograd, eds., *Feminist Perspectives on Wife Abuse.* Newbury Park, Calif.: Sage, 90–113.

Schwartz, M., and W. DeKeseredy. 1993. The return of the "battered husband syndrome" through the typification of women as violent. *Crime, Law, and Social Change* 20: 249–265.

Stark, E., and A. Flitcraft. 1988. Personal power and institutional victimization: Treating the dual trauma of woman battering. In F. Ochberg, ed., *Post-traumatic Therapy and Victims of Violence*. New York: Brunner/Mazel, 115–151.

———. 1995. Killing the beast within: Woman battering and female suicidality. *International Journal of Health Services* 25: 43–64.

Stets, J., and M. Straus. 1990. Gender differences in reporting marital violence and its medical and psychological consequences. In M. Straus and R. Gelles, eds., *Physical Violence in American Families: Risk Factors and Adaptations to Violence in 8,145 Families*. New Brunswick, N.J.: Transaction, 227–244.

Straus, M., and C. Smith. 1990. Violence in Hispanic families in the United States: Incidence rates and structural interpretations. In M. Straus and R. Gelles, eds., *Physical Violence in American Families: Risk Factors and Adaptations to Violence in 8,145 Families*. New Brunswick, N.J.: Transaction, 151–166.

Vivian D., and J. Langhinrichsen-Rohling. 1997. Are bi-directionally violent couples mutually victimized? A gender-sensitive comparison. In K. Hamberger and C. Renzetti, eds., *Domestic Partner Abuse*. New York: Springer, 23–52.

Vivian, D., and J. Malone. 1996. Relationship factors and depressive symptomatology associated with mild and severe husband-to-wife physical aggression. *Violence and Victims* 12: 1–19.

Williams, O. 1994. Group work with African American men who batter: Toward more ethnically sensitive practice. *Journal of Comparative Family Studies* 25: 91–103.

Williams, O., and R. Becker. 1994. Domestic partner abuse treatment programs and cultural competence: The results of a national survey. *Violence and Victims* 9: 287–295.

Yllo, K., and M. Bograd, eds. 1988. *Feminist Perspectives on Wife Abuse*. Newbury Park, Calif.: Sage.

CHAPTER 3

LETI VOLPP

Feminism versus Multiculturalism

────────────── ABSTRACT ──────────────

In chapter 1, Sokoloff and Dupont argued that feminist theory was crucial in challenging both individual and familial pathological models previously used to understand domestic violence. However, multicultural and multiracial scholars and activists question the universality of the feminist principle and claim that domestic violence neither affects all women the same nor treats gender inequality as the only or primary factor in determining domestic violence. But to posit feminism and multiculturalism as oppositional is to assume that minority women are victims of their culture, according to Leti Volpp. She illustrates in chapter 3 that this assumption is achieved by a strategy that constructs gender subordination as integral only to certain cultures—particularly non-Western cultures.

Elsewhere Volpp (2001) traces the origins of the ubiquitous claim that minority and Third World cultures are more subordinating (and more patriarchal) than culture in the West to the history of colonialism, the origins of liberalism, the negative and demeaning depictions of the feminist subject, and reliance on dualist thinking. In this chapter she shows how pitting feminism against multiculturalism has certain consequences. Most important, placing feminism and multiculturalism in opposition to one another obscures the influences that in fact shape cultural practices, hides the forces—most especially social structural, economic, and political—that affect women's lives, ignores the ways women exercise agency within patriarchy, and masks the level of violence within the United States.

As you read this chapter, consider how culture is often described as the "reason" for domestic violence among immigrant members of your own community. Likewise, elaborate the reasons typically given for why domestic violence is said to be "not as bad" in the United States. After you have read this chapter, consider how you might counter these arguments.

INTRODUCTION

The political theorist Susan Moller Okin recently posed the provocative question: Is multiculturalism bad for women?[1] According to Okin, until the past few decades minorities were expected to assimilate; now such assimilation is "considered oppressive." This, she suggests, raises a dilemma: What should be done when claims of minority cultures or religions contradict the norm of gender equality that is at least formally endorsed by liberal states?

After proffering examples of practices subordinating immigrant women and children,[2] Okin concludes that we have too quickly assumed that feminism and multiculturalism are both good things that are easily reconciled. Although she acknowledges that Western cultures still practice many forms of sex discrimination and notes that "virtually all" of the world's cultures have distinctly patriarchal pasts, she asserts that some cultures—mostly, she says, Western liberal cultures—"have departed far further from [these pasts] than others." Thus, Okin concludes: Female members of "a more patriarchal minority culture" may "be much better off if the culture into which they were born were either to become extinct (so that its members would become integrated into the less sexist surrounding culture)," or if the culture were encouraged to alter itself so as to reinforce the equality of women.[3]

But is Okin correct to posit multiculturalism and feminism as contradictory? I argue here that posing multiculturalism and feminism as oppositional results in a discourse of "feminism versus multiculturalism" that is premised on serious and fundamental logical flaws. Such a discourse relies upon a particular subject, the immigrant woman victim of minority culture.

An example might help to illustrate the troubling nature of this discourse. I was asked to present a talk at a certain university. As I described its contents and tentative title, "Feminism versus Multiculturalism," an organizer of the event suggested changing the name of the talk to "Is it OK to Beat My Wife?" She asserted that the graphic title would draw more people than my far more abstract and confusing title of "Feminism versus Multiculturalism." But why would this be so? The proposed title reinscribed certain popular assumptions: there exist communities of people who think it may be perfectly appropriate to engage in domestic violence; namely, those communities are too ignorant, too primitive, too backward to know any better. The revised title also pointed to the parameters of the debate that normally frames the discussion of feminism and multiculturalism: Group one argues it is OK for me to beat my wife, and the other group argues no, we have universal feminist principles that would never allow you to beat your wife.

The argument between these two positions has limited utility. What is much more interesting to explore is the question of why this binary discourse so frequently structures the parameters of the debate. My criticism of the structure of the discourse of feminism versus multiculturalism does not stem from the perspective of cultural relativism. Rather, it starts from the position that we can make normative choices, such as, it is never "OK to beat one's wife." The thrust of my argument is not that we ought to eliminate or dismiss feminist values but to suggest they broaden and shift when we examine immigrant and Third World women in a more accurate light. The first section of this chapter illustrates how feminist discourse on particular forms of patriarchy assumes that non-Western women are situated within cultural contexts that require their subordination, achieved by a discursive strategy that constructs gender subordination as integral to their culture. The second section addresses the problematic consequences of the feminism versus multiculturalism discourse. I conclude by suggesting the basis for a constructive dialogue beyond the discourse of feminism versus multiculturalism.

DEATH BY CULTURE

The discourse of feminism versus multiculturalism presumes that minority cultures are more patriarchal than Western liberal cultures.[4] Because representations of minority women are often interchanged with those of Third World women, the depiction of minority cultures in this discourse often reflects assumptions about Third World cultures. Thus, both immigrants of color and Third World communities are necessarily the subject here.[5] Since the vision of the suffering immigrant or Third World woman and the liberated Western one has so strong a hold on the American imagination, I attempt to demonstrate that the presumption of Western women's liberation depends upon the notion that immigrant and Third World communities are sites of aberrant violence. Part of the reason many believe the cultures of the Third World or immigrant communities are so much more sexist than Western ones is that incidents of sexual violence in the West are frequently thought to reflect the behavior of a few deviants—rather than a integral part of our culture. In contrast, incidents of violence in the Third World or immigrant communities are thought to characterize the cultures of entire nations.[6]

The specific case of dowry and domestic violence murders provides an example of this phenomenon. Dowry murders take place when a new wife is murdered, usually burned to death, in connection to escalating dowry demands. Dowry murders are thought of as a peculiar indicator of the extreme misogyny of India and are frequently confused with *sati,* the widow immolation supposedly justified by Hindu scripture that rarely takes place in contemporary India. An article in *The New Yorker* about arranged marriages in South Asian communities suggested that dowry murders are the cultural alternative to Western divorce—a way to exit relationships. Instead, the more appropriate analogy is to equate dowry murders with domestic violence, specifically, domestic violence murders in the United States.[7] The philosopher Uma Narayan has calculated that death by domestic violence in the United States is numerically as significant a social problem as dowry murders in India.[8] But only one is used as a signifier of cultural backwardness: "They burn their women there." As opposed to: "We shoot our women here." Yet domestic violence murders in the United States are just as much a part of American culture as dowry death is a part of Indian culture. In the words of Narayan, when "cultural explanations" are given for fatal forms of violence only in the Third World, the effect is to suggest that Third World women suffer "death by culture."[9]

We identify sexual violence in immigrants of color and Third World communities as cultural, while we fail to recognize the cultural aspects of sexual violence that affect mainstream white women. This is related to the general failure to look at the behavior of white persons as cultural,[10] while always ascribing the label of culture to the behavior of minority groups. Thus, to bolster her claim that we cannot embrace both feminism and the values of minority cultures, Okin invokes the recent Nebraska case of two sisters, thirteen and fourteen years of age, who were forced by their Iraqi immigrant father to marry, respectively, twenty-eight and thirty-four-year-old men.[11] But why are only the child marriages of nonwhite immigrants and not those of white Christian sects believed to threaten feminism? Okin fails to discuss another well-publicized case that took place in a splinter Mormon sect in Utah, where a sixteen-year-old was forced by her father to marry her thirty-two-year-old uncle, as his fifteenth wife.[12] The tension believed to exist between feminism and multiculturalism, or universalism and cultural relativism, not only relies upon the assumption that minority cultures are more sexist, but it also assumes that those cultures are frozen and static entities. Within these discourses, only minority cultures are considered traditional, made up of unchanging and longstanding practices that warrant submission to cultural dictates. There appears to be an inverse correlation between full citizenship and cultural visibility.[13] Those with power appear to have no culture; those without power are culturally endowed. Western subjects are defined by their abilities to make choices, in contrast to Third World subjects, who are defined by their group-based determinism. Because the Western definition of what makes one human depends on the notion of agency and the ability to make rational choices, to thrust some communities into a world where their actions are determined only by culture is deeply dehumanizing.[14]

These assumptions preclude the understanding that minority cultures, like all cultures, undergo constant transformation and reshaping.[15] Also forgotten about culture in this bifurcated discourse is that culture and claims to cultural identity are always contested within communities. The culture we experience within a particular community will be specific and affected by our age, gender, class, race, disability status, and sexual orientation. The "culture" Okin assumes must be recognized through multiculturalism is comprised primarily of male articulations of gender-subordinating values. But minority cultures encompass feminist values as well. Recognizing that feminism exists within communities of color breaks down the equation between multiculturalism and antifeminism inherent in the notion of "feminism versus multiculturalism."[16]

The manner in which culture is hybrid and contested is often not recognized. This happens, in part, because people within a community explain their actions through their cultural identity.[17] Alternatively, people outside a particular community may mistakenly identify certain practices within that community as the result of culture.[18] Often these two occur in tandem, so that, for example, a criminal defendant invokes "culture" as the explanation for his sex-subordinating behavior.[19] The media happily picks up the defendant's claim (or proffers its own claim) that this problematic behavior is a product of a certain community's culture because the idea that nonwhite others engage in primitive and misogynistic cultural practices fits preexisting conceptions. Unfortunately, the "culture" targeted in the feminism versus multiculturalism debate is often an indiscriminate lumping of self-serving claims by elites of communities or nations, the claims of anthropologists that are truly relativistic, and the claims of those who, from a feminist perspective, seek to explain that minority and Third World women should be understood as more than victims of their culture. This problematic aggregation of very different assertions about culture has forestalled constructive discussion.

HOW CULTURE OBSCURES

The excessive focus on minority and Third World sex-subordinating cultural practices has at least four detrimental effects. First, it obscures the degree to which many "Third World women's problems" are rooted in forces beyond one's individual community, so that structural forces shaping cultural practices are hidden from view. Second, it directs attention away from issues affecting women that are separate from what are considered sexist cultural practices. Third, by positioning "other" women as perennial victims, it denies their potential to be understood as emancipatory subjects. And fourth, it diverts one's gaze from the sexism indigenous to United States culture and politics.

First, in concealing structural forces that shape cultural practices, what can be erased are *forces that make culture.* Specific cultural practices are connected to forces that deny women economic and political agency. These forces include global inequalities; new articulations of patriarchies in specific regions that are, for example, the result of emerging religious fundamentalisms; the legacies of colonialism and racism;[20] and the flows of transnational capital.[21] Our culture is not constructed within "hermetically sealed" boxes that travel with us from cradle to grave.[22] While culture is often represented as the product of timeless ritual insular to particular communities, such forces profoundly shape culture.

For example, amid the concern about gender apartheid under the Taliban, there has been little focus on the relationship between the intensification of religious fundamentalism and geopolitical economics.[23] The United States gave aid to various mujahideen forces in Afghanistan to fight the Soviets, as religious fundamentalists were believed to be more effective anticommunist fighters. From these mujahideen groups, the Taliban emerged. The United States aided General Zia of Pakistan—whose government adopted the notorious hudood ordinances that among other provisions criminalized extramarital sex, so that women who accuse men of rape or become pregnant risk punishment for adultery—for the same reason. Feminists in the United States need to think critically about the relationship of this aid to states with policies inimical to women's concerns, instead of abstractly condemning Islam as the font of patriarchal oppression.[24]

The second point is that the extreme focus on what is commonly conceptualized as cultural violence or subordination makes it difficult to see *forces beyond culture.* There are other important social, political, and economic issues affecting women's lives other than the cultural practices that garner so much attention. Only certain problems receive coverage or generate concern, namely those used to illustrate the alien and bizarre oppression of women of color; for example, *sati,* dowry death, veiling, female genital surgeries, female infanticide, marriage by capture, purdah, polygamy, footbinding, and arranged marriages. Other problems—which raise questions of the role of dominant individuals, communities or states in shaping gendered subordination, such as ongoing relationships of economic inequity, development and community policies, exploitation by transnational corporations, or racism—are ignored.

As an illustration of this, Alice Walker and Pratibha Parmar made a film critical of female genital surgeries called "Warrior Marks," which has been the target of both intense praise and criticism. In the book they wrote to accompany the film, they recount an anecdote that describes a meeting between the filmmakers and a group of women who run a collective garden. Asked about their feelings about "female genital mutilation," the response of these women is to ask the "rich Americans" for a refrigerated truck they badly need to get their produce to outlying areas. The filmmakers, not perceiving themselves as rich by their own cultural standards, joke that they could probably only pay for one tire of such a truck. The women do not mention the truck again.[25]

The issues affecting immigrant or Third World women that receive the greatest attention are those that appear most easily identifiable as concerns to relatively privileged women in the West. These concerns include violations that threaten the freedom of movement, freedom of dress, freedom of bodily integrity, and freedom of control over one's sexuality, rather than violations of the right to shelter or basic sustenance. Thus, self-conception, in terms of what one fears for oneself, may play a role in generating concern about specific violations of women's rights.

The decision to focus on the issue of the cultural origins of violence against women rather than their material well-being also reflects a specific history. The focus on violence was a strategic one made by the "women's rights as human rights" movement.[26] Male violence against women was believed to be the universal experience that could tie together women across the world, in the face of North-South divides that presented too much conflict among women regarding the issue of transnational economic equality.[27] But the enormous success in creating a transnational "women's rights as human rights" movement that coalesced around the problem of the woman subject to male violence has served to shape what we envision as gender subordination. This strategy may contain limits as to what gains it can produce.[28]

The insistent focus on immigrant and Third World women as victims also leads many to deny the existence of *agency within patriarchy*, ignoring that these women are capable of emancipatory change on their own behalf. The binary assumption that women in the West have choice, and that those in immigrant and Third World contexts have none, in part reflects the limits of our language in describing choice: Either one is an agent, or one is a victim. This binary also reflects historical representations of the West as the site of rugged individualism, and the East as the repository of passivity and culture. Furthermore, it reflects a legacy of feminist politics and theory that presents Third World women as bound by culture, as described above. This conceptualization has bled into discourses that can deny the subjectivity of immigrant and Third World women, both in terms of feminist empowerment and in terms of their enjoyment of pleasure.

A fourth effect of this intense focus on other women's sexist cultures is that it *obscures violence at home,* namely specific practices of violence against women within the United States, including those perpetrated by the state. The First World is seldom depicted as a violator in discussions of women's international human rights. For example, the obsessive focus on Muslim countries' "Islamic" reservations to the Convention on the Elimination of All Forms of Discrimination Against Women (CEDAW) obscures the fact that the U.S. government has made reservations in the same manner.[29] Both Muslim countries and the United States have entered sweeping reservations based on domestic law to the principle of equality—Muslim countries on the basis of Islamic law, and the United States on the basis of the U.S. Constitution. Although the specific U.S. reservations made are not identical to those made by Muslim countries, it has been argued that through these reservations, both countries refuse to recognize international obligations due to a domestic "sacred law."[30]

Thus, the excessive focus on the cultural devaluing of "other" women obviates the fact of sexism among majority communities or in Western states. The negative image of "other" women is used as a mirror of progress, so comparisons between women, as opposed to comparisons with men, become the relevant frame of reference for the discussion of human rights. By accepting the contention that their lives are superior to the lives of women from "other" cultures, the attention of many women is diverted from the fact that they continue to be subordinate to men within their own culture.

CONCLUSION

It may be easier to think of problems affecting minority and Third World women as solely the product of religious fundamentalism and barbaric culture than to shift the focus of feminist practice in the manner I suggest above. It does not seem coincidental that the way some feminists have depicted gender oppression in immigrant and Third World communities reflects a failure to think about how women's concerns in those communities might implicate their own identities. There is a strong desire for innocence in many strands of feminist politics,[31] supported by the definition of the essential female identity of woman as victim of male violence. But an individual can be subordinated in one social relation and dominant in another.[32] There is an ease with which one slips into a position of subordination, for example, as a woman subject to the discrimination of the glass ceiling, without seeing how this very subordinate location may simultaneously reflect privilege, for example, as one that relies on domestic labor and child care by immigrant women of color. The missionary impulse to save immigrant and Third World women from their subordination is rarely turned to uplift domestic workers from exploitative work situations. The repressive cultures of these women, however, are a subject of feminist concerns. Thus, women in the First World can feel as though they have autonomy and agency in contrast to women in the Third World, at the same time that they feel victimized by men in the First, but will not conceptualize themselves to be agents of subordinating practices. This absolution of responsibility rests on the assumption that relations between women are presumed to be non-oppressive, whereas the bonds of race are presumed to oppress women of color. But this ignores the oppression of race and class among women. While to some extent this is understood in the context of the domestic politics of the United States, the innocence of the category "woman" seems to have been repackaged in the wrapping of the discourses of feminism versus multiculturalism and transnational women's rights.

A missionary feminist effort assuming West is Best incurs a defensive reaction from members of criticized communities and thus plays into the hands of those who choose to defend sex-subordinating behavior in the name of cultural nationalism. Resistance then becomes configured as the necessity of preserving culture, leading to the freezing of particular identifications of culture,[33] which keeps women trapped within the binary logic. Blanket condemnation is less helpful in engendering dialogue than acknowledging that women in the West also have a problem with epidemic rates of male violence against women, sharing strategies that have been attempted to combat this violence, and asking how immigrant and Third World women are grappling with violence in their own communities. And beyond the mere equivalence of universal gender subordination, we also must understand and confront how gender subordination is related to other forces of subordination—including racism and transnational economic inequalities. This means paying attention to context, to the meaning of difference, and to global disparities of power.

We cannot simply accept the terms on which many have structured this debate. The assertion that women of color are to be saved from deviant cultures that pose a threat to "our" ideas, and the frequent response that this statement is Eurocentric or imperialist, are both equally impoverished notions. We need to progress from accusation and rejoinder and move beyond the dialectic that emerges from this binary.

To be clear, the question of representation by feminists is far from the only problem plaguing women in immigrant or Third World communities.[34] I am not asking that we have no critical engagement with issues affecting communities in the Third World and communities of color. I call for, not a refusal to criticize, but a more careful examination of the particularity of women's relationships to specific patriarchies, as well as to geopolitical and economic relationships. Attempts to make normative judgments and to change behavior must be premised on the understanding that cultures, including our own, are patriarchal—not more or less, but differently, patriarchal. We also need to understand cultures as characterized by resistance to patriarchy. When we consider the role of culture, we must not prioritize culture merely because we respect group rights, but should look to particular contexts in order to determine whether justifications of practices based on culture should be supported or not, depending on what subordination is forwarded or combated through such support. Such an analysis would simultaneously recognize the disenfranchisement due to racism and the legacies of colonialism and recognize that this disenfranchisement has constructed the experiences of minority and Third World women in a way that is bound up with their experience of gender. We need to acknowledge both that culture shapes gender domination in any community, and that specific histories and present-day practices necessarily will mediate the understandings of what constitutes culture and how it shapes, hurts, or benefits our lives.

We must think creatively and in new ways. If, for example, we find that the transnational "women's rights as human rights" alliance constructed to combat male violence against women cannot translate into global organizing against structural economic inequalities, what then? This suggests that we think hard about new alliances or constructs that do not necessarily rely on the notion of the universal female subject.[35] We will not reach new possibilities through a simplistic and binary freezing of difference and sameness, of women vis-a-vis men, and of "us" vis-a-vis minority and Third World communities. We need to learn to see and challenge the multiple, overlapping, and discrete oppressions that occur both within and across white/Western and Third World/nonwhite communities. Otherwise, we remain mired in the battle of feminism versus multiculturalism.

NOTES

1. Susan Moller Okin, Is multiculturalism bad for women? In Joshua Cohen et al., eds., *Is Multiculturalism Bad for Women?* (Princeton: Princeton University Press, 1999), 7, 9.

2. As examples of the clash of cultures that can ensue, Okin proffers Muslim schoolchildren wearing head scarves, polygamous marriages in African immigrant communities, and female clitoridectomy in African immigrant communities in France and the United States. In addition, Okin describes four other types of cases in the United States: the marriages of children or marriages that are otherwise coerced (which she illustrates with an example involving Iraqi immigrants), Hmong marriage by capture, parent-child suicide by Japanese and Chinese immigrants, and "wife-murder by immigrants from Asian and Middle Eastern countries whose

wives have either committed adultery or treated their husbands in a servile way." Ibid., 18. I am not addressing here the claims Okin makes about religion. For a response to these claims, see Martha C. Nussbaum, A plea for difficulty, in *Is Multiculturalism Bad for Women?*, 105.

3. Okin, Is multiculturalism bad for women?, 23.

4. The "minority" cultures depicted in the feminism versus multiculturalism discourse are immigrant, and not African American, cultures.

5. I recognize that there are risks to replicating the blurring of minority immigrant and Third World communities as I do here by describing the fact of this fungibility.

6. I give other examples of this phenomenon that involve adolescent marriage in Leti Volpp, Blaming culture for bad behavior, *Yale Journal of Law and Humanities* 12(2000): 89, 91–93.

7. Uma Narayan, *Dislocating Cultures: Identities, Traditions, and Third-world Feminism* (New York: Routledge, 1997), 95.

8. Narayan's research was based upon FBI statistics that indicated roughly 1,400 U.S. women annually were victims of domestic violence murder—a number that appears to only reflect those cases yielding convictions. The Indian government statistic of roughly 5,000 annual dowry murders includes all deaths suspected to be dowry murders—including deaths that yielded no conviction. India's population is roughly four times that of the United States. Ibid., 99.

9. Ibid., 84.

10. In suggesting there is a general failure to look at the behavior of white persons as cultural, I am not asserting that actions are never attributed to whiteness, only that behavior is more often attributed solely to race when the actor is a person of color.

11. See Okin, Is multiculturalism bad for women?, 18.

12. For a discussion of this case, see Volpp, Blaming culture, 100–102.

13. See Renato Rosaldo, *Culture and Truth: The Remaking of Social Analysis* (Boston: Beacon Press, 1989), 198.

14. On the depoliticizing effects of cultural discourse, see Volpp, Blaming culture, 96–97.

15. See generally, Stuart Hall, Cultural identity and diaspora, in Jonathan Rutherford, ed., *Identity, Community, Culture, and Difference* (London: Lawrence and Wishart, 1990), 222, 225.

16. Whether it makes more sense to make the claim that gender subordination is not part of any culture, or that gender subordination is fundamental to every culture, depends on whether the speaker seeks, in the first instance, to make an aspirational claim, or in the second, to demonstrate the universality of this problem.

17. For example, heads of Asian nations claim that freedom and democracy are not "Asian values."

18. See, for example, the claim of Samuel Huntington that the East does not embrace Western political values where Huntington warns that this will engender a "clash-of-civilizations." Samuel Huntington, *The Clash of Civilizations and the Remaking of the World Order* (New York: Simon & Schuster, 1996), 20–21.

19. On "cultural defenses," see generally Leti Volpp, Talking "culture": Gender, race, nation, and the politics of multiculturalism, *Columbia Law Review* 96(1996): 1573, 1575–1576.

20. As an example of the role of colonialism, British colonial law destroyed communities that gave women more substantive rights than they were then given under colonial rule. See, for example, Sudhir Chandra, *Enslaved Daughters: Colonialism, Law and Women's Rights* (New Delhi, India: Vedams Books, 1998), 1–5, 15–41, 161.

21. For an example of scholarship that links these factors to the existence of female genital surgeries, see Inderpal Grewal and Caren Kaplan, Warrior marks: Global womanism's neocolonial discourse in a multicultural context, *Camera Obscura* 39(1996): 5, 7.

22. Rosaldo, *Culture and Truth*, 44.

23. For example, one could look to the Feminist Majority Foundation leaflet, "Stop Gender Apartheid in Afghanistan," which was widely circulated. While the leaflet does recognize

some geopolitical relationships—mentioning that Pakistan "supports the Taliban with military aid and personnel, Saudi Arabia provides the Taliban with financial support," and that the petroleum industry may provide financial support for the regime—there is not explanation of the U.S. role in training or funding the mujahideen who became the Taliban.

24. For this point, see Inderpal Grewal and Caren Kaplan, Introduction: Transnational feminist practices and questions of postmodernity, in Inderpal Grewal and Caren Kaplan, eds., *Scattered Hegemonies: Postmodernity and Transnational Feminist Practices* (Minneapolis: University of Minnesota Press, 1994), 1, 19–20.

25. For a description and analysis of this incident, see Grewal and Kaplan, Warrior marks, 21–22.

26. See Margaret E. Keck and Kathryn Sikkink, *Activists beyond Borders: Advocacy Networks in International Politics* (Ithaca: Cornell University Press, 1998), 165–198. They describe how the category "violence against women" was constructed through this transnational activism, by unifying many practices that in the early 1970s were not understood to be connected, such as "female genital mutilation" in Africa and domestic violence in the United States. See also 171–173.

27. Ibid.

28. In pointing this out, I in no way intend to diminish the tremendous accomplishments of the "women's rights as human rights" movement. The hope is that transnational networks formed around the question of violence can be deployed to support activism around other concerns and that these networks will not fragment around previous North-South divides.

29. See Ann Elizabeth Mayer, Reflections on the proposed United States reservations to CEDAW: Should the constitution be an obstacle to human rights? *Hastings Constitutional Law Quarterly* 23(1996): 727, 239, 800–805. See also Ann Elizabeth Mayer, Where does the U.S. stand on women's human rights? Reflections in a jaundiced eye, human rights postscript 18, *Human Rights Interest Newsletter* (for American Society of International Law) 6 (Winter 1996).

30. Mayer, Reflections, 738, 743.

31. I mean here by innocence both the desire for the category "women" to be pure and uncomplicated, unsullied by difference, as well as the desire not to be culpable for the disenfranchisement of others.

32. Sherene H. Razack, *Looking White People in the Eye: Gender, Race, and Culture in Courtrooms and Classrooms* (Toronto: University of Toronto Press, 1998), 13–14.

33. As an example of this, anticircumcision efforts by Protestant missionaries in the context of British colonial practices, such as land alienation, hut and poll taxes, and an oppressive labor recruiting system, led female circumcision to become associated with nationalism, independence, and anticolonial struggle. Keck and Sikkink, *Activists,* 69–70.

34. By asserting there are problems other than representation, I do not intend to indicate that representation and materiality are two separate constructs; I see them as imbricated in one another.

35. An example of a new alliance might be the organizing of women under the rubric of "single women," a concept that provides linkages between women who are divorced, deserted, widowed, and never married. This example makes apparent that the assumptions we may have about natural alliances, for example, between lesbians and gay men, and assumptions we may have about alliances that would seem to have no salience, for example, among single women of all sexual orientations, are dependent upon our local context.

CHAPTER **4**

BETH E. RICHIE

A Black Feminist Reflection on the Antiviolence Movement

─────────── ABSTRACT ───────────

B eth E. Richie is a scholar, activist, and member of Incite!—a national activist organization of women of color advancing a movement to end violence against women of color and their communities through direct action, critical dialogue, and community organizing; see chapter 8. Richie critiques the antiviolence movement for discounting race, nationality, class, and sexuality as significant constructs in the analysis of gender violence. Richie argues that violence against women of color is deeply embedded in issues of structural racism and poverty. She questions the "universal risk" theory of domestic violence. This rhetorical paradigm of risk rests on a "false sense of unity" that violence can happen to anyone regardless of their race/ethnicity, wealth, poverty, religion, sexuality, or social location.

Overreliance on the criminal justice system as a response to domestic violence must be reevaluated in terms of its impact on communities of color. Increased use of force, mass incarceration, and police brutality negatively impact on the safety of women of color. The failure of the mainstream anti-violence movement to address these realities contributes to a loss of its credibility and legitimacy in communities of color. Richie calls for new scholars and leadership—advocates and researchers—to create analyses and organizing strategies that acknowledge "the race of gender and the gender of race." As you read this chapter, consider the false assumptions of the "universal risk" theory characterizing domestic violence as a phenomenon that affects all women equally. How do law and policy shaped from experiences of a generic battered woman reflect the needs of economically advantaged women and white women over women of color and economically poor women?

What strategies do you envision that simultaneously place women of color at the center of domestic violence analysis, hold abusers accountable without mass incarceration, and resist racist characterizations of marginalized communities?

For the feminist-based anti-violence movement in the United States, the new millennium marks the beginning of an interesting third decade that poses particular challenges and concerns for Black feminist activists and our work to end violence against women. The mainstream social movement, organized over thirty years ago in response to an emerging consciousness that regarded gender violence as the most extreme point along the continuum of women's oppression, can claim numerous victories, such as legal reforms that protect the rights of battered women and sexual assault survivors, the criminalization of sexual harassment, and legislative moves to call attention to the needs of children who witness domestic violence. In addition, an elaborate apparatus of social services has been developed to provide emergency shelter, crisis intervention counseling, medical and legal advocacy, and ongoing assistance with housing, employment, and custody issues that women who experience violence need. African-American and other women of color have been at the forefront of the most radical dimensions of this work.

Services and support at the individual level have been matched with an array of academic and public policy initiatives designed to address violence against women. There are several journals dedicated to presenting new research and intervention discussions related to gender violence, and at least four university-based research centers focus on violence against women. Each year witnesses a growing number of national conferences, [dedicated to] issues related to gender violence, which attract a range of audiences, some with more activist goals and others with more professional and bureaucratic interests. The National Institute for Justice, the Centers for Disease Control, the Departments of Housing and Urban Development and Health and Human Services, and—paradoxically—even the Department of Defense have established federal initiatives that attempt to reduce or respond to violence against women in this country. The feminist campaign at the grassroots level has influenced government and public policy to a considerable extent, which has resulted in a significant influx of public funding for victim services, law enforcement training, and prevention services. This growth, due in no small part to the grassroots activism of survivors and other women, has deeply influenced the mainstream consciousness. Evidence of

From *Signs* 25, Issue 4 (2000): 1133–1137, © University of Chicago. Reprinted by permission of the author and University of Chicago Press.

this influence appears in several recent public awareness campaigns and opinion polls that suggest that tolerance for gender-based violence has decreased significantly in the past ten years. Feminist activism has paid off; we have witnessed a considerable shift in public consciousness with regard to the problem of violence against women.

Arguably, a critical dimension of the public awareness campaign that has led to this expansion in resources for, and the credibility of, the antiviolence movement in this country is the assertion that violence against women is a common experience, that any woman or child can be the victim of gender violence. In fact, many of us who do training, public speaking, teaching, and writing on violence against women traditionally begin our presentations by saying, "It can happen to anyone." This notion has become a powerful emblem of our rhetoric and, some would argue, the basis of our mainstream success. Indeed, many people in this country finally understand that they and their children, mothers, sisters, coworkers, and neighbors can be victimized by gender violence—that it really can happen to anyone.

The ideas that any woman can be a battered woman and that rape is every woman's problem were part of a strategic attempt by early activists to avoid individualizing the problem of domestic and sexual violence, to focus on the social dimensions of the problem of gender violence, and to resist the stigmatization of race and class commonly associated with mainstream responses to social problems. This approach was based not only on the empirical data available at the time but also on the lived experiences of most women who—at many points in our lives—change our behavior to minimize our risk of assault. This generalized construction helped to foster an analysis of women's vulnerability as both profound and persistent, rather than as particular to any racial/ethnic community, socioeconomic position, religious group, or station in life. As a result—from college campuses to private corporations, from public housing complexes to elite suburban communities, and in all manner of religious institutions—progress has been made in increasing awareness that violence against women is an important social problem that requires a broad-based social response.

And yet, as a Black feminist activist committed to ending violence against women, something seems terribly wrong with this construction at this point in time, something that leaves many African-American women and other women of color still unsafe and renders our communities for the most part disconnected from the mainstream antiviolence movement. I would even argue that the notion that every woman is at risk—one of the hallmarks of our movement's rhetorical paradigm—is in fact a dangerous one in that it has structured a national advocacy response based on a false sense of unity around the experience of gender oppression. For, as the epistemological foundation of the anti-violence movement was institutionalized, the assumption of "everywoman" fell into the vacuum created by a white feminist analysis that did not very successfully incorporate an analysis of race and class.

In the end, the assumed race and class neutrality of gender violence led to the erasure of low-income women and women of color from the dominant view. I contend that this erasure, in turn, seriously compromised the trangressive and transformative potential of the anti-violence movement's potentially radical critique of various forms of social domination. It divorced racism from sexism, for example, and invited a discourse regarding gender violence without attention to the class dimensions of patriarchy and white domination in this country.

Put another way, when the national dialogue on violence against women became legitimized and institutionalized, the notion that "It could happen to anyone" meant that "It could happen to those in power." Subsequently, the ones who mattered most in society got the most visibility and the most public sympathy; those with power are the ones whose needs are taken most seriously. When mainstream attention to the needs of victims and survivors was gradually integrated into the public realm of social service and legal protection and became visible in research studies, "everywoman" became a white middle-class woman who could turn to a private therapist, a doctor, a police officer, or a law to protect her from abuse. She consumed the greater proportion of attention in the literature, intervention strategies were based on her needs, she was featured in public awareness campaigns, and she was represented by national leaders on the issue of violence against women.

So what began as an attempt to avoid stereotyping and stigma has resulted in exactly that which was seen early in the anti-violence movement as a threat to the essential values of inclusion, equality, and anti-oppression work. The consequence of this paradigmatic problem is that victimization of women of color in low-income communities is invisible to the mainstream public, at best. Worse yet, when poor African-American, Latina, Native American women and other women of color are victimized, the problem is cast as something other than a case of gender violence.

Similarly, scholarship and activism around racial/ethnic and class oppression often ignore gender as an essential variable. This argument is supported by the growing body of research on women who use drugs, women in prison, women who live in dangerous low-income neighborhoods, lesbians of color, or young women who are involved with street gangs. Where women and girls are included in these studies or activist campaigns, they are seen as "special cases" within those populations rather than as women per se. Gender is not considered a central, defining part of their identity, and their experiences are subsumed by other master categories, typically race and class. They are essentially de-gendered, which renders them without access to claims of gender oppression and outside the category of individuals at risk of gender violence.

It is here, at a critical crossroads, that I ponder my work in the anti-violence movement as a Black feminist activist and academic. From here I offer critical observations and make recommendations for the future. First, it seems that to continue to ignore the race and class dimensions of gender oppression will seriously jeopardize the viability and legitimacy of the anti-violence movement in this country, a dangerous development for women of color in low-income communities, who are most likely to be in both dangerous intimate relationships and dangerous social positions. The overreliance on simplistic analyses (as in the case of "everywoman") has significant consequences for the potential for radical social change. I suggest that we revisit our analytic frame and develop a much more complex and contextualized analysis of gender violence, one rooted in an understanding of the historical and contemporary social processes that have differentially affected women of color.

I argue for a reassessment of the responses that have been central to anti-violence work—in particular, the reliance on law enforcement as the principal provider of women's safety. For over a decade, women of color in the anti-violence movement have warned against investing too heavily in arrest, detention, and prosecution as responses to violence against women. Our warnings have been ignored, and the consequences have been serious: serious for the credibility of the anti-violence movement, serious for feminist organizing by women of color, and, most important, serious for women who experience gender violence but fall outside of the mainstream.

The concern with overreliance on law enforcement parallels a broader apprehension about the expansion of state power in the lives of poor women of color in this country. Just as the anti-violence movement is relying on legal and legislative strategies to criminalize gender violence, women in communities of color are experiencing the negative effects of conservative legislation regarding public assistance, affirmative action, and immigration. And, while the anti-violence movement is working to improve arrest policies, everyday safety in communities of color is being threatened by more aggressive policing, which has resulted in increased use of force, mass incarceration, and brutality. The conflict between the anti-violence movement's strategy and the experiences of low-income communities of color has seriously undermined our work as feminists of color fighting violence against women.

Obviously, leadership emerges as central to this dilemma. While there is a renewed call for unity and diversity from some corners of our movement, others (women of color who have dedicated years to this work) are appalled at the persistent whiteness of the nationally recognized leadership. As the bureaucratic and institutional apparatus of the anti-violence movement grows—bringing more funding, more recognition, and also more collaborations with partners who do not share our radical goals—there is little evidence of increasing racial/ethnic and class diversity. Despite some notable exceptions, the lack of women of color in leadership roles in anti-violence programs is startling and contrasts sharply with the rhetoric of inclusion, diversity, and commitment to anti-oppression work. While there may be structural excuses for this, the fact that so few national organizations (even feminist ones) have successfully promoted the leadership of women of color is almost a mockery of the values on which the movement was built. Given the similar invisibility of women of color as leaders in struggles for racial justice (again, with some exceptions), the situation can seem dire as we face the new millennium.

Yet, for better or worse, the solutions are not enigmatic; they exist within our core values and the principles on which the anti-violence movement was organized. Feminist women of color need to step forward as never before, re-claiming our place as leaders both in the anti-violence movement and in struggles for gender equality in our communities. The anti-violence move-ment needs only to acknowledge the contradictions between its rhetoric and practice and to deal honestly with the hypocrisy in its work. As members of a social justice movement committed to ending oppression, we must recon-sider the complexity of rendering justice by paying attention to specific vul-nerabilities of race and class. As we claim victories on some very important fronts, our understanding of gender oppression must be broadened to in-clude state-sanctioned abuse and mistreatment of women. If we are prepared to go there, then we can begin the millennium ready to face the really hard, radical work of ending violence against women—for each and any woman.

CHAPTER **5**

SHAMITA DAS DASGUPTA

Women's Realities

Defining Violence against Women by
Immigration, Race, and Class

——————————————— ABSTRACT ———————————————

S hamita Das Dasgupta provides the reader with a comprehensive overview of
the ways in which the many aspects of immigration—personal, institutional,
and cultural—impact battered women from diverse racial, ethnic, and class
backgrounds. Regional conflict, the opening of borders previously closed, persistent political and economic repression, and trends toward rapid globalization
influence high rates of migration worldwide. In 1990, the number of immigrants
to the United States surpassed 1.5 million. In 2000, the foreign-born population
in the United States reached nearly 10 percent of the total population (25.8 million or 9.7 percent). The U.S. Immigration and Naturalization Service estimates a
projected growth of 275,000 undocumented persons each year, based on a 1996
assessment of about 5 million undocumented immigrants residing in the United
States. Immigration is a significant force that state systems need to address.

In this chapter, Dasgupta reviews how migration heightens women's vulnerability. Domestic violence research has frequently ignored the impact of immigrant status and the role that anti-immigrant sentiment plays in law, policy, and
the provision of services to battered women.

Dasgupta explains that, despite the efforts of battered women's advocates,
discrimination remains a significant barrier in all spheres of society greatly affecting the lives of immigrant women, especially those experiencing domestic violence. She suggests that racial and ethnic stereotypes of immigrant women as
"deficient," "inferior," "exotic," or simply different further render them as the
"other," which allows society and its institutions to ignore their concerns and
needs.

Immigrant women seeking to leave abusive relationships face additional
hardships in a mainstream culture that is often hostile to both immigrants and
their cultures. In this process they are often degraded, defined as backward,
subservient, meekly accepting of male domination and patriarchy; immigrant

women are thus said to contribute to their own victimization. The women may also be pressured to hide the abuse from public knowledge in the name of protecting the fragile image of the immigrant community. These barriers make it extremely difficult for immigrant battered women to seek and receive the help that they need.

Given the personal, institutional, and cultural barriers that immigrant battered women face when trying to escape abusive relationships, what are some culturally competent ways to eliminate barriers? How does an understanding of the complexities and hierarchies of race, gender, class, language, and immigrant status influence legal and community remedies available to marginalized groups of battered immigrant women?

A CULTURE OF VIOLENCE

After heart-wrenching deliberations, Najma Sultana,[1] a Pakistani woman in New Jersey, decided to seek a temporary restraining order against her abusive spouse. This was not an easy decision for her. She was going against her family, which urged her be patient; her religion, which affirmed that virtuous women are always tolerant; her two children, who were crying for their father; her community, which sneered at women who invited outside interference into the family; and everything she had learned about marriage, love, and women's role in society. She was also working against her fear of being alone with meager resources in a foreign country. In retaliation, Najma's husband, much more conversant in the ways of this country, secured a restraining order against her. A few days later, when both appeared before their county's family court judge, there were no doubts that Najma was a battered woman and that her husband's claims were baseless. Yet the judge, who vacated both of their restraining orders, stated that such treatment of wives may be an accepted practice in the couple's native culture and that, therefore, the husband has probably acted in accordance with his cultural beliefs.[2]

On September 7, 1987, Jian Wan Chen's husband smashed her skull with a claw hammer after she allegedly admitted to having an affair. Chen's body was discovered by her teenage son in the family's Brooklyn apartment. In March, Brooklyn Supreme Court Justice Edward Pincus sentenced Jian's husband to five years probation on a reduced manslaughter charge. After hearing the testimony of a Hunter College anthropologist, the judge concluded that Dong Lu Chen, a recent immigrant, was driven to violence by traditional Chinese values about adultery and loss of manhood. (Jetter, 1989, p. 4)

These stories are only two examples of the brutal realities of immigrant women's lives. Although the United States takes pride in pioneering legislative and social policy changes in anti-domestic abuse work, many of its residents routinely fall through the cracks of a system that supposedly has been erected to protect victims. Because of the indefatigable efforts of women of color, the anti-domestic violence community has now come to a grudging recognition of the system's insensitivity to race and class. Such recognition is still not forthcoming, however, in regard to immigrant victims.[3] The majority of us refuse to acknowledge even the existence of battered immigrant women, let alone recognize the differences in their circumstances. This attitude of disregard is reflected in all spheres of society: the state constructs laws that generally are detrimental to the safety of immigrant battered women; the legal system does not know how to deal with them; battered women's agencies neglect to institute programs that address their specific needs; and citizen-neighbors pretend not to hear or understand shrieks ostensibly in foreign languages.

The term *immigrant* conjures up various images in our minds. Once, when I asked my class what they thought when they heard the term *immigrant,* a student replied that she generally thought this person could not speak English, had little education, was on welfare, behaved in "foreign ways," and most likely was an "illegal." Many other students nodded their agreement. When I announced to the class that I was an immigrant and then asked how they saw this description fitting me, most were aghast and assured me they did not think of me as an immigrant.

This episode in my class underscores the fact that "immigrant" has become a constructed, rather than a legal, category in this country. Whereas the legal definition demarcates individuals who have entered this country by obtaining certain types of permissions from the government, the socially constructed classification selects only a subgroup of this larger population. One's affluence, educational background, or length of residency has little relevance to this popular determination. To the general populace, an immigrant is an Asian or a Latino regardless of how many generations he or she has lived in this country. White Europeans are rarely viewed as immigrants, as are Africans and Caribbeans at times. Being weird, bizarre, and subnormal complete this picture of an immigrant.

Not only do immigrant women, especially immigrant women of color, chafe under this general perception, but their burden is further increased by being women in a patriarchal society and being women of color in a white supremacist country. As "foreign" women, they are viewed as backward, subservient, and quietly accepting of male domination and patriarchal control. This perception is prevalent even among battered women's advocates who are trained to be tolerant of differences. During a diversity training that I conducted for domestic violence intervention workers, advocates derisively discussed Asian women's passivity (expressed in terms such as "They tend to walk a few steps behind their men") and dependency traits of Latinas ("They will never go against their men").[4]

 Such attitudes emanate from, and in turn reinforce, the fundamental belief that women of "other" cultures are inferior to their American counterparts and perhaps contribute to their own victimization.[5] Such ethnocentrism contributes grievously to the culture of violence that surrounds immigrant women of color in the United States (for further discussion, see Omi and Winant, 1986). The Marriage Fraud Act of 1986 and its later amendments, the Welfare Reform Act of 1996, are but symptoms of this pervasive disposition of neglect and abuse that immigrant women suffer in U.S. society.[6] As long as we think of immigrant women as "other," as long as we believe that their understanding and awareness of domestic violence are substandard, we facilitate an atmosphere that steeps legislation, law enforcement, professional intervention, and community attitudes in violence toward them.

VIOLENCE IN "OTHER" WOMEN'S LIVES

Violence against women is a phenomenon that seems endemic in every society (Heise et al., 1994). Researchers and activists alike, however, generally emphasize the violence that is perpetrated by the individual: the husband, father, brother, or male relative physically chastising his wife, daughter, sister, or other woman in his family. Rarely are we aware of the abuse that occurs beyond this intimate circle. Needless to say, the individual abuser and the victim do not operate in a vacuum; rather, they are nested within the supportive circles of social institutions and culture (see figure 5.1).[7] Ubiquity of both institutions and culture encourages and maintains abuse and victimization at the individual level.

Although all women are victims of this nexus of culture, institutions, and the individual abuser, nowhere is this unholy alliance more distinct than in the

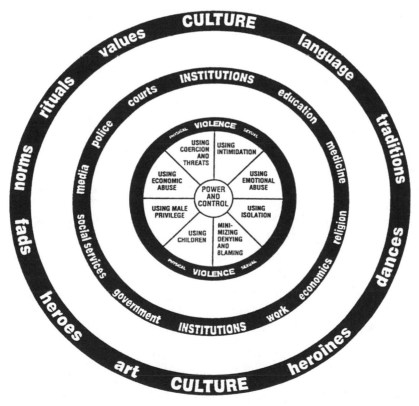

Figure 5.1   The Supportive Circles of Social Institutions and Culture. *Source:* Domestic Abuse Intervention Project, Duluth, Minn.

lives of battered immigrant women. Cultural symbols that abound in the United States promote not only male superiority and female subjection but also deficiency of immigrant women of color and their cultures to white people and their norms. The exoticizing of Latina and Asian women that occurs routinely in our cinema, art, theater, fashion, literature, and language further renders these women "other," a designation that allows us to ignore their concerns and needs at institutional levels. Our attitudinal unconcern gets translated into laws, court proceedings, police behavior, educational curricula, and social service practices. The following case exemplifies this victimization:

> Vanita's parents arranged her marriage with a scientist residing in the United States who had returned to India on a bride-finding mission. Only five days after their wedding, her husband left India to return to the United States. It took her nearly fifteen months to receive the appropriate visa to come to the United States. Almost as soon as they started living together, Vanita's husband began to demand total subordination from her. "You have to listen to me, I am your god," he would say. He restricted her food intake and dictated what she could wear, who she could talk to, and where she could go. He also sexually assaulted and battered her regularly.
>
> The abuse worsened when Vanita became pregnant. Her husband made it clear to Vanita that there was no escape. If she tried to leave him, he would withdraw his permanent residency sponsorship to make her undocumented and initiate deportation proceedings. She would not only have to go back to her parents in ignominy but also lose her newborn son in the process.
>
> Although she has now lived for more than two years in the United States, Vanita's husband has not mentioned anything about removal of her conditional status. Vanita now believes that her husband may not have filed the sponsorship papers at all. This means that she has been undocumented for the past two years. The implications fill Vanita with fear.

A cursory look at Vanita's situation leaves no doubt as to her husband's abusiveness. What may not be quite so apparent is the role that U.S. laws have played in her victimization. By the provisions of the Marriage Fraud Act, only a conditional residency status may be conferred on immigrant spouses of legal permanent residents (LPRs) or U.S. citizens (USCs). Because the process can be initiated only by the LPR/USC spouse, it is obvious how this law can become an instrument of torture in the hands of batterers. By entrusting the power to determine a woman's (il)legality of existence in the United States, the state has literally handed over to an abuser the power to control her. Vanita's husband has used this power cleverly by making her undocumented, which he knows will ensure her dependence on him (see Anderson, 1993).

The situation of Raco a battered immigrant woman from China, also reflects this use of power:

> [Raco] . . . was six months pregnant [last year] when, she said, her husband beat her so badly that she fled into the streets and asked the police for help. . . . Raco, who looks like a teen-ager, fears retaliation from her husband, a Chinese-American who courted her by mail for ten years. Three months after arriving in this country, Raco said, her husband began hitting her in the face because she could not get along with his parents, who lived with them in an apartment

in Manhattan. Then the beatings increased, she said, because she did not want a child right away.

"He threatened not to sponsor me for permanent residence if I didn't carry the pregnancy to term," she said through an interpreter. But the violence continued even after she agreed to have the baby. (Howe, 1991, p. 40)

When an immigrant woman gathers strength and resources to leave her abusive relationship, the disdain of the mainstream toward her culture adds further obstacles to the usual hurdles she would have faced at such a time. Once, I had gone to a New Jersey police station to pick up a South Asian battered woman who had been turned out of her home by her husband. She was a frightened young woman who did not speak much English and had already spent half a night on the streets in her nightgown. The two police officers had been extremely solicitous and had provided her with food and a warm jacket. When I entered the station, however, they let loose a tirade about my "culture" (I, too, am a South Asian woman) and the approval of battering in it. Although sorely tempted, I judiciously decided to refrain from reminding them of the statistics on the batterings, rapes, and murders of American women by their intimate partners. I wondered whether the police officers would have as easily held the U.S. culture responsible for these atrocities against women!

This quick allocation of blame to an immigrant's "culture" is not singular to these police officers. Many white Americans presume that "other" cultures, especially minority ones, are far more accepting of woman abuse than the U.S. culture.[8] The African American culture is a culture of violence, Latin cultures are based on brutal machismo that flourishes on wife abuse, and Asian cultures train women to pleasure their men to the point of disregarding abuse from them. I have lost count of how many times I have fielded questions on "bride burning" and "dowry-death" (even when the topic of discussion was other than violence against [South Asian] women) where the inquirer's intentions were to underscore the peculiarities of my "culture." When I have pointed out, albeit differences in weapons, that these are extreme cases of wife abuse similar to the ones in the United States, many have remained unconvinced, and some have even become angry. How dare I compare and suggest similarities between an "other" culture and the normative one! American mainstream society still likes to believe that woman abuse is limited to minority ethnic communities, lower socioeconomic strata, and individuals with dark skin colors. The impact of this public violence of imperialism, classism, and racism on battering in the private sphere of home and intimate relationships has, unfortunately, received little research attention (for a discussion on this issue, see Almeida et al., 1994).

A TRAP NAMED IMMIGRATION

The chronicle of peoples' immigration to the United States is neither benign nor fair. The policies that historically have regulated migration, especially from nations of color, were hardly based on generosity and a sense of justice. U.S. labor and foreign policies have always guided formations of U.S.

immigration policies. For example, in the early 1800s, when the United States needed cheap labor to build railroads, immigration from China was encouraged; during the 1960s, with a dearth of scientists and technically educated people in the country, immigration policies were relaxed for Asians so trained. Furthermore, until 1980, the admittance of refugees to the United States was regulated by U.S. foreign policy interests, which led to the conferring of refugee status mainly on individuals from communist countries. In fact, in a 1990 lawsuit, the Immigration and Naturalization Service (INS) admitted that most of the decisions it made were politically based.[9]

Although INS policies have been universally prohibitive regardless of gender, women have had to bear the brunt of its inherent misogyny, racism, and xenophobia. From the days of early Chinese immigration, U.S. migration policies have been expressly restrictive to women of color. Wives of men who were living and working in this country were routinely denied entry visas. Even today, it may take more than two years to secure entry visas for wives of legal permanent residents (LPRs) from Third World countries.

Much of this misogynist flavor is a result of the impact of the doctrine of coverture on U.S. immigration procedures.[10] The concept of "coverture" entails women's subordination to their husbands and the surrender of all legal power. Historically, married couples were not seen as equal partners; rather, the husband was considered to have legal authority over his wife and children. Impressions of coverture are still visible in the recent Marriage Fraud and Welfare Reform Acts. Although these acts are supposedly gender-blind, in actuality, men, the primary immigrants to this country, become vested with inordinate powers due to them. Thus, by the dictates of the Marriage Fraud Act, the man ends up being the sponsor and controller of his wife. The "deeming" provisions of the Welfare Reform Act bestow a man with the power to command his wife's eligibility for securing public assistance.[11]

Although the Welfare Reform Act and the 1990 and 1994 amendments to the Marriage Fraud Act have provided relief for battered women by specifying "battered women's waiver," "self-petitioning," and "deeming" exemptions, these have also created an atmosphere of unprecedented terror for battered women by reinforcing the imbalance of power already existing in such relationships (see Ho, 1990, 1991). Furthermore, these acts reveal a deep lack of understanding of the dynamics of intimate violence. For instance, one prerequisite of being exempted from deeming is that a battered woman leave her abusive relationship. Yet, practitioners in the field are aware that obtaining resources may be the precondition for leaving an abuser, rather than vice versa. Furthermore, these requirements lack the recognition of battered women's safety issues.[12]

IN THE NAME OF "CULTURE"

Activists and experts in the field of domestic violence now recognize that, rather than any particular apparent reason, gender inequality inherent to patriarchal social orders may be to blame for woman abuse in families (Bograd, 1988; Dobash and Dobash, 1979; Straus et al., 1980). When immigrants arrive on the shores of the United States, they do not leave behind the socialization and conditioning they have already received (Dasgupta and Warrier, 1996). The patriarchal cultural structures in which they grew up have already instructed the majority of immigrants in gender roles that are inherently inequitable. In the United States, however, complexities of the dynamics of abuse increase manifold.

Although most of us like to believe that migration to the United States automatically improves women's status and safety, it is not inevitably so. Immigration may help women escape from some structural oppressions of extended families; however, immigration may deprive them of protections that such family constellations offer. A case in point is the situation of South Asian immigrant women. In South Asia, abusive behavior of a man may, to some extent, be checked by other family members, neighbors, and in-laws. Community shame can also be evoked to restrain an abuser. Furthermore, additional safety valves—such as women's temporary escape to their natal families when conjugal tensions increase—have developed in social-familial structures to offer women some degree of security. These trips have been ritualized in the culture as women going to *maike* (mother's home) or *baaper bari* (father's home). Such routine ways of diffusing stress or curbing abusive behaviors are, of course, lost to the immigrants. Moreover, being in a country where a strong sense of family and community is absent may actually pressure immigrant women to cling more tenaciously to their nuclear families.

I have often been asked why a community, which can be oppressive at times, is so important to an immigrant woman. A community may not only meet the psychological needs of an immigrant woman but also may supply her a lifeline. "If she doesn't speak much English, can she leave her community? Where can she go? Especially if she has to worry about economic survival. If you ask 'your life or your community?' for some women it's the same thing" (Lum, 1988, p. 50). This need to belong to a community has, in fact, jeopardized the safety of many immigrant women within their families. A close look at the case of immigrant women in the South Asian community may illustrate this point more clearly.

The South Asian community visible in the United States today started forming in the early 1970s, after the passing of the Immigration and Naturalization Act of 1965, which eased immigration from Asia. At that time, INS policies selected specifically for a highly technologically oriented population and thus artificially created a homogenous Western-educated South Asian community in the United States. Because of its quick financial success, the community soon earned recognition as a "model minority" from the mainstream. Soon, South Asians embraced this heady reputation and became preoccupied with projecting a flawless image back to the mainstream. Maintenance of this unblemished facade required masking intracommunity problems, such as domestic violence, poverty, unemployment, intergenerational conflicts, drug abuse, and mental illness. Although all community members have suffered for this deceit, women have been particularly victimized by the ensuing repression. Women who have dared to speak out against spousal abuse or other intracommunity problems have been either perfunctorily exiled by community leaders or pressured to preserve their silence (Dasgupta and Dasgupta, 1997). Consequently, the majority of battered women who seek external help express great fear of being psychologically and literally banished from the communal fold.

> Steven Shon, a psychiatrist [said] . . . that, often, the battered Pacific Asian woman may perceive the risks of talking about her abuse as far out-weighing the advantages. If she reveals that she has been beaten—to the social worker, outside family member, her minister—the woman runs the serious risk of bringing a great deal of shame upon herself, her husband, and her family. In cultures where lineage, family integrity, and the strict adherence to role obligations are highly valued, "losing face," or bringing disgrace upon self and family, is no small matter. It can be the mark of grave *personal failure* for many Pacific Asian women. (Bush, 1982, p. 10)

In addition to this demand from the community to present the image of intact and cohesive families, most battered women feel obligated to protect their relatives who may be miles away in their natal countries. Women often believe that a divorce would bring such disgrace to their families that it may jeopardize the marital eligibility and social status of their siblings. Being distanced from day-to-day realities of their daughters' lives, the parents, too, may insist that the women try harder to please their husbands, to be more tolerant, or at least to postpone leaving until the children grow up. Furthermore, many battered immigrant women are afraid that separation or divorce might risk their own children's educational opportunities and future happiness, the very reasons they may have migrated to the United States in the first place.

> The woman believed that to be a "good mother" she had to keep the family intact. The presence of a father, abusive or not, was regarded as essential to the proper upbringing of children. Gurpreet, a mother of two who had suffered physical beatings for more than a decade, justified her decision to remain with her husband, "For children, I will sacrifice all. I can't take the children away from [their] security." Vimala echoed her sentiments. "Parents must be there for children always and do what is best. I have sacrificed my life this long and stayed in this abusive relationship for my children's sake." (Dasgupta and Warrier, 1996, p. 252)

ESCAPE FROM ALCATRAZ

The dream of living a safe and peaceful life may remain removed from a battered immigrant woman trapped in this labyrinth of individual, institutional, and cultural violence. Escaping the cycle of violence is an extraordinary feat for any woman, and for immigrant women the obstructions may seem insurmountable. Being an immigrant and a woman of color complicates and exaggerates the barriers to ending violence in one's life, as does socioeconomic status. The following lists are a summary of impediments within three categories that battered immigrant women may experience in the United States:[13]

Personal

- *Shame:* The feeling of shame may encompass losing face, disgracing affinal and natal families, failing in domestic and marital responsibilities, and letting one's community down. All of these may also span one's country of origin and the United States. This shame can be powerful enough to imprison a woman in her abusive relationship forever.
- *Fear:* This fear may involve leaving a familiar situation and moving into the unknown, as well as practical safety issues.
- *Financial impoverishment:* Financial insolvency is one of the most paralyzing problems that battered immigrant women encounter when leaving their abusers. Many are poor to begin with, and others may face uncommon poverty as a result of their migration. As a direct result of their abusers' efforts to isolate them, many immigrant women may also be unskilled in conducting financial transactions in this country. In many traditional societies, men tend to take care of the money even when the women work. Thus, many immigrant women sincerely assume that they cannot have access to their own earnings without their husbands' permission.
- *Lack of support system:* Most immigrant women have come to the United States alone, depending solely on their spouses. When experiencing abuse, they may not have any emotional or physical support and thus feel reluctant to leave the only haven they know.
- *Dearth of survival skills:* Many immigrant women may lack basic wherewithal to survive in this country. For example, they may not know how to drive a car, use public transportation, shop, use banks, use a telephone, find jobs, or read a newspaper.

Institutional

- *INS and public benefit policies:* As discussed above, stringent immigration and welfare policies restrict battered immigrant women's ability to leave abusive spouse-sponsors, as well as to find resources to ease separation.
- *Cultural insensitivity:* In the United States, battered women's flight from abusive situations is greatly facilitated by shelters, police (who often make the first contact), and other experts. At all these intervention points, immigrant women may meet with insensitive comments, derision, xenophobia, and racism. Many immigrant women who have taken the initial trouble to go to a shelter soon return to their abusers, swearing never to enter a shelter again. I have heard from battered women that they have been exhorted by shelter workers to "act as Americans, now that you are here" (see Metz, 1993) or quizzed scornfully about their "arranged marriages." All such experiences inhibit

battered immigrant women from accessing the few resources that may be available to them.

- *Financial requirements:* The initial legal procedures, as well as setting up a new household, may require finances that are beyond the reach of most immigrant women. In addition, many women may financially support their parents, siblings, or other relatives in the country of origin and believe that they should not cut off this support for their own "selfish" reasons.
- *Child custody issues:* Although gaining custody of children is an issue with which most battered women struggle, in the case of an immigrant woman it may gain added complexity. A child born in this country is a U.S. citizen by birth, yet his or her mother may be undocumented because of withdrawal of sponsorship. Thus, theoretically, a mother may be deported but the courts disallow her young children to accompany her. Recently, a New Jersey court rejected the request of an Indian mother to take her children to India for a visit; the judge believed that India would be an unsafe/unhealthy place for American children.
- *Language barrier:* An immigrant woman whose native tongue is other than English may face tremendous difficulties in communicating at all levels in the United States. Even when a woman is fluent in English, during crisis she may want to speak with someone in vernacular.

Cultural Ideology

- *Meaning of marriage:* Many traditional cultures find divorce unacceptable. Marriage is supposed to be permanent in many religions and cultures.
- *Keeping family intact:* Many immigrants who come from traditional societies strongly believe that children can be brought up well only in an intact family. Many regret that they cannot provide their children with an extended family, especially if they themselves grew up in one. Thus, breaking down a nuclear family further to a single-parent family may be unthinkable to many immigrant women.
- *Unacceptability of divorce:* In many societies, divorce is unacceptable, and a divorced woman is thought to be tainted. Many women prefer to live in abusive relationships than to tackle the stigma of divorce.
- *Acceptability of "fate":* Predestination of life events is a strong motif in many ancient cultures. Thus, a violent relation may be accepted as one's "fate" or reprisal for one's past misdeeds.
- *Tolerance toward abuser:* Beliefs such as that the batterer may have a change of heart and "a good woman can change a man" are common themes in all cultures. Cultures that overemphasize tolerance and compassion in women's gender role, as it happens in many traditional nations, may predispose women not to seek divorce or separation from their abusers (Dasgupta and Warrier, 1997).

One other issue that needs attention in this discussion of intimate violence from immigrant women's perspectives is a legal one: the issue of "cultural defense" in courts.[14] Should the U.S. justice system take the cultural background of an immigrant, both as defendant and as plaintiff, into account? Interestingly, the opposite camps of this argument are not necessarily populated by the same members all the time. Although most progressives support multiculturalism, they balk at decisions that allow domestic violence to go unabated (see examples at the beginning of the chapter). Opponents, supposedly conservatives and nativists, propose that an individual's cultural background should have no bearing in the court of law because "when in Rome" thinking prevails. Feminists and battered women's advocates have bounced uncomfortably between being for and being against this issue. Although most acknowledge that cultural socialization may significantly affect the way women perceive, respond to, express, and ameliorate abuse, they are not ready to allow the same latitude to batterers. On this point, they side with conservatives.

The reason for this vacillation is a fundamental misunderstanding of other cultures. In fact, I believe that many feminists and battered women's advocates secretly suffer from gnawing suspicions that "other" cultures do actually support woman abuse.[15] Thus, they are not sure where to land on this argument. The question that goes begging is, What do we mean by culture?

Regardless of its degree of traditionality, every culture has its historical, local, and individual variations. Although the structure of judicial arguments presumes a culture to be static and monolithic, it is hardly ever so. Furthermore, cultural motifs are rarely stripped of exceptions, contradictions, and complexities. For example, every culture has tenets that disenfranchise women, as well as empower them. Islamic cultures, which are considered to be misogynist, provide a wealth of rights for women, such as the right to education and occupation; to own and control property; to choose a marital partner; and to claim sexual satisfaction. Similarly, Hindu cultures encompass widow immolation, as well as the role of *Virangana* (woman warrior-leader). Judeo-Christian cultures also have comparable discrepancies. The key issue to scrutinize here is why beliefs and customs that oppress women gain recognition as "culture" in society and the aspects that enable women are doomed to obscurity. As advocates, feminists, and activists, it is incumbent on us to articulate this disparity and to query whose purpose such biases serve.

SO, IS THERE A SOLUTION?

Culture is an important part of immigrant women's lives and identities. To presume that immigrant women will shed their cultural backgrounds as easily as their residences is to disrespect women's very existence. If U.S. courts are to provide "individualized" and "particularized" justice, then they have to be sensitive to people's cultural backgrounds (Coleman, 1996). Yet, multiculturalism without an understanding of culture or cultural nuances is bound to yield decisions that reek of society's misogyny, xenophobia, ethnocentrism, and racism. Ignoring culture, of course, leads to a form of generic justice that has little resemblance to justice. The remedy may lie in a thorough campaign of education and training. Although the task seems daunting, it is not without precedence. Battered women and their advocates have already accomplished a similar crusade that has modified the country's attitude and awareness about battering.

The tripartite barriers that battered immigrant women face can hardly be demolished overnight. The complexities of the problem demand simultaneous attack and unraveling at various levels. Overwhelmed by the enormity of issues, many a sympathetic soul has wavered and asked the inevitable questions, Why do these women migrate? Why don't they stay in their own countries, or at least go back? The answers will not easily satisfy. Responses must include examination of individuals' aspirations to better themselves and to make better lives for their children. Simultaneously, we must dissect the colonial histories of immigrants and comprehend the issues that have driven them out of their native countries to seek stability elsewhere. The postcolonial devastation of economy, politics, safety, and families that many nations of color have experienced need to be in the foreground when we consider explanations of peoples' migrations.

In the meantime, as activists and academics focus on ending violence in all women's lives, we must understand and grasp the depths of battered immigrant women's despair. Only by carefully listening to the voices of immigrant women of color and by following their lead can we successfully change the lives of women who have suffered our negligence and ignorance for so long.

NOTES

1. Throughout this chapter, names of individuals have been changed to protect their privacy.

2. I became aware of this particular case in my work with Manavi as a battered women's advocate. Manavi, established in 1985, is the first organization that focuses on violence against South Asian women in the United States.

3. I use the term *immigrant,* not as a legal marker, but to indicate individuals who have chosen to enter this country as students, workers, spouses, refugees, and so on. I use it as a catch-all term that does not refer to one's legal status.

4. The stereotype of (ultra)feminine Asian women and their willing subjugation to men is common in the West. For a discussion of this issue, see Rivers (1990).

5. During a training session with domestic violence advocates, a participant commented that the helplessness and dependence that she has witnessed in South Asian women are unparalleled in other "American" women. I presented the idea that many immigrant battered women in this country face deep isolation. Separated from family, friends, and familiar surroundings, they may feel paralyzed to take action and thereby appear more helpless than they really are. Another participant caustically retorted that, although it may be true that an immigrant woman has no family here, no one had stopped her from making friends. She implied that many immigrant women—in this case, South Asians—choose to isolate themselves. The remark reeks of victim blaming, as well as a serious lack of understanding of the dynamics of battering.

6. The Marriage Fraud Act is a provision of the Immigration Reform and Control Act (IRCA) of 1986. It was passed to reduce immigration through fraudulent marriages to U.S. citizens (USCs) or legal permanent residents (LPRs). It imposes a two-year conditional residency requirement on an "alien spouse." The condition applies only to individuals who have been sponsored by their USC or LPR spouses. Conditional status is

removed by the INS after two years from the date of application for permanent residency of the "alien spouse" if the couple can prove "good faith" marriage. Provisions of the 1990 amendment and 1994 Violence Against Women Act (VAWA) rectify some problems of the 1986 act by allowing battered women to flee abusive spouses (known as battered women's waiver), apply for permanent residency without sponsorship (self-petitioning), and request stay of deportation in cases where the individual is undocumented (cancellation of removal). None of the procedures is user-friendly, however, to say the least.

The Welfare Reform Act of 1996 has many provisions that demonstrate little understanding of the dynamics of battering, and the act is especially insensitive to the realities of immigrant battered women.

7. This wheel of concentric circles was developed by the Domestic Abuse Intervention Project, 206 West Fourth Street, Duluth, MN 55806, (218) 772–2781. I thank them for allowing me to include it in this chapter.

8. I deliberately have *not* written "the U.S. culture" in quotation marks to draw attention to the contrast. Most Anglo Americans believe that only "others" have "cultures" (read: tribelike qualities, different/difference, weird), whereas they themselves are normative and, therefore, devoid of the limitations of culture.

9. In 1990, the U.S. Immigration and Naturalization Service settled a lawsuit erupting from its selective disapproval of asylum requests by agreeing to reconsider 200,000 asylum applications from Guatemala and El Salvador.

10. The principle of *coverture* is based on English common law.

11. *Deeming* ensures that the sponsor of an immigrant is held financially responsible for all public assistance sought by the latter. This, of course, places the husband (sponsor) of a battered woman (immigrant) in a position to control her access to medical help or other public benefits. Battered immigrant women who have not paid Social Security for at least forty quarters are exempt from deeming only if they are not residing with their batterers and their need for assistance is caused directly by the abuse.

12. More than 40 percent of battered women who are killed by their spouses meet with lethal abuse when they have left or are considering leaving their relationships. Severance of relationship may heighten risk of injury for battered women.

13. This section has been adapted from Dasgupta and Warrier (1997).

14. It is also disheartening to see that "cultural defense" and the affirming decisions occur mostly in cases of woman abuse. The implication of this bias is that courts are more likely to accept misogyny as integral to "other" cultures but not other criminal behavior. Such "culturally sensitive" decisions are less likely to come forth in cases of stranger rape, murder, and other crimes.

15. See Shon and Ja (1982) and Rimonte (1991). Unfortunately, most academic and popular inquiries tend to focus on those traditions in a culture that affirm women's low status and assume these to be fixed phenomena. Rather than challenge the validity of these customs as true cultural symbols, most investigators unquestioningly accept their authenticity. I dispute this basic assumption and believe that researchers need to ask the deeper question: Who are the beneficiaries of popularizing a particular culture from this angle?

REFERENCES

Almeida, R., R. Woods, T. Messino, R. J. Font, and C. Heer. 1994. Violence in the lives of the racially and sexually different: A public and private dilemma. *Journal of Feminist Family Therapy* 5(3/4): 99–126.

Anderson, M. J. 1993. A license to abuse: The impact of conditional status on female immigrants. *Yale Law Journal* 102: 1401–1430.

Bograd, M. 1988. Feminist perspectives on wife abuse: An introduction. In K. Yllo and M. Bograd, eds., *Feminist Perspectives on Wife Abuse*. Newbury Park, Calif.: Sage.

Bush, V. 1982. The silent crisis of Pacific Asian women. *Western States Shelter Network Review* 6(10, July/August).

Coleman, D. L. 1996. Individualizing justice through multiculturalism: The liberals. *Columbia Law Review* 96(June): 1093–1167.

Dasgupta, S. D., and S. Dasgupta. 1997. Women in exile: Gender relations in the Asian Indian community in the U.S. In S. Maira and R. Srikanth, eds., *Contours of the Heart: South Asians Map North America.* New York: Asian American Writers' Workshop.

Dasgupta, S. D., and S. Warrier. 1996. In the footsteps of "Arundhati": Asian Indian women's experience of domestic violence in the United States. *Violence Against Women* 2(3): 238–259.

———. 1997. Barriers to making change. *In Visible Terms: Domestic Violence in the Asian Indian Context.* 2d ed. Union, N.J.: Manavi.

Dobash, R. E., and R. P. Dobash. 1979. *Violence against Wives: A Case against the Patriarchy.* New York: Free Press.

Heise, L., J. Pitanguy, and A. Germain. 1994. *Violence against Women: The Hidden Burden* (World Bank Discussion Paper, No. 255). Washington, D.C.: World Bank.

Ho, V. 1990. Double jeopardy, double courage. *Ms.,* October, 46–48.

———. 1991. Illegal aliens fear INS more than fists of abusive spouses. *Arizona Republic, Valley and State,* August 31, pp. B1–B2.

Howe, M. 1991. Battered alien spouses find a way to escape an immigration trap. *New York Times, Metropolitan,* August 25, p. M1.

Jetter, A. 1989. Fear is legacy of wife killing in Chinatown: Battered Asians shocked by husband's probation. *New York Newsday,* November 26, p. 4.

Lum, J. 1988. Battered Asian women. *Rice* (March): 50–51.

Metz, H. 1993. Asian, American, feminist. *Progressive* 57(6, June): 16.

Omi, M., and H. Winant. 1986. *Racial Formation in the United States from the 1960s to the 1980s.* Boston: Routledge & Kegan Paul.

Rimonte, N. 1991. A question of culture: Cultural approval of violence against women in the Pacific-Asian community and the cultural defense. *Stanford Law Review,* 1311, 1317–1320.

Rivers, T. 1990. Oriental girls. *GQ* (British ed.), October, p. 158.

Shon, S. P., and D. Y. Ja. 1982. Asian families. In M. McGoldrick, J. K. Pearce, and J. Giordano, eds., *Ethnicity and Family Therapy.* New York: Guilford.

Straus, M. A., R. J. Gelles, and S. Steinmetz, eds. 1980. *Behind Closed Doors: Violence in the American Family.* Garden City, N.Y.: Doubleday.

CHAPTER 6

VALLI KALEI KANUHA

Compounding the Triple Jeopardy

Battering in Lesbian of Color Relationships

ABSTRACT

In this classic contribution to the domestic violence literature, Valli Kalei Kanuha raises the concerns of lesbian women of color who have experienced domestic violence. Because of their multiple disadvantages as women, people of color, and lesbians, they are triply oppressed. Through the combined effects of racism in feminist and lesbian communities, and sexism and internalized oppression in communities of color, these women are silenced and made invisible.

In lesbian communities, the voices and concerns of women of color have traditionally been excluded, ignored, or somehow diminished. There has also been a tendency to view homophobia as the primary or even sole oppression that they face. However, lesbians of color face multiple oppressions because of the impact of racism. Feminists of color have at times distanced themselves from lesbians of color to avoid homophobic retaliation. Lacking support from other women, lesbians of color face many hardships when abused by their partners. Lack of legal protections for lesbians may also lead to greater efforts to demonstrate togetherness, which makes separation more difficult.

Lesbians of color feel alternately accepted and rejected in their ethnic communities, given the pervasive nature of racism, sexism, and heterosexism. Because of this triple jeopardy, lesbians of color take enormous risks when seeking help. They may struggle with conflicting loyalties and fears of hostile responses from police and service providers. They also face the considerable hurdle of finding service providers who are both culturally competent to deal with issues facing lesbians of color and practically competent to act in the area of domestic violence. It thus becomes more crucial than ever for services to be explicitly welcoming to lesbians of color and to be prepared to work with both lesbian survivors and batterers in appropriate ways.

Violence between lesbian partners differs significantly from violence in heterosexual couples owing to the powerful effect of societal homophobia that silences and obstructs help-seeking. This chapter addresses the unique challenges faced by lesbians of color in violent relationships, given not only the interface between violence and homophobia but also racism and homophobia. Kanuha discusses community responses to lesbians of color and clinical issues presented in therapy by lesbians of color who are battered.

Although it was once assumed that battered women represented a small segment of society, it is now conservatively estimated that almost two million women in the United States are abused by their male partners every year (Walker, 1979). Owing to the courage of many battered women and the support of women's advocates who together have worked to end violence in the lives of men, women, and children, a growing network of shelter and non-shelter services as well as extensive legislative and judicial reform have begun to address this longstanding social problem (Schecter, 1982).

One aspect of domestic abuse that has been receiving more attention in women's communities and in programs that serve women and lesbians is violence in lesbian relationships. Due to societal heterosexism and its effect in closeting lesbians who are experiencing violence, research and analysis on this very complex issue are still in the formative stages (Paisley and Krulewitz, 1983). Most literature on lesbian battering, available through women's and gay/lesbian publications, is primarily anecdotal in nature (Irvine, 1984; Kaye, 1984; Klauda, 1984; Western Center on Domestic Violence, 1984). Meyer and Hunter (1983), Chapman and Karcher (1983), and Livingstone (1982) have conducted [early] surveys of lesbians who have been abused by their partners. These reports indicate some similarities between battered lesbians and their heterosexual counterparts, such as the range of violent behaviors exhibited by batterers and possible correlations between violence and chemical abuse. Kerry Lobel (1986) edited the [first] anthology on lesbian battering in which a number of lesbians describe their experiences of being battered, and workers in the battered women's movement offer theoretical analyses of violence in lesbian relationships.

Most of the discussion on lesbian battering cited above had been limited to perspectives by and of white lesbians. While battered lesbians share many of the same experiences that all battered women face, the *combination* of being women, battered, lesbians, and people of color creates significant barriers for lesbians of color in the writing and telling of their battering experiences. Because battered lesbians of color are women, they are the victims of societal sexism that pervades all women's lives. Because they are battered, they struggle to maintain a sense of their physical, emotional, and spiritual selves in the midst of daily terrorization. Because they are lesbians, they are a stigmatized, invisible group often silenced by powerful influences of homophobia. And

From *Diversity and Complexity in Feminist Therapy*, eds. Laura S. Brown and Maria P. P. Roots (Binghamton, N.Y.: Harrington Park/Haworth), 169–184. Copyright © 1990 by The Haworth Press, Inc. Reprinted by permission of the publisher.

finally, because they are women of color, they have survived a centuries-old legacy that oppresses them based solely on the color of their skin.

This chapter is based on extensive clinical experience with lesbian abusers and battered lesbians, but with more limited experience specifically with lesbians of color in battering relationships. I begin by exploring lesbians of color, the combined effect of racism in feminist and lesbian communities, and sexism and internalized oppression in communities of color in silencing these women. I also discuss the implications these issues have for the ways communities and lesbians of color address violence in their intimate relationships.

THE ROLE OF RACISM IN LESBIAN AND FEMINIST COMMUNITIES IN SILENCING LESBIANS OF COLOR

In the United States, the liberation movements of the 1960s and 1970s began a process whereby many oppressed classes of people, including lesbians and their communities, were empowered to live with strength and pride. Despite the continued and growing prevalence of societal homophobia in the 1980s [and beyond], lesbians have maintained their visibility through active participation in all aspects of society, including childbearing and childrearing, social and professional associations, political work, and the full range of activities that were once solely the public domain of heterosexuals.

While the development of a distinct lesbian culture is evidenced by music, art, literature, and research that is reflective of lesbian lifestyles, most of the cultural artifacts that supposedly represent "the" lesbian community have been white (Roberts, 1981; Vida, 1978). This predominantly white lesbian perspective has been broadened in the last few years through the articulate voices of many lesbians of color and others who have written and spoken about their experiences (Allen, 1981; Moraga and Anzaldúa, 1983; Noda et al., 1979; Smith, 1983; Walker, 1982).

The relative absence of lesbian of color perspectives in the definition of lesbian culture can be attributed primarily to racism that manifests itself in a variety of ways. First, lesbian communities are not immune from the pervasive effects of societal racism, which results in the exclusion of lesbian of color perspectives in social, political, economic, and academic institutions. This is not to imply that lesbians of color are not present in those institutions; rather, lesbians of color and their experiences are not actively and publicly included with the same frequency as white lesbians.

Another effect of racism is evidenced by the social-political analysis of many white lesbian-feminists that heterosexism is the primary or even sole oppression that lesbians must face. This assumption commonly manifests itself by either white lesbians' insistence that homophobia overrides racism as a system of oppression or by their completely overlooking the interface of racism with heterosexism (Combahee River Collective, 1986; Smith and Smith, 1983). While affirming the premise that discrimination against lesbians and gay men is based on heterosexism, the assumption that *all* lesbians suffer equally from homophobia denies the very existence of lesbians of color and other groups of lesbians that are affected by other forms of oppression, such as ageism, classism, anti-Semitism, and ableism.

Related to the above is the fact that the racial solidarity and privilege among white people, which maintains the institution of racism, allow most white lesbians the free choice to dissociate themselves on the basis of lesbian and gender identity from men (white and non-white), whether or not those lesbians define themselves as separatists. *Due to racism and the concomitant need for people of color to bond together against it, however, lesbians of color are inextricably bound to their racial-ethnic communities and therefore to men of color.* While such an alliance does not preclude many lesbians of color from strongly identifying with lesbian culture and white lesbians, the threat that accompanies this association cannot be overstated. For lesbians of color, embracing a lesbian lifestyle makes them vulnerable not only to homophobic attacks (which they share with white lesbians), but also to *homophobic and racist* attacks (which they do not share with white lesbians).

Throughout the history of the women's movement nationally and internationally, male-dominated institutions have viewed the development of feminism and feminists as threats to well-entrenched patriarchal systems. As a defensive tool of heterosexism, "lesbian baiting" has been devised to intimidate anyone who is committed to the elimination of sexism by the suggestion and/or accusation that "feminism equals lesbianism." The use of homophobia as a mechanism to maintain sexism is critical in our analysis of women's oppression (Clarke, 1983; Pharr, 1988). However, the power of the patriarchy is witnessed by the fact that the mainstream women's movement has, until recently, been remiss in its active support of lesbians and their contributions to feminism (Steinem, 1978).

What I would suggest, however, is that the fear and hatred manifested against lesbians by the patriarchy is of *white* lesbians, and not a fear of lesbians of color. If racism functions to oppress non-white people, it interacts with sexism to deny the mere existence of lesbians of color. On a "hierarchy of oppression," lesbians of color are not deemed a threat to the white, male, heterosexual system because by their identity as *non-white, female, and homosexual,* they hold very little power and status in society. As a result, heterosexism relegates lesbians of color to a much lower status than that of white lesbians, and works effectively to silence them not only in the larger society but in lesbian and feminist communities as well.

Many women of color have confronted white feminists about the subtle and direct manifestations of racism within feminist scholarship, analysis, and political organizing (Giddings, 1984; Hull et al., 1982; Smith, 1983; Yamada, 1983). . . . While Lorde (1983), Smith (1985), and other lesbian-feminists have affirmed the role of lesbians of color in the development and actualization of feminism, few white feminists have spoken with the same fervor on behalf of lesbians of color in the women's movement.

However, although lesbians of color in the early years of the movement almost came to expect that white feminists—lesbians or straight—would not acknowledge them, there had always been the hope that feminist women of color—many straight—would do so. Unfortunately, even as many feminist women of color began to advocate for a separate and distinct identity from the class of "all women," the celebration that has accompanied the affirmation of women of color has not always included their lesbian sisters (Clarke, 1983). Because the gains made by women of color on behalf of women *and* men of color have been hard sought against a racist, sexist society, the figurative (and literal) embracing of lesbians of color has been perceived as compromising those accomplishments due to the fear of homophobic retaliation upon already-vulnerable women of color. This is not an indictment of the politics of women of color, as we are well aware that some of our most articulate non-white feminists are open lesbians such as Audre Lorde, Barbara Smith, and Merle Woo. For these women and other lesbian-feminists of color, however, their analysis of racist oppression has *always* included its effect on both gay and straight, men and women of color, which has not been true with other people of color who call themselves feminist.

The preceding analysis demonstrates the power of racism, sexism, and all other forms of oppression to undermine what should be natural alliances among the dispossessed. For lesbians of color, racism has certainly compromised the affirmation that they have expected from the lesbian and feminist communities, both of which have purported to speak on behalf of women as an oppressed class. For lesbians of color in battering relationships, that lack of support only further jeopardizes their ability to seek sanctuary from their violent relationships.

INTERNALIZED OPPRESSION IN COMMUNITIES OF COLOR AND ITS IMPACT ON LESBIANS OF COLOR

For many lesbians of color, the contradiction in feeling both inherently safe yet afraid as lesbians in their ethnic communities is evidence of the pervasive nature of both racism and sexism. There are a number of ways that both forms of oppression work independently and simultaneously to silence lesbians of color.

As stated in the previous section, there is such a critical tie between homophobia and sexism that perhaps it is unnecessary to make any distinction between the two concepts. Hatred of feminists is hatred of women who are not dependent on maintaining the patriarchy—that is, women who do not *need* men for their daily survival, sense of self, or raison d'etre. By extension, lesbians are also perceived as living independent of the patriarchy, and therefore are also hated (whether or not they are "feminists"!).

In a complex combination of sexism and racism, many communities of color identify feminists and therefore lesbians as white phenomena (Clarke, 1983; Giddings, 1984; Smith, 1983). While partially justified in their attribution of the mainstream, political-social feminist movement to white women, it is more likely that the powerful influence of sexism in communities of color results in many people of color "blaming" the existence of lesbians on white feminism. In addition, by relegating lesbians to "whiteness," people of color can protect themselves from further racist attack by dissociating themselves from "social deviants" that not even white people want to have in their midst.

At the opposite end of the same racist-sexist continuum, however, the adherence by communities of color to sexism as a means of controlling women actually becomes a point of commonality with the oppressor—that is, white, male, heterosexual systems. The fact that sexism is an institution that both white and non-white communities support is one of the ways that men of color, in particular, can maintain a sense of equal status to white men. The existence of lesbians, however, is evidence that the patriarchy—whether in white or non-white communities—is fallible. That there would be a class of women who could exist and thrive independent of males implies that sexism as an institution has not been totally effective in controlling all women. When communities of color—that is, men of color—acknowledge the existence of lesbians of color, it forces them to acknowledge not only that they have failed to control "their" women but also that they are not as equal in status to white men as they believe. As a result, communities of color are reluctant to recognize, much less affirm, lesbians of color.

Another way that lesbians of color threaten their communities is the implication that they are obviously choosing same-sex bonding for reasons other than reproduction of the species. Especially for communities of color, this perception becomes interpreted as having serious ramifications for continuation of the race as many ethnic minority groups historically have been subject to mass genocide due to racism. Homophobic attitudes about lesbians of color become focused on the perceived betrayal that lesbians manifest by not adhering to heterosexism and therefore, to perpetuation of the race. It is clear, however, that the perpetuation of non-white races is not incumbent on heterosexual *or* lesbian women of color having babies. Rather, the fear of extinction, which is deeply rooted in racism, so threatens communities of color that sexism is used to scapegoat lesbians of color in order to defend against white, male, heterosexist institutions.

The dual effect of racism and sexism on lesbians of color is that they are silenced in the very communities which should be havens from the racist, sexist, classist institutions that comprise majority culture. If racism compromises the ability of lesbian communities to support lesbians of color, and if heterosexism in combination with racism prevents feminists from acknowledging their lesbian of color sisters, there is always the expectation of a historically viable, ethnic culture that lesbians of color can "belong" to. Unfortunately, the rejection of lesbians within their ethnic communities is very common (Hidalgo and Hidalgo-Christensen, 1979). As Smith and Smith (1983) so painfully state about homophobia in the Black community, "There's nothing to compare with how you feel when you're cut cold by your own" (p. 124).

In summary, it is somewhat surprising that lesbians of color would ever feel safe in the world. The triple jeopardy they face as women living in a sexist society, as lesbians living in a homophobic society, and as people of color living in a racist society forms a complex web of silence and vulnerability with very little protection. In this oftentimes isolated existence, lesbians of color in violent relationships are further hidden due to the shame and fear associated with domestic abuse.

COMMUNITY RESPONSE TO THE PROBLEM OF BATTERING IN LESBIAN OF COLOR RELATIONSHIPS

For all the reasons previously discussed, and perhaps others, lesbians of color take enormous risks to come out in lesbian, feminist, or ethnic communities, and of course, in society-at-large. For lesbians of color who are in violent relationships, "coming out" about being battered is further compromised owing to the history that many of the communities mentioned above have had in dealing with the problem of domestic abuse in male-female relationships. For battered lesbians of color, their abusers, and all of us who are concerned about violence and its relationship to complex institutions of oppression, we are facing the uncovering of another class of people whose presence blatantly reminds us of the continuing impact of sex, race, class, and other forms of oppression in our society.

The acknowledgment of lesbians of color in battering relationships will threaten many of us in the communities that we have so carefully nurtured over the years to protect us from those painful effects of oppression. For feminists, the existence of violence in lesbian of color relationships represents the failure of the mainstream women's movement to adequately address the interface of sexism, racism, violence, and homophobia. If the women's movement during the last twenty-five years has built a credible base against white, male patriarchy at least in part by minimizing non-white and lesbian perspectives in the early development of feminism, then acknowledging lesbians of color in battering relationships will surely shatter some of that stability.

For the battered women's movement, the discussion of violence in lesbian of color relationships raises the same questions and criticisms as did the acknowledgment of lesbian battering, about our heretofore well-founded analysis of sexism and male violence. In addition, the progressive sexual assault and battered women's movements will undoubtedly be forced to confront the role of lesbians of color—as clients, residents, participants, staff, and as leaders—in our local, state, and national programs.

For lesbian communities, the exclusion of lesbians of color in many of the lifestyle norms of lesbian culture becomes more apparent when battering in lesbian of color relationships is recognized. While domestic abuse is now more widely viewed as a social problem, it still has implications of deviancy not only for the victim ("Why does she stay?") but also for the abuser ("batterers are sick"). With the stigma of pathology that is still attached to homosexuality, as well as the . . . conservative backlash which has marked the U.S. social-political climate . . . since the 1980s, the fear of increased homophobic retaliation toward the entire lesbian and gay community will surely be intensified by lesbians of color coming out about their abusive relationships.

Finally, for communities of color that have built strong ties based on ethnic pride and solidarity against racism, dealing more openly with lesbians of
color in battering relationships will make those communities more vulnerable to racist attacks by attributing lesbian violence in non-white populations
to "problems in the race." In addition, those communities will have to confront the sexism and homophobia in their own neighborhoods that continue
to hurt lesbians of color who are their mothers, daughters, and sisters.

CLINICAL PERSPECTIVES ON BATTERING IN LESBIAN OF COLOR RELATIONSHIPS

There has not been adequate study or research on lesbian battering to make
definitive comparisons between lesbians and heterosexuals who experience
violence in their primary relationships. Many clinicians and battered women's
advocates who have worked with both populations suggest that there are
more similarities than differences (Hart, 1986; Kanuha, 1986; Klauda, 1984;
Lobel, 1986). Violence in lesbian of color relationships, however, has not
been examined in much depth owing to the small number of lesbians of color
that have sought assistance from domestic abuse and other service providers.

For many lesbians of color in violent relationships, the isolation connected with racism in both the lesbian and women's communities makes it
exceedingly difficult to seek help. While many lesbian communities are holding educational-discussion sessions on lesbian battering, along with offering
support groups for battered lesbians, outreach to lesbians of color has not
been very effective (Knollenberg et al., 1986). Not only are many lesbian
events targeted towards "the lesbian community" as one seemingly homogeneous group, but the small and connected nature of many predominantly
white lesbian communities often results in lesbians of color feeling uncomfortable and out of place. For lesbians of color who are in battering relationships, seeking help within the lesbian community for a problem as serious as
partner abuse is only another barrier to overcome.

While more therapists, battered women's programs, and gay/lesbian social service agencies are becoming sensitive to racism issues and working
with people of color, very few have received training about lesbian battering.
Even less have a solid base in both antiracist and lesbian violence work. Besides The Gay and Lesbian Anti-Violence Project in New York and individual
therapists and support groups scattered in different cities around the country
there are few programs that are specifically focused on services for either lesbian abusers or survivors (Lobel, 1986; NiCarthy et al., 1984; Porat, 1985).
One severely battered lesbian of color stated firmly that she would never go
to a battered women's shelter; however, she was unsure whether or not her
reluctance was due to racism or homophobia in that particular shelter. Other
lesbians of color have preferred to seek help from therapists—lesbian or
straight, white or non-white—due to the relative privacy and confidentiality
of the therapeutic context. In every case, however, the task for lesbians of

color in battering relationships always involves a troubling balancing act in finding providers who are not only sensitive to the issues of lesbians, women of color, and domestic abuse, but who are also competent. Most women are not faced with that same complexity of barriers when seeking help in dealing with battering relationships.

In the United States, the violence against women movement was begun [now more than three decades ago] largely through the efforts of white feminists. Recently, however, people of color have been challenged by feminist women of color to acknowledge the existence of domestic abuse in their communities (Burns, 1986; Richie, 1985). Due to institutionalized racism, most people of color are well aware of the subtle and direct repercussions that will result from their admission to the dominant white society that their communities are experiencing a serious social problem such as domestic violence. History has proven that whites need very little rational justification to label non-white people as pathologic, and thereby to maintain systematic oppression against them. Not only is there legitimate fear of punishment by white society for "just having a problem," but attempts to then seek help from the very systems that should be helping them (police, courts, hospitals) are often fraught with insensitivity, hostility, and incompetence (American Indian Women Against Domestic Violence, 1984; White, 1985; Zambrano, 1985).

If we consider the racist society in which we live, and place within it the heterosexist attitudes and practices of some communities of color, lesbians of color have good reason to believe that their ethnic communities will not provide them safety from the domestic violence they are experiencing. While escape from racism in society-at-large usually reinforces among people of color loyalty to one's ethnic community, the sense of belonging and protection for lesbians of color in battering relationships is usually compromised due to their sexual preference. In addition, many lesbians of color who are experiencing relationship violence express a need to protect both their communities and themselves from the retaliation of the dominant white and heterosexual society that would use lesbian battering to further stigmatize and oppress them.

In the final analysis, the conflicting loyalties to their community, to their relationships, and to themselves become so overwhelming that lesbians of color are oftentimes trapped into remaining in battering situations. Dealing with these conflicts by clearly delineating the multiple issues involved in "coming out" about being women of color, being lesbians, and experiencing violence, along with identifying appropriate responses to each of those situations would empower lesbians of color to alleviate the violence in their relationships.

A number of lesbians of color who have been in battering relationships with white women have suggested that the power issues inherent in biracial relationships had an effect on the violence with their partners. One battered lesbian of color stated that her partner, who was white, verbally abused her using racial epithets and negative racial stereotypes while also physically abusing her. Another woman of color described an S & M ritual based on a master-slave scenario with her white partner that eventually deteriorated into nonconsensual sexual and physical abuse.

Because there are no studies of the effects of racism on the dynamics of relationship violence (in either heterosexual or lesbian couples), we can only speculate on its impact and/or meaning. For white lesbians who are in battering relationships, the power implied in white privilege may manifest itself either by rationalizing the use of violence to control their partners or by justifying the battering by their partners who are women of color as an irrational attempt to "equalize" the relationship. For lesbians of color who are in battering relationships with white partners, one of the results of institutionalized racism could be a form of internalized oppression where violence is well understood as one of the behaviors that people of color are accustomed to experiencing. This is not to imply that lesbian relationships with/between women of color are more violence-prone; there is absolutely no evidence to support such a conclusion. Rather, lesbians of color who are in biracial relationships have often reported that the use of violence to control others is part and parcel of racism, and, therefore, is sometimes used to explain why one could batter, or be battered. In work with lesbians of color who are either abusers or survivors, [service workers] need to be aware of the possible effects that racism has on the dynamics of violence and control in intimate relationships.

Many of the public agencies that deal with domestic abuse—police, courts, social services—have notoriously poor training or sensitivity not only about women, but certainly about women of color and lesbians. The rampant heterosexism and racism of these key service providers in domestic abuse intervention always jeopardize women, but even more so women of color and lesbians. For lesbians of color in battering relationships, their legitimate fear of these systems cannot be underestimated. Many lesbians of color will refuse to call the police, obtain orders for protection, or press charges against their abusers due to the retaliation that they will have to endure by those agencies. It is important to understand the critical role of systems advocacy, in addition to supportive counseling when working with lesbians of color who are attempting to access these services. [Community services] must be careful and thorough in assessing the inherent dangers to lesbians of color who utilize traditional institutions that work with heterosexual battered women and should respect the choices that lesbians of color must make with regard to those systems.

Finally, the role of psychotherapy in the "treatment" of domestic abuse has received mixed reviews by many feminists due to the traditional tendency of the male-dominated mental health profession to blame women who are the victims of violence (Bograd, 1984; Schecter, 1982). . . . Training and monitoring of therapists who work in the area of domestic abuse has given therapy more credence as an option for battered women and their families (Edelson, 1984; Walker, 1984). However, there is still an absence of training on issues related to women of color, lesbians of color, and lesbian battering throughout the various mental health disciplines. Therapy for lesbians of color in battering relationships requires that the therapist not only be competent in evaluating the appropriateness of psychotherapy (vs. support, advocacy, or self-help), but that she have an understanding of all areas that affect the lives of lesbians of color, that is, racism, sexism, and domestic abuse. *reminded me of a turn about therapy for racism/race trauma*

CONCLUSION

The multiple issues that affect lesbians of color in violent relationships are complex, confusing, and always painful. Therapists working with lesbians of color must be able not only to acknowledge this myriad of issues but also, more important, to understand the interface between them. The isolation, silence, and fear that many lesbians of color must live with daily can only be broken through that acknowledgment and understanding. By continued research, analysis, and clinical observation, the feminist therapy profession can make significant contributions in ending violence in the lives of this vulnerable group of women.

REFERENCES

Allen, Paula Gunn. 1981. Beloved women: Lesbians in American Indian cultures. *Conditions: Seven,* 67–87.

American Indian Women Against Domestic Violence. 1984. Position paper. (Available from the Minnesota Coalition for Battered Women, 435 Aldine St., St. Paul, Minn. 55104).

Bograd, Michele. 1984. Family systems approaches to wife battering: A feminist critique. *Journal of Orthopsychiatry* 54: 558–568.

Burns, Maryviolet C. 1986. *The Speaking Profits Us: Violence in the Lives of Women of Color.* Seattle: Center for Prevention of Sexual and Domestic Violence.

Chapman, Marilyn, and Kim Karcher. 1983. Draft-support group summary. Paper.

Clarke, Cheryl. 1983. Lesbianism: An act of resistance. In Cherríe Moraga and Gloria Anzaldúa, eds., *This Bridge Called My Back: Writings by Radical Women of Color.* New York: Kitchen Table/Women of Color Press, 128–137.

Combahee River Collective Statement. 1986. New York: Kitchen Table/Women of Color Press.

Edleson, Jeffrey L. 1984. Working with men who batter. *Social Work* (May–June): 237–242.

Giddings, Paula. 1984. *Where and When I Enter: The Impact of Black Women on Race and Class in America.* New York: William Morrow.

Hart, Barbara. 1986. Lesbian battering: An examination. In Kerry Lobel, ed., *Naming the Violence: Speaking Out about Lesbian Battering.* Seattle: Seal Press, 173–189.

Hidalgo, Hilda, and Elia Hidalgo-Christensen. 1976. The Puerto Rican lesbian and the Puerto Rican community. *Journal of Homosexuality* 2: 109–121.

Hull, Gloria, Patricia Bell Scott, and Barbara Smith, eds. 1982. *All the Women Are White, All the Men Are Black, But Some of Us Are Brave: Black Women's Studies.* Old Westbury, N.Y.: The Feminist Press.

Irvine, Janice. 1984. Lesbian battering: The search for shelter. *Gay Community News,* January 14, pp. 13–17.

Kanuha, Valli. 1986. Violence in intimate lesbian relationships. Paper.

Kaye, Janet. 1984. Breaking the silence on lesbian battering. *Los Angeles Herald Examiner.*

Klauda, Ann. 1984. Violence in intimate lesbian relationships. *Equal Time,* May 16, pp. 1, 3.

Knollenberg, Sue, Brenda Douville, and Nancy Hammond. 1986. Community organizing: One community's approach. In Kerry Lobel, ed., *Naming the Violence: Speaking Out about Lesbian Battering.* Seattle: Seal Press, 98–102.

Livingstone, Betty. 1982. Domestic violence in the Madison lesbian community. Paper.

Lobel, Kerry, ed. 1986. *Naming the Violence: Speaking Out about Lesbian Battering.* Seattle: Seal Press.

Lorde, Audre. 1983. The master's tools will never dismantle the master's house. In Cherríe Moraga and Gloria Anzaldúa, eds., *This Bridge Called My Back: Writings by Radical Women of Color.* New York: Kitchen Table/Women of Color Press, 98–101.

Meyer, Pat, and Phoebe Hunter. 1983. Iowa City survey and results. Unpublished report. Iowa City, Iowa: Domestic Violence Project.

Moraga, Cherríe, and Gloria Anzaldúa, eds. 1983. *This Bridge Called My Back: Writings by Radical Women of Color.* New York: Kitchen Table/Women of Color Press.

NiCarthy, Ginny, Karen Merriam, and Sandra Coffman. 1984. *Talking It Out: A Guide to Groups for Abused Women.* Seattle: Seal Press.

Noda, Barbara, Kitty Tsui, and Z. Wong. 1979. Coming out: We are here in the Asian community: A dialogue with 3 Asian women. *Bridge: An Asian American Perspective* (Spring).

Paisley, Christine A, and Judith E. Krulewitz. 1983. Same-sex assault: Sexual and non-sexual violence within lesbian relationships. Paper presented at the National Conference of the Association for Women in Psychology, Seattle, Wash., March.

Pharr, Suzanne. 1988. Sexism and homophobia. Paper.

————. 1997. *Homophobia: A Weapon of Sexism.* Includes afterword and annotations. San Francisco: Chardon Press/Jossey Bass.

Porat, N., ed. 1985. Lesbian issue [Special issue]. *WCDV Review* 10(2). (Available from Western Center on Domestic Violence, 870 Market Street, San Francisco, Calif. 94102).

Richie, Beth E. 1985. Battered black women: A challenge to the black community. *The Black Scholar* 16(2): 40–44.

Roberts, J. R. 1981. *Black Lesbians: An Annotated Bibliography.* Tallahassee, Fla.: Naiad Press.

Schecter, Susan. 1982. *Women and Male Violence: The Visions and Struggles of the Battered Women's Movement.* Boston: South End Press.

Smith, Barbara, ed. 1983. *Home Girls: A Black Feminist Anthology.* New York: Kitchen Table/Women of Color Press.

————. 1985. Home truths on the contemporary Black feminist movement. *The Black Scholar* 16(2): 4–13.

Smith, Barbara, and Beverly Smith. 1983. Across the kitchen table: A sister-to-sister dialogue. In Cherríe Moraga and Gloria Anzaldúa, eds., *This Bridge Called My Back: Writings by Radical Women of Color.* New York: Kitchen Table/Women of Color Press, 113–127.

Steinem, Gloria. 1978. The politics of supporting lesbianism. In Virginia Vida, ed., *Our Right to Love: A Lesbian Resource Book.* Englewood Cliffs, N.J.: Prentice Hall, 267–269.

Vida, Virginia, ed. 1978. *Our Right to Love: A Lesbian Resource Book.* Englewood Cliffs, N.J.: Prentice Hall.

Walker, Alice. 1982. *The Color Purple.* New York: Harcourt Brace.

Walker, Lenore E. 1979. *The Battered Woman.* New York: Harper and Row.

————, ed. 1984. *Women and Mental Health Policy.* Beverly Hills: Sage Publications.

Western Center on Domestic Violence. 1984. *Lesbian Battery: Selected Articles.* (Available from Western Center on Domestic Violence, 870 Market Street, Suite 1058, San Francisco, Calif. 94102).

White, Evelyn C. 1985. *Chain, Chain, Change: For Black Women Dealing with Physical and Emotional Abuse.* Seattle: Seal Press, New Leaf Series.

Yamada, Mitsuye. 1983. Asian Pacific American women and feminism. In Cherríe Moraga and Gloria Anzaldúa, ed., *This Bridge Called My Back: Writings by Radical Women of Color.* New York: Kitchen Table/Women of Color Press, 71–75.

Zambrano, Myrna Z. 1985. *Mejor Sola que Mal Accompanada: For the Latina in an Abusive Relationship.* Seattle: Seal Press, New Leaf Series.

CHAPTER **7**

JYL JOSEPHSON

The Intersectionality of Domestic Violence and Welfare in the Lives of Poor Women

———————————— ABSTRACT ————————————

Domestic violence and poverty are intimately linked in the United States. Angela Browne, a well-known domestic violence researcher, compiled impressive statistics linking domestic violence and poverty (1997, 1998):

- 92 percent of homeless women experienced severe physical and/or sexual assault at some point in their lives;
- 63 percent of women in poverty have been victims of intimate partner violence, and 32 percent are currently in abusive relationships;
- Poor women who have been victimized face significant barriers to employment; abusive partners often sabotage training and employment efforts;
- 65 percent of women on public assistance have experienced partner violence at some point in their lives.

In addition, 57 percent of mayors in a recent survey, included in the U.S. Conference of Mayors' *Status Report on Hunger and Homelessness* (1999), identified domestic violence as a primary cause of homelessness; almost half of the women who receive funds from Temporary Assistance to Needy Families (TANF) cite domestic violence as a factor in their need for assistance (Raphael, 1995); and female-headed households are six times poorer than male-headed households—a huge issue for women who escape violent relationships (Strategy Alert, 1996)

Jyl Josephson's chapter applies the lens of intersectionality to domestic violence and welfare reform. She explores how social welfare legislation racializes and criminalizes poverty and reinforces dominant hierarchies of power and social control by regulating the lives of poor women.

With the passage of "welfare reform" legislation in 1996 in the form of the Personal Responsibility and Work Opportunity Reconciliation Act (PRWORA), women below the poverty line who experience domestic violence are regularly endangered by eroding public assistance. There are few choices in this "welfare reform" legislation: women must make a rapid transition to either employment or marriage.

In 2003, the U.S. Congress agreed to invest a total of $1.8 billion over six years in programs that encourage poor women to marry. More than 2 million low-income single mothers across the country are targeted for marriage promotion programs, which will place many lives at risk. The majority of people receiving welfare assistance are women who have been victims of domestic violence. For one-third of these women, the abuse is ongoing. Women need support to escape and recover from the abuse, not incentives to stay in unsafe relationships. Indeed, structural supports—education, training, child care, and services for domestic violence, mental health, and substance abuse—are programs that need financing. These initiatives are known to help lift women out of poverty and support their resilience. Josephson challenges reductionist causal relationships used to describe the lives of "welfare moms." She interrogates the complexities of being poor, battered, and a woman of color.

As you read this chapter examine how state regulation of social benefits has become racialized and evolved to exercise increasing control over women of color in poverty. Later, in chapter 22, this theme is revisited, as Donna Coker writes about state intrusion in women's lives by governing through an ideology of control. Policies of welfare reform, child removal, immigration, and a "war" on drugs disproportionately victimize women marginalized by race, class, and culture. Josephson and Coker help us understand how new policies—welfare reform and marriage incentive programs—interact with preexisting state control to sustain an ethic of criminalizing social problems like poverty and domestic violence.

This chapter explores the utility of an approach to examining the interaction of such categories as race, class, and gender developed by critical legal theorists and African American feminist scholars—the use of the heuristic concept of "intersectionality"—and applies the approach to one aspect of contemporary social policy in the United States: the domestic violence provisions of the 1996 federal welfare law ([Personal Responsibility and Work Opportunity Reconciliation Act of 1996] hereafter PRWORA). The chapter discusses contemporary manifestations of gender- and race-based social control via social welfare policy as they interact with the individual control experienced by victims of domestic violence. Utilizing the concept of intersectionality, the chapter also discusses the evidence which documents the relationship between domestic violence and welfare receipt, and analyzes the interaction between state, social, and individual partner's efforts to control women receiving Temporary Assistance for Needy Families (TANF).[1]

From *Journal of Poverty* 6(1) 2002 (Binghamton, N.Y.: Haworth), 1–20. Copyright © 2002 by The Haworth Press, Inc. Reprinted by permission of the publisher.

The analysis presented here offers an alternative to the simplistic, unidirectional linear causal relationships that are often used to describe the lives of women who utilize social services programs. For example, poor women who receive TANF are often described as "dependent" (Fraser and Gordon, 1994); wage work or workfare is then the solution that will make them "independent." This description defies reality, in part by assuming any type of work, even at minimum wage, leads to independence, and in part by defining child care as nonwork. After all, women who receive these benefits do so because they are engaged in the work of caring for their children, in addition to working to retain their benefits and earn whatever they can in addition to their benefits (Edin and Lein, 1997). The chapter suggests that intersectionality is a useful device in efforts to understand the complexities faced by women subject to the social control of social services and domestic violence, offering a way to avoid being coopted into simplistic modes of thinking about women, social services, and domestic violence.

INTERSECTIONALITY AND DOMESTIC VIOLENCE

Feminist scholars have long recognized the multiple aspects of individual identity and the complexity of the interactions between multiple forms of oppression and social hierarchy. Legal scholar Kimberlé Crenshaw developed the idea of intersectionality to analyze the relationship between race and gender in discrimination in the labor force and elsewhere. Crenshaw initially used this analysis to highlight the problems that minority women experience in trying to demonstrate workplace discrimination on the basis of both race and gender: courts have generally required that claims be made on either one ground or the other, but not on the combination of race and gender (Crenshaw, 1991a). In a subsequent article and essay, Crenshaw argued that intersectionality is also a useful tool to understand the interaction of racism and sexism in the experiences and lives of women of color who are victims of domestic violence (Crenshaw, 1991b, 1997). With respect to domestic violence, Crenshaw uses this concept to analyze the ways in which mainstream discourse on domestic violence, as well as services for victims of domestic violence, are targeted toward white women and ignore the particular nature of domestic violence for women of color.

Other scholars have subsequently developed this concept for a variety of uses, to analyze phenomena as disparate as films in popular culture and state and federal legal decisions, and with respect to many different types of social hierarchies, oppressions, and power relationships (Collins, 1998; Grillo, 1995). Intersectionality tries to analyze the many categories of identities in terms of their complex and often conflicting interactions. For our purposes here, four key aspects of intersectionality theory are useful.

First, as Collins argues, the process of constructing group identities is usually seen in binary terms: male/female, white/Black, heterosexual/homosexual. However, intersectionality "problematizes this entire process of group construction" (Collins, 1998, p. 205). Intersectionality offers a means for analyzing and describing the experiences of individuals within a system of interlocking hierarchies (Collins, 1998, pp. 201–228). This does not mean that group identities or group-based experiences disappear; rather, intersectionality is a concept that can help to understand how experiences of domination can change and can vary for different groups and for different individuals within groups, even while they are reproducing long-standing inequalities and hierarchies. Intersectionality thus provides a means of understanding the experiences of individuals within a context of hierarchical power relations and is, thus, particularly useful in understanding the complexity of the lives of women who are both recipients of public benefits and victims of domestic violence.

A second aspect of intersectionality that makes it particularly useful for the purposes used here is the concept of "structural intersectionality" developed by Crenshaw: "The ways in which the location of women of color at the intersection of race and gender make our actual experience of domestic violence, rape, and remedial reform qualitatively different than that of white women" (1991b, p. 1245). With respect to domestic violence, poor women and women of color often have additional problems which must be addressed if battered women's shelters are to meet their needs (Crenshaw, 1991b). Crenshaw discusses the reluctance of the minority community in Los Angeles to release data to her regarding domestic violence, given that it would reinforce stereotypes about minority men as violent (Crenshaw, 1991b, p. 1253). Other problems include a higher incidence of poverty among minority women and the lack of available jobs in their neighborhoods. Poor women and women of color are also less likely to have networks that can provide necessary financial support to help them leave their abusers (Crenshaw, 1991b, p. 1246). Immigrant women also face additional problems in dealing with domestic violence, especially when their immigration status is dependent upon their relationship with their abuser (Crenshaw, 1991b; Narayan, 1997). Anna Santiago and Merry Morash also note that Latina women who are victims of domestic violence may find family members or Latino/a-run social service agencies more helpful than domestic violence shelters, particularly when shelters do not have bilingual personnel and are not located in Latino communities (1995).

These analyses highlight the ways in which the particular social locations of women based on race, ethnicity, class, immigrant status, and familial relationships, shape their experiences of domestic violence and demarcate the available options for dealing with their situations. If services that are available are not responsive to the particular needs of women in minority communities, then they are unlikely to have access to or choose to utilize those services. Understanding the means to provide intervention strategies to victims of domestic violence thus requires an understanding of the ways in which race, class, gender, ethnicity, immigration status, and status with respect to welfare receipt interact in women's lives.

A third key aspect of intersectionality that can aid analysis of PRWORA and domestic violence is what Crenshaw terms "political intersectionality," which occurs when political movements that should address the particular concerns of poor women and women of color—specifically anti-racist politics, anti-poverty advocacy, and feminist politics—instead operate in ways that marginalize these concerns. A number of scholars have analyzed this problem, which is evidenced in feminist efforts to gain recognition for domestic violence as a public problem, in anti-racist politics, in the provision of domestic violence support services (Crenshaw, 1991b), in the work of poverty lawyers (Margulies, 1995), and in the clash between the discourse of feminist advocates of domestic violence and advocates for the poor (Meier, 1997). The basic point is that political movements that fail to take account of the multiple intersecting identities of those they seek to empower end up marginalizing all but those in the dominant category. Emphasizing that domestic violence occurs to women of all races and social classes was a useful political strategy, but it also served to limit the availability of services that would address the specific needs of women of color and poor women.[2] (See Richie, chapter 5, this volume.)

Similarly, in an analysis of the discourse of domestic violence, Kathleen Ferraro argues that the existence of both a public discourse and state interventions in domestic violence constitute both a "feminist victory" and "nightmare," "in which emancipatory ideals collide with repressive mechanisms of social control" in a way that ignores social hierarchies based on gender, race, and class (1996, p. 77). Crenshaw, Linda Ammons, and Beth Richie discuss this problem of intersectionality in relation to the reluctance in some minority communities to recognize domestic violence as a serious problem, critiquing an anti-racist politics that either sees gender-based domestic violence as a manifestation of racism or seeks to suppress acknowledgment of this problem as a means to combat racism (Ammons, 1995; Crenshaw, 1991b; Richie, 1996). Peter Margulies and Joan Meier critique the failure of poverty lawyers and analysts to address the problem of domestic violence, as well as the lack of communication, until recently, between the battered women's movement and the anti-poverty movement (Margulies, 1995; Meier, 1997). Thus, each of these movements, which could address the concerns of poor and minority women who are subject to state control through social policy and domestic violence on the part of their partners, has in the past failed to recognize the specific concerns of these women.

A fourth way in which intersectional analysis can be useful is implicit in the concept of political intersectionality: it can help us to see what is wrong, but also point the way toward policies that might be more effective. For example, Crenshaw, Margulies, and Meier all argue that there are ways to address the problems exposed by intersectional analysis, in part through a coalitional politics that brings together advocates regarding these issues, and in part through centering analysis on the particular and individual circumstances of poor women and women of color who are victims of domestic violence. It was this sort of coalitional politics that brought about two legislative initiatives that provide the basis for some services to poor women whose lives are also affected by domestic violence. (See Coker, chapter 22, this volume.) Thus, intersectional analysis highlights the way that policy responses could more effectively address the many and varied intersectional identities and lives of poor women and women of color who are affected by PRWORA and by domestic violence. In what follows, I will outline the provisions of PRWORA that are of particular significance for women who are victims of domestic violence.

STATE REGULATION VIA SOCIAL BENEFITS

Feminist analysis of social welfare policy in the United States indicates a long history of social control of women through social policy. Much recent feminist scholarship has discussed the role that gender and race played in the development of the state-based mother's pension programs and the Aid to Dependent Children program that grew out of these pensions (Gordon, 1990; Mink, 1998). Scholarship on the U.S. welfare state consistently documents the division between deserving and undeserving recipients of public assistance and the long history of social control of those deemed undeserving.

What is meant here by social control is the imposition of specific behavioral requirements that must be met by recipients of public benefits in order to maintain their eligibility for those benefits. Even in the state-level programs that preceded the ADC program behavioral requirements were extensive, and mothers' pension recipients were supervised through home visits and mandatory training courses (Nelson, 1990). The 1996 welfare law is thus a continuation of long-standing distinctions in U.S. social policy between the deserving and the undeserving poor and of the racial and gendered nature of these policies (Gordon, 1990; Mink, 1998; Quadagno, 1994). But, whereas single mothers who were widows were viewed somewhat sympathetically during the New Deal era, the pervasive imagery of single mothers as irresponsible black teenagers that has been cultivated since the late 1960s has successfully moved single mothers from their tenuous place among the deserving poor to a firm location among those who are undeserving (Josephson, 2000; Williams, 1997). Given their place among the undeserving poor, extensive state supervision of the lives and behaviors of AFDC/TANF recipients is seen as justified and justifiable.

It is not incidental that the development of increased supervision of the behaviors of women receiving AFDC came about at the same time that policies that had explicitly excluded minority women from AFDC were challenged by the civil rights and welfare rights movements. Work requirements, begun with the 1967 amendments to the Social Security Act and greatly expanded in subsequent legislation, occurred as more minority women were eligible to receive benefits. As Williams notes, "African American women had always been expected and required to do wage work in U.S. society, predominantly as domestic and agricultural workers. Thus as the new image of the welfare recipient was constructed as African American, it was only to be expected that they (unlike white women) should be required to work" (1997, p. 5).

The aspects of AFDC/TANF that indicate increasing levels of state-based social control are unmistakable. However, I do not wish to suggest here a simple model of social control, in which social control by the state is problematic, while societal and familial forms of social control are benign or acceptable (Gordon, 1990, p. 194). Rather, I wish to suggest that the increased social control evidenced in the AFDC/TANF programs intersects with other forms of social control, including domestic violence. These intersecting forms of control are complex, and intersectional analysis can help to see the interaction between existing social hierarchies, state forms of social control, and the control manifested by intimate partners through violence. Poor women, who are the objects of these forms of control, are not lacking in subjective agency and may respond to various kinds of control in multiple ways depending upon their circumstances. To analyze these women's lives and ultimately to find strategies that address the effects of both poverty and domestic violence, we need to see the intersection of multiple valences of social control as well as resistance to that control.

An example of this view of social control and resistance is in the interaction between child support policy and AFDC/TANF. Women who receive AFDC/TANF have been required since 1967 to assign their child support benefits to the state and since 1975 to cooperate in the establishment of paternity and of a child support order. From 1984 through 1996, these women could receive, at most, $50 per month from an established and paid child support order; the remainder was collected by the state and federal governments (Josephson, 1997).[3] That both women and men see this as a form of social control is evidenced in Edin and Lein's study of low income women (1997). Edin and Lein found that, although 60 percent of the welfare reliant mothers in their sample did cooperate fully in the case of at least one of the fathers of their children, an equal percent also indicated that they had either lied or withheld information in the case of at least one father (1997, pp. 159–160). Many of these mothers made arrangements with the child's father to receive covert payments or in kind support in exchange for not "turning them in" to the child support agency. Edin and Lein also note that the child support system provided an important means of leverage for some of these women: they were able to induce fathers to provide support because of the threat of "put[ting] the law" on them (1997, p. 162). Thus, the social control of state-enforced child support is not only both complied with and resisted by custodial mothers but also used as a tool to obtain support from their children's fathers. In this, they were fairly successful: one-third of welfare reliant mothers in this study received cash assistance from noncustodial fathers; another third received in-kind support. Thus, social control is complex and has many valences, some of which can be and are deployed by those subject to it to improve other aspects of their lives. In this instance, the fact that federal and state child support provisions place specific legal requirements on *both* parents provides women with some leverage in relation to their children's fathers. Most of the social control mechanisms in the AFDC/TANF program, however, are directed only at custodial parents: that is, primarily, women.

The 1996 Welfare Law and Social Control of Recipients

PRWORA constitutes a major change in U.S. social policy, and a summary of its provisions is not my intent here. I will focus on those provisions that constitute increased social control of women and that are of particular importance for women who are both recipients of welfare benefits and victims of domestic violence.

PRWORA ends the entitlement status of programs that assist needy families, requires work participation, and provides for lifetime time limits on the receipt of benefits. The law also increases the pressure to cooperate with child support establishment and collection, while eliminating the monetary benefits provided under previous law. Sanction mechanisms have been increased, both in terms of state sanctions for individual recipients and federal sanctions for states that fail to meet program goals. The law is intended to provide recipients with strong incentives to engage in work activity and to provide states with strong incentives to require work activity of as many recipients as possible, whether or not it is work that can provide sustainable support for a family with children. The law clearly emphasizes short-term movement into employment and movement of recipients off the rolls, over long-term employment and self-sufficiency strategies. Through sanctions against recipients and states the law increases state control over recipients of benefits.

The PRWORA law did contain one provision that recognized the connection between domestic violence and welfare receipt: the Family Violence Option (FVO), also known as the Wellstone-Murray amendment. This option was originally introduced by Senator Wellstone as an amendment to H.R. 4, the Personal Responsibility Act, passed by the 104th Congress in 1995 and vetoed by President Clinton; the amendment was struck by the conference committee (Pollack, 1996). The FVO is an amendment to the 1996 welfare law that permits states to temporarily exempt women who are victims of domestic violence from the work requirements and time limits under PRWORA, as well as the paternity establishment and child support cooperation requirements, through "good cause" waivers. The Family Violence Option emerged out of efforts of the National Task Force on Women, Welfare, and Abuse to make the welfare law less damaging to poor women who are victims of domestic violence (Kittay, 1998; Meier, 1997). In the 1996 law, it was originally a requirement, but was converted to an optional provision in conference committee (Meier, 1997). States that adopt this option must confidentially screen applicants for current or past domestic violence, and provide referrals to support services as appropriate. States have the option of whether to adopt the Option; as of May 1999, thirty-six states had adopted the FVO, six states had not adopted the FVO but had domestic violence provisions in their state welfare plans, five states were in the process of adopting the FVO, and two states had adopted the FVO but left its implementation up to individual counties in the state (Raphael and Haennicke, 1999).

Initially, some states hesitated to adopt the Family Violence Option in part because the draft regulations issued by the Department of Health and Human

Services [DHHS] indicated that domestic violence waivers should be counted as part of the 20 percent of caseload limit on the total number of hardship waivers that states are permitted to grant. But the intent of the authors of the Wellstone-Murray amendment was to provide a separate category for victims of domestic violence *in addition to* the hardship exemptions. However, the effort to clarify this via legislation in 1997 was blocked (NOW Legal Defense and Education Fund, 1997). Obviously, this provision would have significantly reduced the impact of the Family Violence Option, given the data on rates of domestic violence among TANF recipients discussed below. Fortunately, in 1999 the Department issued regulations indicating that states will not be penalized for failing to meet the work participation rates if the reason is that participants have received temporary family violence waivers, as long as the waivers granted meet certain federal requirements (Raphael and Haennicke, 1999).

An additional piece of legislation that should be noted is the Violence Against Women Act of 1994 [VAWA], which was the first comprehensive federal legislation intended to address the problem of domestic violence in the United States. The Act is significant for many reasons; for present purposes, what is important is that the legislation initiated a nationally coordinated effort to study the problem of domestic violence. Some funds appropriated under VAWA have been utilized to study the problem of domestic violence and welfare.

DOMESTIC VIOLENCE AND WELFARE RECEIPT

Recent research has shown that many women receiving public assistance are or have been subject to the individual control of violent domestic partners. The research discussed here provides empirical evidence regarding the multiple and interacting strands of oppression that many poor women experience. One way that gender hierarchies are maintained is by strategies of direct control of "the proximate other" (Collins, 1998, p. 223); domestic violence is a physical form of this control. As the evidence discussed below indicates, many women who receive TANF are subject to conflicting mechanisms of social control via program requirements for work versus the violence they experience at the hand of an intimate partner. The empirical evidence points to the importance of understanding the specific circumstances of individual women, which is clarified, I will argue, through the use of intersectional analysis.

Studies of domestic violence consistently show that poverty increases the risk of domestic abuse, especially of severe violence (Browne and Bassuk, 1997). Feminist scholars, critical of these figures, have noted that what may actually be occurring is that poor women are more likely to report domestic violence than are women with higher incomes.[4] Whether or not women who are poor are in general more likely to experience domestic violence, it is certainly the case, as Crenshaw argues, that poor women's experiences with domestic violence and their ability to escape from situations of domestic abuse are different than those of women with more resources and more affluent social networks. Regardless of one's assumptions regarding the relative frequency of domestic violence among women of different income categories, it is important to see the specificity of circumstances of poor women who experience violence at the hands of their intimate partners.

The prevalence of domestic violence among women on welfare was brought to widespread public attention by Jody Raphael of the Taylor Institute. The first report by the Taylor Institute was issued in 1995 and included data from grassroots programs that established a connection between domestic violence and the long-term receipt of AFDC. The second report also included data from social service providers and individual women (Raphael, 1996). The third report cites evidence from more rigorous research, including the Better Homes Fund study, the McCormack Institute study, and the Passaic County study (Raphael and Tolman, 1997). In addition, a number of scholarly publications have appeared since the initial Taylor Institute report. Raphael has also published a book on the subject (Raphael 2000). What has emerged is a fairly clear picture of some aspects of the relationship between poverty, welfare receipt, and domestic violence, as well as questions that remain to be answered about other aspects of these relationships. After discussing the general parameters of the relationship between domestic violence, poverty, and receipt of social services benefits, the discussion here focuses on work requirements and on exemptions from child support cooperation.

Domestic Violence, Poverty, Receipt of Social Services Benefits

The studies are very clear on one point: women who receive social services benefits are much more likely to have been victims of child abuse and/or domestic violence than are women in the general population. It is important to note that the studies of domestic violence that specifically focus on recipients of welfare benefits do not include all women who are poor; women may experience poverty without utilizing social services programs. Thus, if it is correct that rates of domestic violence are higher among poor women than among women in the population as a whole, this may explain part of the problem of domestic violence and welfare, but it does not explain the particularly high rates of violence for women on welfare that are demonstrated by these studies. What may be happening is that women who have nowhere else to turn, or who have exhausted what support is available to them from family and friends, utilize TANF benefits to escape domestic violence (Davis and Kraham, 1995). Thus, while Bureau of Justice Statistics data seem to indicate that there is a *correlation* between *poverty* and domestic violence, the relationship between domestic violence and *welfare receipt*, at least for some women, may well be *causal*: women may utilize social services benefits as their means of support in the process of escaping their abusive partners.

One clear finding across all studies is that women recipients of AFDC/TANF report a much higher incidence of physical abuse at some time in their lives than is true for women in the general population.[5] The studies discussed in the third Taylor Institute report, for example, found that between 33.8 percent and 64.9 percent of respondents had experienced violence at the hands of an intimate partner at some time in their adult lives (Raphael and Tolman, 1997, p. 21).[6] Respondents also reported high levels of abuse during childhood. When respondents were asked about recent abuse, the proportion reporting physical abuse ranged from 14.9 percent to 19.5 percent for abuse within the last twelve months to 32.3 percent for abuse within the last two years (Raphael and Tolman, 1997, p. 21). By contrast, the National Crime Victimization Survey found the rate of violence against women by intimates within a one-year period to be about 9.3 per one thousand, or 0.93 percent (Bachman and Saltzman, 1995, p. 3).[7] Another study also shows a correlation between *recent* experience of domestic violence and receipt of AFDC and food stamps, which indicates the possibility that some women utilize AFDC as a means to leave situations of domestic violence (Lloyd, 1997). It is clear that women who receive AFDC/TANF are much more likely to have experienced domestic violence at some time in their adult lives and more likely to have experienced abuse during childhood, than have women in the general population (Lyon, 1997).

This finding also holds true for poor women who receive other kinds of social services. For example, a study of poor homeless and housed women (all of whom had one or more children) conducted in Worcester, Massachusetts, found that 60 percent of the total sample of 436 women had experienced domestic abuse by a male partner during adulthood, and 32.4 percent had been subject to severe violence at the hands of their most recent or current partner. Many of these women had also experienced violence in childhood: more than 60 percent experienced violence at the hand of a caretaker, and 42 percent reported sexual molestation in childhood. The authors found, in keeping with many studies of child abuse, that the experience of violence in childhood was a strong predictor of abuse in adulthood. And, of those reporting domestic abuse in adulthood, 78.7 percent had sustained physical injuries (Browne and Bassuk, 1997). Significant numbers of women in the sample also resisted the abuse to which they were subjected: many of these women did leave or try to leave their abusive partners, half had sought police protection, and one-third had obtained restraining orders. However, the prevalence of both childhood and adulthood abuse means that "in sum, across the lifespan, the majority of these young mothers had experienced only brief—if any—periods of safety" (Browne and Bassuk, 1997, p. 275).

The studies also provide some anecdotal evidence regarding the relationship between domestic violence and welfare receipt. For example, women in the Maine Coalition for Family Crisis Services study said that they feared poverty and that the fear of poverty as a result of the TANF time limits made them more fearful of leaving their abusive partners. One woman said that, after receiving her notice regarding the new TANF requirements, "she thought she had better stay with her abusive partner." She said, "I felt more trapped" (Cooley et al., 1997, p. 3).

Some elements seem to hold true across the variety of studies, despite the different approaches in terms of sampling and interviewing techniques. Some of these findings reflect similar findings in other studies of domestic violence and thus are not unique to low income women; for example, women who were abused as children are more likely to suffer abuse as adults. Other findings, however, point to the unique problems faced by poor women who are subject to state control via the regulation of their behavior as recipients of AFDC/TANF.

Work Requirements and Domestic Violence

Although the evidence regarding the specific relationship between ability to work and recent experiences of domestic violence is mixed, several recent studies indicate that some women do indeed have more difficulty working as a result of domestic violence. Lloyd and Taluc's study of low-income women in Chicago found that women who had experienced domestic violence had more job turnover and had experienced more spells of unemployment than women who had not been victims of violence (1999). They also had more health problems and lower incomes. However, they were not less likely to be currently employed, at least when the authors utilized the aggregate data on domestic violence. When the authors examined separately the effects of specific acts of aggression, they found that women whose partners had threatened to kill them, and women whose partners had prevented them from going to work or school or had threatened to harm their children were indeed less likely to be currently employed. Thus, as the authors note, women who experience violence may be in very different circumstances depending upon the nature of the abuse and may respond very differently to their circumstances (Lloyd and Taluc, 1999).

Browne, Salomon, and Bassuk also address the question of the relationship between recent (within the twelve months prior to the interview) experiences with domestic violence and work activity (1999). In this study the authors observed a relationship between recent experiences of violence and ability to work at least thirty hours per week for a six-month period: women who had experienced recent violence were about one-third as likely to have worked this amount as women who had not. The authors specifically controlled for other factors, such as mental health variables and other factors that were negatively associated with ability to work. This finding did not hold true for women who had ever experienced violence, but only for women who had recently experienced violence (Browne et al., 1999, pp. 416–417).

The anecdotal evidence also seems to indicate that some male partners who are abusive engage in behavior intended to sabotage women's efforts to become self-sufficient through work or participation in work training and education programs (Raphael, 1996). Women in many of the studies reported direct controlling behaviors related to their attendance at work training activities required by AFDC/TANF programs. Abusive partners tried to sabotage women's work by coming to their workplace, calling the workplace constantly, or physically abusing them on the day before a test or an interview. Women noted that their partners either seemed threatened by the possibility that they would have increased independence through improving their work skills or were simply jealous of any contact that the women had with other people in the work or work training setting.

Many of the anecdotes reported in these studies, especially in relation to work activity, seem to indicate that the kind of violence experienced by some women is more akin to what Michael Johnson has termed "patriarchal terrorism" than to what he terms "common couple violence." Patriarchal terrorism "involves the systematic use of not only violence, but economic subordination, threats, isolation, and other control tactics" (Johnson, 1995, p. 284). This clearly describes the controlling behaviors discussed by some of the women in these studies regarding their partners' efforts to sabotage their work or educational activity. For women affected by this type of violence, compliance with work requirements may be nearly impossible, and may put them in greater danger.

Domestic Violence and Child Support

Only one published study to date has examined the experiences of women applicants for TANF benefits with the child support good cause exemption. Prior to the passage of PRWORA, scholars had noted that rate of requests for the good cause exemption, and the rate at which such requests were granted by the child support enforcement system, was almost certainly lower than the rate of domestic violence among these applicants (Josephson, 1997; Mannix et al., 1987). The child support study conducted by the Center for Policy Research of Denver seems to support this conclusion (Pearson et al., 1999). The authors sought to determine the incidence of violence among applicants for TANF, as well as how frequently the perpetrator of the abuse was the father of one of the applicant's children for whom child support collection was being pursued. They also asked applicants whether they wished to have a good cause exemption to their child support cooperation requirement.

Of the 1082 women respondents, 40 percent had experienced domestic violence at the hands of a current or former partner. Among those who had experienced violence, 70 percent reported that the abuser was the father of at least one of their children. This is the group of women that was provided information about the good cause exemption to the child support cooperation requirement. Interestingly, these women overwhelmingly opted to cooperate with child support; only 6.7 percent stated that they were interested in applying for the good cause exemption. Those who declined were asked why they chose not to take the option; the reason most women gave was that they wanted the child support. Many also stated that they already had an existing order or that the abuser already knew where they lived so this was not a reason to not pursue child support (Pearson et al., 1999, p. 440). One problem revealed by this study was that only about one-third of the women who expressed interest in the child support exemption actually received it, partly because many women did not have the required documentation (for example, an affidavit, a police report, or a court order), and partly because women are only given a week to assemble all necessary documents for the application (Pearson et al., 1999, pp. 441–443). This study seems to indicate that the child support exemption provision is an important protection for some women, that most women will still wish to pursue child support enforcement, and also that more effective implementation might include accepting women's own statements in addition to court records (Pearson et al., 1999; Raphael and Haennicke, 1999).

The studies to date thus seem to indicate the following key points. Women receiving social services have much higher rates of lifetime violence than do women in the population as a whole. Women receiving social services also have higher rates of recent (usually defined as within the last twelve months) violence than do women in the population as a whole, and this violence seems to interfere with their ability to maintain work, although more details of this latter relationship need to be fleshed out by the evidence. Women who report experiencing violence also have higher rates of other problems such as health-related problems and mental health problems than are found in representative samples of women in the United States. There is some anecdotal evidence that some partners engage in intentional behavior meant to sabotage women's work opportunities. Women with recent experiences of abuse have lower wages and are more likely to utilize social services programs. The violent partner or former partner is also frequently the father of some of these women's children, and for a small percentage of these women the child support good cause exemption, if effectively implemented, could provide an important protection from future violence. Collectively, these studies document the serious effects that domestic violence has on these women's lives, from their ability to simply live in safety, to their ability to work or complete work-training programs, to their physical and mental health and well-being. Thus, public assistance and domestic violence seem to intersect in multiple ways in women's lives. Although we have begun to understand these relationships, there is a need for more research, including both nationally representative samples and studies of the implementation of the Family Violence Option.

THE INTERSECTIONALITY OF DOMESTIC VIOLENCE AND WOMEN'S POVERTY

The intersection of domestic violence with poverty is not merely an analytic tool; for the women who are subjects of the studies discussed above, domestic violence constitutes an additional barrier to the possibility of escaping poverty while living in safety. The women interviewed for these studies identified many instances in which their abuser sabotaged their efforts to gain greater independence through acquiring skills or working for wages. Although they were working at rates similar to nonabused women, they had more difficulty maintaining work effort over time. And most currently or formerly abused women choose to pursue their child support enforcement cases despite abuse by their children's father. Thus, the way that domestic violence and welfare receipt intersect for these women is complicated. Intersectionality helps in understanding the complex ways in which individualized, violent control by male partners interacts with the social regulation inherent in social welfare programs.

First, intersectionality helps to analyze the interlocking hierarchies that structure the lives of the women affected by poverty, welfare reform, and domestic violence and the many valences of control to which they are subject. Thus, individual experiences of these hierarchies may vary greatly depending upon the woman's particular circumstances. In some instances the social control that the state exerts may help women to gain power in relation to their partners or former partners, as in the example of child support enforcement noted earlier. In other instances state control may operate to disempower women by making it less likely that they will leave an abusive partner. In those instances where states are implementing the Family Violence Option and the child support good cause exemption effectively, and women are referred to domestic violence service providers for assistance, this portion of the law may provide women with an avenue out of the individual control of a violent partner. However, women may be reluctant to reveal that they have been abused to case workers who also have the power to make determinations regarding their eligibility for benefits and may experience the implementation of the FVO as itself an invasion of their privacy by case workers (Raphael and Haennicke, 1999). The avenues of empowerment, and what empowerment means, may differ for different women, depending upon their circumstances—the nature and extent of the abuse, their work and educational backgrounds and experiences, the job opportunities available based on such factors as location, transportation, and race- and gender-based employment discrimination.

Second, intersectional analysis helps to show that women who experience domestic violence are not all the same and do not have the same experiences, nor do they respond to their circumstances in the same way. As discussed above, the interaction between poverty, domestic violence, and work activity is complex, and different women may respond differently (for example, by increasing their work activity) to experiencing domestic violence. So, as advocates noted early on in the implementation of the FVO, forgoing work requirements temporarily should not mean that women are not provided with work training and job assistance opportunities. In analyzing the intersection of poverty and domestic violence, we need not paint a simple picture of a singular woman victim; rather, we need to understand the various ways in which both the social control of male abuse of women and state control via welfare policy interact in individual women's lives. This understanding must be attentive to the effects of race, ethnicity, disability, and other factors in shaping women's experiences. Such attentiveness will be crucial to implementing effective strategies to enable poor women to leave both violence and poverty behind.

Third, political intersectionality can be used to outline the ways that the complexity of the lives of women receiving TANF was not represented by the policy design inherent in the 1996 welfare law. Political intersectionality provides a critique of the description of women that is embedded in public policy. For example, women with depression and physical disabilities are unlikely to be helped in the long term by short-term interventions aimed at placing them in the work force as quickly as possible. This point has been made in many ways by feminist scholars who study welfare; intersectionality provides a way to describe the multiple kinds of oppression and social hierarchies that affect women on welfare. For the most part the law assumes that women need only short-term assistance, and the motivation of benefits cuts, to obtain paid employment (Josephson, 2000). Further, it assumes that getting a job will solve the problem of recipients and their families, an assumption which is refuted by a great deal of empirical evidence (Edin and Lein, 1997). Thus, political intersectionality shows the limitations of some aspects of PRWORA. As the law is assessed in the period leading up to the law's expiration in 2002, the coalitions that have formed around the issue of domestic violence and welfare need to ensure that public officials attend to the evidence discussed above regarding the complexity of poor women's lives.

Finally, intersectionality points to the difficulty of implementing provisions such as the FVO in a way that actually assists the women it is intended to assist without providing further mechanisms for the state or their partners to exercise more extensive control. Some of the literature that analyzes implementation notes these complexities, and the difficulty of providing notice of the FVO and child support good cause exemption, as well as screening for domestic violence, in a way that does not discourage women from reporting their circumstances. Raphael and Haennicke note that screening mechanisms should be directly linked to the benefits that can be provided by FVO and good cause; they argue that this is likely to both increase self-reporting and invade women's privacy as little as possible (1999). As implementation of these portions of PRWORA continue, the evidence regarding variations in state procedures should be weighed carefully to balance the interests of ensuring that women are protected from further violence and are also provided the opportunities and assistance that they need to improve the conditions of their lives.

CONCLUSION

Recognizing intersectionality bears fruit in a number of ways. It leads us to a more complex and nuanced analysis than the discourse surrounding the 1996 welfare law permitted. The evidence regarding welfare receipt and domestic violence requires a more complicated understanding of poor women's lives. Intersectionality also leads us to a more complex view of the services and interventions that are necessary to provide a real social safety net for women whose lives are affected in complicated ways by multiple hierarchies and forms of discrimination. Services intended to assist poor women will inevitably fail if they fail to recognize the actual circumstances of women's lives. Intersectional analysis allows advocates, policymakers, scholars, and practitioners to see the reality of women's lives, and, hopefully, to utilize the instruments of public policy to empower women to live lives freed from domestic violence.

NOTES

1. The program was called Aid to Dependent Children (ADC) when it was created in 1935; the name was changed to Aid to Families with Dependent Children (AFDC) in 1962. The 1996 legislation discussed below terminated the AFDC entitlement program and renamed the new program Temporary Assistance for Needy Families (TANF). Many of the studies discussed in this essay were conducted before the 1996 change in the law. In the discussion that follows, I refer to the title of the program appropriate to the time period to which the text refers.

2. As discussed below, this should not be taken to mean that women of color are more likely to experience domestic violence. The nationally representative evidence indicates that this is not the case. What Crenshaw is critiquing here is the erasure of the particular concerns of women of color in the discourse, politics, and practices of domestic violence advocacy, as well as the failure of minority communities to acknowledge domestic violence as a significant problem.

3. PRWORA abolished the $50 pass through requirement; most states have now eliminated it.

4. For example, the National Crime Victimization Survey shows that women with incomes under ten thousand dollars per year are more likely to report domestic violence (Bachman and Saltzman, 1995). However, since the study is based on self-reports, it is not clear whether the actual incidence of violence is higher among women with lower incomes, or whether they are simply more likely to report the violence that does occur.

5. One of the problems with drawing generalizable conclusions from these studies is that they have been conducted in a wide variety of ways. The initial evidence came from studies initiated by domestic violence service providers and studies conducted by or among providers of social services. Other studies have been conducted by researchers utilizing a variety of methods, but generally not including nationally representative samples. Thus, the evidence discussed here is described in fairly broad terms, drawing on the most consistent findings.

6. The wide range likely stems from differences in the definition of physical abuse utilized in the studies; the study which found a rate of 33.8 percent did not include slapping, pushing, and shoving in the definition of physical aggression.

7. It should be noted that the numbers are not directly comparable, as some of the behaviors specifically mentioned in the welfare studies (e.g., slapping, pushing, and shoving) are not specifically mentioned in the questions on the NCVS.

REFERENCES

Ammons, L. 1995. Mules, madonnas, babies, bathwater, racial imagery, and stereotypes: The African American woman and the battered woman syndrome. *Wisconsin Law Review* 5: 1003–1080.

Bachman, R., and L. Saltzman. 1995. *Violence Against Women: Estimates from the Redesigned Survey*. Washington, D.C.: U.S. Department of Justice, Bureau of Justice Statistics.

Browne, Angela. 1998. Responding to the needs of low income and homeless women who are survivors of family violence. *Journal of American Medical Association* 53(2): 57–64.

Browne, A., and S. Bassuk. 1997. Intimate violence in the lives of homeless and poor housed women: Prevalence and patterns in an ethnically diverse sample. *American Journal of Orthopsychiatry* 67: 261–278.

Browne, A., A. Salomon, and S. Bassuk. 1999. The impact of recent partner violence on poor women's capacity to maintain work. *Violence Against Women* 5: 393–426.

Collins, P. H. 1998. *Fighting Words: Black Women and the Search for Justice*. Minneapolis: University of Minnesota Press.

Cooley, T., E. Jones, A. Onge, and L. Wilcox. 1997. Safety and self-support: The challenge of welfare reform for victims of domestic abuse. Bangor, Maine: Maine Coalition for Family Crisis Services.

Crenshaw, K. 1991a. Demarginalizing the intersection of race and sex: A black feminist critique of antidiscrimination doctrine, feminist theory, and antiracist politics. In K. T. Bartlett and R. Kennedy, eds., *Feminist Legal Theory: Readings in Law and Gender*. Boulder, Colo.: Westview Press, 57–80.

———. 1991b. Mapping the margins: Intersectionality, identity politics, and violence against women of color. *Stanford Law Review* 43: 1241–1299.

———. 1997. Intersectionality and identity politics: Learning from violence against women of color. In M. L. Shanley and U. Narayan, eds., *Reconstructing Political Theory: Feminist Perspectives*. University Park: Pennsylvania State University Press, 48–67.

Davis, M., and S. Kraham. 1995. Protecting women's welfare in the face of violence. *Fordham Urban Law Journal* 22: 1141–1157.

Edin, K., and L. Lein. 1997. *Making Ends Meet: How Single Mothers Survive Welfare and Low-Wage Work*. New York: Russell Sage.

Ferraro, K. 1996. The dance of dependency: A genealogy of domestic violence discourse. *Hypatia* 11(4): 77–91.

Fraser, N., and L. Gordon. 1994. A genealogy of dependency: Tracing a keyword of the U.S. welfare state. *Signs* 19: 309–336.

Gordon, L., ed. 1990. *Women, the State, and Welfare*. Madison: University of Wisconsin Press.

Grillo, T. 1995. Anti-essentialism and intersectionality: Tools to dismantle the master's house. *Berkeley Women's Law Journal* 10: 16–30.

Johnson, M. 1995. Patriarchal terrorism and common couple violence: Two forms of violence against women. *Journal of Marriage and the Family* 57: 283–294.

Josephson, J. 1997. *Gender, Families, and State: Child Support Policy in the United States*. Lanham, Md.: Rowman & Littlefield.

———. 2000. Gender and social policy. In S. Tolleson-Rinehart and J. Josephson, eds., *Gender and American Politics: Women, Men, and the Political Process*. Armonk, N.Y.: M. E. Sharpe Publishers, 133–159.

Kittay, E. F. 1998. Dependency, equality, and welfare. *Feminist Studies* 24: 32–43.

Lloyd, S. 1997. The effects of violence on women's employment (Working Paper WP-97-4). Chicago: Northwestern University and University of Chicago, Joint Center for Poverty Research.

Lloyd, S., and N. Taluc. 1999. The effects of male violence on female employment. *Violence Against Women* 5: 370–392.

Lyon, E. 1997. *Poverty, Welfare, and Battered Women: What Does the Research Tell Us?* Washington, D.C.: National Resource Center on Domestic Violence.

Mannix, M. R., H. A. Freedman, and N. R. Best. 1987. The good cause exception to the AFDC child support requirement. *Clearinghouse Review* 21: 339–346.

Margulies, P. 1995. Representation of domestic violence survivors as a new paradigm of poverty law: In search of access, connection and voice. *George Washington Law Review* 63: 1071–1104.

Meier, J. 1997. Domestic violence, character, and social change in the welfare reform debate. *Law & Policy* 19: 205–263.

Mink, G. 1998. *Welfare's End*. Ithaca, N.Y.: Cornell University Press.

Narayan, U. 1997. "Male-order" brides: Immigrant women, domestic violence, and immigration law. In P. DiQuinzio and I. M. Young, eds., *Feminist Ethics and Social Policy*. Bloomington: Indiana University Press, 143–158.

Nelson, B. J. 1990. The origins of the two-channel welfare state: Workmen's compensation and mother's aid. In L. Gordon, eds., *Women, the State, and Welfare*. Madison: University of Wisconsin Press, 123–151.

NOW Legal Defense and Education Fund. 1997. Family violence option clarification "dumped" by House Republican conferees. Washington, D.C.: Author.

Pearson, J., N. Thoennes, and E. A. Griswold. 1999. Child support and domestic violence: The victims speak out. *Violence Against Women* 5: 427–448.

Pollack, W. 1996. Twice victimized: Domestic violence and welfare "reform." *Clearinghouse Review* 30: 329–341.

Quadagno, J. 1994. *The Color of Welfare*. New York: Oxford University Press.

Raphael, J. 1995. Welfare women, violent men. *The Christian Science Monitor*. April 20.

———. 1996. *Prisoners of Abuse: Domestic Violence and Welfare Receipt*. Chicago: Taylor Institute.

———. 2000. *Saving Bernice: Battered Women, Welfare, and Poverty*. Boston: Northeastern University Press.

Raphael, J., and S. Haennicke. 1999. Keeping battered women safe through the welfare-to-work journey: How are we doing? *Final Report to the Department of Health and Human Services*. Chicago: Taylor Institute.

Raphael, J., and R. M. Tolman. 1997. *Trapped by Poverty, Trapped by Abuse: New Evidence Documenting the Relationship between Domestic Violence and Welfare*. Chicago: Taylor Institute.

Richie, B. E. 1996. *Compelled to Crime: The Gender Entrapment of Battered Black Women*. New York: Routledge.

Santiago, A. M., and M. Morash. 1995. Strategies for serving Latina battered women. In J. A. Garber and R. S. Turner, eds., *Gender in Urban Research*. Thousand Oaks, Calif.: Sage, 219–235.

Strategy Alert. 1996. Community information exchange, Spring.

United States Conference of Mayors. 1999. A status report on hunger and homelessness in America's cities.

Williams, L. 1997. *Decades of Distortion: The Right's Thirty-Year Assault on Welfare*. Somerville, Mass.: Political Research Associates.

CHAPTER **8**

INCITE!–CRITICAL RESISTANCE STATEMENT WITH AN INTRODUCTION BY JULIA SUDBURY

Gender Violence and the Prison Industrial Complex

Interpersonal and State Violence against Women of Color

―――――――――――――――――― ABSTRACT ――――――――――――――――――

Incite! Women of Color against Violence and Critical Resistance are two U.S. national activist organizations founded in 1998 and 2000, respectively, to fight against the violence toward and oppression of women and men of color. Incite! works toward developing community accountability models that do not depend on the criminal justice system for addressing violence against women of color. Critical Resistance (CR) seeks to build an international movement to end the Prison Industrial Complex (that is, the mass imprisonment of poor people and people of color) by challenging the belief that the criminal justice system and its prisons make communities safe.

As Josephson discusses in chapter 7, an increasingly punitive attitude toward women of color has dramatically affected the legal systems with which poor women interact most: welfare, criminal justice, and family courts. In each of these arenas poor women are stigmatized; their behavior is viewed with suspicion and hostility; and state efforts to control their sexual and maternal behavior become ever harsher. One little noticed form these policies have taken is a lifetime ban on cash assistance and food stamps, as well as loss of public housing and education benefits, to women with felony drug convictions.

The Incite!–CR statement is preceded by an introduction by Julia Sudbury, a member of both collectives. She provides a history and context for understanding how the Incite!–CR statement is born out of the experiences of women of color as radical bridge builders between diverse movements (for example, Women, Black Power, Prisoner Rights, and Workers Rights movements). It is within an intersectional analysis that such grassroots people's movements must be situated.

The Incite!–CR statement expresses the outrage and call to activism that punitive social policies engender. Incite! and CR encourage us to think beyond the single issue of domestic violence to build power and community capacity for structural change across institutions. Incite! and CR reflect vibrant grassroots movements seeking enforcement accountability in the U.S. Immigration and Naturalization Service, border patrol, prison system, law enforcement, and other social institutions by way of confronting the racist and classist limitations of the criminal justice approach to domestic violence.

Incite!–CR entreat us to break tight silences about violence at home, in the streets, and by state agents by informing and engaging the community both to promote social, environmental, and economic justice and to build a collective consensus about safe communities with the absence of domestic violence and institutional violence as the pillar of public safety. These organizations also challenge the professionalization of the domestic violence movement. These ideas are more fully explored by Andrea Smith in chapter 24.

As you read this chapter, identify the myths and stereotypes held in popular culture that the statement by Incite!–Critical Resistance debunks. What broader social institutions are linked and rendered complicit in domestic and institutional violence? Which of your own values are confronted?

INTRODUCTION: TOWARD A HOLISTIC ANTI-VIOLENCE AGENDA—WOMEN OF COLOR AS RADICAL BRIDGE BUILDERS

The publication of the twentieth anniversary edition of *This Bridge Called My Back* was a cause for celebration and reflection among women of color in the United States (Moraga and Anzaldúa, 2002). First printed in 1982, the bridge metaphor captured the challenges facing women of color as they negotiated the radical social movements of the 1970s and 1980s in the United States. Expected to act in feminist spaces (as if gender were the primary oppression structuring their lives), in radical movements of color (as if the struggle against white supremacy were the only meaningful engagement), and in leftist organizations (as if gender and race were distractions to the fight against capital), women of color struggled to generate a politics that could honor the complex intersections of race, class, and gender in their lives. Working with white women to challenge violence against women, and with men of color to defend their communities against police brutality and institutional racism, women of color frequently found themselves acting as the bridge between a multiplicity of social movements. Yet this role, while critically

From *Social Justice* 30, no. 3 (2003): "Toward a Holistic Anti-violence Agenda: Women of Color as Radical Bridge-Builders" by Julia Sudbury, 134–140; Critical Resistance Statement, 141–150. © 2003 Social Justice. Reprinted by permission.

important as a basis for coalition-building, was also draining—as Kate Rushin (2002) succinctly communicated in "The Bridge Poem":

> I'm sick of seeing and touching
> Both sides of things
> Sick of being the damn bridge for everybody.
> . . . I explain . . .
> the white feminists to the Black church folks the Black church folks
> To the ex-hippies the ex-hippies to the Black separatists
> the Black separatists to the artists the artists to my friends' parents
> I do more translating
> Than the Gawdamn U.N.

Women of color who identified as feminists or addressed gender issues in communities of color risked being labeled "traitors," "lesbians," or "white identified." If they challenged racism or admitted working alongside men of color in feminist spaces, they risked being labeled "male-identified" or "divisive."

Twenty years later, much has changed. The intersectional politics elaborated by women in *This Bridge*, once a marginal and controversial perspective, have been mainstreamed and there are even textbooks to explain them to the beginner (Andersen and Collins, 2001). Women writers of color, who once were limited to small radical publishers like Kitchen Table Press, are now published by mainstream imprints that expect to sell significant quantities to women's studies programs across the country. Anti-racist white feminists and pro-feminist men of color have joined women of color in critiquing racism in the women's movement and sexism in the anti-racist movement. The Critical Resistance–Incite! statement that follows is testimony to the living legacy of women of color as bridge builders.

In the post–September 11 era, many women of color have tired of seeking to transform liberal identity-based movements that claim to represent all "women" or "African Americans," for example, but remain entrenched in the politics of imperial feminism or patriarchal and heterosexist rights for black men. Instead, our own organizations are based on an intersectional analysis of violence, and participate in and build coalitions within issue-based movements, such as the antiwar, prison abolitionist, political prisoner, police brutality, racial profiling, and domestic violence and sexual assault movements.

Walking in the footsteps of the contributors to *This Bridge*, activists from the prison abolitionist and domestic violence and sexual assault (DVSA) movements have come together to write the Critical Resistance–Incite! statement . . . The seeds of the statement were sown at the first Critical Resistance conference, which took place in Berkeley, California, in fall 1998. Among the organizers of that conference were women of color who had been active in both the prison abolitionist and DVSA movements. The conference brought together 3,500 activists, students, academics, former prisoners and their families, former political prisoners, and cultural workers to launch a new broad-based abolitionist movement based on a critique of the prison-industrial complex. Women were predominant in the organizing and were integrated into the conference panels and workshops. Nevertheless, some DVSA activists who attended the conference felt that there was insufficient seriousness attached to the question of how women's safety would be guaranteed in the "world without prisons" envisioned by many of the participants. Nor did they feel that the prison movement was always serious enough about holding men who had perpetrated violence against women accountable for their actions. At the same time, those working in communities of color were highly critical of the actual impact of initiatives designed to protect women, such as mandatory arrest, zero tolerance campaigns around domestic violence, and enhanced sentencing, concluding that these had contributed to a prison-building boom that was increasingly capturing both men and women of color in its net. Surely it was irrational, they argued, to expect protection from a system that was itself a key perpetrator of violence against poor communities and communities of color.[1] This difference in opinion, rooted in real experiences of the prison abolitionist movement and the criminal justice system, created barriers between the two movements that potentially threatened the effectiveness of both. Two years later, some of the women of color who had been involved in Critical Resistance, along with many who were involved in the DVSA movement, came together to form Incite! Women of Color Against Violence. The Critical Resistance–Incite! statement was thus birthed by two mutually overlapping collectives. . . .

Incite! was founded as "a national activist organization of radical feminists of color advancing a movement to end violence against women of color and their communities through direct action, critical dialogue, and grassroots organizing."[2] Instead of establishing a hierarchical structure that might lead toward cooption, Incite! members conceptualize it as a movement that emerges out of grassroots struggle. Local Incite! chapters are generated organically around local issues, but are infused with an analysis that emerges from its conferences and task forces, the latter focusing on issues ranging from reparations for survivors of Indian Boarding Schools to violence against queer [includes lesbian, bisexual, transgendered, intersexed] women of color.

Critical Resistance is a national organization dedicated to fighting the prison-industrial complex and building genuine and durable forms of justice and security. The organization was established at the conference entitled "Critical Resistance: Beyond the Prison-Industrial Complex" that took place in Berkeley in 1998. The conference was organized by a racially diverse group that included former prisoners, prison activists, students, academics, sex workers, homeless advocates, queer, youth, and HIV/AIDS activists and aimed to build a broad-based radical prison abolitionist movement. Critical Resistance advocates the abolition of prisons. They define abolition as "a political vision that seeks to eliminate the need for prisons, policing, and surveillance by creating sustainable alternatives to punishment and imprisonment."

The organization calls instead for sustainable alternatives that generate safety and security, while refusing to rely on law enforcement. Critical Resistance argues against investing more money into the prison system, calling instead for the diversion of funds from punishment and retribution into social welfare and community development. [Critical Resistance works] . . . in partnership with broad-based coalition[s] including environmentalists, farm worker unions, Latino and immigrant advocates, and anti-prison activists. . . . [Its work] . . . has generated a national debate about the failure of the "prisons as public works" policy that presents prison construction as a form of economic regeneration for stagnant small towns. Other work includes airing a radio show that reaches inside prisons throughout California, organizing local campaigns, movement building through large national and regional gatherings, and public education through film festivals, publications, and media work.

Engendering Organic Theory

The process by which the Critical Resistance–Incite! statement came to be written differed significantly from the usually solitary pursuit of writing theory. It was written by a group of six women of color and one pro-feminist man of color. The group included founder members of both organizations, as well as activists involved in prison abolition or anti-violence work for at least two decades. Their stories of the lessons learned during years of activism in a range of contexts were invaluable. . . .

The statement inspired significant debate and concern from activists who felt it was either overly critical, or they were not ready to embrace its implied disengagement with the state. Where possible, our goal was to incorporate these concerns and to ensure a broad-based commitment to . . . the statement. For domestic violence organizations, [this] . . . required a rethinking of their services, their level of involvement with the local police, and the options they provided to women escaping violence. It was therefore extremely significant when the National Coalition Against Domestic Violence signed on, since the organization plays a major leadership role in the DVSA movement.

. . . The statement stands as an important model of organic theory and an alternative to the individualizing model of academic theory production. Electronic mail has taken collective involvement in theory-making to a level hitherto unknown. Hundreds of activists read, debated, and commented on the statement before it reached print. The statement is available to social movements as uncopyrighted material. It belongs to no individual and can be reproduced or even rewritten as necessary. . . . Like organic matter, organic theory has a life of its own. Both unpredictable and fluid, it emerges from activist collectives and evolves through interaction and debate. Morphed from individual pursuit to organizing project, writing theory becomes a radicalizing process, generating unexpected outcomes and transforming the political consciousness of [those involved].

Autocriticism as a Basis for Radical Coalitions

Reading the Critical Resistance–Incite! statement may elicit a number of emotions. Those who were involved in the pioneering days of the DVSA movement may feel defensive. The statement is highly critical of what the authors deem an overreliance by anti-violence activists on the criminal justice system and argues that this has backfired in many cases, causing further harm to women of color, and to queer, immigrant, and native women. For women who have dedicated years to forcing the police and judiciary to take violence against women seriously and who viewed the Violence Against Women Act as a significant personal success, this may be difficult to hear. For those who have uncritically embraced incarceration as punishment for harming women, the idea that "prisons don't work" may lead to anxiety and even despair. What are we left with to keep women safe if we do not have the prison? Incite!'s Community Accountability taskforce has been working with organizations like Brooklyn's Sista II Sista and Seattle's Communities Against Rape and Abuse to identify and disseminate community-based models for challenging violence against women, but much more needs to be done before these are widely available. (See A. Smith, chapter 24, in this volume.) However, prison activists may feel unfairly criticized. Those who work with women in prison may feel that the claim that the prison abolitionist movement conceptualizes men of color as the primary victims of state violence makes their work invisible. Similarly, prison activists in general may feel that they pay more attention to issues of gender violence than is allowed for in the statement.

In writing the statement, we took risks in making these criticisms about the two movements. We recognized that there were generally exceptions to the trends we pointed out. Nevertheless, we felt that an honest autocriticism needed to point to our weakest areas, not to hide behind our best practices. We recognized the diversity of actors and organizations that make up any movement and that it was possible, from our experience as well as from research, to make valid statements about the limitations of our work. These criticisms are made in the context of an immense commitment to both the DVSA and the prison abolition movements. They are made with love and respect and with the goal of generating an honest dialogue between actors in both movements. It is our belief, implicit in this statement, that autocriticism can be a powerful tool for breaking down the barriers that keep diverse social movement activists from working together. With our differences on the table, and a mutual commitment to addressing our limitations, we have the potential to build a unified anti-violence movement to end both state and interpersonal violence.

Julia Sudbury

INCITE!–CRITICAL RESISTANCE STATEMENT

We call on social justice movements to develop strategies and analyses that address both state *and* interpersonal violence, particularly violence against women.[3] Currently, activists/movements that address state violence (such as

anti-prison, anti-police brutality groups) often work in isolation from ac-
tivists/movements that address domestic and sexual violence. The result is
that women of color, who suffer disproportionately from both state and interpersonal violence, have become marginalized within these movements.
It is critical that we develop responses to gender violence that do not depend
on a sexist, racist, classist, and homophobic criminal justice system. It is also
important that we develop strategies that challenge the criminal justice system and that also provide safety for survivors of sexual and domestic violence. To live violence-free lives, we must develop holistic strategies for addressing violence that speak to the intersection of all forms of oppression.
The anti-violence movement has been critically important in breaking the silence around violence against women and providing much-needed services to
survivors. However, the mainstream anti-violence movement has increasingly relied on the criminal justice system as the front-line approach toward
ending violence against women of color. It is important to assess the impact
of this strategy.

1) Law enforcement approaches to violence against women *may* deter
   some acts of violence in the short term. However, as an overall strategy for ending violence, criminalization has not worked. In fact, the
   overall impact of mandatory arrests laws for domestic violence have
   led to decreases in the number of battered women who kill their partners in self-defense, but they have not led to the same decrease in the
   number of male batterers who kill their partners.[4] Thus, the law protects batterers more than it protects survivors.

2) The criminalization approach has also brought many women into
   conflict with the law, particularly women of color, poor women, lesbians, sex workers, immigrant women, women with disabilities, and
   other marginalized women. For instance, under mandatory arrest laws,
   there have been numerous incidents where police officers called to domestic incidents have arrested the woman who is being battered.[5] Many
   undocumented women have reported cases of sexual and domestic violence, only to find themselves deported.[6] A tough law and order agenda
   also leads to long punitive sentences for women convicted of killing
   their batterers.[7] Finally, when public funding is channeled into policing
   and prisons, budget cuts for social programs, including women's shelters, welfare, and public housing are the inevitable side effects.[8] These
   cutbacks leave women less able to escape violent relationships.

3) Prisons don't work. Despite an exponential increase in the number of
   men in prisons, women are not any safer, and the rates of sexual assault
   and domestic violence have not decreased.[9] In calling for greater police
   responses to and harsher sentences for perpetrators of gender violence,
   the anti-violence movement has fueled the proliferation of prisons
   which now lock up more people per capita in the United States than in
   any other country.[10] During the past fifteen years, the numbers of
   women, especially women of color in prison has skyrocketed.[11] Prisons
   also inflict violence on the growing numbers of women behind bars.
   Slashing, suicide, the proliferation of HIV, strip searches, medical neglect, and rape of prisoners has largely been ignored by anti-violence

activists.[12] The criminal justice system, an institution of violence, domination, and control, has increased the level of violence in society.

4) The reliance on state funding to support anti-violence programs has increased the professionalization of the anti-violence movement and alienated it from its community-organizing, social justice roots.[13] Such reliance has isolated the anti-violence movement from other social justice movements that seek to eradicate state violence, such that it acts in conflict rather than in collaboration with these movements.

5) The reliance on the criminal justice system has taken power away from women's ability to organize collectively to stop violence and has invested this power within the state. The result is that women who seek redress in the criminal justice system feel disempowered and alienated.[14] It has also promoted an individualistic approach toward ending violence such that the only way people think they can intervene in stopping violence is to call the police. This reliance has shifted our focus away from developing ways communities can collectively respond to violence.

In recent years, the mainstream anti-prison movement has called important attention to the negative impact of criminalization and the buildup of the prison industrial complex. Because activists who seek to reverse the tide of mass incarceration and criminalization of poor communities and communities of color have not always centered gender and sexuality in their analysis or organizing, we have not always responded adequately to the needs of survivors of domestic and sexual violence.

1) Prison and police accountability activists have generally organized around and conceptualized men of color as the primary victims of state violence. Women prisoners and victims of police brutality have been made invisible by a focus on the war on our brothers and sons. This emphasis fails to consider that state violence affects women as severely as it does men.[15] The plight of women who are raped by INS [Immigration and Naturalization Service] officers or prison guards, for instance, has not received sufficient attention. In addition, women carry the burden of caring for extended family when family and community members are criminalized and warehoused.[16] Several organizations have been established to advocate for women prisoners;[17] however, these groups have been frequently marginalized within the mainstream anti-prison movement.

2) The anti-prison movement has not developed strategies for dealing with the rampant forms of violence women face in their everyday lives, including street harassment, sexual harassment at work, rape, and intimate partner abuse. Until these strategies are developed, many women will feel shortchanged by the movement. In addition, by not seeking alliances with the anti-violence movement, the anti-prison movement has sent the message that it is possible to liberate communities without seeking the well-being and safety of women.

3) The anti-prison movement has failed to sufficiently organize around the forms of state violence faced by Lesbian, Gay, Bisexual, Transgendered, Two-spirited, and Intersexed (LGBTTI) communities. LGBTTI street

youth and trans people in general are particularly vulnerable to police brutality and criminalization.[18] LGBTTI prisoners are denied basic human rights such as family visits from same sex partners, and same-sex consensual relationships in prison are policed and punished.[19]

4) While prison abolitionists have correctly pointed out that rapists and serial murderers comprise a small number of the prison population, we have not answered the question of how these cases should be addressed.[20] The inability to answer the question is interpreted by many anti-violence activists as a lack of concern for the safety of women.

5) The various alternatives to incarceration that have been developed by anti-prison activists have generally failed to provide sufficient mechanisms for safety and accountability for survivors of sexual and domestic violence. These alternatives often rely on a romanticized notion of communities, which have yet to demonstrate their commitment and ability to keep women and children safe or seriously address the sexism and homophobia that is deeply embedded within them.[21]

We call on social justice movements concerned with ending violence in all its forms to:

1) Develop community-based responses to violence that do not rely on the criminal justice system *and* which have mechanisms that ensure safety and accountability for survivors of sexual and domestic violence. Transformative practices emerging from local communities should be documented and disseminated to promote collective responses to violence.

2) Critically assess the impact of state funding on social justice organizations and develop alternative fundraising strategies to support these organizations. Develop collective fundraising and organizing strategies for anti-prison and anti-violence organizations. Develop strategies and analyses that specifically target state forms of sexual violence.

3) Make connections between interpersonal violence, the violence inflicted by domestic state institutions (such as prisons, detention centers, mental hospitals, and child protective services), and international violence (such as war, military base prostitution, and nuclear testing).

4) Develop an analysis and strategies to end violence that do not isolate individual acts of violence (either committed by the state or individuals) from their *larger contexts*. These strategies must address how entire communities of all genders are affected in multiple ways by both state violence and interpersonal gender violence. Battered women prisoners represent an intersection of state and interpersonal violence and as such provide an opportunity for both movements to build coalitions and joint struggles.

5) Put poor/working-class women of color in the center of their analysis, organizing practices, and leadership development. Recognize the role of economic oppression, welfare "reform," and attacks on women workers' rights in increasing women's vulnerability to all forms of violence and locate anti-violence and anti-prison activism alongside efforts to transform the capitalist economic system.

6) Center stories of state violence committed against women of color in our organizing efforts.

7) Oppose legislative changes that promote prison expansion, criminalization of poor communities and communities of color, and thus state violence against women of color, even if these changes also incorporate measures to support victims of interpersonal gender violence.

8) Promote holistic political education at the everyday level within our communities, specifically how sexual violence helps reproduce the colonial, racist, capitalist, heterosexist, and patriarchal society we live in as well as how state violence produces interpersonal violence within communities.

9) Develop strategies for mobilizing against sexism and homophobia *within* our communities in order to keep women safe.

10) Challenge men of color and all men in social justice movements to take particular responsibility to address and organize around gender violence in their communities as a primary strategy for addressing violence and colonialism. We challenge men to address how their own histories of victimization have hindered their ability to establish gender justice in their communities.

11) Link struggles for personal transformation and healing with struggles for social justice.

We seek to build movements that not only end violence but also create a society based on radical freedom, mutual accountability, and passionate reciprocity. In this society, safety and security will not be premised on violence or the threat of violence; it will be based on a collective commitment to guaranteeing the survival and care of all peoples.

NOTES

1. For a thoughtful discussion of this complex debate, see Sen (1999) and Special Report, The color of violence (2000–2001).

2. At www.incite-national.org, accessed August 22, 2003.

3. Critical Resistance and Incite! Women of Color Against Violence are U.S.-based organizations that participate in transnational networks and alliances. Although many of the critiques of the anti-violence and anti-prison movements in the statement may be relevant to non-U.S. contexts, the authors do not make any claims of universality and recognize that movements in other countries have developed from distinct histories and political contexts.

4. In a twenty-year study of forty-eight cities, Dugan et al. (2003) found that greater access to criminal legal remedies for women led to fewer men being killed by their wives because women who might otherwise have killed to escape violence were offered alternatives. However, women receiving legal support were no less likely to be killed by their intimate partners and were exposed to additional retaliatory violence.

5. See McMahon (2003), Osthoff (2002), and Miller (2001). Noting that in some cities, more than 20 percent of those arrested for domestic violence are women, Miller concludes: "An arrest policy intended to protect battered women as victims is being misapplied and used against them. Battered women have become female offenders."

6. Women's dependent or undocumented status is often manipulated by batterers, who use the threat of deportation as part of a matrix of domination and control. Although the Violence Against Women Act (VAWA, 1994; 2000) introduced visas for battered immigrant women, many women do not know about the act's provisions or are unable to meet evidentiary requirements. Since the Illegal Immigration Reform and Immigrant Responsibility act

made domestic violence grounds for deportation, women may also be reluctant to subject a legal permanent resident spouse to potential deportation proceedings by reporting him to the police. In addition, women arrested under mandatory arrest laws could themselves face deportation. See Raj and Silverman (2002) and Jang et al. (1997).

7. For example, former California Governor Grey Davis, whose tough "law and order" platform included a promise that no one convicted of murder would go free, rejected numerous parole board recommendations on behalf of battered women incarcerated for killing in self-defense (Vesley, 2002). For further information and testimonies of incarcerated survivors of domestic violence, see www.freebatteredwomen.org.

8. Christian Parenti (1999) documents the shift in government spending from welfare, education, and social provision to prisons and policing.

9. The U.S. prison and jail population grew from 270,000 in 1975 to two million in 2001 as legislators pushed "tough on crime" policies, such as mandatory minimums, three-strikes-and-you're out, and truth-in-sentencing (Tonry, 2001: 17). More than 90 percent of these prisoners are men, and approximately 50 percent are black men. Despite claims that locking more people away would lead to a dramatic decrease in crime, reported violent crimes against women have remained relatively constant since annual victimization surveys were initiated in 1973 (Bureau of Justice Statistics, 1994).

10. In 2001, the United States, with 686 prisoners per 100,000 residents, surpassed the incarceration rate of gulag-ridden Russia. The United States dwarfs the incarceration rate of Western European nations, like Finland and Denmark, which incarcerate only 59 people out of every 100,000 (Home Office Development and Statistics Directorate, 2003).

11. The rate of increase of women's imprisonment in the United States has exceeded that of men. In 1970, there were 5,600 women in federal and state prisons; by 1996, there were 75,000 (Currie, 1998).

12. Amnesty International's investigation of women's prisons in the United States revealed countless cases of sexual, physical, and psychological abuse. In one case, the Federal Bureau of Prisons paid $500,000 to settle a lawsuit by three black women who were sexually assaulted when guards took money from male prisoners in exchange for taking them to the women's cells; prisoners in Arizona were subjected to rape, sexual fondling, and genital touching during searches, as well as to constant prurient viewing when using the shower and toilet; women at Valley State Prison, California, were treated as a "private harem to sexually abuse and harass"; in numerous cases, women were kept in restraints while seriously ill, dying, or in labor, and women under maximum-security conditions were kept in isolation and sensory deprivation for long periods (Amnesty International, 1999).

13. See Smith (2000–2001).

14. Mary Koss (2000) argues that the adversarial justice system traumatizes survivors of domestic violence. For a first-person account of a rape survivor's fight to hold the police accountable, see Doe (2003). Jane Doe was raped by the Toronto "balcony rapist" after police used women in her neighborhood as "bait."

15. For a comprehensive account of state violence against women in the United States, see Bhattacharjee (2001).

16. Added burdens on women when a loved one is incarcerated include dealing with the arrest and trials of family members, expensive visits and phone calls from correctional facilities, and meeting disruptive parole requirements (Richie, 2002).

17. In the United States, see Justice Now Legal Services for Prisoners with Children, at http://prisonerswithchildren.org; Free Battered Women, at www.freebatteredwomen. org; California Coalition for Women Prisoners, at http://womenprisoners.org; and Chicago Legal Advocacy for Incarcerated Mothers, at www.c-l-a-i-m.org. In the United Kingdom, see Women in Prison, at www.womeninprison.org.uk; and Justice for Women, at www.jfw.org.uk. In Canada, see the Canadian Association of Elizabeth Fry Associations, at www. elizabethfry. ca/caefs_e.htm.

18. According to transgender activists in the Bay Area, the police are responsible for approximately 50 percent of all trans abuse cases. The Transaction hotline regularly receives

reports from TG/TS survivors of police violence who have been forced to strip to "verify gender" or subjected to demands for sex from undercover police officers (*San Francisco Examiner*, 2002; *Bay Area Reporter*, 1999).

19. See Faith (1993: 211–223).

20. The response of abolitionists Thomas and Boehlfeld (1993) to the question of what to do about Henry, a violent rapist, is an example of this problem. The authors conclude that this is the wrong question because it focuses on a small and anomalous subsection of the prison population and detracts from a broader abolitionist vision.

21. Alternatives to the traditional justice system such as Sentencing Circles are particularly developed in Canada and Australia, where they have been developed in partnership with indigenous communities. However, native women, critical of these approaches, have argued that they fail to address the deep-rooted sexism and misogyny engendered by experiences of colonization and may revictimize women (Monture-Angus, 2000). See also Hudson (2002).

REFERENCES

Amnesty International. 1999. *Not Part of My Sentence: Violations of the Human Rights of Women in Custody*. New York: Amnesty International.

Andersen, Margaret, and Patricia Hill Collins. 2001. *Race, Gender, and Class: An Anthology*. 4th ed. Belmont, Calif.: Wadsworth.

Bay Area Reporter. 1999. Another transgender murder. April 8, pp. 29 and 14.

Bhattacharjee, A. 2001. *Women of Color and the Violence of Law Enforcement*. Philadelphia: American Friends Service Committee and Committee on Women, Population, and the Environment.

Braman, D. 2002. Families and incarceration. In M. Mauer and M. Chesney-Lind, eds., *Invisible Punishment: The Collateral Consequences of Mass Imprisonment*. New York: The New Press, 117–135.

Bureau of Justice Statistics. 1994. National Crime Victimization Survey Report: Violence Against Women. NCJ-145325.

Chesney-Lind, M. 2002. Imprisoning women: The unintended victims of mass imprisonment. In M. Mauer and M. Chesney-Lind, eds., *Invisible Punishment: The Collateral Consequences of Mass Imprisonment*. New York: The New Press, 79–94.

Combahee River Collective. 1995. A Black feminist statement. In Beverly Guy-Sheftall, ed., *Words of Fire: An Anthology of African American Feminist Thought*. New York: The New Press. First published in 1977.

Crenshaw, K. W. 1994. Mapping the margins: Intersectionality, identity politics, and violence against women of color. In M. A. Fineman and R. Mykitiuk, eds., *The Public Nature of Private Violence*. New York: Routledge, 93–118.

Critical Resistance. 2002. What is abolition? Available at: www.criticalresistance.org.

Currie, E. 1998. *Crime and Punishment in America*. New York: Henry Holt.

Coe, J. 2003. *The Story of Jane Doe: A Book about Rape*. New York: Random House.

Dugan, L., D. S. Nagin, and R. Rosenfeld. 2003. Exposure reduction or retaliation? The effects of domestic violence resources on intimate-partner homicide. *Law & Society Review* 37(1): 161–198.

Faith, K. 1993. *Unruly Women: The Politics of Confinement and Resistance*. Vancouver: Press Gang Publishers.

Home Office Development and Statistics Directorate. 2003. World prison population list. Online at: www.homeoffice.gov.uk/rds/pdfs2/rl88.pdf.

Hudson, B. 2002. Restorative justice and gendered violence. *British Journal of Criminology* 42(3): 616–634.

James, J. 1996. *Resisting State Violence: Radicalism, Gender, and Race in U.S. Culture*. Minneapolis: University of Minnesota Press.

Jang, D., L. Marin, and G. Pendleton. 1997. *Domestic Violence in Immigrant and Refugee Communities: Assessing the Rights of Battered Women*. 2d ed. San Francisco: Family Violence Prevention Fund.

Koss, M. 2000. Blame, shame, and community: Justice responses to violence against women. *American Psychologist* 55: 3–14.

McMahon, M. 2003. Making social change. *Violence Against Women* 9(1): 47–74.

Miller, S. 2001. The paradox of women arrested for domestic violence. *Violence Against Women* 7(12): 1339–1376.

Monture-Angus, P. 2000. The roles and responsibilities of Aboriginal women: Reclaiming justice. In R. Neugebauer, ed., *Criminal Injustice: Racism in the Criminal Justice System*. Toronto: Canadian Scholars' Press.

Moraga, C., and G. Anzaldúa, eds. 2002. *This Bridge Called My Back: Writing by Radical Women of Color*. 3d ed. 1982; Boston: Kitchen Table Press.

Osthoff, S. 2002. "But Gerturde, I beg to differ, a hit is not a hit is not a hit." *Violence Against Women* 8(12): 1521–1544.

Parenti, C. 1999. *Lockdown America: Policing and Prisons in the Age of Crisis*. New York: Verso Books.

Raj, A., and J. Silverman. 2002. Violence against immigrant women: The role of culture, context, and legal immigrant status on intimate partner violence. *Violence Against Women* 8(3): 367–398.

Richie, B. E. 2002. The social impact of mass incarceration on women. In M. Mauer and J. Chesney-Lind, eds., *Invisible Punishment: The Collateral Consequences of Mass Imprisonment*. New York: The New Press, 136–149.

Rushkin, K. 2002. The bridge poem. In C. Moraga and G. Anzaldúa, eds., *This Bridge Called My Back: Writing by Radical Women of Color*. 3d ed. 1982; Boston: Kitchen Table Press.

San Francisco Examiner. 2002. Transgender sues police. August 9.

Sen, R. 1999. Between a rock and a hard place: Domestic violence in communities of color. *Colorlines* 2(1).

Smith, A. 2000–2001. Colors of violence. *Colorlines* 3(4).

Special Report. 2000–2001. The color of violence. *Colorlines* 3(4).

Thomas, J., and S. Boehlefeld. 1993. Rethinking abolitionism: "What do we do with Henry?" In B. Maclean and H. Pepinsky, eds., *We Who Would Take No Prisoners: Selections from the Fifth International Conference on Penal Abolition*. Vancouver: Collective Press.

Tonry, M., ed. 2001. *Penal Reform in Overcrowded Times*. Oxford: Oxford University Press.

Vesely, R. 2002. Davis' right to deny parole to abused women upheld. *Women's ENews*, December 19.

PART II

Culture, Resistance, and Community

Part 2 of this anthology examines how culture and community interact with social structural, economic, and political conditions to shape women's experiences of violence, the individual, institutional, and state responses to violence, and, most important, women's patterns of resistance to domestic violence.

As discussed in the introduction to part 1, culture is fluid and complex, not something that can be summed up in a word (like "Latino" or "Anglo" or "gay" culture; see Perilla, 1999). This section of the anthology explores examples of how specific cultures intersect with race, class, immigration status, sexuality, and the particular experiences of individuals within different groups in the United States to create what Jyl Josephson (chapter 7) describes as "interlocking hierarchies of oppression," as well as unique sets of strength and support.

Leti Volpp (2003, see also chapter 3) gives an example of how culture is often mistakenly used only in reference to "Others." In newspaper and other popular accounts of the case of a Hmong immigrant, Khoua Her, who strangled her six children and then hanged herself in a failed suicide attempt, "Hmong culture" was said to be responsible in explaining her acts. However, individual psychology or mental illness (for example, postpartum depression and failure to take medications) was used to explain similar behavior on the part of Andrea Yates—a white, Christian woman born in the United States—who killed her five children. This psychological explanation was offered despite the fact that in Yates's case, she and her family made specific, numerous references to how their Christian beliefs shaped her family's actions and her own.

There is a certain tension in the examination of the intersection of culture and violence (see Volpp, chapter 3). Both advocates and academics too often essentialize and universalize the experience of violence. To fight against racism and cultural stereotypes that insist on placing violence in the domain of "Others," Volpp (chapter 3) and Dasgupta (chapter 5) recognize the understandable appeal in emphasizing that violence against women is epidemic in most societies, that no racial, ethnic, or socioeconomic group is immune. As the authors in part 2 reveal, however, ignoring the specificity of violence ignores the experiences of both individual women and communities and fails to provide adequate tools for combating violence.

In chapter 9, Robert L. Hampton, Ricardo Carrillo, and Joan Kim discuss family violence in African American communities. Historically, research on family violence has found higher rates of domestic violence among communities of color, particularly African American communities. The authors argue, however, for a more *contextual* understanding of the findings and better research questions; they demonstrate the difficulty of distinguishing from degree of poverty, family disruption, housing density and segregation, embeddedness in social networks, and the social organization of communities because race is so firmly embedded in racist structures. Community-level social processes may in fact be more predictive of family violence than race. Although it is improving, high-quality, contextually embedded research on communities of color is still sorely lacking. Hampton and colleagues (chapter 9) call for research in which African American families are viewed as neither deviant from nor equivalent to the middle-class white family, but different and equally valid. While acknowledging the many strengths of families in Black communities under great stress, they caution us not to paper over destructive conditions and behaviors in African American communities.

A number of researchers have confirmed what Hampton and coauthors assert: that factors other than race explain the disproportionate impact of domestic violence in communities of color. For example, recent analysis of the National Crime Victimization Survey finds that lower income, not race, best predicts rates of intimate partner violence (Rennison and Planty, 2003). Jacquelyn Campbell and colleagues (2003) similarly found that male unemployment explained differences in intimate partner femicide that initially appeared related to race. These analyses fail to take into account, however, the multidimensional, intersectional nature of race, culture, class, income, and the like. As Hampton and colleagues (chapter 9) point out, African American families are disproportionately likely to live in extreme poverty, which makes it difficult to truly separate the effects of race and income. Even community-level analyses of the effects of race and income are not conclusive, as the United States's legacy of racism in urban policy means that very few predominantly white neighborhoods in the United States evidence the same degree of poverty and social disorganization as the most disadvantaged predominantly African American communities (see McNulty, 2001; Rusk, 1995).

Whereas Hampton and coauthors lay out a structural framework for understanding domestic violence in very poor African American communities, Neil Websdale (chapter 10) provides a case study of this situation in Nashville, Tennessee. He elaborates on the lives of poverty-stricken African American women who are abused by their partners and live in communities that have been badly hurt by globalization, the history of slavery, and the contemporary racist conditions that exist in the United States. Websdale describes the impact of intense racialized poverty on Black communities, families, and individuals and details how this makes it difficult for abused women to protect themselves from violence in the home. For example, he finds that the women simply cannot afford to pay for costly divorces or child custody battles; rather, they may leave and lose benefits of child support, or they may become involved in some kind of criminal activity (for example, drugs or petty theft), which therefore precludes asking for help from police, shelters, or other service providers. Moreover, encouragement to leave a violent home fails to consider the reality: the situation one enters in the larger community and society may be equally if not more violent because of the unsafe neighborhood one lives in and/or the violence and discrimination a poor Black woman might experience outside her own community. According to Websdale, this dilemma is intensified for many women who either are or have been in prison for domestic violence-related reasons or for other offenses, commonly drugs and drug-related crimes.

In chapter 11, "Domestic Violence in Ethnically and Racially Diverse Families," Carolyn M. West addresses the reluctance of both individual women of color and their communities as well as some activists, survivors of violence, and researchers within marginalized communities to discuss domestic violence. C. West suggests that some officials have pressured marginalized communities to keep private potentially damning information about violence to protect the community from harmful stereotypes and oppressive social policies. Zanita Fenton (2003) notes that, while keeping violence in the realm of the private can protect male privilege, it is important to understand the implications of speaking out for particular communities. In the United States, for example, Fenton argues that Blacks are invisible as victims and whites are invisible as perpetrators of violence. Because of the multiple layers of stereotypes pertaining to Black women (for example, that they are more able to withstand violence and more likely to be violent than white women) and the multiple forms of racism embedded in the criminal justice system (for example, Black men are more likely than whites to be arrested, and the police are less active in responding to the complaints of Black women), there are real dangers to individuals and the community when speaking out about violence. C. West (chapter 11), like Fenton (2003), believes that the self-imposed "gag order" has been lifted. Given the problems engendered by breaking the silence, it remains imperative for scholars to situate discourse on race and ethnicity at the intersections of multiple forms of oppression. When breaking the silence, it is necessary

to simultaneously work to eliminate racism, homophobia, and class oppression and to understand the ways that particular contexts necessitate
individualized solutions. Thus, C. West reviews population-based studies
that have examined the prevalence of violence among the four largest
ethnic groups in the United States: African Americans, Latina/Latino
Americans, Asian Americas, and Native Americans.

The debate among Native American communities discusses whether
colonization was "the cause" of domestic violence or whether domestic violence existed in different tribes prior to colonization (see
Kanuha, 2002). Given the different experiences of more than five hundred Indian tribes in the United States, a case can still be made that colonization played a major role in disrupting the lives of Native American people so thoroughly that the process either caused or intensified
greatly the violence against women. Colonization refers to the removal
of Native people from their ancestral lands as well as a purposeful and
tremendous reduction in size of Indian peoples and the ensuing prohi-
bition against traditional religious practices. Colonization also has
meant the forced movement from a group orientation to an individual-
based society, from land-based to cash-based profit-oriented economy,
from greater equality between men and women to male-dominated
Judeo Christian hierarchy in the family and society, from pride in one's
own people and culture to frequent removal of Native children into
boarding schools that tried to "brainwash" them against their own language, culture, and people (see McEachern et al., 2000; Murray, 1995).

Sherry L. Hamby (chapter 12) underscores the importance of community organization and culture in understanding domestic violence
among Native Americans. Although often portrayed as a monolithic
group ("Native Americans"), Hamby emphasizes the need to recognize
both tribal differences related to the various ways in which gender and
authority interact in Native American communities and the great variations in geography, land base, wealth and resulting marginalization.
This diversity has far-reaching consequences for the community context of domestic violence. To be effective, advocates must understand
not only the ways that Native communities might be similarly affected
(such as racism, colonialism, and concerns about majority culture domination and control of resource and power) but also the ways that each
community might offer unique combinations of strengths and challenges in confronting domestic violence. Hamby does not dismiss the
need for feminist approaches; rather, she argues that feminist analyses
are meaningful only when firmly rooted in the specific circumstances
and social conditions of each Native American community. Thus, she
argues, like Hampton (chapter 9) and C. West (chapter 11), that severe
poverty and unemployment of Native Americans in many different
communities are important parts of the equation in explaining domestic violence in Native American communities. Because of colonialism,
many Native American communities experienced abrupt changes from

hunter/gatherer or agrarian societies to cash-based economies and the forced moves experienced by some communities have resulted in a cycle of extreme poverty and indebtedness that continues to this day. She also argues, as do most authors in this volume, that racism and colonialism coupled with poverty restricts access to numerous services.

With regard to Native Hawaiian experiences, Sally Engle Merry (2000) provides an historical ethnography of the colonial transformation of Hawaiian law and culture. Within this context, she shows how the American colonizers remade "the Hawaiian *ohana* kinship system into the privatized Christian Victorian nuclear family centered on male authority enforced through violence" (Adelman, 2003, p. 2).[1] Merry describes how many protections for Hawaiian women (for example, divorce for women who had been violated by husbands, punishment of men who assaulted their wives) were supplanted by the "rule of coverture" and the criminalization of desertion by a wife. "In other words, while physical violence and men's control over women clearly existed throughout the nineteenth century, colonization transformed the meaning and possibly the practice of the violence and intensified husbands' 'natural' authority. Merry traces the loss of public concern with men's violence in the family and increased legal efforts to contain women in marriage" (Adelman, 2003, p. 6).

Battered women, members of marginalized communities, share to some extent the anguish of negotiating between the protections available through the court systems and advocacy communities of the dominant culture while not trusting those systems to truly serve them. Sherene Razack (1998) describes the inaction of what she calls the Aboriginal (that is, Native Canadian or First Nations) communities in Ontario, Canada, in the face of sexual violence as being "between a rock and a hard place." Abusers in Aboriginal communities in Ontario are simultaneously perpetrators of crimes and victims of oppression in the dominant culture. Razack argues that the choice of this particular community to remain silent on violence against its women, while wrong, can be understood in the context of tremendous anger related to the multitude of injustices done to the community. Women find themselves reluctant to be seen as "traitors" to their communities at the same time they desperately need safety. This theme is echoed throughout the work of a variety of authors. African American, Latina American, Asian American, Pacific Islander, Native American, and other women of color fear turning their abusers over to a criminal justice system with a long history of brutality toward men of color.[2] Immigrant women face the additional fear of scrutiny by immigration authorities and intrusion into their private lives by the state without providing safety. They also fear deportation.

Sharon Angella Allard, in chapter 13, reveals one particular way in which African American women are poorly served by the criminal justice system. Through her analysis of the "battered woman syndrome" she also questions the very definitions of battered women that are centered on white, middle-class women. The premise of the "battered woman syndrome" is fundamentally flawed and does not reflect the current state of knowledge about battered women (for more discussion, see Dutton, 1996). However, this language appears in statutes and case law in some states and is still used by some defense attorneys. The syndrome is based on the concept of "learned helplessness," a concept that does not apply to most, possibly not any, battered women. The implied passivity conforms, however, to the prevailing societal image of middle-class white women as opposed to African American women, who are stereotypically viewed as angry and violent or too strong to be a "victim." Because of this clash of stereotypes, Allard argues that jurors and judges in the case of African American defendants are less likely to find persuasive "battered woman syndrome," which thereby limits their available defense strategies.

In addition to racial and ethnic communities, religious communities within the United States also present multiple layers of oppression and strengths that change the form and meaning of violence for women and affect their ability to access support in ending the violence. As Native people reminded us earlier, the attempt to "civilize" them was grounded in a Christian ethic that espoused the virtues of patriarchal families within a male-dominated society (for example, see Merry, 2000; Razack, 1998; Murray, 1998). While domestic violence in the dominant white Christian world is discussed elsewhere (see Alsdurf and Alsdurf, 1989; Fortune, 1995; Nason-Clark, 1997), this anthology focuses on the experiences and challenges in Jewish and Black Christian church communities.

Dena Sadat Hassouneh-Phillips (1998), in her discussion of how culture and systems of oppression intersect in the lives of abused women, notes that religion can be used to support male authority over women. For some women of faith, failing to submit to abuse is framed as lacking religious faith; thus, the decision to leave an abuser becomes a moral choice as well as a practical and emotional one. For others, their spirituality is a source of strength as well as vulnerability. Thus, in a small sample of Muslim women in the United States, Hassouneh-Phillips (2002) found that the women's relationship with Allah provided them an important means of coping with ongoing violence through Koranic recitation, prayer, and meditation. For many, Allah was a sustaining force when they had no one else to whom they could turn, a move that allowed them to maintain some of their dignity amidst desperately abusive situations.

In the abstract to chapter 14, Madelaine Adelman, a scholar in the area of domestic violence in Jewish and Arab communities, offers a context within which to analyze the dilemma faced by abused Jewish women. Her insightful comments frame the questions and answers

facing these women. Chapter 14, written by Beverly Horsburgh, outlines the plight of Orthodox Jewish women who are abused. Should a
woman decide to leave her abuser, she may also have to leave behind
her religious practice, her family, and her community, without being
able to easily access the support and safeguards of the traditional or
mainstream domestic violence advocacy community. Orthodox Jewish
women cannot obtain a divorce without the consent of their husbands,
a rule that leaves the women particularly vulnerable to an abuser. If she
chooses to leave without the "get," or religious divorce decree, then
she cannot marry within the Orthodox faith. Because the role of Orthodox women in active religious practice has traditionally been almost
entirely within the home, she therefore cannot be a functioning member of her Jewish community. Moreover, if a woman chooses to leave
despite these challenges, few women's shelters allow her and her children to observe Jewish dietary laws and other religious behaviors. In
making the decision to leave her abuser, a profoundly difficult action in
most circumstances, she also leaves all that has given her life meaning
up to that point. This chapter outlines the particular ways that Orthodox Jewish women face multiple barriers to leaving violent relationships. Members of other religious communities in the United States,
however, face the similarly difficult choice between their faith, family
and community, and their personal integrity (see T. West, chapter 20).

Horsburgh emphasizes the manner in which public and private
interact within the Orthodox Jewish community to limit battered
women's choices (see Battajarchee, 1997). Because Orthodox Jewish
women tend not to have public status—their social roles and religious
practice are restricted to the private realm—they cannot petition for a
"get," and the husband's battering behavior is seen as private, and
therefore not open to the intervention of others. Like numerous other
authors in this anthology (for example, Volpp, chapter 3; Hampton
et al., chapter 9; C. West, chapter 11; Hamby, chapter 12), Horsburgh
touches on the ambiguity of making domestic violence public. Orthodox women cannot count on the support of neighbors, who may feel
shamed to see violence in their community. They cannot count on the
usual advocacy systems to provide culturally and religiously appropriate services. They rightly fear anti-Semitic reactions from the police and
court systems. Recognizing this, Horsburgh ends with a call for the Jewish community itself to grant women public status.

In chapter 15, Lois Weis and her colleagues specifically examine how
race and class intersect with battering in the lives of white working-
class women. Whiteness is usually invisible. It is an unmarked category
in discussions of domestic violence as in most of society. Some members
of the white working class in the United States once had access to well-
paying, secure jobs, which allowed male bread-winners to earn a "family wage" while women took care of the home and children. Weis and
coauthors, however, describe a situation in which men's employment

options are less abundant and less remunerative; and most women now work outside the home for small wages and few benefits, while they are still expected to carry the same burdens of caring for the home and the family. The authors describe two patterns experienced by these women: "settled lives" for women who remain within intact nuclear families and "hard living" for women who move through multiple family configurations and jobs and more often rely on welfare. Interviews revealed, however, that despite the outward differences, these women were similar in organizing their lives around men's violence and poverty. The "settled living" women worked hard to maintain at least the appearance of a traditional, harmonious family but were often victims of multiple forms of violence from parents and from previous and current boyfriends and husbands. The "hard living" women were different mostly in that they had *left* a violent situation—a solution that possibly provided temporary relief from violence, but not from poverty, and often lead to experiencing even more violence. The authors report that the most striking difference between the two groups is that the "settled living" women were reluctant to reveal experiences of violence in contrast to the "hard living" women who spoke about violence in their homes to family, friends, neighbors, and the criminal justice system.

A number of conditions have heightened the desperation and isolation of this group. White working-class women have suffered under an economy that has become increasingly deleterious to all members of the U.S. working class. Rather than reach out in solidarity to Black women, who struggle under similar, and usually worse, economic conditions, the authors describe how racism has successfully divided these groups. Weis and coauthors suggest that because "whiteness" can be measured only in relationship to an "Other" and as white families have found themselves living closer to poverty and over time using welfare benefits, they have increasingly identified African American and other families of color as "inferior," which thereby distances themselves from poor Black women. Additionally, since working-class women have not been able to join with the traditionally white, middle-class feminist movement, these "women have not had available to them the structural conditions [e.g., decent educations and well-paying jobs for themselves and their men] in which to articulate a vocabulary of critique."

Resistance as a theme cuts across race, class, culture, and immigration status, while it simultaneously retains aspects unique to each group. What can appear to outsiders as a passive acceptance of abuse by a woman commonly involves active strategies of resistance. The implicit notion of battered women's passivity in the face of violence exists only because of societal beliefs that women are passive, as evidenced in the frequently heard question, "Why doesn't she just leave?" The active nature of women's resistance has been documented in numerous studies. For example, Jacquelyn Campbell and colleagues'

(1998) longitudinal study of primarily African American women found that the women thought of their strategies of resistance as achieving nonviolence rather than ending the relationship, although often the relationship ended in the process. Their journeys toward nonviolence were most often circuitous and involved trying out a number of strategies before achieving success.

Chapters in part 2 provide numerous examples of the ways that women's strategies of resistance are shaped by their particular combination of culture, ethnicity, social class, language, and immigration status. For example, Margaret Abraham (chapter 16, discussed at greater length below) describes a Pakistani woman, feeling desperately isolated in the United States, used the telephone directory to compile a list of families with South Asian names and began calling people on her list; eventually, someone gave her the number of a South Asian Women's Organization that helped her. Weis and colleagues (chapter 15) describe a working-class, white, Catholic woman calling on her faith in God to give her the courage to call the police and inform on her husband's plans to commit a crime—a strategy that successfully landed her husband in jail. (More strategies are named in the discussion of the chapters below.)

In chapter 16, Margaret Abraham describes how South Asian immigrant women, often despite language barriers, lack of financial resources, and fears about their immigration status, actively resist a spouse's violence by "strategically navigat[ing] within the cultural and structural constraints to end the violence perpetrated against them." Defying cultural stereotypes about "submissive" South Asian women, the women described a variety of resistance strategies within the constraints of their lives. In addition to patriarchal cultural values, Abraham demonstrates how socioeconomic class, ethnicity, legal status, financial resources, and accessibility of alternative support systems help to determine the strategies used by the women and the effectiveness of their tactics. Some women worked through traditional familial relationships and enlisted family support in negotiating with in-laws. Some were able to demand or secretly arrange for some measure of financial independence. Even less effective strategies, such as placating and avoiding the abuser, can be seen as active forms of resistance used by women to obtain some measure of security as they learn new strategies. Abraham's chapter also highlights how some women were able to draw support from their extended ethnic community; for others, the community actually presented another means of oppression.

Resistance does not happen in isolation but within a multi-layered context. Moreover, resistance is communal as well as individual. Thus, Abraham (1995) describes the pivotal role of some South Asian Women's Organizations (SAWOs) in not only helping women to escape abusive relationships but also in raising consciousness and advocating collective-oriented action. For example, SAWOs educate the battered woman and the community to the fact that domestic violence is not only an individual problem but, in fact, is also a socially constructed community problem that requires social solutions. They stress that the individual abuser can never be discharged of his role and responsibilities in domestic violence. In a similar argument in part 3, Traci C. West (chapter 20 and 1999) also elaborates on the many ways in which another community organization, the Black church, must expose and actively resist domestic violence in its congregations, which makes domestic violence a communal, not an individual, problem.

Michelle Fine and her colleagues, in chapter 17, write about the "quiet resistance" of Puerto Rican women to violence. Despite a culture that places a high value on the nuclear family and traditional gender roles, Latina/o households have experienced a rise in the number that are female-headed as well as a rise in the number of Latinas who are working outside the home and seeking higher education. In many ways, these women are bearing the brunt of the same economic pressures as the white, working class women described previously by Weis and colleagues (chapter 15), while also managing the legacies of colonialism and racism. Fine and colleagues' (chapter 17) narratives of abused Puerto Rican women contain stories of resistance that are less "quiet"; they use strategies, such as fighting back physically and committing welfare fraud, to subvert a failed system that cannot support a family. One woman recounted how she retaliated every time she was abused or stalked by her former partner. She slashed his tires, "carved" his car, and beat him in front of his parents; yet she did not go to the police because she did not want to ruin his future career as a lawyer. These women also spoke ambivalently of their support systems within the larger ethnic community. Although some women derived power and liberation in their extended family and faith communities, others found those networks added another layer of oppression that they needed to resist.

Juanita Perilla (1999) has analyzed the case of battering of Latina immigrants within a framework of human rights. She suggests that domestic violence be reframed as terrorism because both involve random acts of well-planned violence, creation of an atmosphere of intimidation, and the deliberate use of aggression to silence opposition. While focusing on a particular subset of issues pertaining to Latina women, Perilla's suggested remedy—development of critical consciousness—has universal applications. The process of learning the history of the set of conditions and structures that relate to a particular group can allow women to transcend their individual situations and join with their larger community. When this process is connected to the more universal history of gender-based oppression, women can weave together the cultural values and traditions that empower and liberate both their individual and collective futures. This, of course, requires simultaneous work at both the local and the global levels. (For examples, see Almeida and Lockard, chapter 18.)

Each chapter in this section makes clear the specific ways that a particular intersection of race, ethnicity, class, culture, immigrant status, and the like influences the meaning of and reactions to violence for women located at specific intersectionalities. The last section of the anthology, part 3—Structural Contexts, Culturally Competent Approaches, Community Organizing, and Social Change—later presents several, albeit incomplete, solutions in response to domestic violence in marginalized communities described here in part 2.

Natalie J. Sokoloff and Kathryn Laughon

NOTES

1. I am indebted to Madelaine Adelman not only for pointing me to Merry's book, *Colonizing Hawai'i The Cultural Power of Law* (2000) but also for sharing her knowledge about the literature in general and her prepublished review of Merry's work (2003).

2. See Sokoloff's (2002) *Multicultural Domestic Violence Bibliography* for a listing of the vast array of articles on women from diverse backgrounds within each of these (and other) communities. Available at: www.lib.jjay.cuny.edu/research/Domestic Violence/.

REFERENCES

Abraham, Margaret. 1995. Ethnicity, gender, and marital violence: South Asian women's organizations in the United States. *Gender and Society* 9(4): 450–468.

Adelman, Madelaine. 2003. Domestic violence and difference. Arizona State University. Paper.

Alsdurf, James, and Phyllis Alsdurf. 1998. *Battered into Submission: The Tragedy of Wife Abuse in the Christian Home.* Downers Grove, Ill.: InterVarsity Press.

Battajarchee, Anannya. 1997. The public/private mirage: Mapping homes and undomesticating violence work in the South Asian Indian community. In M. Jacqui Alexander and Chandra Talpede Mohanty, eds., *Feminist Genealogies, Colonial Legacies, and Democratic Futures.* New York: Routledge, 308–329.

Campbell, Jacquelyn, L. Rose, J. Kub, and D. Nedd. 1998. Voices of strength and resistance: A contextual and longitudinal analysis of women's responses to battering. *Journal of Interpersonal Violence* 13: 743–762.

Campbell, Jacquelyn C., D. Webster, J. Koziol-McLain, C. Block, D. Campbell, M. Curry, et al. 2003. Risk factors for femicide in abusive relationships: Results from a multisite case control study. *American Journal of Public Health* 93(7): 1089–1097.

Dutton, Mary Ann. 1996. Battered women's strategic response to violence: The role of context. In J. L. Edleson and Z. C. Eisikovits, eds., *Future Interventions with Battered Women and Their Families.* Thousand Oaks, Calif.: Sage, 105–124.

Fenton, Zanita. 2003. Silence compounded: The conjunction of race and gender violence. *Journal of Gender, Social Policy, and the Law* 11(2): 101–115.

Fortune, Marie. 1995. *Keeping the Faith: Guidance for Christian Women Facing Abuse.* San Francisco: Harper.

Hassouneh-Phillips, Dena Sadat. 1998. Culture and systems of oppression in abused women's lives. *JOGNN* 27(6): 678–683.

————. 2002. Strength and vulnerability: Spirituality in abused American Muslim women's lives. Portland: Oregon Health Sciences University. Paper.

Kanuha, Valli Kalei. 2002. Colonization and violence against women. In *Domestic Violence in Asian and Pacific Islander Communities National Summit: Proceedings 2002*. San Francisco: Asian and Pacific Islander Institute on Domestic Violence, 30–33.

McEachern, Diane, Marlene Van Winkle, and Sue Steiner. 2000. Domestic violence among the Navajo: A legacy of colonization. Arizona State University. Paper.

McNulty, T. L. 2001. Assessing the race-violence relationship at the macro level: The assumption of racial invariance and the problem of restricted distributions. *Criminology* 39(2): 467–489.

Merry, Sally Engle. 1999. *Colonizing Hawai'i: The Cultural Power of Law*. Princeton, N.J.: Princeton University Press.

Murray, Virginia. 1998. "Traditional" legal perspective: A comparative survey of the historic civil, common, and American Indian tribal law—Responses to domestic violence. *Oklahoma City University Law Review* 23: 433–457.

Nason-Clark, Nancy. 1997. *The Battered Wife: How Christians Confront Family Violence*. Louisville, Ky.: Westminster John Knox.

Perilla, Julia. 1999. Domestic violence as a human rights issue: The case of immigrant Latinos. *Hispanic Journal of Behavioral Sciences* 21(2): 107–133.

Razack, Sherene. 1998. What is to be gained by looking white people in the eye? Race in sexual violence cases. In *Looking White People in the Eye: Gender, Race, and Culture in Courtrooms and Classrooms*. Toronto: University of Toronto, 56–87.

Rennison, C., and M. Planty. 2003. Non-lethal intimate partner violence: Examining race, gender and income patterns. *Violence and Victims* 18(4): 433–444.

Rusk, David. 1995. *Baltimore Unbound: Creating a Greater Baltimore Region for the 21st Century: A Strategy Report*. Baltimore: Johns Hopkins University Press.

Sokoloff, Natalie J. 2002. *Multicultural Domestic Violence Bibliography*. Available at: www.lib.jjay.cuny.edu/DomesticViolence/.

Volpp, Leti. 2003. On culture, difference, and domestic violence. *Journal of Gender, Social Policy, and the Law* 11(2): 101–107.

West, Traci C. 1999. *Wounds of the Spirit: Black Women, Violence, and Resistance Ethics*. New York: New York University Press.

CHAPTER 9

ROBERT L. HAMPTON, RICARDO CARRILLO,
AND JOAN KIM

Domestic Violence in African American Communities

———————————— ABSTRACT ————————————

This chapter reviews the literature detailing the prevalence of domestic violence in African American communities. While more recent statistics are provided in chapter 11 (by C. West), the value of Robert L. Hampton and his colleagues' contribution is its theoretical interpretation of domestic violence in poor Black communities that suffer high levels of structural disadvantage. In chapter 10, Websdale provides an actual study of the principles established here with a particular African American community. These two chapters, as companion pieces, set the stage for part 2 as it explores the issues of culture, community, and resistance—all within a structural context.

The literature review reports the now well-known finding that both lethal and severe forms of domestic violence are disproportionately high in African American communities. What can explain this racial difference (between African American, white, and Latino/a families) in the rates of domestic violence? Hampton and his colleagues argue that socioeconomic factors and racialized social structural inequalities within many African American communities, specific to their historical and contemporary experiences, explain the disproportionately high rates of domestic violence in Black families.

Because most poverty-level whites do not fall into the same category of "extreme poverty" that many Blacks do, simplistic comparisons between ethnic groups can be misleading. The typical residential community for a poor Black family differs significantly from that of a poor white family. For example, Hampton and colleagues find only 7 percent of whites live in areas of extreme poverty while nearly 40 percent of poor Blacks live in such extreme-poverty areas. Even so, when studies control for socioeconomic status, the spousal abuse rate for Blacks was equal or comparable to that of whites. Clearly, poverty largely accounts for the comparably high rate of domestic violence in Black communities. However, poverty itself does not cause higher rates of violence in the home, but social structural conditions within poverty-stricken neighborhoods do: persistent and concentrated poverty; racial, economic, and social isolation; chronic unemployment; social disorganization and family disruption.

The authors urge researchers to conduct studies on domestic violence that go beyond narrow operational definitions of poverty to include a wide range of structural and contextual factors like the extent of involvement in social networks, residential mobility, racial and economic segregation, population and housing density, and the degree of social organization/disorganization in the surrounding community. Keep these findings in mind as you read about the lives of battered women in other marginalized communities described in this section of the book.

Public and political attention to domestic violence has increased in recent decades. Discussion of rape and wife battering has become more prevalent in public media, and services for battered and raped women have become more available (National Research Council, 1996). The societal dimensions of the problem are also now more clearly understood. . . .

Violence and homicide in communities of color, especially in the African American and Latino/Hispanic communities, have also become a focus of public attention. Demand has risen for the prevention and control of violence in these particular communities, partially because of a growing realization that minorities experience disproportionate mortality and morbidity as a direct consequence of violence. . . .

From 1976 to 1993, Black males and females in all age categories had far higher homicide rates than their White counterparts (U.S. Department of Justice, July 1994). In 1992, the homicide rate (per 100,000) for Black males was 67.5, compared to 9.1 for White males. Black females had a homicide rate of 13.1, versus 2.8 for White females and 10.7 for women of color overall (National Center for Health Statistics, 1992). Overwhelmingly, Black males, age eighteen to twenty-four faced the greatest risk for lethal victimization: In 1993, the homicide rate for Black men in that age bracket was 184.1 (per 100,000) versus 17.4 for White men in the same category (U.S. Department of Justice, July 1994). These high homicide rates have led African American men to be targeted for classification as an "endangered species" (Gibbs, 1988).

Within this context, all types of violence in communities of color [become] public health and criminal justice concerns. As reported by the U.S. Department of Health and Human Service's Office of Minority Health

This abridged version was originally published as "Violence in Communities of Color" in *Family Violence and Men of Color: Healing the Wounded Male Spirit*, eds. Ricardo Carrillo and Jerry Tello (New York: Springer), 1–30. © 1998 Springer Publishing Company, Inc. Used by permission.

(1994): "African Americans, the largest minority population in the United States, suffer disproportionately from preventable diseases and deaths." Street (1989) argued that, without a willingness to deal with race, "we cannot make headway in dealing with crime in this country" (p. 29).

The disproportionate representation of Blacks and some other minorities in violent crimes generally extends to intrafamilial violence, as discussed in this chapter. However, despite the growing literature on family violence, recent research still largely ignores traditionally underrepresented groups and communities of color (Asbury, 1993; Hampton, 1987; Hampton and Yung, 1996; Huang and Ying, 1989). This omission not only limits the development of appropriate knowledge concerning the prevalence of violence among these groups but also leaves practitioners without relevant information needed to develop culturally sensitive intervention and prevention programs.

This chapter examines previous research on lethal and nonlethal [couple] violence in an effort to better understand its prevalence, type, severity, and relationship to families. We begin by reviewing homicide differentials and spousal violence in families of color [in general and African American families in particular]. We then examine approaches to data collection and research on families of color by noting any gaps or other research issues.

LETHAL COUPLE VIOLENCE

Overall, intrafamily violence accounted for at least 18 percent of all homicides in 1990 (FBI, 1991) and 54 percent of all child homicides in 1994 (FBI, 1994).[1] According to a 1988 U.S. Department of Justice Survey of murder cases disposed in large urban counties, 16 percent of murder victims belonged to the defendant's family (Bureau of Justice Statistics, July 1994). Some general trends in family violence stand out in survey findings:[2]

- Spousal violence accounted for the largest share of family violence, representing 40 percent of intrafamily murders. In 1992, 18 percent of female homicide victims were killed by their spouse or [former] spouse, and an additional 10.2 percent by other relatives (FBI, 1992). Women were more likely to be victims in spousal violence cases, with 60 percent of the assailants in spousal murder cases being men. Women were disproportionately victimized in family homicide cases, comprising 45 percent of family murder victims, compared to a rate of only 18 percent for nonfamily murders.
- Although wives were more likely to be killed than their husbands in spousal violence cases, men still represented the majority (55 percent) of family murder victims. "Fathers, sons, and especially brothers are more likely to be killed by family members than their female counterparts" (National Research Council, 1993). Two-thirds of assailants in family murders were men. . . .

Many general trends in family violence seem to extend to African American families as well. Evidence indicates that partner homicide accounts for the majority of all lethal interactions among African American families.

Similarly, in the aggregate, the most likely family murder victims and defendants were spouses, who accounted for 40 percent of family murder victims overall (Bureau of Justice Statistics, July 1994). . . .

However, while some general trends in family violence seem to cut across race, the rates of intrafamilial violence have consistently been found to be higher for African American families than for White families. Intrafamily homicide rates have been found to have a high correlation with percent Black (0.605) and percent poor (0.560) (Williams and Flewelling, 1988). Overall, Blacks represented 54 percent of all murder victims in the United States, and 58 percent of all victims in family murders (Bureau of Justice Statistics, July 1994). Blacks comprised the majority of victims and defendants in spousal, offspring, and sibling murders (Bureau of Justice Statistics, 1994).

Local and national studies (Block, 1987; Mercy and Saltzman, 1989; Saltzman et al., 1990; Zimring et al., 1983) have also shown higher rates of spousal homicide among ethnic minorities (National Research Council, 1994). Based on 1976–1985 Supplemental Homicide Reporting data, African Americans comprise approximately 45 percent of spousal homicide victims and have a spousal homicide rate 8.4 times greater than that of Whites (Mercy and Saltzman, 1989). In comparison to White women, Black women face higher risk for intimate homicide (victimization by a spouse or boyfriend), even though the intimate homicide rate for Black women has declined over the past two decades (U.S. Department of Justice, November 1994). The intimate homicide rate for Black women age eighteen to thirty-four fell from 8.4 per 100,000 in 1977 to 6 per 100,000 in 1992, while the rate for their White counterparts remained relatively constant. Currently, however, the intimate homicide rate for Black women (6 per 100,000) is still significantly higher than that for White women (1.4 per 100,000).

Black women are also more likely than their White counterparts to inflict lethal violence against their husbands. While 74 percent of White spousal murder victims were wives, only 59 percent of Black victims of spousal murder were women (U.S. Department of Justice, November 1994). The Bureau of Justice Statistics' 1988 survey of large urban counties found that Black wives were "just about as likely to kill their husbands as husbands were to kill their wives." This survey found that 47 percent of Black spousal murder victims were men and 53 percent women (U.S. Department of Justice, July 1994). However, proportionately larger numbers of Black wives are being killed than in years past: "In 1977, more Black husbands were killed than Black wives. . . . By 1992, fewer Black husbands were killed than Black wives" (U.S. Department of Justice, November 1994). . . .

NONLETHAL COUPLE VIOLENCE

As discussed above, minority families, especially Black families, experience a disproportionate share of lethal intrafamily violence. Ethnic differences in family violence incidence rates extend to nonlethal violence as well. In this section, we review research on the prevalence, distribution, and correlates of nonlethal spousal violence. . . .

Unfortunately, there are no "official" data on couple violence. In spite of potential for obvious biases, official data were they to be available would provide information on an extremely large number of cases known to authorities and service providers. In the absence of these data, researchers must rely on data collected in either clinical or survey samples. Official criminal justice data tend to underreport domestic violence against women because nearly half of all domestic violence incidents found by the National Crime Survey had not been reported to the police (U.S. Department of Justice, August 1986).

The U.S. Department of Justice reports that Black and Hispanic women, as well as never-married women in lower-income and younger age groups, were most vulnerable to becoming the victims of violent crime (U.S. Department of Justice, November 1994). Other studies (Cazenave and Straus, 1990; Hampton and Gelles, 1994; Sorenson et al., 1996; Straus and Gelles, 1986) also indicate that African Americans report physical violence by intimates more frequently than whites (National Research Council, 1996). However, the revised National Crime Victimization Survey (NCVS), administered in 1992, found no statistically significant differences between ethnic groups in violent victimization rates by intimates. (This figure includes rapes, sexual assaults, robberies, and aggravated and simple assaults, but excludes homicides.) The NCVS did find elevated risk levels for violent victimization by an intimate among women with annual family incomes under $10,000 (U.S. Department of Justice, August 1995).

The First National Family Violence Survey (NFVS) (Straus et al., 1980) is generally cited as the first comprehensive source of data on the prevalence and incidence of spousal violence in Black families. Straus and his colleagues reported that Black husbands had higher rates of overall and severe violence toward their wives than White husbands. According to the NFVS, the rate of severe violence toward wives, or wife abuse, in Black families was 113 per 1000, while the rate was 30 per 1000 in White households. Violence in Black families was more likely to be "reciprocal": Black wives responding to the NFVS were twice as likely to engage in acts of severe violence against their husbands (76 per 1000) compared with White wives (41 per 1000).

The Second National Family Violence Survey (1985) was designed to address many of the shortcomings of previous research. A comparison of data from the two surveys revealed that overall husband-to-wife violence was unchanged between 1975 and 1985. Severe violence, or "wife beating," declined by 43.4 percent. Furthermore, these data revealed an increase in the rate of overall and severe wife-to-husband violence (Hampton et al., 1989).[3]

Cazenave and Straus (1990) reported that when income is controlled, Black respondents were less likely to report instances of spousal slapping at every income range except the $611,999 level. Black respondents at both ends of the income scale were less likely to report engaging in these behaviors than Whites with comparable incomes. Cazenave and Straus (1979) noted

that the persistence of higher rates of spousal violence, both for the large income group containing the Black working class and for Blacks in both occupational groups, suggests that, even aside from income differentials, Black
spousal violence is notably high.

Although statistics suggest that Black families represent a significant portion of violent families identified and served by agencies, this may in part
reflect the actions of gatekeepers and not racial differences in the type, nature,
or severity of family violence (Hampton, 1987; Hampton and Newberger,
1985). Cazenave and Straus's (1979) analysis of data from the First National
Family Violence Survey seems to suggest that there is a need to examine further factors associated with spouse abuse among Blacks. . . .

A SECOND LOOK AT THE RELATIONSHIP BETWEEN
RACE AND FAMILY VIOLENCE

As explained earlier, current empirical research has consistently shown higher
levels of family violence and overall violent crime within Black communities. . . . What accounts for the racial differences in rates of family homicide
and other violent crime?

A closer look at the empirical evidence indicates that race is not as strong
a predictor of violence as other social characteristics (Sampson and Lauritsen,
1994). Sampson (1985, 1986) found that rates of violent victimization were
two to three times higher in communities with high levels of family disruption,
regardless of race. When he controlled for percent female-headed families, he
found no significant relationship between percent Black and violent victimization (Sampson, 1985). Other studies (Messner and Tardiff, 1986; Smith
and Jarjoura, 1988) also found that family structure, particularly percent
single-parent families, has a much stronger causal relationship to violent
crime rates than does race (Sampson and Lauritsen, 1994).

In their article for the National Research Council, Sampson and Lauritsen
(1994) report that, while rates of violence are usually higher in Black and/or
other minority communities, "the direct effect of race is often quite weak"
(p. 64). Residential mobility or change was more consistently correlated to
violence, especially in the context of poverty, social dislocation, family disruption, and population density.

Similarly, [although] poverty is almost always strongly correlated with violence, it, too, has a weaker direct effect on violence than other community
factors (Sampson and Lauritsen, 1994). When other community factors are
controlled, the correlation between poverty and community violence becomes
weaker. The crucial aspect of poverty in relation to violence seems to be "in
the context of community *change*" (Sampson and Lauritsen, 1994, p. 63).

Overall, homicide rates in communities are strongly correlated with "population structure, resource deprivation/affluence, and percent of the male
population divorced" (Land, McCall, and Cohen, 1990, p. 947). Resource
deprivation has the greatest effect on homicide rates, followed by male divorce

rate and population structure (Land et al., 1990). Housing and population density is another factor correlated with violent crime. Regardless of age, race, or gender, victimization rates were higher in high-density neighborhoods than in lower-density neighborhoods. The effects of density were independent of other community traits (Sampson, 1985). Another strong predictor of violence is family disruption, as measured by divorce rate or percentage of female-headed families. Block (1979), Messner and Tardiff (1986), Roncek (1981), Sampson (1985, 1986), Schuerman and Kobrin (1986), and Smith and Jarjoura (1988) have all documented the strong, positive relationship between violence and family disruption (Sampson and Lauritsen, 1994).

Similar correlations appear to hold true for intrafamily homicide. Fagan and Browne (1994) found "evidence that marital homicide is an urban phenomenon, more often located in social areas that typify the problems of urban areas: poverty, residential mobility, weak family structures, and concentrations of minority populations" (p. 176). Similar risk factors appear to be at work in both family and nonfamily homicides. The limited research on Black spouse abuse reveals similar variables, including occupation, income, embeddedness in social networks, unemployment; and violence in one's family of origin (Uzzell and Peebles-Wilkins, 1989).

Other studies also suggest a strong relationship between social disorganization and spousal violence and the converse between social stability and decreased violence. In their analysis of data from the First National Family Violence Survey, Cazenave and Straus (1990) found that embeddedness in primary networks is more closely associated with lowered rates of spousal slapping for Black couples than for White couples. For Black couples, the number of years in the neighborhood, the number of children, and the number of nonnuclear family members in the households were all associated with lowered levels of spousal violence. In spite of the small sample size ($n = 147$ Black families), these data provided some important insights concerning violence in Black families. The study revealed that a number of variables must be examined for a thorough comparison. The study also revealed that rates of violence among Blacks vary by family income, social class, and degree of social network embeddedness.

Still other studies suggest that marital violence among Blacks may be partially due to historical experiences of institutional racism. In assessing the effects of race on spousal violence, Lockhart and White (1989) and Lockhart (1991) found that a larger proportion of middle-class African American women reported that they were victims of violence by their marital partners than middle-class European American women. Using data gathered through a proposive sample in a large major southeastern metropolitan city, Lockhart argues that her data support Staples's (1976) conclusions that African American couples were not inherently more violent than European American couples. Higher levels of violence, when they do exist, may be [owing] in part to the particular social predicament of African Americans in American society. By this reasoning, many Blacks have achieved middle-class positions only recently as a result of relatively recent changes in their lives and may have retained the norms, values, and role expectations of their lowered-[socioeconomic status] developmental experiences (Lockhart, 1991). Aggressive and violent problem-solving strategies may be partially related to this background. Many African Americans are also subject to additional stress because of the uncertainty and tenuousness of their newly acquired position; this situation (that is, process of adjustment to social change) may influence their use of violence.

In an ethnographic study of domestic violence against Black women, Richie (1996) proposed a "gender entrapment" model to explain the link between gender, race/ethnicity, social stigma, battering, and crime. In this model, social disenfranchisement conspired with gender inequality to "lure" Black women to seek respect and "success" in a socially constructed "ideal" nuclear family, only to be physically battered, forced into illegal activity, and then finally, incarcerated. Furthermore, she found these dynamics uniquely among Black women and not among the White women in her study. Richie's model links hegemonic cultural values with social disenfranchisement (linked to both race and gender) in explaining how Black women become trapped within abusive intimate relationships.

Similarly, Lockhart (1985) hypothesized that socioeconomic factors accounted for racial differences in domestic violence rates. When ethnicity alone was taken into account, rates of spousal abuse were higher for Blacks. However, when SES among Blacks and Whites was controlled, the spousal abuse rate for Whites was equal to that of Blacks. One possible hypothesis explaining these results is that rates of violence change as a result of the level of poverty. Most poverty-level Whites do not fall into the category of "extreme poverty" that some Blacks do; therefore, comparison rates are misleading.

Risk factors for violent crime like social isolation and concentration effects are more commonly found in high-poverty, disproportionately Black urban areas. As argued by Wilson (1987), poor Blacks—especially female-headed families with children—have been increasingly isolated and disproportionately concentrated in inner-city areas. These communities have suffered the heaviest blows from structural economic changes resulting from the shift from goods-producing to service-producing industries: [decreased] manufacturing jobs and increasing gaps between high-wage and low-wage jobs. The loss of manufacturing jobs led to increased joblessness among Black males and persistent poverty, which in turn disrupted Black family structure in inner-city communities. Furthermore, Wilson argued, "social buffers"—institutions like churches, schools, stores, and recreational facilities—suffered as a result of the exodus of middle- and upper-income Black families from inner-city areas. With the loss of economically and socially stable families and with the disruption of remaining families, informal social controls and economic and social supports for communities weakened considerably. Family and social disruption became concentrated in communities that were increasingly isolated from the mainstream social and economic structures. Hypothetically, this concentrated social and family disruption led to increased violence in predominantly Black inner-city communities (Sampson, 1987).

This concentration of poverty, largely falling along racial lines, has taken a greater toll on Black than White communities and families. In 1980 in the five largest U.S. central cities, 70 percent of poor Whites lived in nonpoverty areas, compared to only 15 percent of poor Blacks. Only 7 percent of Whites lived in areas of extreme poverty, while nearly 40 percent of poor Blacks lived in such extreme-poverty areas (Sampson and Lauritsen, 1994). As a result, the typical residential community for a poor Black family differs significantly from that of a poor White family (Sampson, 1987; Stark, 1987). Even the "worst" White residential communities are significantly better off with respect to poverty and family disruption than the average Black community (Sampson, 1987). Consequently, according to Sampson and Lauritsen (1994), "the relationship between race and violence may be accounted for largely by community context (e.g., segregation, concentration of family disruption and joblessness, social isolation, sparse social networks). We simply do not know, and cannot know, given the typical individual-level research design" (1994, p. 83).

Thus, a closer look at the empirical evidence suggests that social instability and change within a community have more to do with violent crime than race or even poverty. Race and poverty have both been found to have a strong correlation with violent crime, particularly homicide, but they appear to have become confounded with other social variables, such as family disruption, embeddedness in social networks, residential mobility, population/housing density, and the presence or absence of social organization in the surrounding community. Community characteristics, not just individual family characteristics, appear to have a significant impact on the risk for victimization by violent crime. Such family and community-level risk factors are more prevalent among urban minority, particularly African American, communities. The research in minority family violence also suggests that family violence, in particular, is sensitive to social influence such as the availability of social networks, resource deprivation, divorce rate, immigration status, and other forms of family or social disruption. Both family and nonfamily violence rates differ significantly by race; both types of violence also seem to be affected similarly by social context.

DATA COLLECTION AND RESEARCH ON
FAMILIES OF COLOR

The relationship between race and family violence has been demonstrated, but the exact nature of this relationship and the causal variables involved are not as clearly understood. More research—especially methodologically different types of research—needs to be done to address the social processes and community-level characteristics that engender violence (Sampson and Lauritsen, 1994). Simple continuation of current research trends is insufficient for uncovering these social processes (Fingerhut and Kleinman, 1990). Current knowledge of minority family violence is limited [owing] to weaknesses in data collection efforts, methodologies, and research perspectives that often fail to account for the complex social interactions leading to elevated levels of violence in minority families.

Data Collection Needs

Overall, there is a paucity of methodologies for data collection for viewing families of color. To date, there has been relatively little research or data collection on violence within families of color (National Research Council, 1996). National crime statistics collected by the Federal Bureau of Investigation and the National Center for Health Statistics generally classify victims as Black, White, and "Other"; consequently, there is no national homicide data for non-African American minority communities.

Families of color have been victims of benign neglect in community-based studies of spousal violence. While some studies on domestic violence include large numbers of African Americans and/or Hispanics, most concentrate on White families. The First National Family Violence Survey (Straus et al., 1980) was constrained by the small sample of Black families ($n = 147$) and limited sampling frame. The survey did not include Hispanic families in sufficient numbers for comparative analyses. Although Asian Americans represent the fastest growing minority group in the United States (LaFromboise, 1992), the National Research Council (1996) found no survey studies of intimate violence experienced by Asian-American women. In particular, current research remains unclear on the influence of socioeconomic and cultural factors on racial differences in the self-reported incidence of physical violence between intimates (National Research Council, 1996). . . . As explained by the National Research Council (1996): Most studies have used measures and instruments developed on Anglos and simply applied them to members of other ethnic groups, for whom the instruments' validity is unknown. There may be differences in the intent of a question and a respondent's interpretation related to patterns of expression and idioms that may vary across cultures. This may explain, in part, the lack of consistency of results across studies" (1996, p. 42). . . .

Research Perspectives

Not only is current literature on minority family violence limited by insufficient and/or inconsistent data collection, [but] it is also limited by a deficiency in culturally sensitive research perspectives. Research methods that view the world from a Western European perspective and that minimize the importance of collecting data from communities of color seem to assume deviancy and pathologize the rates of violence among communities of color.

Up to recent times, conceptual models for the study of Black families in particular have been heavily influenced by schools of thought that use the traditional White middle-class family as the primary referent and that view differences as "deviancy" or "pathology." Such a "pathologist" approach became particularly influential in the 1960s and 1970s with the publication of Daniel Patrick Moynihan's report (1965) on Black families. Moynihan targeted family disorganization as the principal cause of deterioration in the Black community and "initiated the study of the Black family as a pathological form of social organization" (Staples and Johnson, 1993).

Since that time, while the "pathologist" approach has remained influential, other research approaches for studying families of color have emerged. In social science literature, differences between White middle-class families and African American families have been explained recently in terms of cultural deviant, cultural equivalent, or cultural variant perspectives (Allen, 1978; Fine et al., 1987). These perspectives are easily extended to other families of color.

Researchers holding the cultural deviant perspective recognize that families of color are different from majority-group families. These differences are viewed, however, as deviancy, implying that the values and lifestyles of families of color are pathological. Quality of life for families is viewed through the values of mainstream culture, which often ignores the positive features of families of color.

The cultural equivalent perspective holds that there is no clear cultural distinction between majority families and families of color. Advocates of this perspective argue that differences in socioeconomic status, especially higher rates of poverty among many minority groups, explain group differences in family life. During the 1970s, research shifted predominantly to this perspective (Johnson, 1988).

The cultural variant perspective, which is largely evident in predominantly Black journals, argues that families of color are culturally unique, yet functional and legitimate (Staples and Johnson, 1993). One version of this position holds that among African Americans, the African cultural heritage is viewed as the primary determinant of family behavior. The conditions that African Americans encounter in the United States influence the expression and development of this basic African core (Fine et al., 1987). Similar to an ecological perspective, the cultural variant perspective recognizes the impact of differences in environments, which result in differences both in family structure and in ways of functioning. These family patterns are often necessary adaptations of a group culture to a new set of circumstances.

There is a danger of viewing all differences as healthy, when in fact some differences are pathological (Daniel, 1985). It must be understood that not all adaptations are positive and that to some extent the interpersonal violence we see in many communities of color may reflect negative adaptations.

CONCLUSION

The current literature indicates relatively higher levels of violence within African American families. . . . African American families have consistently been reported to have higher incidence rates of lethal and nonlethal marital and parent-to-child violence. However, the socioeconomic factors implicated in these phenomena are not clearly understood. Large gaps in data exist concerning family violence among all minority communities, in part because of neglect or misunderstanding by the research community, in part because of language and cultural barriers. Because of the sensitive nature of family violence, all forms of family violence, particularly marital violence, tend to be underreported (Bureau of Justice Statistics, 1988, 1993). A lack of culturally sensitive research and data collection methods, a lack of community-level measurement, as well as possible racial biases within the child welfare system and/or other public institutions, also cloud the picture and make conclusive findings difficult to draw.

Research methodologies must reflect the diversity of worldviews and re-analyze data that most notably account for differences from a nonpathological perspective. More sophisticated analyses are needed to explore the complicated variables of race/ethnicity, social class, culture, social networks, acculturation, and communitywide variables such as resource deprivation, residential turnover, family disruption, and other socioeconomic factors and their relationship to family violence. Future research should seek to recognize cultural differences in family functioning without viewing such differences as "deviant" or pathological and should recognize the complex nature of differences between and within ethnic groups. Furthermore, future research should seek to address the large gaps in knowledge concerning violence among families of color, which have been understudied in years past.

While family violence remains tragic for all involved, minority families bear a disproportionately large share of the burden. More concentrated and culturally sensitive research can lead to a clearer understanding of the scope and causes of violence in families of color, which can in turn lead to more effective prevention and intervention efforts in years to come.

NOTES

1. The Federal Bureau of Investigation's Uniform Crime Reports (UCR) system accounts for "most serious crimes committed" (National Research Council, 1993). The UCR conducts data collection on a national level of crimes committed in the United States. The UCR also collects additional homicide data through its Supplemental Homicide Reports (SHR). Homicidal data is codified from death certificates by the National Center for Health Statistics (NCHS), while nonfatal violent crime victimization reports are conducted by the National Criminal Victimization Survey conducted by the U.S. Department of Justice. In addition, the Center for Disease Control has attempted to tabulate homicidal data.

2. Except when noted, all the statistics in the following list come from the Bureau of Justice Statistics, July 1994.

3. The comparison was based on the more limited version of the Conflict Tactics Scale.

REFERENCES

Allen, W. R. 1978. The search for applicable theories of Black family life. *Journal of Marriage and the Family* 40: 117–129.

Asbury, J. 1993. Violence in families of color in the United States. In R. L. Hampton, T. Gullotta, G. R. Adams, E. Potter, and R. P. Weissberg, eds., *Family Violence: Prevention and Treatment*. Newbury Park, Calif.: Sage, 159–178.

Block, C. R. 1987. Lethal violence at home: Racial/ethnic differences in domestic homicide in Chicago, 1965 to 1981. Paper presented at the meeting of the American Society of Criminology, Chicago, November.

Block, R. 1979. Community, environment, and violent crime. *Criminology* 17: 46–57.

Bureau of Justice Statistics. 1988. *Preventing Domestic Violence against Women* (Special Report). Washington, D.C.: U.S. Department of Justice, Office of Justice Programs.

———. 1993. *Murder in Families* (Special Report). Washington, D.C.: U.S. Department of Justice, Office of Justice Programs.

———. 1994. *Sex Differences in Violent Victimizations* (Special Report). NCJ-164508. Washington, D.C.: U.S. Department of Justice, Office of Justice Programs, July. Updated Sept. 1997.

Cazenave, N. A., and M. A. Straus. 1979. Race, class, network embeddedness, and family violence: A search for potent support systems. *Journal of Comparative Family Studies* 10: 281–299.

———. 1990. Race, class, network embeddedness, and family violence: A search for potent support systems. In M. A. Straus and R. J. Gelles, eds., *Physical Violence in American Families: Risk Factors and Adaptations to Violence in 8,145 Families.* New Brunswick, N.J.: Transaction Books, 321–335.

Fagan, J., and A. Browne. 1994. Violence between spouses and intimates: Physical aggression between women and men in intimate relationships. In National Research Council, *Understanding and Preventing Violence: Vol. 3. Social Influences.* Washington, D.C.: National Academy Press, 115–260.

Fine, M., A. I. Schwebel, and L. James-Myers. 1987. Family stability in Black families: Values underlying three different perspectives. *Journal of Comparative Families Studies* 18: 1–23.

Fingerhut, L., and J. Kleinman. 1990. International and interstate comparisons of homicide among young males. *Journal of the American Medical Association* 263: 3292–3295.

Gibbs, J. T. 1988. *Young, Black, and Male in America: An Endangered Species.* Dover, Mass.: Auburn House.

Hampton, R. L. 1987. Family violence and homicides in the black community: Are they linked? In R. L. Hampton, ed., *Violence in the Black Family: Correlates and Consequences.* Lexington, Mass.: Lexington Books, 135–156.

Hampton, R. L., and R. J. Gelles. 1994. Violence toward black women in a nationally representative sample of black families. *Journal of Comparative Family Studies* 25(1): 105–119.

Hampton, R. L., R. J. Gelles, and J. W. Harrop. 1989. Is violence in black families increasing? A comparison of 1975 and 1985 national survey rates. *Journal of Marriage and the Family* 51: 969–980.

Hampton, R. L., and E. H. Newberger. 1985. Child abuse incidence and reporting by hospitals: The significance of severity, class, and race. *American Journal of Public Health* 75: 56–60.

Hampton, R. L., and B. R. Yung. 1996. Violence in communities of color: Where we were, where we are, and where we need to be. In R. L. Hampton, P. Jenkins, and T. Gullotta, eds., *Preventing Violence in America.* Thousand Oaks, Calif.: Sage Publications, 53–86.

Huang, L. N., and Y.-W. Ying. 1989. Chinese-American children and adolescents. In J. T. Gibbs, L. N. Huang, et al., eds., *Children of Color.* San Francisco: Jossey-Bass, 30–66.

Johnson, L. B. 1988. Perspectives on black family empirical research, 1965–1978. In H. P. McAdoo, ed., *Black Families.* 2d ed. Newbury Park, Calif.: Sage.

LaFromboise, T. D. 1992. In obligation to our people: Giving merit to cultural and individual differences. *Focus* 6(1): 11–14.

Land, K., P. McCall, and L. Cohen. 1990. Structural covariates of homicide rates: Are there any invariances across time and space? *American Journal of Sociology* 95: 922–963.

Lockhart, L. L. 1985. A re-examination of the effects of race and social class on the incidence of marital violence: A search for reliable differences. *Journal of Marriage and the Family* 49: 603–610.

Lockhart, L. L. 1991. Spousal violence: A cross-racial perspective. In R. L. Hampton, ed.,

Black Family Violence: Current Research and Theory. Lexington, Mass.: Lexington Books, 85–102.

Lockhart, L. L., and B. White. 1989. Understanding marital violence in the Black community. *Journal of Interpersonal Violence* 4(4): 421–436.

Mercy, J. A., and L. E. Saltzman. 1989. Fatal violence among spouses in the United States, 1976–1985. *American Journal of Public Health* 79: 595–599.

Messner, S., and K. Tardiff. 1986. Economic inequality and levels of homicide: An analysis of urban neighborhoods. *Criminology* 24: 297–318.

Moynihan, D. P. 1965. *The Negro Family: The Case for National Action*. Washington, D.C.: U.S. Department of Labor.

National Center for Health Statistics. 1992. *Vital Statistics of the United States, 1989* (Vol. 3, Pl. A). Hyattsville, Md.: Author.

National Research Council. 1993. *Understanding Child Abuse and Neglect*. Washington, D.C.: National Academy Press.

———. 1994. *Understanding and Preventing Violence: Vol. 3. Social Influences*. Washington, D.C.: National Academy Press.

———. 1996. *Understanding Violence against Women*. Washington, D.C.: National Academy Press.

Richie, B. E. 1996. *Compelled to Crime: The Gender Entrapment of Battered Black Women*. New York: Routledge.

Roncek, D. 1981. Dangerous places: Crime and residential environment. *Social Forces* 60: 74–96.

Saltzman, L. E., J. A. Mercy, M. L. Rosenberg, W. R. Elsea, G. Napper, R. K. Sikes, R. Waxweiler, and the Collaborative Working Group for the Study of Family and Institute Assaults in Atlanta. 1990. Magnitude and patterns of family and intimate assaults in Atlanta, Georgia, 1984. *Violence and Victims* 5(1): 3–18.

Sampson, R. J. 1985. Neighborhood and crime: The structural determinants of personal victimization. *Journal of Research in Crime and Delinquency* 22: 7–40.

———. 1986. Neighborhood family structure and the risk of criminal victimization. In J. Byrne and R. Sampson, eds., *The Social Ecology of Crime*. New York: Springer-Verlag, 25–46.

———. 1987. Urban black violence: The effect of male joblessness and family disruption. *American Journal of Sociology* 93: 348–382.

Sampson, R. J., and J. L. Lauritsen. 1994. Violent victimization and offending: Individual-, situational-, and community-level risk factors. In National Research Council, ed., *Understanding and Preventing Violence: Vol. 3. Social Influences*. Washington, D.C.: National Academy Press, 1–95.

Schuerman, L., and S. Kobrin. 1986. Community careers in crime. In A. J. Reiss, Jr., and M. Tonry, eds., *Communities and Crime*. Chicago: University of Chicago Press, 67–100.

Smith, D. R., and G. R. Jarjoura. 1988. Social structure and criminal victimization. *Journal of Research in Crime and Delinquency* 25: 27–52.

Sorenson, S. B., D. M. Upchurch, and H. Shen. 1996. Violence and injury in marital arguments. *American Journal of Public Health* 86: 35–40.

Staples, R. 1976. Race and family violence: The internal colonialism perspective. In L. Gary and L. Brown, eds., *Crime and Its Impact on the Black Community*. Washington, D.C.: Howard University Press.

Staples, R., and L. B. Johnson. 1993. *Black Families at the Crossroads: Challenges and Prospects*. San Francisco: Jossey-Bass.

Stark, R. 1987. Deviant places: A theory of the ecology of crime. *Criminology* 25: 893–909.

Straus, M. A., and R. J. Gelles. 1986. Societal change in family violence from 1975 to 1985 as revealed in two national surveys. *Journal of Marriage and the Family* 48: 465–479.

Straus, M. A., R. J. Gelles and S. K. Steinmetz. 1980. *Behind Closed Doors: Violence in the American Family*. Garden City, N.Y.: Anchor/Doubleday.

Street, L. 1989. Why focus on communities? In A. J. Reiss, Jr., ed., *Proceedings of the Work-*

shop on Communities and Crime Control. Washington, D.C.: Committee on Research on Law Enforcement and the Administration of Justice, National Research Council, National Criminal Justice Reference Service, 27–34.

U.S. Department of Justice. 1986. *Preventing Domestic Violence against Women.* Bureau of Justice Statistics Special Report. Washington, D.C.: U.S. Government Printing Office, August.

———. 1994. *Violence against Women.* Bureau of Justice Statistics Special Report No. NCJ-145325. Washington, D.C.: U.S. Government Printing Office, January.

———. 1994. *Murder in Families.* Bureau of Justice Statistics Special Report. Washington, D.C.: U.S. Government Printing Office, July.

———. 1994. *Violence between Intimates.* Bureau of Justice Statistics Special Report No. NCJ-149259. Washington, D.C.: U.S. Government Printing Office, November.

———. 1995. *Violence against Women: Estimates from the Redesigned Survey.* Bureau of Justice Statistics Special Report No. 154348. Washington, D.C.: U.S. Government Printing Office, August.

U.S. Department of Justice, Federal Bureau of Investigation. 1995. *Crime in the U.S. 1994.* Uniform Crime Reports. Washington, D.C.: U.S. Government Printing Office.

Uzzell, O., and W. Peebles-Wilkins. 1989. Black spouse abuse: A focus on relational factors and intervention strategies. *Western Journal of Black Studies* 13: 10–16.

Williams, K., and R. Flewelling. 1988. The social production of criminal homicide: A comparative study of disaggregated rates in American cities. *American Sociological Review* 53: 421–431.

Wilson, W. J. 1987. *The Truly Disadvantaged: The Inner City, the Underclass, and Public Policy.* Chicago: University of Chicago Press.

Zimring, F. F., S. K. Mukherjee, and J. B. Van Winkle. 1983. Intimate violence: A study of intersexual homicide in Chicago. *University of Chicago Law Review* 50(2): 910–930.

CHAPTER 10

NEIL WEBSDALE

Nashville

Domestic Violence and Incarcerated Women in Poor Black Neighborhoods

─────────────── ABSTRACT ───────────────

In chapter 9, Hampton and his coauthors provided us with an important structural framework for studying domestic violence in intensely poor and racially segregated African American communities. In this chapter, Websdale describes a case study that takes us into the homes and lives of families in some of the poorer Black neighborhoods of Nashville, Tennessee. The intense poverty is compounded by the violence against and within these communities such that a battered woman trying to find safety from a violent family situation too often must go out into a community that is equally if not more "unsafe." In the words of one woman who works with battered women from the Nashville projects in this study: "Not only is [a battered] woman in danger in her home, but once she steps outside that door, it's like a war zone." It is so bad that a taxi will not go into her area to pick her up as she tries to take steps to protect herself.

Unlike other chapters in this anthology, Websdale also talked with battered women who were incarcerated at the time of this study. The abuse histories of women in prison is one of the most powerful and consistent findings that emerges in the prison literature. This is especially true for Black women in prison, as Beth E. Richie documented in her classic book *Compelled to Crime: The Gender Entrapment of Battered Black Women* (Routledge, 1996), and for the women in Websdale's ethnographic report in this chapter.

Websdale reports on not only the women's deep-seated historical resistance to opening up Black family life to outside scrutiny but also on how more effective and proactive contemporary policing is not adequate, by itself, to protect desperately poor and disenfranchised Black women from domestic violence. Rather, he argues, Black women's plight exists alongside the disadvantage of Black families in general, the ever weakening condition of Black men in the global economy, and the increasingly marginalized position of Black women—in the economy, alongside violence against them in the home. It is the assault on Black kinship systems, in the context of desperate economic conditions, he argues, that renders Black women more vulnerable to both domestic violence and imprisonment.

The problem then, according to Websdale, is not only to empower individual Black women who are battered, as the mainstream Women's Movement has argued, but it is also imperative to empower the Black community and the families within it for systemic battering to stop.

After you read both chapters 9 and 10, compare and contrast the findings that Hampton and his colleagues discovered in the larger literature review on domestic violence in poor African American communities with Websdale's case study in Nashville. Comment on the degree to which Hampton and his coauthors offer explanations that also either validate or disprove Websdale's findings.

Springtime was in bloom as I pulled up in the parking lot of the Tennessee State Correctional Facility for Women. I got out of my car and headed toward the reception area. I was [scheduled] to talk with a group of inmates about their lives, their families, their experiences with the police, and crime in and around the housing projects. The atmosphere at the prison was tense. Two women awaited execution on death row. As I walked toward reception, a startling juxtaposition of images confronted me. The first was a cluster of flowering Bradford pear trees, thick and creamy against the skyline. The night before I had seen similar luxurious blooms as I traveled through a wealthy new subdivision of Nashville to interview a senior police officer at his home. The second image surrounding the prison complex was the concertina wire, confining a motley collection of supposedly dangerous individuals.

Amid laughter, tears, cussing, and poking fun, rich information emerged from the conversations. At some point in their lives, these women's intimate male partners had beaten them. Holly had lived in the Nashville housing projects most of her life. She was serving time for fighting back against her violent husband. Her story provides a neat segue into my discussion of the policing of domestic violence. Holly told her story with great humor and panache. I sensed that she had told it several times before.

> This man got the gun, he's talkin' about how he's fixin' to blow my brains out. I got on the phone to 911, "Please y'all, 911, somebody please hurry, please hurry." I hear the gun click . . . "Pa-ching." Dead blew up the waterbed. The woman on the other end [dispatcher] said, "Madam, what's goin' on? Madam what's goin' on? . . . [laughter] I'm sayin, "Lady help! The man got a fuckin' gun, lady help!" . . . I'm up on the big waterbed, now water goin' everywhere . . . and the woman said, "Don't cuss, lady, don't cuss." [laughter]
> What the hell you talkin' about "don't cuss?" [laughter]

This abridged version was originally published as "Black Kin and Intimate Violence" in *Policing the Poor: From Slave Plantation to Public Housing* (Boston: Northeastern University Press, 2001), 113–129. Reprinted by permission of the publisher.

I was sick of bein' bruised. I can't see. Got to open my eyes with my hand. He said, "Bitch, I'm goin' to bed." He went up an' he went to bed. I pour me some grits and water, like I seen my momma do to my daddy, and I sit there, and I sit there, and grits and the water got together. I put in some sugar. I just pulled the cover back, started pouring from the top of his head all the way down to his mouth. Police come, "Lady . . . why didn't you call us?" I said, "You ignorant motherfuckers, if you check 911 I called y'all three hours ago tellin' you this man is shootin'. . . . This waterbed is blown to hell, holes all in the mattress, great big old holes in the wall, water done just messed up everythin' . . . and that was a sawed-off double barrel, he meant business." Police said, "Well, we gonna have to carry you in." I said, "Carry me in?" They carried me down . . .

Well you call them police, you call police an' you hang up the telephone, they'll get there quicker than you would callin' 'em . . . and tellin' 'em there's somethin' goin' on. They'll call right back to make sure you're okay . . . [laughter] Well this happened just recently. I just found this out. My uncle, he called the police station, and told them that he was gonna blow it up, and they came an' got him immediately. [laughter] They took me to jail for aggravated assault. They told me the sugary grits was the weapon. They said that sugar in that grits was just like glue—it peeled all his skin.

Elaine told her story quietly, without sarcasm, and with a deeply depressed affect lubricated with tears. Elaine perceived that she contributed to her own victimization by giving her abusive partner authority to "take that much possession over my life." She drew much support from people at the table as she recalled her abusive husband's surveillance and torture, and the resistive violence she used against him that eventually led to her incarceration.

He was possessive. I gave him that authority over me to take that much possession over my life. The jobs I had, every job I had while I was with him for eleven years, had to be to his standards, the clothes I wore . . . he had to go to the shopping mall with me and make sure that my skirts wasn't too short . . . my pants wasn't too tight, um, when we went out to eat I had to sit with my face like this in the plate and eat. I couldn't look at nobody. Somebody recognize me and he says, "Who that!?" . . . You know and stuff like that, and then, you know, a lot of times I blame myself for stayin' with him as long as I did because I figured if I hadn't stayed with him as long as I did, he wouldn't been able to continue to abuse me. But, when you in love with somebody you take stuff like that. . . . This man stabbed me in my leg with a butcher knife, he beat me up . . . and then would try to have sex with me. After he done beat me, he talk about how I look beautiful with my face all swelled. I got knots on the top of my forehead, but I look beautiful to him with all these knots and stuff. He like just to see me like that because he knew that nobody else would want me. But he beat me up one time too many, I got hurt. I did like she [Holly] did. I let him go. I made love to him. I let him go to sleep. When he woke up I was sittin' in his chair stabbin' him with a steak knife. . . .

I took him and drug him to the car, took him to Vanderbilt Hospital, called his mom, and told her, "I just almost killed your son for puttin' his hands on me." They handcuffin' me at the hospital. He told the police, he said "Naw, I don't want to press no charges against her." And I looked at him, I said, "You shouldn't! Look at me." An' I told police, I said "Look at my damn face—he done beat me stupid, an' I'm not supposed to do anything to him? And you all gonna take me to jail?" See, that's what I can't understand. When we fight back to protect ourselves, the law wants to lock us up.

I attended domestic disturbances in poorer neighborhoods of Nashville, interviewed two groups of mostly black women from the Tennessee State Penitentiary for Women, and talked with twenty or so other women at domestic violence and homeless shelters. Many of these women had remained silent about their victimization for long periods of time. They attributed their silence to fear of retribution, love of their abusers, shame, embarrassment, wanting to keep the family together, relying on his paycheck, and hope that things might change.

Cecilia, a black woman, endured three violently abusive relationships from 1986 to 1997. She talked about domestic violence in the black community. "I heard my mom talk about how my grandfather abused her and his family. She was from a family of nine children. I've heard other stories like that. In the black community people want to keep it hush-hush. This is a family matter. This is nobody else's business."

One night at a refuge in a run-down neighborhood in East Nashville, I attended a support group meeting for ten black battered women. At the meeting Alicia told me that some black women would not automatically call the police if beaten. She told me that the projects offered little privacy. Calling the police, for whatever reason, violated that privacy. Given the street violence in the projects, one can understand Alicia's sentiment. She also observed that some black female victims of domestic violence engaged in illegal activities that made calling the police problematic. "The environment that they're living in, you don't call all the time, ya know, because everything is everybody's business and you know they don't want people to know what's going on behind closed doors. A lot of times the woman could be involved in some illegal action and she might not speak out about domestic violence."

Bessie, the support group facilitator, talked of the courage of black women coming together to share their victimization.

> When you think about it historically, this whole issue of domestic violence for women of color, and black women in particular . . . was kept hidden, and unless you talked to your doctor, your pastor, unless you were able to speak to your friend next door, you kept it between the family members. This support group is really a new way of fighting back in terms of speaking out, to come and talk about what's going on in their homes. We have to not only work through the mistrust of the system, but we have to . . . trust one another. It's amazing that we have these women who actually are very courageous to even take the steps to enter into that healing process of speaking out and doing whatever they can to keep themselves safe.

Many black women I talked with highlighted a deep-seated historical resistance to opening up black family life to scrutiny. Black women passed down this resistance across many generations, which may indeed trace an unbroken line back to Africa. Black women withheld information about familial conflict and domestic violence as a means of preserving the integrity of black kinship systems in the face of slavery and its aftermath. Given this cultural legacy, it makes sense that black battered women would see the family as a respite from a deeply racist world and would hesitate before calling authorities. It is likely that black family life alleviated the pressures of slavery in different ways for black men and women. During slavery and beyond, black women endured interpersonal violence at the hands of black men within those families, just as they endured rape, sexual assault, whippings, and other forms of ritualized violence and control by white slavers.[1] Though it may have been the case that white planters prohibited slave men from assaulting their partners, white men had the right to beat women to maintain discipline on the plantations. How this affected black women's senses of their families as potential respites and how these understandings influenced their willingness to report their abusive black male partners needs more exploration.

As Herbert Gutman shows, the black family endured many hardships during slavery. Referring to evidence from Mississippi and northern Louisiana slaves, Gutman notes that "about one in six (or seven) slave marriages [was] ended by force or sale." He goes on to observe that most slave sales apart from estate divisions and bankruptcies involved teenagers and young adults. Slave parents hated slave owners for making such sales. Specifically, Gutman comments, " 'Good' masters hesitated making such sales, 'bad' masters did not, all masters poisoned the relationship between slave parents and their children."[2] Undoubtedly, the black family lived with the threat of the potential sale of one or more of its members. Just as it did not recognize slave marriages, the law did not protect the black family. However, Gutman's work established that most blacks lived in nuclear families during slavery and that black men and women sought out marriage during nineteenth-century Reconstruction as a legal way to confirm and sanctify their unions and bolster the black family.[3] He notes that upon emancipation "most Virginia ex-slave families had two parents, and most older couples had lived together in long-lasting unions." Strongly disagreeing with Daniel Patrick Moynihan's influential work on the black family, Gutman argues that the post–World War II migration of blacks northward caused significant family breakup. Gutman attributed this breakup not to the "tangle of family pathology" rooted in slavery (Moynihan's argument) but to the chronically high unemployment and underemployment that greeted blacks displaced from the rapidly mechanizing system of southern agriculture. Put simply, blacks could not earn sufficient money to support family life in northern cities. The rise of global capitalism exacerbated this unemployment and underemployment, particularly from 1980 onward.

That blacks have had to fight to preserve, further extend, and develop their kinship systems in the face of pressures such as unemployment and underemployment reminds us of their deep commitment to family values. In their long and oppressive history, blacks really have put families first. This concern to protect family life is one of the roots of the deep compromise faced by black battered women in the housing projects of Nashville. Only during the twentieth-century redemption (1980–2000) [did] domestic violence in black kinship systems appear on the political radar. Such interest in extending police "protections" to the black community arose partly in response to the calls for police reform articulated by the Kerner Report. However, as my ethnography reveals, protecting black women from violent intimate partners does not simply turn upon the provision of more effective and proactive community policing services. Rather, the plight of black battered women exists alongside the disadvantaged position of black families in general and the ever-weakening position of black men in the global economy. The assault on black kinship systems during the twentieth-century redemption actually renders black women more rather than less vulnerable to intimate violence.

Marcie, a black victim of domestic violence, told me it was difficult to report her abuser. After attending a domestic call at Marcie's home, a detective and I dropped her off at a friend's house in the Edgehill projects on a Saturday night around midnight. Marcie told us she wanted to go in quickly because people might label her a "snitch." Any association between a black battered woman and the police, including turning in a man who beats her, risks housing project residents' applying such labels. The battered woman is more vulnerable still if her abuser sells drugs or engages in street crime. As Marcie walked to her friend's house, a half dozen young black men stood within a few feet openly selling drugs in an Edgehill parking lot. They scrutinized the detective and me closely. We also drew stares from a group of five or six people standing in the front yard of a crack house. At that time of night in Edgehill our unmarked and rather run-down police vehicle did not provide us with what I perceived to be adequate protection. My fear was palpable, and I was glad to leave the scene. I could not help wondering how Marcie and others lived under such conditions.

Bessie talked of how black women feel compromised [when] reporting black batterers because in so doing they must become accusers. These black battered women worry that in identifying their abusers to police they might perpetuate stereotypes of black men as "violent." Bessie believes that the women's movement neglects black battered women and is unable to see how its emphasis on the empowerment of individual women does not take into account black women's concern with the black community as a whole:[4]

> What we have learned is that it's anger about a lot of things. Not just him beating her. It's anger about what she doesn't have access to. It's anger about not having an education. It's anger about not having money. It's anger about not being able to take care of her children. It's anger about the stigmas, the stereotypes, and the system. It's anger about her own situation but also anger about his situation. The inner conflict about "I have to report him and he's a black man. When I report him, what does that do to him? Then I become part of the system." The whole issue of the disproportionate number of black men that are in prison. And the whole black man plight—just dealing with that, is tough. It's tough. Very tough. So when sisters come to our program, we are very respectful of them just for having courage to pick up the phone. You see what I'm saying? She becomes part of the accuser. And that's a lot to deal with.[5] But at the same time, as a victim, I've got to make myself safe. So it's a lot of emotions and a lot of feelings in there. And in terms of fighting back, they say we fight back more, and sometimes I really don't buy that because of our spirituality or our religiosity. And when you're part of a religion that says to you, "Forgive and

forget," there's a part of you that you're denying, and that's the anger. And it takes that last hit. Then you say, "I can't do this anymore." Everybody reaches a place when they say, "No more."

Some battered black women talked of their need to have a father figure to help their sons negotiate masculinity and the streets.[6] These women talked of putting up with domestic violence so that abusers might help their sons survive the dangerous world of the housing projects. Living in safer neighborhoods, although not necessarily safer homes, white women did not face the same kind of trade-off.

During my ethnographic research in Florida and Nashville, a number of black women told me that they see battering as more of a white woman's problem that they, as black women, would not put up with. Alison, a black battered woman from Florida who killed her abusive husband, rendered an eloquent statement of this viewpoint: "White girls are gullible. White girls will put up with centuries of abuse. They will not fight back. It is just the way they've been brought up. They are very soft. They are taught to be obedient. A lot of white girls even let their kids run all over them. Black women are a little smarter."[7] If this view that black women will not or should not put up with battering is pervasive, then black battered women may experience considerable shame. Perhaps this shame is of a different form, degree, and intensity from that suffered by more affluent women of European ancestry.

Domestic homicide rates among blacks are higher than those among whites and Latinos.[8] However, some research reveals that this effect falls away dramatically when researchers control for socioeconomic status.[9] Studies of all persuasions suggest higher rates of domestic violence among poor blacks than poor whites. Noel Cazenave and Murray Straus report that at the lowest income levels "black and white respondents . . . have similar rates of severe spousal violence except at the $6,000–$11,999 income level where the rates are notably higher for blacks."[10] Bureau of Justice Statistics (BJS, 1998) show black women more vulnerable to nonlethal intimate violence than women of all other races.[11] The disproportionate victimization of black women could be the reason more black women commit domestic homicide. Between 1992 and 1996, 11.7 per 1,000 black women experienced intimate male violence, compared to 8.2 per 1,000 white women. Over the same period, 2.1 per 1,000 black men and 1.4 per 1,000 white men reported intimate female violence.[12] According to official sources, intimate partner homicide declined in the black community at a much faster rate than among other races or ethnic groups.[13] This faster reduction might be attributable to increased policing of black communities, the mass incarceration of young black men, who are no longer available to either kill or be killed; the more efficient provision of medical services that reduce the death rate from things like gunshot wounds during domestic disputes; or the fostering of a social climate more critical of domestic violence, a climate promoted by the anti-domestic violence movement and the growth of shelter for women.

One possible reason black women do not report their own interpersonal victimization or that of their neighbors is that they see too much domestic violence in their communities. Without further detailed ethnography it is difficult to know how deeply embedded this desensitization to domestic violence might be among residents in Nashville's housing projects. In a public forum in the James A. Cayce public housing projects, a young woman recently reminded Bessie of some people's complacency toward domestic violence. Bessie explained:

> I was out in Cayce Homes about three weeks ago facilitating a discussion on domestic violence. There was a young lady there that challenged me like I had not been challenged before by a teen in I don't know when. She challenged in that she was so desensitized to a family member who was experiencing domestic violence. It was a lethal situation. She was saying to me, "So what, Bessie, I know exactly what you're talking about." I'm up here doing the power-control wheel and talking about the dynamics, the cycle, doing all that. She says, "I don't care. You can tell me that all you want to but she keeps going back to him and he keeps beating her, so we just leave it alone. We don't do anything about it." So we were going back and forth with one another. I was determined to keep her talking. I wanted to hear that attitude. When I finally presented to her, "What if there were lots of people in the community that feel the way you do about domestic violence and everybody just accepts it?" She said, "That's how it is." And then, right at that moment, I realized how important it is for us to continue to educate in those particular communities because now it's just normal behavior. What that says to me is, if this is normal behavior to a seventeen-, eighteen-, or nineteen-year-old child, the chances of her being a victim . . . are greater.

However, my conversations with Officer Ron Hawkins, a white officer who worked in Edgehill for two years as community policing took off there, had a more positive view of the willingness of black women to report domestic violence:

> Once they found out there were officers at the Edgehill Enterprise Office that were dedicated to making sure that they were safe, they knew they could call us and ask for a specific officer and say, "Listen, he came over again last night. He was beating on my door at three o'clock in the morning, screaming and yelling, cussing me and threatening to kill me." She would know that I have some history with her as far as her past incidents with this boyfriend or husband or whatever. We would say, "Okay, come on over to the office. We will come get you and take you down to get an order of protection," or if the protection order was already there, we would get a warrant for violating that order. They got to the point that they were doing it. And then we would assist them, of course, through the entire process. When they would come into court, we would show up too because we would physically make the arrest or we had some contributing information. Women would come in and say, "Hey, Officer Hawkins." They would come over and sit down next to us and we would tell them what the process was, what was going to happen, this is what we're doing, this is how things are going to happen today in the courtroom process. It made them more comfortable with it. Has it influenced others to call and report domestic violence? I think so. I don't have hard numbers, but I think it has.

In a discussion about the decline in domestic homicides, Detective Bronson offered the following observations, concurring with Officer Hawkins that the rise in community policing has led to an increased call volume on domestics:

> BRONSON: I know that Vanderbilt's Medical Center, for instance, is an excellent trauma center. I've seen them, the EMTs, say, "They're not going to make it." And they would get them to Vanderbilt, and they make it. I think the medical services have had a great impact on reducing homicides. I believe community policing is building more trust. We get a lot more calls a lot quicker. Reporting has definitely gone up. Whereas somebody else would say, "I thought I heard a gunshot next door but I'm not going to call. I don't want to get involved."
>
> WEBSDALE: So it's neighbors reporting as opposed to, say, victims increasingly reporting because of community policing presence? It's not like you're getting into the families but . . .
>
> BRONSON: I would say that both have increased.

However, it remains clear from my ethnographic findings in both Nashville and Florida that there are a significant number of women who do not call the police.[14] In Florida, it was among the ranks of these highly entrapped women that the domestic homicides occurred, with either partner killing the other. My ethnography reveals something of how black battered women feel about calling the police, but we need to learn much more. Clearly, as in Florida, a significant portion of people killed in domestic disturbances came from families that have had little contact with the police. Detective Bronson, concurring with my research into domestic homicides in Florida, which showed domestic deaths to be mostly crimes of escalating violence, intimidation, and entrapment of women, said: "Most of the homicides that are related to domestic violence are victims that we have never dealt with. We have had a few that we have dealt with, but a lot of them we never had the first call. You have to wonder if their family ever knew about any of this violence, and if they did, why didn't they call? People had to know about this after seeing all these injuries, it had to be going on, because the probability of them just shooting or stabbing them to death for the first time is very low. Most likely there is an escalation of bruises or broken bones."

Battered women also talked of their fear of public space,[15] though some appeared tough and street savvy, and said they did not find their particular projects threatening, those women were in the minority. Battered women's fear of the social and physical spaces surrounding their homes makes it difficult to get to shelters or attend support group meetings concerning battering or drug-addiction problems. Regina, who works with battered women from the projects in Nashville, explained:

> One of the things that we have had to deal with is their level of concern for safety, even in terms of being picked up by a cab to get to our program. The cab driver does not come to that area after a certain . . . time on certain days. We used to have support group meetings on Friday. If we didn't call a taxi before twelve noon, the taxi driver would not go into the area. That, to me, said a lot. So if we didn't call to say "pick up this woman at a certain place that is outside

of the housing area," then we would have to make other arrangements to pick her up. Not only is this woman in danger in her home, but once she steps outside that door, it's like a war zone that public transportation will not enter. I'm not hearing from women that we are serving from that area that they feel safe because police officers are there on bikes.

Much of what I have referred to above concerns battered women who live in the poorest sections of Nashville, namely the public housing projects. Most of these women are African American. Most are unmarried and do not need to seek formal legal dissolution of their violent relationships. A conversation with two legal advocates for battered women, Henrietta and Germane, reminded me of the extent to which poverty is a barrier for women who seek to leave their abusers. I had witnessed this phenomenon before in rural Kentucky, where women reported using permanent orders of protection as "makeshift divorces."[16] It was disconcerting to see a similar drama played out in Nashville, where, in the Latino community especially, there is a strong patriarchal imperative against divorce.[17]

WEBSDALE: I attended a "domestic" the other day where a woman was looking for a divorce and was looking to move out of her relationship, and she was telling me that she managed to find a cheap source of a divorce, which was $375. She said it would normally cost $500 to $700 to pick up a divorce.

HENRIETTA: That is pretty standard. I mean, that is uncontested divorce with no property and no children. Just a very simple divorce.

GERMANE: When you get into a custody battle . . . I have a friend who left her abusive husband and she spent over $5,000 divorcing him.

HENRIETTA: Yeah. That's very discouraging for poor women and children especially. Men always threaten to fight for custody whether they want it or not. So it can be very very expensive. If a woman calls an attorney and says, "I have children and I want a divorce and I think he's gonna fight for custody," she will be quoted $1,500 outright.

WEBSDALE: Yeah. I've done some research in Kentucky, and there I heard that women would just not get married again. They will just move away and not get divorced because it so difficult, expensive, and time-consuming. Do you see a lot of that?

GERMANE: I do. Especially in the community that I work with, the Latino community. There is cultural and religious opposition to divorce to the extent that women will just separate and just never even bother to get a divorce.

WEBSDALE: In a permanent state of separation, if you will, which in itself is somewhat dangerous.

GERMANE: It is. It is dangerous. They also limit themselves in terms of what they can actually obtain for things like child support. It becomes very difficult. In the Latino population, we're not known to just have one or two kids. Many have four or five, so it becomes very difficult to support a family that size. They don't want to further their state of danger by asking for child support or asking for a divorce. So many don't even bother with it.

The domestic violence case I initially referred to in my discussion with Germane and Henrietta warrants careful consideration. Andy Baron had abused his wife, Nancy, on a number of occasions, was a drunk, and had problems keeping a job and supporting his family. Nancy was in the process of seeking legal advice regarding divorce and making moves to leave him. On a hot and humid afternoon in August, Andy used his vehicle to ram a car containing Nancy, Kirk (Nancy's brother), and Julie (Kirk's girlfriend). He had followed them to a back street and engaged in a verbal argument with Nancy, following which he rammed their car. Detective Eastwood and I arrived at the scene of what appeared to be a motor vehicle accident. A patrol unit was already there talking with those at the scene. On our way to the scene we had passed under a bridge a hundred yards from the accident, situated near a truck stop in Nashville. There was [a] large dent in the side of Nancy's vehicle and glass all over the road. Kirk told us that if he had not dived back into the vehicle (landing on the backseat) as Andy rammed them, "I would have been killed." While Detective Eastwood talked with Nancy, I chatted at length with Kirk. I asked him if he had engaged in a physical altercation with Andy that afternoon, to which he replied, "No, he knows better than that, I'd have kicked his butt." At one point Nancy told me that she had located a source for a cheap divorce who charged only $375.

Andy had driven away from the scene in his own car. A security guard from the nearby truck stop witnessed the confrontation and took off in pursuit of Andy. At one point Andy stopped his vehicle, drew a gun, and fired several shots at the security officer, who then gave up the chase. Eastwood and I learned of this shooting over the police radio. Eastwood directed the patrol officer at the scene to interview the security officer, who had returned to the relative tranquillity of the truck stop. I spent the next four hours or so with Nancy, Kirk, Julie, and other family members as Eastwood processed this case through the Domestic Violence Unit (DVU) of the Nashville Police Department, the Nashville night court, the emergency room, and the jail.

At the DVU Detective Eastwood filed four charges of aggravated assault against Andy, who, earlier that day, had also attempted to run down one of his own children. I thought to myself that Andy was not that good behind the wheel of a car or that he was playing some kind of sinister game. We then proceeded to transport Nancy and Julie to night court to put these cases to the commissioner; Kirk followed in another vehicle. By the time we arrived at night court, it was dark. I glanced around to check out the scene, knowing that this is not always the most salubrious of places. There were twenty or so people milling around, some in tattered clothes, some in suits and nice dresses (attorneys?). As I continued the surveillance work of the wary and, by now, weary ethnographer, Detective Eastwood's radio blurted out a message: "Do you know of an Andy Baron who is now under medical treatment at the ER after receiving two gunshot wounds?" Eastwood wondered if there was any confusion over the name (Baron is a pseudonym for a very common last name), so he checked in with the dispatcher. Nancy was by now distraught in the back of the police vehicle. Julie was helping to calm her down.

The dispatcher then confirmed that it was the Andy Baron who had reportedly rammed Nancy, Julie, and Kirk hours earlier and shot at the security guard who had pursued him. As if this was not bad enough, the tension built to fever pitch as the dispatcher told Eastwood that one of the nurses at the ER had described Andy Baron's injuries as serious and life-threatening. Nancy began to wail and throw herself around in the back of the police car, saying that Andy is the father of her three children, and that although he is an "asshole at times," she did not want to see Andy die. We slowly helped Nancy into one of the interview rooms at night court amid those charged with DUI, prostitution, and other offenses.

The patrol officer from the scene joined us. The situation had now changed significantly because the patrol officer and the detective were not sure if Andy had shot himself or if Nancy had somehow shot him; the police learned that Andy had told the admitting medical personnel that his wife shot him (we heard then he had two gunshot wounds to the abdomen). The patrol officer entered the interview room, where Nancy was still sobbing. He told her to calm down and then asked her if she had erased any of the harassing calls she claimed Andy had made to her earlier that day threatening to hurt himself if she left him. She answered no, telling the officer that the calls were still on the answering machine. The officer, in a very serious tone, told Nancy, "Don't erase those messages we'll need them as evidence." The patrol officer glanced at me, and we both knew why he needed them, so did Kirk, Julie, and Nancy, all of whom were now paying close attention.

The patrol officer disappeared, leaving me in the interview room with Julie, Nancy, and Kirk. Julie opened a container of pills. As natural as can be, Julie handed Nancy a tablet of Valium from her personal stash, saying, "That should calm you down." Having just witnessed a federal narcotics offense, I smiled rather wickedly to myself: the federal government was paying me as a consultant to work on this project. Being familiar with the effects of Valium, I knew that in approximately thirty minutes Nancy would relax significantly. Indeed, I sensed I had just experienced a rare and transcendent moment of "ethnographic empathy."

The police located Andy's vehicle, and Eastwood and I traveled to examine it. The crime scene analyst found no blood or gun, but did find a large knife under the driver's seat and a collection of empty beer cans. It seems Andy had gotten a ride from where he dumped the van to somewhere close to the hospital. We then visited the ER, where we learned the truth about Andy's medical status. He had two superficial gunshot wounds, seemingly caused by his pinching folds of fat on his stomach and shooting through them. Eastwood and I looked at each other and headed back to night court. By the time we arrived, the patrol officer had listened to Andy's recorded threats to take his own life if Nancy left him.

Behind a thick shield of bulletproof glass and looking down on the courtroom, the commissioner signed out the warrants to pick up Andy. I broke away from the group as we left night court to visit the restroom to urinate. This was clearly a mistake, and if I had not been with a police officer I would probably have been better off finding somewhere quiet at the back of the building to relieve myself. As I left a small, dirty room, that was liberally blessed with a mixture of vomit and fecal material, I ran into Kirk, who took me to one side. I had become quite fond of Kirk as the evening wore on. Indeed, I wondered to myself at the time, somewhat cynically, if this was the kind of male bonding the middle-class men's movement was bleating about. He said he was happy that things worked out right and that his sister was getting justice. It had been clear to Kirk all along that Andy was a game-playing manipulator who had shot himself to get attention. Perhaps at last his sister would see the light and move beyond "this loser." Kirk went on to say that he was due at work in the morning; it was late, and he wanted to get home. I asked what kind of work he did. He told me he delivered flowers and that his boss was already considering him for promotion. According to Kirk, the other drivers were not as quick or reliable as he was. He had been on the job only a month. He then made a strange face and said, "You know, I'm sorry I won't be delivering flowers to Andy at the morgue tomorrow." We smiled and shook hands. People discuss death easily and lightly on the streets.

Police arrested Andy a little while after he left the hospital. We got a call that we needed to book him into jail. As I left the court building and headed toward the jail, I wondered if it was the same jail where police used to beat black men in the elevator. I quickly reminded myself that it was not, that things had doubtless improved in Nashville, and felt a little easier as I rode up the elevator with Eastwood into the booking area. I mentioned the state of the restrooms at the night court to Eastwood, and he looked at me as police sometimes do at academics and said something like, "What do you expect with the prostitutes who work the area, the homeless men, and the drug addicts who sleep in there at all hours?" I reflected on the $375 that Nancy said would pay for her divorce, assuming, as Germane and Henrietta had reminded me, the divorce was straightforward. Eastwood and I went on to the next call. . . .

NOTES

1. See Morris, 1999; Clinton, 1994; A. Davis, 1983; hooks, 1984. Catherine Clinton (1994: 140) notes that even after Emancipation most freedwomen did not bring agents from the Freedmen's Bureau into their domestic lives. At the same time, "White observers condemned husbands who considered wife-beating a 'right' and resisted bureau intervention."

2. Gutman, 1976: 318, 319.

3. It was not until the early 1960s that we began to see the significant rise in female-headed households in the black community.

4. For similar accusations about Asian battered women, see Wang, 1996, discussed in Websdale, 1999: 37–39; for Native American battered women, see Zion and Zion, 1993.

5. As we saw in chapter 1 (Websdale, *Policing the Poor*, 2001), the tension, conflict, and violence between police agencies and the black community dates back to slavery. The fact that the criminal justice system has brutalized blacks affects the willingness of some black women to call police during domestic violence conflicts.

6. Donnell Stewart (2000) makes a similar observation from his experience as a therapist working with batterer treatment groups in Boston through the EMERGE program. I am most

grateful to David Adams for passing on these materials to me and sharing his insights regarding domestic violence and men and women of color. Personal conversation, July 12, 2000.

7. See Websdale, 1999: 153.

8. Websdale, 1999: 216. In my 1994 research into domestic homicides in Florida, I found that 1.58 black women per 100,000 kill their intimate black male partners, compared with 0.23 Latinas and 0.15 white women. I found the black intimate-partner homicide rate in Florida to be six times that of whites and two and a half times that of Latinos. These findings are consistent with those of numerous other researchers, for example, see Centerwall, 1984, 1995.

9. Centerwall, 1984, 1995.

10. Cazenave and Straus, 1995: 326–327. They speculate that there may be some effects of racial oppression which are independent of income and which may cause marital stress and tensions that may erupt in violence"(1995: 336). For a recent discussion of these issues of race, class, and woman battering, see Ptacek, 1999.

11. Bureau of Justice Statistics (BJS), 1998; 2000. Nonlethal intimate violence includes rape, sexual assault, robbery, and aggravated and simple assault.

12. For men, the rate of victimization by an intimate was about one-fifth the rate for women. However, it is important to note that these figures do not address the context of violence, the nature of injuries received, or the meaning of the violence to the men and women involved. Between 1993 and 1998, 11.1 per 1,000 black women experienced violence by an intimate, compared to 8.2 per 1,000 white women. Over the same period, 2.1 per 1,000 black men and 1.3 per 1,000 white men reported intimate violence perpetrated by females (see BJS, 2000, Appendix Table 4: 10).

13. Websdale, 1999: 216–232.

14. Ibid.

15. Renzetti and Maier (1999: 12, 13) report similar fear among women living in public housing in Camden, New Jersey. None of the thirty-six women interviewed by Renzetti and Maier reported feeling safe in her neighborhood at night. When asked about their biggest problem, "every woman mentioned personal safety concerns and fear of crime." Like the women I interviewed in Nashville, many of the Camden women reported "often" hearing gunshots outside their units at night.

16. Websdale, 1999: 202.

17. Germane did most of her work with Latinas, some of whom had entered the United States illegally. In the cases of battered illegal-immigrant Latinas, Germane noted the peculiar complexity of any pending divorce or separation and the way she had to work on the immigration issues to establish legal immigrant status before addressing the divorce issue. For a discussion of the plight of immigrant battered women, see Websdale, 1999: 178; Orloff and Rodriguez, 1997.

REFERENCES

Bureau of Justice Statistics. U.S. Department of Justice. 1998. *Violence by Intimates: Analysis of Data on Crimes by Current or Former Spouses, Boyfriends, and Girlfriends.* NCJ-167237, March. Washington, D.C.: Government Printing Office.

———. 2000. *Intimate Partner Violence.* By Callie Marie Rennison and Sarah Welchans. NCJ-178247, May. Washington, D.C.: Government Printing Office.

Cazenave, Noel A., and Murray Straus. 1990. Race, class, network embeddedness, and family violence. In Murray Straus and Richard Gelles, eds., *Physical Violence in American Families.* New Brunswick: Transaction Publishers, 321–339.

Centerwall, Brandon S. 1984. Race, socioeconomic status and domestic homicide, Atlanta, 1971–1972. *American Journal of Public Health* 74: 813–815.

———. 1995. Race, socioeconomic status, and domestic homicide. *Journal of the American Medical Association* 273(22): 1755–1758.

Clinton, Catherine. 1994. Bloody terrain: Freedwomen, sexuality, and violence during Reconstruction. In Catherine Clinton, ed., *Half Sisters of History: Southern Women and the American Past*. Durham, N.C.: Duke University Press, 136–153.

Davis, Angela. 1983. *Women, Race, and Class*. New York: Vintage.

Gutman, Herbert. 1976. *The Black Family in Slavery and Freedom, 1750–1925*. New York: Pantheon.

hooks, bell. 1984. *Ain't I a Woman?* London: Pluto Press.

Morris, Christopher. 1999. Within the slave cabin: Violence in Mississippi slave families. In Christine Daniels and Michael V. Kennedy, eds., *Over the Threshold: Intimate Violence in Early America*. New York and London: Routledge, 268–285.

Orloff, Leslye, and Rachel Rodriguez. 1997. Barriers to domestic violence relief and full faith and credit for immigrant and migrant battered women. In Byron Johnson and Neil Websdale, eds., *Full Faith and Credit: A Passport to Safety*. Reno, Nev.: National Council of Juvenile and Family Court Judges, 130–148.

Ptacek, James. 1999. *Battered Women in the Courtroom*. Boston: Northeastern University Press.

Renzetti, Claire, and Shana L. Maier. 1999. "Private" crime in public housing: Fear of crime and violent victimization among women public housing residents. Paper presented at the annual meeting of the Academy of Criminal Justice Sciences, Orlando, Florida (March).

Stewart, Donnell Lassiter. 2000. Specialized groups for African American clients. In *Emerge Batterers Intervention Group Program Manual*. Cambridge, Mass.: Emerge, 122–133.

Wang, Karin. 1996. Battered Asian American women: Community responses from the battered women's movement and the Asian American community. *Asian Law Journal* 3: 151–185.

Websdale, Neil. 1999. *Understanding Domestic Homicide*. Boston: Northeastern University Press.

———. 2001. *Policing the Poor: From Slave Plantation to Public Housing*. Boston: Northeastern University Press.

Zion, J. W., and E. B. Zion. 1993. Hozho' Sokee'—Stay together nicely: Domestic violence under Navajo common law. *Arizona State Law Journal* 25(2, summer): 407–426.

CHAPTER **11**

CAROLYN M. WEST

Domestic Violence in Ethnically and Racially Diverse Families

The "Political Gag Order" Has Been Lifted

─────────────── ABSTRACT ───────────────

Previous chapters set the stage for Carolyn M. West's discussion of a self-imposed rule of silence—in the name of solidarity—that historically has weighed upon communities of color regarding domestic violence. To speak out on violence in families of color too often invited excessive state surveillance and the stigma of community betrayal, not safety.

Consistent with the cautions of Hampton (chapter 9) and Websdale (chapter 10), Carolyn West urges the reader to be a critical consumer of social science research on race and culture. In her analysis of studies of prevalence that measure violence in ethnically diverse families, the author reveals measurement issues in domestic violence research that have produced either inconclusive or contradictory outcomes. A summary of past research findings provides a context for the oft-repeated question: Are ethnic minority families more violent than Anglo Americans?

Carolyn West helps the reader understand the structural—or as she calls it "demographic"—factors that trump race and culture in the measurement of domestic violence prevalence. These factors are chiefly poverty, unemployment, and to some extent recency of migration. In line with Hampton's and Websdale's analyses, the author demonstrates how structural explanations are necessary to understand differing rates of violence across ethnic groups.

When race and ethnicity influence and determine access to economic resources, as is the case in the United States, an understanding of abiding histories of exclusion and disadvantage is key to any inquiry on racial and ethnic diversity and domestic violence. Without a structural context for prevalence studies, there is a tendency to consider sociodemographic "variables" in a vacuum. If the analysis of the data disregards social structural context, issues of patriarchy, colonialism, racism, and inequality go unchallenged and social research colludes with these persistent stereotypes.

The author reviews the strengths and protective factors of communities of color and concludes that in fact the self-censoring gag order has been lifted. However, as discussed by Traci West in chapter 20 and Lisa Sun-Hee Park in chapter 21, this is only partly true. As you read this chapter, consider the following questions. What are the benefits and drawbacks of studying racial and ethnic group differences in the prevalence of domestic violence? How might findings from such studies perpetuate or reinforce negative images of some racial and ethnic groups? How might findings benefit the racial and ethnic groups that are studied?

To protect themselves and their communities from stereotypes and oppressive social policies, some people of color have imposed a "political gag order,"[1] which is a form of community pressure to suppress information about partner or domestic violence. As a result, some survivors have been discouraged from revealing their victimization and some community members and leaders have been reluctant to participate in the research process (West, 1998). Fortunately, more researchers, activists, and survivors have broken the silence around violence in ethnically and racially diverse families. As evidence, intimate violence in communities of color has been the subject of more books (de Anda and Becerra, 2000; West, 2002), special editions of journals (Dasgupta, 1999; Williams and Griffin, 2000), and literature reviews (Hampton, et al., 1998; Oates, 1998).

Although the political gag order has been lifted, researchers should continue this important work for several reasons. First, the United States is undergoing a major demographic transformation in racial and ethnic group composition (U.S. Census Bureau, 2001). As a result, investigators assert, "given the range of cultures represented here in the United States today, research on spouse abuse should take into account the ethnicity of respondents" (Gabler et al., 1998, p. 591). Second, to consider new directions for research, we must review the findings of previous research. Finally, researchers face a new challenge. Cultural sensitivity requires them to articulate racial similarities in intimate partner violence; simultaneously they must highlight racial differences without perpetuating the stereotype that ethnic groups are inherently more violent than White Americans. This intricate balance can best be accomplished by considering how the intersection of various forms of oppression (race, class, and gender) converge to create demographic inequalities and cultural factors that may increase the probability of violence in ethnic families (West, 2002).

Accordingly, the first section of the chapter describes the four largest racial groups in the United States: African Americans, Hispanic/Latino/

Latina Americans, Asian Americans, and Native Americans. In the second section I review the literature and discuss recent developments. The final section discusses how the intersection of oppressions may create demographic and cultural factors that increase the risk of violence in families of color.

DESCRIPTION OF ETHNIC AND RACIAL GROUPS

Partner violence occurs in a larger historical and cultural context. I establish this context by reviewing the demographic characteristics of the four largest ethnic groups, highlighting significant historical events, identifying contemporary challenges faced by each group, and emphasizing cultural strengths that may act as protective factors.

African Americans

Approximately 12 percent of the U.S. population, or 34 million people, identify themselves as African American. The Black population is increasing in diversity as greater numbers of immigrants arrive from Africa and Caribbean countries. Many African Americans trace their ancestry to the African slave trade. Their enslavement was characterized by forced separation of families, beatings, sexual assault, and loss of language and culture. As late as 1910, a majority of Blacks continued to be impoverished in the Deep South. Social and economic advancement came with the 1964 Civil Rights Act, which prohibited legal segregation in public accommodations and discrimination in education and employment.

Although African Americans now span all socioeconomic classes and professions, the legacy of slavery and discrimination continues to influence their social and economic standing. For example, in 1999 almost 25 percent of Black families had incomes below the poverty line. Many of these impoverished families reside in urban areas, which are plagued with high rates of community violence (U.S. Department of Health and Human Services, 2001).

Despite these challenges, African Americans have developed adaptive beliefs, traditions, and practices. For instance, religious commitment and prayer are common among this group. The family, both immediate and extended, has been and remains a source of comfort and strength. African Americans, by developing a capacity to disregard negative stereotypes about their group, have acquired some protection from low self-esteem (Oates, 1998).

Hispanic Americans

According to Census 2000, 35 million people, or approximately 13 percent of the U.S. population are categorized as Hispanic/Latino/Latina Americans. Almost two-thirds are persons of Mexican origin, followed by Puerto Ricans, Cubans, and Central Americans. Although the majority of Hispanics (64 percent) were born in the United States it is important to consider the historical events that brought Latinos to the United States. Mexicans have been U.S. residents longer than any other Hispanic ethnic group. After the Mexican War (1846–1848), when the United States took over large territories from Texas to California, the country gained many Mexican citizens. More recently, economic hardships in Mexico and the need for laborers have increased the flow of Mexicans to the United States. After World War II, large numbers of Puerto Ricans began arriving to the U.S. mainland. In the 1980s, the migration patterns became more circular as Puerto Ricans chose to return to the island; however, Puerto Ricans have been granted U.S. citizenship. Between 1959 and 1965, the first wave of Cuban immigrants, who were predominately educated professionals, arrived in the United States. As political refugees, they received economic assistance from the federal government. However, subsequent waves of Cuban immigrants, often less educated and nonwhite, received less economic support. Central Americans, the newest Hispanic ethnic group, arrived in the United States between 1980 and 1990. Many immigrants were fleeing political terror and atrocities in El Salvador, Guatemala, and Nicaragua (U.S. Department of Health and Human Services, 2001).

Different migration histories contribute to demographic variations among Hispanic ethnic groups. For example, Cuban Americans, tend to be older, more educated, and economically advantaged, followed by Puerto Ricans, and Mexican Americans. Furthermore, Hispanic groups vary in their level of acculturation. Some, fourth- or fifth-generation Americans, are very acculturated, but newly arrived immigrants continue to embrace their culture and customs (U.S. Department of Health and Human Services, 2001). Despite their diversity, many Hispanics value familism or family unity, respect, and loyalty. In addition, religion plays an important role in the lives of Hispanics (Oates, 1998).

Asian Americans

Asian Americans make up a diverse group that originates from three major geographic locations: (1) East Asia, which includes China, Japan, and Korea; (2) Southeast Asia, which includes Cambodia, Laos, and Vietnam; and (3) South Asia, which includes India, Pakistan, and Sri Lanka (Oates, 1998). Between 1990 and 2000, the number of people identifying as Asian American reached 10 million people, or 3.6 percent of the U.S. population (U.S. Census Bureau, 2001).

The Chinese were among the first Asian groups to come to the United States. Between 1848 and 1882, the discovery of gold in California and work in the railroad industry drew large numbers of Chinese immigrants. However, the government passed laws, such as the Chinese Exclusion Act of 1882, which limited Asian immigration. Migration to the United States grew following the 1965 Immigration Act, which supported family reunification and discouraged discrimination against Asians. During the late 1970s and 1980s, the U.S. government, for political and humanitarian reasons, accepted large numbers of Southeast Asian refugees from Vietnam, Cambodia, and Laos (U.S. Department of Health and Human Services, 2001).

Asian Americans reflect diversity in terms of ethnicity, culture, and religion (Buddhism, Confuciansim, Hinduism). This group is also linguistically diverse, with more than one hundred languages and dialects spoken. On average, Asian Americans have completed more formal education than other ethnic groups. However, there are ethnic group differences. Descendents from the Indian subcontinent (India, Pakistan, Bangladesh) tend to be more educated than Cambodians, Hmong, and Laotians. The rates of poverty also vary across ethnic groups. Japanese Americans (7 percent) were least impoverished, followed by Chinese, Korean, and Thai Americans who reported poverty rates of 14 percent. Southeast Asians, such as Cambodians (43 percent) and Hmong (64 percent), reported the highest poverty rates (U.S. Department of Health and Human Services, 2001). Despite their diversity, Asians value family relationships, respect for authority, and elders as well as responsibility, self-control, discipline, and educational achievement (Oates, 1998).

Native Americans

According to the U.S. Census Bureau, 4.1 million people, or 1.5 percent of the U.S. population, identify as Native Americans and Alaska Natives (Eskimos and Aleuts). Despite increased willingness to acknowledge Indian ancestry and increased birth rates, this ethnic group remains small. Native Americans and Alaska Natives were self-governing people who thrived in North America. This began to change when Europeans "discovered" and colonized North America. In the seventeenth century, European contact exposed Native people to infectious diseases. Over time, almost every tribe was subjected to forced removal from their ancestral homelands, brutal colonization, and confinement to reservations. As a result, the population began to decline. During the 1970s, Native Americans and Alaska Natives began to demand greater authority in their communities, which led to the reemergence of tribal courts and councils (U.S. Department of Health and Human Services, 2001).

There are hundreds of different native peoples and languages across North America. Limited educational opportunities and high unemployment rates are common community problems. As a result, approximately 25 percent of Native Americans live in poverty. Alcohol-related problems, diabetes, and inadequate health care contribute to premature death; consequently, this relatively young population has an average age of twenty-eight (U.S. Department of Health and Human Services, 2001). In spite of these social and economic challenges, many Native American families value respect for elders, cooperation, group cohesion, and respect for religion (Oates, 1998).

In conclusion, despite economic and social advances, ethnic groups are disproportionately more likely to be young, impoverished, and less educated (U.S. Department of Health and Human Services, 2001). All these demographic factors are associated with increased levels of partner violence. However, each ethnic group has developed cultural strengths, which have enabled them to deal with violence in their families (Oates, 1998; West, 1998).

INCIDENCE OF PARTNER VIOLENCE

The earlier research on domestic violence presents a complex, and at times contradictory, picture of racial differences in the rates of partner violence (see review by West, 1998). To summarize, African American, Hispanic, and White American battered women reported similar rates of partner violence in nonrepresentative samples, such as shelter residents. However, when compared to White Americans, African Americans and Native Americans reported higher rates of partner violence in community samples and large nationally representative samples. In national studies, Latino couples reported both higher and lower rates of partner violence when compared to White couples. "Ethnic lumping," which is the failure to consider ethnic group differences, may explain these conflicting results. When Latino ethnic group differences were taken into account, Puerto Rican husbands reported the highest rate of wife assault and Cuban husbands reported the lowest rate. Methodological problems, including small sample size and ethnic lumping, have made it difficult to draw conclusions about the lifetime prevalence rates of partner violence among Asian Americans and American Indians (West, 1998).

A growing body of research has focused on violence in ethnically diverse families (Hampton et al., 1998; Oates, 1998). Similar to previous studies, investigators found few ethnic differences in nonrepresentative samples. For example, in a community sample of more than seven hundred low-income women, African American, Mexican American, and European American women reported comparable rates of intimate partner violence (Marshall et al., 2000). However, in nationally representative studies, women of color, particularly Black, Hispanic, and Native American women, generally reported higher rates of domestic violence (Tjaden and Thoennes, 2000).

In this section I review the research on ethnic differences in intimate partner violence. Many of these findings are based on four national studies: (1) The National Alcohol and Family Violence Survey (NAFVS) is comprised of face-to-face interviews conducted with a national probability sample of 1,970 persons who were living as couples with a member of the opposite sex. Hispanics were oversampled ($n = 846$). Respondents had the choice of being interviewed in English or Spanish (Jasinski, 1998). (2) The National Alcohol Survey (NAS) was comprised of interviews conducted in forty-eight states with participants who were eighteen years of age or older. Blacks and Hispanics were oversampled (Cunradi et al., 1999). (3) The National Violence Against Women Survey (NVAW) consisted of telephone interviews with a nationally representative sample of eight thousand women and eight thousand men. Participants were queried about their experiences as victims of violence, including intimate partner violence (Tjaden and Thoennes, 2000). (4) The National Crime Victimization Survey (NCVS), which is administered by the U.S. Bureau of the Census. Household members are interviewed annually concerning their criminal victimization during the six months preceding their interview (Rennison and Welchans, 2000).

African Americans

Intimate partner violence among African Americans has been well documented (West, 2002; Williams and Griffin, 2000). Consistent with previous research, African Americans women were somewhat more likely than White women to be assaulted by an intimate partner (26 percent vs. 21 percent, respectively) (Tjaden and Thoennes, 2000). Both Black men and women sustained and inflicted abuse. According to the NCVS, between 1993 and 1998 Blacks were victimized by intimate partners at significantly higher rates than persons of other races. More specifically, Black women experienced intimate partner victimization at a rate 35 percent higher than that of White women. Black husbands were also abused, with rates approximately 62 percent higher than that of White husbands (Rennison and Welchans, 2000). The NAS provided further evidence of this racial pattern. Black couples reported the highest rate (23 percent) of male-to-female partner violence, followed by Hispanic couples (17 percent), and White couples (11 percent). Female-to-male partner violence followed a similar pattern. Black couples reported a higher rate (30 percent) than their Hispanic (21 percent) and White (15 percent) counterparts (Cunradi et al., 1999). Caution should be used when interpreting these gender differences. When rates of severe violence were considered, Black women were frequent victims of wife battering (Kessler et al., 2001). In fact, homicide by intimate partners is the leading cause of death for African American women between the ages of fifteen and twenty-four (National Center for Health Statistics, 1997). Black women may be using aggression as a form of self-defense in retaliation for the abuse perpetrated against them.

Hispanic Americans

According to previous research, when compared to White Americans, Hispanic Americans reported both higher and lower rates of partner violence (West, 1998). More recently, higher rates were reported by Latinos. For example, Hispanic couples reported both male-to-female (17 percent) and female-to-male (21 percent) partner violence, which are higher than the rates for White couples (11 percent and 15 percent, respectively) (Cunradi et al., 1999). Similarly, based on the NAFVS, Hispanic husbands were more likely than White husbands to inflict wife assaults that were both minor (16 percent vs. 12 percent) and severe (5.2 percent vs. 2.7 percent) (Jasinski and Kaufman Kantor, 2001). However, when researchers considered the experiences of battered women, Latinas (37 percent) and White women (34 percent) reported comparable rates of severe violence, defined as beatings or threats with weapons (West et al., 1998).

When ethnic group differences were investigated, researchers discovered important differences. In a large sample ($n = 1,000$) of ethnically diverse women who were recruited from community hospitals, Central American (7 percent) and Cuban American women (7 percent) were least likely to be abused, followed by Mexican American women (14 percent). Puerto Rican women (23 percent) reported the highest rates of partner abuse (Torres et al., 2000). A similar pattern was discovered when researchers used the NAFVS. When severe violence was considered, Mexican American husbands born in the United States (11 percent) were more likely to admit to wife assault than either Puerto Rican (7 percent) or Mexican husbands born in Mexico (2.5 percent). No Cuban husbands reported wife battering. Although not statistically significant, these patterns illustrate the importance of investigating ethnic group differences (Jasinski, 1998).

Asian Americans

Although domestic violence researchers have been criticized for neglecting the experiences of Asian Americans (West, 1998), more recently this population has been the focus of literature reviews (Lee, 2000; Lum, 1998) and special journal editions (Dasgupta, 1999). According to the NVAW survey, physical assault was reported by 12 percent of women who identified as Asian/Pacific Islander ($n = 133$). This is significantly lower than the rate for Native American (30 percent), mixed race (27 percent), and Black women (26 percent). The researchers concluded, "the lower intimate partner victimization rates found among Asian/Pacific Islander women may be, at least in part, an artifact of underreporting" (Tjaden and Thoennes, 2000, pp. 26–27). This political gag order has been attributed to traditional Asian values that emphasize close family ties and harmony. In addition, stereotypes, which characterize Asians as "model minorities," make some survivors and community members reluctant to discuss this problem (Yick, 2000).

Past research has been limited by ethnic lumping and small sample size (West, 1998). Although both these methodological problems continue to exist, researchers have begun to use larger samples to investigate intimate violence in Asian groups. For example, violence in South Asian families (Bangladeshi, Indian, Pakistani) has come to the attention of investigators. Dasgupta (2000) cited a study conducted in Boston with 160 highly educated, professional South Asian women between the ages of eighteen and sixty-two. Nearly one-third had experienced physical abuse in their present relationship. Yoshihama (1999) discovered similarly high rates of abuse when she conducted face-to-face interviews with 211 women of Japanese descent. Approximately 50 percent of the respondents had experienced some form of physical partner violence during their lifetimes. Other researchers used telephone directories to identify and interview approximately 250 Chinese American (Yick, 2000) and Korean American families (Kim and Sung, 2000). In both ethnic groups, almost 20 percent reported minor violence (for example, slapped, pushed, shoved) and 8 percent experienced severe violence.

Native Americans

Previous research on this population also has been limited by ethnic lumping and small sample size (West, 1998). These methodological problems continue to exist; however, the few available studies indicate that partner violence is a serious problem in this population. Based on the NVAW survey, 30 percent of Native American/Alaska Native women ($n = 88$) had been physically assaulted by a male partner. Although not significantly higher, these women reported more victimization than their African American (26 percent) and White women counterparts (21 percent) (Tjaden and Thoennes, 2000).

Considering tribal and regional differences has enhanced our understanding of domestic violence among Native Americans. For example, severe victimization has been found among Native women in rural Alaska (Shepherd, 2001) and Native American women on the Apache and Hualapai reservations (Hamby, 2000). A larger study was conducted at an Indian Health Service comprehensive health care facility. Among the 341 Navajo women who completed the survey, 52 percent had reported at least one episode of domestic violence, with verbal (40 percent) and physical abuse (41 percent) most frequently reported. Almost one-third of the physical abuse was categorized as severe violence (Fairchild et al., 1998).

In summary, using nonrepresentative samples, researchers discovered comparable rates of domestic violence across racial groups (Marshall et al., 2000). However, in national studies, researchers discovered important racial differences, which have been consistent over time. When compared to White Americans and other racial groups, African Americans reported substantially higher rates of partner violence (Rennison and Welchans, 2000). In general, Hispanic couples reported more spousal assault than their White counterparts; when ethnic group differences were considered, Puerto Ricans and Mexican Americans reported more marital violence than Cubans (Jasinski, 1998). More researchers have investigated violence in Asian American families. In a national study, Asian/Pacific Islanders reported less victimization than other ethnic groups, which may be due to underreporting (Tjaden and Thoennes, 2000). Although racial comparisons were not made, based on self-report studies, domestic violence is a serious problem among various Asian American groups, including South Asians, Japanese, Chinese, Korean, and Vietnamese families (Lum, 1998). Finally, the research on domestic violence among Native Americans continues to be limited by small sample size and failure to consider tribal and regional differences. Nevertheless, researchers have documented substantial rates of partner abuse among Alaska Native women (Shepherd, 2001) and Native American women (Fairchild et al., 1998).

FACTORS THAT CONTRIBUTE TO ETHNIC DIFFERENCES

After several decades of research, a consistent demographic profile of the most likely victims and perpetrators has emerged: young, impoverished, and unemployed African American or Hispanic couples (Holtzman-Munroe, et al., 1997; Rennison and Welchans, 2000). However, it would be inappropriate to conclude that ethnically diverse families are inherently more violent. As previously discussed, families of color are disproportionately more likely to be young, impoverished, and less educated (U.S. Department of Health and Human Services, 2001), the very demographic categories at the greatest risk for violence. Although each ethnic group has developed cultural strengths that may act as protective factors, economic marginalization continues to influence the culture of their families. For example, less acculturated individuals are more likely to be impoverished because they lack access to education and job opportunities. Poverty has also been linked to heavy drinking (West, 1998). This section reviews how demographic and cultural factors converge to increase the probability of violence in ethnically diverse families.

Demographic Factors

Similar to previous research (West, 1998), investigators continue to find links between domestic violence and youthfulness (Jasinski, 2000), poverty (Torres et al., 2000), and husband's occupational and employment status (Jasinski et al., 1997). More recently complex associations have been discovered between these demographic categories and partner assault. For example, researchers have begun to investigate stressful events in the lives of young couples, such as pregnancy (Jasinski and Kaufman Kantor, 2001). In addition, the most impoverished families, such as the welfare dependent, are at increased risk for violence (Tolman and Raphael, 2000). Finally, more violence occurs in families when additional factors, such as work stress, occur in conjunction with unemployment and low occupational status (Jasinski et al., 1997).

PREGNANCY.   Researchers have discovered associations between ethnicity and battering among pregnant women. According to research based on the NAFVS, pregnancy was associated with severe wife assault among White women. In contrast, when compared to Hispanic women who were not pregnant, pregnant Hispanic women were more likely to be victims of minor wife assault and to be victimized for the first time during the survey year (Jasinski and Kaufman Kantor, 2001). Using an ethnically diverse sample of women recruited from community hospitals in Florida and Massachusetts, researchers discovered important ethnic group differences. Puerto Rican women were most likely to report abuse during pregnancy, followed by White and Black women. Pregnant Mexican American, Cuban American, and Central American women were less likely to report victimization (Torres et al., 2000). Despite these ethnic differences, pregnancy was not a predictor of wife assault in either study after the researchers controlled for socioeconomic status, stressful life events, and age.

WELFARE DEPENDENCY.   As previously noted, poverty has consistently been associated with higher rates of domestic violence (Torres et al., 2000). However, poor, welfare dependent women are especially vulnerable (Tolman and Raphael, 2000). Although this link has been found across ethnic groups, there are some important differences. Previous relationship violence was associated with lower rates of employment for White women. In contrast, Black and Mexican American women who received public assistance were more likely to report victimization in previous relationships (Honeycutt et al., 2001). Furthermore, battered women of color may face additional challenges while making the transition from welfare to the workforce. For instance, in one study although Black women had more education and work experience than their White counterparts, racial discrimination made it difficult for them to find employment after completing a job-readiness program (Brush, 2001).

HUSBAND'S OCCUPATIONAL AND EMPLOYMENT STATUS.   Unemployment and employment in blue-collar professions has been linked to increased levels of wife assault (West, 1998). Researchers have discovered a more complex association between employment status and domestic violence. Based on the NAFVS, Hispanic husbands were more likely to face extended unemployment in the year prior to the survey, but White husbands were more likely to experience trouble with their supervisors. Although all these men experienced work-related stress, their reaction varied based on ethnicity. Specifically, work stress was associated with increased drinking and wife assault among Hispanic men. In contrast, work stress among White men was associated with elevated levels of drinking, but not violence (Jasinski et al., 1997). Furthermore, Jasinski (2001) suggested that a curvilinear relationship may exist between employment patterns and violence in ethnically diverse families. For example, working overtime may be stressful and thus increases the risk of violence; conversely, working fewer weeks is related to lower income, which may also increase both stress and domestic violence.

Cultural Factors

In some cases, racial differences remained after demographic factors were taken into account. For example, after controlling for sociodemographic factors, severe violence continued to be elevated in a nationally representative sample of Blacks and Hispanics (Kessler et al., 2001). Consistent with previous research, cultural factors, such as level of acculturation and heavy alcohol use, may account for some of these ethnic differences (West, 1998). With additional research, investigators have discovered more complex associations between partner violence and these cultural factors.

LEVEL OF ACCULTURATION.   Intimate partner violence has been associated with the couple's level of acculturation, which is "the process whereby immigrants come to adopt the values and behaviors of the host country" (Jasinski, 1998, p. 173). However, the results have been contradictory. Depending on the ethnic group, both high and low levels of acculturation have been linked to violence. Moreover, inconsistent definitions of acculturation and the failure to consider the confounding effects of socioeconomic status may partially account for these conflicting results (West, 1998). All these methodological problems continue to exist, which may explain why researchers continue to find both high and low levels of acculturation linked to increased rates of partner violence. More recently, researchers have discovered that couples who reported medium levels of acculturation are also at risk.

High Acculturation Level. Based on the NAFVS, highly acculturated Hispanic American husbands were more likely to assault their wives. More specifically, after controlling for age, poverty, and education, third-generation Hispanic husbands were almost three times as likely to beat their wives compared to Hispanic husbands who were born outside the United States (Jasinski, 1998). Similarly, abused Latinas reported higher levels of acculturation, as measured by preference for the English language (Torres et al., 2000).

Researchers suggest that acculturation may present some new challenges. Embracing the cultural values of U.S. society does not protect against racial discrimination. In fact, perceptions of discrimination may increase with longer residence in the United States. As a result, some Latinos may feel alienated from the larger society, which may contribute to frustration and stress, and ultimately conflict and violence (Jasinski, 1998).

Low Acculturation Level. Partner violence is also a common occurrence among less acculturated couples, particularly if they are recent immigrants. Several factors may contribute, as well as complicate, intimate violence in these families (for a review, see Raj and Silverman, 2002). Initially, immigrants may be optimistic about moving to the United States, a "land of opportunity." However, upon arriving they may find themselves economically and socially marginalized. Many recent arrivals, particularly if they come from rural areas, may lack education and job skills that are transferable to the U.S. economy. Consequently, they are often impoverished, which is a risk factor for abuse. Second, isolation can create an environment that both fosters and conceals family violence. Recent immigrants must often adapt to a new country without support from family members and friends. The absence of this support network can increase family stress and decrease the likelihood of intervention in cases of abuse. Battered immigrant women may be further silenced by fear of deportation, especially if they or their partners are undocumented workers, have limited access to social services, lack English language skills, and are faced with oppressive legal policies, which require extensive documentation of abuse.

Medium Acculturation Level. The NAS included a broader measure of acculturation. For example, participants' were asked about their ease of social relationships with Anglos and Hispanics, preference for Hispanic media and music, and their proportion of Hispanic friends, church members, and neighbors. Based on their score, Latino participants' were categorized as low, medium, or high in acculturation level. Overall rates of male-to-female Hispanic partner violence were highest among men in the medium acculturation group followed by those in the low and high acculturation group. Similarly, when compared to the high and low acculturated groups, the overall rate of female-to-male Hispanic abuse was almost twice as high among medium acculturated women. The authors speculated that individuals in the medium range had lost connection with their country of origin and had not yet adopted the values associated with the U.S. culture. Without a strong identification to either culture, these couples may be vulnerable to anxiety, stress, conflict, and potentially violence (Caetano et al., 2000).

To summarize, consistent with previous research, various levels of acculturation have been linked with domestic violence (West, 1998). More recently, increased rates of intimate violence have been linked to high (Jasinski, 1998), low (Raj and Silverman, 2002), and now medium levels of acculturation (Caetano et al., 2000). A variety of factors, such as inconsistent definitions of acculturation, may explain the wide range of results. More empirical research should be conducted before drawing conclusions.

ALCOHOL ABUSE.   By using large nationally representative samples, more research has begun to investigate the link between drinking and domestic violence. Although substance abusers were not oversampled, these studies are valuable because they oversampled ethnic groups (African Americans and Hispanics) where they asked detailed questions on alcohol use and abuse. As a result, complex associations have been discovered among partner violence, substance abuse, and ethnicity. Based on the NAFVS, a large study designed to measure the links between alcohol and family violence, the association between wife abuse and drinking was influenced by work stress, related to being laid off, fired, or unemployed. Among Hispanic men, work stress was linked to increased levels of both drinking and wife abuse. In contrast, White men who experienced work stress were more likely to drink, but not batter their wives (Jasinski et al., 1997).

Intricate associations also were discovered when researchers used the National Alcohol Survey (NAS). Ethnic differences in the links between alcohol-related problems and intimate partner violence remained after controlling for sociodemographic factors, psychosocial variables (childhood victimization, impulsivity), and alcohol consumption. When compared to Black couples without drinking problems, Black couples with either male or female alcohol problems were substantially more likely (ten and five times, respectively) to report wife abuse. Conversely, although White couples with either male or female alcohol problems were at a twofold risk of wife battering, these associations were not significant. Similarly, male and female alcohol problems were not predictive of wife beating among Hispanics (Cunradi et al., 1999). However, when the level of acculturation was considered, the association between alcohol use and partner violence became more complex. For example, medium and highly acculturated Hispanic women who drank report the highest occurrences of intimate partner abuse (Caetano et al., 2000). Taken together, the association between alcohol and intimate partner violence among various ethnic groups is complex and sometimes difficult to interpret. Caetano and colleagues (2000) summarize the literature well: "alcohol's role in partner violence becomes a moving target interacting differently with such factors as couple members' personalities, socioeconomic status, and ethnicity" (p. 42). Clearly more research is required.

SUMMARY AND NEW RESEARCH DIRECTIONS

The first section of this chapter was devoted to describing the cultural, linguistic, economic, historic, and geographic diversity among the four largest racial groups in the United States. Given the major demographic transformation in racial and ethnic group composition (U.S. Census Bureau, 2001), domestic violence researchers must continue to focus on ethnic and racial differences. In the future, researchers should consider partner violence among individuals who identify as "mixed race" and couples who are in interracial relationships. In addition, researchers should explore the diversity among White or European Americans; for example, those who identify as Polish, Italian, or German American. Moreover, much more work needs to be done to study how social class and geography intersect with race, ethnicity, and domestic violence.

The second section reviewed and discussed recent developments in the research. Consistent with previous findings, nationally representative studies revealed higher rates of partner violence among Black, Hispanic, and Native Americans when compared to White Americans. Asian Americans reported the lowest rate of domestic violence, possibly due to underreporting (Tjaden and Thoennes, 2000). Much of this research has focused on violence in heterosexual or cohabiting relationships. There is a need to investigate ethnic differences in dating relationships (Watson et al., 2001) and same sex relationships (Turrell, 2000).

Although ethnically diverse families reported alarmingly high rates of partner violence, it would be a mistake to conclude that these families are inherently violent. Consequently, the third section focused on demographic and cultural factors that may contribute to ethnic differences in partner violence. Consistent with previous research, people of color are overrepresented in demographic categories that are at greater risk for violence, such as couples who experience pregnancy, welfare dependency, or unemployment. Further, the rates of abuse may be influenced by both level of acculturation and alcohol abuse. As the research continues to grow, investigators have discovered a complex association between demographic and cultural factors.

The violence in ethnically diverse families is both very similar and vastly different from the violence experienced by their White counterparts. The next research challenge is to investigate racial similarities without negating the experiences of people of color and to simultaneously highlight racial differences without perpetuating stereotypes about the inherent violence of ethnic groups (West, 2002). This intricate balance can best be achieved by considering how partner violence is influenced by living at the intersection of various forms of oppressions (for example, race, class, gender, sexual orientation, immigration status), as presented in this anthology. Alternatively stated, "a middle-class, African American heterosexual Christian woman is not just African American, not just middle-class, not just Christian, and not just female. Instead, her life is located at the intersection of these dimensions" (Hassouneh Phillips, 1998, p. 682). The victim's location in this system of oppression determines her vulnerability to violence (for example, poor women are more likely to be victimized), societal perceptions toward the victim (for example, ethnic groups are said to be more violent and interventions are said to not be successful), and the victim's access to help (for example, less acculturated women receive less assistance). Further, the legacy of historical violence and trauma, such as forced migration and slavery, as well as contemporary challenges, including poverty, inadequate educational opportunities, and violence both against and within a community can influence how ethnic families experience abuse (Sanchez-Hucles and Dutton, 1999). Despite the substantial rates of intimate violence, most families of color have developed cultural strengths that act as protective factors, which reduce the likelihood of abuse.

In conclusion, the political gag order has been lifted. Consequently, survivors are more willing to reveal the abuse in their lives. In addition, scholars and practitioners are often collaborative partners on research projects pertaining to violence in diverse populations. This is an important beginning; however, much work remains. To advance the research, investigators, community members, activists, and survivors must develop culturally sensitive models that address the complexity of violence in ethnically and racially diverse families.

NOTE

1. The terms *people of color* and *ethnically diverse* are used to refer collectively to the four ethnic groups discussed in this chapter (African Americans, Hispanics/Latino/Latina Americans, Asian Americans, and Native Americans). Also, the terms *African Americans* and *Hispanics* are used interchangeably with *Blacks* and *Latinos/Latinas*, respectively. Where possible, the ethnic group is identified (e.g., Mexican American, Chinese American). The terminology used to refer to racial/ethnic groups may vary based on regional, political, and personal preferences.

REFERENCES

Brush, L. D. 2001. Poverty, battering, race, and welfare reform: Black-White differences in women's welfare-to-work transitions. *Journal of Poverty* 5: 67–89.

Caetano, R., J. Schafer, C. L. Clark, C. B. Cunradi, and K. Raspberry. 2000. Intimate partner violence, acculturation, and alcohol consumption among Hispanic couples in the United States. *Journal of Interpersonal Violence* 15: 30–45.

Cunradi, C. B., R. Caetano, C. L. Clark, and J. Schafer. 1999. Alcohol-related problems and intimate partner violence among White, Black, and Hispanic couples in the U.S. *Alcoholism: Clinical and Experimental Research* 23: 1492–1501.

Dasgupta, S. D., ed. 1999. Violence against South Asian women. [Special issue] *Violence Against Women* 5(6).

———. 2000. Charting the course: An overview of domestic violence in the South Asian community in the United States. *Journal of Social Distress and the Homeless* 9: 173–185.

de Anda, D., and R. M. Becerra. 2000. *Violence: Diverse Populations and Communities.* Binghamton, N.Y.: Haworth Press.

Fairchild, D. G., M. W. Fairchild, and S. Stoner. 1998. Prevalence of adult domestic violence among women seeking routine care in a Native American health care facility. *American Journal of Public Health* 88: 1515–1517.

Hamby, S. L. 2000. The importance of community in a feminist analysis of domestic violence among American Indians. *American Journal of Community Psychology* 28: 649–669.

Gabler, M., S. E. Stern, and M. Miserandino. 1998. Latin American, Asian, and American cultural differences in perceptions of spousal abuse. *Psychological Reports* 83: 587–592.

Hampton, R., R. Carrillo, and J. Kim. 1998. Violence in communities of color. In R. Carrillo and J. Tello, eds., *Family Violence and Men of Color: Healing the Wounded Male Spirit.* New York: Springer, 1–30.

Hassouneh-Phillips, Dena Sadat. 1998. Culture and systems of oppression in abused women's lives. *Journal of Obstetric, Gynecologic, and Neonatal Nursing* 27(6): 678–683.

Holtzman-Munroe, A., N. Smutzler, and L. Bates. 1997. A brief review of research on husband violence: Sociodemographic factors, relationships factors, and differing consequences of husband and wife violence. *Aggression and Violent Behavior* 2: 207–222.

Honeycutt, T. C., L. L. Marshall, and R. Weston. 2001. Toward ethnically specific models of employment, public assistance, and victimization. *Violence Against Women* 7: 126–140.

Jasinski, J. L. 1998. The role of acculturation in wife assault. *Hispanic Journal of Behavioral Sciences* 20: 175–191.

———. 2001. Physical violence among Anglo, African American, and Hispanic couples: Ethnic differences in persistence and cessation. *Violence and Victims* 16: 479–490.

Jasinski, J. L., N. L. Asdigian, and G. Kaufman Kantor. 1997. Ethnic adaptations to occupational strain: Work-related stress, drinking, and wife assault among Anglo and Hispanic husbands. *Journal of Interpersonal Violence* 12: 814–831.

Jasinski, J. L., and G. Kaufman Kantor. 2001. Pregnancy, stress, and wife assault: Ethnic differences in prevalence, severity, and onset in a national sample. *Violence and Victims* 16: 219–232.

Kessler, R. C., B. E. Molnar, I. D. Feurer, and M. Applebaum. 2001. Patterns and mental health predictors of domestic violence in the United States: Results from the National Comorbidity Survey. *International Journal of Law and Psychiatry* 24: 487–508.

Kim, J. Y., and K. Sung. 2000. Conjugal violence in Korean American families: A residue of the cultural tradition. *Journal of Family Violence* 15: 331–345.

Lee, M. 2000. Understanding Chinese battered women in North America: A review of the literature and practice implications. In Diane DeAndea and Rosina Becerra, eds. *Violence: Diverse Populations and Communities.* Binghamton, N.Y.: Haworth Press, 215–242.

Lum, J. L. 1998. Family violence. In L. C. Lee and N. W. Zane, eds., *Handbook of Asian American Psychology.* Thousand Oaks, Calif.: Sage, 505–525.

Marshall, L. L., R. Weston, and T. C. Honeycutt. 2000. Does men's positivity moderate or mediate the effects of their abuse on women's relationship quality? *Journal of Social and Personal Relationships* 17: 660–675.

Oates, G. C. 1998. Cultural perspectives on intimate violence. In N. A. Jackson and G. C. Oates, eds., *Violence in Intimate Relationships: Examining Sociological and Psychological Issues.* Woburn, Mass.: Butterworth-Heinemann, 225–243.

Raj, A., and J. Silverman. 2002. Violence against immigrant women: The roles of culture, context, and legal immigrant status on intimate partner violence. *Violence Against Women* 8: 367–398.

Rennison, C. M., and S. Welchans. 2000. *Criminal Victimization 1999: Changes 1998–1999 with Trends 1993–1999* (NCJ 178247). Washington, D.C.: U.S. Department of Justice, Bureau of Justice Statistics. August.

Sanchez-Hucles, J., and M. A. Dutton. 1999. The interaction between societal violence and domestic violence: Racial and cultural factors. In M. Harway and J. O'Neil, eds., *What Causes Men's Violence against Women?* Thousand Oaks, Calif.: Sage, 183–203.

Shepherd, J. 2001. Where do you go when it's 40 below? Domestic violence among rural Alaska Native women. *Affilia* 16: 488–510.

Tjaden, P., and N. Thoennes. 2000. *Extent, Nature, and Consequences of Intimate Partner Violence: Findings from the National Violence Against Women Survey* (NCJ 181867). Washington, D.C.: U.S. Government Printing Office.

Tolman, R. M., and J. Raphael. 2000. A review of research on welfare and domestic violence. *Journal of Social Issues* 56(4): 655–682.

Torres, S., J. Campbell, D. W. Campbell, J. Ryan, C. King, P. Price, R. Y. Stallings, S. C. Fuchs, and M. Laude. 2000. Abuse during and before pregnancy: Prevalence and cultural correlates. *Violence and Victims* 15: 303–321.

Turrell, S. C. 2000. A descriptive analysis of same-sex relationship violence for a diverse sample. *Journal of Family Violence* 15(3): 281–293.

U.S. Census Bureau. 2001. *Overview of race and Hispanic origin: Census 2000 brief.* Retrieved February 9, 2002, from http://www.census.gov/population/www/socdemo/race.html.

U.S. Department of Health and Human Services. 2001. *Mental Health: Culture, Race, and Ethnicity—A Supplement to Mental Health: A Report to the Surgeon General.* Rockville, Md.: U.S. Department of Health and Human Services, Substance Abuse and Mental Health Services Administration, Center for Mental Health Services.

West, C. M. 1998. Lifting the "political gag order": Breaking the silence around partner violence in ethnic minority families. In J. L. Jasinski and L. M. Williams, eds., *Partner Violence: A Comprehensive Review of 20 Years of Research.* Thousand Oaks, Calif.: Sage, 184–209.

———. 2002. Black battered women: New directions for research and Black feminist theory. In L. H. Collins, M. R. Dunlap, and J. C. Chrisler, eds., *Charting a New Course for Feminist Psychology.* Westport, Conn.: Praeger, 216–237.

———, ed. 2002. *Violence in the Lives of Black Women: Battered, Black, and Blue.* Binghamton, N.Y.: Haworth Press.

West, C. M., G. Kaufman Kantor, and J. L. Jasinski. 1998. Sociodemographic predictors and cultural barriers to help-seeking behavior by Latina and Anglo American battered women. *Violence and Victims* 13: 470–494.

Williams, O. J., and L. W. Griffin. 2000. Domestic violence in the African American community. [Special Edition] *Violence Against Women* 6(5).

Yick, A. G. 2000. Predictors of physical spousal/intimate violence in Chinese American families. *Journal of Family Violence* 15: 249–267.

Yoshihama, M. 1999. Domestic violence against women of Japanese descent in Los Angeles: Two methods of estimating prevalence. *Violence Against Women* 5: 869–897.

CHAPTER **12**

SHERRY L. HAMBY

The Importance of Community in a Feminist Analysis of Domestic Violence among Native Americans

 ABSTRACT

There has been a modicum of research on domestic violence among indigenous people in the United States, much of which includes claims of precolonial harmony and a matriarchal social structure that was said to be beneficial for all women. Sherry L. Hamby argues that the experiences of more than five hundred Native tribes in the United States defies any simplistic notion of Native American universality—either in terms of their social, political, economic, or gender structures or in terms of domestic violence.

Some Native American tribes are matriarchal (societies where the final decision-making power rests with the mother, other senior females in the tribe, or equally with men) while others are patriarchal (where males have final decision-making power). These different social organizations and the gender roles derived from them vary greatly from one tribe to the next. Not enough research has been done to determine the extent to which various social structures and forms of organization impact domestic violence rates in different Native American communities. In addition, whether a society is matrilocal or patrilocal (whether a couple live with the wife's or the husband's family, respectively) and matrilineal or patrilineal (whether inheritance is passed down through the mother's line or the father's, respectively) probably impacts greatly on how women are treated and the degree to which domestic violence is tolerated in a community (Murray, 1998). But we do know that gender relations *are* crucial to understanding domestic violence, but not in isolation.

Nevertheless, European colonization—which included decimation by disease, loss of ancestral lands and way of life, forced relocation to reservations, imposition of missionary practices and religion, and mandatory education of children in boarding schools—has still had a tremendous impact on domestic violence in Native communities as, indeed, has poverty, racism, unemployment, and the like.

Among Native communities today considerable differences still exist that relate to the experience of domestic violence. Hamby emphasizes the need to take into account differences related to how gender and authority interact in Native communities and to consider the great variations in geography, land base, wealth and poverty, and resulting marginalization in any analysis of domestic violence. She calls for a framework that roots a feminist analysis in the specific circumstances and social conditions of each Native American community. Only in this way, she argues, can one understand the colonial and racist legacies in some Native American communities of cycles of extreme poverty and unemployment, which are, in turn, related to the experience of domestic violence and many restrictions to much-needed services.

Here, as in the poor African American communities in Nashville discussed by Websdale (chapter 10), the need to empower Native American communities themselves and their families, with particular emphasis on the unique concerns of individual tribes, becomes paramount if we hope to end domestic violence in their communities. Given the similarities and differences between the Native American, African American, and other marginalized communities of color discussed so far, what key similarities and differences do you find in their experiences of domestic violence, how it is handled, and what is needed to end such violence in these different communities?

There are 512 recognized native groups and 365 state-recognized Indian tribes who speak 200 different languages in the United States alone (Chester et al., 1994). The peoples [who] are defined as a single "American Indian" or "Native American" entity by the majority culture are in fact composed of an extremely diverse and heterogeneous set of communities, many of whom had little or no contact with one another prior to the modern era (Groginsky and Freeman, 1994). American Indians are faced with the same oversimplifications that lump Laotians, Japanese, and others into a single "Asian" category and Puerto Ricans, Brazilians, and many others under a single "Latino" rubric (West, 1998). As with all ethnic and cultural groups, far greater attention needs to be paid to the form and context of individual native communities to advance our understanding of how community structure and identity affect community problems, particularly for American Indians who reside on reservations. This appreciation is especially needed among non-Indian outsiders, who are most likely to see native peoples as a single homogeneous group. While a more community-oriented analysis is needed in a wide range of areas, this chapter focuses on how an appreciation of intertribal differences enhances a feminist analysis of domestic violence in native North America.

Originally published as "The Importance of Community in a Feminist Analysis of Domestic Violence among American Indians" in the *American Journal of Community Psychology* 28, no. 5 (2000): 649–669. Reprinted by permission of the author and Kluwer Academic/Plenum Publishers.

FEMINIST ANALYSIS OF DOMESTIC VIOLENCE

Feminism has contributed much to the understanding of the causes and per-petuation of domestic violence in American, Canadian, and European cul-tures (for example, Dobash and Dobash, 1979; Pence and Paymar, 1993). The most important contribution has been to emphasize that the primary cause of domestic violence is the gendered nature of power and control in in-timate relationships. In Western culture, violence against wives historically occurred in a rigid patriarchal structure that offered almost no legal or social redress to battered wives. According to a feminist analysis, violence against wives is not a problem with anger, but a behavior that has a goal of main-taining male dominance of the social climate. In recent times, Western soci-etal changes have reduced but not eliminated the patriarchal structure (Dobash and Dobash, 1979; Pence and Paymar, 1993). Socialization into gender roles that produce male domination, male violence, and female sub-ordination remains a powerful force. It is still acceptable for men to behave possessively toward their partners and to demand domestic labor. The belief in the sanctity of the family is still valued and produces an unwillingness to intervene in family affairs that helps create a context in which domestic vio-lence can still occur without punishment. This theoretical analysis acknowl-edges that not all men batter women and that not all batterers are the same, but the root cause of violence is seen as gendered definitions of privilege (Pence and Paymar, 1993). Nonetheless, significant gains have been made and evidence suggests that rates of domestic violence may be falling over time, at least in the United States (Straus and Kaufman Kantor, 1994).

More recent feminist analysis has included class along with gender and dominance as crucial to the understanding of domestic violence. Early femi-nist accounts paid little attention to socioeconomic issues and tended to fo-cus on upper middle-class European American females (Ptacek, 1997; Richie, 1996). Domestic violence advocates frequently went even one step further and insisted that there was no association between class and violence in an ef-fort to make clear that domestic violence crosses all class boundaries (for ex-ample, Davidson, 1978). Although it has been repeatedly demonstrated that domestic violence occurs in all socioeconomic groups, it is increasingly ac-knowledged that economic stresses both increase the likelihood of violence occurring and severely curtail victims' abilities to effectively respond to vio-lence once it has occurred (Cazenave and Straus, 1990; Ptacek, 1997).

THE IMPORTANCE OF COMMUNITY CONTEXT

The success of the social movement against domestic violence in American and European countries rests largely on the success of the critique of the status quo that emerged at the beginning of the movement (for example, Davidson, 1978; Dobash and Dobash, 1979). That critique was successful because feminists accurately identified the common threads of experience in the lives of White, middle class, European American women. Some of those common threads included the isolation produced by the suburban nuclear family, an increasingly secular culture that was heavily influenced by Protestant roots, and traditional patriarchal gender roles. Current efforts to extend this movement to other cultural groups face considerable obstacles due to significant religious, social, economic, and cultural differences between those groups and the generally liberal, secular, and middle-class values of most American anti-violence advocates (Richie, 1996; Timmins, 1995).

Many authors with crosscultural experience have noted that the ability to extend domestic violence awareness into new communities is dependent on the ability to appreciate, understand, and respect the cultural values of those communities (compare Timmins, 1995). There are many factors, some centuries old, that are specific to particular tribal groups and that affect the context and definition of domestic violence in native communities (Chester et al., 1994). Additionally, contemporary disparities in land bases, varying geographic locations of reservations, and differences between tribes with reservations and tribes without them, have created new sources of diversity. For example, some reservations, such as Gila River near Phoenix, Arizona, are located near modern urban centers. As a result, the economic marginalization of its members, who have improved access to jobs and casino profits, is not as extreme as found on more geographically isolated reservations. Contrary to popular conceptions among non-Indians, tribal membership is a key defining aspect of most native communities and an important feature of personal identity.

It should also be noted that American Indians have multilayered identities, just as others do. This often does include an identity of "American Indian," and many organizations such as Inter Tribal Councils, the UNITY youth organization, and the Gathering of Native Americans (GONA) promote common political interests and fellowship. The need for respecting tribal differences is emphasized in this chapter both because that is the identity most commonly lost to outsiders and because of the need to find local solutions to the domestic violence problem. Just as the original analysis of domestic violence in the majority U.S. culture focused on commonalties among the community of middle-class White females, so a comprehensive analysis of domestic violence in native North America must start with an appreciation of community identity. Further, although it might be useful to apply the main tenet of a feminist analysis of domestic violence, that of the role of male power and control, to native groups, such application must be sensitive to ethnic differences in the meaning and expression of the concept.

DOMESTIC VIOLENCE IN NATIVE NORTH AMERICA

Existing survey data indicate that rates of domestic violence are currently quite high in most native communities. Within a generally elevated range, there is also evidence for significant variability, although unfortunately most data are not tribal specific. A study of women who had sought various programs for American Indians in the Rocky Mountain region showed 46 percent had a history of domestic violence (Norton and Manson, 1995). A survey of pregnant native women in Minnesota indicated that 60 percent were currently with an abusive partner (Bohn, 1993). Both of these studies took place in centralized health care centers that provide services to many tribes in those regions. A qualitative study of three Alaska communities found that informants believed domestic violence to be occurring in 15 to 36 percent of the homes in their community (Shinkwin and Pete, 1983). Unfortunately, though, this studied relied on publicly known incidents. The only community-based study of domestic violence victimization found a yearly incidence rate of 48 percent and a relationship prevalence rate of 75 percent for female residents of an Apache reservation (Hamby and Skupien, 1998). Other lifetime estimates range from 50 to 80 percent (West, 1998).

Medical and shelter data also suggest that rates of domestic violence are high. A study on the Hualapai Indian Reservation in Arizona showed that domestic violence accounted for 56 percent of all female assault victims who received medical attention (Kuklinski and Buchanan, 1997). In Minnesota, American Indians comprise less than one percent of the population but 11 to 14 percent of women in shelters (Bohn, 1989; Wolk, 1982). There are some data suggesting that domestic violence rates are higher for American Indians than for other U.S. ethnic groups. One national study found that rates of severe domestic violence were higher for American Indians than for European Americans (Bachman, 1992), while another found that lifetime rates of all physical assault and rape were higher for American Indians than any other U.S. ethnic group (Tjaden and Thoennes, 1998). In New Mexico, statewide data showed that domestic violence-related homicide rates were higher for American Indians than for others (Arbuckle et al., 1996).

Although these data suggest that rates of domestic violence are generally higher in most native communities compared to other U.S. communities, the quality of information is sometimes poor. Much of this limitation is due to the use of telephone or mail surveys that are appropriate for middle-class suburban homes but do not include homes that are too poor or isolated to have telephones or communities whose members have relatively low levels of English fluency. Other methodological drawbacks include a tendency to focus on clinic samples, use of measures with unknown properties in native populations, and use of interviewers who are unfamiliar with the community (Chester et al., 1994). Data based on nationally representative surveys often include very few American Indians with which to make group comparisons. Much of the literature is still impressionistic and anecdotal (West, 1998). Further, even studies of groups who are primarily American Indian (for example, Maguire, 1987) may attend little to issues of race or culture. There is a great need for more investigations of domestic violence among American Indians that takes into account the culture and context of Indian life (LaFramboise et al., 1995b).

It is debated whether domestic violence is a new problem in American Indian communities. Some authors believe that domestic violence has been present for a long time, while others assert it dates after the introduction of Western European influences. Many [authors] state that while domestic violence did occur prior to Western contact, it was rare and severely sanctioned. Documented cases do date from the mid-1860s but these also postdate missionary contact (Chester et al., 1994), although it seems possible that European influence on communities at the time of first contact was modest. Assessments of native cultures before Western contact are difficult because of the lack of written or visual records (DeBruyn et al., 1990), and oral histories have received insufficient attention. It is likely that, as in other areas, there was considerable variability among tribes and that unrecognized cultural differences account for some of the disagreement. The one area of agreement is that rates of domestic violence appear to have risen dramatically in the last 150 years (Chester et al., 1994; DeBruyn et al., 1990; Gunn Allen, 1990; LaFramboise et al., 1995b). Contact with Westerners has had many negative consequences, including increased domestic violence rates, probably due in part to profound losses in the traditional statuses and roles of both men and women (Wolk, 1982). Participants in one study reported an increase in domestic violence during a ten-year period of oil business development (Durst, 1991). There are anecdotal accounts of U.S. agents forcing violent couples to remain married (Levinson, 1989). While there has been little formal examination of the influence of Western contact and oppression, few question that the poverty and social and economic marginalization of many American Indian communities has contributed to the severity of the current domestic violence problem.

THE ROLE OF DOMINANCE IN DOMESTIC VIOLENCE AMONG AMERICAN INDIANS

There is some research evidence, unfortunately rather limited, that the feminist analysis of domestic violence has relevance for American Indian communities. One recent quantitative study found that ratings of partner's control over finances was associated with increased physical assault and injury victimization for Apache females (Hamby and Skupien, 1998). There have been several feminist efforts to intervene against domestic violence in native communities (for example, DeBruyn et al., 1990; Maguire, 1987; National Training Project, 1997). Although some advocates believe that power and control models have an even deeper meaning for native communities that are also faced with external domination by U.S. society (DeBruyn et al., 1990), in general, data on the relevance of a feminist analysis have not been offered. The historical record is composed primarily of qualitative ethnographic accounts, which unfortunately often contain only sparse descriptions of marital relationships (Bohn, 1989). Observers in some native communities have reported that punishment for infidelity was a major control technique and closely tied to domestic violence. Apache tradition, at least in the nineteenth century, permitted men to cut off the noses of unfaithful wives (Cochise, 1971; Stockel, 1991). Disfigurement was also sometimes the punishment for female infidelity among the Dakota and Ojibway (Bohn, 1989). Many tribes encouraged women to stay in violent marriages if they had children by their husbands (LaFramboise et al., 1995a). However, abuse that was perceived as unjustified was not tolerated by Ojibway extended family (Bohn, 1989).

Levinson's (1989) ground-breaking crosscultural work is still the main source of quantified information in this area. His results indicate that patterns of dominance between husbands and wives can help explain both high and low levels of domestic violence. He reviewed the ethnographic records of ninety societies worldwide. Of these, seventeen were native communities in North America. Of those seventeen, three were found to have no or minimal levels of family violence: Iroquois, Fox, and Papago (also known as Tohono O'Odham). The others, such as the Arapaho, showed evidence of domestic violence at least back to the nineteenthth century. Societies that lacked family violence were generally characterized by shared decision making, wives' control of some family resources, equally easy divorce access for husbands and wives, no premarital sex double standard, monogamous marriage, marital cohabitation, peaceful conflict resolution within and outside the home, and immediate social responses to domestic violence. Some of these, such as shared decision making, clearly represent authority aspects of dominance, whereas others, such as divorce access and lack of sexual double standards, indicate that societies that do not restrict or disparage women tend to be less violent. In general, his findings support the feminist conclusion that higher levels of male dominance are associated with high rates of domestic violence. Levinson's work is also consistent with the proposition that variation among native communities exists and can be partly attributed to differences in dominance dynamics.

Although the literature that focuses on domestic violence among American Indians is quite small, there is considerable literature on gender roles and gender dynamics. This body of knowledge can help to illustrate the importance of tribal context in an analysis of domestic violence. While much of this literature has focused on the period before Western domination, the dramatic effects of Western contact indicate that both the traditional and modern eras need to be examined to fully understand today's domestic violence problems. The following discussion first takes up the issue of gender and power using feminist and community psychology principles. Although class issues have received less attention, they are also critical to an analysis of the contemporary situation. A section is devoted to the issues of class and domestic violence. This is followed by conclusions and recommendations for addressing domestic violence in Indian country.

GENDER AND DOMINANCE

Gender and dominance have been topics of increasing visibility in literature about native peoples. Unfortunately, much of the literature is heavily politicized. Early literature on native communities has been criticized for overly negative and skimpy portrayals of native women that were often excessively colored by colonial and missionary attitudes (compare Klein and Ackerman, 1995). In recent years, however, the political pendulum has swung in the other direction and American Indians are often idealistically held up as examples of egalitarian or matriarchal societies (for example, Guemple, 1995; Gunn Allen, 1990). The implication of these portrayals is that violence was not part of male-female relations in matriarchal societies.

Neither portrayal is accurate, and both extreme views tend to paint in broad strokes the gender roles in individual tribes and often for all of Indian country. Current slogans about domestic violence like "It's Not Cultural" (DeBruyn et al., 1990) or "It's Not Traditional" are meant to apply equally well to the Apache as to the Lakota when there are large and important differences in gender roles in these and other native communities. Even more problematically, analyses of single communities are often colored by predetermined conclusions. For example, Guemple (1995) details how Inuit men "exercise ultimate control over decision making in domestic matters" (p. 22), how wives are reprimanded if their housework is not acceptable to their husbands, and how husbands can even arrange sexual exchanges with other men without their wives' consent. She further reports that Inuit women do not have similar reciprocal powers, yet nonetheless concludes that "men and women in Inuit society enjoy relatively equal status, power, and prestige" (p. 27), primarily because the division of labor is so gender specific that they have relatively independent social roles. Although it is important to acknowledge variations in power dynamics among Inuit tribes, as with any other community, such a biased analysis of social relations is doomed to failure despite the authors' apparent good intentions. A more complete analysis would incorporate nonegalitarian features of power dynamics into the authors' final assessment of women's status. Some authors at least acknowledge that their redefinition of reality does not correspond to current attitudes in many tribes. For example, DeBruyn and colleagues (1990) discuss the current problem, common in some tribes, of using the term "Indian love" as a slang term for domestic violence.

In fact, the analysis of gender relations in native communities is a complex and challenging task. There are many frameworks that might be applied, but a feminist analysis of the gendered nature of power relations is key to understanding how gender relations can promote or at least permit domestic violence. The association of gender and dominance will be explored using a tripartite typological model of dominance (Hamby, 1996) to elucidate some of the variations in dominance within and across native groups. The types of dominance that are most closely associated with domestic violence in existing literature can be grouped into three main categories: authority, restrictiveness, and disparagement (Hamby, 1996). An appreciation of the distinctions among forms of dominance has been noted in previous literature (for example, Pence and Paymar, 1993), but this framework is the first formal organization of dominance types. While the existing empirical literature on the dominance-violence link consists primarily of studies with European Americans, the framework provides a beginning place to explore these issues in native communities and highlight areas that need to be changed or adapted in different communities.

Many writers emphasize the complementarity of gender roles in many native communities (compare Klein and Ackerman, 1995). In native societies with highly specialized gender roles, there was often little overlap in work and sometimes even little contact between men and women. Unfortunately, past scholarship has seldom concentrated on areas of overlap and, in particular, on areas of conflict and how conflict was handled. Thus, it is possible to emphasize matrilineal descent or some other feature of women's lives without focusing on their risk for being abused or mistreated, which likely involves their interactions with their husbands and their community at least as much as it involves segregated aspects of their lives.

Gender and Authority

The notion of authority is closely related to decision-making power. In this form of dominance, instead of both partners in a relationship having equal input on decisions about the relationship, one partner holds a majority of decision-making power. He or she is "in charge" of the relationship. Authority is also related to social roles and social status, and is often obtained through wealth, occupational status, or other forms of prestige. The association between authority and domestic violence has been studied extensively, although much Western research has relied on a rather poor measure of decision making. Thus, the size of the association between authority and domestic violence has been found to be only moderate (although positive) in most U.S. and European studies (Hamby and Sugarman, 1996). In his comprehensive crosscultural study, however, Levinson (1989) found that male household decision-making power was one of the most important predictors of rates of violence.

Male and female authority is also the form of dominance that has been most extensively studied in native communities. In scholarship about native communities, it is most often discussed using the anthropological terms for social organization: matriarchy/patriarchy, matrilineal/patrilineal, and matrilocal/patrilocal. Matriarchal societies, in contrast to patriarchal ones, are ones in which the mother is the head of the family, clan, or tribe. Final decision-making power rests with the mother or possibly other senior females in this kind of organization. Most matriarchal societies are also matrilineal; that is, the line of descent or clan membership is passed through the mother. There are, however, far more matrilineal societies than matriarchal ones, both in and out of Indian country. Matrilocal societies are those in which living and social arrangements focus on the woman's family of origin, as when newlyweds reside near the bride's parents. Female authority associated with matrilineal and matrilocal societies is often indirect.

Many outsiders believe that all traditional native cultures are matriarchal and often refer to native women as particularly empowered, but this is an overgeneralization that does not reflect variations from one tribal culture to another and even within single tribes (Klein and Ackerman, 1995). Many observers do not distinguish between matriarchal and matrilineal organization, as well. In fact, gender roles and social organization differ greatly from one tribe to the next (LaFramboise et al., 1995a). The status of women probably varies from one context to another in many tribes more than in most Western cultures. For example, a tribe may be matrilineal while at the same time limiting women's access to political positions and religious ceremonies. Most studies focus on the precolonial period, but contact with European Americans has eroded female-centered social organization in many parts of Indian country. Christian marriage conventions influence many American Indian tribes today, and patriarchal, patrilineal patterns are far more prevalent today than in the past. Boarding schools often participated in the indoctrination of Western values by offering less education to girls than boys and making girls clean the schools (LaFramboise et al., 1995b). Most observers (for example, Gunn Allen, 1990; Wolk, 1982) believe native women have lost status due to Western patriarchal influences, but at least one study attributed a very recent rise in domestic violence to the increasing status of females (Durst, 1991). Informants in those Canadian native communities cited increased tendencies for women to work outside the home and become the primary wage earners as causes of domestic violence.

Although it is not possible to describe all 512 groups in this paper, some flavor of the differences and similarities across tribes can be suggested with a few examples. The San Carlos Apache are traditionally matrilineal and matrilocal. In their case, matrilocal social organization is better preserved than matrilineal clan identity. The Iroquois, Hopi, and Zuni tribes are also matrilineal (Chester et al., 1994). In contrast, the Omaha (V. Phillips, Omaha tribal member, personal communication, 1997), Ojibway (Bohn, 1989), Pima, and Cheyenne (Chester et al., 1994) are all patrilineal. Whereas many matrilineal societies are not matriarchal, most patrilineal societies are patriarchal. Some native societies practiced pure forms of neither, and the common categorizations do not easily fit all native cultures. For example, the Pomos of the west coast traditionally practiced both matrilocal and patrilocal residence, with the same couple often alternating between families, at least for a time (Patterson, 1995). Klein (1995) has described how the Tlingit have both a matrilineal and avunculocal (residing near one's uncle) system that is further complicated by a common crosscousin marriage pattern.

The Iroquois, a confederacy of tribal nations, are a good example of the complexity and variability of social organization. Traditional Iroquois societies are often described as matriarchal (for example, Chester et al., 1994; Gunn Allen, 1986) and approach matriarchy more closely than most societies. Historically, Iroquois women had significant arenas of power, including land ownership, control over horticultural production, and the ability to nominate chiefs. Important powers were reserved for men, however. Women could not be chiefs, although the line of descent passed through women. Women influenced who became leaders but were not in direct leadership roles. They influenced but did not control war making. Thus, they do not represent a full matriarchy (Bilharz, 1995). Rather, traditional Iroquois society may best be described as one with complementary gender roles, matrilineal descent, and matrilocal residence (Bilharz, 1995). The Seneca, one nation of the Iroquois, illustrate some of the changes that modified traditional society during the colonial period. By the late 1800s, Quakers and Federal officials had transformed their matrilineal society into a patrilineal one that emphasized the nuclear family (Bilharz, 1995; Gunn Allen, 1986). The reservation system and disagreements with the United States led to political changes that disenfranchised women. Only men could hold tribal offices and vote. Women did not gain the vote until 1964. At that time, the aftereffects of a flood provided Seneca women opportunities to influence relief programs and obtain more paid employment. More recently, women have held elective offices, but not president (Bilharz, 1995). Thus, some of the status lost in the last 150 years has been regained, although outside patriarchal influences continue.

The complexity of gender status among the Seneca and other tribes needs greater recognition. As best as can be determined, few tribes were absolute matriarchies, and an overly simplistic portrayal of them as such can mask important gender issues. Even further caution should be exercised in concluding that domestic violence is absent from societies with matriarchal, matrilineal, or complementary social organization. Male and female authority is only one aspect of gender roles. Authority probably best represents what resources women can access to help stop domestic violence. Matrilineal descent or matrilocal residence may speak little to the question of how much freedom women have to choose their friends, take on the roles they want, or divorce as they wish. A broader analysis of dominance can shed more light on the role of gender in domestic violence. Other forms of dominance are more centrally tied to the dynamics of domestic violence in European American countries (Hamby and Sugarman, 1996), and deserve some exploration in native contexts as well.

Gender and Disparagement

Disparagement occurs when one partner fails to equally value the other partner and has an overall negative appraisal of his or her partner's worth. For example, one partner may feel that he or she is more deserving, skilled, and attractive than the other is. Typical beliefs include "My partner is not a very good person." The egalitarian opposite occurs when both partners in a relationship equally value each other's worth and personal attributes (Hamby, 1996). Spousal disparagement is correlated with frequency of conflict and divorce (Shackelford and Buss, 1997) as well as with abusive behavior (Hamby, 1996; Shackelford and Buss, 1997). Although this aspect of dominance has been less studied than authority and restrictiveness, it appears to be linked to authority and at least moderately related to violence (Hamby and Sugarman, 1996).

Many accounts of native communities suggest that disparagement was not historically common. Observers often note the valuation of both male and female contributions to the maintenance of the social fabric of tribal communities. The complementarity of gender roles and the necessity of many forms of labor to the success of a community tend to promote an appreciation for each person's contribution. Descriptions of the Tlingit (Klein, 1995), Inuit (Guemple, 1995), Blackfoot (Kehoe, 1995), Lakota (Wolk, 1982), and many other groups emphasize the value of both men's and women's contributions to family and society. Women's role as bearers of children is also typically honored. Spirituality is an extremely important aspect of most American Indian cultures and typically also emphasizes respect and honor. This aspect of egalitarian social relations appears to be a strength of many native cultures.

There is very little written on contemporary patterns of disparagement, but it is likely that the loss of traditional roles has led to less mutual valuation of the roles of men and women. Anecdotally, the devaluation of both male and female status has been much commented upon (for example, Gunn Allen, 1990). Men's traditional roles have eroded more than women's traditional roles in many communities, as jobs outside the home have become scarce and hunting and fishing activities are sometimes restricted (Wolk, 1982). It has been noted that role loss and internalized oppression have had a profound negative impact on men's self-esteem and contribute to the level of violence in native communities (Duran et al., 1998). Meanwhile, women's roles as caregiver and food preparer may be better preserved. It is possible that the relatively greater devaluation of men's roles has led to frustration and jealousy of women, perhaps especially of those who have paying jobs. This could be one mechanism for the increase in domestic violence found by Durst (1991) during a period when women increased outside employment. One qualitative study found that some battered Navajo women felt men could not handle their wives' success when faced with unemployment or similar stresses (Maguire, 1987). These outside pressures may contribute to a sharpening of gender-based distinctions and contribute to the increases in disparagement and domestic violence of the last 150 years.

Gender and Restrictiveness

Restrictiveness refers to the extent to which one partner feels the right to control and limit the other's behavior. For example, the restrictive partner may prohibit a partner from spending time with certain individuals or going certain places. The restrictive partner usually feels that he or she has a right to know and be involved with everything his or her partner does. The egalitarian opposite of restrictiveness occurs when both partners in a relationship respect the other's right to some individual autonomy concurrent with their mutual commitment (Hamby, 1996). Jealousy is often a main cause of restrictiveness. Restrictiveness is a prominent feature of many clinical descriptions of battering (for example, Pence and Paymar, 1993). A meta-analysis showed that restrictiveness had the strongest association with domestic violence of the three dominance types (Hamby and Sugarman, 1996). These studies consisted of primarily European American participants. Restrictiveness has received less attention in the literature on gender and native communities, yet the importance of the construct in Western samples suggest it may have potential to contribute to an understanding of domestic violence in native communities.

As with other aspects of native communities, an appreciation of marked variation across groups is the key to understanding restrictiveness. Individual autonomy, which is the opposite of restrictiveness, is highly valued among the Blackfoot (Kehoe, 1995). As a result, Blackfoot women could potentially depart from traditional gender roles of submissiveness and docility and seek other lifestyles. There is a concept called *ninauposkitzipxpe,* or "manly hearted woman" in traditional Blackfoot society. Such women owned property, tended to be active in religious ceremonies, and were assertive in public, in their homes, and as sexual partners. The term "manly hearted" derived from gender stereotypes that considered boldness and ambition to be ideal male attributes, but the designation was available to many, especially older, women (Kehoe, 1995). Among the Ojibway (Wolk, 1982) and Apache (Stockel, 1991), some women became healers and warriors, but it was not generally accepted for men to take on women's roles.

Modern attitudes toward restrictiveness in intimate relationships are affected by a complicated interplay of many issues. Many tribes currently show the influence of Christianity with resultant restrictions on women's behavior, particularly access to divorce. For example, members of Pueblo tribes, which are heavily Catholic, are often very resistant to women's efforts to leave abusive relationships and may be told that they should tolerate such abuse (DeBruyn et al., 1990; LaFramboise et al., 1995a). In one study, Navajo women reported that their own parents and their in-laws frequently encouraged reconciliation after violence (Maguire, 1987). Women who work to help domestic violence victims on some reservations have received death threats in efforts to intimidate them (DeBruyn et al., 1990).

Rigidity in gender roles is one aspect of restrictiveness and is the only aspect that has been extensively described in the literature. There are many other important aspects of restrictiveness, however. Control over social contacts and movements outside the home are two primary characteristics in many cultures, including those influenced by Christian and Muslim religions. It seems possible that they are important to native communities as well. Some Inuit women had no control over their own bodies (Guemple, 1995). Jealousy was apparently common among the Apache around the time of early Western contact, supported by social prohibitions restricting access between married men and women. A man whose wife was unfaithful was considered unmanly if he did not take strong action, which usually meant beating and often disfiguring his wife (Opler, 1941/1996). A more recent study of battered Navajo women found that they often thought jealousy or the desire for control was the motive for violence (Maguire, 1987). Anecdotally, today many native battered women report such control tactics as being locked in their homes, forbidden to speak with their friends or even family of origin, and not being allowed to have money. Whether these are general patterns in some tribes needs further study.

SOCIOECONOMIC ORGANIZATION
AND DOMESTIC VIOLENCE

Violence in male-female relationships comes not just from gender roles but also from the stresses placed on both genders. American Indian and other ethnic minorities continue to be disadvantaged in a society in which race determines access to economic resources. Current poverty rates of American Indian communities range from 20 to 47 percent, compared with 12 percent of the total U.S. population (LaFramboise et al., 1995b). Numerous sources document the lower income, education, and employment of American Indians in contrast to European Americans and even compared to some other minority groups (West, 1998). There is consistent evidence that lower socioeconomic status places one at greater risk for domestic violence (Ptacek, 1997). Racism also makes it more difficult for American Indian victims to access the resources they need to escape domestic violence, such as assistance from legal and social services agencies (Maguire, 1987). Other communities beset by extreme poverty and racial discrimination, such as Black women in ghetto communities, also have high rates of battering (for example, Richie, 1996). No study of American Indians can be complete without an acknowledgment of their socioeconomic situation.

Socioeconomic change has been dramatic in the last 150 years. Many native tribes were hunting and gathering societies prior to Western contact, but others, such as the Pueblo tribes, were primarily agricultural-based farming communities (Wolk, 1982). In some societies, such as the Apache, raiding held significant economic importance (Opler, 1941/1996). Most communities did not adhere to a concept of individual land ownership. Some tribes moved seasonally to maintain the best access to food and water, but others lived in single locations with year-round access to food. Lack of food and other necessities was not unknown, but differential lack of resources was fairly uncommon. There were not marked disparities between the wealth of different tribes that approach the differences between Anglo and Indian communities today. Nonetheless, the individual accumulation of wealth and the consequent ability to be generous were important in some tribes, such as the Tlingit, and women with greater socioeconomic status enjoyed greater freedoms in some groups (Klein, 1995).

In the last century, increases in poverty rates and changes in socioeconomic organization are thought to have contributed to the current high rates of domestic violence. The forced transition from hunting, gathering, and farming to a cash-based economy threw most native groups into a cycle of poverty and indebtedness from which most have not emerged (Bohn, 1989; Chester et al., 1994; DeBruyn et al., 1990). The ability to develop economically strong communities has been severely damaged by other forms of economic and social marginalization. These include the removal of Indian peoples from their ancestral lands, prohibitions against traditional religious practices, frequent removal of Indian children into foster homes and boarding schools, and a drastic reduction in the native population from the time of Western contact until the creation of the reservations. Some authors also believe that stereotypical images of Indians, which emphasized the physical threat that Indians posed to U.S. residents, have become a self-fulfilling prophecy over time and have affected native peoples despite their struggles to oppose them (Gunn Allen, 1990). In fact, the persistence of these images contributes to some reluctance to provide more data on domestic violence that potentially could be misused to reinforce negative stereotypes (Wolk, 1982). This is another reason why it is extremely important to provide textured, contextualized accounts of domestic violence that avoid racist stereotypes.

Socioeconomic problems, including the loss of social roles due to unemployment and lifestyle restrictions, have also promoted alcoholism in native communities (Duran et al., 1998). Although most participants in one study saw alcohol as a major cause of domestic violence (Hamby and Skupien, 1998), it also seems likely that both problems stem from the social conditions created by Western oppression. It should also be noted that the use of alcohol and other drugs varies considerably from one native community to another (Koss and Chester, 1997; Pego et al., 1996), and, as with other areas, blanket generalizations should be avoided.

Despite the importance of socioeconomic issues and the effects they have on many aspects of native life, the association between socioeconomic status and domestic violence has been even less studied in native communities than the link between male dominance and violence. In a rare study of socioeconomic factors, Durst (1991) found mixed effects in a study of two native Arctic communities. He reported that domestic violence rates appeared to increase with industrial development but also that the communities' willingness to discuss and respond to the problem increased. Norton and Manson (1995) did not find socioeconomic differences within their native sample, but differences between violence levels in native and non-native communities are often attributed to socioeconomic differences (Chester et al., 1994). In other minority communities, poverty often helps create violent situations and keeps women in them (Richie, 1996). Thus, it likely that American Indians are not inherently more violent than other groups, but are more likely to be overrepresented in demographic categories that are at greater risk for violence.

SUMMARY AND IMPLICATIONS

Many factors contribute to the current domestic violence situation in Indian country. Although there is evidence that current rates of domestic violence are very high in Indian country, insufficient attention has been paid to tribal differences in rates, causes, and contexts of violence. The several hundred communities that are identified as American Indian by the majority United States and Western culture encompass the gamut from matriarchal, matrilineal societies to patriarchal, patrilineal societies and many forms in between. Possible responses to domestic violence will also depend on specific tribal cultures and the varying degrees of Western influence. Contextualized, community-oriented feminist analyses need to take these differences into account. In addition, class, another important element of an ecological, feminist analysis, is a hugely important factor in tribal communities that have often lost their traditional sources of sustenance and wealth. The stress of poverty contributes to the high rates of domestic violence and should be part of any contextualized or ecological analysis.

The implications of such an analysis are numerous.

1) Although it may seem frustrating to outsiders to have to individually approach each community, many of which are fractions of their precolonial size, this is nonetheless needed. The feminist analysis of gender, class, and power will vary tremendously from cultures such as the Iroquois, who traditionally gave women considerable power, to the Pueblos, who have been influenced by Catholicism and its patriarchal ideology for more than four hundred years. The frequency of domestic violence and the ability to respond to it will vary from the Fox, who have historically experienced low levels of domestic violence, to the Apache, for whom domestic violence was sometimes an acceptable punishment. Analyses of these communities need to be as accurate and culturally congruent as the critiques that initiated the domestic violence movement in European American cultures, or they will have little impact. For example, in one Apache community, presentations on the historic lack of domestic violence in Indian country are often greeted by questions about the Apache practice of cutting off a nose for infidelity. These questions may not be offered to the speaker but discussed only among community members. Overgeneralizations, no matter how positive, diminish the credibility of both speaker and intervention.

2) As with most nonmajority communities, we need more information on prevalence rates, antecedents, and outcomes of domestic violence (West, 1998). Research should assess tribal identification, and residence (on and off reservation) and should not aggregate data across diverse groups.

3) The small postcolonial size of most American Indian communities affects what interventions will be seen as congruent with preserving community identity. According to the 1990 census, only nine tribes have more than fifty thousand members. While the 1990 census is generally considered an undercount of tribal populations, this still illustrates how tribal survival is a real issue for many American Indians. The choice of marriage partners from one's own tribe may be quite limited. Although many interracial marriages occur, some women may be reluctant to marry outside their tribe and especially to marry a non-Indian. The dilution of bloodlines is a sensitive issue in some communities (Sprott, 1994). A contextualized analysis suggests that divorce—a recommendation of many domestic violence advocates—may be viewed quite differently by American Indians who will not have the same options for intraracial remarriage that most other women have. Advocates from other ethnic groups may see such attitudes simply as prejudice against interracial marriages rather than as cultural survival issues.

4) Local cultures should be viewed as resources and potential sources of strength (Trickett, 1996). For example, autonomy, highly valued among

Blackfoot (Kehoe, 1995), could play a central role in formulating community-based domestic violence interventions. Other values are more central to other native groups. Among the Apache, strength, especially in the sense of endurance, and respect are primary values, and any community intervention would do well to emphasize those attributes. The importance of making specific tribal adaptations is increasingly recognized by groups such as National Training Project (1997), which addresses this issue when they share a batterers program developed among the Lakota with other native groups. The lack of disparagement that characterizes many American Indian cultures is also a resource.

5) Interventions in American Indian communities need to be sensitive to the history of oppression and domination by outsiders. Using materials or resources developed for the majority culture can raise issues of domination. At the same time, tribal communities should not be forced to reinvent the wheel in some outsider's interest of developing an emic approach. Starting from scratch may seem like a luxury of academic privilege, and many American Indian communities are interested in more immediate solutions. They may be happy to borrow from existing work if they feel that will be effective and efficient. There can also be advantages to outsider participation; for example, some tribal members perceive greater confidentiality with outsiders. Such factors should be considered and be openly acknowledged.

How can these goals be accomplished? It is mostly among outsiders that more attention needs to be paid to these recommendations. Feminist standpoint theory (for example, Hartsock, 1998) points out that subordinate groups have information about social relations that are not available to members of the dominant group, as subordinate members must learn the social mores of both groups. One Blackfoot woman expresses this idea by calling American Indians "bicultural warriors" (Newbreast, 1998). Oppression should not be romanticized, but members of subordinate groups may be less likely to see themselves as "universal man." Standpoint theorists also discuss how achievement of a standpoint is not an automatic by-product of group membership, but often intentionally sought (Hartsock, 1998). Although no European American can entirely escape his or her dominant ethnic position, it is perhaps possible to at least increase one's awareness of what that means. Most American Indian reservation communities have distinct cultures. They offer unique opportunities to get away from the White experience of being perceived as the universal norm—to get away from the overwhelming experience of being treated as lacking race or culture that is so pervasive in American society.

Unfortunately, most non-native researchers and providers interact with American Indian cultures from a position of power and privilege. They spend only brief periods, sometimes hours, on reservations, interact only as professionals, and leave. It is possible to do otherwise. In the spirit of community psychology, one can become involved in anti-domestic violence movements, or one can attend community social activities. Unlike other U.S. minority communities, tribes typically have their own government, and one can often attend political rallies or town meetings. European Americans can experience firsthand what it is like to be a statistical minority, what it is like to not know the appropriate social behavior or catch all of the jokes, what it is like to be regarded with uncertainty or suspicion about the reasons for your presence, and what it is like to hear frequent references to the problems caused by your own cultural group. European Americans who are willing to do so will learn that American Indians indeed have a culture and an ethnic identity. This will, I hope, promote more culturally congruent violence research and more active programs against domestic violence with American Indians.

REFERENCES

Arbuckle, J., L. Olson, M. Howard, J. Brillman, C. Anctil, and D. Sklar. 1996. Safe at home? Domestic violence and other homicides among women in New Mexico. *Annals of Emergency Medicine* 27: 210–214.

Bachman, R. 1992. *Death and Violence on the Reservation: Homicide, Family Violence, and Suicide in American Indian Populations.* Westport, Conn.: Auburn House.

Bilharz, J. 1995. First among equals? The changing status of Seneca women. In L. Klein and L. Ackerman, eds., *Women and Power in Native North America.* Norman: University of Oklahoma Press, 101–112.

Bohn, D. K. 1989. Roles, status, and violence: Ojibway women in historical perspective. Paper.

———. 1993. Nursing care of American Indian battered women. *AWHONN's Clinical Issues* 4: 424–436.

Cazenave, N. A., and M. A. Straus. 1990. Race, class, network embeddedness, and family violence: A search for potent support systems. In M. Straus and R. Gelles, eds., *Physical Violence in American Families: Risk Factors and Adaptations to Violence in 8,145 Families.* New Brunswick, N.J.: Transaction Publishers, 321–340.

Chester, B., R. W. Robin, M. P. Koss, J. Lopez, and D. Goldman. 1994. Grandmother dishonored: Violence against women by male partners in American Indian communities. *Violence and Victims* 9: 249–258.

Cochise, C. N. (with Griffith, A. K.). 1971. *The First Hundred Years of Niño Cochise.* New York: Pyramid Books.

Davidson, T. 1978. *Conjugal Crime: Understanding and Changing the Wifebeating Pattern.* New York: Hawthorn Books, Inc.

DeBruyn, L., B. Wilkins, and K. Artichoker. 1990. "It's not cultural": Violence against American Indian women. Paper, presented at the 89th American Anthropological Association Meeting, New Orleans, La., November.

Dobash, R. E., and R. P. Dobash. 1979. *Violence against Wives: A Case against Patriarchy.* New York: The Free Press.

Duran, E., B. Duran, W. Woodis, and P. Woodis. 1998. A postcolonial perspective on domestic violence in Indian country. In R. Carrillo and J. Tello, eds., *Family Violence and Men of Color: Healing the Wounded Male Spirit.* New York: Springer, 95–113.

Durst, D. 1991. Conjugal violence: Changing attitudes in two northern Native communities. *Community Mental Health Journal* 27: 359–373.

Groginsky, L., and C. Freeman. 1994. Domestic violence in American Indian and Alaskan Native communities. *Protecting Children* 11: 13–16.

Guemple, L. 1995. Gender in Inuit society. In L. Klein and L. Ackerman, eds., *Women and Power in Native North America.* Norman: University of Oklahoma Press, 17–27.

Gunn Allen, P. 1986. *The Sacred Hoop: Recovering the Feminine in American Indian Tradition.* Boston: Beacon.

———. 1990. Violence and the American Indian woman. *Newsletter: Common Ground—Common Planes.* The Women of Color Partnership Program, July, 186–188.

Hamby, S. L. 1996. The Dominance Scale: Preliminary psychometric properties. *Violence and Victims* 11: 199–212.

Hamby, S. L., and M. B. Skupien. 1998. Domestic violence on the San Carlos Apache Indian Reservation: Rates, associated psychological symptoms, and current beliefs. *The Indian Health Services Provider* 23: 103–106.

Hamby, S. L., and D. B. Sugarman. 1996. Power and partner violence: A meta-analytic review. In S. L. Hamby (chair), *Theorizing about Gender Socialization and Power in Family Violence.* Symposium conducted at the American Psychological Association Annual Meeting, Toronto, Ontario, August.

Hartsock, N. C. M. 1998. *The Feminist Standpoint Revisited and Other Essays.* Boulder, Colo.: Westview Press.

Kehoe, A. B. 1995. Blackfoot persons. In L. Klein and L. Ackerman, eds., *Women and Power in Native North America.* Norman: University of Oklahoma Press, 113–125.

Klein, L. F. 1995. Mother as clanswoman: Rank and gender in Tlingit society. In L. Klein and L. Ackerman, eds., *Women and Power in Native North America.* Norman: University of Oklahoma Press, 28–45.

Klein, L. F., and L. A. Ackerman, eds. 1995. *Women and Power in Native North America.* Norman: University of Oklahoma Press.

Koss, M. P., and B. Chester. 1997. Alcoholism prevalence and gene/environment interactions in American Indian tribes. Paper.

Kuklinski, D. M., and C. B. Buchanan. 1997. Assault injuries on the Hualapai Indian Reservation: A descriptive study. *The Indian Health Services Provider* 22: 60–64.

LaFramboise, T. D., J. S. Berman, and B. K. Sohi. 1995a. American Indian women. In L. Comas-Diaz and B. Greene, eds., *Women of Color: Integrating Ethnic and Gender Identities in Psychotherapy.* New York: Guilford Press, 30–71.

LaFramboise, T. D., S. B. Choney, A. James, and P. R. Running Wolf. 1995b. American Indian women and psychology. In H. Landrine, ed., *Bringing Cultural Diversity to Feminist Psychology: Theory, Research, and Practice.* Washington, D.C.: American Psychological Association, 197–239.

Levinson, D. 1989. *Family Violence in Cross-cultural Perspective.* Newbury Park, Calif.: Sage.

Maguire, P. 1987. *Doing Participatory Research: A Feminist Approach.* Amherst: University of Massachusetts.

Murray, Virginia. 1998. A comparative survey of the historic civil, common, and American Indian tribal law responses to domestic violence. *Oklahoma City University Law Review* 23: 433–547.

National Training Project. 1997. *Walking in Balance: A Native Approach to Domestic Violence.* Duluth, Minn.: Author.

Newbreast, T. 1998. The challenge of FAS in Native American communities. Presented at FAS: Train the Trainer, San Carlos Apache Reservation, Ariz. January.

Norton, I. M., and S. M. Manson. 1995. A silent minority: Battered American Indian women. *Journal of Family Violence* 10: 307–318.

Opler, M. E. 1941/1996. *An Apache Life-way: The Economic, Social, and Religious Institutions of the Chiricahua Indians.* Lincoln: University of Nebraska Press.

Patterson, V. D. 1995. Evolving gender roles in Pomo society. In L. Klein and L. Ackerman, eds. *Women and Power in Native North America.* Norman: University of Oklahoma Press, 126–145.

Pego, C. M., R. F. Hill, G. W. Solomon, R. M. Chisolm, and S. E. Ivey. 1996. Tobacco, culture, and health among American Indians: A historical review. *The Indian Health Services Provider* 21: 19–28.

Pence, E., and Paymar, M. 1993. *Education Groups for Men Who Batter: The Duluth Model.* New York: Springer.

Ptacek, J. 1997. Racial politics, class politics, and research on woman battering. Paper, presented at the 5th International Family Violence Research Conference, Durham, N.H. July.

Richie, B. E. 1996. *Compelled to Crime: The Gender Entrapment of Battered Black Women.* New York: Routledge.

Shackelford, T. K., and D. M. Buss. 1997. Spousal esteem. *Journal of Family Psychology* 11: 478–488.

Shinkwin, A. D., and M. C. Pete. 1983. Homes in disruption: Spouse abuse in Yupik Eskimo society. Ph.D. diss., University of Alaska, Fairbanks.

Sprott, J. E. 1994. "Symbolic ethnicity" and Alaska Natives of mixed ancestry living in Anchorage: Enduring group or sign of impending assimilation? *Human Organization* 53: 311–322.

Stockel, H. H. 1991. *Women of the Apache Nation: Voices of Truth.* Reno: University of Nevada Press.

Straus, M. A., and G. Kaufman Kantor. 1994. Change in spousal assault rates from 1975 to 1992: A comparison of three national surveys in the United States. Presented at the 13th World Congress of Sociology, Bielefeld, Germany. July.

Timmins, L. 1995. *Listening to the Thunder: Advocates Talk about the Battered Women's Movement.* Vancouver: Women's Research Centre.

Tjaden, P., and N. Thoennes. 1998. *Prevalence, Incidence, and Consequences of Violence against Women: Findings from the National Violence against Women Survey.* Washington, D.C.: U.S. Department of Justice (NCJ 172837).

Trickett, E. J. 1996. A future for community psychology: The contexts of diversity and the diversity of contexts. *American Journal of Community Psychology* 24: 209–234.

West, C. M. 1998. Lifting the "political gag order": Breaking the silence around partner violence in ethnic minority families. In J. L. Jasinski and L. M. Williams, eds., *Partner Violence: A Comprehensive Review of 20 Years of Research.* Thousand Oaks, Calif.: Sage, 184–209.

Wolk, L. E. 1982. *Minnesota's American Indian Battered Women: The Cycle of Oppression.* St. Paul, Minn.: St. Paul American Indian Center.

CHAPTER **13**

SHARON ANGELLA ALLARD

Rethinking Battered Woman Syndrome

A Black Feminist Perspective

──────────────── ABSTRACT ────────────────

The concept "Battered Woman Syndrome" was coined by Lenore Walker in 1980. Battered Woman Syndrome, a legal defense, has been used to explain to jurors why a battered woman felt compelled to kill her abuser. This psychological interpretation rests on Walker's idea of learned helplessness; because of the traumatic stress of living in a constant state of fear, a woman may feel unable to escape from the relationship and may resort to violence to survive. Battered Woman Syndrome redefined the assertion of self-defense in some cases of assault or homicide by offering an explanation of the effects from repeated physical, sexual, and/or psychological abuse by a partner against women. This syndrome also makes a case as to why women find it difficult to leave their abuser. Expert testimony on Battered Woman Syndrome is usually introduced in court to bolster self-defense cases where the circumstances under which a battered woman kills her abuser do not meet the traditional standards of imminent danger.

Gondolf and Fisher (1988), however, in their classic work, *Battered Women as Survivors*, refute Walker's theory of "helplessness"; they provide a markedly different "survivor" theory that takes into account the multiple ways in which battered women actively seek help and cope throughout the abusive relationship.

In this chapter, Sharon Angella Allard explains that the Battered Woman Syndrome legal defense has been denied to poor Black women. Racist stereotypes and media-demonized images of Black women put them in a disadvantaged position when trying to defend themselves in court. Black women do not fit the cultural stereotype of the passive, weak, fearful, white middle class victim of domestic violence. These dominant cultural stereotypes, informing Walker's concept of Battered Woman Syndrome, are most likely to influence jurors' decision making. "Rethinking Battered Woman Syndrome: A Black Feminist Perspective" helps the reader understand more fully that harsh penalties are applied to a

Black woman when a jury interprets her behavior as acting out of anger rather than fear.

Allard makes clear that larger structural forces—racism, sexism, and class inequality—directly impact battered women seeking assistance in the courts. As you read this chapter, review the ways in which Black and white women have been differentially treated and perceived by the legal system. How does the history of differential treatment in the courts impact Black battered women defendants today? What is the role of the media in perpetuating unequal treatment of battered women of color in the legal system?

INTRODUCTION

The plight of battered women gained national attention when Farrah Fawcett portrayed a battered spouse in the television movie, *The Burning Bed.*[1] The program depicted the physical and psychological torture that leads a battered woman to take the life of her batterer and the subsequent legal challenges that she faces when claiming self-defense in response to a murder charge. Viewers observed a woman in the throes of a psychological breakdown and in fear of losing her life. But viewers never saw her anger. The lack of any hostility in the act of killing her husband made her actions appear justifiable, excusable, or at least sympathetic.

This perception of battered women as psychologically impaired and lacking hostility is not limited to the confines of television programs or movies. Consider, for example, the real-life stories of Hedda Nussbaum and Geraldine Mitchell. Each woman claimed to have been battered by her companion, and each woman was charged with the battering death of the child in her care. The charges against Nussbaum were dropped because "she was so beaten down—emotionally and physically—that she had been powerless to stop her companion."[2] Mitchell, in contrast, "was not given a chance to testify in return for the dropping of charges" and pleaded guilty to manslaughter.[3] Despite almost identical factual situations, Mitchell's story was silenced while Nussbaum's was publicized and accepted. According to Mitchell's attorney, Mitchell was treated more harshly than Nussbaum because Mitchell was Black and poor while Nussbaum was white and middle class.[4] The courts' different treatments of these cases perpetuate a view in the public that the impact of battering on a woman's life varies, depending on whether a woman is Black or white.[5]

The . . . plight of battered women led to a general theory of how a battered woman responds to her situation. In an effort to educate the court about why a battered woman might respond by killing, battered woman syndrome is often introduced at trials. As articulated by Lenore Walker, the syndrome is characterized by a cyclical pattern of psychological and physical abuse which can be broken down into three phases.[6] The first phase is marked by minor battering incidents, when tension builds and the woman exhibits complacent behavior to appease the batterer. The second phase is marked by an acute battering incident, when the woman feels completely isolated and helpless. The third phase is marked by a period of conciliation (the "honeymoon" period), when the batterer expresses his remorse and the woman is forgiving and understanding. Battered woman syndrome theory rests on the notion that a battered woman may suffer from "learned helplessness," whereby the psychological pressures of living in a constant state of fear limit her responses to coping with each individual attack rather than focusing on a way to escape her circumstances.[7] Expert witnesses testify to educate the jury about the reasonableness of the battered woman's conduct. In a homicide case, expert testimony on battered woman syndrome can comprise an essential part of a battered woman's case for self-defense.

To claim self-defense, a defendant must show that she "reasonably" believed that she was in "imminent" danger of serious bodily harm or death. For a belief to be reasonable, the threatened harm must be imminent. The prevailing definitions of reasonableness and imminence, however, exclude a battered woman. Without testimony on battered woman syndrome, the court will not admit evidence of prior abuses against the woman by her batterer on the grounds of irrelevance to the homicide. Consequently, a jury is unlikely to find that a battered woman's use of deadly force was based on a reasonable belief that she was in danger of imminent death or serious bodily harm. Yet, the circumstances under which a battered woman kills her batterer often do not reflect standard notions of imminent danger: a battered woman might strike out against her batterer when his back is turned or when he is asleep or [otherwise] inattentive. Such an action may be perceived as unreasonable because the woman was not necessarily in imminent harm. The classic, male orientation of the law of self-defense, coupled with gender stereotypes, limits the ability of judges and jurors to perceive a battered woman's conduct as reasonable.[8] Testimony on battered woman syndrome, therefore, makes an enormous difference in convincing juries that a battered woman's response was, in fact, a reasonable exercise of self-defense.

While battered woman's syndrome furthers the interest of some battered women, the theory incorporates stereotypes of limited applicability concerning how a woman would and, indeed, should react to battering. To successfully defend herself, a battered woman needs to convince a jury that she is a "normal" woman—weak, passive, and fearful. If the battered woman deviates from these characteristics, then the jury may not associate her situation with that of the stereotypical battered woman. Therefore, it is possible that the difference in perception as to the reality of Nussbaum's and Mitchell's experiences with battering was shaped by cultural notions of who are "good" women and [who are] "bad" women.[9] Race certainly plays a major role in the cultural distinction between the "good" and [the] "bad" woman. The passive, gentle white woman is automatically more like the "good" fairytale princess stereotype than a Black woman, who as the "other" may be seen as the "bad" witch. White women have the benefit of this dual stereotype of "good" and "bad" women. If a woman is perceived as being a "good" woman, she can expect greater protection, while Black women are seen as "bad" and as deserving victims.[10]

This chapter demonstrates that while theories such as battered woman syndrome explain why a battered woman's behavior is reasonable, the definition of "woman" that guides such theories is based upon limited societal constructs of appropriate behavior for white women. This mythological standard, however, does not apply to the historical experiences of women of color, particularly Black women. The first section of this chapter addresses the need for an intersectional analysis of battered woman syndrome based upon race and gender. Such an analysis is needed to free all women from subordinating stereotypes. The second section of this chapter compares the different historical legal treatment of Black and white women. The fact that Black and white women have been subordinated in different ways has resulted in distinct normative definitions of their roles as women. Finally, the third part of this chapter explores media portrayals and images generated by the historical experiences of Black women. These images define Black women in a manner that excludes them from the "feminist" critiques of either self-defense or battered woman syndrome. This chapter concludes that theories such as battered woman syndrome provide, at best, only a partial solution for explaining the conduct of battered women. By relying on prevailing definitions of "women," the theory does not address the law's refusal to recognize a battered woman's conduct as reasonable unless her conduct falls within a very narrow set of stereotypical behaviors and circumstances.

THE NEED FOR AN INTERSECTIONAL ANALYSIS OF BATTERED WOMAN SYNDROME

An intersectional approach, one which incorporates a gender and race analysis, of battered woman syndrome is needed if the law is to address adequately the needs of all battered women.[11] Existing studies on the sexual biases in the law of self-defense and battered woman syndrome include little, if any, analysis as to how race and gender shape women's experiences of violence. Ideally, theories about battered woman syndrome should not marginalize any group of women but should incorporate those experiences shaped by race and gender.[12] Racism alone does not cause the disproportionate conviction of Black women who kill their batterers. We must expose why stories about battered Black women are less credible to a jury than stories about battered white women.

Battered woman syndrome relies on prevailing gender characterizations of dominant, white society. A study identified forty-one sex role stereotypes.[13] A number of these stereotypes about women can be found in the battered woman syndrome characterization of women: very emotional, very submissive, very excitable in a minor crisis, very passive, very uncomfortable about being aggressive, very dependent, very gentle.[14] Each of these characterizations reflects traditional notions of what society considers appropriate behavior for "normal" women.

In contrast to these stereotypes, both the stereotypical images and the historical reality of Black women's experiences in the United States are interpreted by the dominant society as a manifestation of Black women's deviance from "normal" women. This deviance is reflected in the omnipresent images of the hostile Sapphire,[15] the wanton Jezebel,[16] and the strong and assertive Sojourner Truth.[17] The characterizations of the antagonistic yet subordinated Sapphire and the promiscuous Jezebel reaffirm society's belief that Blacks are less human and less individualistic than whites, while the strength found in the characterization of Sojourner is a direct challenge to the prevailing definitions of "passive" womanhood. Consequently, Black women must overcome the demeaning stereotypes of both race and gender.

To the extent that battered woman syndrome theory is based on stereotypes of white women, the theory is inapplicable to women of color. For instance, Black women's exclusion is evident in Lenore Walker's discussion of battered women and anger.[18] Walker stresses that for a battered woman to present a successful defense to a charge of killing her batterer, the woman must not appear angry. If the jury perceives that a woman killed out of anger, rather than fear, the jury is likely to give her a harsher penalty. This has disturbing implications for Black women, who Walker acknowledges are subject to the stereotype that all Black women are "angry."[19] Given that the legal system legitimizes these perceptions,[20] there is a greater likelihood that a jury would believe a prosecutor's story that a battered Black woman acted out of revenge and anger, as opposed to fear, in taking the life of her batterer.

While Walker recognizes that such perceptions greatly affect a Black woman's chances for acquittal when she kills her batterer, Walker does not offer an analysis of how battered woman syndrome, by its own terms, fails to address this problem. Consider the story of Sarah Smith, a Black woman who shot and killed her abusive husband to save her own life. Smith was convicted of second degree murder.[21] When asked by the prosecution if she considered leaving her husband when he was lying down, Smith responded: "Not without chancing that he would catch me at the door and blow my brains out, no."[22] Smith's story arguably would have been accepted by the jury if battered woman syndrome did not limit a battered woman's motivation to a response based solely on a woman's fear. Moreover, Smith's story would have been more "believable" to a jury under a theory which legitimized a battered woman who acted from a position of strength rather than of weakness. Such a theory does not now exist; such a theory is needed.

THE HISTORICAL LEGAL VIEW OF "WOMEN" IS RACE-BASED

The Anglo-American legal tradition initially viewed women as property. This view was based on the patriarchal gender stereotypes of active, masculine, powerful, and authoritative men and passive, feminine, powerless, and deferential women.[23] In 1897, British jurist William Blackstone held that men were responsible for the actions of their wives and therefore authorized to control them.[24] Included within men's responsibility was a duty to protect their wives. Therefore, "good" women were not expected to have to defend themselves in any fashion. Women were certainly not permitted to kill their protectors for any reason.[25]

Feminist theorists criticize these traditional laws as reflecting the "origin of law as a form of male authority and power."[26] These theorists argue that the adoption of sexist images results in paternalistic laws designed to protect women.[27] But such critiques ignore the distinct impact of race in the assignment of gender definitions. Sexist as these protectionist images may have been, they were not meant for Black women. Throughout history, Black women's experiences with patriarchy differed from those of white women.[28]

Black women's historical and social experiences under slavery and thereafter resulted in images that define Black women as deviant. While the Victorian notion of "true womanhood" defined white women as possessing unquestionable moral character, Black women were defined as immoral.[29] This race-based difference in stereotypes made it easier for white men to justify the sexual exploitation of Black women. Such stereotypes also made it easier for white women to accept the exploitation of Black women. Because exploitation was ignored or justified, Black women were not perceived as deserving of male protection.[30] For example, the law historically denied that Black slave women could be raped because they were regarded as immoral. This perception continues to influence the investigation and prosecution of rape charges brought by Black women today.[31]

The difference between how Black and white women are treated and perceived also stems from the fact that Blacks as a group have not received the protection of the law and have historically been denied all rights.[32] While laws formally changed, recent statistics continue to reflect that crimes committed against whites have higher prosecution rates and result in longer sentences than crimes committed against Blacks.[33] Again, Black women are saddled with dual stereotypes of race and gender. As women, they have to overcome the presumption that the law provides sufficient protection for them. As Black women, they must further prove that they are deserving of such protection.

This difference in stereotyping makes battered woman syndrome all the more damaging; not only does the theory perpetuate dominant gender role stereotypes, but it does so to the exclusion of Black women. Therefore, when a jury hears a story of a downtrodden woman completely overwrought by the circumstances of her situation and in fear for her life, it is less likely that they will accept this story as applied to women whose history and present day images deny their need for protection. It is true that white women may face this risk due to the "good" woman/"bad" woman dichotomy. However, while white battered women have to transcend one set of stereotypes to achieve the "good" woman status, Black women, who are in a sense twice removed from this status, have a far heavier burden.

MEDIA IMAGES AND SOCIAL PERCEPTIONS OF BLACK WOMEN: THE IMPACT OF RACE AND GENDER IN THE LAW OF SELF-DEFENSE AND BATTERED WOMAN SYNDROME

Black women generally fall outside the dominant gender definitions upon which battered woman syndrome and feminist analyses of self-defense rely. The media provides much of the information about persons outside of the majority population.[34] Deviant images of Black women abound in society. Images which accurately represent the experiences of Black women exist, but nonetheless remain outside the dominant view of who is a "real" woman.

One image of the Black woman is that of an immoral, promiscuous being.[35] This image arose from a perverted reversal of the historical sexual exploitation of Black women. Current media images perpetuate this perversion. . . . [Many media images of Black women] deviate from or directly challenge those of the traditional passive woman. Because battered woman syndrome is based on the traditional view of the "normal," passive woman, the theory does little to help Black women who are excluded from this stereotype. The dominant images of Black women as domineering, assertive, hostile, and immoral may hinder a judge's or juror's ability to comprehend a Black woman's act of self-defense as based on "learned helplessness" in much the same way that gender definitions of white women serve as an obstacle in the law of self-defense.[36] While a white woman's conduct in killing may be viewed as inapposite to traditional gender roles, the same conduct by a Black woman may be viewed as typical of her character. . . .

The historical acceptance of wife beating also makes it less likely that a jury will perceive any present or prior beating as indicative of bodily harm sufficient to justify the use of deadly harm by any woman.[37] This is particularly likely to be the case for Black women who are considered "strong and suffering."[38] The perception that Black women possess more physical strength than white women may decrease the likelihood that a Black woman reasonably believed that she was in danger of serious bodily harm.[39] This perception of Black women is further perpetuated today in theories that assert either implicitly or explicitly that Black women are emasculating or matriarchal. For example, the current policy debate concerning the status of the "underclass" tends to focus on the plight of Black men, which implies that Black female-headed households are the real problem for the underclass.[40] Moreover, the moralistic overtones of this debate contributes to the perception that Black women are sexually immoral.[41]

The relevance of the differences in the normative definitions of Black women and white women may not be significant with regard to self-defense if neither woman's behavior is considered reasonable. The distinction is significant, however, in the context of battered woman syndrome theory. The theory's use of characterizations that reflect traditional gender role stereotypes appears to be an attempt to restore the battered woman's image to reflect society's normative definition of a normal woman. But this definition does not apply to women who are considered "other." "Black men and women live in a society that creates sex-based norms and expectations which racism operates simultaneously to deny; Black men are not viewed as powerful, nor are Black women seen as passive."[42] Thus, battered woman syndrome essentially excludes Black women.

CONCLUSION

Battered woman syndrome presents a troubling paradox. For some battered women, the theory is a viable tool for satisfying the legal standard of self-defense and for explaining their behavior as reasonable. For others, the theory's use of standard gender definitions may not only exclude some battered women but may actually impose an additional obstacle. To the extent that battered woman syndrome restores a battered woman's image to that of a "good" woman, the theory implicitly embraces the notion that there are "good" women and "bad" women. This dichotomy necessarily implies there is an "other" who can be pointed to as lacking in the characteristics of "true womanhood." Therefore, to assert battered woman syndrome successfully, a woman must avoid association with any of the images of "other."[43] Such avoidance is especially difficult for a Black woman, who is viewed as "other" simply by virtue of her skin color. Thus, battered woman syndrome fails as a viable theory for all battered women.

While it may be possible to expand the characterizations or terminology upon which battered woman syndrome relies, this would also be a limited solution. The problems which spawned the need for theories such as battered woman syndrome still remain. The law of self-defense is a narrow vehicle for accommodating the specific circumstances in which women may find it necessary to take defensive action. Battered woman syndrome explains the behavior of battered women within fairly strict categories, that is, that a woman is fearful, weak, and submissive. Yet, the theory provides no means for assessing the reasonableness of the woman's act of killing unless she is given the "excuse" of learned helplessness. "Excuse connotes personal weakness and implies that the defendant could not be expected to function as would a 'normal' person."[44]

Even an analysis that criticizes battered woman syndrome for pigeonholing the battered women's behavior as unreasonable relies on dominant gender-based experiences.[45] Gender-based theories that do not incorporate race and class will be as problematic as battered woman syndrome. As long as such theories rely on majority gender definitions, the majority will marginalize the experiences of the minority.

Measures must be taken to isolate and redefine established gender norms. The lack of a comprehensive analysis incorporating the effects of race, class, and gender on the legal system reinforces the necessity of "multiple consciousness as jurisprudential method."[46] This is not to suggest that the existing studies and theories are without merit. Rather, it is a call to recognize the harm which will continue in the absence of an intersectional analysis of feminist legal principles.

NOTES

This essay was conceived in Professor Kimberlé Crenshaw's seminar, "Race and Gender in the Law," given at UCLA School of Law in the spring of 1990. The seminar provided the unique opportunity to develop theory through application. In addition to Professor Crenshaw, I would like to thank Callie Glanton, Victor Cannon, and Laura Reece for their time, comments, and encouragement. I am especially grateful to Elvina and Lincoln Allard who taught me that knowledge opens doors others would rather leave closed.

1. *The Burning Bed,* 1984, NBC television broadcast, Oct. 10.

2. Tumulty and Drogin, 1989, Steinberg convicted in girl's death; Jury returns manslaughter verdict, rejects murder count, *Los Angeles Times,* Jan. 31, A4, col. 1.

3. Fried, 1991, Queens mother pleads guilty in fatal battering of boy, 3, *New York Times,* Jan. 24, B2, col. 5.

4. Ibid.

5. My chapter capitalizes "Black" while not capitalizing "white." I mean to distinguish between Black as a cultural group as opposed to a skin color. "Blacks, like Asians, Latinos, and other 'minorities,' constitute a specific cultural group and, as such, require denotation as a proper noun." K. Crenshaw, 1988, Race, reform, and retrenchment: Transformation and legitimation in antidiscrimination law, *Harvard Law Review* 101: 1331, 1332 n.2. Inherent devaluation is communicated by the term "black," and so the capitalization also seeks to empower the cultural group.

6. See generally L. Walker, 1979, *The Battered Woman.*

7. See ibid.

8. The chief criticism of the law of self-defense has been that it is inapplicable to the sociological experiences of women. In this context, as well as in the area of battered woman syndrome, the analysis employed is not wholly transferable to the experiences of Black women. Discussions on the sex biases in the law of self-defense point to the differences in the socialization of men and women with regard to the use of physical force and violence. "A woman who has spent twenty, thirty or fifty years absorbing the message that she is, and ought to be, gentle, weak and helpless; that she needs to be protected from pain and injury; that she cannot really rely on her own strength to save her from danger . . . is bound to view a violent assault differently than a man whose own training in these matters is likely to have been so very different." C. Gillespie, 1989, *Justifiable Homicide: Battered Women, Self-Defense, and the Law.* This characterization applies to all women to some degree. However, the dominant perception of Black women, coupled with their actual socialization, may render the above characterization inapplicable. See the third section of this chapter.

9. Feminist scholars have developed the idea of "good" as opposed to "bad" women in the context of gender stereotypes. See, for example, A. Dworkin, 1974, *Woman Hating.* The racial component of this concept, however, has not been widely explored. I am expanding upon the concept set forth by Kimberlé Crenshaw that "racist ideology . . . arranges oppositional categories in a hierarchical order; historically, whites represented the dominant antinomy while Blacks came to be seen as separate and subordinate." Crenshaw, 1988, 1373.

10. See Murray and Stahly, 1987, Some victims are derogated more than others, *Woman's Journal of Black Studies* 11: 177. The results of this study confirm that "the derogation of Black women relative to white women seems to be both a general and a pervasive phenomenon." Ibid. See also McClain, 1986, Cause of death—Homicide: A research note on Black females as homicide victims, *Victimology* 7: 204, 205. Although this chapter focuses on the experiences of Black women, the underlying arguments apply to all women who fall outside of the standard gender definitions described by current battered woman syndrome theory.

11. See Crenshaw, 1989, Demarginalizing the intersection of race and sex: A Black feminist critique of antidiscrimination doctrine, feminist theory and antiracist politics, *University of Chicago Legal Forum,* 139, for an analysis of how race and gender are viewed as exclusive of one another and are treated as such in antidiscrimination law, feminist theory, and antiracist politics. This exclusive analysis results in the exclusion of Black women's legal claims.

12. See b. hooks, 1981, *Ain't I a Woman: Black Women and Feminism;* P. Giddings, 1984, *When and Where I Enter: The Impact of Black Women On Race and Sex in America.* Both works offer an historical analysis of the impact of Black women on race and gender in American society. hooks's introduction presents the problem: "No other group in America has so had their identity socialized out of existence as have black women. . . . When black people are talked about, sexism militates against the acknowledgment of the interests of black women; when women are talked about, racism militates against a recognition of black female interests. When black people are talked about the focus tends to be on black men; and when women are talked about the focus tends to be on white women" (p. 7).

13. See Gillespie, 1989, 106, n.8.

14. Ibid.

15. Sapphire is the name of the Black female character in the television comedy Amos 'n' Andy about two Black males. Sapphire was the loud and sassy wife of one of the men. She regularly fought with her husband about his annoying behavior. The show was eventually discontinued after civil rights organizations complained about the stereotypical and derogatory depiction of Blacks. Today the term "Sapphire" conjures up images of a shrill, nagging, hostile, and aggressive Black woman. See Austin, 1989, Sapphire bound! *Wisconsin Law Review* 539, 540 n.1; B. Andrews and A. Julliard, 1986, Holy mackerel! The Amos 'n' Andy story, 1516; *New Dictionary of American Slang,* 1986, ed. R. Chapman, 368.

16. Jezebel is defined as a woman who is "impudent, shameless, or abandoned." *Webster's New Collegiate Dictionary,* 1981, 150th ed., 616. "Jezebel was the wanton, libidinous black woman whose easy ways excused white men's abuse of their slaves as sexual partners." Austin, 1989, 570, n.15; D. White, 1985, Ar'n't I a woman? Female slaves in the plantation South 46, 61.

17. Sojourner Truth freed herself from slavery to become an active abolitionist and suffragist. Her bold spirit and unswaying convictions became a touchstone within the 1970s women's rights movement. Truth is widely known for her response to a heckler at a women's rights convention in 1871: "Truth asserted that women were not inherently weak and helpless. Raising herself to her full height of six feet, flexing a muscled arm, and bellowing with a voice one observer likened to the apocalyptic thunders, Truth informed the audience that she could outwork, outeat, and outlast any man. Then she challenged: 'Ain't I a woman?'" P. Giddings, 1984, 54, n.12; B. Loewenberg and R. Bogin, eds., 1981, *Black Women in Nineteenth-Century American Life: Their Words, Their Thoughts, Their Feelings,* 234.

18. See L. Walker, 1989, *Terrifying Love: Why Battered Women Kill and How Society Responds.*

19. "The ratio of Black women to white women convicted of killing their abusive husbands is nearly two to one in one of my studies. My feeling is that this is the result of our society's misperceptions of Black people in general, of women in general, and of Black women in particular. The 'angry Black woman' is a common stereotype in many white minds; subtly, but no less powerfully, white society in America fears 'Black anger.'" Ibid., 206.

20. The courts have permitted prosecutors to use peremptory challenges to strike prospective Black jurors on the basis that such persons appeared to be hostile. See S. Johnson, 1985, Black innocence and the white jury, *Michigan Law Review* 83: 1611. Similarly, it is unlikely that a potential employer will be found to have discriminated on the basis of race if she can point to specific deficiencies in an applicant's interview even when these deficiencies may reflect cultural biases.

21. Golden, 1991, Abused wife is found guilty of murder; Self-defense plea rejected, *New York Times,* Jan. 24, A16, col. 4. One juror commented, "We didn't believe her."

22. Ibid.

23. D. Wareha and R. Castillo, 1985, Afro-American and Mexican-American women who have been victims of domestic violence (battered) in Los Angeles County shelters (June), thesis, Graduate School of Social Welfare, UCLA; L. Gilbert and P. Webster, 1982, *Bound By Love: The Sweet Trap of Daughterhood,* xvi.

24. "Husband and wife, in the language of the law, are styled baron and feme. . . . If the baron kills his feme it is the same as if he had killed a stranger, or any other person; but if the feme kills her baron, it is regarded by the laws as a much more atrocious crime, as she not only breaks through the restraints of humanity and conjugal affection, but throws off all subjection to the authority of her husband. And therefore the law denominates her crime a species of treason, and condemns her to the same punishment as if she had killed the king. And for every species of treason . . . the sentence of women was to be drawn and burnt alive." Schneider, 1980, Equal rights to trial for women: Sex bias in the law of self-defense, *Harvard Civil Rights-Civil Liberties Legal Review* 15: 623, 629 (quoting 1 W. Blackstone, 1987, *Commentaries on the Laws of England,* ed. R. Welsh and Co., 418, n.103).

25. Ibid.

26. Rifkin, 1980, Toward a theory of law and Patriarchy, *Harvard Women's Law Journal* 3: 83, 87.

27. The conventional policy wisdom of the eighteenth and nineteenth centuries regarded women as appropriately dependent on men. Women were thought incapable of determining important matters for themselves, too virtuous to be exposed to the rough and tumble of the larger world. D. Kirp, M. Yudof, and M. Franks, 1986, *Gender Justice,* 30.

28. Family life during slavery presents but one example of this difference. While white women's experiences were marked by a paternalistic protection in the domestic sphere, Black women were subjected to the sexual and economic desires of their captors.

29. P. Giddings, 1984. Giddings discusses how economic expansion in the 1830s resulted in the growth of a new middle class seeking to reach upper-class status. "For women, the vehicle for these aspirations was what became known as the 'cult of the lady' or the 'cult of true womanhood.' . . . A woman had to be true to the cult's cardinal tenets of domesticity, submissiveness, piety, and purity in order to be good enough for society's inner circles. Failing to adhere to any of these tenets—which the overwhelming number of Black women could hardly live up to—made one less than a moral, 'true' woman." Ibid., 47.

30. See third section of this chapter, 13, for a discussion of the masculine characterization of Black women.

31. See Wriggins, Rape, racism, and the law, *Harvard Women's Law Journal* 6: 103, for a discussion of the law's failure to address the rape of Black women. Wriggins traces this denial through slavery (rape of Black women by both Black and white men legal) and the post–Civil War period (fact of Black defendant only relevant to prove intent to rape a white woman). She notes recent studies showing both that white judges and juries impose harsher sentences when the victim is white and that decisions to prosecute for rape are based on differences in the perceptions of chastity based on race.

32. Both during and after slavery, Blacks were subjected to white discipline and control as a matter of law; first through the use of slavery codes and then through "Black" codes. For a more expansive treatment of these issues, see A. Higgenbotham, 1978, *In the Matter of Color;* D. Bell, 1980, *Race, Racism, and American Law,* 85.

33. See McCleskey v. Kemp, 481 U.S. 279, 312 (1987) (statistics show that the race of the defendant and the victim are often factors which lead to disparities in death penalty sentencing); Bureau of Justice Statistics, U.S. Department of Justice, 1984, *Sourcebook of Criminal Justice Statistics,* 692, table 6.70 (data indicates that a larger number of nonwhites than whites are executed).

34. Mass media contributes to the "public's conceptions of reality, the 'facts', concepts, and definitions from which people construct their beliefs about the world in general and about social reality in particular." G. Smitherman-Donaldson and T. Van Dijk, ed., 1988, *Discourse and Discrimination,* 24.

35. "After slavery ended, the sexual exploitation of black women continued, in both the North and the South. . . . To sustain it, in the face of the nominal freedom of black men, a complex system of supportive mechanisms and sustaining myths was created. One of these was the myth of the 'bad' black woman. By assuming a different level of sexuality for all Blacks than that of whites and mythifying their greater sexual potency, the black woman could be made to personify sexual freedom and abandon. A myth was created that all black women were eager for sexual exploits, voluntarily 'loose' in their morals and, therefore, deserved none of the consideration and respect granted to white women." G. Lerner, 1973, *Black Women in White America: A Documentary History,* 163.

36. Walker, 1979. See note 7 above and accompanying text.

37. See Schneider, 1980, for a discussion of the legal origins of the sanctioning of woman abuse based on a notion that women were property to be protected by men.

38. Gloria Naylor in an essay on the myth of the strong Black woman also traces the roots of this imagery to the role of Black women during slavery: "They were stronger creatures; they didn't feel pain in childbirth; they didn't have tear ducts." Naylor, 1988, The myth of the matriarch, *Life,* Spring, 65. Naylor also points out that Black women themselves may have adopted this perception at great cost to their personal well-being by feeling that if they are not able to withstand all things they are somehow inadequate. This observation provides an interesting perspective from which to evaluate the experiences of Black women who are battered.

39. The image of the strong Black woman arose during slavery to justify the disparate treatment of Black women and white women with regard to labor. "To explain the black female's ability to survive without the direct aid of a male and her ability to perform tasks that were culturally defined as 'male' work, white males argued that black slave women were not 'real' women but were masculinized sub-human creatures." b. hooks, 1981, 71.

40. "Anti-feminists argue that changing sex role patterns have threatened males so that they are demonstrating their anger by domestic brutality. As supporters of male dominance they assert that violent acts against women will continue until society returns to the good old-fashioned days of sharply delineated sex roles." Ibid., 105. See also W. Wilson, 1987, *The Truly Disadvantaged: The Inner City, The Underclass and Public Policy;* D. Moynihan, 1965, *The Tangle of Pathology in The Negro Family: A Case for National Action;* this controversial report asserted the existence of a matriarchal family structure among Black households was the reason for the low socioeconomic progress of Blacks in America.

41. McGrory, 1986, Moynihan was right 21 years ago, *Washington Post,* Jan. 26, B1, col. 1; Will, 1986, Voting rights won't fix it, *Washington Post,* Jan. 23, A23, col. 5. Both articles point to irresponsible sexual conduct as the primary cause of the underclass.

42. See Crenshaw, 1989, 155.

43. Such images include those based on ethnicity, class, and sexual orientation as well as race.

44. Sagaw, 1987, A hard case for feminists: People v. Goetz, *Harvard Women's Law Journal* 10: 253, 256 n.21.

45. See Littleton, 1989, Women's experience and the problem of transition: Perspectives on male battering of women, *University of Chicago Legal Forum,* 23. While this work provides a legitimate critique of battered woman syndrome, it is nonetheless a gender-based analysis; it is suggested that another explanation for why a battered woman remains in an abusive relationship is the connection thesis which describes women as connected to others (materially in the context of pregnancy), and as fearing abandonment and isolation.

46. M. Matsuda, 1989, When the first quail calls: Multiple consciousness as jurisprudential method, *Women's Rights Law Reporter* 11: 7.

CHAPTER **14**

BEVERLY HORSBURGH

Lifting the Veil of Secrecy

Domestic Violence
in the Jewish Community

──────────────── ABSTRACT ────────────────

Although unacknowledged, what we know about domestic violence in the United States is implicitly based on research conducted within a majority Christian society on several levels. First, Christians numerically outnumber the non-Christian population in the United States, and, second, Christian perspectives on gender, race, sexuality, marriage, and divorce are built into and permeate U.S. law and society. In fact, a sense of difference/Otherness is assigned to people who are not Christian. Think back to previous chapters. No one was labeled "Christian" to describe their individual or community identity, in part because Christianity in the United States attains an unmarked dominance or insider status. Perhaps, also, most Americans who identify themselves as Christians think about their participation in Christianity as a religion instead of considering social or cultural, as well as spiritual, identification with their religion. This is the case, for example, among Orthodox and ultra-Orthodox Jews in the United States for whom identifying as a Jew (individual identity), being Jewish (cultural identity), and practicing Judaism (religious identity) converge to form a communal way of life. Given this identity difference, a Jewish battered woman disclosing negative information about her community runs the risk of betraying that community. Moreover, leaving the community might mean losing her identity altogether.

Judaism and Jewish life in the United States can be categorized into various schools of thought: Secular Humanist, Reconstructionist, Reform, Conservative, Orthodox, and ultra-Orthodox. Some Jews may identify with none or more than one of these approaches. The community of Orthodox and ultra-Orthodox Jews that you read about in chapter 14 number approximately 10 percent of American Jewry; they organize themselves, their families, and their communities around maintaining strict adherence to Jewish law. Part of this social organization is based on an ideology of gender complementarity: that is, men and women possess distinct strengths and responsibilities that, when combined, create a functioning whole. Scholars suggest that because gender complementarity differentiates between men and women (and some would argue supports a hierarchy of men over women) this system of social relations is inherently sexist or patriarchal. Others explain that gender complementarity allows for the full expression and valued contribution of each gender. (See Hamby, chapter 12, for a discussion of this issue for some Native American tribes.)

In analyzing how religion, community, and culture structure domestic violence—what Beverly Horsburgh terms a "battering culture"—this chapter powerfully illustrates why an individualistic approach to the study of domestic violence leaves so much unexplained. At the same time, be aware that the author weaves into the structural framework a rather psychological accounting of why individual men batter. She offers an extensive collection of resources to document her analysis; this chapter provides a basic framework of Horsburgh's citations, and a complete list of footnotes is available on Lexis Nexis.

Horsburgh's analysis leads us to ask certain questions, which you might keep in mind as you read this chapter. For example, how do community-based tensions between majority and minority communities shape men's battering and women's experiences and responses to domestic violence? What place does economic stability or mobility play in the lives of Orthodox and ultra-Orthodox battered women? How do members of the Orthodox and ultra-Orthodox communities examined here attempt to manage what they consider to be intolerable levels of domestic violence and male dominance in the home?

Madelaine Adelman

[handwritten annotation: individual approach to battered women / domestic violence not enough, we must also examine how culture / community influence]

INTRODUCTION

. . . I spoke with many Jewish battered women. This is the testimony of Rachel,[1] an Orthodox Jewish woman:

I am Israeli, the youngest of eleven children in an Orthodox family. I was seventeen when I met my husband. He was also Orthodox, an American exchange student, a medical student at Hadassah Hospital.

You can't know my life. My story would be a bestseller. He hit me before we married—chased me around the room when I refused to marry him. After we married it was much worse. He drank a lot and took drugs. He became even more violent when he was drinking. He was two different people. In public he was the famous doctor, holier than God, loved by all. In private he was a monster. He controlled absolutely everything. At our home on Miami Beach he wanted the air-conditioning at 72 degrees. If I changed it, he would scream, hit, carry on so. The radio station he liked had to be on in every room. I wasn't allowed to touch it. It was his way or no way. He also beat the children. We have six children. When the children talked in bed past bedtime he would make them do push-ups. Those poor little kids, trying to do push-ups, so young. If they stopped, he would get out the strap or a hanger from the closet. I couldn't interfere. I would get such a smack across the face, my nose would bleed.

I couldn't leave him. It would break my parents' hearts to know that I was unhappy. I had six children. I was not educated. I didn't speak good English. I had no job skills. Where could I go with six kids? I told no one. If I told the rabbi, he would want to talk to my husband and then he would really kill me. I was raised not to complain about your personal problems. You don't hang your dirty laundry outside. It would hurt his practice if I told our friends. Besides, he threatened if I left him he would kill me, himself, and the children. Also, he told me he would disappear and I would never see a cent. Once he showed me a newspaper article about a husband who murdered his wife. He told me he would do this too.

In 1979 I became pregnant with my seventh child. He insisted I have an abortion even though it was dangerous because I was four months pregnant. I am a religious woman. I told him I cannot. He made me miserable, started hitting me. . . . I called the rabbi and told him that my husband wants to kill my baby. The rabbi came over and cried. He tried to convince my husband to let me have my baby. He said, "This child is nachas. This accident is a blessing. You're an Orthodox person, you can't do this!" My husband went crazy. He turned on the television—it was Rosh Ha-Shanah! "We're no longer Jews" he tells the children. "Your mother is a selfish woman who wants to destroy me!" Finally, on the eve of Yom Kippur, the holiest evening, he takes out a gun and points it at me. He told me to have the abortion or else everybody will be dead: me, the children, him. He told me to tell the doctor it is what I want to do. My own doctor wouldn't do it. So he found another doctor. On Yom Kippur, I had an abortion. I cried. I was lying in bed bleeding and fasting because it is the day of atonement. I prayed to God to give me strength to leave him.

Eventually, after twenty-seven years of marriage, I gained a little strength. I went to my brother who moved from Israel to New Jersey. I didn't tell my husband where I was. I wouldn't tell the children either because he would beat them if he thought they knew where I was staying. I told him on the telephone that I want a divorce. My brother flew to Miami to talk to him. My husband said, "Over my dead body she'll get the get (religious bill of divorcement)." My brother told me my husband is a dangerous man. He would definitely kill me if I divorce. Also, I had a boyfriend, and my husband told me that in the Bible, a man is allowed to kill his wife if she sees another man.

I spoke with my husband every day by phone. I promised him if he would just give me the get, I would still be his wife. I just needed some independence. We would date and be boyfriend and girlfriend. I signed an agreement in which he took custody of the two youngest children—the rest were adults and out of the house. Also, he would live in the house. His lawyer told him to give me some money in the agreement or the judge would be suspicious. He wouldn't let anyone examine his books. I have no idea how much money he has. I had to promise to remarry him. Anything, in order to have the get. He threatened he would schmooze my name in the community and tell everyone I abandoned my children and have a boyfriend if I didn't promise to remarry him. Of course, that's not in the agreement.

"You don't hang your dirty laundry outside"

"if i left him he would kill me"

It took five months for me to receive the get. I got my civil divorce the same day. So I came home to Miami, anxious to see my children. He is there, in the house! He put up a sign "Welcome Home My Sabbath Queen!" Dangling from the chandelier is a necklace, spelling out my name in diamonds! He tells me that everyone thinks I was in Israel. He insists we go out for dinner. I said "You're crazy! We're not married, I have a get." He threatened suicide and pushed me into the bedroom. He locked the door and raped me. That get was just a piece of paper. I thought I never would be rid of him. The next month he took me to a hotel at gunpoint, drugged me, and raped me in a hotel room.

The kids are afraid of my ex-husband. If he tells them not to talk to me, they don't talk to me. I never got my personal possessions. Everything is gone—my sterling silver, my dead father's *tallis* (prayer shawl), the ancient artifacts that Moshe Dayan gave my family. I have been fighting him in court for five years. He won't let the children visit, telling the judge my second husband isn't religious enough. We are trying to overturn the agreement. The judge doesn't believe I was forced to sign it in order to receive the get. I told the judge that my ex-husband abused me and the kids. The children swore to the judge that their father never hit them. They also said that he didn't really hit me—maybe just a slap. I know! My ex-husband told the children if you want to stay alive, say nothing. The judge decided that because I got my get, nothing is wrong with the agreement. He is an idiot! Would an Orthodox woman agree to leave her children?

This is the testimony of Hannah, a non-Orthodox Jewish woman:

In growing up, it was unheard of that a Jewish man beats a Jewish woman. That was not even a remote possibility. Jewish men make the best husbands. I was raised to believe that being Jewish is the same as being "good." Even after my divorce, I was told by my family to find a nice Jewish boy. It still angers me because my family knew my ex-husband was not "good." My husband came from a supposedly religious family. He was raised Conservative and went to shul (congregation) fairly regularly. I met him in high school. In those days I didn't know anyone who wasn't Jewish. All my friends were Jews. Now I see a connection between religion and violence. When my husband went to synagogue he would feel exalted. That sense of self-uplift does not come from within but from an external structure. The organization gives you status. So when he came home, shame would set in and he would get in touch with his lack of self-esteem. He needed to regain control and would take his feelings of shame out on me. He beat me more after going to synagogue. He got stirred up in synagogue and came home to reality where he hated himself. He never told his rabbi he had a problem.

There was no way to disagree with him. I could say anything or nothing and that would set him off. He also intimidated me. He would say, "I hope your parents die so I can walk on their graves." He called me a whore and accused me of having affairs when I went to the basement of the building to do wash. He had plenty of affairs. He told our son—actually bragged about it—that he was unfaithful on our honeymoon. He has no sense of boundaries.

After he beat me he would indulge in lavish apologies. He brought me roses, and I said, "I don't want flowers." He beat me with the roses and the thorns. He hit me when I was pregnant and called me an unfit mother. I was not a woman because I didn't want a second child. I left him for the first time when my son was five months old. He threatened to commit suicide. Even my father was worried about him. My family did believe me, however. My father and brother helped me move back into my parents' home. We saw a marriage counselor exactly once. I was terrified to see my husband in the therapist's office, so my brother escorted me. I think my husband bribed that therapist. He cried throughout the session. I couldn't cry. He said he had no reason to change unless I came back. The therapist told me it was only fair to give him a chance. I didn't want to go back. My ex-husband is very charming. He charmed that therapist. I did move back. My parents told me I was on my own. They were disgusted that I returned and were not supportive after that.

The beatings were worse now because I took his son away from him. Now I was really alone. I couldn't tell my parents or my friends. I felt so ashamed. If I'm a Jewish woman and Jews don't beat their wives, who am I? I had no framework to identify with. I didn't know anyone who was abused. Jews and abuse, the two do not go together. I felt this way all the time. As a Jewish woman, I had to keep the home and hearth. I was raised to keep peace and make my marriage work. Finally I told my friends. They said it doesn't happen in Jewish families.

In that year and a half before I left again, I almost died. He would stay out all night and come home and beat me senseless. I was afraid I would drop the baby. I saw a doctor because I had a concussion. The neighbors called the police several times, hearing shouting and screaming. He would leave the police station and beat me because he had to go to the station. I couldn't press charges. I didn't want my son's father in jail. I thought I could handle it. I used to wish that I could be an alcoholic or that I could fall down and someone would take care of me. I took care of my son, but no one cared for me.

Eventually I broke out of it. He pushed me against a kitchen cabinet. He was right up against my face. I reached behind and pulled a knife out of the drawer. I wanted to stab him, but I knew that if I didn't kill him, he would kill me and my son would only have him. What came through was my rage. I never before felt so angry and afraid I would not survive. I was feeling it, not intellectualizing the problem. Now I am a psychotherapist, and I tell other women about this. That moment you intensely feel it all. . . .

I write on behalf of these women, aware that they relived their pain in their conversations with me and did so willingly, in order to help others who are abused. Their stories, as women and as Jews, suggest we should broaden the feminist dialogue on domestic violence to include those who are set apart from others and who have been mostly silent victims. The narratives also reveal that battering is symptomatic of gender subordination in general and, at the same time, a unique experience, grounded in particular, individualized concerns.[2]

Although commentators have discussed some of the particular and general problems associated with domestic violence, relatively little attention has been paid to Jewish battered women. Even a well-publicized case, such as the tragic story of Hedda Nussbaum,[3] prompted little public interest. Contrary to the idealized vision of Jewish family life as warm, loving, and nurturing, in many Jewish homes a woman experiences physical violence, emotional abuse, and terror. Like other battered women, a Jewish woman must deal with the general problem of sexism. She is ashamed to admit she is abused and worries that the police will fail to protect her. She also worries that she will lose *"to some Jews she is nothing more than a traitor"*

custody of her children as well as her only means of support if she should divorce her abuser. In addition, Jewish women encounter anti-Semitic stereotyping in the outside world. Stamped as an abrasive, emasculating, and overbearing mother or a pampered, demanding, and self-centered shrew, a Jewish woman hardly evokes sympathy from the public or a court of law. She also incurs hostility within her own community in accusing a Jewish man of physical abuse. Exposing Jewish misconduct to the Christian majority is a *shanda,* a shame that brings disgrace upon all Jews in that each shoulders the burden of representing an entire people. To some Jews, she is nothing short of a traitor who undermines efforts to combat the more pressing issue of anti-Semitism.

For an Orthodox Jewish woman, the problems are even more overwhelming. In naming herself battered and identifying with other non-Jewish women, she must risk the loss of her Jewish self and the fulfillment that comes from belonging to a religious community with deeply felt shared values. She might have few contacts with the outside world. She could actually fear representation by a non-Jewish lawyer or even a non-Orthodox Jewish lawyer. In many cases, regardless of secular law reforms and despite her courageous willingness to end her marriage and obtain a restraining order, she might never be able to extricate herself from her batterer. She is anchored to him for the rest of her life, unless he dies or is willing to grant her a divorce according to Jewish law.

The Jewish woman's problems are exacerbated by the scarcity of statistical evidence on domestic violence among Jews. Both the Jewish and non-Jewish worlds make her officially nonexistent. Although studies document domestic violence in 15 to 30 percent of Jewish families,[4] as far as both cultures are concerned, Jewish men never abuse the women in their lives. Popular images enshrine them as the perfect husbands. The popular culture also assumes Jewish women to be spoiled by their fathers, catered to by their mates, and that they exercise control over their intimate relationships. As a result, Jewish women suffer the stigma of supposedly dominating their meek, obliging boyfriends and husbands. Jewish women internalize the stereotyping of Jewish male/female relationships and are less able to picture themselves as battered. They are also unlikely to be believed by family, friends, social workers, or the courts. Many rabbis discount their claims of abuse, telling them to try harder, for the sake of *shalom bayit* ("peace in the home"). The Jewish community's denial of domestic violence and the tendency to hide the issue within the confines of religious courts contribute to the oppression of Jewish women and underscore the ineffectiveness of secular authorities to combat woman-beating on their own. In the end, fewer social services are available to these women.

its not just about being believed by others

Furthermore, Jewish academics, who are uniquely in a position to publicize the plight of battered Jewish women and thereby educate others to understand their situation, have ignored the issue. Law professors who are drawn to Jewish law in their scholarship minimize or ignore altogether the degree to which rabbinical justice is an expression of patriarchy. The very same regime of law that refuses to release a battered Jewish woman from her pain is extolled by Jewish intellectuals in the academy as a paradigm of enlightenment and a source of inspiration for the secular legal system. Ignored by the Jewish intelligentsia, alienated by her religious leaders, friends, and family, as well as unknown in the outside world, a Jewish battered woman can be truly alone.

It is important to lift the veil of secrecy, render visible what has been made invisible and tell the stories of Jewish battered women. To help these women we must first get to know them through their narratives and through exploring Jewish law, traditions, and social practices that are contributing factors in the development of a battering culture. In this chapter, I attempt to accomplish this task and to introduce you to the world of Jewish battered women.

In this chapter, I examine the blatant and more subtle forms of intragroup oppression in Jewish culture that foster the mistreatment of women. In the first section, I discuss Jewish law (halakhah) and Jewish religious/social practices from a feminist perspective, indicating the many ways in which certain interpretations of the law reflect a belief in the inferior status of women and sustain an environment conducive to woman-abuse. I focus on the exclusion of women as meaningful participants in the Jewish tradition, the toleration of woman-beating in the rabbinical commentary, and the inability of women to initiate a divorce under halakhah. In the second section, I attempt to describe the recurring problems facing Jewish battered women.

JEWISH LAW AND SOCIAL PRACTICES: FOSTERING A BATTERING CULTURE

The Impact of Halakhic Gender Distinctions on Woman-Abuse

The traditional Jewish way of life is governed by the *mitzvot,* obligations that pertain to nearly all aspects of human conduct. The obligations are derived from the Torah, the Jewish Bible, believed to be given to the Jews at Sinai, and rabbinical commentary on the Torah. The word Torah denotes either the five books of Moses or the entire Hebrew Bible. It also more broadly refers to all the teachings and writings in the Jewish legal tradition. *Halakhah* comprises both the written law and the oral law stemming from biblical obligations. The Talmud is commentary—written complications of the oral law.

In Judaism, the daily performance of or forbearance from performing certain acts infuses even the most mundane of everyday activities with spiritual significance and celebrates our wonder at the greatness of creation. Rabbinical law, however, exempts women from many mitzvot because of biology, childrearing responsibilities, and a belief that women are intellectually incapable of committing themselves to a life immersed in halakhah. Daily devotions become constant reminders of gender differences. Thus, to live by the law in Judaism is to ground oneself in patriarchy. Indeed, the very word patriarch denotes the founders of the Jewish faith. In a religious culture in which the actual practice of ritual is often more important than faith, depriving women of performing religious obligations limits them to the periphery of Jewish life.

Presently, not all Jews adhere to Jewish law. Only Orthodox Jews faithfully follow halakhah, committed to a belief that the Torah is the word of God and that the rabbinical sages were divinely inspired.[5] Reform Judaism eliminated many rituals, dietary restrictions and other customs. Conservatives hold to the traditional ceremonies and the use of the Hebrew language in prayers. Conservatives, however, are more flexible than the Orthodox in their observance of the dietary laws and other rituals. The elimination of some gender distinctions in Jewish rituals has alleviated obvious signs of sexism in non-Orthodox ceremonies. Nevertheless, even though the non-Orthodox no longer follow Jewish law in its entirety, Jewish law and rituals are only some of the ways in which the Jewish cultural tradition conveys the notion that women occupy a different and inferior status to men. Ingrained attitudes can outlive symbolic rituals and these attitudes might well continue to influence the upbringing of many nonobservant Jews. As Jewish cultural identity is important to the non-Orthodox as well as the Orthodox, Jewish sensibility is cultivated in both subgroups by emphasizing Jewish family values and distinguishing the value of the traditional Jewish mother.

In addition, traditional Orthodox families have more children than other Jews. Since non-Orthodox Jews are more likely to assimilate into the larger society and forego all ties to their Jewish past, the proportion of traditionalists in the Jewish community has increased. At the same time, many secular Jews, seeking their roots and a sense of communal spiritual identity, are returning to the fold of Orthodoxy. The Reform movement is also demonstrating a renewed interest in halakhah. Furthermore, given the intensity of Jewish opposition to intermarriage and the sheer number of eligible Orthodox men and women, some non-Orthodox Jews might marry into the Orthodox community and find they are expected to observe a traditional Jewish lifestyle. Due to the growing numbers of Orthodox Jews, the Orthodox perspective on women may well begin to predominate in Jewish circles or to play an increasingly significant role. No matter the number of women affected, the sexism inherent in Jewish law reflects on all women and involves all non-Jewish as well as Jewish feminists. To the extent that Jewish law tolerates the beating of women, it is a problem for everyone.

I begin my discussion of halakhah in the same way an Orthodox Jewish man begins his day, with the traditional morning prayer. Each morning an observant Jew thanks his Creator for not having made him a woman. The day commences with a commitment to the maintenance of hierarchy. Other gender distinctions are also immediately apparent in morning observances. Only men are required to wear fringed four-cornered prayer shawls (*talit katan*) and to don phylacteries (black boxes containing scripture that are bound to one's arm and forehead). In general, women are expected to pray in private or among other women. It is men who join together to pray publicly in the synagogue. Public prayer requires the presence of a *minyan,* defined by the Orthodox and some Conservatives as a quorum of ten adult males.

[handwritten margin note:] An important concept here & elsewhere. The number is irrelevent; the mere practice (reflects poorly on the whole. Which 1 woman can be beat, all remain in danger.*

Other exclusions are also painful reminders of women's second-class status in traditional Judaism. A Jewish court (a *Bais Din*) will not admit the testimony of women except in a few emergency situations. Women may usually recite prayers during Jewish services but are not obliged to recite the Shema, the prayer beginning "Hear O Israel, the Lord our God, the Lord is one," although it has been invoked for centuries as the central tenet of Jewish faith. Halakhah also does not bind women to hear the reading from the Torah on the Jewish Sabbath, to dwell in a *sukkah* (a shed or tent open to the sky) on the Feast of the Tabernacles (*Sukkot*), or to hear the shofar blown on the Jewish New Year (*Rosh Ha-Shanah*) and the Day of Atonement (*Yom Kippur*). Exemption from specific religious obligations commanded by God means that women are not part of the religious community and that gender roles are not socially created. They are enscribed in the divine plan of the Almighty.

Consequently, since halakhah precludes women from numerous obligations and does not count them as members of the congregation, it also prohibits them from participating in traditional synagogue rituals. Women cannot be called to the Torah, recite blessings, or read passages of scripture, all of which are great honors. In Orthodox synagogues, women sit separately behind a mechitza (partition) so that the men are not tempted to drift away from holy thoughts by the sight of a female. To the ultra-Orthodox, even the voices of women during prayer are a possible sexual distraction. The custom of gender separation is not in the strictest sense a Jewish tradition, in that the *mechitza* was originally introduced by assimilated Jews living in Moslem countries to resemble the majority, weakening arguments for its preservation as a Jewish tradition.

Furthermore, despite the popular portrayal of the Jews as the people of the Book, women in the past were not allowed to study Torah. The notion that Jews value education more than others, consecrating reading as a sacred obligation, turns out to be only a half-truth. Halakhah commands fathers to teach only their sons to read the law. Historical Jewish exegesis on the Bible has been largely the efforts of highly respected male rabbis answering the questions of other male rabbis. A lack of literacy has for centuries stopped Jewish women from exercising religious authority and ensured male control over legal interpretation. The Orthodox also do not permit women to become rabbis. A woman leading a religious service violates the honor of the community.[6]

Other exclusions exist as well. When a male child is born in a Jewish family, there is a special ceremony for friends and relatives. The child is given a Jewish name and circumcised (the brit milah or bris) eight days following his birth. However, there is no traditional ceremony in honor of the birth of a baby girl. If anything, in the past, a daughter's birth was a disappointment to a Jewish family. Fortunately, today, the non-Orthodox Jewish community has developed special ceremonies to honor the naming of a baby girl.

Later in a child's life, in traditional Judaism only a male becomes *Bar Mitzvah* and formally assumes adult responsibilities at the age of thirteen. A ceremony at the synagogue celebrates the first time he is called to the Torah to recite blessings and chant the *haftarah* (writings from the prophets pertaining to that week's reading of Torah). Thirteen-year-old girls enjoy no traditional formal rite of passage.[7] No fanfare, ceremony, or applause marks their entry into adulthood.

On the other hand, certain mitzvot in Jewish law pertain only to women. Women's obligations reinforce domesticity and female biology. The most significant is the obligation of the mikveh. In traditional Judaism the mensturating woman is a *niddah* ("one who is ostracized"). Because she is unclean, sexual intercourse with a niddah is forbidden for fourteen days. To become pure and able to resume sexual relations with one's husband, an observant Jewish woman must immerse herself in the mikveh, a ritual bath partaken in a specially designed structure for women. She must clean every area of the body scrupulously.

Oddly enough, the mikveh ritual is gaining in popularity among otherwise nonobservant Jewish wives who portray it in glowing terms as an advantage for women. For them, the mikveh is positively feminist. They enjoy being able to count on a special time each month to take leave of their husbands, relax in the company of other women, and develop their own spheres of autonomy. Some Orthodox women insist that the forced separation between husband and wife enhances sexual desire. Nevertheless, associating women with contamination is degrading. The mikveh obligation suggests that the normal female biological cycle is a dirty and shameful experience.

Other social customs also maintain gender hierarchy. Despite evidence that Jewish women attend college at the same rate as Jewish men, some Jews tend to be ambivalent over the education of women. Even today, many non-Orthodox families hold out marriage as the ultimate goal for a daughter, whereas they encourage a son to pursue higher education. In general, Jewish families raise women to believe that their role in life is to preserve the Jewish family and transmit Jewish traditions to the children. In 1980, a Bais Din blamed the rise in Jewish divorces on Jewish women receiving too much education.[8]

The practices of one particular sect in Orthodox Judaism are notably at odds with the popular stereotype of the Jewish regard for education. In the Orthodox Lubavitcher community, schooling is strictly segregated. Boys study Hasidic philosophy for three hours a day; girls, for forty-five minutes. In high school, a boy's day ends at 9:30 p.m.; a girl's at 4:45 p.m. A girl's entire education primarily consists of studying the Bible, the religious holidays, and the Jewish dietary laws. Although most of the boys continue their studies at various yeshivas (Jewish colleges), the girls are given a smattering of higher education at the same school they attended since kindergarten. Lubavitchers view secular learning for both genders as a distraction from religious texts.

Orthodox interpretations of halakhah also cultivate female modesty in dress. The ultra-Orthodox insist on gender-distinct clothing to further reinforce gender roles. Married women wear scarves or wigs to cover their hair when in public to symbolize female modesty and family responsibilities. Dresses must fall close to the ankles, and sleeves must cover the arms. Only opaque stockings are worn, and women are not allowed to wear trousers. Mixed-sex dancing is prohibited. An ultra-Orthodox man will not shake hands with a woman when introduced, lest she arouse sexual longings. Similarly, married women are instructed not to have extended conversations with men who are not their relatives. All of these ingrained sex-based practices, intended to preserve family stability, also inhibit sexuality, constrain self-expression, encourage female passivity, and perpetuate a "separate spheres" philosophy.

In the employment realm, a recent study indicates that Orthodox women require flexible working hours. Because of the demands of the dietary laws and the need to observe the Jewish Sabbath as well as other holidays, they tend to hold part-time positions. They frequently work in Jewish institutions that are willing to accommodate their strict religious practices. Most women remain in female-dominated professions such as library jobs, teaching, nursing, and social work. Hasidic women are less likely than other Orthodox women to have a bachelor's degree and are less able to be employed.

Hasidic women are also seldom involved in activities outside the religious community. They spend more time in informal women's groups that study the Torah, focusing on its dictates on parenting and other family matters. They seldom attend civic, political, or cultural events. They do not subscribe in general to a broad range of secular newspapers or magazines, limiting their reading to a small selection of Jewish publications and family-oriented magazines, such as *Women's Day or Organic Gardening*. Since the *Lubavitcher Hasidim* look to their *Rebbe* (spiritual leader) for advice and guidance on virtually all aspects of their lives, and since the late Rabbi Schneerson, the leader of the Lubavitcher community, denounced commercial television, most Lubavitchers do not own television sets. The lives of Orthodox and ultra-Orthodox women alike are defined almost exclusively by religion and the family.

As a result, there is no role outside of marriage for Jewish Orthodox women. Few adult women are single or divorced, and nearly all are expected to have children. Abortion and contraception are forbidden to the ultra-Orthodox except in limited circumstances. Orthodox women tend to believe they have an ethical and communal responsibility to bear children in light of the Holocaust. The preoccupation with domesticity and religion, which for Orthodox women are one and the same, makes maintaining close social relationships outside their own religious circles difficult. Many newly Orthodox women admit that they feel compelled to distance themselves from their parents and their own extended families because of various tensions that surface over their chosen way of life.

The Orthodox lifestyle engenders deferential women, docile appurtenances to male authority who only serve to complement their men, and lays the groundwork for a battering culture. While feminists bemoan the tendency to view domestic assaults as expressions of private lovemaking and work to break down a secular legal system based on the difference between private and public conduct, a religious subculture within our society enhances gender hierarchy and the private/public distinction through religious ritual, apparel, daily habits, and social interactions. At the same time, this subculture isolates women from possible sources of assistance. In this world, if a woman should resist authoritative cultural uniformity, batterers—experts at rationalizing their behavior—may find excuses within halakhah. . . .

The Impact of the Jewish Divorce System on Woman-Abuse

The refusal of the rabbinical authorities to permit halakhic changes has also caused serious problems for the many Jewish women who need to obtain a Jewish divorce. No area of halakhah has been more contested by Jewish women. Furthermore, although Jewish law and secular law seldom are at odds in this country, a Jewish religious divorce raises secular issues. Many Jewish women, who require both a civil and a religious divorce, ask the state to intervene in the religious tribunal's proceeding and redress their grievances. The interaction between religious law and secular law in the divorce arena demonstrates the limits on state power to empower Jewish battered women. They are sacrificed by the secular system out of constitutional respect for private religious practices and forsaken by the religious authorities for the sake of upholding tradition. Caught between both legal systems, abused women, who surmounted other obstacles to obtain civil restraining orders and civil divorce decrees, find they are still chained to their abusers under Jewish law.

Halakhah permits divorce under certain conditions. This has been an advantage for both women and men in that some unhappy unions may be dissolved. To protect a woman, Jewish law requires that she consent to a divorce proceeding. In addition, it mandates an elaborate premarital agreement (*ketubah*) in which the man promises to pay the woman a sum of money if he should divorce her. In the Jewish legal system, however, only a man creates the marriage and only he has the unilateral power to end it. A marriage cannot dissolve until the husband delivers a get to his wife. Both parties must appear before the Bais Din (usually composed of rabbis, or a male rabbi and two male witnesses). A scribe writes in Aramaic: "I release and set aside you, my wife, in order that you may have authority over yourself to marry any man you desire. . . . You are permitted to every man. . . . This shall be for you a bill of dismissal, a letter of release, a get of freedom. . . ."

The husband then literally places the get into the woman's hands and she formally receives it. After the ceremony, the get is sliced with a knife so that it cannot be used again and turned over to the custody of the officiating rabbi. Both parties receive a petur, a statement of release attesting that they have received a Jewish divorce.

Since battering is a means of control, Jewish law places the Jewish batterer in a unique position to ensure that a woman's fate remains in his hands. Some battered Jewish women, knowing that only the husband is empowered to divorce, view their situation as hopeless. For them, there is no point even in attempting to leave. A civil divorce cannot save her from a tragic and humiliating fate, for without a get, she is an agunah, a woman enchained. An agunah has virtually no standing in the community. As a woman who is neither married nor unmarried (under Jewish law), she still legally belongs to her husband, although they no longer live together as husband and wife.

Unless she has been issued a *get,* an *agunah* is not free to enter into a Jewish marriage even if she has acquired a civil divorce and even if the first marriage only involved a civil ceremony. Any children born of a second marriage, without having first acquired a get, are *mazerim* ("bastards"), the offspring of an adulterous union. Mazerim are shunned and forbidden to marry Jews (although they are Jews) for ten generations and may only marry other mazerim or converts to Judaism. In contrast, the children of a Jewish father who has not obtained a Jewish divorce are not illegitimate. In Jewish law the status of the children depends on the status of the mother. For observant Jewish women whose very identities are centered in marriage and children, obtaining a get is a matter of great importance. They are trapped, unable to rebuild their lives as long as the get issue remains unresolved.

The Babylonian Talmud does allow one procedure for relief. To avoid the fate of becoming an agunah, a woman may appeal to the Bais Din to force her husband to initiate a divorce. Three circumstances warrant a court's intervention: if the husband is afflicted with a disease that is deemed unendurable, if he neglects his marital obligations, or if the couple experiences sexual incompatibility. A diversity of opinion exists in the commentary on whether wife-beating is grounds to compel a divorce. The most respected authorities, Joseph Caro, Maimonides, and Moses Isserles, countenance some degree of woman-hitting and do not permit divorce under all circumstances in which there is evidence of wife-battering. Although a generous reading of Talmudic sources would include domestic violence as sufficient grounds for compelling the issuance of a get, there is no certainty that the exclusively male decision-maker[s] will believe the woman's claim of abuse.

Many communities do not have a standing Bais Din. The laypersons chosen are not always experts on Jewish law and disrespecting its ruling is not an uncommon occurrence. The traditional purpose for requiring the parties to appear before a Bais Din is to persuade the couple to resolve their differences. Furthermore, the husband is in a better position to make sure the all-male court is composed of social or business colleagues who will decide in his favor. Corruption in Batei Din proceedings is notorious.[9] If he is unable to control the court, as a last measure, a husband can simply fail to appear or refuse to comply. A Jewish court, outside of Israel, has no authority to compel adherence to its orders. Empowering religious courts to enforce their rulings would not, in any case, resolve the problem.

Moreover, forcing the husband to deliver the get presents halakhic problems. In theory, he must act voluntarily, forcing a tortuous reasoning process. For example, Jewish law considers the court's order to be a legal obligation. Since a Jew in his heart would not wish to violate religious law by disobeying a rabbinical tribunal, a man has consented to deliver a get of his own free will when ordered by the religious authorities. He complies with the court's

[margin handwriting:] exclusively male decision makers in the divorce appeal process

directive, "rather than the execution of the get per se." In addition, a man acts voluntarily if the coercive circumstances are unrelated to the get. For instance, in the rabbinical commentary, a man thrown into debtor's prison was released by his wife's relatives on condition that he obtain a get. Because he was not imprisoned for failure to issue the get, he was found to have acted of his volition.

The woman victim and her community may also indirectly exercise coercion. Orthodox women have become particularly skilled in this area. They live near each other in small communities in which they share similar lifestyles. They spend most of their time in the company of other women and have developed a strong sense of sisterly solidarity. They have been known to resort to self-help, such as posting the husband's name and picture in public places, organizing economic boycotts, and even hiring gangs to beat up recalcitrant husbands. A group of Orthodox women in Montreal refused to attend the mikveh bath until the men in their community persuaded an obstinate husband to deliver a get. One Orthodox woman went to the Committee to Free Agunot, a local group of residents and Orthodox rabbis. It organized more than two hundred people to gather in front of her in-law's home in Brooklyn, New York. Rabbis told the crowd of the shame this man brought to the community. Rallies and demonstrations continued for weeks. Six years after the woman first asked her husband for a get, she finally received it. In 1987, an Orthodox rabbi, president of the New York Board of Rabbis, urged the one thousand rabbis in the organization to take action against men who refuse the get, including denying them synagogue membership and honors.

Women have no choice but self-help in these situations insofar as the secular authorities hesitate to intervene. The traditional constitutional function of religious freedom in this country respects the right to practice religious beliefs in conformance with that particular faith's forms of worship and customs. In Judaism, this necessarily includes the right to maintain a religious legal system because the religious law is integral to practice. Since respecting religious rights usually amounts to a secular court's withdrawal from a religious conflict under the rubric of the Establishment Clause, the secular system has made refusal easy for these men. A husband need only couch his refusal to deliver a get as a defense of his religious freedom. If a civil court directly orders the issuance of a get, the court arguably advances one particular theology, and the action is thereby impermissibly entangled in religion.

A husband's refusal to deliver a get is not likely to be motivated by a sincere religious conviction, however. Rather, he is more likely to be motivated by spite or the desire to punish his wife. Oftentimes the husband uses his power to extort custody or money in exchange for the get of freedom. This is *chutzpah,* not religion. Respecting religious faith under the Establishment Clause should not grant men the right to keep women in dead marriages. By failing to act, courts privilege criminal assaults in the name of private religious freedom. At such times, the state must become involved in religious practices for women to receive the equal protection of the law. In fact, the state is already embroiled in the get controversy because Jewish women have raised the *not to mention the inadequacies of secular responses to issues of domestic violence overall*

issue in civil divorce cases and Jewish authorities in some areas have requested that legislation be passed to alleviate the plight of the agunot. . .

In conclusion, until all Jews acknowledge women as the equals of men, secular law reform is only a partial solution to the get problem. <u>Jewish women today must bargain with their batterers, buy their freedom, and accept less than they deserve</u>. Regardless of civil laws aimed at protecting battered women, many Jewish women will continue to remain hostages as long as the various Jewish denominations refuse to unite. By clothing power in the garb of religious faith, Jewish traditionalists circumvent the society's attempts to curtail violence against women: Jewish law constructs gender relationships along lines of authority and control, Jewish rituals can encode negative gender references, Jewish cultural upbringing can often reinforce traditional, rigid, gender-role boundaries, and Jewish religious texts at times tolerate woman-abuse. Lastly, the Jewish legal system undermines the escape attempts of its own battered women. In the next section, I place battered Jewish women in the forefront and attempt to describe their reactions to their battering situations.

EXPERIENCING A BATTERING CULTURE

Imagine the difficulties facing Orthodox battered women.[10] First of all, <u>it may be difficult for them to interpret their situation as abusive, given their submissive role in life.</u> They must see past a belief system in which devotion to one's family and the honor of one's husband define a woman's identity. <u>Even if willing to leave their batterers, quite often they are ill-equipped to become self-supporting.</u> They <u>lack money</u> and have <u>restricted career options</u> because of their religious practices. They have <u>limited contacts with the non-Orthodox and secular worlds</u>. Hasidic women in particular, trained to be totally dependent on men, are frequently not sufficiently educated to survive on their own. <u>Community mores dictate that Orthodox women turn to their rabbis</u> for advice, instead of calling the police, a social worker, or a psychologist. Unfortunately, these rabbis rarely suggest that a woman should obtain a restraining order or see a therapist.[11] More often, <u>rabbis tell them to try harder to please their husbands for the sake of *shalom bayit*</u>. Orthodox rabbis tend to discount the pervasiveness of woman-beating in their own communities.[12] These women are also reluctant to pursue professional help because they <u>believe they harm the reputation of all Jews.</u> Because Jewish law forbids lies, gossip, and defamatory speech, in publicizing their abuse, Jewish women are seen as violating Jewish law.

Additionally, Jewish women could fear contact with a non-Jewish professional or even a non-Orthodox Jew. Conversing with a nonrelative, especially a man, about one's intimate life is a strange and shameful experience. A newly Orthodox Jewish woman who is estranged from her parents could feel she cannot return to her former home, thus denying herself this avenue of relief. A shelter is only a possibility if Orthodox women are able to continue their

religious and dietary observances. Hasidic women also need assurance ¡
their children will not be exposed to television.[13] Few shelters can meet th{
needs; however, a growing number of groups such as Safe Homes Advice ar
Legal Aid for Victims of Abuse (SHALVA) in Chicago, *Shalom Bayit* in San
Francisco, as well as a number of groups in Los Angeles, have established
shelters and other services which accommodate Jewish women's needs.[14] Despite the presence of such services in a select group of communities, if an Orthodox woman decides to end her marriage, her batterer controls the Jewish
divorce proceeding and a religious court, less understanding than the secular
system of her contributions to the marriage, decides her entitlements.

Moreover, <u>suggesting divorce to an Orthodox woman is akin to directing
her to shed her identity and Judaism itself</u>. A life of abuse among her own
people could seem preferable to risking the loss of all that has shaped her existence. These women are often embedded in unusually close-knit communities tied together by a value system in which their roles as wives and mothers
give coherence and sanctity to daily living. We ask them to forfeit their place
in an extended family rooted in social stability in exchange for secular chaos,
moral uncertainty, and economic insecurity. It is difficult, indeed, for us to be
sure we are right in telling them to leave.

The situation of non-Orthodox Jewish battered women more readily lends
itself to relief. Nonetheless, there is no reliable statistic that would justify assuming woman-abuse is more severe in Orthodox communities. In fact, one
study suggests that higher income Jewish families have a greater number of
violent incidents than lower income Jewish families.[15] Although ritual observances are long forgotten, sexist cultural attitudes may still prevail, as seen in
one study by Mimi Scarf.[16] Like their Orthodox sisters, more assimilated
Jews are raised to believe that the Jewish husband is intelligent, generous,
and seldom violent. Parents instill the romantic myth of the perfect Jewish
family, depicting the home as a haven of domestic peace in which all Jews are
ensconced, safe from the outside world. Wife-beating seems alien, something
beyond the Jewish experience. Families caution Jewish women against anti-
Semites, racists, and neo-Nazis—not Jewish men. Yet, there are telling signs
in Jewish culture that suggest the fallacy of these myths. Jewish men created
caricatures about Jewish women, and these gender stereotypes are symbolic
representations of actual power relationships. Jewish men manifest sexist resentment and hostility by reducing Jewish women to a joke. . . . The Jewish
wife or girlfriend is also the scapegoat for the rage and frustration a man feels
as a member of a minority group, an anger that he cannot ventilate in public.
Even worse, Jewish women tend to internalize their negative stereotyping
and learn to hate themselves.

Furthermore, romantic myths concerning Jewish family life paralyze many
Jewish battered women, preventing them from obtaining help and stopping
professional caregivers from recognizing that they are battered when they
eventually seek counseling. Unable to believe what is happening in their lives
and afraid to confide in parents, friends, or therapists, they live with tremendous guilt and shame. Raised to assume sole responsibility for maintaining

the family and preserving the Jewish people, their battering signifies their failure to be good Jewish wives and mothers.

Partly due to the hostility of the larger societies in which they have lived, Jews tend to place heavy emphasis on family life and stress the importance of the woman's role in ensuring that Jewish values and Jewish traditions are imparted to the children. The wife/mother is also the bulwark against trends to assimilate into the greater culture. Cast into the position of perpetuating the existence of the Jews and judged according to their performances as wives and mothers, Jewish women inevitably fail to measure up to such impossible standards.

Moreover, Jewish women are burdened with powerful images of their immigrant foremothers, those formidable *yiddishe mamas.* The traditional immigrant Jewish mother, starved for food, for love, and for an education, sacrificed herself for the sake of her husband and sons. Also, many Jewish women have learned to place their marriages ahead of their careers, and they may be financially dependent on their husbands. The batterer may even be supporting his wife's parents. It might be difficult to contemplate living without a husband's economic support. Seeing no point in seeking help and too ashamed to discuss their beatings, they remain silent victims.

The women in Mimi Scarf's study also keep their abuse secret from their children. She found that Jewish women insulate their sons and daughters from witnessing their beatings. They precipitate approaching battering incidents so that the beating is over before the children come home from school. At night, they muffle their screams when hit by their men rather than upset the children. If a Jewish woman eventually divulges her secret, she might seem only the complaining, over-indulged Jewish princess, unaccustomed to the hard work and daily grind that a marriage plus children entails. If she informs her family of her abuse, she is likely to be told he is a "nice Jewish boy" from a good family, hardworking, makes a good living, and so on. Her in-laws tell her it is all her fault.

Jewish women also face other difficulties that deter them from revealing their abuse. They worry that they will encounter anti-Semitism at non-Jewish agencies and are reluctant to discuss their intimate lives with non-Jewish professionals. They also are concerned with damaging their husbands' reputations in the community. For the same reason, modern Jewish women seldom discuss their abuse with rabbis. Uncomfortable with strangers and unwilling to disclose their problems to other Jews in the community, these women are truly alone.

In addition, some Jewish women who are battered are also Holocaust survivors. For them, physical abuse is modest consideration in return for the opportunity to create new Jewish lives. Their families symbolize the resurrection of the Jews despite attempts at genocide. Many accept their beatings, seeing them as trivial in comparison to what they have already endured. Holocaust consciousness, on some level, could influence all battered Jewish women. At times, the overwhelming hold of this tragic experience on Jewish sensibility causes Jews to downplay and avoid other more immediate issues.

Holocaust consciousness could lead Jewish battered women to feel guilty if they complain and possibly to assume that they deserve less sympathy than those who suffered in the past.

When their beatings require medical attention, some Jewish women find physicians or emergency care away from their own local communities. They adopt false names and pay in cash out of the small amounts they have managed to hoard away from their batterers who often strictly monitor and control family finances. They would not dare call the police, unable to conceive of flashing lights and a husband being led away in handcuffs in the middle of the night in a "nice" Jewish neighborhood. That is a great *shanda,* a blight on the family that could destroy a husband's good name. It is also an open admission that the woman is a failure. For these reasons, Jewish women remain in their abusive situations longer than [many] other women.[17]

If they eventually divorce, Jewish wives are unable to prove in court that they have been abused. Frequently, there is no history of arrests or restraining orders documenting their abuse. These middle-class, relatively affluent abusers seldom possess criminal records and do not appear violent. Often they are the social acquaintances of the sitting judges and are rabbis, accountants, doctors, college professors, neighbors, and lawyers. The negative imagery surrounding Jewish women can also work to their disadvantage in deciding custody, alimony, and property. Society again assumes that Jewish men revere their stereotypically undeserving wives. Moreover, because Jewish men have largely succeeded in assimilating into the greater middle-class, they cannot be distanced into the violent Other. In acknowledging the Jewish batterer, we implicate ourselves. For Jewish battered women to become visible, the middle class must admit that they are the batterers. . . .

CONCLUSION

Battered and disenfranchised Jewish women deserve more from their Jewish brethren than pretty pictures of halakhic reasoning to serve as models for the secular system to emulate. They need an identity politic that remembers that they too are Jews. That would be an authentic *nomos* for all in the Jewish community. The religious impulse felt by many men and women—a sense of spirituality and a belief in a creator as the source of morality—is worthy of respect. We do not respect that impulse when we create social and religious practices that exclude women or constrain them from escaping physical and emotional harm.

I believe Jews are obligated to grant Jewish women public status. The problem of battering in the Jewish community cannot be addressed as long as Jewish women are viewed as private persons, hidden from public scrutiny. In light of the many problems these women encounter, one would expect the Jewish legal community to have rushed to their defense. One would assume that law school professors and legal scholars, in particular, would have the insight and knowledge to underscore the deadly combination of factors—insular cultural traditions acting in combination with a gender-biased secular law—that leads to the oppression of Jewish women. Legal scholars should be in the vanguard, suggesting changes and challenging discriminatory attitudes that reflect poorly on all Jews. [Thus,] I criticize the neglect of women's issues in the writings of Jewish professors and point out that Jewish identity politics, the tendency to present rabbinical thought as a flawless, archetypical jurisprudence, also plays a role in maintaining a battering culture. [This too must change.]

NOTES

I thank my colleague Peter Margulies for all his good advice. I also thank Janice Weintraub and Joan Childs, psychiatric social workers who helped me contact Jewish battered women in my community. I appreciate the dedication of my research assistants, Jacki Cannavan and Julie Shapiro, as well.

1. In order to protect the privacy of the women I interviewed, I have given them biblical names. I am grateful to the many Jewish psychiatric social workers who helped me contact the women I interviewed.

2. See Elizabeth M. Schneider, 1992, Particularity and generality: Challenges of feminist theory and practice in work on woman-abuse, *New York University Law Review* 67: 520, 568, urging us to link battering to the general problem of sexism without losing sight of the particularity of an individual battered woman's experience.

3. Hedda Nussbaum was beaten for years by her lover, Joel Steinberg, who eventually murdered their illegally adopted daughter Lisa Steinberg. See Ann Jones, 1994, *Next Time, She'll Be Dead: Battering and How To Stop It* (1994: 167–198), for a vivid account of Hedda Nussbaum's injuries. Yet despite her suffering, some writers blamed her for failing to save her child. See, for example, Susan Brownmiller, 1989, Hedda Nussbaum, Hardly a heroine, *New York Times,* Feb. 2, A25. Others were more understanding. See, for example, Martha Minow, 1990, Words and the door to the land of change: Law, language, and family violence, *Vanderbilt Law Review* 43: 1665, 1678–1683.

4. Estimates vary depending on the study and the year in which it occurred. See, for example, Jewish Family Service [Ft. Lauderdale, Fla.], 1994, *What Is Family Violence?,* which states that between one-fourth and one-third of all American Jewish families experience domestic violence. . . .

5. There is no single authoritative system in Judaism. Even within Jewish denominations practices may vary. Lines between modern Orthodox, Conservative, and Reform are not firm. Cultural factors influence practices as well. The Sephardim (those of Spanish descent) have different customs than the Ashkenazim (those of German descent). Any classification is, to some extent, an oversimplification.

6. See Susan W. Schneider, 1985, *Jewish and Female: A Guide and Source Book for Today's Jewish Woman,* 52. The Jewish Theological Seminary (the Conservative school) voted in 1983 to allow women to be ordained after years of lobbying and pressure. The Reform movement officially accepted women as rabbis in the nineteenth century. However, a woman was not actually ordained until 1972 (53). Reconstructionist Jews also permit women to become rabbis. They are also more acceptable to these congregations than to other sects in Judaism. Women, however, have played an active part in synagogue ritual since the onset of the Reconstructionist movement (73).

7. Ibid., 134–135. In Orthodoxy, a girl automatically becomes an adult one day after her twelfth birthday. Reconstructionist, Reform, and some Conservative congregations have introduced the Bat Mitzvah, a ceremony for girls paralleling the Bar Mitzvah. Even though some Orthodox daughters become Bat Mitzvah, it is controversial. See Moshe Meiselman, 1978, *Jewish Women in Jewish Law,* 61, maintaining that Bat Mitzvah "mock[s] the entire structure

of Judaism . . . to invest these celebrations with . . . detailed rituals." Some Reform temples have abandoned the Bat Mitzvah and instead hold Confirmation ceremonies at the end of high school. S. Schneider, *Jewish and Female,* 134.

8. E. Schneider, Particularity and generality, 554. Schneider argues that a Jewish woman tends to be raised to believe that intellectual achievement matters less than one's marriage. Furthermore, she is cautioned that if she appears to be extremely intelligent, she alienates men. She should be smart, but not too smart.

9. This information has been provided to me anecdotally by several rabbis and Jewish attorneys who have been involved in Batei Din procedures. Irving Breitowitz notes: "[I]t cannot be denied that in more than a few cases, litigants' contentions that the . . . judges are not neutral or are not learned have been borne out. . . . Even litigants acting in bad faith escape the wrath of their communities by alleging bias. . . ." S. Schneider, *Jewish and Female,* 328.

10. I realize I risk gender essentialism in classifying all Orthodox women as exhibiting the same or similar reactions to domestic abuse. Individuals within a social group defy categorization; nonetheless, identifying group interests and concerns may enable us to help these "special" battered women overcome problems they share that are connected to their Jewish upbringing. I therefore take license to engage in what I hope will be some useful generalizations.

11. See Rabbi Julie Ringold Spitzer, 1991, *When Love Is Not Enough: Spousal Abuse in Rabbinic and Contemporary Judaism,* 25. One woman, beaten for years, was sixty years old when she left her husband and entered a shelter. The rabbi called her and convinced her to return home. When she again entered the shelter after another beating, the rabbi convinced her to give the husband a second chance. The third time she sought refuge (she suffered a broken rib), the rabbi again advised her to come home. He told her that her husband wanted to repent by taking her to visit the Holy Land (24).

12. For instance, one rabbi asked a battered woman how many times she had been beaten. He went on to say, "Let's assume once a month. That's only twelve times a year. That does not make sense to get divorced." See ibid., 24. Another told an audience that in the thirty years he had been a rabbi he had never heard of a single incident of spousal abuse. At the time he spoke, three women in his congregation were clients of the Family Violence Project in Los Angeles. See Naomi Levy, 1988, Two shelters, one threat, *Lilith,* Summer, 8.

On the other hand, there are caring rabbis and Jewish women's organizations who play an active role in educating the Jewish community. B'nai B'rith Women, for example, mailed a sermon and fact sheet on woman-beating to rabbis nationwide before the 1994 October High Holidays, encouraging them to speak out on the topic (on file with the Harvard Women's Law Journal).

13. Telephone Conversation with Carolyn Fish, director of a shelter that cares for Jewish battered women in Rockland County, New York, Apr. 19, 1994.

14. See Elizabeth R. deBeer, 1988, Wife abuse, drugs, and silence, *Lilith,* Summer, 9. In Chicago, SHALVA provides private homes as havens for these women. It was started by a group of Orthodox women leaders after hearing a rabbi's wife speak on the topic of Jewish domestic violence. [A further list of domestic violence help for Jewish battered women can be found in San Francisco at Shalom Bayit; in Los Angeles Orthodox Jews staff a noncrisis phone line called Ezras Bayit ("Help in the Home") and a shelter, Shiloh. Other shelters and resources exist in Far Rockaway, New York, Toronto, Houston, Baltimore, Boston, Minnneapolis, and Philadelphia.

15. See Marlene Adler Marks, 1988, Abuse in Jewish families is no secret anymore, *Jewish Journal,* Nov. 27–Dec. 3, 15. There is no reliable statistic on whether woman-abuse is more severe in one particular Jewish community over another. Others maintain the problem may be especially acute among the Orthodox, particularly the Hasidim. See Lynne Ames, 1991, B'nai B'rith assisting battered Jewish women, *New York Times,* Oct. 6, 6. . . . In Israel, domestic violence is believed to be a problem in all religious, ethnic, and socioeconomic subcultures. See Shira Leibowitz, 1988, Two shelters, one threat, *Lilith,* Summer, 8. Powerful social pressures lead two-thirds of the women who seek refuge in a shelter to return to their husbands. Ibid.

16. See Mimi Scarf, 1988, Marriages made in heaven? Battered Jewish wives, in *On Being a Jewish Feminist,* 51, 61–62, emphasizing the disadvantages Jewish battered women face because they are influenced by idealistic myths concerning Jewish family life and cannot overcome the community's denial of the problem of domestic violence. Mimi Scarf interviewed two hundred people and nearly one hundred Jewish battered women; see ibid., 63 n.2.

17. Jewish women remain in the home on the average of eight to ten years. Non-Jewish women begin to take action three to five years after the initial battering episode. Spitzer, *When Love Is Not Enough,* 26.

SELECTED REFERENCES

[Please note that for a full listing of references, go to Lexis Nexis. Below are a few key references suggested by the author for your perusal.]

Adler, Rachel. 1983. The Jew who wasn't there. In Susannah Herschel, ed., *On Being A Jewish Feminist.* New York: Schocken, 12–17.

Biale, Rachel. 1984. *Women at Jewish Law: An Exploration of Women's Issues in Halakhic Sources.* New York: Schocken.

Breitowitz, Irving. 1992. The plight of the Agunah: A study in Halacha, contract, and the first amendment. *Maryland Law Review* 51: 312–421.

Greenberg, Blu. 1977. Jewish divorce law: If we must part, let's part as equals. *Lilith,* Spring/Summer 1(3).

Harris, Lis. 1985. A reporter at large: Lubavitcher Hasidim part II. *New Yorker,* September 23, 57, 85–87, 98.

Horsburgh, Beverly. 1993. Jewish women, Black women: Guarding against the oppression of surrogacy. *Berkeley Women's Law Journal* 8: 29, 57, 61.

Leibowitz, Shira. 1988. Two shelters, one threat. *Lilith,* Summer, 8.

Lipstadt, Debra. 1983. And Deborah made ten. In Susannah Herschel, ed., *On Being A Jewish Feminist.* New York: Schocken, 207–209.

Scarf, Mimi. 1988. *Battered Jewish Wives: Case Studies in the Response to Rage.* New York: Edwin Mellen.

Spitzer, Rabbi Julie. 1991. *When Love Is Not Enough: Spousal Abuse in Rabbinic and Contemporary Judaism.* New York: Women of Reform Judaism, National Federation of Temple Sisterhoods.

CHAPTER 15

LOIS WEIS, MICHELLE FINE, AMIRA PROWELLER, CORRINE BERTRAM, AND JULIA MARUSZA

"I've Slept in Clothes Long Enough"

Excavating the Sounds of Domestic Violence among Women in the White Working Class

──────────── ABSTRACT ────────────

Just as Christianity was an unmarked category in chapter 14's discussion of domestic violence in the Orthodox Jewish community, so too whiteness is typically an unmarked category—the assumed norm—in most discussions of domestic violence in the United States. In this chapter we learn about poor and working-class white women whose embodiment of whiteness is gendered; that is, they tell us that to be a white working-class woman, in part, means to desire a stable, intact family, with a husband able to support it within a globalized economy that has increasingly made that goal difficult, if not impossible, to achieve. Moreover, in their hopes to be self sufficient, some women try to hold on to their whiteness by stereotyping and disparaging African-American women who obtain state assistance to survive. How this impacts on white working-class women's own safety is also a matter of concern.

In this study of thirty white women from two cities in the northeastern United States, two distinct groups of white working-class women emerge: "settled lives" women and "hard living" women. The "hard living" women have left their violent homes, thereby exposing their "private troubles" to public view; the "settled lives" women have not left because, if they did so, then they could pay the price of becoming "hard living." Both groups talk about violence and despair, resistance and hope. And both groups talk about violence in their lives from very early on—whether against themselves or other women and girls in their families.

The women from both groups reported disturbingly high rates of domestic violence. Although settled living women seldom criticized men or the idealized family, hard living women spoke readily about the violence. But they were too often teetering on the brink of poverty and homelessness to be heard. As the settled lives women remained with their partners, they tried hard to hang on to the ideal image of the stable, intact family despite their lived realities of being abused, overworked, burdened by the majority of household responsibilities, and stressed to financially make ends meet. They tended to characterize the abuse as something that had only occurred in the past.

But even the women who had left abusive relationships continued to experience violence and abuse in their lives. For some, exiting the traditional family led to a temporary respite from violence—and almost assuredly poverty—at least in the short run. However, the authors note, they did not talk about violence in *new* relationships since they left their former abusive partners.

With the substantial loss of decent paying jobs in their communities, cuts in social programs, and the subsequent necessity for women to work as wage-earners as well as primary caretakers in the family, these women represent a generation of white working-class women who are suffering as women of color have long suffered under an economy that is crushing the working class. Rather than reach out in solidarity with poor and working-class Black women, Weis and her colleagues describe how racism successfully divides these groups.

As you read this chapter, think about how whiteness acts as a barrier to safety for these women. Be clear about how racist perspectives on poverty inform these white working-class women's responses to violence. And think about comparisons between white working-class women's experiences of domestic violence and those of Black, Native American, Orthodox Jewish, and lesbian women of color you have read about thus far.

I didn't have the luxury of sleeping in pajamas as a kid. I always slept in my pants and in my shirt because you never knew what time of the night the fight was going to break out and what you had to do. Because you might have to run out of the house and go call the cops because they [my parents] ripped the phone out of the wall and are choking each other to death. You never knew. So I never had that relaxing point of crawling into bed, which is part of my other phobia now. I don't sleep with any clothes on.
      —Suzanne, a thirty-one-year-old white mother of four

INTRODUCTION

In this chapter, we analyze the lives of white working-class women in two contemporary, deindustrialized urban communities. Drawing from qualitative narratives gathered from individual and group interviews with poor and working-class white women in the urban Northeast, we listened to and analyzed the experiences of violence and despair, and resistance and hope,

From *The Urban Review* 30, no. 1 (1998): 1–27. Reprinted with kind permission from the authors and Kluwer Academic Publishers.

articulated by the women in this race and class fraction. In our two-city sample, it was, initially, quite easy to distinguish between women living in these two presumably distinct domestic scenes. According to Howell's (1972) categories, "settled lives" women survive within what seem to be stable, intact family structures. In deceptively simple contrast, "hard living" women float between different types of households, move in and out of welfare, and have less education and more (low-paying) employment. Despite these apparent differences, however, our analysis led us to conclude that almost all of these poor and working-class white women and their families were negotiating lives disrupted by an inhospitable economy, and almost all of these women were also surviving within scenes of domestic violence that had spanned generations. The distinction between the "settled lives" women and the "hard living" women may, sadly, be determined only by whether the woman has *left* her violent home. While current political debates romanticize the "settled lives" woman (the good woman who stays home, cares for her children and husband, and "plays by the rules") and demonize the "hard living" woman (the bad woman who leaves her home, lives in poverty, flees her husband/boyfriend, and relies intermittently upon social services), our data suggest that both of these groups of women come from the same communities, have endured equivalent levels of violence, and differ only in the extent to which they expose their "private troubles" to public view (Wright Mills, 1959).

That these two groups of women actually live very similar domestic contexts is particularly disturbing as welfare "reform" debates contend that "hard living" women are lazy, irresponsible, and unwilling to commit to family life. Our data contest these claims and suggest, instead, that poor and working-class white women, whether they "stick it out" or "leave," are faced with high levels of domestic violence. Those women who leave the "ideal" (if violent) married domestic space for a "safer" public sphere on welfare are today being disparaged in part because they expose the fundamental *fallacies* of the family wage and domestic ideologies—ideologies which have been so sacredly believed in the United States. Because of the "hard living" women, the image of the comfortable and stable white working-class family is beginning to shatter.

In this analysis, social class is understood as individual and collective relationships to the means of production (Sennett and Cobb, 1972; Halle, 1984). We categorized the participants in this study as coming from working-class backgrounds based upon an analysis of area census tract data spanning close to a century as well as individual oral histories of family relations to work. The narrations of these white women, moreover, indicate historical connections to working-class life in terms of education and periodic reliance on public assistance. Because of a restructuring economy, however, many of these women and their families had also experienced poverty and thus had frequently shifted between working-class and poor modes of existence. In describing some of these women as poor, we include those individuals (themselves and their families) who stood completely outside the U.S. occupational system or those who had experienced long-term unemployment (Wilson, 1987).

This analysis of working-class and poor women reflects feminist thinking on this subject. Feminist scholarship has taken very seriously the dominance of men in the working-class family and the ways in which the historical struggle for the family wage has privileged white men in both the site of the wage-earning workplace and the home/family space. This scholarship, however, represents a specific look at *white* working-class women. Middle-class white women and women from other cultural backgrounds across classes have a very different set of struggles revolving around the wage-earning sector and the home/family sphere. For African-American women, for example, a wage-earning male in the household could never be assumed insofar as racism prevented African-American men from obtaining the types of jobs that white working-class men were able to obtain. Thus the dynamics for these two groups were, and remain, very different (hooks, 1981, 1989; Weis, 1990; Davis, 1981; Giddings, 1984).

CONTEMPORARY WHITE WORKING-CLASS WOMEN AND DOMESTIC VIOLENCE

While the white women whom we interviewed did not see themselves living in an "ideal" family structure—that is, they admitted that they worked too much, that their partners earned too little, and that "home work" was still theirs—they also reported, with far less criticism, extraordinarily high rates of domestic violence. Across both cities [Jersey City, New Jersey, and Buffalo, New York] and both types of "living," we documented abuse in 92 percent of the interviews. These women had been severely, and in many cases repeatedly, abused by a parent, an early lover, or a current husband/boyfriend and/or had a sister that was currently being abused. These poor and working-class white women, however, seldom criticized men and family, and all discussed abuse as if it had been experienced only in the past. Although "hard living" and "settled lives" women negotiate the secret of male violence in different ways, the data suggest that women from both groups learn to arrange their lives around the violence that erupts behind closed doors.

The literature on male violence against women spans a number of areas: discussions of the battered women's shelter movement (Shechter, 1982); manuals on how to escape violent situations (White, 1985; Nicarthy, 1989); legal issues surrounding such violence (Fineman and Mykitiuk, 1994); and empirical and theoretical explorations involving what domestic violence is, what causes it, and to what it is related (Dobash, 1979; Walker, 1984; Steinmetz and Strauss, 1974; Jones, 1994; Roy, 1977; Hanmer and Maynard, 1987; Hoff, 1990). In the last category, discussions cover stressors that are linked to domestic violence such as alcohol abuse, satisfaction with one's life situation and partner, and the extent to which such violence is linked to social class. While it is widely argued that violence in the home appears across social classes, it is now generally acknowledged that there is more of it in poor and working-class families. While alcohol abuse is linked to violence, the removal of alcohol does not necessarily guarantee that violence will end (Downs et al., 1993).

Rare in the literature are portraits of male violence against women drawn from *within* communities, across race/ethnicity and social classes. Specifically, we do not have research that locates white women at the intersection of their own class, race, and gender, producing both lived realities regarding violence in the home and women's responses to such violence. While we recognize individual variation in such responses, we also wish to emphasize that the intersectionalities explored in this analysis may lead to important questions and generalizations about raced and gendered communities. In addition, there is very little literature that explicitly explores the relationship between gendered violence and race, especially among those who are white. Very few studies focus specifically on the experience of violence in the home within racial groupings and the ways in which racially distinct life experiences may be linked to expressions of violence and reactions to such violence (White, 1985; Marsh, 1993; Coley and Beckett, 1988).

One study that did attend closely to dynamics of class and race, within gender, was conducted by Kurz (1995), who randomly sampled divorced women from Philadelphia (*n* = 129) and found that *across classes and races,* a full 70 percent of these women had experienced violence at the hands of their husbands at least once. What started out as a study of divorce quickly and dramatically evolved into a study of domestic violence. Within her sample, Kurz also identified a set of family characteristics that included violence, alcohol abuse, drug abuse, and husbands' absence from the home. Kurz found these characteristics to be disproportionately reflective of life in poor and working-class white homes. Concerned about the effects that alcohol and drugs, in particular, had on themselves and their children, many of these women left their partners. Kurz's sample is strikingly similar in narrations and demographics to our sample, in which an overwhelming majority of the white women we interviewed reported childhood abuse (physical or sexual) and/or adult domestic abuse at the hands of a father, a mother's boyfriend, or the woman's husband or her boyfriend. In our research, however, the conditions of "hard living" spanned the seeming "stability" of families, whether the woman was currently married or not. In order to contribute to the debate over the need for public services to serve women and children in flight from violence, we need more in-depth studies of the ways in which communities of women within class and race groupings narrate their experiences with violence in the home as well as their responses to this violence. Spaces ultimately need to be located and then pried open in which women can participate in a collective discussion of the violence that emanates from gender arrangements inside some poor and working-class white families.

URBAN WHITE WORKING-CLASS WOMEN TODAY: A CONTEMPORARY SAMPLE

Our data derive from a large-scale Spencer Foundation project that was designed to capture the narrations of low-income white, African-American, and Latino/Latina men and women, ages twenty-three to thirty-five, as to what their life had been like since leaving high school. As part of this project, we probed their early family life as well as their current situations concerning issues of family, schooling, employment, social activism, religion, and neighborhood/community. One hundred fifty-four individuals were interviewed in Jersey City and Buffalo. Interviews were between three and five hours long. Interviewees were drawn from "self-selected and meaningful urban communities," such as Head Start programs, welfare offices, literary centers, churches, parenting groups in schools, and community organizations such as Hispanics United and the Urban League. In addition, extensive focus group interviews were held among targeted groups. For example, we held focus groups with white working-class women who currently had their children enrolled in a Diocesan elementary school. All interviewees were selected by the gatekeepers of each of the organizations with which we worked or were nominated by their peers. We highlight this set of points only to indicate that all of our interviewees were currently connected to meaningful networks and did not represent, in all likelihood, the most alienated individuals within any given community. Many of these poor and white working-class women, however, were self-described as estranged from kin insofar as they were the ones "left behind" in communities of concentrated poverty, while more fortunate siblings had fled "up" and out to the suburbs. These, then, were poor and working-class white women from varying communities, who continued to find themselves ensnared in the structural inequities of the U.S. class system.

For this analysis, our sample included thirty white women from Buffalo, New York, and Jersey City, New Jersey. Buffalo is a community of relatively "stable" working-class households, in which white men, until quite recently, enjoyed a rich economy of manufacturing and other unionized blue-collar positions. Hit by a dramatic sweep of deindustrialization in the 1970s and early 1980s, Buffalo's white working class today has suffered from downward mobility relative to the previous generation. In vivid contrast, Jersey City is a port city on the northeast coast, textured in languages, cultures, and dense communities of recent immigrants, suffering since the 1950s the loss of working-class and blue-collar jobs. A much more transient and less "stable" city, Jersey City prides itself on ethnic diversity and access to New York City and has become one of the "experimental" sites for new "welfare reform" policies.

FAMILY WAGE LITERATURE

As the white women at our sites narrated their experiences, they revealed that they had historical relationships to working-class life, most having had fathers and grandfathers who worked in factories and plants and mothers who stayed home to raise children. Dorothy Smith (1987) and others have argued that the working-class family has been characterized by a marked subordination of women to men. An implicit contract between husband and wife stipulates that she will provide the household and personal services demanded, in return for which he will provide for her and her children whatever he deems appropriate. Thus the household is organized in relation to his needs and wishes: mealtimes are when he wants them; he eats with the children or alone, as he chooses; sex is when he desires it; the children are to be kept quiet when he does not want to hear them. The wife knows at the back of her mind that he could take his wage-earning capacity and make a similar "contract" with another woman.

Over the past two decades, numerous scholars interested in class and gender have attested to the conditions of white working-class women's lives, focusing on the notion of the "family wage" as a contributing factor to their experience. Martha May (1987) suggests, on the basis of a study of the Ford Motor Company, that the family wage as ideology became and remained important because it appeared advantageous to *all* family members. To achieve this goal, however, this ideology rigidly deployed and maintained existing gender distinctions in work/domestic roles. For employers, the ideology of the family wage held out the possibility of lowered wages for some workers (mainly women) and a stable workforce whereby industry could amass long-term profits. By linking gender roles and subsistence for the working class, the family wage ideology successfully reinforced the notion that women should receive lower wages than men or stay at home. Woodcock Tentler (1979) contends that, although many white working-class women historically were in the wage labor force before marriage, their wage work experiences failed to alter their dependence on the family since nearly all jobs available to women offered less security and status than did the role of wife and mother, and many jobs were no longer available to women once they became wives and/or pregnant. Thus, for white working-class women, life outside the family offered little economic protection and was not seen as being as respectable as work within the home.

While the family wage literature presumes a situation in which the man works full time with benefits, and the wife stays at home with the children, our data reveal this was not the case for our sample of contemporary poor and working-class white women. Most of the women in this sample were employed, with jobs that were mostly clerical and did not pay well, to be sure. At the time of our study, *all* married/attached women had husbands/boyfriends who were currently employed in blue-collar jobs or civil service blue-collar work such as security and other city employment. The prospects for employment for these men, however, seemed to be dwindling. So, too, were the women's expectations that men would support their wives and children. Some of these women and their families, in fact, continually fell in and out of working-class and poor modes of existence. Donna, the oldest woman in our sample at forty, narrated what she saw as a decline in gender role expectations evolving since she was growing up:[1]

> I was taught to stay home, cook, clean, take care of my children. These girls—nah, they're taught to just go out, dress up, leave their kids with other people. They're not taught anything. Well, I'm glad my daughter doesn't do that.

I mean, we take my granddaughter at times and keep her with us, but there's times that she—ya know—she'll take her and spend a couple of weeks with her, and then we'll—she'll come back with us for a couple of days. So we help her out a lot. They worked [men in the past]. They had jobs. I mean, they didn't stay in school. They quit as soon as they were of age and they worked. The men today don't work. Teenagers, rather. They don't work. They just bum off their girlfriends, or their mothers. There's—there's mothers that are goin' to school with me, that have their seventeen-year-old sons livin' with them, cuz they have to. But they don't work, and their mother's givin' them money, buying their clothes, and they don't go to school; they play hooky from school. The one girl [in another class], she quit because her son was hangin' out on the street corner, all night. She said her son was tellin' her, "I'll punch the shit out of you; you can't tell me what to do." I said, "If my son ever—" And she said, "Well he's big. I'm afraid of him." "As soon as you show you're afraid, he's gonna come at you," I just said. "Take a baseball bat and crack him with it, ya know."

For Donna, the ideal male still provided for his family, but lived reality fell far short of this ideal. Young men, she described, were no longer fulfilling their obligations to their families.

Joan, another white woman from Jersey City, expected only the minimum from any man in a relationship. That is, he must "contribute":

First of all, I would never accept any man into my home who is not going to contribute. Physically we can contribute to each other; that has nothing to do with it. Material, yes, has a whole lot to do with it. You know how they say material does not? It does. They also say money doesn't buy you love. Well, but I'm sorry to say, money buys everything else [*laughs*]. Money is a necessity, no matter how you look at it. Without it, where are you? Where could you even begin, you know? Love is not going to bring you bread to eat.

Joan, like Donna, is upset by men's lack of contribution to their families. In these poor and working-class white families, women work and men are employed, but their family contributions are neither steady nor reliable. The romance of the family wage is fading fast. Many of these women, in their interviews, were critical of the inadequate money brought in by the men in their lives and the inequitable division of labor within the household. They complained that while they (the women) worked, the men did little around the house. Katlin explained the difference between the attitudes of her abusive former boyfriend and the father of her children (George) and Mack, her current boyfriend:

George felt that I was supposed to take care of him. My job was to take care of him. My job was to take care of the house. His job was to go to work. Mack doesn't feel that way. You know, Mack is like, if he comes here and there is food there, I be like "Mack, you hungry?" He be like "Yeah." I be like "Well, go serve yourself." George, on the other hand, if I said, "George, you hungry?" he be like "Yeah, serve me." Yeah, George was taught that that's what a woman was supposed to do; a woman was supposed to serve you, a woman was supposed to. Mack was taught, if you can do for yourself, you get up and do it for yourself; you don't wait for nobody else to get up and do it for you.

These women's lives begged the question of how well the historically situated family wage literature represents their contemporary experiences. With the rapid decline of the U.S. steel industry and other areas of manufacturing and production over the last few decades (Bluestone and Harris, 1982), in the span of a few years white working-class males were left without the means of securing a steady family wage. Although symbolic forms of the family wage ideology remain intact within homes—for example, George upheld the marked subordination of women to men—today both women and men struggle in the public world of work to make material ends meet.

WHOLE CLOTH: WOMEN'S LIVES OF VIOLENCE

We now take you into the private worlds of three of our narrators—Suzanne, Kathy, and Anna—in order to open up the pain, passion, and violence that festered beneath the surface of this raced and gendered class fraction. Suzanne was a thirty-one-year-old white female. She might be considered among the "settled lives" women. Married, she was currently a volunteer in a local school, was unemployed and had four children. She and her husband had applied for public assistance but had been denied funds because they fell over the designated income line for qualification. Her story of growing up with two alcoholic parents weaves through the ways in which alcohol abuse and violence saturated her family of origin and all who were associated with this family:

> I grew up in an alcoholic family. Both parents were alcoholics, so we basically were left alone a lot. We were raised, basically, in the back room of a bar. We didn't have a good home life as far as that goes. That's probably why I'm the opposite. There was no—there was always degrading things said to us. There was none of the self-esteem stuff [no attempt to build the children's self-esteem], or anything else like that. We were always called dumb and stupid and told we weren't going to amount to anything. I have two, well, I had three sisters and one brother. One sister died of SIDS [sudden infant death syndrome] when she was three months old. And my brother committed suicide when he was twenty-seven because he just couldn't handle—he, he was one of those kids that never felt like he fit in. So, he did everything, what everybody dared him to. And one kid, when he was twenty-one, somebody dared him to jump into the creek, in the middle of winter. And he did. And he became paralyzed. So, when he was twenty-seven, he killed himself because he couldn't handle the fact that being paralyzed and not getting married and not, you know, having anything else— My other sister turned out to be an alcoholic because she followed my parents' steps. And my other sister is an oddity. Because they usually say if you come from an alcoholic family, you're either an alcoholic or you're totally against it. I'm totally against it [drinking]. My sister turned out to be an alcoholic, and my other sister is a social drinker [*laughs*]. Which they say doesn't happen.

Suzanne drew attention to the ways in which alcohol and violence were, for her, linked. According to Suzanne, her siblings were, in hindsight, unaware of the family's dysfunctions while growing up and, today, were living lives filled with the same forms of abuse:

> [My nonalcoholic sister] lived in la-la land. I always tell her, I don't know where she lived, because she didn't live in our house. You know, she's so condemning of my [alcoholic] sister. And I told her, "But look at what we were raised in." And that's the first thing my other sister [the alcoholic] will say is "Well, Mom and Dad did it, and we're all here." But we're not all here. You know, my brother killed himself because of it. And she actually lost her life because of it, because she's so busy drinking. She's not raising her kids either. So her kids are going through the same thing, basically, all over again. And she also: My mother was abused by my father all the time. And my sister let men beat her up, too. She used to get beat up terrible all the time. So, her kids have seen that already, too. And they say that's another trend—the abuse. You try to find somebody like your father and you end up in that type of situation. And just like my brother, my brother hated to see my father beat up my mother. But at the same time, he beat the hell out of his girlfriends. So it's a thing, after you see it, you think it's normal even though it's not. I'm against [alcohol], because I saw my mother [who also was an alcoholic]. My father used to tell my mother, "Who would take you with four kids? What would you do [if you left me or I left you]?" And he used to call her fat and ugly, and she was beautiful and thin. But it's a game they play to keep you in your place.

She commented further on how she used to defend herself from the outbreaks at home and how those experiences affected her today:

> And with me, with my father, he tried once. He used to try to, used to fondle me. And that was about it. So, and then one time he grabbed me and I smacked him. It was the only time I ever hit my father because I don't believe that you should ever hit your parents, but I swore that he was not going to do to me what he did to the rest of that family. And since that time, he never touched me because I'm bigger than him. And my mother [is the same size]. I used to tell my mother, "Why didn't you sit on him? He was so thin and so little, you could have just sat on him instead of getting beat up all the time." But my mother wouldn't. She was afraid of him. Yeah, I used to get to the point where I stood in between the two of them, praying that neither one of them would hurt each other, and I'd end up getting punched in the middle because I couldn't stop them and get them parted. But they were both as sad, as far as my father would come home drunk. He would go out on the couch and go to sleep, and my mother would wake him up and drag him off the couch. Well, you're asking for a fight, you know. I don't want him hitting her. Just like I don't want her hitting him. I mean, there was blood in our house just about every day. Somebody was always whacked with something. And dinnertime, to this day, I still don't sit at the dinner table with my kids. We eat in the parlor in front of the TV, or whatever. I can't sit at a table and eat with my kids. Because every time we sat and ate, we had to sit there. And you weren't allowed to leave, and just as you're getting ready to eat, a fight broke out and you couldn't leave the kitchen. So you had to sit there and listen to it. So I can't sit at the table.

Contrary to the Norman Rockwell images of the nuclear family sitting down to eat dinner, Suzanne, as a child, was entangled in a set of family relations that drowned in alcoholism and, according to her, violence associated with drinking. As she stated, "The scariest thing is never knowing if you were going to wake up and have a mother and father," or facing what would be going on when she awoke. She recounted sleeping in her clothes every night of her life in the event that she would have to flee her house in the middle of the night. The fact that she now slept without clothes was seen and felt as an act of immense liberation. Suzanne's stories, however, are not the only examples of such abuse and are not even necessarily the most extreme. As evidenced in the data, these white working-class women's lives were saturated with fear and violence that seemed to mount from the moment that they were born. Although not every white working-class household looks this way, the violence that does exist is rough and hard and has a lingering presence.

Kathy was twenty-four years old and white. She was currently unemployed, having worked previously at Our Lady of Victory Infant Home as an aide to profoundly physically and mentally handicapped adolescents. Kathy was not married but was in a relationship. She had an infant son and a five-year-old daughter, neither of whom were the children of the man she was seeing currently. Kathy received (WIC) benefits but had not applied for welfare. Her savings amounted to $1,500, and this was what she was living on at the moment. Kathy's life had been filled with violence from every direction. A prototype of the "hard living" woman, she had been raised by an abusive father, raped when she was twelve, and brutally assaulted by the father of her first child when she was eighteen. Kathy remembered the things that frightened her while she was growing up:

> My father terrified me. He had a very bad temper. And my mother's drinking. My father would never physically hurt my mother because she would have packed us up in a heartbeat. But he mentally abused her. Nothing was ever good enough, nothing was ever right. Um, she wanted to go back to work. He kept telling her, "No, no, no. Your place is here." Like—like, no matter which way she turned, he was there with a blockade, trying to stop her from being her own person, developing her own will. She started drinking. I don't remember when she started, but I do remember one instance very vividly. My brothers don't remember this. I was ten. We were down in Georgia, visiting my father's sister and her husband. My mother had a glass and it was half full of wine, and what she kept doing was drinking it and filling it back up to half when my father was home. And I saw this, like, well, my father caught onto her. And my father was a big man, he was probably about six-one or six-two. He grabbed all three of us, picked us up and threw us in the Winnebago and took off. And he was going to leave her there. And I remember screaming. We must have gone about four or five miles out and maybe even more than that. We were screaming, screaming, "We don't want to leave mama. We don't want to leave mama." He was just going to leave her down there and take us with him. At that point, I didn't care if he hit me or not. I just kept screaming and screaming and screaming. And if he hit me, I was going to scream even louder. I wanted to go back, and I didn't care what he did. You know, if he slapped me for screaming, I was going to scream louder. I screamed myself hoarse, and he finally turned around.

In Kathy's case, it was her mother who was the alcoholic. The scenario of violence, however, was similar to that of Suzanne. Both Kathy and Suzanne narrated lives filled with shock and shame, surrounded by hitting, crying, verbal abuse, and insecurity. The small Kathy did not know whether or not her mother would be abandoned by her father in Georgia, and Suzanne slept in clothes each night of her young life in case she had to escape for help or safety.

Anna was twenty-six years old and white. A single mother, she had one son, age 8. She was on public assistance and was unemployed at the time. She had been in and out of abusive relationships throughout much of her young life. One of the "hard living" group, Anna had sought therapy for the past year and said that she had found it helpful for understanding her tendency to pursue and stay in abusive alcoholic relationships. She stated that she could live without a man—that for her own sanity was worth living by herself if that turned out to be necessary. As she reflected on her life through therapy, she said she had been forced to confront her past:

> My father worked at a place called J. H. Williams, and they made tools. He was making pretty good money. The only problem was my father was a miser. Actually I really couldn't say he was a miser because he would spend money, but he would spend money on himself. He would order things out of these magazines that were junklike. I used to get one from Spencer, one from—I don't even remember the names of these places—but he would order things that were just—one thing I can remember was a calendar where it was like a lifetime calendar. You could just change the months on it and the days. When my father passed away, I think we had about thirty of them, all the same. Coasters. There were tons of them, just stupid little things he would buy by quantities. He would save everything from twist ties to bags to the Styrofoam packages from meats, and I can understand saving some of it. I save certain things like that. But my father—they were in the upstairs apartment, which we could have been renting it if we could have fixed it or cleaned it up, because when I was young, probably about one, we had a fire, and he started fixing the downstairs, but he never finished the upstairs, and all of his stuff was just up there. It was in my bedroom [she never had a bedroom because there was too much "garbage" in it—she slept in her parents' room]; it was in the pantry; it was in the kitchen. There was just stuff everywhere—on the kitchen table, in the bathtub, just junk that he would buy or save. And he used to buy himself lots of clothes. He never bought me any clothes or my mother any clothes. My uncle used to go and get me clothes from the Goodwill.

At a later point, Anna described her family as follows:

> My father's an alcoholic, and my mom is mentally ill. She's schizophrenic, and it was tough. My father was also abusive in some ways. He wasn't real abusive compared to what you hear about some kids going through, but he was abusive and he was also—he had a big belief that the man runs everything and the woman belongs home barefoot and pregnant. I was kind of the caretaker. I did the cooking from, I can remember seven years old, making dinner and cleaning. It was more or less I was to take care of my mother instead of her taking care of me.

At school, Anna explained she had been picked on by the other children because of her lack of hygiene. This lack of cleanliness was a result of her father's obsessive control over the household. Anna also remembered a few instances of sexual abuse, while perhaps dismissing others from memory:

> [The teacher] would call me "piggy," "smelly," "dirty," names like that, and the kids started following along with it. And I'd say, by the fourth grade, I started cleaning myself out. I didn't care anymore, but my father had this thing that you were allowed to take a bath once a week. He would measure the shampoo, he would measure the soap, and if he thought somebody was using the shampoo when he said you shouldn't, you'd get a beating [this contradicts her earlier statement that he didn't hit her, only verbally abused her]. But I got sick of it, and the beatings almost became to be painless when hit with a belt or punched. It almost didn't phase me any more. I figured I'd rather be clean and go to school and have friends because it hurt more to not have friends than to be hit by my father. I know that we all slept in the same bed, which was another thing. I didn't have my own bedroom. My bedroom was filled with garbage, and I remember when I started developing, my father would put his arm around me and touch me on my breasts, and I always wondered; he would make it look like he was sleeping, but sometimes I thought that he was awake because I would move his hand, and it would go back up. But I don't remember anything more than that. I suspect that things had happened when I was in foster homes, and that I blocked it out because I do have a lot of hard time with any intimate relationships.

Growing up in poor and working-class white homes, these women had been subject to various forms of violence throughout their lives. Their bodies carried the marks of abuse. Suzanne, Kathy, and Anna described sexual abuse, verbal abuse, and physical abuse. Kathy, the daughter of an abusive man who attempted to leave his wife in Georgia, recounted that she was beginning to suspect that her father had killed his first wife. Through self-reflection, she was beginning to piece together the emotional fragments of abuse in her own life and that of her half-sister and was coming to believe that her father could have shoved his first wife down a flight of stairs; in the fall, she suffered an aneurysm the next morning and died. (Apparently she did die from an aneurysm; the only question is the extent to which his beating precipitated it). Kathy could, however, imagine that it was true—that her father was such a violent man that it was conceivable to her that he did, in fact, do this. As she approached her teens, she used to run by the railroad tracks to get away from home. There, one day, she met another sixth-grader—a boy—who raped her in her secret hiding place, that private space to which she would run to escape her abusive father. He left her with a "surprise package": She was pregnant at the age of twelve, and her friend's mother arranged for her to have an abortion. Kathy had been lurched from one violent encounter to another, as had many of the women we interviewed. If they had not been beaten, as a child or now, it was their sisters who were being abused by current husbands or lovers.

The hand of the male is not soft and supportive for Suzanne, Kathy, and Anna; it is instead large, violent, and brutal—a force to be feared. Therefore, one would expect that poor and working-class white women would voice some criticism of men and family. The most striking point here is that they do so only rarely. As we will argue below, the intimacies shared in an interview do not translate into collective sharing, nor do they spur a critical analysis of the role of family, heterosexuality, and/or men in ways that begin to break the cyclical patterns of violence that have programmed and continue to regulate gender relations inside some poor and working-class white families. While white women were willing to tell us a great deal in the secret space of our interviews, they left relatively unaltered the tone of reconciled contentment in which they wrapped narratives of the family as loving and supporting, and little scratches the surface as these women attempt to raise the next generation.

These three women came from very similar childhood spaces and lived in very different adult worlds, and yet all carried histories and endured the pain of domestic violence. As we reviewed the narratives of all thirty women, a set of recurring themes emerged as the poor and working-class white women managed the "shared secret" of male violence. While "hard living" and "settled lives" women negotiated the secret differently, they were all managing their lives around male violence and impending poverty.

"HARD LIVING" WOMEN

Very much like their presumably "settled lives" sisters, "hard living" women reported long histories of violence at the hands of men—from childhood forward. Whether describing fathers, stepfathers, or "neighborhood boys" who molested them as children, these "hard living" women, as girls, often turned to their mothers seeking care, attention, and resolution. Many women noted with disappointment that their mothers, caught in the ideology and finances of the family wage, "didn't want to" or "couldn't" talk about it. Stranded in a world in which family life was assumed to be private life and sexual violence was assumed to be a woman's problem, many of these mothers tried to be as responsive as they could be—within the fixed space of heterosexual domestic life. This meant, typically, attending to their daughters' needs while ignoring the guilt of the boys/men involved. In many instances, mothers tried to maintain "stable" homes amidst a gendered violence which was crushing their daughters.

Sherile, a twenty-two-year-old white woman who was sexually molested by a neighborhood boy when she was just a child, sought comfort and conversation from her mother. Sherile reported, as many did, "My mom—I tried to find out what really happened, but she doesn't. It's like everybody feels uncomfortable talking about it to me, and that bothers me, because they were old enough to know and could tell me, whereas my memory is kind of foggy about it." Lorraine shared a similar story:

> One of my mother's boyfriend's friends molested me. And, um, another man that my mother had baby-sit me, he had molested me when I was a kid. When

I was a kid I tried to tell my mother, but she didn't believe me at the time. So then I just, like, didn't say anything, like I said, like when I was a kid, I, I never did anything about it; I just accepted it. When I went to college I went to counseling for it and stuff. I'm still going.

Rose told a slightly different story, with a similar theme. She also could not turn to her mother for help. Rose also explained how her neighbors chose to ignore her abuse:

Like I said, my mother's boyfriend used to beat us. And then my mother was, on and off—she'd be violent too. I was silent about it. I guess at the time I just didn't feel like there was anything I could do. Like I remember as a kid trying to tell my mother to leave him. He was violent towards her, too. And she never did. So, um, like I said, I guess I just felt like there was nothing I could do. When I was young, it was kind of like everybody knew? Like, everybody on the block knew, well, he hits those kids, or whatever. But nobody ever did anything. Actually I remember one time family services had come to our house. I don't remember who called or why they had come, but I remember they had to talk to me, to ask me how I was getting along with my mother's boyfriend. And I remember before that they [mother and boyfriend] were threatening me, saying, "Oh, we'll beat you if, you know, if you say anything. Pretend like we get along fine." And so that's what I did.

Most women tried, in vain, to talk to their mothers. And most mothers, caught in the web of threatened poverty and domestic ideology, chose not to hear. It is well documented that children in homes where mothers are battered are at great risk for physical harm and are also likely to be adversely affected by some of the ways in which their mothers struggle to cope (Straus, 1983; Jaffe et al., 1990). In two cases, young girls turned to mothers who were, indeed, helpful. But even here, the girls worked with their mothers *around* the accused man, never confronting or holding him accountable for his actions. Susan, now age twenty-seven, described her family as "Great family life. Me and my brothers and sisters. We were close." Further into the interview, however, she explained what happened when she learned she was pregnant as a teenager:

I guess I was too young to really know. I'd skip my period, and I said I think I'm pregnant, and I said there's one way to find out; I'll talk to my mother. So it was me and my best friends, two very good friends of mine. We went, and my mother's very open about sex. You know, if you ask any questions, she'll explain it to you point-blank. So we were like we're having a problem with somebody. I didn't tell my mother I was pregnant though. But afterwards, my father hit me, and he had punched me on the side, and I peed blood, and I went and told my mother I was peeing blood; and when I went to the hospital they kept me for observation for twenty-four hours or whatever, and they did blood work and everything. Then the doctor told my mother I was pregnant and she came into the room she told me. And I was, like, I knew that, Mom; I just didn't know how to tell you. She was, like, why were you hiding it? I was, like, because I didn't want Daddy to kill me, and we hid it from my father. My mother took me and got the abortion; my father never knew.

Susan's story showed by far the best attempt to tell and be heard by her Mom. But even here, her father's abuse, horrific as it was, was overlooked. Her mom did double duty: working "around" him and his temper, and saving her daughter.

Moving into adult domestic abuse among "hard living" women, we found similar patterns of attempts to speak, amidst fear of reprisals and/or the absence of an audience. While very few "settled lives" women actually told family members or friends about their abuse, we did see a number of the "hard living" women speaking aloud—be it to friends, neighbors or kin, through religion, psychotherapy, or the justice system. These women were, for the most part, unmarried, on their own, and had fled violence and were teetering on the edge of poverty and homelessness. These women appeared to feel more *free* to speak about domestic violence. In comparison, "settled lives" women—living in what appeared to be intact, stable marriages—were relentlessly silent about their own stories. "Hard living" Gena described how when her boyfriend beat her, he would find her to blame:

> [He would say] it was my fault. I made him do that, because I yelled at him and he couldn't handle it. I threw him out. I'd block the door; he'd kick the door right in. And when I would call the cops, he would hide in the building; they couldn't find him and they would leave. And then, he'd stay away for a couple hours or all night, go to his friends' or his mother's. Then come the next day: "I'm sorry I messed up again. I won't let it happen again." And this went on for a year. I told him the next time you hit me don't go to sleep here cuz I will chop you up. I sat in my chair with an axe in my hand and said I was gonna chop him up that night. He wasn't gonna touch or hurt me again. He wasn't gonna steal anything. He wasn't ever gonna hit me. And he wasn't gonna ever tell me what to do. Then I—I'd just sit. Who were you to hit me and then tell me you wanna make love to me? Please. And it's my fault? That's sick. Every time he fought or stole somethin' the cops never did nothin'. They would say, "We can't do nothin' cuz we can't find him." So what are you gonna do? Press a complaint to—he ain't gonna show up in court.

Gena also explained that when she got pregnant, his violence erupted. Among this sample there were a number of women for whom the onset of pregnancy and the reassertion of violence co-occurred. Pregnancy and the first few years after the birth of a child can be a time of heightened financial, physical, and emotional stress, all which has been linked to an increase in the potential for violence (Gelles, 1988; Parker and McFarlane, 1991; Campbell, et al., 1992; Helton et al., 1987). As Gina described, a restraining order helped at first, but it did not stop the violence from continuing:

> That helped. He went and stayed with his mother. And he wouldn't come near me, because he was afraid to go to jail. That [lasted] for three months. Because when he came back, it was good. And that's when he was doin' really good. And then I got pregnant with Jessica. And then when Jessica was born, it started all over again. The same cycle. With the drugs, him stayin' out. But then he started—instead of takin' things from the house—he started just usin' his

whole pay. You know, borrowin' all week, and then come payday he didn't have a full pay. I'd have to go down and meet him at the job just to get the money, or else, if he got his pay, he'd be done [*laughs*].

For other "hard living" women, the courts offered other forms of temporary salvation. Julia remembered that pregnancy also brought out violence in her child's father:

See, with my second son, their father used to beat me up. And he broke my ribs, and I was two months pregnant with my second one, and I had gone to the hospital. I didn't know I was pregnant. I put criminal charges against him. He went to jail because what they did was they arranged for him to remain in jail until I had the baby because they didn't know whether I would survive or something would happen with the baby during the pregnancy, whatever, and indeed if anything happened to either one of us, he was going to be charged with first-degree murder because it was inflicted on me. He was incarcerated for, I think it was—which time? Cuz I had him locked up several times for no child support. Oh, when he hit me, he served three years.

A few women turned to counseling, although the costs typically exceeded their resources. Quite a few also testified that God was their salvation. In complaining about Mike, Jana, a woman of white and Puerto Rican parentage, revealed that she relied on God in a clever, life-saving move:

Mike would beat me; he beat me up all the time. Take sex, and I didn't want to give it to him. I was scared of him. He said if I fought back, he would kill me. Look, I'm not talking about a slap. It came to a point where he hit me like I was a man. Plenty of times [I would call police]. There were lots of times I did. Mike was the type of man that he would tell the cop to mind his own fucking business. Mike was the kind of guy, he would play you off, he would have you on his side. Any male species he would have on his side. Oh yeah, he used to say, "She's a bitch. You know what she did to me?" He would make up stories. Oh, Mike was good, he was a good actor. He was a good con artist. He was a con. He was good. My mom didn't know for years. I was ashamed. "Oh, Mom, I got something to tell you. I'm getting beat up now." No, I didn't tell her. "Oh Mom, well, I'm not getting raped this time or anything. I'm getting beat up now." It was something that I didn't say. I had nothin' good to say. He was a drug addict. Mike was into heroin.

As for her children, she described how she would do all she could to protect them from his rage:

I loved them. They were mine. Regardless if I planned them, I took care of them. I did everything in the several years' relationship with Mike. Getting beat up, protecting them, crying, telling them it's OK, Mommy is all right. I would get better. I was my kids' savior. I protected them for it. [He] never hit them. Never yelled at them. I would get beat up for them. They did something wrong, I took their beatings.

Jana now gave full credit for her escape from the abusive relationship to her reliance on God. As Jana explained, her faith gave her the courage to make a big decision:

> I was in a shelter with nuns: St. Francis in downtown Jersey City. I overheard a conversation he was having with a friend. Mike was a car thief. He would steal car radios. I heard [Mike] was going to New York to steal a car, hijack a car and bring it to New York and sell it. So I dropped the dime on him. It was like God told me to. I don't know. I think God saved me. I think God put him in jail. I think God wanted me to hear the conversation. God dared me into doing this. God knows everything. He knows everything about me, inside and out.

Through extensive bouts of violence, from childhood through adulthood, these "hard living" women sought an audience, found few who will listen, and ended up with therapy, the police, or God. Given the depth and pain of violence in these women's lives, it is curious that even these women, willing to seek a remedy outside their homes, *did not talk about violence in current relationships.* This was a noticeable absence, considering that these women were at various stages in their lives, with and without children, in and out of work.[2] Indeed, we began to notice that many of these women described current relationships as "good" and then elaborated by explaining that their current partners did *not* beat them. The absence of reported current violence was presumably evidence of a "good" relationship. For example, Sandra reported:

> It's good. I mean, he's there for me. It's good. I don't know what to say [*laughs*]. He listens to me. He's a friend. I don't know. I guess I got all the conveniences of a nice relationship. I don't get beat up; I don't get put down. He listens to me. He gives me advice. He's a friend and he doesn't do drugs, he doesn't drink, so that's good, you know. He is a good father. He's just got to pay a little more attention to his son, but overall he's good.

Sandra, a twenty-one-year-old, described the "good" aspects of her relationship in the negative: Her fiancé didn't beat her, and therefore the relationship must be good. The absence of a definition of a good relationship suggests that these women had expectations of relationships that were abusive, feeling that any partner who did not abuse them seemed like a "good" partner. The "hard living" women were on the move, but never free—for long—from violence.

"SETTLED LIVES" WOMEN

Unlike the "hard living" women, the women surviving in what appeared to be "settled lives" were far more reluctant to reveal evidence of violence to anyone. While we opened a relatively silenced space in the private interviews, information about domestic violence, by their own admission, was rarely shared. Abuse remained a *well-known, shared family secret* in its worst form. One had to protect oneself and one's children, insofar as one could. When things got too bad, of course, there were shelters that could take these women in, but most "settled lives" white women did not avail themselves of these services unless absolutely necessary. Given that the women's role was to sustain family life, with stories of abuse came embarrassment and, ironically, evidence of *her* failure. Silence cloaked abuse in the hope that its biting reality would soften and eventually fade away: Keep it private, and then maybe it will go away. Maybe today will be different. Maybe he (or she) will not come home drunk and set off a series of encounters that will result in beatings, in violence, in our sleeping in our clothes, in our thrown plates of food, in our blood, in our screams, in our terror. Will my sister have a knife? Will she be drunk? Will she set Dad off? Will Mom leave? Can I use soap? Why don't the "settled" women, white and working class, scream in rage about the family that allows this to go on? Why is this all so guarded an event in the discourse of this class fraction? For whom, among poor and working-class whites, does the myth of the harmonious family survive? Living in violence may be better than living on the streets or losing custody of one's children. If she speaks, the "settled" woman could pay the price of becoming "hard living."

For "settled lives" white women, like Suzanne above, domestic violence is a domain of muted criticism that has difficulty breaking through. We offer some theoretically based observations and speculations as to why this is the case. Working our way through theory, we argue in this section that this is tied to the ideology of the family and the way in which this ideology has historically worked through married white working-class women's lives, as well as the ways in which family, as an ideal, is cross-valorized with the construction of race through the marking or nonmarking of white as a race marker that intersects with the ideology of the family.

As noted earlier, white working-class women's lives have been largely defined and contained by the family. The struggle for the white family wage was a struggle that solidified men as breadwinners, as individuals who were responsible for the support of dependent women and children. While this is certainly true in every white class fraction, white working-class women had virtually no means of escape from this position in that they could not acceptably obtain employment outside the secondary labor sector where [low] income levels conventionally frustrated possibilities for financial independence and autonomy. Thus their existence was almost totally dependent on the male wage of father and/or husband and the way in which this male wage established patterns of male dominance in the home. There has not been, then, any historically based critique from within the white working class of the nuclear family and/or of male dominance, as has been the case for white middle-class women, for example. The resurgence of the feminist movement in the 1960s was clearly spearheaded by and aimed at a white middle-class audience, at women who would be able to support themselves if they so chose. White working-class women were in no such position, and there has been little critique of men or the nuclear family arrangement emanating from within the white working-class community. In other words, these women have not had available to them the structural conditions in which to articulate a vocabulary of critique.

Certainly feminist language and analysis has reached deeply within the white working class in some ways (Weis, 1990; Sidel, 1990), but the sense of a collective movement was not (and is not) lodged within this class fraction. Thus there is nothing internal to the class that would lead white working-class women to critique and challenge male dominance and its potential link to violence. (Indeed, it can be argued that its very "middle-classness" caused working-class white women to reject the women's movement in the same way that some black women have rejected the women's movement because it was seen as white.) White working-class women who rejected the ideology of domestic life and its attendant violence sacrificed their "respectable" place in the class fraction. They became seen as—that is, painted as—"hard living" women who experienced within-class violence and expulsion from the standards of gendered life. As a result, gender/class/race ideology stays intact, as the dissenters exit—and are punished.

Since the "settled lives" women evidence that, at all costs, they perpetuate the myth of stable and agreeable home life, it is here where the possible cross-valorization of the ideology of family and the production/maintenance of whiteness as a racial identity marker becomes relevant within this class fraction. At this juncture, we find total silence in the literature on violence in the home. As Ruth Frankenberg (1993), Chakravorty Spivak (1984), Toni Morrison (1992), and others have argued, the construction of the dominant white self cannot be understood except in relation to the construction of the "other." Scholars of colonial discourse such as Said (1979) have argued powerfully that the construction of the dominant white self can be understood only in relation to the co-construction of the inferior colonial other. Thus dominant whites were constituting themselves discursively at the same time that they were constituting the colonial "other." Frankenberg (1993) states:

> Colonial discourse (like racist discourse) is in many ways heterogeneous rather than univocal, not surprising given the extent and geographical dispersion of European colonizing projects. However, if a common thread runs through the whole range of instances of colonial discourse, it is the construction of alterity along racial and/or cultural lines—the construction of others conceived as fundamentally different from, and inferior to, white European, metropolitan selves (Said, 1979). It must also be noted—and this is a point perhaps more difficult to grasp upon first encounter with it—that it is precisely by means of the construction of a range of others that the self or dominant center constitutes itself. White/European self-constitution is, in other words, fundamentally tied to the process of discursive production of others, rather than preexisting that process. (p. 63)

Frankenberg (1993) suggests that it is the legacy of colonial discourse that generated a sense of whiteness as an "empty" space, but one that is simultaneously normative. Whiteness is appropriated as the norm, as that against which all others should be judged. It is, then, an unmarked signifier—a marker only full in relation to the constructed other. Its fullness, then, inscribes, at one and the same time, its emptiness and presumed innocence. It is here, then, that the co-construction of the African American becomes so important. The African American, according to our informants, is largely lazy and prone to violence and does not want to work. While this is a largely male critique (Weis et al., 1997), white women express similar sentiments. Among the white women in this study, negative images of those of African and Puerto Rican descent circulated throughout descriptions of the other, as Carol narrated:

> Like I said, I'm sure there's quite a few out there that are pretty good. It's just a lot of people won't give themselves a chance to know them because they're afraid, or just so sure that they're bad because they're black or Puerto Rican. What can you do? It's hard to say, but sometimes that's all you see in the paper, is they're black or Puerto Rican. Granted, there are white ones that are white trash, too. But the majority of the time, the ones that are causing trouble are them [black and Puerto Rican]. And I can understand why people feel that way. And it's too bad that not everyone can get along, but that's just the way it is.

Although Carol recognized that there is "white trash, too," she added that "the majority of the time, the ones that are causing trouble are them [black and Puerto Rican]." This line of thinking was sustained in conversation with Judy, whose ready association of black folks with criminal activity undermined any possible space for a notion of the black family as a "good family." She saw such families only as white: "I guess we think of black people as more involved in crime [than they are], people who are going to hurt you, not couples who are the same as you [white], with families, trying to make ends meet like you are."

These projections of the social deviant coupled with that of the "nonworking" African American enable whites to draw the boundaries of what signifies acceptable nonworking at the borders of their own community (Weis and Fine, 1996). Many white working-class men and women whom we interviewed received welfare benefits, but, as they articulated, this was somehow "different" from when African Americans received such benefits: We, the good hard-working whites, only take welfare when we absolutely need it; they—African Americans—take welfare all the time and do not make an effort to find work. There is a material dimension here as well. White women, if they are married, have husbands who have had a better chance to obtain a white male wage, thus offering the possibility of securing greater financial stability. For those women living with male wage earners, the steady family income that their husbands brought home drew, for them, the line between them and African-American women, for whom this possibility was all too often ruled out in the face of stark levels of unemployment among poor black males.[3] Although many white women work outside the home, and white men do not earn (or share) the kind of wage that they (or their fathers) may have had in days of heavy industry, it is still the case that a white male wage can mean the difference being working-class and destitute (Oliver and Shapiro, 1995).

Note, then, that the "settled lives" women, who endure domestic violence in smarting secrecy and who belittle African-American women-headed families, may be voicing their anxieties about falling into the "hard living" pit. For the "settled lives" white women, the black family becomes the discursive trash bin, but the white "hard living" woman may be the embodied terror.

Given what we heard from women who were "hard living," we saw that exit from the traditional family was no escape from violence, just temporary respite, and almost assuredly poverty—at least in the short run. Many of the "hard living" women had to reinvite once violent men, the fathers of their children, back into their homes, even if they were on welfare, in order to make financial ends meet. And yet, just as poignantly, the "settled lives" women had no escape and no recourse. Justifying their decision to stay, they disparaged the black "other" in terror of their white counterparts' lives.

CONCLUDING THOUGHTS

The "hard living" white women whom we interviewed may merely have been the front-runners of a generation of white women suffering, as women of color have long suffered, under a right-wing administration in the context of an economy that is crushing the working class and the poor. They may have been the archetypes of a world yet to come for many poor and working-class white women. Merely an admission of violence away from those females who appeared to be thriving in "intact" families, the "hard living" white women lived and spoke more like the African-American women in our sample. Although still privileged by whiteness, the "value" of a white working-class man has been diminished in both the economic and domestic spheres, just as the "value" of an African American man has always been circumscribed in the United States by a racist labor market (Oliver and Shapiro, 1995). And so white family forms, like those of African Americans and Latinos, take shape in political response to the economy, the rise of jails, the dwindling presence of men, and diminished resources for children and women—married or not.

As the public sphere collapses—or more aptly is collapsed—by a Congress eager to universalize cutbacks for the poor and abatements to the rich, women of the poor and working classes are being squeezed into tighter and tighter domestic corners and pushed out of the public world of work, welfare, and battered women's shelters. While escape from violence appears easy to those onlookers who ask, "Why doesn't she just leave?" we hear from these women that they can barely *afford* to leave, especially if they have children. They forecast family homelessness and more violence. As the public sphere shrinks, women will get beaten with more regularity, fewer options, and more muzzled critiques. They will be swept into the corners of a reinstitutionalized "private" sphere, secured in its violence by the hollowing of the economy and the retreat of public sector services for women and children.

The poor and working-class white women we interviewed experienced lives saturated with domestic violence, from childhood up to the present. The question remains: To what extent do family members, neighbors, friends, clergy, and, in particular, educators leave the issue of abuse uninterrupted, thus aiding the perpetuation of the "cycle" of abuse? Lorraine, for instance, described how when she was a child, she was abused by a family friend, but her mother did not believe her. After a while, said Lorraine, "I just didn't say anything." Rose told how her mother's boyfriend used to abuse her and her siblings, and although "everybody on the block knew, nobody ever did anything." In yet another example, Anna remembered that while she was growing up, her home life was filled with physical and sexual violence. School was also a hurtful place; as Anna recalled, her teacher called her derogatory names relating to her poor hygiene, and soon "the kids [other students] started following along with it."

As the white females in this research narrated, in the process of growing up they had been conditioned to expect that people would turn their backs on their problems or would be compliant in their pain. The lessons they learned were that abuse was to be kept a secret, males were not accountable for their actions, and females must "work around" this violence. Guided by such worlds of pain, we argue that educators must contemplate the issue of domestic violence as they look at the faces of the children in their classrooms. We must begin to understand what it means when so many of these students are raised in violence and/or have parents that grew up with abuse. The violence that today's parents experienced while growing up is likely to cast a long shadow over the current home lives of youth. As the literature indicates, not only does domestic violence impede school performance, but it also wages war on the healthy emotional growth of children (Elkind, 1984; Hughes, 1988; Jaffe, et al., 1990; Afulayan, 1993). Educators can no longer ignore this pervasive problem.

In most states, teachers are mandated to learn about and report on child abuse. We argue, however, that responses that cut closer to the core of this issue are needed. We contend that domestic violence must be openly discussed in classrooms as a sweeping social problem, an aspect of gender relations that is played out behind the closed doors of many homes and in many communities. For example, through studying history and/or literature, both girls and boys can begin to talk about domestic violence, critique such behavior, and learn to hold males more responsible for abuse. In addition, high school students can be led to serve internships in domestic violence shelters, on hotlines, and in advocacy groups. Through these connections, young people can begin to see themselves as linked to a larger social movement. This can be an emboldening experience for teens—particularly those who are growing up in abusive households—as they can develop a critical voice and reach out to services on their own.

Today, Suzanne makes a point not to sleep in any clothes as a form of resistance to those many years when she kept her clothes on day and night in fear that she would have to flee unexpected outbursts of family violence. Held hostage to the impossibilities of criticism and escape, she and other women are left to defer yet unrealized dreams for the next generation. As the poor and working-class white women in this analysis indicate, domestic violence is painful, emotionally tattering, *and* commonplace. Educators and others in the lives of those who live in violent homes must begin to think seriously about significant ways in which they can assist in disrupting the "cycle" of abuse.

NOTES

This research was supported with funds from the Spencer Foundation.

1. Although our sample specifications were ages twenty-three to thirty-five, we did interview this one forty-year-old.

2. The violence that these women did narrate was a violence of the past, not current. This raises important theoretical and methodological cautions about women's self-reports of current violence. As Fine and MacPherson (1995) describe in research with adolescent girls, a critique of heterorelations is more likely to be narrated *in retrospect* than about a current relationship. Stories take time to construct, and stories of trauma take much time to utter, let alone construct. Becky Thompson (1994), in a study of women's experiences of eating problems, writes, "Like many qualitative anthropologists and sociologists, I am not sure there is such a thing as a complete story: future experience keeps adding to and revising what the present offers. Partial truths and circuitous narratives of lived experience are often the closest approximation of the whole story available" (p. 24). Lived stories take time and space to construct, and these women piece together what little they have had the time and space to construct, telling stories of the past. A woman in a study conducted by Kidder, Lafleur, and Wells (1995), who examined women's recollections of "the sexual transformation of professional relationships," later recalled "sexual harassment" and offered more clues to the lack of current violence narrations. She described her feelings of guilt and shame after a professor sexually harassed her and added, "I can say this now that it's history." She wondered if she could have avoided the incident. The women in Jersey City and Buffalo had a language for domestic violence, as evidenced by their descriptions of past abuse, a language to which women of previous generations may not have had access. They were therefore not "preverbal" in Kidder et al.'s sense. However, like the woman in Kidder et al.'s sample, they may have sought safety in history, a place where guilt and shame were not as immediate emotions. To criticize current circumstances of violence may have been unaffordable for these women without plans and resources for escape from that violence.

3. At least in recent history, although the current movement toward globalization has shifted many of these once secure white male jobs out of the country, out of the unions, and out of the Northeast.

REFERENCES

Afulayan, J. 1993. Consequences of domestic violence on elementary school education. *Child and Family Therapy* 15(3): 55–58.

Bluestone, B., and B. Harris. 1982. *The Deindustrialization of America.* New York: Basic Books.

Campbell, J., M. Poland, J. Waller, and J. Ager. 1992. Correlates of battering during pregnancy. *Research on Nursing Health* 15: 219–226.

Coley, S. M., and J. O. Beckett. 1988. Black battered women: A review of the empirical literature. *Journal of Counseling and Development* 66(6): 266–270.

Davis, A. 1981. *Women, Race, and Class.* New York: Random House.

Dobash, R. E. 1979. *Violence against Wives: A Case Study against the Patriarchy.* New York: Free Press.

Downs, W. R., B. A. Miller, and D. D. Panek. 1993. Differential patterns of partner to woman violence: A comparison of samples of community, alcohol abusing, and battered women. *Journal of Family Violence* 8(2): 113–135.

Elkind, P. 1984. *All Grown Up and No Place to Go.* Reading, Mass.: Addison Wesley.

Fine, M., and P. MacPherson. 1995. Hungry for an Us: Adolescent girls and adult women negotiating territories of race, class, and gender difference. *Feminism and Psychology* 5(2): 181–200.

Fineman, M. A., and R. Mykitiuk, eds. 1994. *The Public Nature of Private Violence: The Discovery of Domestic Abuse.* New York: Routledge.

Frankenberg, R. 1993. *White Women, Race Matters: The Social Construction of Whiteness.* Minneapolis: University of Minnesota Press.

Gelles, R. 1988. Violence and pregnancy: Are pregnant women at greater risk of abuse? *Journal of Marriage and Family* 50: 841–847.

Giddings, P. 1984. *When and Where I Enter: The Impact of Black Women on Race and Sex in America.* New York: Morrow.

Halle, D. 1984. *America's Working Man: Work, Home, and Politics among Blue-Collar Property Owners.* Chicago: University of Chicago Press.

Hanmer, J., and M. Maynard, eds. 1987. *Women, Violence, and Social Control.* Atlantic Highlands, N.J.: Humanities Press International.

Helton, A., J. McFarlane, and E. Anderson. 1987. Battered and pregnant: A prevalence study. *American Journal of Public Health* 77: 1337–1339.

Hoff, L. A. 1990. *Battered Women as Survivors.* New York: Routledge.

hooks, b. 1981. *Ain't I a Woman: Black Women and Feminism.* Boston: South End Press.

———. 1989. *Talking Back: Thinking Feminist, Thinking Black.* Boston: South End Press.

Howell, J. 1972. *Hard Living on Clay Street: Portraits of Blue Collar Families.* New York: Anchor Books.

Hughes, H. 1988. Psychological and behavioral correlates of family violence in child witnesses and victims. *American Journal of Orthopsychiatry* 58: 77–90.

Jaffe, P., D. Wolfe, and S. Wilson. 1990. *Children of Battered Women.* Newbury Park, Calif.: Sage.

Jones, A. 1994. *Next Time She'll Be Dead.* Boston: Beacon Press.

Kidder, L., R. LaFleur, and C. Wells. 1995. Recalling harassment, reconstructing experience. *Journal of Social Issues* 51(1): 53–67.

Kurz, D. 1995. *For Richer for Poorer: Mothers Confront Divorce.* New York: Routledge.

Marsh, C. E. 1993. Sexual assault and domestic violence in the African-American community. *Western Journal of Black Studies* 17(3): 149–155.

May, M. 1987. The historical problem of the family wage: The Ford Motor Company and the five dollar day. In N. Gerstel and H. E. Gross, eds., *Families and Work.* Philadelphia: Temple University Press.

Mills, C. Wright. 1959. *The Sociological Imagination.* London: Oxford University Press.

Morrison, T. 1992. *Playing in the Dark: Whiteness and the Literary Imagination.* Cambridge, Mass.: Harvard University Press.

Nicarthy, G. 1989. From the sounds of silence to the roar of a global movement: Notes on the movement against violence against women. *Response to the Victimization of Women and Children* 12(2): 3–10.

Oliver, M., and T. Shapiro. 1995. *Black Wealth, White Wealth: A New Perspective on Racial Inequality.* New York: Routledge.

Parker, B., and J. McFarlane. 1991. Identifying and helping battered pregnant women. *Maternal and Child Nursing* 16: 161–164.

Roy, M., ed. 1977. *Battered Women: A Psychosociological Study of Domestic Violence.* New York: Van Nostrand Reinhold.

Said, E. 1979. *Orientalism.* New York: Random House.

Schechter, S. 1982. *Women and Male Violence: The Visions and Struggles of the Battered Women's Movement.* Boston: South End Press.

Sennett, R., and J. Cobb. 1972. *The Hidden Injuries of Class.* New York: Knopf.

Sidel, R. 1990. *On Her Own.* New York: Viking.

Smith, D. 1987. Women's inequality and the family. In M. F. Katzenstein and C. M. Mueller, eds., *The Women's Movements of the United States and Europe.* Philadelphia: Temple University Press.

Spivak, G. C. 1984. The Rani of Sirmur. In F. Barker, ed., *Europe and Its Others,* Colchester, U.K.: University of Essex Press.

Stack, C. 1972. *All Our Kin.* New York: Anchor Press.

Steinmetz, S., and M. Strauss, eds. 1974. *Violence in the Family.* New York: Dodd Mead.

Straus, M. 1983. Ordinary violence, child abuse, and wife-beating: What do they have in common and why? In D. Finkelhor, R. Gelles, G. Hotaling, and M. Straus, eds., *The Dark Side of Families: Current Family Violence Research.* Beverly Hills, Calif.: Sage.

Thompson, B. 1994. *A Hunger So Wide and So Deep: American Women Speak Out on Eating Problems.* Minneapolis: University of Minnesota Press.

Valentine, B. 1980. *Hustling and Other Hard Work: Lifestyles in the Ghetto.* New York: Free Press.

Walker, L. A. 1984. Battered women, psychology, and public policy. *American Psychologist* 39(10): 1178–1182.

Weis, L. 1985. Without dependence on welfare for life: The experience of Black women in the urban community college. *The Urban Review* 17(4): 233–256.

———. 1990. *Working-class without Work: High School Students in a De-industrializing Economy.* New York: Routledge.

Weis, L., A. Proweller, and C. Centrie. 1997. Re-examining a moment in history: Loss of privilege inside white, working class masculinity in the 1990s. In M. Fine, L. Weis, L. Powell, and M. Wong, eds., *Off White.* New York: Routledge.

Weis, L., and M. Fine. 1996. Narrating the 1980s and 1990s: Voices of poor and working class white and African-American men. In *Anthropology and Education Quarterly* 27(4): 493–516.

White, E. 1985. The psychology of abuse. In *Chain, Chain Change: For Black Women Dealing with Physical and Emotional Abuse.* Seattle: South End Press.

Wilson, W. J. 1987. *The Truly Disadvantaged: The Inner City, the Underclass, and Public Policy.* Chicago: University of Chicago Press.

Woodcock Tentler, L. W. 1979. *Wage Earning Women: Industrial Work and Family Life in the US, 1900–1930.* New York: Oxford University Press.

CHAPTER **16**

MARGARET ABRAHAM

Fighting Back

Abused South Asian Women's Strategies of Resistance

 ABSTRACT

Stereotyping is harmful to all battered women; and yet it is common in the dominant heterosexual, white, Western European model facing battered women of color, immigrants, and lesbian, gay, bisexual, and transgendered people in the United States. Asian women, for example, are defined by alternative stereotypes: passive and submissive women, who are unable to hold their own or be assertive in the patriarchal family; or the hard working "model minority" women who could not possibly be abused by a husband.

In this chapter, Abraham challenges the idea that abuse and passivity are synonymous. Despite their lack of resources and relative isolation, she finds that South Asian battered women in this study utilized many creative strategies in resisting the abuse throughout their marriages. They employed a wide range of coping skills, help-seeking behaviors, and other actions to challenge their abuser, seek assistance, or leave the abusive relationship. Resistance strategies included silence, confrontation, hiding, talking back, hitting back, challenging the abuser's fiscal control, contemplating and resisting suicide, and seeking informal and institutional help. Of the women who sought outside help, most turned to other South Asians, their families, friends, neighbors or community members—at least in part a recognition of the need for cultural understanding or support.

Abraham argues that the women in the study "strategically navigated within the cultural and structural constraints to end the violence perpetrated against them." For example, cultural values emphasizing the importance of marriage and cultural cohesiveness influenced many of the South Asian women to remain in the abusive relationships, at least initially. In addition, the socioeconomic class, ethnicity, legal status, financial resources, and accessibility of alternative support systems determined both the kinds of strategies women utilized and the extent to which their tactics were effective. And yet, despite their lack of resources and relative isolation, almost all the women in this study ultimately took the courageous step of leaving their abusers. As you read this chapter, consider the following issues. Abraham alerts the reader to forms of resistance—hiding, avoidance, silence, and contemplating suicide—that many people from mainstream American society might fail to recognize as positive forms of resistance. Can you think of other culturally specific forms of resistance that might be misinterpreted by outsiders, particularly service providers? How can such misinterpretations impact battered women utilizing these strategies? Finally, what were some ways in which the women's financial, legal, and social circumstances impacted their choices?

There are people who hear of incidents of domestic violence and respond: "Maybe it was her fault. It can't be just his fault. What is wrong with these women? Why don't they fight back? They are not children! They could have gotten out or done something about it! Why do they go back? I don't understand these women, why do they just lie down and take this stuff? Why do they suffer in silence?" Often it is easy to blame women and assume that they passively accept abuse. Studies have shown, however, that abused women do employ a number of techniques in an effort to stop the abuse, to get assistance, or to leave the abuser (Pagelow 1981; Bowker 1983; Gelles and Straus 1988; Mehrotra 1999). My research too indicates that despite the lack of resources and relative isolation, abused South Asian women engage in a variety of strategies of resistance that challenge assumptions of passivity and submissiveness. Sometimes these acts of resistance are for immediate gains, but ultimately they are a part of the empowerment process that helps many women retain or regain a sense of self (Lempert 1996).

In this chapter I focus on individual women's strategies of resistance—all the tactics that a woman uses to challenge her abuser's power and control and prevent her abuse. Although I use incidents as examples, it is important to keep in mind that women's strategies of resistance cannot be reduced to specific incidents but must be understood in the context of the multiple strategies most women use in a relationship. Class, ethnicity, legal status, socioeconomic viability, and the accessibility of alternate support systems also play a major role in determining a woman's use of strategies of resistance and their efficacy. It is not only the patriarchal relations within the marriage that influence abused immigrant women's strategies of resistance in the United States. Issues such as perceptions of ethnic and class discrimination shape women's response. For example, while a woman may resist her abuser by talking back or by seeking the help of a South Asian friend, she may be more reluctant to call the police, if her perception of them is that they are racially or class biased. In addition, the need to belong to one's ethnic community may sometimes take precedence over gender-based abuse within the marriage. Thus, for various cultural and socioeconomic reasons, many South Asian immigrant women initially feel that it is important to try to keep their marriage together or at least to try personal strategies prior to seeking informal or formal help. Initially some are also torn between their resentment toward their abuser and their sympathy to the economic and social frustrations that the abuser experiences because of his ethnic and class position in the United States.

This is not to say, however, that abused immigrant women do not use multiple strategies of resistance against their abusers from early on in the marriage. Rather their strategy is partially determined by the resources and alternative opportunities they have available. Although the decision to get out of a relationship permanently usually did not occur until the woman felt the situation was untenable, nearly all women I interviewed did take the courageous step of leaving the abuser. Thus they not only resisted their abuser but also challenged the normative order that assumes a married woman's place is with her husband and his family. Throughout the marriage these immigrant women used creative ways to challenge their abuser, seek help, or leave the abusive relationship. They strategically navigated within the cultural and structural constraints to end the violence perpetrated against them.

Time and again in my interviews, I heard of the great risks abused immigrant women took to challenge their abuser despite their relative isolation and the limited resources available to them. Women's strategies of resistance included silence, avoidance, confrontation, hiding, talking back, hitting back, challenging the abuser's fiscal control, contemplating and resisting suicide, and seeking informal and institutional help. Often women had to resist not only their abuser but also those others who deliberately or inadvertently contributed to the abuse.

With some variation within categories, I will draw on Lee Bowker's (1983) threefold typology to categorize strategies of resistance. These are: (1) *personal strategies,* such as talking, promising, hiding, avoidance, and passive or aggressive defense; (2) *using informal sources of help,* such as family members, in-laws, neighbors, friends, and shelters; and (3) *using formal sources of help,* such as the police, social service agencies, and lawyers. To Bowker's personal strategies, I have added contemplating and resisting suicide and challenging the abuser's fiscal control.

PERSONAL STRATEGIES

Placating and Avoidance

One of the most common strategies, especially in the early stages of abuse, is to placate the abuser, particularly when the abuser is the husband. This is done by trying to do what he wants, praising him, apologizing to him, wearing the clothes he likes, cooking what he desires, and generally engaging in the activities most perceived as minimizing the abuse. Many of the women I interviewed initially used this strategy of resistance with the hope that it would make the abuser feel good, diffuse the tension, and reduce the probability of an immediate abusive episode. This was particularly the case with women who came to the United States as dependents. This strategy of placating should not always be seen as passivity or merely giving into the abuser. Rather, it is a type of resistance women engage in while trying to negotiate a relationship in a new country where they are isolated, dependent on their abusers, and perceive themselves as not having many other viable options.

For example, Geeta, an economically dependent spouse in an alien country, tried to placate her husband in the early stages of their marriage by dressing the way he liked. Often he would make her change her clothes a number of times before deciding what she should wear. To appease him she adhered strictly to his demand that she cook daily for him and be bathed before he arrived back from work. With no family support and what she perceived as extremely limited options, she used this behavior as a strategy to attempt to reduce the probability that her husband would abuse her. In reality, such a strategy is rarely effective, and most women move away from it once they realize they have other options.

In a couple of cases, placating as a strategy of resistance was an indirect method of disproving the abuser or enhancing a woman's own self-worth. For example, for Mary's husband, George, the notion of Mary's large student loan, common in the United States, was a culturally alien concept. The debt, when translated from dollars to Indian rupees, seemed a tremendous amount and was a constant source of tension in their arranged marriage. George had married Mary believing her to be professionally well placed with a corresponding level of earnings. The realization that she had a huge loan, coupled with his own occupational downward mobility since arriving in the United States, brought on a large degree of marital discord. Thus, when Mary's husband used the loan as a catalyst to abuse her, Mary attempted to placate him by promising that she would somehow drastically reduce the amount of the loan. To do so, she saved as much as she could from her salary and borrowed a large sum of money from her sister. This, from Mary's point of view, was not just a way of placating her husband but also a strategic way of taking away what she perceived to be a major source of tension in the marriage.

In some cases the strategy of placating is combined with avoidance, as was the case with Shehanaz, a twenty-two-year-old Muslim woman married to her thirty-nine-year-old cousin.

> He would verbally abuse and also hit me. I had become so used to this that I considered it trivial. I used to try and please him. Whenever we got that junk mail, saying you have become a millionaire, tell him that. But he would still keep fighting with me. Sometimes when I couldn't take it anymore, I would go out for a walk hoping things would calm down by the time I returned. Sometimes he would be in a pleasant mood when I came back.
> . . . Then he started bothering me to take up a job as all his pay was going toward the mortgage payment. It was very difficult for me to apply as the phone was disconnected and he never gave me money for bus fare. I tried to do

whatever I could by walking. He used to get very angry saying everybody works and I was sitting home. I asked this person I knew to help me but he had bad intentions. He tried to take me to a motel. I somehow ran back home . . . I could not talk about it to anybody as they were already against me.

Other women I interviewed employed the strategy of avoidance by using another room, trying to minimize the time spent in common space. Often women's language barrier, isolation, and lack of money compel them to find ways to resist within the constraints they encounter. Many abusers take advantage of a woman's lack of familiarity with the new country to intimidate her and instill unnecessary fears about unknown others, including neighbors and the police. Thus placating and avoidance are the first line of resistance for abused women who do not have a support system and are dependent on their spouses. They feel that the least confrontational approach at this stage, though limited, may be the only viable strategy. Here again language barriers and lack of a sense of community play a role in compelling the woman to work and resist within the parameters of the spousal relationship. At some point in the relationship, however, the abused woman usually realizes that placating is not always effective because there is no way to predict the abuser's actions or reactions. Thus she begins using additional strategies.

Talking Back

Many of the women I interviewed also resisted by talking back. Talking back here includes all forms of verbal resistance. It involves questioning the abuser's attitude and behavior, denigrating his family if he has denigrated hers, telling him to stop the abuse, screaming, and confronting him about his relationships. For example, Reena says: "When my husband forced me to have sex I would say to him that he was a dog. I would tell him that I was not a dog. . . . He would say nothing. Just do it." While Reena's denigration of her husband did not have much of an impact on him, it is still an important form of resistance. It articulates her disgust at his behavior and communicates her need for respect. In another instance, Malti, who tried to appease her husband by doing things the way he liked and tolerated his emotional abuse, talked back the first time her husband physically abused her. She recounts:

He was in the family room and got a call from his answering service . . . he said the telephone number aloud. I was cooking and I did not pay any attention. As soon as the answering service hung up, he said, "What was the telephone number?" I said, "I don't know. . . ." He got so furious, that I have no brains, I am not of any use. I think that was the first time he hit me or he did something violent. I told him at that time. This time I will tolerate this because it is the first time, even the second time probably I would let you go. The third time you touch me I am out of this house.

In Yamuna's case, when all her pleading and placating did not stop her husband from sexually abusing her, she resisted by scaring him with her screams. She recalls:

All the time I was thinking of how to get out of there and then one night when he initiated sex, I just couldn't take it. I just screamed. I mean I started getting hysterical. I just started screaming and that frightened him a little bit, I think. I said, Don't come anywhere near me. I think I must have been down on the floor. I think he did not know what was happening. He called his brother and that's when things got out of his control and I guess he was helpless. The brother was upset and called my parents and that started the ball rolling.

Many of the women I interviewed, including Mallika, Geeta, Jayathi, Shahida, Wahida, Usha, and Mary, talked back to abusers. One of the strongest cases of talking back among my interviews, however, and one that resulted in one of the most serious cases of battering, was that of Tara. This type of talking back, though extremely dangerous, shows the extent to which a woman resists her abuser.

. . . Tara, despite her husband's brutality, challenged his demands and talked back to him by saying she would not do what he asked. She defied her husband by telling his woman friend that he was coercing her to lie. Nearly all the women I spoke with resisted by talking back at some point in the relationship, although not many talked back under the type of conditions that Tara did. Talking back is an important strategy of resistance because it voices a woman's resentment at her treatment and challenges her oppressor's power and control. Among the women I spoke with, talking back had varying effects on the abuser. In Malti's case, it led to her husband's taunting her by asking where she would go with a baby and no job. For some of the other women it resulted in their abuser resorting to some form of further verbal denigration or violence. In general, however, the women rarely took a submissive attitude and often at great risk to themselves resisted their abuser's attempts to exercise power and control.

Challenging the Abuser's Fiscal Control

Another extremely important personal strategy of resistance and one much more difficult for immigrant women, especially dependent spouses, is to limit the power exercised by the abuser through his financial control. Many women mentioned the abuser's complete control over the finances as a major mechanism of abuse and an obstacle in getting out of the relationship. Yet some of these women resisted their abuser's control by trying to open a separate bank account, using money from a hidden stash, seeking money from a relative or friend, or appealing for and obtaining some personal allowance.

. . . Usha challenged her husband and his family's control of her finances by refusing to close her independent bank account, even when her husband beat her for asserting her independence. Shehanaz, similarly resisting her husband's financial control, demanded that he give her the money her father had sent for her. Shahida too resisted her husband's financial control by first taking money from his secret stash for an emergency and, later, when her husband accused her in front of his friends of stealing, explained to them her state of penury. As a result, her husband's friends were able to persuade him to give her an allowance that she was not accountable to him for. Prior to this, her husband had not even given her a dollar. Such personal strategies, especially shaming, though at times dangerous, can be an effective form of resistance, given the constraints under which these women live.

Some of the women resisted by demanding joint accounts. Though not always successful, the very process of insisting on a joint account challenges the abuser's financial control. In addition to the husband's financial control, the need for a minimum balance and other banking costs are structural impediments that limit women's chances of starting independent accounts, especially for those who have very little money. Such structural impediments make it harder for women to resist the financial control of the abuser. Michael Strube and Linda Barbour's study (1983) found that women who are economically dependent are more likely to stay with an abusive husband. Strategies are needed through which abused immigrant and lower socioeconomic women can obtain financial benefits such as no minimum balance requirement and free personal banking.

Hitting Back

A few women defended themselves by hitting back, but this strategy was least used. This could be because women were afraid to use physical force or were intimidated by the sheer physical strength of their abuser. It could also be that a woman feared that taking a more aggressive defense tactic such as hitting back might exacerbate the violence against her, with a greater chance of jeopardizing her own life. This issue needs further research. Only three of the women talked of hitting back. Tara was one of them. One day when Tara's husband began sexually abusing her, Tara, after months of encouragement from her young son, finally began hitting her abusive husband. She recounts:

> He was starting to force me to have sex, and I said no. I don't want you to touch me. He started asking why, do you have a new boyfriend? I said no. Actually I had my period at that time. I gave him that excuse but it didn't work. He still started forcing me. He pushed me down. I said no, the reason I don't want you to touch me is because you have touched that girl and I saw you, and that is enough. He said you have no proof. She was just there to borrow some money. So we had verbal confrontation back and forth.
>
> Then he started pushing me down. I started pushing him back, I started punching him back, for the first time, after all these years. I started kicking him back. That strength actually I got it from my son. . . . Actually September till December I was abused, three days a week. Every time he abused me, my son would say, mom why do you take it, why don't you hit him back. All these three months he brainwashed me. So when he hit me that time, I hit him back, I kicked him with my feet, I punched him, I tried to bite him.

Tara's attempts at hitting back only exacerbated her husband's violence against her, and as a result she had to be hospitalized with a ruptured bladder. Thus while hitting back is a strategy of resistance, its outcome can be extremely dangerous. Tara's experience, however, did lead to police involvement and to her finally leaving her husband.

Suicide

When escape tactics fail, in desperation some women contemplate or attempt suicide. Usually this occurs when women are feeling extremely depressed, isolated, and appear to have lost hope of either changing the relationship or getting out. Isolated and alienated, the women I interviewed who contemplated suicide perceived this as a last resort when all else seemed to fail. Yamuna, Wahida, Jayathi, and a young woman called Deepa, whose husband had not only been abusive but also at one point decided to leave her, all contemplated suicide. Jayathi was the only one who attempted it, although she did not succeed. Contemplation of or attempting suicide demonstrates the sense of desperation that some of these women feel and their perception that death will release them from their abuse.[1] Suicide here is an extreme strategy of resistance, and a tragic one. Some women contemplate suicide because they see it as the only remaining means of ending the abusive relationship. This is especially the case when women perceive themselves as having absolutely no external alternative support system. As Yamuna comments: "All I needed was to get out of there. Whether it meant killing myself or running away to a safe place. I needed to get away from that place and from this man."

Similarly, Jayathi explains how three months after her arrival in the United States in 1982, frustrated and depressed, she tried to commit suicide as a way out of her oppressive life with her husband.

> He had been to [a coat store] to buy him a coat. He came back and said something to me. I yelled back at him. I was just waiting for an opportunity like this. I gobbled down all the pills, including the sleeping pills. Of course, because we had had the fight I was sleeping with the children in the other room and he was in the master bedroom. . . . I told the kids. I had my son on one side and my daughter on the other. I told them that mommy is going. Please be good. God will watch over you. I will watch you from upstairs . . . the pills must have started reacting. I was moaning and groaning. He heard me from the next room. He came and called the ambulance and the doctor at the same time. They took me and pumped my stomach and I was at the intensive care unit for four or five days.

Jayathi's suicide attempt was diagnosed as a drug overdose from depression. Counseling was recommended for her and her husband, but her husband only attended one session, where he was questioned about his abusive behavior. Despite the recommendation for continued counseling, Jayathi was forced to stop after the twenty sessions covered by her insurance because her husband was unwilling to pay for more out of his own pocket. Once the counseling stopped and most probably knowing that her avenues of support were limited, Jayathi's husband started abusing her again. Jayathi, on her part, slowly began resorting to multiple strategies, including silence, avoidance, and finally obtaining a divorce. In this case noncompliance by the abusive spouse with strategies of formal intervention and the abused spouse's lack of financial ability were a major hindrance to the prevention of abuse.

Wahida's contemplation of suicide poignantly reveals the way in which women, even in the depths of desperation, cling to the possibility of more viable options for themselves. At the time Wahida contemplated suicide, she felt that she was no longer getting any support from her family. She had struggled to get off welfare, get vocational training, and had found a job that barely provided for her children. She had left her husband and gotten herself an apartment, only to have him come back into her life and destroy all that she had struggled to build. To make matters worse, he was slowly trying to alienate her children from her. Desperate, lonely, and demoralized, Wahida contemplated suicide as a way out of her misery:

There was so much mental abuse, so much torment, and so much emotional abuse. He started accusing me that I want to go out to work, because I want to flaunt around, I want to play around with guys. He couldn't stand to see that I was supporting my kids and myself. His manly ego couldn't sit there and take it. He used to purposely make me late to work. I used to try very hard. I wanted to keep this job. No matter what the pay is, I want to keep this job. I started out at fifteen thousand. It wasn't enough for the kids and me but it was something. Something is better than nothing. It was better than welfare. I said, no, I have to go. There was so much, so much, so much, mental abuse now.

So much emotional abuse. I couldn't take it any more. He would say bad things to the kids. He would say your mom is no good. Your mom is bad. He would tell me that your kids hate you. So I said, now you are trying to turn the kids away from me. And he was driving me so insane, that I thought that I was going insane. I was totally mad. It was not even six months of my job, and I was totally mad. I said I can't take it any more. He drove me to commit suicide.

In 1991, I left the kids. My oldest had gone to school, I left the other two with him at home, and I walked out. I thought that I was really going to kill myself that day. And I went and just sat on the lake. It was a cold February morning, below twenty degrees weather, cold and snow. I didn't think of anything. My mind wasn't thinking straight. I was so distressed . . . . I had given him hundred and fifty dollars, and he said that he is going to give it back right away, as he had to pay the lease on his cab. I said O.K. I am giving it to you, but I need it back, I don't have a single penny to go to work. And he promised me that he would give it back to me. He didn't [and I could not go to work that day]. I was so frustrated. On top of it, he is talking all these things with me, trying to torture me more. I didn't have anything. He wanted me to lose this job. He wanted me to be helpless again. He wanted me to be dependent on his way of life and I refuse to do that. I didn't want to lose the job. I thought that I was just going to kill myself. So I went to the lake, sat there for three hours. I sat there thinking and thinking and thinking. I thought I am really going crazy.

Then I thought I am not the one who is crazy. He is. I work too hard to get here, to be on my feet again, and I am not going to lose it. The kids are small. I constantly kept thinking of the kids. The kids don't deserve him. Because if something happens to me, my mom is not going to take them in. He will just take them to India, dump them in his parents' house and he will be off. So I thought about the kids. I thought that I am not going to prove to the world, that I was really crazy, and he is all right. I said that I am not going to do this. I was sitting there, and I remembered I read it in [an] Indian newspaper about an association started for Indian domestic violence women. So I walked into a SAWO [South Asian women's organization] and [a staff member] was there. I told her what I was about to do. She was glad that I came in. First thing she told me, go get your kids. So I went and got my kids. And stayed in the shelter for two months. I left the house. All I did was take my immediate belongings, and some important documents, like my passport, citizenship paper, and the kids' birth certificates. I just took my immediate clothes, and some of my work clothes. I didn't take anything else and I went back to work.

Although some of the women I interviewed contemplated suicide, none of the women took an aggressive defensive stance such as threatening their husband that when he was not on guard that she would kill him, as did the women in the studies of Bowker (1983) and Pagelow (1981). The most aggressive threat I encountered was an effort to intimidate the abuser by telling him that she would call the police.

USING INFORMAL AND SEMI-FORMAL SOURCES OF HELP

Despite their lack of resources and extreme isolation, many abused immigrant women, feeling the inadequacy of personal strategies, begin trying to get help from informal sources. This is usually the first level of looking outward as a strategy of resistance. Among the women I interviewed, many repeatedly tried to get external help. Some were successful; some partially successful; and some unsuccessful. The success depended on various factors, including the geographic distance of the persons whose help was sought, their attitudes, and the type of assistance they were willing to give. Almost all the abused women who sought help went first to South Asians, their families, friends, neighbors, or community members, at least in part due to a need for cultural sensitivity or support from one's own. Here the notion of "one's own" varied, based on social ties and accessibility.

Family

With the exception of two of the women, women who had their parents or siblings in the United States sought their families' support in their strategy of resistance. Women were more likely to contact their families, temporarily move in with them, or seek their support during a crisis or in its immediate aftermath. Family members intervened and used the family as a mechanism of social control and accountability against an abusive husband in the case of Mary, Tara, Shehanaz, and Mala.[2] In Tara's case, while her family members, particularly her sister, were always there for her in a crisis and in its immediate aftermath, they made no active attempt to dissuade her when she returned to her husband. In contrast, Mary's family was willing to actively intervene. Her brother even took an aggressive defensive position, saying that he would "settle" her husband by intimidating him with a baseball bat. Mary herself was against such intervention, however, as she hoped she could still salvage her marriage and change her husband's behavior. Although the process of seeking the help of family and demonstrating to the abuser that a woman has options is an important strategy of resistance, it is limited depending on the family's response and the woman's current attitude toward her abuser.

Some of the women who did not have any family or friends in the States reluctantly sought the help of their families back in South Asia. . . . However, geographic distances make it hard to explain all the issues or to get concrete help. What was extremely interesting were the ways women whose own family members were not accessible strategically used informal sources of help such as in-laws, their husband's friends, and neighbors.

In-laws

I found that some immigrant women, despite their isolation and lack of social networks, sought the assistance of others, including the abuser's kin or friends. While not always successful, seeking such help illustrates women's efforts to engage in resistance by whatever means possible. For example, having faced three months of abuse from her husband and with no support network of her own. Reena stayed temporarily with her husband's aunt. This aunt, her husband's mother's younger sister, was sympathetic to Reena's plight as she had been abused by Reena's father-in-law twenty years earlier when he sponsored her to the United States. While Reena was staying with the aunt, her husband came demanding that she return to him. Reena explains:

> He asked me to come back to the same house but I refused to return. I continued to stay with the lady. He used to come and curse. He said I didn't like him and liked the man of this house instead. He told me, "You like him. Is he your husband? I know he already has one wife and now he wants a young girl." The couple was old. When he said all this I felt unwell [fainted]. The ambulance came and took me to the hospital and from there we later went to stay with my father-in-law. However, my father-in-law would get upset if I cooked something that he did not like. I was pregnant at the time and so we parted on bad terms.

Reena left her husband three times, once with her daughter, whom she then left in India for three months while she tried to organize her life. All three times, Reena stayed away from her husband for a period of time, only ultimately to be persuaded to return. When I interviewed Reena, her husband was living with her and their child, violating the court order that prohibited his contact with them. She told me that this time her husband called on their anniversary and took her to the temple. There he gave her a new *tali,* a symbol of marriage, and vowed that he would treat her well. Reena told me that her decision to return was determined by the belief that her husband was a good father and that her daughter was being deprived of his love and attention. In my interviews I noticed that the impact of the abuse on a woman's children and the husband's attitude toward the children played a major role in determining whether to stay or leave the husband.

The notion of staying with an abusive husband or returning to him can be partially explained as a type of attitude that Barnett and La Violette (1993) call "learned hopefulness." The battered woman continues to believe that her partner's abusive behavior will stop and that his personality will change for the better. I also believe that in the immigrant context, the reason why women such as Reena frequently return to their abuser can be attributed to the ethnic and class barriers women encounter in their day-to-day lives. For immigrant women, language barriers and lack of social interaction can create a sense of loneliness and a need to identify with someone, in this case, even the abuser. This is especially true when the abuser manipulates this loneliness so that the abused woman begins to hope that the relationship will improve and alleviate her loneliness, as with Reena.

Like Reena, Yamuna too tried a range of strategies to protect herself, including an unsuccessful attempt to persuade her mother-in-law to come and live with them in their studio apartment. She hoped that the elderly woman's presence would act as a buffer and prevent her husband from sexually abusing her.

> I tried to get my mother-in-law to come and stay with me. I told her that I am new to this place and I have never set up house and things like that. Why don't you come and stay with me? She said, it is not practical since it's a studio and also her eldest son has small kids that he needs her to be with. I literally begged her to stay.

However, unlike Reena, Yamuna was adamant that the abuse should stop immediately and that there was no way that she could continue living with her husband. Thus all her strategies were aimed at somehow getting away from her abuser's control.

Friends and Neighbors

When parental support was unavailable or inaccessible and in-laws were unhelpful, women sought the help of friends, acquaintances, coworkers, or neighbors.

Tired of her husband's abuse and his threat to send her back to Pakistan as a failed wife, Shahida sought temporary assistance from her husband's friend and his wife. Initially wary of seeking their help because they were primarily her husband's friends, Shahida gradually sought their assistance as the wife became sympathetic to Shahida's plight. For Shahida, getting the help of her husband's friend also entailed resisting this man's efforts to take advantage of her vulnerability. In general, however, friends in the community who empathize tend to help within the purview of what they think is culturally or socially desirable. A narrative that demonstrates the creative ways used by immigrant women to seek informal help is that told by Mallika:

> I don't have any relatives here. I know somebody in [another state]. Even my husband has no friends here. Even my father-in-law has no friends. He has three daughters and his daughter has three sisters-in-law. We only interacted with these six families. They are his relatives, so they won't help me.
>
> My husband has never taken me to anybody's house. Therefore I don't know anybody. By God's grace. I thought up this idea. I took the telephone directory

of my area, and made a list of all the Indian families listed there. I thought I would call them and somebody could help me. I talked to Mr. S. I told him that I don't know anybody in America. I don't have any relatives and I am not aware of all the things here so I need some help and could he help me? He said that he empathized with me, and he would talk it over with his wife and call me over to their house and discuss the ways that they can help me. So I went to his house.

I was alone. He wanted me to compromise with my husband, so that we could start our life together. Usually people are not for divorce. He said that he would call my husband over to his house and we could talk. From what I told him, he could make out that my husband did not have any friends, that we never visited anybody. He said that he would invite us and also introduce us to other people. He thought that once my husband started having his own friends and saw how other people lived, he would change and my life would be better.

Later I talked to some woman and she gave me the phone number of a SAWO. I called the president of the association. She asked for all my history. She works with women who come to this country and are abandoned by their husbands. She helped me a lot.

Mallika's narrative is a good example of the way in which women, despite tremendous obstacles, do not passively accept abuse but actively engage in efforts to end it. Often the attitudes and behaviors of those from whom they seek help impede their resistance. In Mallika's case, the limited support she received from the family she approached did not deter her from seeking further help. The notion of abused women calling a friend or someone within the South Asian community for support is closely linked to an immigrant's notion of an imagined community. By calling someone within the community, abused women hope to place some social pressure on their husband to be accountable in a context where there are frequently no other traditional buffers to stop the abuse.

For some women, the problem is not only resisting their abuser but also not succumbing to those individuals who try to persuade them that the issue is not marital violence but a matter of adjusting as a new immigrant. Yamuna narrates:

I don't know what would have happened if the brother [of her husband] had not called my parents. My parents called me back. Of course they tried talking to me. I said I want to come back home. My father said, "Don't worry, this is a new country and I will come in a month and stay with you for a couple of months." For me this month was an unendurably long time. I could not take another day, let alone another month to wait for somebody. I knew I couldn't talk to them. So, later when my husband was not there, I made a call to my friend and asked her to talk to my mother and tell her this is very important. She did that. Then my parents called me right back and said O.K. you can go to [the home of an acquaintance in another city]. They called my in-laws and politely said she is not well, so let her go to [this person's place] for a while. In the meantime, they called this friend, no not a friend but somebody we happened to know and these people sent me a ticket. . . . I went and stayed with them for a while.

At some point, all the women sought some informal help, including shouting out for neighbors or calling a friend when the husband was not home. Seeking informal help has multiple effects. It not only allows a woman to go beyond personal strategies but also indicates to the abuser that there are others beyond the abuser and the abused woman who know about the violence. This can act as a partial deterrent in some situations.

South Asian Women's Organizations

South Asian organizations were usually the most important contact for abused immigrant women.[3] These organizations, for those who approached them, usually became the first source of culturally identifiable collective support. They not only provided tangible support but also by their activities challenged the silence surrounding domestic violence within the South Asian community. [Chapter 8 in Abraham (2000) is devoted to these organizations.]

FORMAL SOURCES OF HELP: THE POLICE AND THE COURTS

While informal sources were the primary source for seeking external help, a few of the women did call the police. More often, however, the police were called either by neighbors, a family member, or a friend. Women who were at least partially raised in the United States or who were more familiar with the institutional services available tended to be more likely to seek the help of the police or to threaten to call the police. For example, when Mary's husband hit her, she threatened to call the police and told him that in this country the police would not tolerate such things. Similarly Malti, who had lived and worked in the United States for some time, called the police when her husband physically abused her and his stepson:

> The third time [Malti was physically abused] my son [from a previous marriage] had a phone call after 11 at night and [my husband] did not want anybody to call my son, period. He told my son to make a list of all his friends, with all their telephone numbers. So that he can call them and warn their parents to tell their children not to call. My son was in college and thought this was too childish. So I said, "Let us drop this." So my husband pushed me away with his hand. My baby was sleeping. My son said, "You can do anything to me but do not touch my mom." I think he pushed me again, and my son got furious. He pushed him and said, "Get away from my mom, don't hit her." My husband got hold of my son's hand. I don't remember what happened but he bit my son to the extent that it was bleeding. I didn't know what to do. I called the police. The police said he could be arrested for that. They asked me whether they could arrest him and put him in jail for the night. I could not see that, so I said no. But they said he can't stay here for at least twenty-four hours. My husband said I should get out of the house. The police said no. She is with a baby. She will not get out of the house. Somehow he got out and came back after twenty-four hours. He could not forgive me for not sticking up for him. He thought I should have told the police that he could stay here.

Once when Malti could not get to the phone, she alerted the police by pressing the silent house alarm in her home, knowing that would bring them. In general, however, women rarely called the police directly. Multiple factors may be involved, including concern about the outcome, wariness stemming from beliefs about negative police attitudes toward minorities, and fear of ostracism by the community. I asked many of these women why they did not call the police and some replied that they simply did not think of it or were worried about the outcome for themselves or their children. Women's hesitancy in calling for formal sources of help probably also stems from both a cultural preference for informal mediation and negative perceptions of police attitudes in their country of origin. Even Malti, who called the police, was reluctant to have her husband spend even one night in jail.

However, when women decide to leave the relationship, they usually contact a lawyer at some point. Of the women I interviewed, fewer than a third first contacted a lawyer on their own. Many of the women sought a lawyer with the help of a South Asian women's organization. Women who did not contact lawyers on their own were primarily deterred by financial constraints, lack of information and accessibility, language barriers, cultural conceptions about divorce, and the difficulties of negotiating their way through structural barriers as new immigrants.

TAKING CONTROL AND GETTING OUT

Although some of the women I interviewed did hear about South Asian women's organizations and used their support in getting out of their marriages, women like Malti, Prema, and Usha did not have such support as these organizations had not yet been created. . . . [In Abraham (2000), chapter 8] I include the narratives of women who sought the help of South Asian women's groups; here I will focus on women who left their relationships prior to the creation of these organizations. These women resisted their abusers and worked out ways to leave and regain control over their lives without much community support. For women like Prema and Usha, the need to get out was also motivated by the impact of the abuse on their children. For Malti, it was the emotional pressure. Their narratives are testimony to the types of struggles women encounter and their will to resist their abuser's control even without any major source of external support. Malti describes how she finally got out:

> Once when there was a conference, he left town. I went to my previous work and said I needed my job. It was already a year and half since I had left it but fortunately they had an opening. I filled in an application and my boss said to take me in. But I had to explain this to my husband. When he came back I told him, my job called me. They have an opening and they want me to come back. He said, "No I don't want you to go back." I said, "They said at least for a month I should go and help them until they find a replacement. Since I know this place why don't I help them out." At that time my daughter was a year and

a half. He said, "What are you going to do with the child?" I said that I would find somebody to take care of her. He said that I had to leave home just half an hour before work and be back half an hour after work. During lunchtime I took the opportunity and started looking for an apartment. I didn't tell him it was a permanent job. He did not know anything. At lunch I would say I am at the cafeteria. People would say she is out for lunch. Nobody knew that anything was going on.

I secured an apartment. You know how apartments go through your credit check. They asked for my current address. I gave my work address. They did not know it was a company. Twice a week in the evenings he would go to another place to work. On that evening I went out to a truck place, rented a van. There was an office building near where I worked. I went there and parked the van at seven at night. I walked home with my baby. The next morning I had taken a day off from work. He did not know that. As soon as he left, I had my son and two of his friends come and help me remove some stuff, put it in the truck and moved out. I said that I am leaving and I left [almost three years after the marriage]. . . . He called me at work. He said he wanted me to come back as this is not the way things should be. He said, "I have nobody to help me." I said, "I couldn't care less." I couldn't take the pressure anymore.

Similarly Prema, who had been abused by her husband for a number of years, finally realized that the only way to stop her husband's abuse of her and her children was to take back control and get out of the marriage. Married in 1962 in India, Prema left India in 1964. Her husband initially had a job in England and later they migrated to the United States. She has worked in the same company for nineteen years. At the time I interviewed her she was completing her undergraduate degree and working as a program analyst, earning approximately $30,000 a year.

Prema's husband had started abusing her very soon after the marriage. From 1968 until the time she left him, Prema's husband did not work. Prema was the sole earning member of her home, although her husband controlled the money. The South Asian community itself was quite small, and she mentioned in her interview with me that the family was relatively socially isolated. They did not have many friends, and most of the time there was only her husband, their two children, and herself. Over a period of time, Prema began seeking ways to get out of the abusive relationship. In 1967 and a couple of times later Prema had tried to seek counseling and leave the marriage. Ultimately in 1982 she succeeded in getting out and began rebuilding a life for herself and her children. The process of getting out was not easy, as she explains:

In 1980 I started taking control, slowly. I started taking control of the money. I quit the second job I had, from which I was making good money because it was an overtime job. I quit that job and started staying home more. Staying with the kids. The more I stayed home, the more control I took over. He lost control of the kids, over the money, over me. So that got him real angry. So the fights instead of being every month or every other week were now every day. And the beatings really accelerated and suddenly everything went haywire. . . . Then I planned I was going to leave him. I had to get some money first. Collect some money of my own. He wouldn't give me any money that was in the bank then. It was all his. It was fine. I don't want it. I opened my own account. Savings account and checking account and started saving money. I paid the rent, whatever needed to be paid I paid and I gave him the money. That is when the fights accelerated because I would ask him why he wants to eat outside when he could eat in the house and then go out instead of spending ten dollars on lunch everyday. Which he wasn't spending anyway. I think he was saving. He just wanted to take it from me. . . .

In 1982, I told him I am getting an apartment, since he is not going. I had got an apartment, paid security deposit and a month's rent on it. I went into the apartment, cleaned it, packed my boxes over at his house and I was going to move. This friend of mine he was going to help me move. He is my best friend's husband. He came to the house and my husband told him that he can't do that. You can't take my wife and kids away from me. You can't move my furniture from my own house. I wasn't moving furniture. It was just my personal things. Otherwise I will have you arrested for taking my wife and kids. So this man couldn't do anything. He was scared and he left me right there. So I said, well, if he is not going to help me, I am going to get out of this place with my kids, with or without these things. Then he knew I was determined. So I had another friend come over, we rented a van and we were going to move out. He told her the same thing but he did promise her that he would go for counseling. The same thing happened with counseling. I went for counseling and the counselor told me that there was no help for him because he is not willing to get help, so what you need is to go ahead. If you want to get divorced, go ahead and start planning. So this was in September 1982. I started looking for an apartment in January, because he had stopped counseling and was getting worse. He had beaten up my kids by then. He had really beaten them up.

He had beaten up my kids, and I talked this to a counselor, and he reported it to my doctor and my doctor reported it to [the authorities, and their] people came in. I had to either give up the kids, or leave the house. That was the choice. I told them I was going to leave the house and that I had already tried once . . . .

About February or March [1983] I started looking for apartments without telling him. I felt I was committing robbery every day of my life after that. I couldn't tell him anything because if I told him, he would have a plan of his own and would ruin my plan. So I decided I was going to move out of this place, without telling him, without taking anything. Just me and my kids. Find another apartment and start all over again. I looked for [an] apartment for two months, February and March. Finally in March I did find an apartment that was going to be vacated by May. I paid the lease and one month rent and moved into this place. That [getting out] was another experience in itself.

Trying to get out of there, just getting your personal things out was really bad. We didn't think he would let us get out first of all without beating us up. He was there when we moved but I had got legal help in February . . . through the yellow pages and talking to lots of other lawyers. The people at work were very helpful. I told them what was happening toward the end. They couldn't believe it. They said, "We thought you had a perfect marriage." I said so did I. . . . After that it was easy going. He was served the day after I left. He found out and didn't show up at the court or anything. Within six months, I got my divorce. I signed off all my rights. I didn't want anything from him for my kids or for myself. I just wanted to get out of his life. I wanted to get out of his life.

While Prema's and Malti's narratives point to the physical and emotional trauma involved in the process of getting out, they also show that getting out is most effective when a woman ultimately recognizes that the abuse must stop now. The departures of Prema, Usha, and Malti, though extremely difficult, were partially possible because they were economically independent, had no major language barrier, and were citizens or LPRs [Legal Permanent Residents]. Economic independence and the ability to communicate in the dominant culture must be considered when assessing women's ability to get out of an abusive relationship in the immigrant context. Thus class position must be linked to ethnicity and gender when addressing women's strategies of resistance.

The narratives in this chapter clearly contradict assumptions that South Asian women passively accept their abuse. Rather, they actively engage in resisting their abuser. The internalization of norms surrounding the institution of marriage coupled with external economic, social, legal pressures, and cultural dislocation all have to be taken into account in seeking to understand the strategies of resistance abused women use. All the women I spoke with resisted their abuser at some point. The amount of time they stayed with their abusers was, to a large extent, contingent on both cultural factors and practical constraints. Isolation and the inability to obtain access to effective informal and formal sources of help influenced the choice of strategies of resistance.

In my interviews, I found that the decision to stay or leave was based on a number of factors, including children, perception of alternate economic options, fear of loss of legal status, fear of deportation, impact on the family, and perception of the lack of availability of resources and support systems. Not having their own bank account, being forced to give up their entire salary, financially relying on their abuser, and all forms of economic dependency impede abused women's strategies of resistance. Women do resist, but it is difficult to fight a battle on one's own, especially when one faces both cultural and structural constraints.

Often it is not that women don't reach out for help, but that the help they receive is symbolic or inadequate. Many women not only have to resist their abuser but also must overcome cultural disapproval for violating the sanctity of the institution of marriage. However, such attitudes are slowly changing. Since the 1990s there has been a gradual shift in the South Asian community toward greater sensitivity to gender roles, especially to the problem of marital violence. There are many individuals, particularly other South Asian women, who do care and want to help abused women. These individuals are often limited, however, by their own socialization in certain cultural values, their lack of knowledge of available resources in the United States, and their inability to provide tangible help given their own socioeconomic circumstances.

One of the common themes throughout my interviews was an abused woman's need for support within her community. That many South Asian women in the early 1980s did not come out in public to denigrate their abusers thus should not be misconstrued as passivity. Their silence was rather due to the atomization of immigrant women, their individual struggles to redefine their cultural and material lives in the United States, and the lack of public acknowledgment of domestic violence as a social problem by the South Asian community.

The immense increase in the number of women who reported domestic violence in late 1980s and the 1990s, including most of the women I interviewed, can be attributed to the birth during this period of South Asian women's organizations that address domestic violence. Their emergence marks a shift from private individual struggles to a more collective, publicly oriented system of resistance against martial abuse.

NOTES

1. In a survey conducted by Mildred Pagelow, approximately 50 percent of the abused women in her sample contemplated suicide, and 23 percent attempted suicide at least one time. See Pagelow (1981).

2. This is Mary, the woman I interviewed, and not Mary Mathew who was battered to death by her husband. One of the women who sought the help of family was Shehanaz, the young Muslim woman. When her husband and mother-in-law abused her, she called her father, who was visiting Canada, and told him of her situation.

3. It is important to note here that my research was only conducted after the formation of these South Asian women's organizations and that my contact with many of the women I interviewed was through these organizations. Therefore, a large number of the women I interviewed were women who had contacted these organizations as a source of support.

REFERENCES

Abraham, Margaret. 2000. Making a difference: South Asian women's organizations in the United States. *Speaking the Unspeakable: Marital Violence among South Asian Immigrants in the United States.* New Brunswick, N.J.: Rutgers University Press, 154–173.

Barnett, O. W., and A. D. LaViolette. 1993. *It Could Happen to Anyone: Why Battered Women Stay.* Newbury Park, Calif.: Sage.

Bowker, L. H. 1983. *Beating Wife-Beating.* Lexington, Mass.: Lexington.

Gelles, R. J., and M. A. Straus. 1988. *Intimate Violence: The Causes and Consequences of Abuse in the American Family.* New York: Simon & Schuster.

Lempert, L. B. 1996. Women's strategies for survival: Developing agency in abusive relationships. *Journal of Family Violence* 11: 269–289.

Mehrotra, M. 1999. The social construction of wife abuse: Experiences of Asian Indian women in the United States. *Violence Against Women* 5(6): 619–640.

Pagelow, M. D. 1981. Secondary battering and alternatives of female victims to spouse abuse. In Lee H. Bowker, ed., *Women and Crime in America.* New York: Macmillan, 277–300.

Strube, M., and L. Barbour. 1983. The decision to leave an abusive relationship: Economic dependence and psychological commitment. *Journal of Marriage and the Family* 45(4): 785–793.

CHAPTER **17**

**MICHELLE FINE, ROSEMARIE A. ROBERTS,
AND LOIS WEIS**

Puerto Rican Battered Women Redefining Gender, Sexuality, Culture, Violence, and Resistance

———————————— ABSTRACT ————————————

As part of a larger study, published in *The Unknown City* (Michelle Fine and Lois Weis, 1998), the authors interviewed women and men across racial and ethnic groups in Buffalo, New York, and Jersey City, New Jersey, to learn about the distinct resistance and agency of Puerto Rican women in the face of a triple menace of violence—at home, in their neighborhoods, and by the state in poor and working-class communities of color.

Oral histories with thirty-four poor and working-class, predominantly Puerto Rican, women reveal how the traditional role performance of gender and culture is at once affirmed, contested, and resisted in the contemporary generation of young urban Latinas in the Northeast. Experiences of domestic violence, joblessness, and culturally bound assertions about gender and sexuality are among those shared by the women interviewed. Each woman's story is deeply interwoven with the women of her family—generations past, present, and future. Caught in the grip between violence and welfare, as described by Josephson (chapter 7), Puerto Rican women struggle to create change while holding on to traditional ideals of family. These women refuse to surrender themselves or their children to violence or social injustice.

This chapter represents one of the very few articles published on Puerto Rican women as a distinct cultural and ethnic group with a unique colonial past and present. Through the women's narratives, the authors uncover, how, far from passive, Latinas resist abuse and contest gender, sex, family, and home arrangements despite the considerable cultural and structural constraints they face.

The narratives of Puerto Rican women reveal stories of oppression on many levels—economic, colonial, state, family, and relationship-based—as well as testimonies of strength, survival, and resistance. As you read this chapter, think about the competing narratives expressed on the part of Puerto Rican women and men. How is violence at home, in the streets, and with state initiation differentially experienced by Puerto Rican women and men interviewed in this study? How do these struggles compare with those described by Websdale (chapter 10) in his ethnography of poor Black women and men in Nashville or by Weis and her colleagues (chapter 15) in their description of poor and working-class white women?

A s part of a larger study, published in *The Unknown City* (Fine and Weis, 1998), we conducted 154 life history interviews and focus groups with men and women across racial and ethnic groups in Buffalo, New York, and Jersey City, New Jersey, in order to write a history of urban Northeast America from the vantage point of poor and working-class young adults. Out of this sample, we spoke with thirty-four Latinas, median age twenty-four years old, from Puerto Rico, Cuba, Ecuador, and Colombia. One hundred percent of our Buffalo respondents and approximately 70 percent of our Jersey City respondents identified themselves as Puerto Rican. All of the Jersey City and 70 percent of the Buffalo sample completed high school or a GED program. In addition, one quarter of our Jersey City sample had some college. Eighty percent were working at the time of the interview; all but five had children.[1]

Each woman brought with her a strong sense of what gender means within her cultural context. We take seriously Juan Flores's (1996) proposition that Puerto Rican identities are deeply and particularly influenced by the colonial relationship between Puerto Rico and the United States and should not be masked with a broad Latina sweep. Thus, we analyze these interviews given the specificities of the Puerto Rican experience, most profoundly the impact of colonization on ethnic and gendered identities.

As you will hear in their own words, these women believe deeply in family, religion, and culture, even as they raise significant and profound questions about economic and colonial oppression, violence drawn at the hands of men, churches filled with more hypocrisy than spirit, culture built on the backs of their mothers, the cruelty of the state, and the subordination of women. And yet, in the face of this—because of this—they persist, narrating, creating, and holding *themselves* accountable for families and communities that thrive in peace. They fight for physical survival, even as their personal well-being is compromised. These women are producing a version of "living Latina" in which gender and culture as traditionally lived are being rewritten with neither economic nor domestic subordination of women assumed. As Hurtado explains, "Chicana feminists also want to remain in their communities and make their struggle as women part of the struggle that affects all oppressed peoples" (1996, p. 90). These women stretch the borders of gender *within Latino culture* and dare to raise their sons and daughters within reclaimed definitions of culture. With a radical reshaping of resistance, they insist upon remaining in their homes, with their children, and in their communities, voicing a quiet but profound critique, and always producing hope. No surprise, the rubs of gendered relations *within* Latino homes, churches, and communities grow more and more contested.

Listen to a focus group of Puerto Rican women who are in the midst of contesting these gender, sex, family, and home arrangements.

> BEATRICE: [I had] security [with him], but when I was about eight months pregnant, I decided things weren't going right between us, and I decided I don't care what he does. This is mine. He's never going to take this away from me. He gave me something that nobody could give me that I would always have regardless of whether he stayed with me or not. But after she was born, and I saw him with her and stuff like that, they got close and I could see that, but it still wasn't close between me and him. So he was the proud father with his only daughter, still it's his only daughter and that's like my little trophy, she's like my little trophy, and that's something he doesn't have anyway anymore. But, when a man abuses you physically, he's also doing verbally, emotionally and sexually. Many times it's all connected. Okay, so in my mind at the time, everything was my fault. *Everything was my fault.* If you're told that enough, you believe it. You believe everything you're told. If you're told repeatedly, you believe it. So I was brainwashed. I was with him for ten years. For those ten years, he brainwashed me. So every time I felt that I wanted to gain his life, it was through a child. So when I had my daughter, I said great. I have my little girl. I had this princess. But I want a boy because, what does a father want most? A son to carry his name. . . . I got pregnant again. But it was still, in my mind, the same thing. If, I give him—the more children I give him, the more he'll love me. Eventually he'll have to love me because I'm the mother of his child. That was my thinking.
>
> ROSEMARIE [interviewer and author]: Did that happen?
>
> BEATRICE: No, it didn't happen. *But you never give up hope,*[2] because that's the only . . . I didn't want to be with him. My mother always had me at home. He was my first boyfriend, my first lover, my first everything. O.K. He was the first in all aspects. Now, the way my mother and my father through thick and thin they had been together. He was her own. Now they're going to be together twenty-three years. And now, that we're all grown, they look back, remember when you were like this. They say to each other, "Remember when you were like this? All the problems we had back then? . . . always wanted . . . ten, fifteen years from now to look back and say, 'You remember when you used to give me all that hard time? And look at us now.'" It would be like I accomplished something. I stuck by a man who was hard to be with, but I stuck by him.
>
> ROSEMARIE: Was that your job? Did you feel like that was your job?

BEATRICE: *I felt that was my job,* yes. I was raised in the type where . . . I cooked everything. But it depends. . . . As a female, that was my job. This is why, this is like a trade school where I would be taught what to do for the future. So, now I had this man.

ROSEMARIE: Did you have that experience at home also?

MERCEDES: But I went through the same thing you did, since I was little. As soon as I turned eight, I learned how to cook. I learned how to do everything in the house. But what did my father always think? Me and him could never get along, because he always wanted to be the little boy in the house. I could have a man, but I'm not gonna take the abuse. I know that's what they teach you and everything, but I don't play that way. I deserve respect just as much as you have respect. I really do. Right now, I have two kids from different guys, and maybe it's because I want respect, and they don't feel like that. They feel like I should be at home with the *chankla* (slippers), and be like an old lady. No. It's not like that. *I always wanna hold my own.* I wanna do things. I wanna do them for me, not for anybody else.

BEATRICE: Once you let him hit you once, he'll do it again and again and again. Because he feels that, oh, I did it once and it was all right. I could keep doing it. And that's when you gotta put your foot down and be like, "I love you and everything, but this is where it stops. Cause I deserve respect. This is my home."

ROSEMARIE: Mm hm.

BEATRICE: It's easier now to teach my daughter that. Now the relationship that I'm in now, I don't look at people and think well do you regret your ten years with him. I think no, because life is experience. And I have three children that live . . . those are my kids. He was just there. But I won't ever trade . . . I don't regret those ten years because those ten years made me who I am today. Now he thinks I'm a bitch. Yes. But you made me who I am. I don't teach my daughter anything bad. But I do teach my daughter in the house. In the situation that I'm in now. What you said, if a man respects you, you respect him right back. *But you are nobody's, nobody's pillow. You are nobody's hitting toy.*

Discussions with individuals and small focus groups of Latina women foreshadow a set of emergent dynamics narrated by the larger sample of women: histories of state (i.e., government), community, and domestic violence witnessed and endured; a personal sense of responsibility and hope; and an urgent duty to challenge when the children witness. Herein lies the power—often smashed and resisted by the state, the economy, men, and sometimes other women—that Latinas reveal battling oppression again, as always, at the beginning of the twenty-first century.

I (Rosemarie Roberts, author), a second generation Latina of Puerto Rican and Cuban parents, resonate with Beatrice, Mercedes, and the other Latinas' experiences of being Latina. I hear our culturally bound "promise" and the subsequent betrayal of that "promise" as Latinas struggle through a reworking of gender, sexuality, and motherhood. With many walking a tightrope in the U.S. between violence and welfare, we find ourselves in the midst of a quiet revolution.

[Rosmarie Roberts continues] Latinas have traditionally lived with a cultural expectation about gender and (hetero)sexuality. We are expected to love and honor our man, cook his meals, clean his house, be available and ready when he wants to have sex, have and care for his children, and look the other way at marital infidelities, all the time working *una doblé jornada* (inside and outside the home). In return, he agrees to protect us and our children, work, pay the bills. Even if our mothers worked, which was often the case, our fathers were supposed to be treated as if they were the primary wage earners. Indeed in the 1940s and 1950s and as early as the 1930s, men migrated here for better job opportunities. Jobs for both our mothers and fathers were easier to come by then. But times have changed. The loss of manufacturing jobs in the U.S. and the lack of social mobility between our mothers' generation and our own have created a radically different experience for us, Latinas coming of age in the 1980s and 1990s.

The economic and social conditions necessary for women to be able to fulfill the traditional role of the "ideal" wife, worker, cook, cleaner, and mother no longer exist. The predominantly Puerto Rican women we interviewed were raised to be "focused on making men the center of [the] universe" (Trujillo, 1998, p. 11). Except soon they learned that the economic conditions for "their" men had slipped. It became increasingly difficult for the men to fulfill their end of the promise. The women watched their men get sucked into the dangerously seductive, momentarily lucrative street life of drugs and violence. Dead-end menial jobs with no opportunities for advancement dealt small and consistent blows to their sense of self. *Ser un hombre* (be a man) so rigidly defined becomes much harder. The blows accumulated. Anger and seething rage turned inward toward self. And against the women and children they love. Increasingly conflicted about the rigid gender and sexual arrangements in their homes and the violence within them, these narratives indicate that Latinas are protesting quietly but maneuvering quickly to get themselves and their children out of the way of danger.

ON GENERATIONS OF WOMEN

Listening to these narratives, we, like Rina Benmayor and her colleagues (1987), Oliva Espin (1996, 1999), Marixsa Alicea (1997), Aida Hurtado (1995), and Jennifer Ayala (2000) were struck by how each woman tells a story of oppression—economic, colonial, state, and family-based—deeply woven with the lives of her family: generations past, present, and future. With a soft but firm refusal of individualism, the stories told across women—connected, betrayed, catching each other, defending one another (Ginorio et al., 1995). These are stories of men whose hands are too fast, whose hearts are too cold.

Some would argue that in Puerto Rican culture, as with other marginalized groups, the passing of stories from mother to daughter and father to son crosses generations and is constitutive of cultural survival (Lykes, 1985; Ward, 1996). We, too, heard stories of pain, understanding talk, and wisdom passed on to generations, carrying politics, cultural memory, pain, loss, and connection. As Carmen explains,

> She [mother] was thirty-nine. She was so beautiful at thirty-nine. She looked very young. A lot of the people could not believe that she passed away. . . . I was like a gum to her. I stuck through my mother through everything. I stuck by her. Yes, we did. In fact, oh, I don't even have the chain with me. My baby brother, I tell you, he doesn't speak about it, but he'll react to it. He brought a heart, a gold heart. It's broken in three pieces and that heart symbolizes my mother's heart. So at Christmastime we separated the heart in three pieces, so each one of us [my brother, sister, and I] has a piece of that heart.

Placing oneself in a "line" of women, with a third of the heart to signify, Carmen authors a kind of loving unwillingness we heard from so many, an unwillingness to see herself or be interviewed as if she were separate, autonomous, or concerned merely with her own personal interests. Rather, as Brinton Lykes (1985) has described in her analysis of "social individuality," the self as narrated by Latinas swims amidst an easy fluidity between and among women within a family, a community, across generations. Carmen remains connected to her mother, and her brother, and her sister.

Most of the women we interviewed were born on the mainland and grew up in the 1960s and 1970s version of urban America. Surrounded, still, by low-paying factories, most grew up in homes where both mother and father were employed.

> DENISE: My mother worked in the Coca-Cola factory, until it closed down, on her feet for ten hours a day.
>
> MARTA: My mother, she had a job—you know, the Colgate-Palmolive clock? It used to be a factory. I waited for her at the back entrance.

At some point, for most, *papi* left. He may have returned to Puerto Rico with his "American money," inviting a reluctant family to accompany him. Or, he may have left to create another family with another woman. He may have drifted off, for a while, perhaps no longer wanted. Regardless of how he left, more often than not, he left. Suddenly, the family of many, which had survived with two inadequate but combined incomes, was left without *papi*. Connections were violated. The abuse of colonialism echoes in the economic and domestic unprotectedness of "my father leaving." The "whole family" is affected and has to reimagine itself; and it is women's job to assure that culture, economics, and hope are left intact. The gendered interdependence of domestic roles collapsed as families grew impoverished.

> MARINA: It affected the whole family all together. Because it was my father, my mother, my sister, my grandmother, and me. My grandmother is my father's mother. So when he left, my mother expected him to take his mother with him. He didn't. He left my grandmother with us. So my mother was like, "Oh, on top of everything you did to me, now I have to take care of your mother, too?" Then my grandmother said, "No. I raised," she raised me. She goes, "I can't leave her. She's like a

daughter to me. She needs, you know, she still needs me. My son is a grown man. He has his own money, his own future. He could do with his life whatever he wants. But she's still young. I can't leave her." And I know my grandmother's here because of me. But it's a conflict between my grandmother and my mother. That is her son.

ANDY [INTERVIEWER]: Um hm. That must be hard.

MARINA: And if my mother wants to go on with her life, she can't do it in front of my grandmother, because that's *a lack of respect*.

ANDY: Right.

MARINA: So it's kind of hard. And then my father paid for everything in the house. My father paid for the rent, the phone bill, the light bill, the shopping. My father paid for everything. Once my father was gone, it was like we couldn't live on my mother's paycheck alone. Then everything, we were so used to having it all, that it came a time when we didn't have it any more. We got so used to my father giving us money once a month to go shopping. If we needed a pair of sneakers, "Dad, I need a pair of sneakers." "Here you go." "Dad, I need this." We were so used to that. Then it came to a point that we didn't have it any more. And we couldn't tell our mother, "Mom, can I have this?" because she didn't have it.

ANDY: Right.

MARINA: So I started working and then my mom took another job. So now she's working two jobs, and I'm working one job. So I help my mother out. My sister is graduating high school. So she needed a prom dress. She needed everything. So now in my house the money is very tight. You know, every little, you know we have to save each and every penny and make sure that we don't misuse the money on stupid things. You know, my mother doesn't tell me what to do with my, with the money I make. I help her out. Every week I give her $50, $100. But she doesn't tell me what I do with my money. But she has to make sure that she has enough money for the rent, for the phone. If the phone goes up too high, she'll tell us. "Girls, stop making these phone calls. Don't, you know, the phone is pretty high this month. Don't turn on the air conditioner too much. When you turn on the iron, make sure you don't leave it on too long." Things we were never used to.

With economic and domestic upheaval, no loss of responsibility but only a substantial loss of capital, "my mom" had to figure out how to survive with *respect* for all left behind. She endured and took care. In hard times, as these women witnessed so often, "mom" almost always rose to the occasion. She worked extra hours, took in neighborhood children, skipped meals, did laundry. She kept the family together. And all the while, the daughters were watching and trying to give a hand. Never wanting to burden *mami* further. Consuelo explains.

The reason we came here, my mother had a lot of problems, money situations. But again, my family was always there for us too. But she felt like kind of, um, embarrassed to ask for help. But, um, my family was always there for us anyway. And I'm very proud of her. Because even though it was only her, some friends and family. She had it rough. She had it rough. And I'd try to help her as much as possible, right, you know, like taking care of my little sister while she was working. She had two jobs. She was working during morning and nights, to support us. And even though it was very hard, she wanted us to go to a private school. She always tried to give us the best, the excellent education for us.

Keeping the family together was women's work—as was the embarrassment of being left behind. And yet, mothers in these narratives mostly did it well. But for more than a few, their mothers were sick when these women were children. Some died young. By the time these young women grew into adolescence, most were going to school and working. Until they got pregnant—which most (82 percent), but not all, did in their late teens or early twenties. More than a few were pregnant from an abusive boyfriend, scared or embarrassed to tell *mami* or their father about the abuse or the baby. Our focus group picks up again:

> BEATRICE: And it's always up to us. It's always up to a woman. Never . . . I don't trust no man to tell me . . . my ex-husband. "Yeah, baby, you won't get pregnant. O.K. I'll take it out." That's how I got my daughter. Of course, I didn't know. I didn't know. He says, "Oh, don't worry. You don't need that." I was young. I was fifteen, sixteen when I started having intercourse with him. So I was so scared. Never mind that my mother would find out that I was sleeping with this boy. But to go to her and say, "Ma, can I go to the doctors and get some birth control?" Are you stupid? No, that would be the end of me right there. I could not. I didn't have that family. That . . . My mom's not Roseanne Barr on the show. No, I didn't have her. My mother would seriously do damage. My parents. My father! You know so, to me that was an embarrassment. It was embarrassing to tell my parents, "Mom, I'm having sex with David." It's not what they expect from their daughter. So it's not something I could go up there and tell them.
>
> MERCEDES: That too.
>
> BEATRICE: So everything I did would have to be *hidden*. I had to do it *behind their back*. I had to do stuff secretly.
>
> MERCEDES: That's what happened to me. . . . When they found out that I was pregnant, they did not even want to know. But they kicked me out of the house . . . He [father] called me a *puerca* (pig) and *puta* (whore) and, what else was it? And a *perra* (dog). Because only a *perra* would do what I did. So and then he started calling me names.
>
> MARINA: Um hm. So by this time, the neighbors saw everything. They called my mother over. They go, "Your daughter's getting beat up by her boyfriend." So of course my mother's like, "Oh, my God." So my sister and my mother, they ran outside. And I wasn't there. So when I finally got home, my mother was like "We can't keep," you know, "We can't keep going like this. Why is he doing this to you?" At that time my father was in Colombia because my grandfather had died. But when my father came back, the neighbors talk a lot and they told him. So he confronted me and he was like, "Did this really happen? Has he really abused you? How long has this been going on?" And then I had

no answers for him. Because in a way, I was so in love with him, that I protected him. And I always fabricated excuses. Well, I deserved it. It was my fault. And it really wasn't my fault, you know. All along, it was his fault. And then my father was like, "I'll kill him." You know, and I was so scared for that. I was so afraid that my father was going to find him one day.

With their mothers living between the church, neighbors, embarrassment, hopes, men who may "kill him [or her]" and the desire to protest, these young women felt they could turn to no one—except, maybe, their mothers. A few of these women surrendered their babies to adoption. One had her baby taken from her by the state. The rest kept their babies, while many families asked them, the daughters, to leave. At least for a while. Living with a boyfriend, his family, or on her own, she had to contend with violence, protecting him, negotiating his mother, and sheltering the children. Now the young women begin to "protect" their men—both out of economic necessity, a blind "respect," "embarrassment," and the cruel mandates of heterosexual "love."

> MUN [interviewer]: Did you press charges?
> YOLANDA: He told me, "Please, please don't say it. That I did it." And I did, you know, being stupid I. . . . Because the policeman did ask me what happened. And I said, "Oh no. I fell." But, you know, it's funny because. *I guess maybe I believed it.* I don't know why I didn't just say, "Yeah. He did it," you know, and let him go to jail. I don't know.
> MUN: Did you go back home when he was being too abusive?
> YOLANDA: Go back home?
> MUN: Yeah, to your mom?
> YOLANDA: To my mom? You've got to be kidding. [laugh] There was no where to run.

Even more than the white women and African American women whom we interviewed (Fine and Weis, 1998), the Latinas, when describing their first love, narrate a form of uncontested gender relations firmly embedded within rigid assumptions of heterosexuality, machismo, and "traditional" formulations of family. When families of origin would not or could not support her, she felt as if she had no options.

> WANDA: Right, wash clothes, iron clothes, or wash dishes, like my brother . . . and that's why my brother's like that. My brother . . . my father wouldn't even let him throw the garbage out.

Puerto Rican women grow up understanding that women's tasks sweep across nurturance and feeding of young and old, socialization for subordination to men, learning that they have responsibility for controlling men's anger, self-consciously "over protecting" children (especially daughters), and assuring that the next generation is imbued with a sense of optimism despite the overwhelming evidence to the contrary. Latinas have long had to pick up the pieces of colonialism, economic and state violence, and domestic abuse.

And as Yolanda and Beatrice explain, sometimes they convince themselves it is "my job."

BEATRICE: *I felt that it was my job,* yes. I was raised in the type where . . . I cooked everything. But it depends, as a female that was my job. This is why, this is like a *trade school* where I would be taught what to do for the future. So, now I had this man.

DINA: What . . . uh, yeah. He was the type that if things did not go his way, he was very dominant. He had to be served. He had to be obeyed like he was some father or god or something, and that's when the beating started.

MUN: His hand was easy, just smacked you?

DINA: He was hitting me when I was pregnant, but I never, never told my mother. Never told her cuz she was hurt by what I did so I said I'm never gonna tell her that he's abusing me.

His mother, she felt what he was doing was right, yes. If I wasn't a *disciplined woman to him and if I had a bad mouth and talked back to him, I deserved to get hit.* Oh yes, you just don't know . . . [laugh] . . . Yeah, and being the way I was raised and how I have so much respect for older people, how I learned not to act like one of those wild crazy women. I was the type that . . .

MUN: Quiet?

DINA: Yeah, I just took what hit me . . . *I felt like I deserved it anyway.* I put myself in that situation.

MUN: When he hit you?

DINA: Hey, when he hit me, I felt like I didn't deserve to get hit, but I didn't deserve either to make my mother feel the pain I was going through.

The women seem to endure, until the children begin to notice.

MUN: Did at any time, did you call the police?

DINA: *I never called the police on him, only until . . . My daughter*—well, my daughter was born and she was in the play pen in the kitchen and I had this . . . no, he never touched her until one day, he did touch her, and that's when I practically almost killed him. I picked up the knife, and I said, "This is it."

MUN: He slapped the girl?

DINA: He hit my daughter, but he hit her, not on her face, but he bent over because she started . . . she was teething. She had two baby front teeth and she started biting on the kitchen chairs. He bent over and started hitting her. He hit her so hard, like she was three, four, five years old. Boy, I climbed on him like a cat. I scratched his neck and everything, and he threw me against the refrigerator. He took me, and he hit me and I fell to the floor. He kicked me in my stomach. I got up and picked up a knife.

MUN: Did you stab him?

DINA: No, I didn't get to stab him. I was swinging the knife. I said, "Please," I said, "Come over and hit me again. Please come and hit me again."

The promise of *una familia Latina* (a Latino family), in all its tradition of gender roles, has been washed away by "shifts in economy, and state policy and shifting consciousness among women." As Marixsa Alicea has argued powerfully,

> Because the women need a sense of stability and security in their own individual family to resist the race oppression and disadvantaged class conditions that accompany migration, they have to put up with gender oppression. Caring work and kin work bring with them power and recognition and are important to building a sense of belonging and connectedness, and at the same time they are oppressive because women are held accountable for doing an unfair share of this work. (p. 621)

As these young women witnessed and endured this betrayal, somewhere, quietly, they tucked away a plan to care for themselves and their children. And yet they kept watching, hoping for a change. Not all leave—with "welfare reform," we would predict painfully that fewer can. But those who leave often do so to "protect the children."

WITNESSING . . . LISTENING TO THE SCREAMS

Among the most painful experiences narrated by this generation of Latinas is the work of *witnessing*. That is, witnessing violence in their families that their mothers, sisters, and sisters-in-law endure; witnessing other Latinas neglect their children from their windows; witnessing boys and young men turn against family; witnessing the loss of lives in streets and neighborhoods invested with drugs and crime.

> LUISA: Yeah . . . a lot of times, well actually . . . when it's really bad, I call DYFS [Division for Youth and Family Services] when it's really bad. And then I get worried because when DYFS comes . . . you know, the parents clean up the kids and dress them up in their cutest little outfit and DYFS says, "Oh, there's nothing wrong here." Just because they look decent from the outside, they don't stop to talk to the child and see how the child is on the inside or anything . . . that really pisses me off. But, um, it's, you know, you look the other way. A lot of times now I look the other way, you know. I can try to take them to the store . . . buy them some ice cream, for the kids that I know can't afford it, and stuff like that. *But there's only so much you can do, you know? It continues . . .*

Marina explains to Andy a similar set of witnessings:

> ANDY: But what about if someone were like strung out on something? You don't think that you might get hurt [if you helped]?
> MARINA: But it will happen. I mean, I've seen it happen so many times and I just say to myself, "Oh, my God. Somebody else." I mean, *you*

hear the screams. But there's nothing you can do.

ANDY: Screams from what?

MARINA: People. Like sometimes they mug them and if it's a lady, you hear her screaming. And then I go, "Oh my God. Somebody else got mugged." *You'll be looking out the window like, "Come on. Let that lady go." But they won't listen to you.* If they really need the drugs or they really need it, they're going to do whatever it takes. And you hear the fights with other kids. And then they have their own little gangs. And then the other gangs come over. And then the shoot-outs. You know, that's the biggest problem, in between that line, because you know you'll get shot and you'll die over nothing. It's a very bad neighborhood. It's not a good neighborhood. I mean, you have to tell them, "Listen. I've got a new boyfriend. He's such and such and such, so when you see him coming up the block, please don't mug him." And they go, "Alright, alright, we got ya."

Despite the witnessing, the screams, and across the fluctuations of optimism and self-blame, Puerto Rican women re-embody resistance: they carry a *grounded sense of responsibility in place*, boiled in a low level critique, braided with radiant hope that things will work out, that family, church and community will prevail. The more they witness, the more they experience, the more they conclude that it is *their responsibility* to set things right, to restore, in their own terms, family and community. Through both self-blame and responsibility, they refuse the betrayal. Puerto Rican women, of all the women we interviewed in the larger study of 154 women (including white, African American and Latina), voiced the most profound and, for us, the most disturbingly high levels of self-blame and beliefs that it is women's responsibility to tame men, to care for mothers, and to protect children.

CARMEN: Cuz I'm afraid that if anything does happen to them, I feel like it will be my fault.

MUN: Why?

CARMEN: Because I would feel that I could have prevented them from doing, and, *being my mother is not here, I feel that I should do it in my mother's place, and I should do it for them.*

Carmen continues her righteous anger:

CARMEN: Oh, okay. *Well women provoke . . .* So I say that if you keep teasing the man and keep yelling and complaining and telling him, you're provoking him so you building it up in him to get mad and snap back at you. That's wrong. Maybe women should learn to like try to understand a little more as far as not to get the man too hyper.

If you listen closely you will hear that the women do not precisely blame themselves for the violence, although some do, but that they do see themselves as responsible for not being able to protect and maintain peaceful, loving, and adequate homes for their children. They endorse the ideology of the safe, nurturing family as though it were real, and then hold themselves and other women accountable when they cannot achieve this goal. And yet whispers of resistance can be heard.

> LUISA: I'm sorry, *we've come too long*. If it's equal rights for everyone, I don't think that *you should stay home*. I don't know . . . I . . . this is me. I think you should, you know, stand up for your rights. If you know your husband is doing you wrong, you know, you give him an ultimatum. You know, you really don't need him. You're on welfare anyway.[3] It doesn't matter. It's not like his money is helping you. The government pays your, you know, you're on Section 8. You have welfare. They're paying, you know. Why are you supporting this man, you know? And that's basically how it goes. They work, take the other women out, and don't do shit for their wives . . . you know just be . . . their husbands . . . ohh . . . these women don't care. They just sit there, and most of them are physical . . . abusive, physically abusive . . . and you see them like treating . . . treating their wives like shit . . . calling them names and "Get inside" and, you know hitting them when they get inside, like they're little kids. Like, you know, like it's their property. It's like and then you hear them, the women, like, you know. . . . "Oh, but it was my fault". . . . "Oh, he hit me, but it was my fault." I'm like, "It's never your fault to get hit. You don't ask to be hit." It's not like . . . no matter what you do, you shouldn't get hit, you know, especially husband and wife. *I don't see why [you] should get your butt whipped every time you do something wrong.*

Witnessing, over time and through windows, enables the bubblings of quiet resistance.

QUIETLY RESISTING

While the Puerto Rican women we interviewed could easily be seen as "traditional" or relatively "conservative" in their gender and sexuality arrangements and judgments, it would be misleading to presume that they are unconflicted about the dance of power/gender/sexuality that unfolds in their histories, their homes, and on their streets. Each generation takes up the next front line of the gendered revolution. Their grandmothers battled colonialism; their mothers battled economic and family disruption. With no struggle or victory complete, this generation of young women knows all too well the torture of gendered role prescriptions, the violence sewn into the fabric of their classed and racialized relations with the state, economy, church, and men. Oliva Espin (1999) has written,

> Groups that are transforming their way of life through a vast and deep process of acculturation, focus on preserving "tradition" almost exclusively through the gender roles of women. Women's roles become the "bastion of tradition." Women's bodies become the site for struggles concerning disorienting cultural

differences. Gender becomes the site to claim the power denied to immigrants by racism. The control of women becomes the means of asserting moral superiority in a racist society. As a consequence, women of all ages in immigrant families face restrictions on their behavior. While men are allowed and encouraged to develop new identities in the new country, girls and women are expected to continue living as if they were still in the old country. . . . They are more often than not forced to embody cultural continuity amidst cultural dislocations. (p. 12)

With the blended passions of Latina sisterhood and spirituality, the muted legacy of U.S. feminism and the dismantling of the economy for their men (and themselves), they are fighting at home and in public with their men, their mothers, and their mothers-in-law to incite change. Those who resist patriarchy and/or heterosexuality (Espin, 1996) pay a particularly severe price. We see evidence of this quiet revolution not just in the narratives but also in the census data we tracked.

As is evident in the spiked rates of Latina female-headed households (1980–1990), Latina entry into the labor force (1980–1990), and Latina enrollment in higher education (1980–1990), this is perhaps the first generation of Latinas to pour their anger and disappointments out onto the streets, courts, and into welfare offices and direct their energy toward jobs, college, and their own apartments. These women are refusing the violence toward which they have been socialized and rejecting the jealousy that riddles their intimate lives. They are willing to leave the homes of their men (although we cannot know the extent to which female headed household status is initiated by women) in order to bring their daughters and sons into family spaces free of violence. (See Fine and Weis, 1998, for more detailed information.)

For entrance in the labor force, pursuit of higher education, and rise in female headed households among white, African American, and Latina women, Puerto Rican women have taken the lead, even if they face lower salaries. Even though these data reveal perverse discrimination on the bases of both gender and ethnicity, these women have witnessed much and are on the move. Seeking independence, self-sufficiency, and physical safety, they yearn to make good on "the promise" to their sons and daughters. All the time looking back and forward, as they narrate identities embedded in personal and social histories of violence, colonization, and survival. And yet, as Aida Hurtado (1995) notes, there may be serious consequences for these acts of resistance and survival.

Salient contradictions between the competing economic demands that force women into the labor force and then demand that they remain loyal to outmoded norms for proper "female" conduct. Women are more likely to feel the contradiction when they join the public realm, such as when they enter the labor force or when they become politically involved. . . . The contradiction between economic and educational accomplishments and "proper" conduct for women is especially salient for Latinas who pursue higher education. (p. 57)

We hear, in our interviews, gendered tensions rumbling within and tumbling outside their homes. Luisa explains her maneuvering out of violence, even as she refuses to turn him into the police:

MUN: Did you involve the courts at all?

LUISA: No, I threatened to, but I didn't have to. Because it got to the . . . well, during this period in time, he had begged and begged and begged and begged and begged and begged and whatever, so I decided to go out and have a talk with him and explain to him that things have changed, what have you. During this time, he was trying to show me that he had changed so much. . . . At that point, I didn't want to change men anymore. I was like so reluctant to start a new relationship, and go through all that . . . so I figured, "Hey, I'm just going to try this again" . . . you know. And I did, which was my mistake. Because I had a friend of mine who kept telling me, "Everyone deserves a second chance . . . everyone deserves a second chance . . . he really might have changed . . . he must love you . . . he's still [here] or whatever" . . . so I kind of, you know, used that as an excuse to go back with him. Big mistake. During the time I was with him, he forgot to tell me that during the time he was stalking me, he had a relationship and was staying with someone who was staying in his house, which was a friend of mine. He also forgot to tell me that she was pregnant, okay. He forgot to tell me a *lot* of things! So by this point, I was so rebellious towards him. . . . I hated him, that I started . . . every time he was stalking me, or came around or anything, I would do something to his car. I carved his car. I slashed his tires. I beat the shit out of him in front of his parents, and I told him, "Now, I'm fighting back." I said, "I'm not scared of you. If you harass me again, you're going to live to regret it." I said, "If I ever see you crossing the street, I will run you over." I said, "That's how bad it's gotten." I said, "I don't want you in my life. I don't want to go to the police with this. I don't want to do . . . No I just want you to stay out of my life." And I told his girlfriend, I said, you know, "You keep him away from me" I said, "If you want to keep him long enough to see his child, you keep him away from me" and after that, he was so paranoid . . . [laughs] . . . He was like, "If I knew that, I would have done it a long time ago." He was so scared, but he still tried. Until this day, he calls me. I mean this is two years later, he still calls me. "How you doin'?" "I still love you." blah, blah, blah.

MUN: Well what was your . . . what was the reason that you didn't want to involve the police?

LUISA: Because he's now a senior in college, and he's going for law, and that's something he really, really wants. And I may be, you know, I may have changed and become a lot colder toward men, stuff like that, but I don't want to be the reason to jeopardize anybody's future in that way. I mean that's something he really wanted, and I knew how badly he wants it. And he's very bright for . . . when it comes to law, and he can really make it, you know. Besides all the flaws that he has, when it comes to law, he knows what he's doing. And I figured if I would press charges against him, if he did get near me, because I know he would have broken them, you know, tried to go against them, and stuff like, and that would ruin his career . . . you know, might, as a lawyer. So I thought about his best interest at that time, *while he was making my life a living hell, I'm still thinking about his best interest. That's why I didn't do it.*

The anger and protectiveness that Luisa talks about can be understood in terms of the within-group solidarity Puerto Rican women experience and assume. As Aida Hurtado (1996) has written about Chicanas, the women with whom we spoke view their world through multiple positions and allegiances. Embodying shared histories of colonialism and economic abuse, these women experience a solidarity with Latino men which often binds them to the abuses they suffer. Keenly aware that economically, politically, and socially there is no such thing as an even playing field for themselves or Latino men, Hurtado says unequal power relations based on ethnicity makes it difficult for Latinas to critique, in "productive ways, the internal functioning of the ethnic . . . group even on the issues that negatively affect women in these groups, such as sexism, incest and battery." Experiencing violence at the hands of Latinos, Latinas also witness their deaths, incarceration, and unfair treatment. Hurtado continues, "the awareness of the relativity of merit leads to anger and to intergroup conflict and almost simultaneously to extreme intragroup solidarity" (p. 13). Women pay a price. They know it. They tell their daughters. The church encourages their silence and endurance. And, usually, at least in the past, they have remained quiet.

Understanding the nuances of gendered, heterosexual power in homes and on the streets perhaps more astutely than many, these women are, however, in the midst of a cultural shift. Trying to realign gendered relations within the Latino community, they seek to assure that domination, jealousy, and abuse are no longer constitutive of family life.

ROSEMARIE: How did you get out of that situation?

BEATRICE: Well, one day, I was at . . . my youngest was about eight months, no, a year old. And, um, he, he had just hit me so bad that day. He had been beating me for no reason. So bad, that when he was leaving, I picked up my kids, called a cab, and I left. And I didn't come back.

ROSEMARIE: But what happened? He had beat you before. What was the, no, what happened?

BEATRICE: The turning point was that I thought in my mind that if he was gonna do that one more time, one of us was not gonna wake up. One of us was not going to wake up. And I knew, I had, I feared about how to do it. I had good ideas about how to do it. "But then my kids would be left without a mother." Or without a father, not that they would have cared for him. But I wanted to see my kids grow up. And then I was thinking, my daughter was about four years old, she feels it throughout her whole life! And the thing that bothered me was that whole week, was that . . . he hit me that whole week . . . was that, god, *my daughter is seeing this and she's gonna grow up thinking a family is supposed to be like this*. Then that was my . . . they say a cycle repeats itself. That's what happened in my home. That's what I saw. That's what I got into. I was just so angry at myself for letting that continue. Now my daughter is getting older. She's already had four years of this. She is already indoctrinated in a certain way because this is her home life. This is the norm for her. This was the norm. But I started thinking like that. I left and I said . . . it was the morning and if my daughter. . . . "I'm gonna let her live like this?" It would be my fault if this happens to her. And I said, "Hell, no!" And while he was asleep, I just packed the kids. Cause it was, he had a little gun, he always kept at home. That was gonna be for me.

These women have not wholly internalized gender subordination. While they do not voice much of a critique of heterosexuality or marriage as institutions, they do insist on dignity and respect, especially in front of their children. This posture puts them at odds with men, sometimes with their mothers, often with their mothers-in-law, but very much in relation with sisters, daughters, and, to their own delight, often with their sons who have witnessed too much violence. To quote Alicea again (p. 599), "While it is true that the women in this study are victims, they are also 'nurturant weavers' who create 'networks of relationship on which [they in turn rely]' " (Gilligan 1982, 17; see also Di Leonardo 1992). The kin work and caring work that Puerto Rican women carry out across the transnational field is not equitably distributed and is burdensome, but it is a means of experiencing love, creating a sense of family, and can bring women power and recognition (Di Leonardo 1991; Hill Collins 1996; Thorne 1993)." These are, then, mothers who engage in the kin work and caring work Alicea (1997) describes, who embody what Patricia Hill Collins (1990) and Janie Ward (1996) define as the "duty to resist." Even as they resist the traditional role of *wife,* they exit violence as *mothers* protecting the children. The duty to resist means doing whatever is necessary to protect the physical survival of your mother and your children—even going on welfare.

As Benmayor and others have determined, we, too, found that poor and working-class Puerto Rican women were committed to the strategic use of welfare and the appropriation of educational and employment opportunities, to the extent that such services enabled them to maintain and advance the standings of their families. Seeing these women as "resource strategists" rather than "dependent poor," Benmayor extends our social consciousness of the public safety net as a vehicle deployed by women, poor and working class, to sustain self and children. Though welfare was fundamentally inadequate, as Lisa explains, it was essential.

It stinks! How do they expect you to live? I've been on welfare. My first daughter, she's seventeen years old, my daughter. I went on welfare with her. I went on welfare for a minute when I had Shantee. And I was on welfare with Alicia. And I'm gonna tell you right now, all the years I collected welfare, I worked. I did not sit and wait on the damn mailman. I did the damn fraud, whatever. Take me to jail now, I don't care. You can't live off that stuff. When I first moved out and I rented my apartment, my apartment was $275 a month. My welfare check was $273. I mean, there is not an apartment anywhere in the world for the amount that welfare gives you. If you don't have Section 8, you can't live. Cause then you have to have three jobs plus a husband and a boyfriend on the side. . . [laughter] . . . That's the only way you can live. You can't do it. It's not physically working.

The rub comes, of course, when these same women confront welfare and educational bureaucracies hostile to their notions of what it takes to secure their children's survival.

MERCEDES: You want to know what they did to me once? I was at welfare, with my little baby now. And I went to this black lady and I was like, "Listen, right now I don't have a place to stay. My father won't take me back. I need a place to stay. I need furniture. I need everything." "Well, honey, all I can tell you is to beg, borrow, and steal." What? Now if I woulda went and did that, I woulda . . . Nah . . .

"Welfare reform"—creating a limit on numbers of years women can be on welfare, demanding work (without child care) and not education—bodes tragically for women trying to exit violence in their homes and may contribute, indeed, to further abuse of women and children (Fine and Weis, 2000).

QUIET RESISTANCE: PUERTO RICAN WOMEN'S LEGACY

Write with your tongues of fire. Let no one smother the flame. We are not reconciled to the oppressors who whet their howl on our grief. We are not reconciled . . . . Your skin must be sensitive enough for the shyest kiss and thick enough to ward off the sneers. And, if you are going to spit in the eye of the world, make sure your back is to the wind. (Gloria Anzaldúa, 1987)

With strong desire and passionate commitment, these Latinas bring what Gloria Anzáldua terms their "tongues of fire"—a particular blend of whispered critique and deep optimism—to securing their own and their children's survival within the family, church, and school. Refusing the betrayal of these institutions, these women quietly author an expanding critique. To each institution, they import an almost incomprehensible, compelling, and contagious belief that change is possible; that good things can flourish; that justice is right around the corner. They are going to make good on the promise of a future, on their own terms, alone if necessary. So, for instance, despite much abuse, heterosexual Latinas still look for a good man. Despite much evidence of church-based hypocrisy, many pray in their own houses over candles and incense in keeping with the traditions of their African ancestors, with a vengeance. Despite much evidence of school-based inadequacies and in-equities, they are deeply involved in their children's schools, searching for pa-rochial schools, volunteering in public schools, and working with children on homework.

The depth of these women's culturally bound beliefs reflects profound ambivalence. These women carry, and give to their children, a shining sense of possibility. Things will get better. Trying to create change, they will not sur-render self or their children to social injustice. Unwilling to accept the be-trayal, they will fight to restore what is their due and their children's. And yet, this sense of possibility bumps into culturally bound beliefs about being women. Their search for the "peaceful family" and their protectiveness of Puerto Rican men may blunt their sight of, and therefore exit from, violent domestic relations. Their insistence on blaming themselves for the ruination of their communities and their home lives may keep them from seeking op-tions. To this end, we share the ambivalence expressed by Benmayor and col-leagues (p. 49): "On the one hand, the assertion of family values and gender roles was a source of strength; on the other hand, these roles could also hold women back. At the same time that the women were struggling for change, they were struggling to recreate the cultural structures that supported them. Consequently, working from within the parameters of the culture could be both empowering and restrictive."

With all the effort, and all the belief, there are still times when the burden of the betrayal, and attempts to keep children from feeling the assault, weighs too heavy.

> YOLANDA: Sometimes I think it's like too late for me. I really think that. I do, but I'm trying. I'm trying. But I think I'm too old, man. I can't . . . those questions like they . . . the guy asked me, "What do you think of five years from now?" It's like, give me a break. I don't know. I don't know what I want to do in. . . . I want to be doing something, but ex-actly what it's hard, you know. How much money would I want to be making? If it was up to me, $100,000 a year; but . . .

Keeping their attention focused on a better life for themselves and their children, engaging in the hard work of maneuvering around state-based obstacles and negotiating across cultures, generations, and genders, these women struggle to survive. They continue and transform the work of their mothers, creating options for self and children.

Today's poor and working-class Puerto Rican women seek further educa-tion, work, care for children. Those connected to men want men to do their share. Demanding that culture not be defined exclusively through gender subordination, these women are packing from scenes of violence and uncer-tainty. The shredding of the public safety net makes it increasingly difficult for these women to endure. Nevertheless, they are boldly redefining gender and sexuality in quiet but collective moves toward redefining culture without violence.

NOTES

1. The small number of women from Central and South America shared similar histories with the Puerto Rican women of conquest and (im)migration. Experiences of domestic violence, joblessness among men and women, and the spirit of resistance embodied by Latinas are among those shared by all the women we interviewed.

2. Italicized text has been translated from Spanish to English. Where translation changes the meaning, the Spanish terms were left in the text with the English translation next to it.

3. See Fine and Weis (2000). The name of the law is the so-called Personal Responsibility act. "With the draconian disappearance of a social safety net for women—not that a very good one ever existed—we witness a twinning of state and domestic violence against women (see Gordon's 1993 analysis of women's complex relations to the state). Women's access to sustained welfare and public higher education have narrowed to a choke. These two social projects, as we (and many others) have learned, have been quietly and profoundly the primary strategies by which poor and working-class women have been able to interrupt what has been perversely called the 'cycle of violence'" (p. 1141).

REFERENCES

Alicea, M. 1997. A chambered nautilus: The contradictory nature of Puerto Rican women's role in the social construction of a transnational community. *Gender and Society* 11(5, October): 597–626.

Anzaldúa, G. 1987. *Borderlands: La Frontera, the New Mestiza*. San Francisco: Aunt Luta Books.

Ayala, J. 2000. In whose voice shall I write? In L. Weis and M. Fine, eds., *Speed Bumps: A Student-Friendly Guide to Qualitative Research*. New York: Teachers College.

Benmayor, R., A. Juarbe, C. Alvarez, and B. Vazquez. 1987. *Stories to Live By: Continuity and Change in Three Generations of Puerto Rican Women*. New York: Centro de Estudios Puertorriquenos.

Collins, P. H. 1990. *Black Feminist Thought*. New York: Routledge.

DiLeonardo, M. 1991. *Gender at the Crossroads of Knowledge: Feminist Anthropology in the Postmodern Era*. Berkeley: University of California Press.

Espin, O. 1999. *Women Crossing the Boundaries: The Psychology of Immigration and the Transformations of Sexuality*. New York: Routledge.

———. 1996. The immigrant experience in lesbian studies. In B. Zimmerman and T.A.N. McNaron, eds., *The New Lesbian Studies: Into the Twenty-first Century*. New York: Feminist Press.

Esteves, S. M. 1990. *Bluestone Mockingbird Mambo*. Texas: Arte Publico Press.

Fine, M., and L. Weis. 2000. Disappearing acts: The state and violence against women in the 20th century. *Signs* 25 (4, Summer): 1139–1146.

———. 1998. *The Unknown City*. Boston: Beacon.

Flores, J. 1996. Pan-Latino/trans-Latino: Puerto Ricans in the "new Nueva York." *Centro* 8 (1, 2): 171–186.

Gilligan, C. 1982. *In a Different Voice: Psychological Theory and Women's Development*. Cambridge, Mass.: Harvard University Press.

Ginorio, A., L. Guitierrez, A. M. Cauce, and M. Acosta. 1995. Psychological issues for Latinas. In H. Landrine, ed., *Bringing Cultural Diversity to Feminist Psychology*. Washington, D.C.: American Psychological Association.

Gordon, L. 1993. Women's agency, social control and the construction of rights by battered women. In S. Fisher and K. Davis, eds., *Negotiating at the Margins: The Gendered Discourses of Power and Resistance*. New Brunswick, N.J.: Rutgers University Press, 122–144.

Hurtado, A. 1996. Strategic suspensions: Feminists of color theorize the production of knowledge. In N. Goldberg, M. Belenky, B. Clinchy, and J. Tarule, eds. *Women's Way of Knowing Revisited.* New York: Basic Books.

———. 1995. Variations, combinations and evolutions: Latino families in the U.S. In R. E. Zambrana, ed., *Understanding Latino Families: Scholarship, Policy and Practice.* Thousand Oaks, Calif.: Sage.

Lykes, B. M. 1985. Gender and individualistic vs. collectivist bases for notions about the self. *Journal of Personality* 53(2): 356–383.

Thorne, B. 1993. *Gender Play: Girls and Boys in School.* New Brunswick, N.J.: Rutgers University Press.

Trujillo, C., ed. 1998. *Living Chicana Theory*. Berkeley: Third World Woman Press.

Ward, J. 1996. Raising resisters: The role of truth telling in the psychological development of African American girls. In B. J. Ross Leadbeater and N. Way, eds., *Urban Girls: Resisting Stereotypes, Creating Identities*. New York: New York University Press.

PART III

Structural Contexts, Culturally Competent Approaches, Community Organizing, and Social Change

D uring the past forty years, the anti-violence movement thrust into public consciousness many types of violence, including many forms of domestic violence, whose existence had been previously denied or trivialized. The achievements of domestic violence organizations are historic and reflect a direct result of feminist activism. Police and court practices are significantly changed; legal standards and public awareness have been transformed.

Deborah Epstein (2002) outlines these gains for us:

> When the battered women's movement grew out of the broader feminist movement in the late 1960s and early 1970s, victims of domestic violence faced monumental practical and political obstacles. No term for intimate abuse existed in the popular lexicon; virtually no shelters or safe houses devoted to battered women had been established; no civil laws had been enacted to deal with the emergency aftermath of an abusive incident; and the government had a long track record of ignoring the problem or even protecting perpetrators. Over the past thirty years, movement activists have focused their energies on revolutionizing the terms of the debate, turning domestic violence into a widely condemned practice, and transforming the responses of police, prosecutors, and the courts. Their efforts resulted in major legal reforms that have substantially expanded and improved the justice system's responsiveness to victims.

In fact, today, mainstream or dominant cultural domestic violence practices celebrate retributive criminal justice approaches to domestic violence; acts of interpersonal violence are now considered to be violations of the state, and punishment of the wrongdoer has now become the state's prerogative.

Historically, there prevailed an underlying conviction among white middle-class mainstream feminist activists that there was value in making domestic violence a "law-and-order" problem.[1] The domestic violence movement sought to protect women from battering by advocating for a more active response from police agencies and the criminal justice system. Consequently, owing to training and collaboration with domestic violence organizations, police have improved their responses. Today, however, this strategy of reform has all too often backfired, especially for battered women from marginalized communities.

Women who turn to the police for protection still face wrongful arrest, degradation from officers, and deportation in the case of immigrant families. Overall, the state disproportionately arrests and oppresses men of color. Research indicates that in some communities, women of color are initially reluctant to call the police and are significantly deterred from making a second call for help, given the impact of incarceration on men in their neighborhoods (Richie, chapter 4; Coker, 2002, chapter 22). Today, communities of color are mobilizing around issues such as the violence and bias of law enforcement, immigration agencies, and the larger criminal justice system (Incite!–Critical Resistance, chapter 8; A. Smith, chapter 24).

The chapters featured in part 3 reorient and reorganize the locus of social change and place community in the foreground as the axis for organizing, mobilizing, and conceptualizing anti-violence work. In recent years elaborating the connections among women's multiple identities has advanced the intersectionalities of gender and race, gender and sexual orientation, gender and ethnicity, gender and immigrant status, and, most important, all these social locations together. We think in more complicated ways about violence and harassment and identity-based discrimination.

An international human rights framework has emerged as a useful tool and an approach that creates the space to make connections around violence in various sectors in women's lives. Freedom from violence is every woman's human right.[2] Violence against women is rooted in identity-based discrimination and reinforces isolation. Social and cultural norms and laws articulated through structural conditions that deny women equal rights with men render women more vulnerable to physical, sexual, mental, social, and economic abuse. The common threads are individual and institutionalized discrimination against women and the denial of basic human rights to individuals simply because they are women.

The historic prioritizing of home and individual over community in the West and the demand for more law enforcement and state protection has displaced critical and innovative thinking and action about alternative community-based strategies for promoting public safety. How women's safety is best achieved is differently conceptualized in the various community-organizing initiatives represented in this section.

Grassroots community organizing differs substantially from white middle-class domestic violence practices that focus on service provision, law enforcement training, and national policymaking. Grassroots community organizing builds capacity for structural change and differs substantially from the dominant practices that "manage" domestic violence through service provision to individual women (see T. West, chapter 20; A. Smith, chapter 24).

Today vibrant grassroots movements operate across critical issues— including the environment, living wage, peace and human rights movements—and build power across institutions to confront the limitations and violence of criminal justice approaches to domestic violence. There is a demand for greater enforcement accountability as provisions for women's safety are undermined by legal biases in the Immigration and Naturalization Service, border patrol, police and prison systems where one agency can intimidate by invoking the powers of another collateral law enforcement agency. Annanya Bhattacharhjee (2002) argues:

> Organizing, at its best, requires the creation of thoughtful and mutually beneficial relationships through a process of confrontation and negotiation, among bodies and institutions that form the community. Through such relationships, the community develops the capacity to bring about change in the way business is done within it and towards it . . . . Consent to eradicate domestic violence would need to arise from a process that determines the absence of such violence to be as integral to the welfare and survival of the community as a living wage, good public education, police accountability, or removal of toxic dumps (p. 5).

Evident in the diverse strategies that follow, many groups are pursuing alternatives to criminalization. They are breaking tight silences that protect patriarchy and racial and sexual privileges of dominant groups as well as ideals of individualism that reinforce isolation and privacy. The focus is on community awareness, advocacy, and social action for material and structural supports—housing, education, employment, child care, safety—while holding batterers accountable through community censure (see Coker, chapter 22, and Websdale and Johnson, chapter 23 on structural supports; Almeida and Lockard, chapter 18 on batterer accountability; A. Smith, chapter 24 on strategies of community censure and social change).

Many authors argue that economic justice and environmental justice are linked to ending domestic violence (Coker, chapter 22; Websdale and Johnson, chapter 23; and A. Smith, chapter 24). These constructs of engaging community through collective strategies for structural change form a common thread throughout the chapters in part 3. As Andrea Smith (chapter 24) argues, a broad array of forces are needed to engage community resolve to denounce violence against women and build a collective consensus about safe communities with the absence of domestic and state violence as pillars of safety. Evidence of the state's interest in ending domestic violence is weak; furthermore, there is no logic in the assumption that state violence can solve gender violence particularly when considered within a global context of armed conflict in the world, streets, and homes of communities of color (see Josephson, chapter 7; Incite!–Critical Resistance, chapter 8; A. Smith, chapter 24).

Part 3 spotlights innovative programs, culturally competent practices, and large-scale social change that place social justice concerns at the heart of domestic violence interventions. For example, in chapter 18, Rhea V. Almeida and Judith Lockard's "Cultural Context Model" acknowledges the role culture plays in perpetuating violence against women. Almeida and Lockard refuse to bolster cultural justifications for domestic violence while simultaneously understanding how culture operates within the context of structural constraints. The goal, of course, is to move us to develop models of social change, not just to provide wider services that are culturally relevant to marginalized communities (see A. Smith, chapter 24).

In this book, an explicit gender equality framework links battering with issues of power and control. Chapters in part 3 expose attitudes of disrespect and verbal abuse of women at home (see B. Smith, chapter 19), in communities of faith (see T. West, chapter 20), in the workplace, in government policies on housing, welfare, and childcare (see Coker, chapter 22) and place deeply felt personal injuries within the context of structures of oppression, racism, and homophobia. This complicated and layered analysis is necessary for any possibility of meaningful social change at the structural level. At the same time, a gender equality framework alone is not sufficient to ensure the state's genuine accountability to battered women. For grassroots innovations in gender justice, the contradictions of engaging with the state on domestic violence continue (Schneider, 1999). Anannya Bhattacharjee (2001) argues that a "community-centered perspective challenges us to go beyond a conventional human rights framework." We cannot best support the safety and self-determination of communities without fully understanding how violence—street violence, enforcement violence, the violence of mass incarceration, and domestic violence—affects communities of color and poor women, both immigrant and U.S.-born, both heterosexual and lesbian, gay, bisexual, and transgendered (LGBT) (see Fine and Weiss, 1998; Incite!–Critical Resistance, chapter 8). As Battacharjee (2001) questions the project: "How do we fight violence against women of color while simultaneously addressing the structural violence faced by the larger community?" (p. 43).

The initiatives described in part 3 are important steps toward developing new strategies to redress the impact of violence and domestic terrorism. Placing men in the larger social structural context offers the opportunity for change in spite of all the forces that support violence or pressure them not to be accountable. The following chapters offer models for intervention that combine society, community, family, and the individual with critical education about racism, colonialism, class bias, sexism, and homophobia.

Janice Ristock (2002) notes that lesbian communities are very diverse and are not as bounded to or by culture in the same ways as other marginalized groups. Community is important to lesbians where families are chosen, self-created, and often inclusive of networks of former partners as significant social supports. Here, lesbian communities offer a powerful example for social change. As Ristock makes clear, relationship violence is a *community* problem, not a private issue, and community is the central stage for making relationships more safe (pp. 182–185). This is particularly true for communities of color in the United States.

Organizations and social movements that have come together around domestic violence include faith-based and grassroots organizations, reproductive rights, LGBT human rights, freedom from sexual assault groups, immigrant rights groups, police accountability, and prisoners' rights. Working through differences, sometimes in opposition, new complexities emerge to construct a multilayered agenda, with marginalized groups of women of color at the center of the development of just and practical action.

One strength of a universal human rights approach to domestic violence is the extent to which it intertwines compulsory legal action and reporting systems that oblige government accountability, transparency, and public dialogue. At the same time, human rights principles demand limits on state power that remedy wrongs by coercive means and selectively apply state power against vulnerable or marginalized groups (Miller and Faux, 1999).

However, problems identified with the human rights framework include a history of exempting human rights violations in the United States and targeting violations of individual human rights in "Other" cultures. Some critics point to the elitist language of human rights and intersectionality scholars as indicative of privilege and advanced education as well as divisive, if not disrespectful of grassroots, collective, "bottom-up" strategies for structural change (see A. Smith, 2003, chapter 24).

A focus on universal human rights strips normative culture to its barest and exposes the collusion of male privilege, racism, colonialism, class privilege, and heterosexism. Inquiry at this level demands that we look at how we each internalize societal oppression and participate in that which stigmatizes, divides, and conquers our "intersected" identities.

New notions of agency and transdisciplinary analyses in theory and practice call for transformative politics that imagine new ways in which women can organize to form alliances to address violence against women—a human rights framework that embraces all of our socially constructed identities and lived realities.

Does "solidarity in multiplicity" (Lugones, as cited in Donaldson, 1992) threaten the very core of feminism? Gloria Anzaldúa (1990) entreats that to "combat racism and sexism and . . . 'work through' internalized violence . . . we must attempt to decolonize ourselves and find ways to survive personally, culturally, and racially" (p. 142).

Andrea Smith (chapter 24) asks: What would it take *to end violence against women of color*? What would this movement look like? And Beth E. Richie (chapter 4) argues that we must ultimately be accountable, not to those in power, but to the powerless.

Donna Coker (chapter 22) reiterates this organizing principle and action strategy by noting that if we hold "poor women of color as the standard," the ineffectiveness of mandatory arrest laws becomes clear: using state violence to curb private violence ultimately fails all women.

Increasingly, multicultural and multiracial domestic violence advocates are recognizing the criminal justice system's limitations, reflected in many chapters in this book and especially in this section (for example, Richie, chapter 4; Almeida and Lockard, chapter 18; B. Smith, chapter 19; Coker, chapter 22; Websdale and Johnson, chapter 23; A. Smith, chapter 24). One group that has attempted to organize around the intersections of state and interpersonal violence is Korean American Women in Need (KAN-WIN), described by Lisa Sun-Hee Park (see chapter 21). KAN-WIN organizes around not only domestic violence but also the impact of global and domestic militarism on survivors of violence. This dual strategy enables the group to collaborate with activist organizations in other communities of color.

Brenda V. Smith (chapter 19) and Traci C. West (chapter 20) remind us that women understand their situations and solutions better than the experts. In fact, many policies and practices developed for battered women during the past thirty years contradict the explicit safety plans of women in peril (see also Josephson, chapter 7).

Brenda Smith makes the point that women are denied agency when mandatory arrest and vertical prosecution proceed without their consent (see Abrams, 1999). In writing about the role of forgiveness and redemption, Brenda Smith notes that the process of forgiving is intensely personal. It is, however, a process that offers the possibility for growth, healing, and insight for the victim, the offender, and the community.

Restorative justice interventions, often rooted in spiritual traditions, described by Brenda Smith, are not without problematic biases, as Andrea Smith warns (chapter 24). These strategies may seek to involve other institutions—like the church, community, or tribal elders—in resolving family violence conflicts. Caution is required to protect victims of violence from intimidation or religious or tribal coercion that require her conformity to community norms that may jeopardize her safety and freedom. Inherent power imbalances exist between victims and perpetrators of interpersonal violence. Restorative justice approaches to domestic violence may imperil women's safety and collude with deeply ingrained beliefs that will continue unless confronted by political, legal, and religious structures. Hence, the batterer is not the only agent of violence and control that a woman faces. Traci West (chapter 20), Donna Coker (chapter 22), Websdale and Johnson (chapter 23) and Andrea Smith (chapter 24) calculate the structural inequalities that shape state and tribal interventions in the lives of women.

The authors in this book contribute to a multilevel dialogue on societal change whereas others primarily look for either individual means to a personal healing and protection or the state response of the criminal justice system to provide protection from domestic violence. How we respond to violence against women depends on our understanding of the underlying causes of inequality, our conception of the parameters of justice, and our beliefs about how communities change.

In this anthology, we argue for the need to recognize differences and solidarities, to value local struggles and global alliances, to examine intersections between the global and the local, and to accept the contradictions and differences among divergent groups and cultures. This requires a solidarity that both embraces and negotiates differences.

The chapters in this anthology communicate outrage and activism by scholars who attach importance to women situated in multiple crosscutting identities, social locations, and status hierarchies—women who are active agents and interpreters of their experiences—with family, community, the state, and the broader project of globalization.

Christina Pratt and Natalie J. Sokoloff

NOTES

1. See Schneider (2000) for the history of and early critique against this approach.

2. The United Nations Declaration on the Elimination of Violence against Women (CEDAW), Article 4 reads: "States should condemn violence against women and should not invoke any custom, tradition or religious consideration to avoid their obligations with respect to its elimination. States should pursue by all appropriate means and without delay a policy of eliminating violence against women." Adopted by the General Assembly in 1994; it remains unsigned by the United States. Available at www.un.org/womenwatch/daw/cedaw/

REFERENCES

Abrams, Kathryn. 1999. From autonomy to agency: Feminist perspectives on self-direction. *William & Mary Law Review* 40: 805–846.

Anzaldúa, Gloria. 1990. *Making Face, Making Soul: Creative and Critical Perspectives by Women of Color.* San Francisco: Aunt Lute.

Bhattacharjee, Anannya. 2002. Putting community back in the domestic violence movement. Available at: www.freeindiamedia.com/women/5_aug_women.htm and http://www.zmag.org/content/Race/bhattacharjee_domestic-violence.cfm.

———. 2001. Whose Safety? Women of Color and the Violence of Law Enforcement. Philadelphia: American Friends Service Committee. Committee on Women, Population, and the Environment.

Coker, Donna. 2002. Presentation at City University of New York Graduate Center. October 23.

Epstein, Deborah. 2002. Procedural justice: Tempering the state's response to domestic violence. *William & Mary Law Review* 43(5): 1843–1904.

Fine, Michelle, and Lois Weis. 1998. Crime stories: A critical look through race, ethnicity, and gender. *Qualitative Studies in Education* 11(3): 435–460.

Lugones, Maria C. 1992. Sisterhood and friendship as feminist models. Cited in Laura Donaldson, ed., *Decolonizing Feminisms: Race, Gender, and Empire Building.* Chapel Hill: University of North Carolina Press.

Miller, Alice M., and Meghan Faux. 1999. Reconceiving responses to private violence and state accountability: Using an international human rights framework in the United States. *Georgetown Journal of Gender and Law* 1(1): 67–93.

Richie, Beth E. 2000. Plenary Address, Color of Violence: Violence Against Women of Color Conference. Santa Cruz, Calif. April.

Ristock, Janice L. 2002. *No More Secrets: Violence in Lesbian Relationships.* New York: Routledge.

Schneider, Elizabeth. 1999. Engaging with the state about domestic violence: Continuing dilemmas and gender equality. *Georgetown Journal of Gender and Law* 1(1): 173–184.

———. 2000. *Battered Women and Feminist Lawmaking.* New Haven, Conn.: Yale University Press.

Smith, Andrea. 2003. Violence against Women and Human Rights. Columbia University School of Law, Amnesty International Ralph Bunche Scholar Presentation.

United Nations Declaration on the Elimination of Violence against Women (CEDAW), Article 4. Available at: www.un.org/womenwatch/daw/cedaw/.

CHAPTER **18**

RHEA V. ALMEIDA AND JUDITH LOCKARD

The Cultural Context Model

A New Paradigm for Accountability, Empowerment, and the Development of Critical Consciousness against Domestic Violence

ABSTRACT

The chapters in part 2 provided numerous illustrations of women's sources of strength and strategies of resistance that are shaped by culture, ethnicity, social class, language, and immigration status. In chapter 17, Michelle Fine and her colleagues described the experiences of Puerto Rican women who place a high value on the nuclear family and traditional gender roles while simultaneously managing legacies of colonialism and racism. Some Puerto Rican women derive power and liberation from their extended family and faith communities, while others experience more oppression from these extended networks.

In chapter 18, Almeida and Lockard posit a new model of accountability and empowerment as a community remedy to end domestic violence. Their Cultural Context Model (CCM) explicitly challenges patriarchy and racism by placing social justice principles and practice at the center of domestic violence intervention. This model is rooted in principles of universal human rights and practices that foster the development of "critical consciousness." This idea of critical consciousness was first developed by Paulo Freire (*Pedagogy of the Oppressed*, 1972) as a strategy to resist hierarchical social inequalities. Freire asserts that education and dialogue hold the potential to transform the human condition and counteract oppression. This process calls forth a political analysis achieved by learning the history of cultural conditions and class structures that support and frame experiences of poverty, racism, marginality, and exclusion.

Working with Freire's concept of critical consciousness to overcome domination and oppression, Almeida and Lockard demonstrate at their center in New Jersey how new practices of both empowerment for women and accountability for abusers help women, men, and their families recover from violence and influence change in the larger community. Through individual, family, group, and community interventions based on critical consciousness of cultural narratives, the Cultural Context Model seeks micro- and macro-level systems change. This model distinguishes between culture and domestic terror, acknowledges the role that culture plays in perpetuating violence against women, and rejects simplistic cultural explanations of domestic violence.

As you read about and analyze the seven major components of the Cultural Context Model, consider the benefits as well as dangers of using this model instead of traditional interventions—that is, shelters, protection orders, arrest, probation, jail. Under what circumstances might the use of Cultural Context Model be unwise or unsafe? Do women in various cultural contexts have the equality, supports, and social capital necessary to engage in the dialogue and encounter that this model demands?

The *Cultural Context Model* is a system of clinical theory and practice that offers solutions to the many dilemmas facing families and communities today. This expanded family paradigm offers a clear analysis of societal-based patterns that contribute to the lack of physical and emotional safety in family and community life. Solutions are created for families through the construction of a community that supports a collective consciousness of liberation (Freire, 1972). This collective knowledge is necessary to dismantle linkages of power, privilege, and oppression.

The major objective of the Cultural Context Model is to create a collective experience that moves systems and individuals within those systems. A guiding premise is that the liberation of women is intrinsically tied to the accountability of men. Therefore, dismantling the power imbalances and restructuring the power that exists between men and women is a critical aspect of change. The Cultural Context Model addresses gender, skin color, ethnicity, spiritual practice, sexual orientation, age, and socioeconomic class in a manner that places these issues at the core of family intervention.[1] "The Cultural Context Model (CCM) was initiated as a means to engage men who use violence, to help battered women, and to assist couples addressing normative issues of gender/racial imbalance. The model continues to have special relevance and success in intervening with both men who have been abusive as well as those who seek help for the range of less extreme problems" (Parker, 2002).

Standpoint epistemology approaches theory and practice by connecting families to larger systems of community and society that shape and control family life (Fox, 1993). Thus, this discourse encompasses concepts of race, class, and sexual orientation (Almeida, 1994, 1998; Almeida and

Dolan-Delvecchio, 1999; Almeida and Durkin, 1999). Linking the interior of family life to the larger social structures that determine family interaction situates families within the very social context that shapes and defines them. At the heart of this conceptualization of family systems therapy is the notion that both accountability and empowerment—traditionally seen as competing moral stances—can coexist simultaneously in the same family. It is from this discourse of moral inquiry that the CCM was born. This definition of the CCM expresses well the way in which a multicultural approach includes both cultural components of a "race/class/gender" intersectionalities analysis as well as a social "structural" analysis as described by Sokoloff and Dupont in chapter 1.

The unique contributions of the Cultural Context Model are threefold: situating conversations about domestic violence within the larger social context of privilege, power, and oppression; countering the segregation of this problem from others; and above all else, privileging the safety of women, children, and men in their homes and community. Interventions begin at the sociopolitical level, in which domestic violence is viewed in a larger context as but one form of social control and oppression. Other examples of such abuses of power include racism, genocide, homophobia, and class entrapment. Therefore, dismantling the power imbalances and restructuring the power that exists—not only between men and women, but power differentials among men and women according to skin color, spiritual practice, sexual orientation, age, socioeconomic class, and the preferential status accorded to different immigrants—are central to individual, family, and community change.

TOWARD A SOCIAL JUSTICE MODEL OF MENTAL HEALTH

Traditional mental health approaches locate domestic violence within the interior of family and individual psyche. This creates an experience of segregation around the presenting problem in a way that is neither helpful to the family/community nor fostering safety for the victims. In traditional models, the structure of individual, couple, or even family therapy limits the experience of change to the interior boundary of family life. This supports the notion of change as a force driven by individual action. Within the CCM the individual woman is provided with a coalition of women increasing her power. Further, she is connected to a coalition of men with whom to challenge male privilege. Men, on the other hand, are connected with sponsors who are men from their community who support nonviolence. This linking offers a network of accountability, while creating expanded notions of masculinity. This coalition building alters the very boundaries and power distribution of family life.

While the battered women's movement has long established the relevance of groups as the only structure within which change for batterers can occur, there continues to be a separation of "therapeutic intervention" from other problems such as depression, marital/relational discord, addiction, work, or parenting issues. As a social justice model designed to confront any problem that interferes with the safety and healthy values of family/community life, the CCM views all these issues within the larger social context that includes experiences of privilege and oppression. By insisting that violence and other presenting issues are located in this larger context, the Cultural Context Model shifts the question, "Why does violence occur?" to "Under what conditions do those with power over others abuse that power?" Further, this philosophy compels us to ascertain the link between client's social location and their "presenting problem." Thus, the Cultural Context Model necessitates a greatly expanded view of domestic violence that calls into question the polarized separation of men into groups of those who are violent and those who are not. It calls into question the very language that positions men who batter versus men who do not. Further, it challenges the entire gamut of mental health descriptors that separate classes of families based upon their diagnostic categories.

Implementation of the Cultural Context Model for service provision requires a team of therapists who are willing to share responsibilities and work collaboratively; share cases and supervise one another using live video or one-way-mirror technology; treat a broad range of client problems using a systemic and not exclusively intrapsychic perspective; learn from each other and from their clients; and work with colleagues, community members, and clients who are both similar to and different from themselves.

In this chapter we outline the philosophy of the CCM as it informs our work with families and communities. Our goal is twofold: first, to inspire readers to question their assumptions about pathology and violence, and, second, to embrace a more diverse and expanded vision of the problems and possibilities therein. We begin with the *intake* and *socioeducation,* then move on to *sponsorship, culture circles, accountability,* and some of the more traditional clinical interventions.

Intake

At the point of *intake,* families are introduced to at least two, if not more, therapists, one of whom will be behind the mirror while the other is in the treatment room. A basic genogram is then constructed. Genograms are tools used by family therapists to record, illustrate, and interpret data about the family over time. (For a more detailed description of genograms, see Bowen, 1978; McGoldrick and Gerson, 1985; McGoldrick et al., 1999.)

In preparation for the socioeducation process we separate families by gender at the first interview. If children or adolescents are present they are connected with others of their age. Although families might happen to share different parts of their problems, such as some might be experiencing difficulty at work while others may not have work, they are *not* grouped by diagnostic category or presenting problem. It is our belief that segregation around presenting problems, while intended to create community through shared experience, in fact further compartmentalizes the client's sense of being. Further, it builds the identity of a family/individual around "pathology" and punctuates time around the problem, rather than around alternate life stories and themes of liberation.

In another departure from traditional models in the CCM, gatherings of men and women create a community emphasizing the notion of a family as an open unit. This shifts the mantel from which a client narrative is told. Instead of a hierarchical structure in which the therapist is the expert and the client is pathologized, the story emerges through skilled questioning, as part of a larger collective. The immersion into the group also rapidly shifts the psychology of individual autonomy to that of a collective consciousness: the collective of social origin within which all families are located.

Socioeducation Process

Socioeducation is the presentation of didactic materials to clients in an effort to raise critical consciousness around issues of gender, race, culture, and sexual orientation. A combination of video clips, books, articles, and music lyrics creates the stimulus to activate discussion that expands the therapeutic conversation. Critical consciousness (Freire, 1972) is exemplified by an experience of living, within which historical/cultural prescriptions for choice making are recognized for what they are and not blindly followed as though they are "the natural order of things." For example, an unexamined belief in the idea that males are aggressive by nature is the antithesis of critical consciousness, which requires an inquiry into this "cultural myth," and a recognition of the fact that adherence to this notion is an act of choice and not simply fate or nature. Freire ties critical consciousness to economic and political systems, noting that domination essentially relies upon a social order within which critical consciousness is suppressed. Education for critical consciousness, on the other hand, dismantles indoctrination and oppression, supporting inquiry and dialogues instead; it is therefore the foundation for liberation and democracy.

To facilitate this process, we ask clients numerous questions regarding the continuum of male and female norms that helped shape their family over time. For example,

- How did the men respond to issues of work, or lack of work?
- Did the women also work outside of the home? How were these issues handled by the men and women in the family?
- How did the impact of race and class control life choices for both, men and women?

The process of dismantling these stories becomes central to constructing alternate life choices.

The socioeducation process takes place, over the course of eight weeks, in small same-sex groups, referred to as *culture circles*. Within these culture circles there is usually a same-sex *sponsor*. The point of this connection is to mentor the new clients into the process of building a critical consciousness.

The clients are then invited into the larger, same-sex culture circles. It is within these larger circles that much of the therapeutic work is accomplished. Couples and families, as subsystems of a larger community, are brought into these circles and assisted with finding solutions that liberate through empowerment and accountability. We find that this structural intervention supports the possibility of a family as an open system; change within this context is community driven. Change for women and families occur at multiple levels and not solely at the personal level.

Scenes from *Sleeping With the Enemy* and *Straight Out of Brooklyn,* two mainstream movies that include domestic violence, are used in conjunction with each other to explore the intersection of class, race, and gender. (Films mentioned are available through Women Make Movies.) *Sleeping With the Enemy* is about an upper middle-class white couple. In the film clip the husband is shown using all of the forms of abuse available to him—physical, emotional, intimidation, sexual and male privilege—in order to control his wife. The "Power and Control in Heterosexual Relationships Wheel—Private Context" (see figure 18.1; Pence and Paymar, 1986; Almeida et al., 1992) is used to help the clients identify these forms of abuse within the interior of the family. Then scenes from *Straight Out of Brooklyn,* a movie about a working-class Black couple struggling with multiple dimensions of poverty and

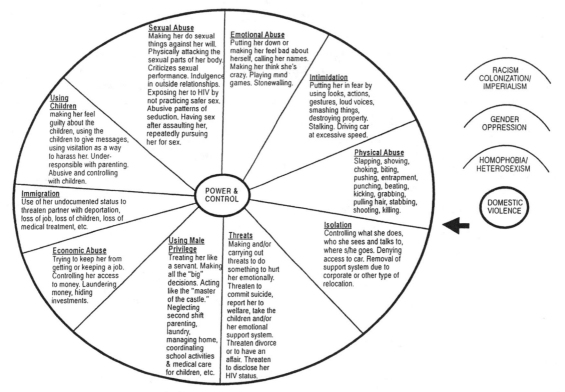

Figure 18.1   Private Context: The Misuse and Abuse of Power within Heterosexual Relationships. *Source:* Power and Control Wheels (Almeida, R., et al., 1992). Reprinted by permission of the Institute for Family Services.

racism, are shown. In these scenes the husband is also extremely abusive of the wife and threatens his son. During the violence he references the many forms of racism that he struggles with each day. In the following scene his wife finds herself in the role of culture bearer, having to explain the impact of racism to her daughter who is challenging her father's violence. In the final scene of the clip the mother's employer is firing her because she will not get "help" for the battering. While holding the father accountable for his abuse, the "Power and Control toward People of Color Wheel—Public Context"[2] (see figure 18.2, Almeida et al., 1992) is used to identify the ways in which the family is subjected to the violence of racism by society. Through questions about the options open to the two women, the future of the African American couple after the wife loses her job, and the disparity in the pressures that racism places upon the African American couple, the definition of violence is expanded to include social violence as well as personal violence. At the same time, the conversation about the film does not minimize or excuse the violence within the family. We use this conversation to introduce a more multilayered analysis of the social location of men within a hierarchy of oppression. Films such as *The Wedding Banquet* (focusing on Taiwanese, Euro-American, and Japanese cultures), *The Joy Luck Club* (focusing on Chinese culture), and *Mississippi Masala* (focusing on Asian Indian and African

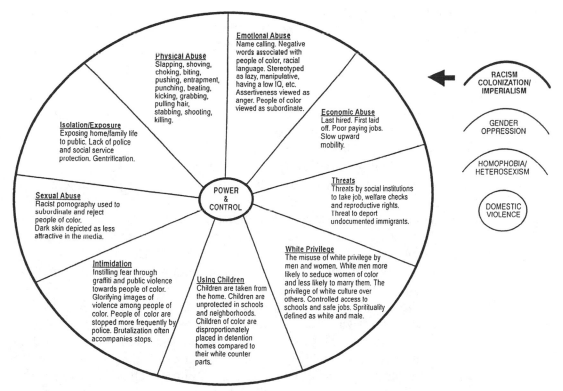

Figure 18.2   Public Context: The Misuse and Abuse of Power toward People of Color.
Source: Power and Control Wheels (Almeida, R., et al., 1992). Reprinted by permission of the Institute for Family Services.

American cultures) are introduced as well, in order to emphasize the universality of these patterns of domination and control often misnamed culture. Since much work has been done on diversity and family therapy (see McGoldrick et al., 1996) we are restricting this discussion to the larger themes of culture and tradition as they impact domestic violence. As providers of change, we cannot comfortably define all men's experiences as being identical with respect to class, ethnic history and racial discrimination. CCM holds a moral and ethical responsibility to define the different social locations that punctuate power, privilege and oppression for men. This is especially so since we are in the business of ending violence.

Conversations about the video between the members of the culture circle and the team of therapists are extremely useful in dismantling traditional norms of family life for girls, boys, men, and women. For instance, if an African American man raises the need for his wife to honor his status given the history of slavery and the larger context of racism, then selected scenes from *This Boy's Life,* in which a downwardly mobile mother tries to protect her family and find a role model for her son by accommodating to an abusive new husband, become a vehicle for exposing that, in most cultures, wives/mothers are expected to excuse the behavior of the man in the house. Traditionally, in the culture at large, women who challenge that role are seen as less than perfect mothers, wives, or daughters. They are particularly ostracized if they attempt to explain the behavior of the man in terms that do not elevate traditional male norms. Articulating the norms that maintain patterns of domination and subordination in all families is crucial to experiences of liberation in CCM.

Of course, based on the different types of cultures represented in the room, the discussion might go in the direction of how culture shapes certain responses. For example, an Asian Indian woman might say that in her culture it is important to support the dowry system and maintain the economic joint system of her husband's family (Almeida, 1996). She might also add that as an honorable wife she is to respect her husband and model such respect for the children—a hallmark of family/patriarchal hierarchy. To address this cultural dilemma, we carefully select video clips and writings by Indian feminists as well as Asian Indian men who hold a critical consciousness. These diverse narratives demonstrate a range of expanded norms for women and men, depicting powerful women who challenge tradition and maintain cultural legacies that do *not* support male domination. The movie *Montreal Massacre,* a documentary that explores the aftermath of the murder of eleven women at the Polytechnic Institute in Canada, is excellent for numerous women who are "other." It exposes the continuum of violence against women in all of its forms and defines this violence as a human rights issue. Numerous women of color challenge the mythology of tradition as being a veil for male domination; also numerous men of color, including Indian and African men, present staunch positions in support of women's rights. Films such as *Warrior Marks,* a documentary produced by Alice Walker and Pratihma Pahbar, that examines genital mutilation and places it in a continuum of patriarchal practices around the globe, is an excellent resource for distinguishing the notion of "culture" from customs of domination. Members of the culture circle can then draw from this knowledge to challenge the traditional proscriptions for women, while simultaneously creating a strong context of support for difference.

Because all of our work is done in the same culture circle, only separating those who have language requirements, the white members of the circle are routinely educated about diverse cultures; for example, the commonly held mythology that all Asian women are comfortable with subordination or that heterosexuality is the only type of partnering within that culture is challenged.

Another frequently presented dilemma is the cultural doctrine of religion. For example, many women and men of the Islamic faith will argue about the religious necessity to veil their adolescent daughters or ascribe some aspect of female enslavement to the Koran. In such situations, we utilize *cultural consultants,* that is, individuals within a particular culture who have a critical consciousness about race and gender, class and colonization. It is indeed a racist assumption that any individual, just by cultural match, is sufficient to create a partnership that reshapes these norms of gendered violence. Not all whites promote nonviolence; similarly, not all members from a particular cultural group are homogenous with regard to a heightened sense of gendered equality. Cultural consultants play similar roles to sponsors, although they participate only as needed. For example, an Imam that we know who supports gender equity in family life might be called upon when a Muslim client is persistent about the idea that the Koran says that women must obey men. A Muslim sponsor can also serve as a cultural consultant if they are versed in the teachings of Mohammed and can challenge the client with respect to the difference between the original writings and subsequent patriarchal interpretations. We have also relied on writings by Muslim feminists (Mernissi, 1982, 1992) and documentaries that can serve the same function.

Another example of a cultural consultant is the use of liberation theologians who offer alternative interpretations of scriptures in many different religions. This form of theology has questioned certain practices in formal religion, such as the accumulation of wealth by Catholic/Christian churches as well as the lower status of women. Battered women are supported in their endeavor to challenge the patriarchy of the church, while being permitted to practice the faith, without ostracism.

The assessment process thus consists of evaluating one's location within the hierarchy of gendered/racial/domination/subordination norms. By using the films, the power and control wheels (figures 18.1 and 18.2), and other tools on the traditional norms of the male role (Green, 1998; Font et al., 1998), we assess for the continuum of violence from control to lethality. When we speak of lethality we mean men who, for example, torture animals, use weapons, abuse a range of substances, have a history of criminal and domestic violence, are on the police force or F.B.I., have the support of militia on their sides, and openly threaten lethality to their partners.

Men who support traditional norms are challenged by a community of men and are required to be accountable to a different set of norms and morality. These new norms represent *gender equity* within diverse cultures and prescribe a relational *ethic of caring.* This is the point at which the traditional norms of patriarchy can be challenged and transformed into expanded ways of being male (Dolan-Delvecchio, 1997). Change is embraced through an opportunity for reviewing different constructs of masculinity (Font et al., 1998). This is crucial to the liberation of women in all spheres of their lives and for the greater spiritual embodiment of men as well.

Socioeducation begins to shift clients' awareness toward a balancing of the personal and the political, the intrapsychic and the social, moving from the interior of experience to the exterior, and further defining one's relational impact on loved ones.

Sponsorship

An example of community participation toward nonviolence is the use of *sponsors*. Men who have not used violence as well as men who have stopped past violence are recruited from the community as sponsors. Sponsors serve multiple roles, but all contribute to a context of accountability and support within the therapeutic encounter. The specifics of a sponsorship program are described elsewhere (Almeida and Bograd, 1990; Almeida and Durkin, 1999), however several fundamental concepts deserve mention here:

- Sponsors are men from the community who support nonviolence in all relationships.
- Sponsors form partnerships with men who engage in violence with the goal of mentoring men into a life of nonviolence.
- Sponsors serve to break down the secrecy surrounding violence, expand conversations about family life to a community process, and break the isolation that informs the relational choices that men make.
- Sponsors model an expanded notion of masculinity that includes vulnerability, nurturing, gentleness, empathy, and an understanding of others. They also model respect for women, children, people of color, sexual minorities, and others who are different.
- Sponsors help other men to view their problems and their choices by taking into consideration their partners, their children, and their families. They teach other men to always evaluate the impact their choices have on others.

Sponsors are brought into the circle in different ways. Usually, they are citizens in the community interested in doing activist work. They are recruited based on their interest in ending violence of all types within the community and then encouraged to participate with that as their goal. Volunteers are trained for three months; they participate exactly like the clients. Through the socioeducation we engage men by connecting them to the larger social context in which we are all embedded. This locates individuals within their multiple experiences of power, privilege and oppression: gender, race, sexual orientation, and cultural stereotyping. We further obtain complete genogram information on sponsors and their families and then assist with discussion of the materials and the social location of power and control. After each session there is an extensive discussion with the sponsors about the culture groups, in which feedback from the team heightens their critical consciousness. Because they are in training, we expect them to go through the same process of learning as therapists, even though they may have participated in prior activist work. They serve as sponsors for one year and then help train new sponsors.

We have found that good sponsors are truly committed to a life of nonviolence. They have chosen to participate with others who struggle to maintain lives of tolerance for difference and embrace nonviolence in *all* aspects of their lives. They are men who continue to learn to expand their expression of masculinity at work, at home, and in the community. They are open about their struggles with other men at work and in their social context, and those with whom they are sponsoring. Sponsors meet regularly together and seek assistance from the pool of other sponsors and staff.

Maintaining a life of nonviolence must include a support system that embraces such values over one's entire life. No one program by itself has the capability of creating such change.

Culture Circles

Most of the work of therapy within the Cultural Context Model continues in same-sex gatherings that we term *culture circles,* except for the intermittent family and/or couple sessions within the entire community, which consists of both men's and women's culture circles. Within these circles there will be partnered as well as single adults. The term culture circles, borrowed from Freire (1972), describes a heterogeneous helping community that includes a team of skilled CCM therapists and sponsors.

In traditional family therapy, the therapeutic circle is most often the family itself in various permutations of the system. While feminist family theory has embraced the notion of the family as an open system, the physical closure of this system within the therapeutic encounter preserves, certainly in heterosexual families, the very fabric of male hierarchy and privacy. Dismantling this structure, or healing this system, depends on opening up the system as much as possible. This creates an experience of the family as an open system. Intervention with mothers, fathers, uncles, brothers, sisters, grandparents, partners, and children is all done as subsystem work, thereby defining the family system not as autonomous but as open and connected—a boundary within a boundary. Knowledge gained from these therapeutic experiences is knowledge held within the family as well as the community.

We use the language of "culture circles" rather than "groups" to describe the work in our community. We made this shift after it became apparent with professional trainees that the theory and language of traditional group therapy ran counter to the ideology of *social activism.* While traditional group theory in mental health was helpful in managing many of the differences of individuals within and out of groups, it still retained a politic of segregation and pathology. For example, various tenets of group theory, such as the roles of the "leader," "monopolizer," or "scapegoat," enhance individual power rather than generate collaboration. While intended to create community or "group cohesion," group membership organized around a diagnostic category (that is, sexual abuse) or presenting problem (that is, domestic violence) further isolates and compartmentalizes one's sense of being. A presenting problem is not the sole organizer of a person's life. In one of our culture circles, members may include a man who raped or battered his partner, a man suffering from a chronic deteriorating illness, and a man who has misused his gender or racial privilege. As such, the culture circles consist of men with a variety of presenting problems. Furthermore, in traditional group therapy participants are required to have *no* out-of-group contact. To build community support toward nonviolence, we encourage participants to build relationships and contact the sponsors often.

Last, the building of compassion and relatedness through active listening is a fundamental value of the CCM. It is operationalized from the first point of contact, when clients are not given much time to focus on their own personal construction of the problem but instead are encouraged to listen to the stories in the films as well as the stories of other men. They are encouraged to ask questions about the experiences of others. We shift the traditional paradigm where work on oneself is accomplished solely by taking group time or controlling the agenda. Rather, male clients are supported to become *actively involved in each other's change process.* This is a powerful tool in dismantling some of the more rigid norms of masculinity, such as focus on self, being in control, and a lack of attention or failure to remember the experiences of others.

Accountability

Accountability, a central theme of the Cultural Context Model, is threaded into all of the components. It is being addressed here as a separate category to place it within the discourse of domestic violence. We view accountability as a fluid, relational concept that informs a way of being in relationship to others; it is a central tenet to liberation. It is not a singular apology, statement, or letter. Rather, accountability is a patterned way of relating to others that challenges the rigid norms of masculine and feminine behavior, and locates collaboration and respect as central norms. In our definition, accountability is broader than links to the criminal justice system and/or battered women's shelters. It includes men and women in the community within which the batterer lives and works who hold him accountable for his violence. The criminal justice system acts as a backdrop to ensure that legal constraints are enforced. However, systems of accountability must include alternatives to the justice system, due to the white heterosexual bias inherent in that structure. In fact, systems of accountability must address the multiple institutions that maintain and perpetuate racism and sexism and the ways those forms of oppression are manifest in family life.

Because we shift the boundary of family life in an attempt to make it a more open system, we frequently engage in conversation about the misuses of power in the public context for people of color and gays and lesbians. Clients thus begin to think about systems of privilege and oppression in contexts other than their intimate lives. Another example of bringing accountability to systems outside of their families is when we assign the men to inquire about various wages that men and women earn in their places of work relevant to the job and educational background. It frequently illuminates the disparity that exists, both between men and women, and men from different class and race backgrounds. Once their awareness has shifted, they are encouraged to attempt to bring some sort of change to this context.

This task may feel overwhelming to the reader. However, there was a time not long ago when the notion of protecting battered women and children seemed overwhelming; there were no laws to protect them. While many of the goals of the domestic violence movement have been realized, the methods of intervention that have evolved (that is, shelters and batterers programs) have not been connected with other institutions that share the same goal. In becoming institutionalized, they have lost their original grassroots mission, thereby becoming more isolated. For example, evolving systems in the community have expanded norms of masculinity, such as gay churches, churches of people of color, temples, and the National Organization of Men Against Sexism (NOMAS) organization. Linking with such organizations can begin to create structures that can support the challenge regarding equity within systems of criminal justice. Currently, more white heterosexual women are protected by the system. Complacency with regards to expanding the service system and creating new forms of networking, as suggested above, would maintain their position of privilege in relation to women of color, whose partners, sons and fathers are incarcerated at a rate that far exceeds that in the white community.

Accountability, then, is not just an expectation for the client. We who embrace this paradigm must adopt a systemic analysis that incorporates social activism, both in and out of the CCM encounter. Historically, change was encouraged in the client while therapists and institutions that provide the services maintain the status quo of inequity. Larger systemic change like building coalitions with those who are "other" and integrating these coalitions into the delivery system are often dismissed as "too burdensome," "not professional," or "not essential to a high standard of care." Perceiving it as a diversion from the "real" issue of male violence further dismisses this larger systemic analysis. The Cultural Context Model expands the concepts of power and oppression, linking the intimate experience to the social and political environment in which families are embedded.

The Cultural Context Model and 12 Step Programs

The following case draws attention to the incidence of the addictive use of alcohol and other substances and domestic violence and the complications associated with the intersection of these distinct, but closely tied, problems. These complications pose a danger to the families of batterers as well as ethical dilemmas for optimal treatment.

Much of the wisdom of the 12 Step Recovery programs is very compatible with the philosophy of CCM. We strongly advise every client with a substance abuse problem to attend AA (Alcoholics Anonymous) and NA (Narcotics Anonymous) meetings regularly and consistently and to adhere to the fundamental principles outlined in the twelve steps and *The Big Book of Alcoholics Anonymous.* However, we monitor the advice that gets handed down by individuals in the fellowship and recommend that the clients who are both addicts and batterers stay in close touch with sponsors in the CCM who are veterans of negotiating the two programs.

Despite the overwhelming evidence that there is a high correlation between the misuse of alcohol and other substances and domestic violence (NCADI, 1995), these two issues are frequently treated separately and with little or no coordination between treatment agencies. The compartmentalizing of treatment for these two lethal problems creates some grave dilemmas. In the addiction treatment community, as well as in the general population, there is a longstanding belief that the ingestion of alcohol/drugs causes violence. This fosters the myth that violence will end once abstinence is achieved and its corollary, that the violence is being addressed in the process of treating the addiction. In that context, victims may then let down their guard, miss key signals that the violence is escalating and/or remove safeguards (that is, restraining orders, physical separations, safety plans). Furthermore, the conventional wisdom of the addiction recovery community is that addiction is primary and thus every issue in an addict's life can only be addressed after sobriety is stabilized. It may be true that a second order shift in family relationships cannot be achieved while clients are under the influence. However, when there is domestic violence, consideration for the safety of the victims must be the driving engine and overarching blueprint for treatment. This means that the social and structural interventions that comprise the early stages of domestic violence must be activated as soon as domestic violence is assessed. At the same time, a plan to facilitate recovery must be put in place. However, this plan is not in lieu of treatment for domestic violence, and the recommendations can never be privileged over the interventions addressing the violence. To illustrate, the recovery community often advises its members to postpone, to an indefinite later date, any activities that would threaten recovery. Any activity that makes the addict uncomfortable can be labeled as threatening. Clearly, writing an accountability letter, being challenged by a group of men about his violence, being confronted with the discrepancy between his version of the history and his partner's narrative are all examples of activities that would raise the addict's level of anxiety. However, these activities must be engaged in for the treatment of domestic violence to begin. If the addict is refusing to do these things, which often happens with the support of the recovery community, the family must understand that no change in the level of risk for violence has occurred.

Another fundamental conflict in the philosophies of CCM and the 12 Step Recovery programs is their opposing positions on privacy and confidentiality. To challenge the principles of privacy and privilege that underpin violence, batterers must be publicly challenged and begin the process of acknowledging violence in community. In the 12 Step Recovery programs, especially as they are currently interpreted through the culture of the fellowship, the private nature of the relationship between an AA member and his sponsor is sacrosanct. The disclosures, even of current violent behavior, between a sponsor and the person being sponsored (a sponsee) in AA and NA are treated with the same privilege as that accorded to those divulged in the confessional. According to the twelve steps the inventory of his alcoholic behavior, including acts of violence, need only be shared with "God and another human being." Furthermore, the tradition of "no cross-talk" at AA and NA meetings, while not part of the original scripture, has become conventional wisdom and is seen as providing the "safety" required for an addict to attend and participate in the meetings. This contradicts the fundamental principle of the domestic violence movement: without the open system of challenging the narrative of the batterer there will be no lasting change. The sponsors in the CCM community provide nurturance, support, mentoring, and connection to the newer men as sponsors in the 12 Step fellowship do. However, the CCM sponsors expand the definition of support to include challenging them on their controlling and abusive behaviors and coaching them on considering the impact of these behaviors on their partners. Further, CCM sponsors value the safety of partners and families over privacy and confidentiality. Thus, information shared with a CCM sponsor is always brought back to the community.

Another distinction between the 12 Step sponsors and the CCM sponsors is that the former, in the guise of neutrality, do not coach sponsees on their behavior toward their families. CCM sponsors advocate for the safety of children and partners by elevating their narratives over that of the batterer. And CCM sponsors honor the need for the safety and the healing of families to take precedence. This means that the work of stopping the violence, taking inventory, and making amends must privilege the timing of the family's needs, not the addict's comfort.

A related difficulty when treating addiction and domestic violence separately is the convention, in recovery circles, of prescribing Alanon for the partners of addicts. When they are also battered women, the Alanon principle of focusing on oneself obscures the need for the victim to hold her partner one hundred percent responsible for his violence. Furthermore, as women are universally socialized to take responsibility for every aspect of a relationship, this adds more weight to the tendency for her to blame herself for the violence. In addition, addiction counselors and rehabilitation programs emphasize the need for spouses of addicts to stop "enabling the addict." This obscures the existence and impact of the violence and places the responsibility for change on the victim.

A fundamental part of treatment, for families who have experienced domestic violence and have been socialized in the 12 Step model as well, is understanding the dangers of that model. To aid in deconstructing the differences between the 12 Step philosophy and the CCM, The "AA and Domestic Violence Power and Control Wheel" was devised (figure 2 in Almeida et al., 1997). This wheel is a powerful tool in delineating the ways in which violence gets minimized, confidentiality misused, and the woman/victim blamed and pathologized when addiction is seen as the sole, or primary problem, and battering or other oppressive practices as the result or bi-product of the addiction.

ASSESSING RELATIONSHIPS: HOLDING OTHERS ACCOUNTABLE FOR MISUSES OF POWER/MEN CHALLENGE OTHER MEN

The expanded paradigm provided by the CCM for thinking about men's' behavior allows for a broad assessment of their relationships, rather than the narrow construction of male to female physical abuse. In our work, men and their families have benefited greatly by applying this notion of "accountability" as "a way of being in relationship." This counters the patriarchal prescription to obscure the work of women in families and leads to a greater enhancement and understanding of those relationships. We often employ the technique of *letter writing* to foster this process.

Letter writing, as narrative method, is used for various purposes in different family therapy models (for example, see Epston and White, 1992). Letter writing as we use it encompasses many different therapeutic tasks. It is used foremost as a document of accountability; this document of accountability is written in the culture circle over time with feedback from sponsors and community members. When it is complete, often after many months, the victim of abuse or other victims in the community then witness it. The letter of accountability is intended to be one major form of truth and retribution, borrowed from strategies used by activists in situations of war crimes and apartheid. Abuses of power historically sanctioned a loss of memory, allowing a range of heinous crimes and behaviors toward those with less power to continue. The remembering of abusive acts and abuse of privilege is released by the perpetrator to the community, who hold the memory while the writer gradually moves to a position of shared memory and responsibility.

These letters are used in addressing parents who are abusive to their children as well as members of the community who may use common forms of racial and gendered patterns of assault towards one another. They serve as a useful tool when family members are unable to have an expanded conversation. Because our work is so focused on breaking down the barriers of privacy that maintain abusive behavior, much of our family and couples work is done in the context of the culture circles. For example, we may bring a woman with several members of her culture circle into the men's circle to have a difficult conversation; the women would enhance her voice and provide support, while the members of his circle would challenge and support him, as well as hold the memory of her experience. This collective conscience alleviates a great emotional burden for women, who come to understand that there are others, particularly men, who can hold and articulate her experience to her partner.

After the letters are read, the community of men are asked to articulate their understanding of the relationship experience, with its varied dimensions of power and control. The commonality of these narratives adds to the collective dismantling of patriarchal and racist ways of being.[3]

CONCLUSION

In this chapter, we have presented an approach to working with men and their families that regards as essential the social location of individuals within the contexts of power, privilege, and oppression and the building of communities that support collaboration and nonviolence. We have given specific examples of the ways in which the politics of self can be deconstructed through the use of socioeducation, sponsors, and cultural consultants. This process of unwrapping the parts of a person's individual and political identity then allows for the gradual rebuilding of a new collective conscience, one that upholds both accountability and liberation.

We expand upon the family therapy techniques of genograms and letter writing to foster this therapeutic work and help clients move toward greater accountability; this takes places within the context of culture circles. Since power over others is maintained through a refusal to remember specific acts of abuse, the power of remembering claimed by the community of culture circles balances the power necessary to create change. For many battered women, this system of intervention offers a range of new options: the possibility of returning to their now nonviolent partners, the possibility of children rebuilding relationships with their abusive parent, the possibility of having a civil and safe divorce, and last, the possibility of maintaining safety through community rather than criminal justice intervention.

We also demonstrated the ways in which abuse of power and control becomes obscured when working with other presenting problems. Owing to the very high incidence of violence and the use of alcohol and other drugs, we specifically addressed the issue of addiction and recovery in 12 Step Programs. Noting that the involvement in 12 Step Programs is imperative to sustained recovery, we then discussed the ways in which the philosophy of these programs poses ethical dilemmas when domestic violence is also present. Because alcohol and other drugs are present in 50 percent of all incidents of domestic violence (NCADI, 1995), it is a serious and critical issue. Ideas about preserving privacy and confidentiality embedded in the 12 Step Programs run counter to the need for public disclosure of abuse. To aid in assessing and maintaining the safety of all family members, and to illustrate the gender bias inherent in the programs, see the AA/DV Power and Control Wheel (Almeida et al., 1997).

The Cultural Context Model is unique in that it situates conversations about domestic violence and other presenting problems within the larger social context of privilege, power, and oppression. The interventions of the CCM counter the segregation of domestic violence from other presenting problems, such as addiction. Above all else, the CCM privileges the safety of women, children, and men in their homes and community.

This conceptual shift regarding where the problem is located opens up a variety of possibilities for intervention and systemic change. If we view the problem of domestic violence solely as located in the interior of the family, disconnected from other forms of oppression, our solutions would be limited as well. In this chapter, we challenge the reader to think beyond programmatic concerns and limitations to question the very definition of domestic violence as well as the efficacy of separating men into groups of men who have used violence and those who have not.

At the heart of the Cultural Context Model is the effort to build communities within which all members of families are ensured safety and respect, fundamental human rights, and conditions necessary for optimum growth and empowerment. Because nearly all institutions in our culture include traditions that marginalize people of color, women, gays and lesbians, as well as other "minorities," an essential element within the construction of communities of support is the reexamination and dismantling of these oppressive institutional traditions.

Although the battered women's movement began as a grassroots, activist group, it has through the years become largely institutionalized. Perhaps dangerously so, it operates within the "mythology of activism." This poses a huge dilemma with respect to understanding the multilayered analysis of gender, race, and culture and how those dimensions of our lives are linked to one's access to structures that promote and ensure safety. White middle-class feminism as a mainstay advocacy forum for battered women is conceptually flawed and unsafe for women on the margin (Crenshaw, 1994; Richie, 1996).

Given the racism, classism, sexism, and homophobia inherent in the criminal justice system, heavy reliance on that structure to end family violence is problematic. Although necessary as a backdrop to ensure protection for victims, we must create alternatives both within and outside of this subculture of patriarchy.

Change thus requires a social context that promotes nonviolence in all forms. Indeed, this needs to be the guiding principle, so that all institutions in the community address an ethic of caring that includes nonviolence as a core norm. However, given that we live under patriarchy, in which not all institutions are committed to such evolution, the therapeutic context that requires that perpetrators of violence change can and should be the foundation from which such communities are created. For example, if we consider that batterer programs are just about the only institution in our culture in which men are forced to change, we can begin to expand upon the potential therein—potential not just to change individual men, but rather to challenge the patriarchy, creating more expanded norms of masculinity and fostering a cultural morality toward nonviolence. Imagine, if you will, the notion of "compliance" in this context. Traditionally, this has meant such things as attending a batterer's group, better managing one's anger, and ceasing to batter one's partner. In the broader context of the Cultural Context Model, compliance is defined as awareness and deconstructing of the links between patriarchy and family abuse as well as ceasing the battering within an individual family. From this perspective, compliance is linked to social activism and might include going into high schools to socialize boys to a life of nonviolence, evolving different norms within the criminal justice system, or shifting norms within corporations. For example, how is corporate crime similar or different from domestic violence with regard to the norms of violence and regard for human rights?

NOTES

Films of Liberation. An excellent resource for films on diversity, gender, race, class, and sexual orientation issues as well as culture, tradition, and violence against women is: Women Make Movies, 462 Broadway, Suite 500D, New York, N.Y. 10013.

1. In this chapter we address heterosexual battering. Therefore, the language of men as batterers is used.

2. Typically, a traditional Power and Control Wheel focuses on private relationships (figure 18.1). Here we include the public arena to ground power and control in race, class, and gender structures (figure 18.2).

3. For research that indicates the efficacy of the CCM for both court-mandated and voluntary clients, see Parker (2002).

REFERENCES

Almeida, R. 1993. Unexamined assumptions and service delivery systems: Feminist theory and racial exclusions. *Journal of Feminist Family Therapy* 5(1): 3–23.

———, ed. 1994. *Expansions of Feminist Theory through Diversity.* Binghamton, N.Y.: Haworth.

———. 1996. Hindu, Christian, and Muslin families. In M. McGoldrick, J. Giordano, and J. Pearce, eds., *Ethnicity and Family Therapy.* 2d ed. New York: Guilford.

———. 1998. The dislocation of women's experience. In R. Almeida, ed., *Transformations of Gender and Race: Family and Developmental Perspectives.* New York: Haworth.

Almeida, R., and M. Bograd. 1990. Sponsorship: Men holding men accountable for domestic violence. *Journal of Feminist Family Therapy* 2(3–4): 234–256.

Almeida, R., and K. Dolan-Delvecchio. 1999. Addressing culture in batterers intervention: The Asian Indian community as an illustrative example. *Violence Against Women* 5(6): 654–682.

Almeida, R., K. Dolan-Delvecchio, and L. Parker, eds. In Press. *Just Families/A Just Society: Transformative Family Therapy.* Boston: Allyn and Bacon.

Almeida, R., and T. Durkin. 1999. The cultural context model: Therapy for couples with domestic violence. *Journal of Marital and Family Therapy* 25(3): 313–324.

Almeida, R., R. Woods, R. Font, and T. Messineo. 1992. Power and control wheels. Reprinted by permission. Institute for Family Services.

Almeida, R., R. Woods, R. Font, T. Messineo, and J. Lockard. 1997. The AA and DV power and control wheel. Paper.

Almeida, R., R. Woods, T. Messineo, and R. Font. 1998. Cultural context model. In M. McGoldrick, ed., *Revisioning Family Therapy: Race, Culture, and Gender in Clinical Practice.* New York: Guilford, 404–432.

Almeida, R., R. Woods, T. Messineo, R. Font, and C. Heer. 1994. Violence in the lives of the racially and sexually different: A public and private dilemma. In R. Almeida, ed., *Expansions of Feminist Family Therapy through Diversity.* New York: Harrington Park, pp. 99–126.

Bowen, M. 1978. *Family Therapy in Clinical Practice.* New York: Jason Aronson.

Crenshaw, K. W. 1994. Mapping the margins: Intersectionality, identity, politics, and violence against women of color. In M. A. Fineman and R. Mykitiuk, eds., *The Public Nature of Private Violence.* New York: Routledge.

Dolan-Delvecchio, K. 1997. The foundation of accountability: A linking of many different voices. *American Family Therapy Academy Newsletter* 64: 20–23.

Epston, D., and M. White. 1992. *Experience, Contradiction, Narrative, and Imagination: Selected Papers.* South Australia: Dulwich Centre.

Font, R., K. Dolan-Delvecchio, and R. Almeida. 1998. Finding the words: Instruments for a therapy of liberation. In R. Almeida, ed., *Transformations of Gender and Race: Family and Developmental Perspectives.* New York: Haworth, 85–98.

Fox, D. R. 1993. The autonomy-community balance and the equity-law distinction: Anarchy's task for psychological jurisprudence. *Behavioral Sciences and the Law* 11: 97–109.

Freire, P. 1972. *Pedagogy of the Oppressed.* New York: Herder and Herder.

Gondolf, E. 1997. Batterers' programs: What we know and what we need to know. *Journal of Interpersonal Violence* 12: 83–98.

Green, R. J. 1998. Traditional norms of masculinity. In R. Almeida, ed., *Transformations of Gender and Race: Family and Developmental Perspectives.* New York: Haworth, 81–84.

Guerin, P. J., and E. G. Pendagast, eds. 1976. *Family Therapy: Theory and Practice.* New York: Gardner.

McGoldrick, M., and R. Gerson. 1985. *Genograms in Family Assessment.* New York: W. W. Norton.

McGoldrick, M., J. Giordano, and J. Pearce, eds. 1996. *Ethnicity and Family Therapy.* 2d ed. New York: Guilford.

Mernissi, F. 1982. Virginity and patriarchy. In A. Al-Hibri, ed., *Women and Islam.* Elmsford, N.Y.: Pergamon, 183–191.

———. 1992. *Islam and Democracy.* M. J. Lakeland, trans. Reading, Mass.: Addison-Wesley.

(NCADI) National Clearinghouse for Alcohol and Drug Information. 1995. Alcohol, Tobacco, and Other Drugs and Women's Health. Spring 1995. NCADI Inventory Number ML011.

Parker, L. 2002. Addressing oppression, power, and privilege in family therapy: A case study. Paper.

Pence, E. and M. Paymar. 1986. *Power and Control: Tactics of Men Who Batter.* Duluth: Minnesota Program Development.

Richie, B. E. 1996. *Compelled to Crime: The Gender Entrapment of Battered Black Women.* New York: Routledge.

CHAPTER 19

BRENDA V. SMITH

Battering, Forgiveness, and Redemption

Alternative Models for Addressing Domestic Violence in Communities of Color

────────────── ABSTRACT ──────────────

Brenda V. Smith asks, "Is there a place for words like forgiveness and re-demption in our discourse on battering and domestic violence?" Smith's chapter can be linked with Almeida and Lockard's approach to domestic violence in chapter 18. Both chapters present alternative practices outside the criminal justice system. And both chapters portray models that are quite controversial and open to critique on the basis of women's safety issues. In this chapter Smith argues that she is outlining some alternatives that poor women of color actually use—in the face of a criminal justice system that does not and cannot solve the problems of domestic violence.

The integration of restorative justice philosophies with domestic violence intervention creates an uneasy mix. Rather than seeking punishment for a crime, restorative justice tries to find ways to repair relationships through reconciliation and reassurance. Historically, restorative justice approaches have not been used to intervene in domestic violence because of the very real power imbalance between survivor and abuser and the related concerns about safety for victims/survivors. Domestic violence occurs between people in intimate relationships that are ongoing and nested within a context of patriarchy that is ingrained in abusers' thinking and action. Change seldom occurs for batterers without significant confrontation by key political, legal, or religious institutions. Moreover, historically, restorative justice models have failed to address these complex dynamics.

Brenda Smith, like Almeida and Lockard in chapter 18, reframes the question of domestic violence and places it within a holistic context—historical, cultural, ethical, racial, social, economic, and political. Violence is thereby defined as a violation of both the individual and the domestic relationship with the goal of intervention focused on relationship repair, abuser responsibility, and repentance.

How appropriate are these alternative models for marginalized groups of women caught at the most disadvantaged intersections of race, class, gender, and sexuality? Carolyn M. West (chapter 11) and Lisa Sun-Hee Park (chapter 21) stress the impossible dilemma faced by women of color who are required to either sacrifice their own safety in the service of family and community and continue in a state of oppression or risk isolation and defamation for speaking out. The yoke of silence regarding domestic violence, in the name of racial and cultural solidarity, weighs heavily upon women connected to communities of faith, especially in neighborhoods of color. Traci C. West examines this dynamic more fully in the next chapter.

As you read this chapter, consider Brenda Smith's definition of forgiveness. Is it the first step or the last step for survivors of domestic violence? What are the advantages and limitations of restorative justice approaches to domestic violence? How does Brenda Smith's model differ from that of Almeida and Lockard?

INTRODUCTION

Is there a place for words like forgiveness and redemption in our discourse on battering and domestic violence? In the thirty-year history of the domestic violence movement, these words have been conspicuously absent from the dialogue and the debate (Schneider, 2000). The absence of discourse on even the possibility of forgiveness or redemption has made many, including me, uncomfortable with engaging in the work and the debate around domestic violence (Coker, 1999; Crenshaw, 1991). Without understanding, acknowledging, and accepting principles of forgiveness or redemption, there is little hope for successful intervention in lives affected by domestic violence. Without discussion of these principles, it is difficult to understand the cyclical nature of relations between batterers and battered women and to craft strategies and interventions that are effective and healing. Without an understanding of forgiveness and redemption, individual wrongdoers and victims alike may remain focused on vengeance and blame, missing important opportunities to proceed as successful—albeit fallible—human beings.

The words, "forgiveness" and "redemption," are loaded in this context. We have been nurtured on the belief that some acts are unforgivable—battering, murder, abuse of children—and that people who commit these acts are irredeemable (Bridgewater, 1997). Not only is forgiveness not a part of the discussion in the domestic violence movement, but most scholars are very critical of even introducing the concept of forgiveness. They believe that focusing on forgiving detracts from the seriousness and unacceptability of the act and opens the possibility that women will return to situations that are dangerous and dysfunctional.

Yet the precepts of many religious (Postawko, 2002; Pope John Paul II, 2001) and psychological principles (Cohen, 1999) are based on forgiveness and redemption. These principles are premised on the belief that forgiveness is a good in and of itself, that it is strengthening and, importantly, that it is necessary for the salvation and healing of the injured person. These principles, both of religion and psychology, leave open the possibility of redemption no matter what the individual has done. Both religious leaders and psychologists believe that without the possibility of forgiveness and redemption, individuals lose hope and motivation to change their lives.

What is forgiveness? Joanna North, in *Wrongdoing and Forgiveness* (1987), offers that "people upon rationally determining that they have been unfairly treated, forgive when they willfully abandon resentment and related responses to which they have a right and endeavor to respond to the wrongdoer based on the moral principle of beneficence, which may include compassion, unconditional worth, generosity, and moral love (to which the wrongdoer by nature of the hurtful act(s), has no right)" (p. 502). Martha Minow (1998a, 1998b) frames her discussion of forgiveness in the context of choices to punish or reconcile. She explains that a punishment model would be consistent with what is now the predominant response to domestic violence—retribution or vengeance through prosecution. Minow suggests that another model would be a restorative justice model that focuses on reconciliation. "Restorative justice emphasizes the humanity of both offender and victim, and repair of social connections and peace as more important than retribution" (p. 969). A focus on reconciliation in the domestic violence context would look at ways to include forgiveness in the lexicon of possible outcomes.

Again the language in this context is loaded, because reconciliation, which is widely used in restorative justice models, runs contrary to a central tenet of domestic violence work—that women should not return to situations where battering has occurred. So reconciliation in the restorative justice model means situating the wrong in the context of the community and having appropriate community based solutions to the offense. It does not necessarily mean, as we often think in the domestic violence context, that the parties will reunite, reconcile, or renew their relationship. Indeed, Minow notes that "forgiveness . . . seems to rule out retribution, moral reproach, nonreconciliation, a demand for restitution, and in short, any act of holding the wrongdoer to account" (Minow 1998, p. 9).

Yet, forgiveness can include both accountability and remembrance. Being forgiven opens up opportunities for accountability because the focus is on the conduct of the offender and not on the offender as a person. The offender is forgiven for his actions, but is still held accountable either through judicial intervention, community and family disapprobation, loss of important rights such as liberty and family interaction, or through alternative forms of dispute resolution.

Why even discuss forgiveness or redemption in this context? Many would say that the decision to forgive depends upon whom you are talking about forgiving and who or what is capable of redemption. There are many spaces for forgiveness in the discourse on domestic violence: forgiveness of self for permitting oneself to be battered; forgiveness of self for exposing children to violence; forgiveness of the batterer; and forgiveness of an unresponsive justice system. While often the focus of the discussion on battering centers on the fallibility of male batterers and abused women forgiving them, this movement has only recently begun to identify battered women's needs for forgiveness.

While there has been some understanding as to why battered women might kill (Browne, 1987), there has been less acknowledgment that some battered women may neglect or even abuse their children (Schneider, 1992, 2000). Battered women who abuse alcohol and other drugs are ignored at best and, at worst, excluded from the discourse on battering (Richie 1996). And what of the many battered and abused women in prisons and jails (Bureau of Justice Statistics, 1999; Browne, 1999) who have been arrested for some other offense (Richie,1996)? Can those fallible women be "forgiven" for their offenses and allowed to receive the community affirmation, validation, social services, and protection that other battered women receive?

This chapter focuses on a topic that while discussed, has been more often than not dismissed in the discourse: battered women's forgiveness of batterers and women's process of forgiving themselves for participating in the relationship.[1] I will use the device of a personal narrative taken from my own experience to explore these two issues.[2]

WHY TALK ABOUT FORGIVENESS AND REDEMPTION?

Why do I talk about forgiveness and redemption? Well, I come from a tradition of love, forgiveness, and redemption. I was raised in a Black Pentecostal church in South Florida.[3] A foundation of that experience was that you could always come back. No matter what you had become; drunk, prostitute, murderer, abuser, or who you were; child, man, or woman, there was always space for you. It was never too late to repent your misdeeds, seek forgiveness, redeem yourself, and come back.[4] It was understood that the breadth of God's abundance and forgiveness included you, no matter what you had done, no matter where you had been.

At the same time that the church exerted this powerful influence on my thinking, I lived in a household where my father beat my mother regularly. The police came on Fridays or Saturdays and locked my father up. My father's girlfriends would bail him out of jail each weekend, and he would return to our home. My mother reminds me of how she used to sleep with either my sister or me, or put both of us in bed and sleep between us so that my father would not try to either beat her or have sex with her. It is only as I have become older that she has referred to my father's conduct as rape. I forget, and she reminds me of how we used to sleep under the bed so that he could not reach her.

I have asked my mother why she stayed. She says,

> I stayed because the church told me to stay.[5] They quoted scripture about our heavy burden and told us that we were supposed to endure the abuse. I was not the only one. A lot of us were working like dogs in the fields and being abused

at night.[6] Your Dad used to take my money.[7] I would get all these dimes for picking tomatoes and he would take them and throw them all over the floor. I would be crawling around on the floor trying to get my money.

I stayed because I had been beaten all my life by my mother. I left my mother's abuse because it was more acceptable for a grown woman to be abused by her husband. I stayed because I wanted you and your sister to have a name. In my family, we all had different last names—Mathis, Minatee, this, that. I didn't want that for my children. I said that I would endure in order for you to have better.

Like many battered women, my mother left and returned (Walker, 1979).[8] Her return was motivated both by economic and social factors. In economic terms we were poor; my father's income as a brickmason made the difference in our being able to own a home and have a car. Socially, being married indicated status. Many women in our community were not married and had children from a series of relationships;[9] but my mother aspired to be different—better. She had also been raised in the Pentecostal church and believed that divorce was a sin. Richie (1996) discusses the continuum of oppression suffered by poor, uneducated women of color, who may not perceive domestic violence as the most serious problem with which they have to cope. That was certainly the case with my mother, whose primary concern was maintaining an income sufficient to keep her and her family in their home.

I remember one of the occasions when my mother left and returned. My parents had had a particularly violent fight, and my mother had decided that she could not take any more. She decided to leave the house, furniture, dishes and move to peace and safety. We moved out of our house into a very small house in a neighborhood of other little box houses. There was one bedroom for all of us, where before we had lived in a three-bedroom house and my sister and I had our own rooms. My aunt Josephine, in a tradition of self-help, ejected my father and his current girlfriend from our home, and we moved back to our house, material possessions, and security, not to my father. Shortly after that my parents divorced.

I ask my mother, "How could you still believe in redemption and forgiveness and the church after what he did to you?" She says,

> I forgave him [your father] and them [the church] in spite of themselves. I forgave them for me and for you. I could not continue to hold on to my anger at them and do what I needed to do for myself or for you.[10] [Thus, her narrative was] I forgive you for being fallible, but I don't forgive you for hurting me or others. I hold you accountable for your actions. But I also open up the possibility for redemption—not only that you can prove that you can do better but that you can do better.

I analogize the battered women's movement to a story that I tried to write about my mother. Each time I began writing about her, I ended up writing about my father. I think this analogy is particularly apt for this discussion. So much of the work in domestic violence has been about men, even though we think it is about women. Personally, I could not write about my mother until I forgave my father because much of what I perceived about her was filtered through my response to him and his actions.

I think that in this movement, it has been difficult to craft effective solutions for men and women because the discourse has left out the concepts of fallibility. So, even when women gain resources and relief, they lose when they are not perfect, when they are fallible, when they do not fear (Kohn, 2002); when they harm or fail to protect their children; when they abuse drugs or alcohol; when they commit some other crime; when they go back to their men and their homes (Dowd, 1993).

One aspect that is often overlooked is self-forgiveness. How did my mother forgive herself? How did she forgive herself for putting me and my sister in danger—for exposing us to harm; the possibility of physical abuse; the reality of emotional trauma and abuse? How did she forgive herself for staying in it when she knew it wasn't right?

My immediate response, which is perhaps always the most honest, is that she had to forgive herself in order to get up every day and keep living. In order to get on buses at four and five o'clock in the morning, and pick tons of tomatoes and oranges for dimes and dollars, she had to forgive herself and others. Otherwise, she would not have been able to go on and provide some measure of security for herself and for us. If she had not had a spirit of forgiveness, I imagine that she would have hurt us, herself, or others.

I also imagine that the abuse that my mother experienced from my father did not feel very different from the abuse of poverty and racism that she experienced every day (Crenshaw, 1991; Richie, 1996). She thought that feeling bad and being treated badly was what happened to women in her circumstances. Until she could envision a better outcome for herself and for us, it was hard to move on.

I realized that my mother could not control my father's violence any more than I could. And like her, I placed the violence in the context of a number of other equally "violent" experiences in my life, racial segregation, poverty, and fear for my safety from people outside my home.

PRINCIPLES UNDERLYING A MODEL BASED ON FORGIVENESS AND REDEMPTION

How do we help women to forgive themselves so that they can move on, so they can make better choices? In beginning to think about applying principles of forgiveness in the domestic violence context, I offer several principles.

First, we must accept the fallibility of both women and men. Intimate relationships are incredibly complex and often irrational. It is rare that there is a neat solution or narrative that positions any party as totally in the right or totally in the wrong.

My mother married my father when she was eight months pregnant with their first child, my sister. He was from Long Island, Bahamas, and was not a citizen of this country, though he wanted to be desperately. They admit that the marriage met both their needs—my mother's need for legitimacy and my father's need for citizenship. They both came into the relationship with unspoken expectations and little experience of healthy relationships. My maternal grandmother had a series of relationships which resulted in ten children with four fathers. My father's mother died when he was seven and he had seen his own father go from relationship to relationship fathering at least sixteen children.

My father came from a culture where physical discipline of children and women was accepted. And to some degree, that was the culture in which my mother came of age. It was the rare man who did not feel entitled to hit or chastise his wife. Both my father and mother came of age in a culture where men routinely had other relationships with women outside of their marital relationships. Notwithstanding these norms, women felt empowered to fight back—to give as good as they got. Women defended themselves, either by challenging the conduct, resorting to physical violence, or by "putting men out." These self-help strategies often led to greater violence against women. To some degree, my mother stepped out of role by refusing to accept my father's infidelity and his physical abuse and by ending the relationship.

Second, institutions are fallible. The nature of institutions is that they are best at dealing with generalities. It is difficult for institutions to respond to the particular needs of individual families (Schneider, 1992). That is why the response by courts and law enforcement to particular problems in domestic violence cases—women not wanting to proceed with arrest or prosecution, for example—wreak such havoc in particularized situations. The interventions of courts, prosecutors and police are blunt instruments that do not handle well the fine and subtle distinctions of families and relationships.

Third, the women involved may themselves understand their situations and solutions better than we do. A basic principle of client-centered lawyering is that clients have crucial information about the nature of their problem and the nature of the solutions to their problems (Binder and Price, 1977). Yet, many of the policies that have been developed over the past thirty years to intervene in and prevent domestic violence run contrary to the explicit desires of battered women.

Often, women decide that they do not want the batterer arrested or they do not want to proceed with prosecution (Arias, 2002). However, mandatory arrest and prosecution policies thwart women's wishes and deny their agency (Abrams, 1999). Of course, women may not want the batterer arrested or prosecuted because they fear for their safety—and that may not be an unreasonable fear (Goldman, 1991). They may also believe that the violent incident will not be repeated. They may believe that the violence may not merit institutional intervention; they would prefer to handle the violence outside of the rigid systems available through police or court processes. Women may seek to involve other institutions, like the church, that are more nimble and rooted in their traditions. They may have mixed motives related to status, fear of loss of important economic and social support, and the desire to preserve their families. Finally, women may fear that institutions of control, once unleashed toward battering men, will ensnare them either through criminal or abuse and neglect proceedings (Schneider, 2000).

Fourth, while thus far interventions in battering have been primarily through the judicial systems, there are other models that may provide greater particularity in resolving family violence conflicts. While each of these models has serious imperfections, so too does the current model. They merit serious discussion, study, and in some instances implementation to determine their effectiveness in addressing domestic violence.

Fifth, the process of forgiveness and redemption is personal and evolving, much like the process of addressing family violence. It often takes years for families to resolve to address violence. Likewise, the process of forgiving and changing or redeeming takes time. The challenge for the domestic violence community is to develop and use models that recognize the persistence of violence, yet the possibility for healing and change.

The role of progressive advocates is to provide women with other ways of imagining and actualizing their own healing and to assist women to move beyond their identities as survivors, which keeps them tied and invested in the violence committed against them to thrivers who have integrated and conquered their experiences of violence. The models below hold out some promise in helping women achieve that goal.

ALTERNATIVE MODELS FOR ADDRESSING DOMESTIC VIOLENCE

While the predominant model for addressing domestic violence in this country is through the formal judicial system (either through the use of civil protection orders or criminal justice sanctions), there are a number of other models of dispute resolution that have been used in other contexts. These models, while still to some degree in their infancy, may offer alternate approaches or elements of an approach to address domestic violence. Each has particular strengths and weaknesses that make its application to particular domestic violence situations more or less promising. Yet, each explicitly acknowledges the possibility of forgiveness or reconciliation and redemption.

I am not advancing any of these approaches as a curative; rather I am elevating those approaches that women in specific communities, particularly those in marginalized communities and communities of color, are using themselves. While any approach involves certain dangers, we should evaluate these alternatives not only as to how they compare to the current criminal justice model, but as to how they support the needs of communities of color. These models, which often bypass, or operate parallel to, the criminal justice system have the benefit of situating resolution of violence in institutions that communities of color respect.

The Mediation Model

Mediation, a common form of alternative dispute resolution, is "the process by which the participants, together with the assistance of a neutral person or persons, systematically isolate disputed issues in order to develop options, consider alternatives, and reach a consensual settlement that will accommo-date their needs" (Folberg and Taylor, 1984, pp. 7–8). Mediation has four primary benefits: (1) success in reaching agreements; (2) reduced costs of conflict resolution; (3) court efficiency; and (4) greater responsiveness to parties' psychological and interpersonal needs (Gunning, 1995). Mediation also has four defining features; privacy, procedural informality, absence of substantive rules and compromise (Gunning, 1995).

These features can carry over to mediation in domestic violence cases, and according to proponents, hold out "the prospect of empowerment to the victim, rehabilitation of the batterer, . . . a model of constructive conflict resolution, [and] an opportunity to end the cycle of violence" (Corcoran and Melamed, 1990, p. 311). Yet, the very features of mediation—privacy, procedural informality, the lack of substantive rules, and compromise—evoke strong opposition to and are a caution against using mediation in do-mestic violence matters. Opponents insist that victims have a right to safety, which is not negotiable (Fischer et al., 1993). Opponents also believe that court intervention is necessary in domestic violence cases to ensure the ac-countability of the batterer (Gunning, 1985; Rifkin, 1984). Moreover, oppo-nents of mediation in domestic violence cases suggest that mediation is incompatible with domestic violence, as it is future-focused and does not ad-dress the history of domination and violence in the relationship (Fischer et al., 1993).

While the arguments on both sides have merit, mediation in domestic vi-olence cases could be very difficult to implement. The nature of battering in-cidents is that there is an acute incident that occurs and requires immediate intervention and resolution. In order for mediation to work, both parties would have to be motivated to resolve the problem and committed to the pro-cess. It would be difficult for a mediation program to assess the motivation and commitment of the parties, without working with the parties over a long period of time.

This investment of time runs contrary to one of the core goals of media-tion—efficient and quick resolution of problems. The benefits of efficiency could be lost in the time required to resolve the often complex problems and relationships associated with battering. Moreover, the traditional settings where most mediation occurs, with the parties together with a neutral party and where parties are unrepresented by counsel, could intimidate women who already are intimidated by the batterer.

Changing the prism somewhat, however, and elevating the goals of for-giveness and redemption, could cast mediation in a different light. While problematic in some respects, mediation has the possibility of advancing principles of forgiveness by permitting the parties to mediate or discuss is-sues that are tangential to the violence that occurred, but important to main-taining a cooperative relationship (such as child custody, visitation, support, and counseling interventions). The presence of a mediator could enhance women's sense of power and of being heard, while simultaneously providing a measure of transparency, so that a batterer's actions to intimidate are apparent. It could also provide an important opportunity for a batterer to show that he has changed, that he can manage his anger, and that he can participate as a partner in making decisions about important issues affecting the relationship.

The Restorative Justice Model

Restorative justice models are anchored in the notion of giving something of positive value to the victim, while acknowledging that infliction of pain or incarceration of the offender is not of positive value (Sherman, 2000). The goal is to restore the victim to wholeness and, also, to help the offender accept responsibility for his wrong and in turn make him a more responsive member of society (Sherman, 2000). Restorative justice mobilizes social networks of families and friends to help them respond to domestic violence, thereby encouraging investment in the process. Another principle of restorative justice is to condemn the act, not the actor (Sherman, 2000).

Lawrence W. Sherman (2000), a proponent of restorative justice, has recommended using a restorative justice model to address domestic violence. Sherman supports restorative justice in domestic violence cases, although he has only studied it in settings involving juvenile violence, property crimes, and drunk driving (Wilson, 2000).

Sherman (2000) offers three theories that argue for using a restorative justice model, rather than a traditional justice model, in domestic violence matters. The first, "reintegrative shaming," activates a family or village approach to wrongdoing that condemns the act, not the actor. Restorative justice is also aligned with the theory of "procedural fairness," which Sherman describes as a process that reduces anger, a prevailing trait of abusers. The third theory that Sherman advances is the "theory of routineness," which suggests that family network involvement in the justice process reduces the opportunities for domestic violence's occurrence.

Sherman's process, frequently led by a police officer, includes three steps: (1) the offender's waiver of any claim of innocence; (2) a "diversionary conference" where the victim and others injured by the offenders' acts are heard; and (3) decision making about repairing the harm and preventing its reoccurrence. This process occurs outside the formal structure of the court, is based on consensus, and is only complete after all parties, including the offender, are heard.

Sherman asserts that restorative justice increases accountability of the offender through shaming mechanisms, while also allowing him to feel that he is treated fairly. He also believes that the process provides victims with more closure, as they are integral parts of the justice process and their emotional needs are explicitly addressed.

In a commentary on Sherman's work, Melvin Wilson (2000) proposes several additional considerations that one should examine before using a restorative justice approach in domestic violence cases. Wilson, who has conducted research with men who batter their partners, outlines several contraindications for using restorative justice among the different personality types of violent men. According to Wilson, many abusers do not accept responsibility for their actions and have difficulty expressing themselves.

While improving batterers' understanding and communication skills should be a restorative justice goal, Wilson believes that the most important function of the restorative justice process is to stop the batterer's violence and to facilitate his acceptance of responsibility for his actions. Wilson believes that the therapeutic process can begin only after the violence ends. Wilson also believes that abusers should compensate their victims for the harm done and that any interventions must be attuned to social and cultural factors.

Wilson's commentary suggests that for restorative justice to work, victims must have a strong support system and the opportunity to express the physical and psychological harm they have experienced. Even with these caveats, Wilson fears that a restorative justice model would not address the interpersonal and inherent power imbalance in relationships, and would thereby fail to intervene in these matters in a meaningful way.

Both Wilson and Sherman leave many questions unanswered about the efficacy and advisability of using restorative justice in domestic violence cases. Kay Pranis's work as the Restorative Justice Planner at the Minnesota Department of Corrections is more promising and implicitly incorporates notions of forgiveness and redemption. In *Restorative Values and Confronting Family Violence,* Kay Pranis (2002) employs restorative justice principles concurrent with training, group conferences, and peacemaking circles,[11] for individual and community healing (Strang and Braithwaite, 2002).

Pranis posits that restorative justice is possible in domestic violence cases, even though traditional restorative justice strategies such as face-to-face meetings and the focus on reconciliation may need to be modified. She argues that the restorative justice project is broader than individual cases and really goes to the larger project of healing the web of connectedness between the parties and the community that has been ruptured by domestic violence. Pranis, like Wilson, cautions that meaningful restorative practices in domestic violence situations must also address "long-established power imbalances, secrecy, ongoing relationships, economic dependencies, . . . [and] family pressures" (Pranis, 2002, p. 32).

While it is obviously fraught with challenges, restorative justice holds out the promise of engagement between battered women and batterers. It provides an opportunity for each to situate and acknowledge the harm, but to move forward with a more hopeful project of recreating a nonviolent relationship—one in which they may be able to discuss and decide about the consequences of the violence and its impact on their future interactions.

Yet, neither mediation nor restorative justice seems to adequately address the need and tendency toward remembrance. It is difficult to move forward without remembering and acknowledging the harm that a batterer has caused. Rather than being "unhealthy" and "unhelpful," as mediation and restorative justice principles seem to suggest, remembrance is a tool that helps humans to learn from past mistakes and to assess the risk of future actions.

The Truth Commission Model may assist in this project of integrating remembrance into forgiveness and redemption.

The Truth Commission Model

Truth commissions employ many of the tenets of restorative justice described above. Many of the elements of successful truth commissions that address national incidents of violence, including systemic rape and other violence against women and crimes against humanity, could be modified to address interpersonal domestic violence.

In transitioning governments, such as South Africa in the 1990s (Graybill, 2002),[12] truth commissions filled a gap between the unjust laws and government of old regimes and the transformation to a more just society with new leadership. According to Donald W. Shriver, Jr. (2001), the primary goal of truth commissions is to establish "a new public legal and moral culture" through a restorative process. Shriver makes the distinction between courts of law, which seek to punish offenders and truth commissions that focus on victims' needs and invite them to speak about their suffering. Victims are not limited to the facts, but are allowed to express feeling and emotion as testimony to their suffering. Thus, "under humane leadership, a truth commission can do justice, not just to facts, but to the lives of whole persons and . . . whole communities" (p. 15). Shriver further posits that as truth commissions work to create a just legal and moral culture, they seek to "bring communities, institutions, and systems to moral judgment" (p. 16).

In South Africa's truth commission, the entire system of apartheid was assessed and revealed; vast numbers of people were found to have some level of responsibility, and individual citizens could no longer deny knowledge of individual and government wrongs (Shriver, 2001). Ongoing dialogue between victims and offenders led to the accumulation of evidence of the wrongs committed (Shriver, 2001). Hearings took place throughout the country and received broad press, radio and television coverage to increase public education, acknowledgment and thereby, healing (Shriver, 2001). They also provided a very visible forum for shaming and vindication. Thus, wrongdoers were shamed throughout the country, indeed throughout the world, and more important, in their own communities. Likewise, victims were vindicated and heard throughout the country, world, and in their own communities.

Shriver continues by describing the South African Truth and Reconciliation Commission ("TRC") process, which gave individual offenders "amnesty for truth" but held out the threat of judicial sanctions if they were noncompliant (p. 17). The TRC assumed the restorative goal of returning both the offenders and the victims to society. The offenders suffered the "informal sanctions of ostracism, disapproval, and disadvantage," while the entire process sought to heal the individuals and the nation (p. 18). Truth commissions have a prospective mission that involves unveiling the past or remembrance to ensure that bad acts will not occur again. Although the TRC did not seek full forgiveness from victims, it did try to reconcile the harm done to restore all parties as productive members of society (Shriver, 2001).

The truth commission model could be useful as a tool to educate the public and the community about the prevalence and impact of domestic violence on the community and families. Specifically, this could be particularly effective if introduced into significant community settings: childcare centers, schools, churches, salons, barbershops, and recreation centers. The primary goal of this intervention would be to increase communities' awareness of domestic violence through increasing its visibility and stimulating the dialogue around the problem and its consequences. It could also engage stakeholders from different communities in the response to violence against women. Importantly, the integration of remembrance as a core component of the truth model offers a significant counterweight to mediation and restorative justice models, which seem to dismiss the critical importance of remembrance.

The Religious Model

In the discourse on domestic violence, religious institutions are most commonly associated with the subordination of women and their rights (Ammons, 1999; McDonald, 1990; Ragsdale, 1995).[13] In *The Role of Religious Institutions in Responding to the Domestic Violence Crisis* (1995), Reverend Katherine Hancock Ragsdale suggests three theological approaches to understanding the role of the church in the context of domestic violence. The first is a hierarchical and patriarchal understanding of our society that derives from the Bible. This construct suggests "men have not only the right but also the responsibility to dominate, discipline, and control their wives and children" (p. 1154). Another understanding of the role of religion focuses on God's omnipotence: God is aware of and wills the abuse and thus a victim of domestic violence should not defy God's doing. Rather, she should endure. A third approach draws on Jesus' martyrdom and suggests that victims achieve salvation by yielding to suffering and powerlessness.

Ragsdale describes these constructs as a means for people to cope with and understand the world through religion. In practice, however, religious leaders employ these constructs subject to their own interpretations, and thus have a choice about whether to dilute, modify, or reinterpret these constructs—either to further their historical meanings and the subordination of women, or to reinvest these constructs with a meaning that recognizes the equality of all individuals and their right to be free from violence and other forms of subordination.

While social movements have reconfigured society, particularly the Civil Rights and Women's movements, and redefined the roles of women, many religious institutions continue to promote fundamental beliefs grounded in male dominance. These beliefs, combined with the fact that the vast majority of Americans practice religion, suggest the continued potency of religious institutions in the subordination of women (Ammons, 2001). The focus of religious institutions and parishes rests primarily on the traditional notion of family but fails to address the needs or problems within the family—such as domestic violence—and those families outside of the norm (Curran, 1997).

Yet the response of religious institutions is not hegemonic. Indeed the Black Church may provide an alternative to the lack of leadership in faith-based communities on domestic violence. In many ways, the Black church has existed within the conservative framework of the church hierarchy, while at the same time challenging that construct. For example, Black churches were an important source of sustenance (West, 1999) for slaves and reinterpreted the Bible (which had been used as a means of legitimizing slavery) as a tool of liberation (Hackett, 2000; Gravely, 1997; Raboteau, 1980). The Black church was also a site of resistance during the Civil Rights Movement (Branch, 1988; Roberts, 1983) and has taken a lead role in other social justice issues.

However, the Black church has been, for the most part, curiously silent on the issue of domestic violence (West 1999)—no doubt for complicated reasons including complicity in shielding men in their congregations from liability for battering and its acceptance of patriarchal norms of conservative religious teachings that were also imbedded in the broader culture. There may be another reason as well; namely the Black church's opposition to institutions, such as the criminal justice system, which continue to disproportionately sanction poor people and people of color (West, 1999). Given the predominant use of the criminal justice system to sanction men for battering, the silence of the Black church may have been more in opposition to using the justice system as a strategy to end violence against women, rather than opposition to protecting women from violence

Several religious groups have been less equivocal in embracing more progressive and reform-based principles in their efforts to reduce community and domestic violence and address the needs of victims. For example, The Franciscan Peacemakers (2003) offer a comprehensive guide to educate and prepare clergy for domestic violence in their ministries.

While acknowledging the complex histories of battering relationships and the importance of confidentiality, the Franciscan guidelines for clergy emphasize that safety must always be the primary concern when taking a stance that directly confronts domestic violence. The Franciscan Peacemakers caution that abuse may not be obvious and insist that clergy who "uncover abuse" listen without assigning blame and "unequivocally challenge the violence." The guidelines provide that clergy should encourage women to find safe environments for themselves and their children and offer abused women choices such as "individual counseling, career counseling, support groups, education, separation, divorce, legal aid or counsel."

The guidelines provide that clergy should not confront the abuser, but should maintain contact with him and be willing to discuss the violence (within the bounds of confidentiality promised to the woman) if the abuser raises it. Contrary to many religious beliefs, the Franciscan Peacemakers emphasize that the primary goal is not to salvage the marriage, but to end the violence. The guidelines suggest "if the abuse is ongoing, it means that the abuser has not repented and that therefore, forgiveness is not appropriate." While incorporating concepts of forgiveness, the Franciscans emphasize the battered woman's need for strength and independence and that "forgiveness is the end, not the beginning of the healing process."

While the religious approaches to domestic violence are varied, they may also be limited due to established religious constructs regarding the preservation of family, the role of women and the role of men. Yet of all the approaches, the religious approach is the one that most clearly speaks to forgiveness and redemption. It is also perhaps the institution that has the best standing to speak to these issues.

CONCLUSION

There are many processes that institutions and individuals have used to resolve deeply felt injuries and harms to other individuals and sometimes, to entire nations. As described above, each model has strengths and weaknesses, as does our current system of addressing domestic violence. Yet, each model shares goals of truth telling, justice, and reconciliation. Appropriately, none of them demand victims' forgiveness of their abusers, realizing that the process of forgiving is acutely personal and cannot be scripted or required. And while none of these processes explicitly refers to redemption, they have implicitly recognized that people can and do change, particularly if they are heard and respected. These processes also share a quality of hopefulness—they recognize that with attention and resources, people and situations have the potential to change and often to improve. Finally, these processes offer something that the current model does not: the possibility for growth, healing, and insight for the victim, offender, and the community.

I would like to end this article as I began it, referring to my own journey to forgive my father. In my struggles to place my father's violence and my mother's forgiveness in context, I am often reminded of a conversation I had with my mother about why I should forgive my father. My question was, "Why should I put up with conduct from him that I would not accept from an acquaintance or friend?" Her response was,

> Because he is your father. You can change friends or acquaintances, but you can't change your family. You are as much a part of him as you are of me. You are just as capable of doing what he did and as vulnerable to abuse as I was. You need to be able to look at both of our weaknesses, accept what happened and move on. You need to try not to repeat the same mistakes that either of us made. And you need to let go of your anger. It is taking up a lot of energy that could be put to better use.

That answer was quite unsatisfactory at the time. It seemed simplistic and frankly, trite. Over the years (however, in that way that we all hate to admit) I have come to agree with my mother. Regardless of whether we like it or want it, we are all connected. In the same way that oppression of a person or people can create individual and cultural privilege, subjugation and disenfranchisement creates bonds of shame and guilt, which tie the oppressor to the oppressed symbiotically (West, 1999; Ball, 1998). For me, anger at my father kept me connected to him and the past in a way that was counterproductive.

Anger takes a great deal of energy, and I am fortunate in being unable to hold grudges—even for deeply personal injuries. Yet forgiveness is more difficult because forgiveness in some way means that perhaps I should no longer remember the terrible things my father did—the beating, the verbal abuse, and the psychic abuse through infidelity, disinterest, and dismissal. Or perhaps, I need to remember his actions and hold on to my anger about it because, if I forget, I may have to forgive. And then I would have to do the arduous work of rebuilding the relationship free from grudges, resentment, and guilt.

While I advocate forgiveness and redemption, I realize that it requires more courage and effort than most people can muster. Thus far, the biggest step I have been able to take is to allow my children to know their grandfather free from my telling of his history. What they know of him is based on his behavior toward them. In this way, I have given my father an opportunity to recreate and redeem himself—if not with me, then with my children.

So he plays games with them that he never played with me and gives them gifts that he never gave me and demonstrates a love and pride that he felt, but could not show for me. And slowly in those random interactions he tells his story. He speaks of his love for my mother, even though he has remarried. He talks of his pride in me and my sister, what we have accomplished, and his regret at not being a part of it. And he admits that he beat my mother, even though he loved her. And sometimes, I am able to love him because I forget not to.

NOTES

1. In this chapter, I address only the interactions between battered women and male batterers. However, this limitation is not to minimize domestic violence that crosses gender, sexual orientation, and age lines.

2. I offer this narrative only as my experience and the experience of my family. It is explicitly anecdotal and speaks to my understanding and integration of those experiences. It is meant to be illustrative and not authoritative. Certainly other women and children affected by domestic violence have different experiences and perspectives. I offer it as one way to look at the concepts and processes of forgiveness and redemption.

3. I am sure that for some the notion of Pentecostals as "forgiving" is somewhat incongruous. Yet for all of its contradictions—women not being able to wear pants (I did); not listening to secular music (I did); not dancing (I did); and being subservient to men (I wasn't)—my church was very accepting of people who had overcome or were still struggling with problems including abuse, alcoholism, drug addiction, and prostitution. More recently, my church has been dealing openly with AIDS and adultery among the congregation.

4. In my church, there was a public space during the service called "testimony" service. During that time, anyone could stand and "testify" about God's goodness or even confess a "sin" or misdeed and ask for forgiveness. Usually when this happened, the church would as one offer affirmation for the individual's statement and display publicly its acceptance of her.

On a visit home last year, I saw this practice in action. The minister asked an estranged couple to come forward. He publicly asked her if she would forgive her husband for his actions (infidelity, drunkenness, deceit, and abuse). Women and men elders from the church came and stood around them. The women indicated that she would forgive him, but that he could not return to their home. So on the one hand the woman offered forgiveness, but held her husband accountable for his actions. She asserted her own personal power to forgive, while at the same time holding her husband accountable for his actions. She also used a very hierarchical and patriarchal institution to shame her spouse.

5. See Merry (2001) and Ragsdale (1995).

6. Like many poor people in the rural South, my mother and five of my aunts were migrant farmers. My mother, her sisters, and their children worked in farms all over Florida and several other states. Depending on age, my cousins and I worked alongside our mothers or ran errands like getting water, preparing lunch, or keeping up with the money.

7. If you worked "by the piece" you earned money for each basket of produce you picked. One basket was a dime. Two baskets were a quarter. If you worked "by the day," you earned minimum wage—at that time $10 to $12 per day.

8. Harder questions about the availability or advisability of forgiveness exist for women who return to situations were abusive conduct continues. Yet many women return and remain in physically and psychologically abusive relationships. Whether they forgive or not is difficult to determine. More often, women hope that the batterer will change or stop the abuse. Alternatively, women think they will be able to change or control the conduct that they believe causes the abuse. In that way, battered women may not ever believe that the batterer engaged in behavior that requires forgiveness.

9. There was little societal stigma attached to having children without being married to the children's father. Yet the community aspired to a more traditional family structure and in subtle ways privileged intact families.

10. See Minow (1998) who discusses the role of restorative justice models in coping with mass domestic violence as in South Africa, as "help[ing] victims move beyond anger and beyond a sense of powerlessness" (p. 969) and posits that these principles may also be useful in domestic violence, on a smaller scale, in the home.

11. Coker (1999) argues that peacemaking and group conferencing are models of dispute resolution that may incorporate traditional indigenous jurisprudence principles focusing on a communitarian goal of improving the lives of individuals and the community through healthy, egalitarian relationships.

12. Following the Pinochet military coup in Chile, which led to the disappearance and murder of more than 3,000 people, Chile established one of the first truth commissions. The commission sought to cope with the loss of human life, government distrust, lack of public awareness, and lack of accountability for the losses that affected the entire nation. South Africa carefully studied the commissions established in Chile, Argentina, and eastern and central Europe when deciding upon the form that its commission would take. South Africa democratically implemented the commissions and "was the very first example of a process officially encouraging public debate and input on the goals, makeup and procedures of a truth commission" (Graybill 2002, pp. 2–3).

13. My discussion here primarily related to Judeo-Christian religions. It does not speak to other religions that may offer more promising approaches to addressing domestic violence.

REFERENCES

Abrams, Kathryn. 1999. From autonomy to agency: Feminist perspectives on self-direction. *William and Mary Law Review* 40: 805.

Ammons, Linda L. 1999. What's God got to do with it? Church and state collaboration in the subordination of women and domestic violence. *Rutgers Law Review* 51: 1207.

Ball, Edward. 1998. *Slaves in the Family*. New York: Farrar, Straus and Giroux.

Binder, David A., and Susan C. Price. 1977. *Legal Interviewing and Counseling: A Client-Centered Approach*. St. Paul, Minn.: West.

Branch, Taylor. 1988. *Parting the Waves: America in the King Years, 1954–1963*. New York: Simon & Schuster.

Bridgewater, Pamela. 1997. Connectedness and closeted questions: The use of history in developing feminist legal theory. *Wisconsin Women's Law Journal* 11: 351.

Browne, A., B. A. Miller, and E. Maguin. 1999. Prevalence and severity of lifetime physical and sexual victimization among incarcerated women. *International Journal of Law and Psychiatry* 22(3–4): 301–322.

Cohen, Jonathan. 1999. Advising clients to apologize. *Southern California Law Review* 72: 1009–1069.

Coker, Donna. 1999. Enhancing autonomy for battered women: Lessons from Navajo peacemaking. *UCLA Law Review* 47: 311.

Corcoran, Kathleen O., and James C. Melamed. 1990. From coercion to empowerment: Spousal abuse and mediation. *Mediation Quarterly* 7: 311.

Crenshaw, Kimberlé. 1991. Mapping the margins: Intersectionality, identity politics, and violence against women of color. *Stanford Law Review* 43: 1241.

Curran, Dolores. 1997. Is your parish a good friend of the family? *U.S. Catholic,* June 1. Available at: http://www.uscatholic.org/1997/06/fearb9706.htm.

Dowd, Michael. 1993. Battered women: A perspective on injustice. *Cardozo Women's Law Journal* 1: 45.

Fischer, Karla, et al. 1993. The culture of battering and the role of mediation in domestic violence cases. *Southern Methodist University Law Review* 46: 2153.

Folberg, Jay, and Alison Taylor. 1984. Mediation: A comprehensive guide to resolving conflicts without litigation. San Francisco: Jossey-Bass.

Franciscan Peacemakers. 2003. Mission. Available at: http://www.franpax.org/index.html. Accessed February 20.

Goel, Rashmi. 2000. No women at the center: The use of the Canadian sentencing circle in domestic violence cases. *Wisconsin Women's Law Journal* 15: 325.

Goldman, Daniel. 1991. Do arrests increase the rates of repeated domestic violence? *New York Times,* November 27, C8.

Gravely, Will B. 1997. The rise of African churches in America (1786–1822): Re-examining the contexts, in William H. Becker, *The Black Church: Manhood and Mission.* In Timothy E. Fulop and Albert J. Raboteau, eds., *African-American Religion: Interpretative Essays in History and Culture.* New York: Routledge.

Graybill, Lyn S. 2002. *Truth and Reconciliation in South Africa: Miracle or Model?* Boulder, Colo.: Lynne Rienner.

Gunning, Isabelle R. 1995. Diversity issues in mediation: Controlling negative cultural myths. *Journal of Dispute Resolution* 1: 55.

Hackett, David G. 2000. The Prince Hall Masons and the African American Church: The labors of Grand Master and Bishop James Walker Hood, 1831–1918. *Church History* 69: 770–802.

Honeyman, Catherine. 2002. Gacaca jurisdictions: Transitional justice in Rwanda, Observations from June 10–Aug. 8. Rwanda Observations. Available at: http://www.fas. harvard. edu~socstud/rwanda/titlepage.html. Accessed February 9.

Kohn, Laurie. 2002. Domestic violence victims, credibility assessments, and the expectations of fact finders. Presented at Symposium: Confronting Domestic Violence and Achieving Gender Equality: Evaluating *Battered Women and Feminist Lawmaking* by Elizabeth Schneider, April 19–20. Transcript available at the American University, Washington College of Law, Women and the Law Program Office.

McDonald, Kathleen A. 1990. Battered wives, religion, and law: An interdisciplinary approach. *Yale Journal of Law and Feminism* 2: 251.

Merry, Sally Engle. 2001. Rights, religion, and community: Approaches to violence against women in the context of globalization. *Law and Society Review* 35: 39.

Minow, Martha. 1998a. *Between Vengeance and Forgiveness: Facing History after Genocide and Mass Violence*. Boston: Beacon.

———. 1998b. Between vengeance and forgiveness: Feminist responses to violent injustice. *New England Law Review* 32: 967, 969.

North, Joanna. 1987. Wrongdoing and forgiveness. *Philosophy* 62: 499–508.

Postawko, Robert. 2002. Towards an Islamic critique of capital punishment. *UCLA Journal of Islamic and Near East Law* 1: 269.

Pranis, Kay 2002. Restorative values and confronting family violence. In Heather Strang and John Braithwaite, eds., *Restorative Justice and Family Violence.* Cambridge: Cambridge University Press.

Raboteau, Albert J. 1980. *Slave Religion: The "Invisible Institution" in the Antebellum South.* New York: Oxford University Press.

Ragsdale, Katherine Hancock. 1995. The role of religious institutions in responding to the domestic violence crisis. *Albany Law Review* 58: 1149, 1154.

Richie, Beth E. 1996. *Compelled to Crime.* New York: Routledge.

Rifkin, Janet. 1984. Mediation from a feminist perspective: Promise and problems. *Journal of Law and Inequality* 2: 30–31.

Roberts, Wesley A. 1983. The Black revolution and the churches. In Mark A. Noll et al., eds., *Eerdman's Handbook to Christianity in America.* Grand Rapids, Mich.: Eerdmans.

Schneider, Elizabeth M. 1992. Particularity and generality: Challenges of feminist theory and practice in work on woman abuse. *New York University Law Review* 67: 520, 552–556.

———. 2000. *Battered Women and Feminist Lawmaking.* New Haven: Yale University Press.

Sherman, Lawrence W. 2000. Domestic violence and restorative justice: Answering key questions. *Virginia Journal of Social Policy and Law* 8: 267–268.

Shriver, Donald W., Jr. 2001. Truth commissions and judicial trials: Complementary or antagonistic servants of public justice. *Journal of Law and Religion* 16: 13.

Strang, Heather, and John Braithwaite, eds. 2002. *Restorative Justice and Family Violence.* Cambridge: Cambridge University Press.

U.S. Department of Justice, Bureau of Justice Statistics, Office of Justice Programs. 1999. *Prior Abuse Reported by Inmates and Probationers.* Washington, D.C.: Government Printing Office.

Walker, Lenore. 1979. *The Battered Woman.* New York: Harper.

West, Traci C. 1999. *Wounds of the Spirit.* New York: New York University Press.

Wilson, Melvin, et al. 2000. Reconciliation, justice, and domestic violence: Commentary on Dr. Lawrence W. Sherman. *Virginia Journal of Social Policy and Law* 8: 292.

CHAPTER **20**

TRACI C. WEST

Sustaining an Ethic of Resistance against Domestic Violence in Black Faith-Based Communities

 ABSTRACT

In the previous two chapters, Rhea V. Almeida and Judith Lockard (chapter 18) and Brenda V. Smith (chapter 19) recognized the limitations of the criminal justice system and urged the use of noncriminal justice solutions in dealing with and transforming violence against women. So, too, Traci C. West argues for the centrality of the Black church in organizing forces against domestic violence in Black communities. In this way, the church remains true to its mission of care and social justice, enables grassroots organization for change, and provides battered women and church-centered communities hope and support for nonviolence at both individual and communal levels.

What would this look like in the Black church? Traci West calls for an "ethic of resistance" against violence toward African American women. This ethic requires the church and its congregants to take violence against Black women seriously by declaring that their anguish genuinely matters and that the violence constitutes significant moral harm which must be accounted for, addressed, and challenged. Communal opposition to the violence must be structured as a social movement to infuse communities with an alternative moral consciousness that condemns violence against women and invents strategies to eliminate it. This social movement must include both political and spiritual aspects because doing so "can counter the barrage of subjugating influences that are a part of so many of the prevailing communal responses to intimate violence."

This social movement must strive to meet several objectives including the need to recognize battered women's spiritual needs and the need to inject feminist political voices into Black church responses to Black men's violence against Black women—all the while appreciating the need to "oppose the silencing of violence against Black women without contributing to the degradation of Black men." Black churches can be a source of tremendous strength for battered women because they can provide immediate support and attention to women who are in the midst of crisis. However, for churches to intervene effectively with this problem, they must stress that religion does not require women to suffer abuse.

West explains the types of resistance strategies in which the church must engage: (1) a continual process of *self-critique* focusing on removing any messages that reinforce the acceptability of violence against women; (2) the integration of rituals to resist violence in internal church practices (for example, eliminate biases in church doctrine or practice) and community outreach efforts (for example, support prayer vigils advocating women's rights; create songs and prayers addressing women's concerns); (3) antiviolence training for relinquishing male dominance in all church forums for youth and adults where ideals about what it means to be a Christian are being taught; (4) increased reliance on communal and peer (especially battered women themselves) approaches to antiviolence education instead of overreliance on domestic violence "expert professionals;" and (5) increased participation of congregations in actively monitoring the treatment of Black victim-survivors by police, health care providers, courts, and other service providers.

These strategies of the Black church to resist domestic violence in the Black community contribute a truly grassroots approach that argues for a community responsibility in the Black church and among its congregants. Can you spell out some strengths and pitfalls that one must notice when forging such a path?

As women initiate resistance on behalf of themselves and in so doing advance the interests of a civil society, it is incumbent upon their communities to continue that momentum. We who are committed to countering the social and intimate violence against Black women must overcome our reluctance to join them. We need to participate in specifying a direction for constructive communal change. Of course, the effort to sustain a deliberate commitment to address violence in women's lives represents a formidable challenge. Some base points for the kind of ethical analysis and practice that can nurture this ongoing work are needed. How do we maintain an ethical vision of human wholeness and well-being that is directly responsive to the converging forms of violence confronted by women?

The ethic that we embrace must not only envision inclusive, truthtelling, moral communities which resist assaults on women; it must also help to build a social movement that brings such communities into existence. These goals have specific implications for the crafting of Christian social ethics [in Black communities]. Those implications will be considered here alongside further elaborations on what the decision to construct this ethic of violence resistance

This abridged version was originally published in *Wounds of the Spirit: Black Women, Violence, and Resistance Ethics* (New York: New York University Press, 1999), 181–207. Reprinted by permission of the publisher.

requires. Concrete strategies for community action will be enumerated as well. They will emphasize ways in which a local church might become involved in this effort. . . .

CASE STUDY IN COMMUNITY ACTION: LOCAL CHURCH INVOLVEMENT IN BLACK COMMUNITIES

In order to suggest even more specific responses, I will focus on the local church as a community organization with the capacity to embody this ethic.

Rationale for Christian Involvement

A primary task of [Black] Christian faith communities is to provide leadership in the midst of desperate and urgent problems such as this one.[1] The requisite Christian engagement in definite practices that uphold women's genuine moral worth can be called "truth-work." Truth-work . . . [and the work of] "knowing and doing" [in the Christian faith] involves an interactive process of becoming empowered.[2] It involves reaching outside oneself to stretch and grow toward the embodiment of justice, and reaching within oneself to tap rich inner resources of courage and passion. To recognize what is truly just, Christians rely upon their ability to access power from God, their communities of accountability, and resources within themselves. They can live out this realization of truth by working to create conditions in the world that reflect it. This process of participating in the incarnation of justice requires literal engagement with distorting human realities such as violence, white supremacy, and male dominance. It means doing the work that enables the truth of human wholeness, worth, and dignity to be fulfilled.

Churches can play a critical role in organizing, sponsoring, and engaging in this truth-work. If they choose to exercise it, they possess an independence from corporate and state control that enables them to play a unique advocacy role in community life. Churches can function as effective and vital organs of the Christian faith by offering victim-survivors needed confirmation of the death-dealing realities that threaten their lives and by opposing those realities. They have the chance to act compassionately by paying direct supportive attention to those caught in the anguishing circumstances and consequences of intimate violence.

When Aisha [one of the women whose experiences West discusses in *Wounds of the Spirit*] founded a church made up primarily of urban Black women, she included a ministry to respond to the neglected concerns of women victimized by violence as a fundamental component of the church's mission. She was convinced that women need reinforcement of the fact that God does not require them to suffer abuse. She explained: "That's why it was important to me to have a different type of ministry than what I see being performed in traditional churches, because of my own pain and the pain of so many women around me that was going unaddressed."

Church Resistance Strategies

SELF-CRITIQUE.   Churches must be engaged in a continual self-critique that focuses on eliminating acts of violence among its members and ferreting out messages that reinforce the acceptability of violence against women within its traditions and practices. Churches need to account for all the ways that their scriptures, liturgies, icons, polities, and teachings uphold the subjugation of women. To identify what their precise participation might be in nurturing these destructive messages, local churches should conduct a regular audit of their practices within their existing committee and organizational structures. For example, the worship committee could audit liturgy, and the trustees could audit icons in stained glass windows and paintings on display. In addition, churches have to distill and reject all theological tenets and organizational strictures that deny women authority and autonomy. This includes explicit affirmations of the integrity and worth of women's bodies and sexuality. Christian traditions that even imply a denial of God's concern for women victim-survivors must be openly challenged and reinterpreted.

Moreover, violence and abuse that occurs at the center of church life, perpctrated by clergy and/or laity against their own family members or other members of the faith community, has to be confronted. When the formal and official practices of the church ignore the extent of abuse against women and children that people in the faith community are well aware of in their own families or in those of their friends and acquaintances, a blatant lie is maintained. The message advocating the cultivation of loving, trusting, right relationships with one another that churches preach on a weekly basis is deeply betrayed.[3] If they fail to activate direct methods of resistance, churches will continue to be thoroughly complicit in male violence, functioning as simply another cultural conveyer of indifference to women's torment.

RESISTANCE RITUALS.   Churches can integrate rituals to resist violence into their internal practices as well as their community outreach efforts. For instance, in a discussion of the need to thwart existing forms of social bias and exploitation, theologian Delores Williams suggests that Black faith communities create resistance rituals based on doctrine that reflects African-American people's experiences and cultural sources. She explains that the doctrine would be "'decoded' of *all* androcentric, gender, homophobic, class and color bias."[4] It should be enacted "as regularly in the African-American denominational churches as the eucharist," so that it is firmly implanted in the community's minds and memory.[5] Though not specifically mentioned by Williams, this proposal could also incorporate opposition to male violence. By naming it and ritually denouncing it on a frequent basis, a recognition of the cultural sanctioning of male violence could be cultivated among church members. Ceremonial affirmations that offer alternatives to debasing and trivializing means of valuing Black women's sexuality and emotional needs might also be woven into these rituals.[6]

Moreover, churches should gather together across racial and neighborhood boundaries for public rituals that give witness to their insistence on women's freedom from male violence. Their witness should emphasize the unique spiritual orientation that faith communities contribute to communal work on this problem.[7] The rituals could include prayer vigils outside police stations, courthouses, town halls, or state legislature buildings. The group would need to offer specific prayers for judges, prosecutors, legislators, and bureaucratic officials who make daily decisions that affect women's safety. They would need to collaborate on the kinds of prayers needed for each and on how issues related to race and gender would be named within the ritual. New songs could be created, in the tradition of 1960s black civil rights movement music, that called out the names of these key officials. Churches in predominantly white suburban communities should also conduct these rituals along the streets of their "secluded" neighborhoods. They would thereby ritually express their opposition to the "privileges" of white supremacy that help to keep the intimate violence occurring in their neighborhoods hidden from public view and reinforce racialized myths about violence against Black women.

TRAINING FOR RELINQUISHING MALE DOMINANCE.   Nothing is more important for churches and the wider community than challenging men to interrogate the relationship between a desire for dominance over others and cultural definitions of manhood, especially those related to male sexual prowess. Of course, this interrogation of male dominance would be inadequate without attending to intersecting issues of social power like race and sexual orientation that appropriately address the particular composition of the group. This training process must involve repeated or continuing opportunities for men to become conscienticized about what constitutes controlling and abusive behavior toward women. Models for the kind of conscientization needed can be found in Latin American Christian-based communities.[8] It is especially appropriate for churches to sponsor this sort of investigation of maleness in Sunday school classes, confirmation classes, or youth group programs, when ideals about what it means to lead a Christian life are initially taught to youth. Adult education forums and men's group meetings should additionally be utilized as venues for male reeducation about violence resistance. Men could be trained as peer counselor-educators to help one another learn behavior toward women based upon equality and respect. Special emphasis has to be given to the topic of sexually appropriate behavior toward children. The scope of this emphasis on sexuality should range from their treatment of female youth within the church to the parenting of their own girl children at home. In addition to fostering concern about routine attitudes and behavior, these male peer educators and other church leaders must directly confront sexually harassing and abusive acts that occur. Again, ongoing opportunities for men to engage in discussions about how to prevent and stop this behavior are critical.

For example, male training sessions could utilize exercises that promote an understanding of the parallels between a male abuser's self-justification of his acts and popular legitimations of white supremacy. Paul Kivel, an activist and writer on antiracism and men against domestic violence, offers categories like denial and blame that are ideal for grasping this concept.[9] For instance, just as abusers refuse to accept responsibility for their actions by blaming the women for "having asked for it" or instigated it by their "henpecking" behavior, whites try to avoid responsibility for racism by blaming Blacks with accusations like "if they weren't so lazy" or "if they didn't spend so much time complaining about racism." In creative exercises based on these types of blaming statements, participants would gain a systemic understanding of the way power interests are defended and sustained. Male training needs to help white men enhance and develop an ability to make connections between the perpetration of male violence and the maintenance of their white privilege. Similarly, it should help Black men deepen their comprehension of the link between male violence and the social nurturance of their internalized racism.

INCREASED RELIANCE UPON COMMUNAL AND PEER RESOURCES IN DEVELOPMENT OF CHURCH RESPONSES.   In every way possible, church education and advocacy efforts need to involve a peer approach. The overreliance on "expert" professionals to present the perspective of women victim-survivors must be actively discouraged. It is essential to invite women to represent themselves, including them as strategists and colleagues, when church resistance efforts are developed. Victim-survivors must not be the mere objects of mission projects to be pitied and "helped" in a paternalistic fashion. The insights that they bring with regard to the experience of violation need to be highly valued.

An acute consciousness of what organizational models churches emulate is imperative as they reach out to women in crisis situations. In what ways is the treatment of a victim-survivor at the church-sponsored program like the process and assumptions she finds at the "welfare" office or the hospital emergency room? How should it be different? Church crisis intervention efforts must consciously attempt to reflect their solidarity with victim-survivors. This commitment requires churches to maintain their independence from state and corporate control. When these interests fund and regulate church programs it is especially difficult (if not impossible) to create a countercultural structure and climate.

TEACHING COMMUNAL ETHICS.   The teaching of ethics must be done from frameworks that illumine the reality of structural power such as male dominance and white supremacy. The systemic character of moral wrong fashioned against specific communities, cultures, and groups of people needs to be taught from a very young age. Therefore, learning how to analyze power relationships and make moral judgments about those relationships should be a crucial component of Christian ethical education. These tools of discernment need to be offered in Sunday school curriculums, weekly preaching, parenting education, and other adult educational opportunities offered to the congregation. Teaching Christian ethical behavior in local churches must intentionally embrace justice education that takes account of past and present acts of corporate sinfulness. This includes the ways that groups of people are marginalized and dehumanized.

Conjointly, the design of basic moral education has to accentuate the recognition of how a communal Christian response can be a sustaining resource in the midst of individual struggles for wholeness that church members face. For instance, teaching about the process of healing in a congregational setting should help people to appreciate the corporate [that is, collective] (rather than merely the individualistic) and participatory (rather than simply the passive) elements that can be tapped in that process. This approach to healing facilitates the faith community's acceptance of its indispensable role in violence resistance. To equip people to speak the truth to violence, a sense of moral accountability derived from an awareness of collective responsibility must be encouraged. Furthermore, in a congregation that retains this enhanced awareness of such corporate [that is, collective] evils as racism and sexism, women victim-survivors may be assisted in shaking off some of the shame they experience. It can perhaps guide them away from self-blame, and toward correctly identifying the potent imprint of those evils in the messages that shape their self-perceptions.

DOCUMENTATION.   Churches need to assist in the documentation of women's stories of abuse and resistance. The distortions contained in the "official transcripts" of women's violation and help-seeking behavior should be countered with subversive record keeping. Documentation is not only a tool of validation for women, but also serves as an inhibitor and sanction against perpetrators.

Churches could devise a means for logging women's depictions of the violence they encounter in their daily lives. It should take every site of community contact into consideration, including interactions within their congregations. For instance, a women's group might sponsor a session for writing prayers of petition about various assaults the women have endured, with an accompanying opportunity to write prayers of thanksgiving that name their concomitant modes of defiance. Another approach might enjoin the appropriate administrative body of the congregation to design a process for receiving written testimony about abusive behavior that may have taken place in the home, church, or community. The design would incorporate guidelines for the content and, when appropriate, a mechanism for response to women's testimony. This process would have to be structured so that it is easily accessed by the women of the congregation. These written statements would be a constant source of accountability to the faith community.

MONITORING.   Congregations should engage in monitoring the public and private neighborhood and community agencies that immediately respond to the crisis of violence against women. There are numerous areas to be evaluated, such as: How promptly do the police respond to women's calls? In their general region, does the police response time differ according to the racial and ethnic makeup of the community or neighborhood? How are women's spiritual and emotional needs attended to by the nearest battered women's shelter? What kind of antiracism training is hospital emergency room personnel provided with? Since church staff must often make referrals in situations of violence to local social service agencies, the quality of those services must be routinely assessed.

One means of doing this is to make personal inquiries of representatives from the community agencies that are the most crucial in providing services to women. Hospital administrators, doctors, police officers, prosecutors, and judges should be invited into the churches and questioned about their practices with regard to violence against women. The results of this monitoring should be publicized through every available means, ranging from the church newsletter to the local news media. Battered women's shelters, rape crisis intervention programs, and even private therapists should also be contacted and their work evaluated in terms of their treatment of Black women victim-survivors. Community service providers have to be held accountable for adequately serving African-American women.

ADVOCACY.   Solidarity with victim-survivors must literally be embodied by advocates who serve in these women's interests. Certain women and men of the congregation could be trained as advocate-friends working against violence and abuse toward women. These individuals would ensure that issues related to this abuse are consistently aired in the congregation and integrated into its mission and structures. Also, in the event that a sexual harassment complaint surfaces against the pastor, this group would provide an advocate to support the woman who brings the complaint.

This group could help generate ideas for political action in the community such as prayer vigils at the local police precinct or posters that voice community concern about violence against women. Advocacy could also include support for progressive national and local legislative initiatives relevant to ending the violence. In its internal monitoring duties, the congregation's violence-resistance advocates would ensure that these legislative concerns were included on the agenda of the appropriate church social concerns committee. Churches should also advocate for connections between violence against women, white supremacy, and patriarchy to be spelled out and incorporated into the law school education and law enforcement training of prosecutors, judges, and police personnel. At the initiative of churches, methods could be devised for monitoring and evaluating the extent to which officials in their communities have received this kind of education. Congregations might also join together to create ecumenical and interfaith coalitions that work with local activists to write local ordinances that contribute to this struggle.

In these advocacy efforts, churches must insistently make the traumatizing consequences of violence a public priority. Churches should track administrative policies and laws that are directly responsive to the anguish visited upon women victim-survivors. They should explore the question of what legislative changes could be made to send a clear signal of community intolerance for this behavior. For instance, what if, in the prosecution of perpetrators of male violence, the traumatizing of a woman was considered one of the crimes that was committed? Testimony about the emotional and spiritual agony involved in incidents of violence could be solicited from neighbors, friends, and relatives and considered pertinent evidence of such a crime.

We need more communities with crisis support teams that are available to be part of the response women receive when they request emergency assistance from the police. These persons can hold the victim-survivor's hand, cry with her, be silent with her, or be supportive in whatever way she wishes. Furthermore, church advocates could press for the cost of a wide range of support services for women victim-survivors of male violence to be established as part of all health care insurance policies, including government-funded health services for poor women. The many details related to these advocacy ideas that need further discussion and debate could be developed by church advocates working in coalition with others in the community committed to this work.

Organizing Strategic Conversations

Churches should initiate consultations to strategize about specific racial and gender issues that reinforce violence against Black women. They could bring together small groups of victim-survivors, service providers, activists, scholars, and community leaders who are already actively working on this issue. These consultations might explore some of the ethical problems that arise in devising community responses that are both feminist and antiracist. One subject for such a consultation should be a candid discussion about how to address the dual realities of white supremacist assaults against Black men and Black male violence against Black women. The session should seek appropriate responses to the competing agendas that these realities create. They could discuss questions like: When launching a public campaign to mobilize community concern, how do you oppose the silencing of violence against Black women without contributing to the degradation of Black men? How should the issue of Black men's violence against Black women be raised with Black audiences? With white or racially mixed audiences? Should whites be spokespersons on this issue? If so, how can they do so in an antiracist manner? Should Black women's photographs be featured in advertising campaigns to raise public consciousness about domestic violence? If so, what are the possible sociopolitical implications of doing this? It is important that such strategic conversations not follow an academic model of one "expert" person delivering a monologue to an audience. Instead, churches should use a consultation model that facilitates dialogue and encourages the joint development of concrete suggestions.

As we face these challenges we can find hope in the reality that society evolves continuously and that shared moral commitment and communal effort can help shape the direction of these changes. We can move toward becoming a less violent environment for African-American women if we seize and hold fast to a radical vision for freedom from the violations that besiege women. This liberation can take place if we commit ourselves to participate in an ethic of resistance that will not give up the struggle. As Denise describes it, this involves a conscious decision.

> And the times that I decided to live and what I wanted to do—you know, like trying to resist, being in the spaces of resistance, were the most empowering. . . . I made a commitment to live and to resist this world's oppression. That is the only place [in which] I could live. I mean, that's the only space of actually living. It is in resistance, or else I give up and that's—it's too terrifying there.

NOTES

1. For a discussion of the critical role of Christian faith communities in developing moral responses to contemporary social crises, see Larry Rasmussen, *Moral Fragments and Moral Community: A Proposal for Church in Society* (Minneapolis: Fortress Press, 1993), especially 150–151.

2. Cornel West, *Prophesy Deliverance! An Afro-American Revolutionary Christianity* (Philadelphia: Westminster Press, 1982), 98.

3. Christine Gudorf, *Victimization: Examining Christian Complicity* (Philadelphia: Trinity Press International, 1992), 92.

4. Delores Williams, *Sisters in the Wilderness: The Challenge of Womanist God-Talk* (Maryknoll, N.Y.: Orbis Books, 1993), 177.

5. Ibid.

6. For a resource that provides rites for women's healing from violence, see Rosemary Radford Ruether, *Women-Church* (New York: Harper and Row, 1985), especially 151–161.

7. For some examples of social justice rituals, see George D. McClain, *Claiming All Things for God: Prayer, Discernment, and Ritual for Social Change* (Nashville, Tenn.: Abingdon Press, 1998).

8. In 1983, I had the privilege of meeting men from a Christian-based community in Nicaragua who described their process of coming to a greater awareness of the destructive impact that the dynamics of "machismo" can have upon women. The women of that community also testified to the behavioral changes taking place in their community that had resulted in increasing men's participation in child care and women's involvement in formal political leadership.

9. Paul Kivel, *Uprooting Racism: How White People Can Work for Racial Justice* (Philadelphia: New Society Publishers, 1996), 40–46. For his work on domestic violence, see *Men's Work: How to Stop the Violence That Tears Our Lives Apart* (New York: Hazelden/Ballantine, 1992).

CHAPTER **21**

LISA SUN-HEE PARK

Navigating the Anti-Immigrant Wave

The Korean Women's Hotline and the Politics of Community

―――――――――――――― ABSTRACT ――――――――――――――

This chapter describes the politics of gender and culture experienced by a feminist Korean women's domestic violence hotline providing a wide range of individual, group, and community services. Lisa Sun-Hee Park outlines the complex tensions between both the hotline and the broader Korean immigrant community and between both the Korean American community and the mainstream feminist domestic violence movement.

The hotline is an all-woman grassroots organization based on feminist and egalitarian principles. The success of the hotline exposed domestic violence in the Korean community. Speaking of domestic violence and drawing attention to its prevalence divided the community. Indeed, the presence of the hotline disturbed the traditional Korean community's sense of unity and family cohesion and invited outside criticism. As you read this chapter, keep in mind the concept of the "political gag-order" in communities of color, which was described earlier by Carolyn M. West (see chapter 11).

This community case study explores the vicissitudes and complexities of alliance and coalition building in immigrant communities. Faced with broader societal hostility in the form of newly restrictive and punitive immigration policies, we learn how the hotline and larger immigrant community joined forces and strengthened connections while, at the same time, mainstream feminist domestic violence organizations distanced themselves from engagement with and advocacy for more humane immigration policies.

Sun-Hee Park argues, as Andrea Smith later does in chapter 24, that social justice requires thinking beyond single issues—for example, domestic violence versus immigration—and, instead, organizing communities to build greater capacity for structural change. Sun-Hee Park provides a picture of a vibrant grassroots movement that breaks the silences that protect abusers. The Korean

Women's Hotline reaches out to publicize in the larger community that domestic violence is not exclusively a women's issue (contrary to how it is regarded in the broader Korean immigrant community). Sun-Hee Park points out that a broad array of forces are needed to deal with the problem of domestic violence to create structural change and social justice.

The passage of California's Proposition 187 in November 1994 produced dramatic tensions in immigrant communities across the country. This bill, which severely restricts the rights of immigrants, was just the beginning of a nationwide wave of anti-immigrant sentiment.[1] The effects of such hostile policies were felt not only by the immigrant community as a whole, but also by immigrant families individually. One aspect of these repercussions is evident in the lives of battered immigrant women. In this chapter, I investigate the impact of anti-immigrant legislation on battered immigrant women by focusing on the relationship between a grassroots domestic violence hotline and the community it serves.[2] I argue that these policies shifted the community boundaries, creating unlikely alliances among adversaries, as well as forming distances between friends.

This chapter focuses on the politics of gender and ethnicity experienced by a nonprofit, community-based, battered women's organization, Korean Women's Hotline (KWH), located in "Koreatown," one of the largest Korean American communities in the nation.[3] Founded in 1990, the Hotline has struggled to survive as a "community-based" entity despite resistance by the larger Korean American community.[4] The tension within this Korean community does not necessarily signify a greater resistance toward domestic violence activists than in other communities. Differences in culture and history may produce some differences in the manifestations of domestic abuse; however, there is no evidence to indicate a greater presence of wife battering in any one community, ethnic group, or class category. According to the Hotline, this resistance on the part of other Koreatown organizations toward KWH stemmed from the fact that KWH members endorsed an alternative model of family unity that challenged the traditional patriarchal and hierarchical Confucian definition of a stable and healthy family.

Four years after its inception, the Hotline found itself at an impasse with the passage of California's Proposition 187 and the subsequent proposal of federal and state anti-immigrant bills. But the threats to restrict immigration and deny documented and undocumented immigrants access to a variety of educational, health care, and social services shifted Koreatown's boundaries to include KWH for the first time. The leaders of this Korean community relaxed their opposition to the Hotline to some degree in an effort to present a united front against the anti-immigrant political climate.[5]

In this chapter, I argue that this shifting of boundaries in response to hostile policies moved KWH from the margin toward the center of the established Korean community. In the process, the Hotline members felt pressure to choose alliances between the Korean American community and the mainstream domestic violence movement. Pulled in two different directions, neither of which adequately encompassed the experiences of Asian immigrant feminist organizations, Hotline members expressed dissatisfaction with both options.

In addressing these topics, I first describe KWH's interaction with the local Korean community prior to the anti-immigrant legislation and then focus on the Hotline's efforts to construct a women-centered definition of a healthy family and community unity. I also discuss local leaders' adverse reactions to this reconstruction of accepted cultural norms. The second part of this chapter presents community life after the passage of anti-immigrant policies. I address the changes that immigrant families, battered immigrant women, and the battered women's hotline experienced, and conclude with a discussion of the implications of the changes for the mainstream domestic violence movement.

ORGANIC-ACTIVIST-RESEARCH

This chapter is the result of three-and-a-half years of weekly involvement with KWH as a member of the organization. I attended board meetings, accompanied women to domestic violence court, wrote grant proposals, provided child care, transportation, language translation, and community education, and directed a volunteer-training program. During my years of involvement with KWH, I gradually became a part of the organization and subsequently became privy to a great deal of "insider" information. My access in this organization was greatly influenced by my personal history as a Korean American woman and activist. As an "organic-activist-researcher," I work within my indigenous population, with which I share intimate cultural understandings and history (Park and Pellow 1996). In this way, my experiences expand the boundaries of participatory research (Stoecker and Bonacich 1992).

My affiliation with two often conflicting arenas of loyalty—the university and the community—provides a unique standpoint from which to witness social behavior (see also Collins 1990). This joint affiliation served as an advantage when interviewing members of the Korean American community, many of whom place significant value on higher education. They viewed their roles as teachers of sorts, helping me with my "schoolwork." Interestingly, this was not the case when I approached the Hotline. Most KWH members had attended a university in the United States and had no romantic notions of academia. In fact, they were initially suspicious of my intentions. In this situation, I overcame a burden of trust (Burawoy 1979) by behaving like a regular volunteer—refraining from interviewing or otherwise acting like a researcher—for eight months. I began the interview process once the KWH members became comfortable with me and after I had established an identity apart from my researcher status.

My work began in February 1992 as a participant observer. I participated in KWH's annual forty-hour volunteer-training program. I then had the opportunity to attend community events and work as a volunteer at KWH. After five months of collecting fieldnotes and gaining trust from KWH, I began conducting formal interviews. I conducted fifty formal interviews ranging from one-half to two hours. Of the fifty community residents interviewed, thirty were KWH members, and ten were community leaders, including two Korean newspaper editors, a pastor, and several heads of Korean organizations. The remaining ten were identified by those previously interviewed in a process defined as "snowball sampling." All the other respondents were first-generation or had immigrated as children. Only one respondent was born in the United States.

The interview structure varied somewhat for Hotline members, community leaders, and community members, in accordance with each group's unique experience. In general, the open-ended questions were organized around five main topics, probing individual awareness and perception of the Korean Women's Hotline, domestic violence, Korean community concerns and problems, women's roles (specifically those of Korean women living in the United States), and the local power structure. I collected much of the data on immigration policy through follow-up interviews, participant observation, and written materials from community groups, as well as mainstream media reports. I conducted interviews in English, Korean, or both, depending upon what was more comfortable for the respondent. In keeping with my promises to respondents in my field research, pseudonyms are used for places, people, and organizations.

LIFE BEFORE THE ANTI-IMMIGRANT WAVE

Korean Women's Hotline and Koreatown

The Korean Women's Hotline, founded by three Korean women, opened its phone lines in 1990 on Korean Independence Day—a symbol of the struggle to attain freedom from violence for Korean American women in the area. KWH's services include not only crisis intervention, referrals, translation, legal advocacy, community education, and leadership development but also domestic violence advocacy training for community volunteers, professional social workers, police officers, and health-care providers. The Hotline is located within a large metropolitan city, in an area called "Koreatown." Approximately 150,000 Koreans live in the city and surrounding suburbs. The Korean community is tightly connected and fairly self-sufficient, acting as a

"micro-society" that offers many of the same services as the larger mainstream society. For instance, the community has a complex communications
system, with three daily newspapers, five weekly newspapers, two television
stations, and two radio stations. There are also sixteen Korean social service
providers, merchants selling everything from Korean food and clothes to Korean movies, and several Korean-owned and -run banks. There are also more
than 160 Korean churches in the larger metropolitan area.

The project initially began with hopes of providing a shelter, but, after
seeking advice from other Asian American social service agencies with similar objectives and evaluating their limited financial and human resources, the
founders resolved to establish a hotline. KWH's mission statement and philosophy, in accordance with the philosophy of the founders, indicates a
strong feminist leaning. Their brochure states

> We, Korean Women's Hotline, are an all-woman, grassroots organization with
> a mission to empower Korean American women who have been abused and
> systematically neglected by our community and rendered powerless by our so-
> ciety. We try to provide an escape from an oppressive situation through inter-
> vention, advocacy, education, self-help, and by promoting leadership among
> Korean American women. (KWH Training Manual 1993, 1)

Similarly, they state their philosophy:

> Korean Women's Hotline is rooted in the belief that all women have the right
> to live free from fear of violence, whether it be psychological, emotional, ver-
> bal, sexual or physical. We believe that violence against women is one symp-
> tom of subordination of women in society. As long as women are not recog-
> nized as equals, violence against them will be perpetuated and tolerated.
> Although those who commit acts of violence against women are ultimately re-
> sponsible for its eradication, we feel that it is women who can best act on be-
> half of the interest of women. Our actions are based on non-hierarchical, egal-
> itarian principles with decisions reached through consensus. (KWH Training
> Manual 1993, 1)

KWH rejects the Korean community's tradition of hierarchy and patriarchy. With a commitment to a democratic decision-making process, KWH
helps promote a sense of leadership among members rather than rely on a
top-down structure. As with many other mainstream feminist organizations,
KWH functions to empower its members as well as to provide a social service. One of the founders describes how the organization affected her and
other women associated with the Hotline:

> I think KWH provided a way for a lot of us to focus more. It clarified a lot of
> issues and became a tool for a lot of us to understand the power structure and
> how things work. 'Cause you know, so many people talk about race and have
> and have-nots, and all this, and many times it stays at a rhetorical level; but I
> think KWH got you to see how it gets to be played out, you know, ultimately.
> So you know, it clarified a lot of issues, at least for me. And I think it happened
> to a lot of other people, too, because through organizing when we didn't have
> any staff, we all did a lot of work, and it was hard, but we all learned a lot of
> skills—how to write a letter, how to take minutes, how to run meetings, how

to contact other people, who the resources are—so, it was an eye-opening experience in a lot of different ways. . . .

KWH provides a forum for Korean women to engage beyond the boundaries prescribed by tradition. Within KWH, women act as pivotal decision-makers, learn new skills, build leadership capacities, and experience camaraderie with other Korean women.

The organization grew considerably in a short time. In three years, KWH hired a second staff member and the number of volunteers increased from zero to thirty. For fiscal year 1993–1994, they reported an annual budget of $83,000, a significant increase from the $1,000 with which the organizers began.[6] From only fifteen to thirty calls a month at its beginning, this organization receives more than one hundred fifty calls a month from the Korean American community.[7] They estimated a 40 percent increase in demand for their services in one year. In response to this increase, the organization moved from their small, one-room office to a larger, two-room office.

On the whole, the domestic violence cases have been severe. The Korean women who call have done so as a last resort. Having endured years of abuse and countless attempts to justify their husbands' behavior, they risked family shame and severe retribution by contacting the Hotline. Some women are in their sixties calling after forty years of abuse, having waited for all their children to marry and have families of their own. However, since KWH does not keep uniform records of the callers to the Hotline, demographics of the callers are not available.

RECONSTRUCTING A HEALTHY FAMILY

KWH's continuing success challenges the Korean community's established norms. For local leaders, the Hotline's presence questions their ability to meet needs of the Korean Americans living in the community. One staff member noted that the dominant view on the pervasiveness of domestic violence within the Korean community is one of denial and that interferes with the general acceptance of KWH. She explained:

> I think they are not ready to accept KWH. Some people appreciate us; but even those who do, do not understand KWH's substance. They don't know about the process and the structure of domestic violence. For example, they think, "Oh what miserable women and children; I cannot believe how the abuser can do that" but at the question of divorce, they always say, "Family is first. We have to save the family." And when they meet an abused woman, they say, "Oh, I cannot believe that. She must have deserved that."

Korean leaders appear apprehensive because KWH's existence may signify a lack of unity within the community. Unity is crucial to maintaining the status quo and a sense of nationalism. Its importance is rooted in Confucianism, a tradition that positions family cohension as the basis of a larger community or state unity. In describing the Korean family system, Chungmoo Choi (1992, 106) writes,

In Confucian culture, filial subordination to the household head is analogous to the subordination of the children-citizens to the father-king. The existence of gender and generational hierarchies within the home conditioned children to accept hierarchy as natural, reinforcing Confucian notions of filial piety and obedience to authority in general and fostering loyalty and obedience to the state.

In accordance with this Confucian philosophy, one community leader said, "in order to have a healthy society, we have to have a healthy family, and the core of that is the mother." Accordingly, a lack of unity in the family is indicative of a breakdown in the ethnic community—a construction that places further blame on women.

One KWH volunteer, however, argues that the outward appearance of unity comes at the expense of women in a domestic violence situation:

> Let's say they have a daughter-in-law and a son and the son is beating the daughter-in-law and suddenly the daughter . . . decides that she is not going to live like this anymore. There won't be harmony in the family and order is going to break down. They just want to keep all the pieces together no matter if she's happy or not. They don't really care about women's lives or happiness, they just want to keep all the pieces together.

A KWH board member adds: "We have to start looking into the fact that the daughter's happiness makes up part of the harmony."

Embedded in these statements is the reconstruction—by KWH members—of what a stable and healthy family and community must look like. KWH's survival legitimates the idea that domestic violence is a serious issue within the Korean American community, and challenges the long-standing ideology of family unity. For Hotline members, presenting this reconstruction of family and community has been an uphill struggle.

In many ways, KWH has had to start from scratch. Many of the significant advances made by mainstream feminists in the domestic violence movement have not been shared by the tightly knit Korean community. As a result of the strict patriarchal and hierarchical culture reinforced by centuries of Confucianism,[8] what constitutes abuse in mainstream American culture may not be viewed as such in Koreatown. What some Koreans define as reinforcing obedience, American culture might define as physical or mental abuse. Asian American activists Margaretta W. L. Lin and Cheng Imm Tan (1994, 323) write, "most people if asked would say that we should not tolerate domestic violence. Yet, many community leaders still say that a little discipline, an occasional beating now and then to teach the woman a lesson, is not domestic violence." KWH members have had to redefine as violence what a Confucian patriarch might view as discipline. As a "community-based" group with little support from the organized community itself, KWH must therefore maneuver carefully in both the Korean and mainstream communities.

KWH is aware that the domestic violence problem is a source of embarrassment, particularly in light of the expectations bestowed upon a community seen as part of a "model minority." According to this myth, Asian Americans are an ideal minority group by comparison to other people of color stereotyped with problems such as domestic violence, crime, and poverty. Much of mainstream American society maintains and accepts the myth with open arms, for if Asian Americans are indeed ideal, they then require no attention or financial support (Suzuki 1989). The myth makes KWH's work all the more difficult because to raise the issue of domestic violence is to air "dirty laundry" and consequently to explode the model-minority myth.

Airing "dirty laundry" is not taken lightly in Koreatown. Fear of embarrassment and shame perpetuates a system of silence. Not surprisingly, KWH's members experience great difficulty in speaking to others about domestic violence. Their actions breach valued rules that dictate "appropriate" behavior for young Korean women. Any deviation from these rules signifies disrespect toward the community elders. These rules create barriers for KWH in their efforts to expand. In fact, the members complain that responding and reacting to such ideology hinders them from fulfilling their mission to assist battered women. In addition to gender roles, KWH actively rejects a number of other norms, including the general perception of the domestic violence problem within Koreatown. This perception was apparent when eight out of the ten local leaders I interviewed acknowledged the existence of domestic violence in Koreatown, but countered that it was less urgent than other "more pressing" problems. They viewed domestic violence as a result of stress due to changes in the economy, rather than as institutionalized male violence: they believe that once a man's economic status improves, he will no longer abuse his wife. Others blamed abuse on mental illness or alcoholism. Although KWH acknowledges the many stresses of immigrant life, they view domestic violence as a persistent part of the community, irrespective of economic class. During a volunteer-training session, one member replied, "Alcohol and the hardships of poverty may aggravate the situation, but the situation was there to begin with. Those who are rich also beat their wives—we just don't hear about them much because they have the resources to protect their privacy. Also, we found that some men who go to Alcoholics Anonymous and become sober continue their abuse."[9] A community leader who described himself as the most powerful Korean person in the geographic region emphasized what he saw as the positive side to domestic violence: "It's the oriental way—to be silent and to suffer. I think that's one of the reasons why women take punches from their husbands and still keep going—taking care of their children . . . and put[ting] them in a nice school. That's strength and that's power." KWH members found this cultural explanation troubling. A board member responded: "We are trying to find an alternative source of power or empowerment for Korean women. It's pretty scary to think that the only way we have power is to suffer. Such thinking doesn't benefit us. It benefits abusers."

The Politics of Community

The Hotline activists' rejection of accepted community ideology has not gone unnoticed. The community has retaliated both directly and indirectly with threats, denial, and negative rumors. For instance, telephone threats by a woman's abuser or an abuser's family members are regular occurrences. In addition to accusations of "brainwashing" women into divorce, KWH is accused of insensitivity to the plight of immigrant Koreans. Not only are the callers angry about the Hotline's interference in their private family lives, they denounce KWH as "Americanized" and as traitors. Threats of lawsuits are also not uncommon.

Local leaders often became hostile when the topic of domestic violence was raised. Several community members I approached for interviews refused to answer any questions directly related to domestic violence in Koreatown and became angry when I mentioned this topic. In an indirect way, community hostility is also shown through the absence of monetary support for KWH. In its second year, the Hotline sent out a mass mailing to all the Korean churches in the area asking for support and offering to visit or conduct community-awareness programs. Only two churches responded, one antagonistically. Interviews I conducted with community members revealed that much of the Korean public is unaware of KWH's activities. While all the community leaders were familiar with KWH, they apparently did not pass this information along to those they served. As it stands, the information passes largely through informal, word-of-mouth means.

In general, Korean American community members avoid speaking of domestic violence and the Hotline. As in the wider society, domestic violence is frequently defined as a "woman's issue." As the president of a Korean organization with more than seven hundred members put it: "I don't know about [KWH]. I just read about that in the newspaper. It's a woman issue and I'm not a woman so I don't know what its function is." He said the topic came up during an association meeting as well: "We discussed that and . . . we thought it was a woman's problem and we just weren't interested about that." This comment presents a false dichotomy of "community" (read "men's") and "women's" issues. As a male, he and his organization see their concerns as separate from women's concerns. According to this organizational leader, economic discrimination against immigrant Korean businesses is the single most important problem—and one which lies only in the "man's" arena. His statements are indicative of the strict hierarchical division of gender roles and concerns in which the term "women's issue" conveniently dissolves any personal involvement.

Closely coupled with the above-mentioned strategy is the official neglect of domestic violence by decision-making and public-opinion-forming institutions in Koreatown. For example, I asked the director of the largest Korean organization (with ten thousand members)—which functions as an umbrella organization for all community groups as well as a representative in mainstream politics—"is domestic violence a community concern at all?" Sidetracking the question, he responded instead by listing the organization's four main goals for the community, which did not include domestic violence. He focused on the importance of community solidarity in achieving greater influence in mainstream politics, particularly in his efforts to combat recent surges in xenophobia. The director of this organization viewed racial/ethnic harmony as vital and the Hotline's goals as inconsistent with his organization's objectives. Unfortunately, without official recognition of the problem, it was unlikely that KWH's concerns would be included in the local agenda.

Rumors constitute the final category of retaliatory action by community leaders against KWH. This may be the most subtle yet most powerful strategy, for word spreads quickly in a close-knit community. Rumors can create a dangerous environment for KWH volunteers, particularly since KWH lacks institutional resources within the community and relies heavily on informal means of communication. While often used as a form of resistance from below (Scott 1990), in this case rumors were employed as tool of repression from above. Rumors that Hotline volunteers enforce divorce and adhere to radical, white, anti-family ideals harm their reputation as legitimate Korean American social service providers. The KWH staff has learned to be cautious. They do not give out their location to everyone who calls. A post office box is available for letters, and advertising is done as discreetly as possible. They leave their brochures in other social service offices and in police stations where the people most in need may obtain the phone number. According to the coordinator, the majority of volunteers became acquainted with KWH through word-of-mouth and personal networks.

Immigrant Families under Fire

Such defensive actions on the part of the Korean American community are understandable given the many stresses evident within immigrant families. The traditional hierarchical boundaries in which husband, wife, children, work, and family are categorized shifted as women entered the workforce upon immigration. In some cases, the women are the only wage earners, having found jobs, as low-paying and dangerous as they may be.[10] This role reversal has challenged the long-standing male authority that promised support and nurturance in exchange for power and control. Lin and Tan state that these factors have aggravated drinking problems and violence in the home, but they are careful to note that "while APA [Asian Pacific American] refugee and immigrant men do have struggles and challenges to cope with, as do the women, this is never an excuse for violence in the home" (Lin and Tan 1994, 330). KWII members reinforce this argument by stating that, although immigration may exacerbate domestic violence, it does not make it inevitable: "There are plenty of immigrant men who don't batter."

Anti-immigrant policies can also exacerbate domestic violence as they limit family resources and disempower the male authority figure. These policies disempower the immigrant community in general and immigrant families in particular by forcing them to rely almost solely on informal networks for survival. With limited access to education, social services, health care, and jobs, the poor and undocumented immigrants may be further isolated.[11] The second half of this chapter will focus on anti-immigrant legislation that affects so many dimensions of immigrant family life, including the well-being of battered women.

LIFE AFTER THE ANTI-IMMIGRANT WAVE

The history of immigration policies in the United States documents the movement of Asian Americans from a despised to a model minority. Restrictive legislation such as the Chinese Exclusion Act of 1882, which ended the first wave of Asian immigration to the United States, is indicative of the portrayal of Asian Americans as the "yellow menace."[12] The doors reopened with the Immigration Act of 1965, creating the second wave of Asian immigration. With the current onslaught of anti-immigrant bills on state and federal legislative agendas, as well as increasing efforts to strengthen the borders of this country, it appears that this second wave is drawing to a close. Given the potential power of immigration policies over so many dimensions of immigrant communities, including the gender ratio (and subsequently the population growth), demographic and social characteristics, and employment patterns, it is not surprising that the mere proposal of an anti-immigrant bill significantly affects the daily routine of immigrant life (Hing 1993). One source of these effects is front-page newspaper articles that report a growing effort to strengthen the nation's borders by making life for those immigrants already here more difficult. For example, the *New York Times* reported [in the mid 1990s]: "With the public growing angry over illegal immigration, the Republican Congress is considering the adoption of the most restrictive changes in the country's immigration laws in seventy-one years" (Holmes 1995, A1).

Fear of anti-immigrant sentiments is evident among Korean Americans who arrived in significant numbers in the 1970s with the passage of the Immigration Act of 1965. Many newcomers were professionals who experienced initial downward mobility upon entering the United States. Many found a niche as small business entrepreneurs catering to Korean ethnic tastes, or entered the African American and Latino consumer markets after confronting job-market barriers, such as glass ceilings in white-collar occupations, difficulties with English proficiency and American customs, and persistent discrimination.[13] Thus, many recent immigrants already lead precarious lives. With anti-immigrant legislation, the family must endure new challenges that leave many immigrant families at risk, and with them the lives of battered immigrant women and the organizations created to assist them.

California's Proposition 187, the 1996 Welfare Reform Bill, and the Immigration Bill HR. 2202 increase the level of stress within immigrant families and communities. These recent U.S. policies affect both documented and undocumented immigrant families. While California's Proposition 187 denies education, health care (including emergency medical care),[14] and social services to undocumented immigrants, the Senate Welfare Reform Bill bars immigrants, including U.S. citizens, from many federal and federally funded needs-based programs. The HR 2202 bill introduced by House Immigration chair Representative Lamar Smith slashes family immigration by one-third, imposes tough restrictions on legal immigrants' access to all federal means-tested programs (school lunches, immunizations, battered women's shelters, Head Start Programs, and so on), and requires hospitals to report undocumented immigrants who seek emergency services.

Immigration Legislation and Battered Women

The sociopolitical context in which this anti-immigrant legislation emerged created a xenophobic reaction toward both documented and undocumented immigrants. The National Immigration Forum, based in Washington, D.C., reported a dramatic increase in discriminatory actions toward people of color one month after the passage of Proposition 187 in California. For instance, a grocery store clerk in Santa Clara examined a legal immigrant's driver's license and refused to sell her anything unless she could produce a social security card verifying her legal status. Other incidents included pharmacies refusing to fill prescriptions unless immigration documents were presented and school security guards barring students of color from entering schools one day after the passage of Proposition 187 (Otto 1994).

The implications of anti-immigrant policies are far reaching for battered immigrant women. KWH members found that battered immigrant women are more fearful than ever of leaving their abusive households as access to legal, medical, and social services is threatened. Almost all the women who call the Hotline are immigrants with limited English proficiency. Most have lived in relative isolation within the Korean community. Their lives consist of home and work, and little else (Rimonte 1989).

Although there are no statistics on exactly how many Korean American women are battered, KWH volunteers agree with others in the battered women's movement that domestic violence knows no boundaries, as it cuts across cultural, racial, political, and socioeconomic divides (Rimonte 1989; Lin and Tan 1994). KWH members speculate that English-speaking Korean women may have other options and seek help from others outside the community, perhaps in an attempt to ensure anonymity. The immigrant women who call KWH, on the other hand, have limited resources and nowhere else to turn. KWH volunteers acknowledge the courage these women have, risking further abuse, family and community ostracism, and possibly deportation (for those whose residence in the United States is dependent on their marriage).

On several occasions, abusers have used threats of deportation as a means of control. In such instances, the law was deliberately misrepresented in order to deter the woman from seeking help, as well as to increase her dependence upon the abuser. In addition, ignorance of legal options, limited English skills, and meager economic resources deter many immigrants from seeking help (Peterson 1988; Abraham 1995). It is apparent that the hostility anti-immigrant policies foster threatens these women's already tenuous well-being.

Immigration Legislation and KWH

As a small community-based organization serving immigrant women, KWH is experiencing a similar fate. Recent government actions have spawned internal strife and funding cuts and have resulted in greater numbers of KWH clientele reporting fear of formal and informal retaliation by mainstream social service providers. The impact of these policies demands a great deal of

KWH's resources. Volunteers have recently focused more of their time and energy on KWH's role as an agent of social change. Members are active participants in anti-Proposition 187 rallies, letter-writing campaigns, and communitywide meetings, in addition to their regular duties. The biannual forty-hour volunteer-training sessions now includes a section on the effect of anti-immigration policy on Asian immigrant women. As mentioned earlier, funding is another major concern during these hostile times. More than one-third of KWH's budget comes from state and federal government sources, a dependence that is increasingly accompanied by official intrusions into KWH affairs. For example, a letter recently arrived from a government office requesting that KWH verify the legal status of all staff members. KWH members understood this letter as a sign of things to come—verification of the legal status of the women and clients who call the Hotline. The strain is apparent as KWH works to remain a strong community-based organization despite thinning resources and greater risks.

Unlikely Alliances

These policies produced an unintended effect on the relationship between KWH and the community leaders. In light of the threats new immigration policies posed, Koreatown leaders developed a heightened awareness of their vulnerable position in the United States. Consequently, concerned community activists drew upon KWH's identity as a Korean immigrant organization to fight against immigration policies. For the first time since the Hotline's founding, some of the community leaders invited KWH to participate in a number of events. The community's need for a unified front in the face of xenophobic legislation diminished the level of resistance toward KWH. One result of this newly formed coalition was the successful organization of a forum entitled, "Developing Effective Strategies in Response to the Recent Anti-Immigration Wave."[15] KWH and nineteen other Korean groups in the area hosted the event. Another unprecedented partnership that emerged in response to imminent government-assistance cuts was a collaboration between KWH and two other Korean social service agencies to diversify, increase, and pool funding sources.

Prior to the current anti-immigrant wave, community leaders tried to dismiss KWH as feminist and therefore foreign to Korean culture. The local leaders' retaliatory actions reflected an effort to place KWH outside of the Korean community—for distance from KWH means distance from domestic violence. In this environment, KWH activists used outside, mainstream sources to maintain a community-based organization and circumvent the barriers local leaders posed. For instance, KWH threatened to air community "dirty laundry" through the mainstream media and to use its legal connections in an effort to force community organizations to listen to its message.

With the introduction of anti-immigration policies, both the wider Korean American community and KWH acknowledged the importance of a unified identity as a defensive measure against powerful institutional forces. With an arrangement to agree to disagree, KWH and the community decided to set aside their differences—as least temporarily—in order to work together against a common enemy. It would be naive to suggest that anti-immigration policies dissolved all past animosities between KWH and other local actors. Despite the opening of the Korean American community boundaries, which have expanded to include KWH, the future of this coalition is uncertain at best.

Creating Distances

The uncertainty that anti-immigrant legislation has caused affects not only KWH's relationship with the ethnic community but also its relationship to mainstream domestic violence organizations. Increased contact with the Korean community has led to a distancing from the larger domestic violence movement. As part of a Korean feminist organization, the Hotline members felt forced to choose between their ethnic and nationalist identity and their feminist identity.

For instance, KWH recently experienced a dilemma when the lease for its office ended and the Hotline needed to find a new home. The Board members conducted a lengthy search involving much discussion among themselves, the women who call the Hotline, and KWH volunteers. Their dilemma centered on whether or not to move closer to other (mainstream) feminist-oriented organizations, or further into the Korean community. Through consensus, the women at KWH decided to move into a building that houses other Korean American social service agencies, in order to sustain their weak but growing ties with the larger Korean community.[16] This move meant that, for the first time, the office would be open to the community. Since confidentiality remained their most important priority, KWH members also secured a private location away from the office where KWH volunteers could meet with Hotline callers should the occasion arise. The Hotline members reasoned that this move would allay some community members' suspicions toward KWH and that confidentiality would remain intact since almost all of their crisis intervention is conducted by the telephone. On occasions when face-to-face meetings are necessary, they are held in courtrooms, shelters, or other, more private locations.

The Hotline's open-house reception in the new office was attended by more than a hundred individuals from various community groups. It was clear that KWH's move to create an "open" environment was well-received by Korean American community members. For the first time, people were welcome to view the office and attend a tour explaining the organization's functions. Also, for the first time, Korean newspaper reporters did not accuse KWH of hiding from the community. However, the reaction was less enthusiastic from some members of the local domestic violence movement. Several individuals, including some of KWH's funders, were openly skeptical about the Hotline's unconventional move. Despite KWH members' attempts to calm their fears, the skeptics remained uneasy about an "open" office.

To a certain extent, this uneasiness is understandable—particularly from the point of view of a funder who wants to protect her "investment." Those working in the domestic violence movement are aware of the importance of keeping shelters confidential, and it is logical to expect others to do the same. The difference here lies in the fact that KWH is a hotline and not a shelter. In addition, KWH is an ethnic, community-based organization that must incorporate lessons learned not only from mainstream domestic violence organizations but also from its own ethnic community. In this way, KWH must find creative solutions to alleviate concerns from two at times opposing arenas of loyalty. The Hotline's move was an effort to take advantage of a fledgling relationship with the larger Korean community while maintaining past alliances with other feminist organizations. Unfortunately, KWH's expectations of better relations with some of the mainstream feminists and funding sources may prove to be ungrounded.

IMPLICATIONS

Ironically, anti-immigrant legislation may present itself as an opportunity to strengthen past alliances as well as to form new ones. Without exaggerating the so-called "positive" side of hostile legislation, one can note that there is evidence that an initial—and temporary—bond created by force can be used productively in forming lasting relationships. In addition, state intervention may expose the gaps or differences between alliances, as is the case for the Hotline's relationship with domestic violence organizations. Nevertheless, this too can be used as an opportunity to explore differences and to find creative ways of working together and forming a closer relationship than that which existed before.

The effects of anti-immigrant legislation, as described in this chapter, are so pervasive in the lives of battered immigrant women that any occasion to strengthen their chances is a chance worth taking. Perhaps we could more easily identify such opportunities if we widened the notion of what constitutes a "woman's" issue or concern. In this respect, both the Korean American and the mainstream domestic violence communities need to expand their respective arenas of concern in order to realize the overlap of issues that they share. For those interviewed in the Korean community, domestic violence was strictly a woman's problem and not viewed as a community issue. In much of the anti-domestic violence community, immigration policy is not viewed as a central concern. As illustrated by the women who call the Hotline, such limitations can have detrimental effects.

It is immigration's embeddedness within economic relationships and institutional inequalities that certifies its status as a feminist issue. Some scholars may have difficulty linking immigration and feminism due to the subtle, pervasive nature of institutionalized phenomena. For example, Kathleen Ferraro (1983, 289) explains that "while there is no longer widespread explicit support for the use of violence to control wives, other macro-level conditions and ideologies perpetuate an environment in which escape from a violent marriage is difficult for women." In this way, immigration law is one such "macro-level condition" that keeps particular women captive in harmful situations.

Similarly, it is domestic violence's embeddedness within economic relationships and institutional inequalities that certifies its status as a Korean American community issue. The economic concerns expressed earlier by community leaders and members are intricately tied to domestic violence. The proposed immigration restrictions that affect the lives of battered immigrant women have a strong connection to economic conditions. This contemporary wave of immigrant scapegoating comes at a time of increasing layoffs and job shortages. It is apparent that immigration restrictions ebb and flow according to economic and political demands (Mohanty 1991, 25) and that these economic and political hostilities are experienced, albeit differently, by the entire immigrant community. The difficulties experienced by the women who call KWH's Hotline are linked to the lives of those in the larger community.

In observing the implications of immigration legislation in the lives of battered Korean American women, the women who serve them, and their community, I have argued that government policies (whether or not a measure is passed) have the power to affect the everyday lives of individuals and to alter relationships with the target community. However, it is also evident that there is considerable activity at the community level in response to government legislation that may open new opportunities. The true test of community-level endurance lies in the ability to recognize allies in different communities and to find creative methods of building a firm foundation of cooperation.

APPENDIX: SPECIFIC STRATEGIES FOR WORKING WITH IMMIGRANT WOMEN

An important preliminary step in working with immigrant women is to be prepared. For many organizations, time and resources are in short supply, but these services are well worth the initial expense. This initiative parallels efforts by proponents of the disabled who have successfully ensured appropriate services in many organizations. I have highlighted four of the most imperative strategies:

1) Language translations (verbal and written): Map out a list of possible resources where same-language counseling and written domestic violence literature are available. Particular ethnic communities (especially those in large cities) will have a variety of written materials.
2) History: To lessen the risk of cultural shock, research a variety of different historical and cultural backgrounds. This effort may ensure a greater mutual understanding. For instance, understanding the history of Korean Comfort Women and other more recent militarized sexual slavery campaigns in Asia may sensitize shelter workers to the reactions of Asian women to the military barracks-like environment of

some shelters. These and other historical facts should be a part of training sessions.

3) Immigration law: Some basic knowledge of immigration law should also be a part of an ongoing training program. This is necessary to protect the rights of immigrant women and children who may not be aware or are misinformed.

4) Basic necessities: Get to know the ethnic communities that surround you and make a list of what is available. For example:

- Food: identify the location of ethnic grocery stores where you can obtain "comfort food."
- Churches: identify nearby or same-language churches, temples, or mosques.
- Job search: identify same-language referrals who can assist survivors in finding a job—particularly those groups well-connected in the ethnic community.
- Bus/mass transit: be prepared to start from the basics—many immigrant women have led very isolated lives.

NOTES

I would like to thank the women at KWH, Allan Schnaiberg, David N. Pellow, Nancy Naples, Elizabeth Clifford, Brett Stockdill, Patricia Zamudio, and Arlene Kaplan Daniels for their valuable comments and encouragement.

1. A September 24, 1995, *New York Times* article reported: "Both [House and Senate Bills] would crack down on illegal immigration and end what has been a thirty-year-old policy of welcoming legal immigrants. For the first time since 1924, there will be a reduction in the number of foreign-born people who are legally permitted to come to the United States" (Holmes 1995, A1).

2. There is no single definition of "community." The term may embody geographic, cultural, religious, and/or political boundaries (Suttles 1972; Hunter 1974; Stoecker 1995). I use this term loosely to designate the boundaries around what I call "Koreatown." Similarly, my use of the term "community" in describing Koreatown denotes the established norms that guide the behavior of those who interact within its boundaries.

3. I use the words "Korean American" and "Korean" interchangeably.

4. My statements concerning Koreans, Korean women, and the Korean community are limited to my arena of study. Statements are not necessarily generalizable to every Korean American person or community.

5. In this case, I make a distinction between community leaders and members. I define the leaders as those who head various Korean American organizations and/or hold an authoritative position within Koreatown. These individuals are almost all male, first-generation immigrants. (The second generation usually moves away from Koreatown.) When asked who holds power or is powerful among Koreans in the larger metropolitan area, my Korean American informants were remarkably consistent in their remarks. Wealthy businessmen, including heads of Korean newspapers, and clergy clearly topped the list. On the other hand, community members are Korean Americans who live, work, worship, or otherwise participate in Koreatown activities, but who do not necessarily hold positions of authority.

6. Approximately 95 percent of the Hotline's funding comes from outside sources such as government agencies and local philanthropists.

7. The number includes all types of calls—emergency and nonemergency.

8. Kim 1981; Chow 1987; Choi 1992.

9. Rimonte (1989, 329) explains, "The community's earlier explanation of domestic violence, blaming the circumstances, is only denying the problem. It also denies the victims the right to look for alternatives and ignores their need to seek help. It also does not question the man's assumed right to beat women during times of stress, or the woman's assumed obligation to respect that right."

10. A part of the reason for this shift may be the increasing decline of traditionally "masculine" unskilled workplaces, such as manufacturing, within the United States. More and more U.S. companies are taking advantage of a shifting global economy that provides lower labor costs in Third World countries (Rubin 1996). Also see Bonacich and Light 1988; Amott and Matthaei 1991; Zhou 1992; Hossfeld 1994.

11. Light 1972; Conzen 1979; Lamphere, Stepick, and Grenier 1994.

12. Miller 1969; Nee and Nee 1987; Takaki 1989; Zhou 1992; Hing 1993.

13. See Suzuki 1989; Yan-McLaughlin 1990; Hing 1993; Bonacich, Ong, and Cheng 1994.

14. Immediately following its passage, a federal restraining order was issued. The order explicitly prohibits state agencies from implementing any regulations until the more than one dozen court cases filed seeking to stop the proposition are resolved.

15. The forum was held on October 21, 1995.

16. The choice was between a building that housed other Korean American social service agencies, located in Koreatown, and a building run by a mainstream feminist organization, located outside of Koreatown.

REFERENCES

Abraham, Margaret. 1995. Ethnicity, gender, and marital violence: South Asian women's organizations in the United States. *Gender and Society* 9: 450–468.

Amott, Teresa L., and Julie A. Matthaei. 1991. *Race, Gender, and Work: A Multicultural Economic History of Women in the United States.* Boston: South End Press.

Bonacich, Edna, and Ivan Light. 1988. *Immigrant Entrepreneurs: Koreans in Los Angeles, 1965–1982.* Berkeley: University of California Press.

Bonacich, Edna, Paul Ong, and Lucie Cheng. 1994. *The New Asian Immigration in Los Angeles and Global Restructuring.* Philadelphia: Temple University Press.

Burawoy, Michael. 1979. *Manufacturing Consent.* Chicago: University of Chicago Press.

Choi, Chungmoo. 1992. Korean women in a culture of inequality. In Donald N. Clark, ed., *Korea Briefing.* Boulder, Colo.: Westview Press, 97–116.

Chow, Esther Ngan-Ling. 1987. The development of feminist consciousness among Asian American women. *Gender and Society* 1: 284–296.

Collins, Patricia Hill. 1990. *Black Feminist Thought: Knowledge, Consciousness, and the Politics of Empowerment.* Cambridge, Mass.: Unwin Hyman.

Conzen, Kathleen N. 1979. Immigrants, immigrant neighborhoods, and ethnic identity: Historical issues. *Journal of American History* 66: 603–615.

Ferraro, Kathleen J. 1983. Negotiating trouble in a battered women's shelter. *Urban Life* 12: 287–306.

Hing, Bill Ong. 1993. *Making and Remaking Asian America through Immigration Policy 1850–1990.* Stanford, Calif.: Stanford University Press.

Holmes, Steven A. 1995. Congress plans stiff new curb on immigration. *New York Times,* Sept. 25, A1.

Hossfeld, Karen J. 1994. Hiring immigrant women: Silicon Valley's "simple formula." In Maxine Baca Zinn and Bonnie Thornton Dill, eds., *Women of Color in U.S. Society.* Philadelphia: Temple University Press, 65–93.

Hunter, Albert. 1974. *Symbolic Communities: The Persistence and Change of Chicago Local Communities.* Chicago: University of Chicago Press.

Kim, Illsoo. 1981. *New Urban Immigrants: The Korean Community in New York*. Princeton, N.J.: Princeton University Press.

Korean Women's Hotline [KWH]. 1993. Training Manual.

Lamphere, Louise, Alex Stepick, and Guillermo Grenier, eds. 1994. *Newcomers in the Workplace: Immigrants and the Restructuring of the U.S. Economy*. Philadelphia: Temple University Press.

Light, Ivan H. 1972. *Ethnic Enterprises in America: Business and Welfare among Chinese, Japanese and Blacks*. Berkeley: University of California Press.

Lin, Margaretta Wan Ling, and Cheng Imm Tan. 1994. Holding up more than half the heavens: Domestic violence in our communities, a call for justice. In Karin Aguilar-San Juan, ed., *The State of Asian America: Activism and Resistance in the 1990's*. Boston, Mass.: South End Press, 321–334.

Miller, Stuart Creighton. 1969. *The Unwelcome Immigrants: The American Image of the Chinese, 1785–1882*. Berkeley: University of California Press.

Mohanty, Chandra Talpade. 1991. Cartographies of struggle: Third World women and the politics of feminism. In Chandra T. Mohanty, Ann Russo, and Lourdes Torres, eds., *Third World Women and the Politics of Feminism*. Bloomington: Indiana University Press, 1–47.

Nee, Victor, and Brett de Bary Nee. 1987. *Longtime Californ': A Study of an American Chinatown*. Stanford, Calif.: Stanford University Press.

Otto, Nancy. 1994. Fax Memorandum. National Immigration Forum, Dec. 5.

Park, Lisa Sun-Hee, and David Naguib Pellow. 1996. Washing dirty laundry: Organic-activist-research inside two social movement organizations. *Sociological Imagination* 33: 138–153.

Peterson, Corinne. 1988. Volunteer Manual. Greehouse Shelter/Chicago Abused Women's Coalition.

Rimonte, Nilda. 1989. Domestic violence among Pacific Asians. In Asian Women United of California, ed., *Making Waves*. Boston: Beacon Press.

Rubin, Beth A. 1996. *Shifts in the Social Contract: Understanding Change in American Society*. Thousand Oaks, Calif.: Pine Forge Press.

Scott, James. 1990. *Domination and the Arts of Resistance: Hidden Transcripts*. New Haven, Conn.: Yale University Press.

Stoecker, Randy. 1995. Community, movement, organization: The problem of identity convergence in collective action. *The Sociological Quarterly* 36(1): 111–130.

Stoecker, Randy, and Edna Bonacich. 1992. Why participatory research? *The American Sociologist* Winter: 5–14.

Suttles, Gerald. 1972. *The Social Construction of Communities*. Chicago: University of Chicago Press.

Suzuki, Bob H. 1989. Asian Americans as the "Model Minority": Outdoing whites? Or media hype? *Change* 21(6): 12–19.

Takaki, Ronald. 1989. *Strangers from a Different Shore: A History of Asian Americans*. Boston: Little Brown and Company.

Yan-McLaughlin, Virginia. 1990. *Immigration Reconsidered: History, Sociology, and Politics*. New York: Oxford University Press.

Zhou, Min. 1992. *Chinatown: The Socioeconomic Potential of an Urban Enclave*. Philadelphia: Temple University Press.

CHAPTER **22**

DONNA COKER

Shifting Power for Battered Women

Law, Material Resources, and Poor Women of Color

———————————— ABSTRACT ————————————

Donna Coker argues that collective strategies to end domestic violence must place poor women of color at the center of the analysis. In accordance with Websdale's (chapter 10) and Websdale and Johnson's (chapter 23) findings, Coker advocates structural supports and material resources that help women escape violence. Attention to the needs of poor women of color effectively benefits all women. She posits a material resource test against which all social policies and domestic violence interventions are measured. Such a test would evaluate how the law or policy being proposed impacted on poor women of color who are battered. If the law or policy harms or is not beneficial to poor and marginalized women of color, then it should not be enacted.

This chapter reviews the influence of race and class in various domestic violence arrest studies and concludes that poor women have not universally benefited from criminal justice interventions. Such interventions are premised on the assumption that separation and arrest create safety for survivors of violence. However, the material resources test is applied to mandatory pro-arrest policies and to increasingly punitive sanctions for batterers and contends that evidence of deterrence is weak and often of limited benefit to battered women in poverty. In chapter 24 Andrea Smith continues this analysis by asserting that domestic violence cannot be solved through more state violence against poor communities of color.

Communities marginalized by race, class, and ethnicity face numerous policies (like state coercion, mandatory arrest, and U.S. Immigration and Naturalization Service deportation procedures) which interact with preexisting social controls to place battered women at greater risk (see Josephson, chapter 7). Child welfare policies, public assistance policies, and associated, ubiquitous random urine screenings sustain a government ideology focused on the social control of poor women of color. The results of these policies are more women arrested and deported and more children traumatized by state intervention. Coker offers an extensive collection of resources to document her analysis; this chapter provides a basic framework of her citations, and a complete list of footnotes and references is available on Lexis Nexis.

The material resources test elevates the standard by which we advance social policy—to benefit poor women of color benefits all women and creates safer communities. As you read this chapter, think about the research on mandatory arrest; examine, as Coker does, data on arrest and recidivism. How might arrest deter some batterers yet inevitably intensify abuse? Conversely, in applying Coker's material resources test, how do pro-arrest policies influence access to and provision of enhanced resources to poor and minority battered women?

L atCrit Theory invites scholarship that centers the experiences of Latinas/ Latinos while tying those experiences to the project of social justice for all. This chapter treats as central the experiences of Latinas and other women of color who are battered by intimate partners and suggests a test for evaluating anti-domestic violence measures that builds on those experiences. I argue that every domestic violence intervention strategy should be subjected to a *material resources test.* This means that in every area of anti-domestic violence law and policy, whether it be determining funding priorities, analyzing appropriate criminal law or arrest policies, developing city ordinances or drafting administrative rules, priority should be given to those laws and policies which improve women's access to material resources. Further, because women's circumstances differ in ways that dramatically affect their access to material resources, the standard for determining the impact on material resources should be the situation of women in the greatest need who are most dramatically affected by inequalities of gender, race, and class. In other words, poor women and, in most circumstances, poor women of color should provide the standard of measurement.

My proposal will not radically reshape structures of racism, sexism, heterosexism, and economic inequality that increase women's vulnerability and limit their responses to violence. Battered women can make few positive claims for material resources because there are few positive claims available for poor people, generally. Rather, in a negative rights world with inadequate and often punitive social services and dramatic inequalities, this proposal is a limited countermeasure designed to increase wherever possible the chances of strengthening women's autonomy. The test is remedial, not revolutionary, but it provides a way to distinguish between different strategies in a manner that accounts for the different material and social conditions that face battered women.

Domestic violence laws and policies may directly provide women with material resources such as housing, food, clothing, or money, or they may increase resources indirectly through the availability of services such as job training, childcare, and transportation. The material resources test requires first that priority be given to those programs, laws, or policies that provide women with direct aid. Second, even when the primary goal of an intervention strategy is not the allocation of material resources, we should prefer methods of implementation that are likely to, directly or indirectly, improve women's access to material resources. Further, we should usually prefer *local* assessment of the impact of law and policy on women's material resources over universal assessments because the impact of a policy will always be mediated by the particular conditions facing women in a given locale. We should *always* prefer assessment that is informed by the circumstances of those women who are in the greatest need. In most circumstances this will be poor women of color who are sandwiched by their heightened vulnerability to battering, on the one hand, and their heightened vulnerability to intrusive state control, on the other. Strategies that increase material resources for poor women of color are likely to benefit—or at least not harm—other battered women in the same locale.

In part I of this chapter, I develop the meaning of a material resources test. In part I.A., I argue that a focus on material resources is likely to empower more women because it addresses four problems of current domestic violence discourse and policy. The first is the tendency to undervalue the importance of race and ethnicity in shaping women's experiences of battering and the institutional responses they receive. The second is the tendency to ignore the way in which poverty makes women more vulnerable to domestic violence. The third is the development of increasingly punitive sanctions against batterers without evidence of increased benefits for battered women. The fourth is the pervasive and incorrect presumption that separation from the abuser equates with safety. Part I.B. describes the importance of the adequacy of women's material resources in their vulnerability to battering. Part I.C. explains the importance of having poor women of color provide the standard for analyzing the effect on material resources of any domestic violence law or policy.

In part II, I apply a material resources test to domestic violence mandatory and pro-arrest policies. I examine the impact of these policies on material resources for poor women of color along two measures: deterrence related effects and nondeterrence related effects. In part II.A. I review the data on arrest and recidivism for batterers of poor women of color. If arrest frequently deters batterers of poor women of color from committing future abuse, then mandatory and pro-arrest policies are likely to be resource enhancing because the result is to diminish the ways in which batterers sabotage women's economic well being. I conclude that while arrest deters some batterers, it may be less likely to deter batterers of poor women of color and may actually increase the risk of abuse for some poor women of color.

In part II.B., I examine the possibility that arrest encouraging policies may be resource enhancing in nondeterrence dependent ways. I conclude that for some poor women of color mandatory and pro-arrest policies result in increased material resources because the police provide victims with information about and referrals to community services and other legal avenues of redress. This information, in turn, assists women in gaining access to increased material resources. The conclusions for poor women of color are uncertain, however, because research often fails to examine the particular experiences of women of color and, when race and ethnicity of victims are considered, only the experiences of African American women and white women are studied. In part II.C., I examine the costs of mandatory and pro-arrest policies for some women of color to determine if the negative consequences of these polices outweigh the potential benefits. I identify a number of potential costs to women but focus my attention on three severe costs: the possibility that the battered woman and her partner may suffer police mistreatment; the possibility that the victim will be arrested; the possibility that noncitizen battered women will be deported. Part II.D. concludes that priority should be given to laws and policies that mandate that police provide assistance and referrals to battered women. These requirements should be expanded to include other assistance such as emergency transportation. With regard to arrest, the gains of *mandatory arrest* policies are frequently offset by the costs for poor women of color. The risks of victim arrest appear to be particularly acute in jurisdictions that have adopted a *mandatory* arrest policy. Therefore, states should adopt policies that allow communities to determine the most appropriate arrest policy for their locale. I outline a method of assessment for local advocacy groups in making a determination of the policies that are likely to increase material resources for poor women of color in their locale. I also suggest changes in police practice that have the potential to further enhance battered women's access to material resources. The conclusion examines the general impact of a focus on women's material resources on federal funding decisions, legislation, and services for battered women.

Throughout this chapter, I examine the particular circumstances for Latinas who are battered. I do this to underscore two related points. First, the use of women of color as the standard by which to apply a materials resource test could operate to create an essentialized "women of color" category that masks important differences that affect the material resources analysis. The literature on battered Latinas illustrates the importance of such differences as immigration status, migration experiences, language, and culture in understanding battered women's experiences. Second, a focus on Latinas also highlights the serious inattention given the study of battered women of color, in general, and Latinas in specific.[1]

I. MATERIAL RESOURCES, DOMESTIC VIOLENCE, AND POOR WOMEN OF COLOR

A. Class, Race, Ethnicity, and Safety in Anti-Domestic Violence Discourse and Law

The material resources test provides a means of operationalizing the feminist goal of empowering battered women through addressing four problems of current domestic violence intervention strategies.[2] The first problem is the tendency to ignore or undervalue the significance of race or ethnicity in shaping the efficacy of universal intervention strategies.[3] A focus on material resources forces an assessment of the impact of intersections of class, immigrant status, race, ethnicity, and gender because these factors will determine the degree to which a policy or law is likely to increase material resources for the women effected.[4]

The second problem with many current domestic violence laws and services is the tendency to ignore the importance of women's economic subordination in their vulnerability to battering. An unstated norm for battered women—those that are white and nonpoor—is created when a policy or law ignores the relationship of poverty to violence and fails to account for racial differences in battered women's experiences.[5] Influenced by the range of services that state and federal funders would pay for, it is this normative client image that is instrumental in constructing battered women's need as primarily psychological, rather than material. Kimberlé Crenshaw's story of the Latina, refused shelter because she was a monolingual Spanish speaker and could not participate in the shelter's English-only support groups, is an extreme example of the devastating effects of this psychological focus.

The third problem a focus on material resources counters is the trend to develop increasingly punitive criminal measures against batterers without evidence that these measures improve the well being of victims. This uncritical resort to increasing criminal sanctions serves to hide the social and political conditions that foster battering. For example, the County Commission in Miami-Dade, Florida, enacted an ordinance in 1999 that, among other provisions, requires the clerk of the court to notify the employer of anyone convicted of a domestic violence offense. The sponsors of the legislation argued that "it sends a message," but regardless of the intended message, the result was direct and predictable harm for poor women of color. Professional men are not likely to lose their jobs if their boss is notified of a misdemeanor conviction, but men working in low-skill jobs, where men of color are disproportionately represented, are likely to be fired. The ordinance takes money directly from poor women and their children by diminishing their possibility for receiving child support. The ordinance probably increases women's danger, as well, since unemployed men may be more likely to engage in repeat violence.

Miami-Dade County is hardly unique in enacting legislation that increases penalties for batterers in ways that provide no benefit—and sometimes positively harm—battered women. Had the county commission assessed the question of the ordinance's impact on battered women's material resources, and had the commission investigated the position of poor women of color in the county, the ordinance never would have been enacted.

The fourth problem with anti-domestic violence discourse and law is the pervasive presumption that women *should* leave battering partners and that doing so will increase their safety. This presumption that separation equals safety is dangerous for women, and particularly so for poor women of color. First, the safety that presumptively flows from separation is largely fictive for poor women. Women with sufficient money to remove themselves some distance from the batterer may increase their safety from all but the most homicidal batterers.[6] Poor women, however, are often simply unable to hide. Further, separation may create catastrophic results for poor women. Separation threatens women's tenuous hold on economic viability, for without the batterer's income or his assistance with childcare, for example, women may lose jobs, housing, and even their children. It is a cruel trap when the state's legal interventions rest on the presumption that women who are "serious" about ending domestic violence will leave their partner while, at the same time, reducing dramatically the availability of public assistance that makes leaving somewhat possible. Thus, failure to acknowledge the manner in which women's access to material resources frames the separation/safety question is the first problem with the focus on separation.

The second problem with equating separation with safety is that legal actors frequently believe a corollary presumption: women's use and full cooperation with legal remedies increases their safety. Women may be less sure than are lawyers and judges that legal orders and safety are equivalent, however. Interviews with battered women demonstrate that women sometimes drop protection orders or refuse to cooperate with prosecution because they were *successful* in using the threat of legal intervention to gain concessions from their abuser.

The third problem with equating separation with safety is that frequently the laws and services based on a separation premise devalue women's connections with their partner and their investment in building family. The application of specialized legal remedies for battered women almost always presupposes separation. For example, though courts may order that respondents to restraining orders refrain from harassment and abuse without ordering the "stay-away" provisions, courts sympathetic to battered women are likely to see this accommodation as counterproductive. But some marriages are worth saving. Sometimes women are successful at getting their partner to stop the violence.[7] Making safety a primary way of assessing intervention strategies frequently results in policies that undermine women's abilities to evaluate various strategies for themselves because it invites law and policymakers to determine what women *should* do to be safe.

The material resources test does not require the state to make judgments about what choices are in battered women's best interest. It operates on only one important presumption: inadequate material resources render women's choices more coerced than would otherwise be the case. Thus resources should be made available to women so that, with assistance, they can make a determination about the best course of action based on their own set of circumstances.

B. Material Resources and Domestic Violence

Inadequate material resources render women more vulnerable to battering. Inadequate resources increase the batterers' access to women who separate, and inadequate resources are a primary reason why women do not attempt to separate. Some battering men appear to seek out women that are economically vulnerable, but even were this not so, the batterer's behavior often has a devastating economic impact on the victim's life. Abusive men cause women to lose jobs, educational opportunities,[8] careers, homes, and savings. Battering renders some women permanently disabled and puts others at greater risk for HIV infection. Women become homeless as a result of battering, their homelessness is made more difficult to remedy because they are battered, and they are more vulnerable to further battering because they are homeless. They frequently become estranged from family and friends who might otherwise provide them with material aid.

Cris Sullivan's research suggests that victims' resources have a relationship to experiencing renewed violence and to increased victim well being.[9] Sullivan compared two sets of women leaving a battered women's shelter. The groups were matched in terms of demographics including race, age, employment status, and severity of violence. Each group contained roughly the same number of women cohabitating with their abuser and women separated from their abuser. The experimental group members were provided with an advocate who met with them twice weekly for ten weeks to assess their needs and set priorities. Advocates assisted women in gaining access to educational resources, legal assistance, employment, services for their children, housing, child care, transportation, financial assistance, health care, and social supports. Participants in the experimental group were compared with the control group on a number of measures at different intervals over the course of two years. The women in the experimental group reported significantly less psychological abuse and depression and significantly higher improvement in quality of life and level of social supports than did those in the control group. Most impressive were the differences in the physical abuse measures: one out of four women in the experimental group experienced no abuse during the twenty-four-month follow up, while this was true for only one out of ten women in the control group. Sullivan believes that what made the advocacy program succeed was that participants, not advocates, guided the direction of the intervention, and the "activities were designed to make the community more responsive to the woman's needs, not to change the survivor's thinking or belief system." Thus, connection to material resources in areas that the women identified as necessary made significant differences both in terms of their ability to improve their lives and in reducing their victimization.

JoAnn Miller and Amy Krull examined victim interview data gathered in three studies of police response to determine the relationship between the victim's employment status and batterer recidivism. They found that unemployed victims in one study were the victims of significantly more recidivistic violence than were employed victims. While this unemployment effect was not borne out in the other two studies, the length of time the victim was unemployed correlated with recidivism in all three studies: the longer the victim was unemployed, the higher the level of recidivism.

Initial inquiries regarding the importance of battered women's material resources focused on the relative economic position of women vis-à-vis their battering partner and found that economic dependency on the partner was a significant predictor of severe violence and a primary reason women gave for re-uniting with their abusive partner. These studies of relative economic power may inadvertently rest on a middle-class norm in which nuclear family households are understood to be autonomous economic units and the dynamic between the couple is the focus of inquiry. Absolute rates of poverty are likely to be equally critical, if not more so, for many battered women. The ability to relocate or hide, for example, is related as much to absolute rates of poverty as it is to women's relative economic resources compared to that of their abuser. The importance of familial and neighborhood networks for economic survival—networks which are likely to be heavily geographically dependent—are critical in determining a woman's ability to relocate.

Despite the vulnerability of poor women to domestic violence, programs for battered women sometimes fail to address the needs of the very poor, particularly those that are perceived as "deviant." For example, some battered women's shelters refuse admission to "homeless" women because they are believed to be too manipulative, "street-wise," or antisocial. Women with substance addictions may find it particularly difficult to obtain shelter that is safe and that treats addiction. Thus, women's poverty renders them more vulnerable to battering, battering deepens their poverty, and extreme poverty may place a woman outside the scope of services designed to assist battered women.

C. Poor Women of Color as the Standard

Domestic violence intervention strategies frequently fail to appreciate the ways in which race, ethnicity, immigration status, culture, and language structure the responses women are likely to encounter from helping institutions, the manner in which battering is understood by those around them,[10] and the manner in which women understand the abuser's behavior. Establishing poor women of color as the standard for assessing the impact on material resources ensures that their needs are no longer marginalized. Poor women of color should be at the center of assessment for a second important reason. The experience of poverty, and hence the manner in which poverty shapes the experience of battering, is further shaped by experiences directly linked to race and ethnicity. For example, the experience of poverty for urban African American women is qualitatively different than the experience of poverty for many white urban women. Poor African American women in urban areas are much more likely to live in neighborhoods in which *overall* poverty rates are high. Thus, even when white women and African American women have similar incomes, their access to social services, police protection, and their exposure to general violence are significantly different. The experience of battering differs, also, because of the failures of helping institutions to meet the needs of battered women of color. Therefore, one cannot assess the likelihood that a given domestic violence intervention strategy will provide material resources for battered women without assessing whether it does so for poor women, who are disproportionately victims of battering, and for women of color, who are both disproportionately poor and whose experiences of battering and community responses to battering is shaped by experiences linked to race and ethnicity.

BATTERED LATINAS. The problems that current universal anti-domestic violence policies create for many Latinas illustrate the value of the material resources test. Scholarship by Latina writers describing the experiences of Latinas who are battered by intimate or former intimate partners focuses on Latinas' material conditions, the social networks and varying family structures within which they live, and the antisubordination struggles with which they engage. These antisubordination struggles involve hierarchies of race, gender, class, language, and immigrant status. Battered Latinas may be forced to fight governmental institutions that are historically hostile to Latinas/ Latinos, as well as social and legal structures of racism/sexism that limit their opportunities for economic stability.

Little domestic violence research focuses on the experiences of women of color and even less on battered Latinas. Research purportedly about "battered women" or "domestic violence" frequently rests on data gathered only or mainly about white women. When research purports to study the experiences of "women of color" it often involves only or mainly African American women. Thus the research on battered women suffers from a black/white paradigm problem in which the experiences of white women represent all women, the experiences of African American women represent "women of color," and differences in experience between African American women and white women represent all racial/ethnic differences.

An additional problem arises in the scholarship that does focus on Latinas/ Latinos: the tendency to group Latinas/os together without regard to important differences between groups. For example, the largest random sample study of domestic violence rates among Latinos/as only interviewed those who spoke English. The National Institute of Justice ("NIJ") study of police response in Miami-Dade Country, Florida, a locale with significant numbers of immigrants from Caribbean and Latin American countries, grouped offenders into just three categories: "White, Black, and Hispanic." This leaves one uncertain as to which category black Cuban Americans are placed, for example, and unable to identify the importance of potentially significant differences of language, culture, or economics between immigrants from Haiti, Jamaica, or Cuba and African Americans.

Domestic violence research on Latinas also frequently ignores the impact of immigration status. Undocumented women may fear that police intervention will lead to deportation proceedings. Batterers who are themselves legal permanent residents or citizens use the threat of deportation to control women.

> Having left the relative safety of extended family and social networks in their countries of origin, immigrant Latinas must take the very difficult first steps into totally unknown circumstances. Their vulnerability in terms of language,

documentation, education level, knowledge of laws and services, and work skills is often used by their abusers as ammunition in their terrorist practices.[11]

For many undocumented women, deportation means not only economic deprivation, but also separation from children, and the probability of more and even greater violence in their home country. In addition, the experiences of political repression or civil war may affect the responses to battering of some Latina immigrants. These experiences may foster distrust of governmental authority and most especially of the police. Additionally, this kind of multiple trauma may result in post-traumatic stress disorder in some women, further complicating the victim's ability to gain economic stability.

Undocumented women are at greater risk of facing violence or the threat of violence at numerous sites including work and their neighborhood. Unless domestic violence becomes severe, it makes little sense to target for criminal intervention only the violence that is perpetrated by an intimate partner. Additionally, immigrant Latinas who do not speak English are seriously disadvantaged in the courts, in their encounters with police, and in the offices of social service agencies.

II. APPLICATION OF THE MATERIAL RESOURCES TEST TO ARREST ENCOURAGING POLICIES

A. Deterrence Related Resources

Battering men frequently sabotage women's attempts at economic self-sufficiency. An arrest policy that deters violence, even if it did not deter psychological abuse and other controlling behavior, would likely have some impact on this diminishment of women's material resources. Therefore, if arrest encouraging policies result in specific deterrence, those policies are likely to be resource enhancing for battered women. This section analyzes the data on the specific deterrence effects of arrest for men who batter poor women of color. Arrest policies in domestic violence cases operate in three variants: no specified policy, pro-arrest (modified police discretion), and mandatory arrest (arrest is mandated where police find probable cause to believe domestic violence has occurred). I refer collectively to pro-arrest and mandatory arrest policies as *arrest encouraging policies.*

The biggest problem for poor women of color with regard to police response has been in getting the police to respond *at all.* Police often believe that violence is an unremarkable event in the households of poor people of color and that police intervention is therefore likely to be ineffective or unnecessary. This may be explained, in part, by a police culture that constructs categories of "normal" and "deviant" people, with poor people of color more likely to be placed in the latter category. Thus, battered women's advocates conceived of arrest encouraging policies, and particularly mandatory arrest polices, as a mechanism for diminishing police discretion that frequently operated to deny protection to battered women, especially poor women of color.

The results of the now famous Minneapolis arrest study—that arrest deterred repeat violence better than did police mediation or separation of the parties—provided tremendous support for the pro-arrest movement.

The National Institute of Justice (NIJ) commissioned studies in six other cities to determine if the Minneapolis findings could be replicated. Though the findings regarding the relationship between recidivism and police intervention varied across sites in the NIJ studies, some findings were consistent: recidivism rates are high regardless of the form of police response, and much of the recidivism violence goes unreported; police intervention stops the immediate violent episode in most cases but is more likely to do so when there is an arrest; disproportionate numbers of African Americans and somewhat lower but still disproportionately high numbers of Latinas/os are the subject of criminal justice intervention in domestic violence cases.

Researchers in only one locale—Miami-Dade, Florida—reported finding the main results of the Minneapolis study across all measures: arrest deterred violence more than did nonarrest. In the remaining sites, researchers concluded that arrest was no better on average at deterring repeat violence than were other police actions studied. More troubling were the conclusions of Lawrence Sherman that arrest had an *escalating* effect on the recidivism of some unemployed batterers.

Research that examines the relationship between community characteristics and batterer recidivism finds similarly disturbing results. A reassessment of the Milwaukee arrest study data found neighborhood characteristics to be more strongly related to recidivism postarrest than were the individual characteristics of the arrestees. Men arrested for domestic violence were more likely to recidivate if they lived in neighborhoods characterized by a combination of high rates of the following: unemployment, divorce, single mother-headed households, households below the poverty line, and households receiving government assistance than were men who did not live in such neighborhoods.

In conclusion, arrest appears to have, at best, a modest deterrence effect and this effect may be less likely for some of the men who batter poor women, whether these recidivists are understood as unemployed batterers or batterers who reside in particularly unstable neighborhoods.

B. Arrest Encouraging Policies and Nondeterrence-Related Resources

The arrest studies focused narrowly on police response and offender behavior. Battered women's advocates argue that apart from specific deterrence, mandatory, and pro-arrest policies help provide victims with other benefits. For example, arrest may result in a woman's immediate safety through cessation of the violence. Arrest may provide support for the victim through police moral solidarity and disapproval of the batterer's behavior. Arrest may assist women in connecting with community resources and other legal remedies and may encourage women to use those resources. As a result of lobbying by battered women's advocates, many police departments that have adopted mandatory or pro-arrest policies have also adopted requirements that officers provide women with information and assistance. These efforts are apparent in the studies of arrest.

Significant numbers of women interviewed in the NIJ studies stated that they were satisfied with the police response. Much of this victim satisfaction relates directly to police practices of providing women with information regarding community resources and assisting their connection with those resources. For example, the victims in the NIJ study in Milwaukee whose batterers were arrested expressed much higher satisfaction rates with police response than did victims whose batterers were merely warned. The difference appears to be related to the degree to which victims believed officers gave them useful information and the degree to which warning group victims felt that officers did not listen to their side of the story. Two-thirds of victims reported that officers gave them information on their legal rights or how to get assistance, and 56 percent reported that officers recommended that victims pursue legal assistance. Even more impressive are the 83 percent who reported that officers gave them information on shelters and women's support groups and the 65 percent for whom police recommended or assisted in contacting shelters. By comparison, most victims in the warned (nonarrest) group did not recall that officers even told them of their right to press charges.

A number of smaller studies in jurisdictions with arrest-encouraging policies show similar results.[12] For example, victims interviewed in a study assessing the coordinated community response in Quincy, Massachusetts, where police are subject to a pro-arrest policy reported that police regularly provide referrals for restraining orders and transport victims and children to shelters and medical care. The Quincy study also finds high victim satisfaction with police response, even though significant numbers of victims opposed arrest. Further, victim satisfaction appears related to whether or not the victim was informed of her rights and given information about restraining orders. In a Canadian study, researchers asked battered women for suggestions to improve police response. The most common response was that police should give victims more information regarding court processes and community services available for women.

In jurisdictions that have adopted mandatory or pro-arrest policies, police are frequently mandated or encouraged to provide women with information regarding community resources and legal remedies, and sometimes with direct assistance in securing resources. Interviews with victims demonstrate that battered women value this aspect of policing and further evidence suggests that the information results in enhancing women's access to resources.

Conclusions regarding these findings are hindered, however, because of the inattention to women of color, particularly non–African American women. Few studies examine Latinas' use of police. Most published accounts of arrest study data fail to examine possible race/ethnicity differences in victim interview responses. Therefore, it is impossible to know how many Latinas initiated the call to police or how many Latinas were satisfied with the police response. A few smaller studies have looked at Latina help-seeking behavior. For example, Gondolf and Fisher reviewed data regarding shelter residents in Texas, comparing Latinas with African American women and white women. The study found similar rates of overall help seeking and, specifically, similar rates of seeking legal assistance. In a study of fifty women in a Texas shelter, Mexican American women were more likely to recommend contacting the police than were white women. However, another small study of pregnant Spanish-speaking Latinas who sought prenatal care in a public clinic and who reported spouse abuse found that only 23 percent had called the police.

C. Negative Effects of Arrest Encouraging Policies that May Diminish Their Resource Enhancing Possibilities

For some poor women of color, the risks of arrest encouraging policies may outweigh the potential benefits. For example, the evidence that arrest may escalate violence for certain unemployed batterers or for those who reside in certain neighborhoods suggests that arrest may increase the danger for a group of women who are the least able to relocate. The risks of arrest-encouraging policies go beyond potential escalation effects, however. For many poor women of color, those risks include the risk of police brutality, primarily against the batterer, but also against the victim; the risk that the victim will be arrested; the risk that police intervention will result in increased and ongoing state intrusion in the life of the victim; the risk of financial loss resulting from the batterer's arrest; and the risk of relationship loss. In addition, for some immigrant women, there is the risk that the victim, abuser, or both will be deported. These potential risks of arrest must be examined in determining whether arrest encouraging polices are likely to, on balance, enhance access to material resources for poor women of color. My analysis will focus on three serious risks: the risk of police mistreatment; the risk of victim arrest and/or ongoing police monitoring of the victim; and the risk of deportation.

THE RISK OF POLICE MISTREATMENT.   Mandatory arrest policies can hardly be said to empower women of color if the result is that police physically or verbally abuse the victim, her abuser, or both. Therefore, arrest-encouraging policies cannot be evaluated without reference to the history of police misconduct toward people of color. For example, "Latinos in the United States have had a long, acrimonious history of interaction with . . . law enforcement agencies. This history is marked by abuse and violence suffered by the Latino community at the hands of police officers who have indiscriminately used excessive physical force against Latinos." Marie de Santis, an attorney who represents immigrant Latinas in California, provided a compelling example of why a battered Latina may not trust the police:

> In the midst of a difficult struggle to escape her husband's violence . . . Claudia called us one day enraged at what police had done with her teenage son. He and a group of his Latino friends had skipped school early one day and gone to one of their homes. . . . The parents weren't home, and neighbors called the police.

Squads of police came and a helicopter, too. Police barged into the house, pushed the kids to the floor, put guns to their heads, and when the kids tried to explain they weren't burglars, police screamed at them to shut up or they would be killed. At the police station, when the homeowners arrived and told the police that, indeed, these kids were all friends of their son and were always welcome in their home, police still did not stop the process, and the DA filed charges. It was only months later when a judge looked at the case that charges against the boys were dropped. Claudia escaped her husband's violence, but she and her children are left with a bitter distrust of police.[13]

De Santis concluded, "women see how some police treat their brothers, sons, husbands, and neighbors, and conclude that police are the last people they'd call for help."[14] Thus, arrest encouraging policies are unlikely to empower poor women of color unless there are strong programs to prevent police mistreatment and well-publicized remedies available for when it occurs.

THE RISK OF VICTIM ARREST AND OTHER FORMS OF STATE CONTROL.   The percentage of women arrested for domestic violence increases sharply when arrest-encouraging policies are adopted. Given the mandate to arrest, officers resort to dual arrests (arresting both parties), trusting the prosecutor and/or the courts to sort it out. Many of the women arrested are battered women whose violence is either in self-defense or is responsive to their partner's repeated violence against them. In addition to dual arrests, sole arrests of women also climb dramatically in these jurisdictions. As Cecelia Espinoza describes, the combination of mandatory arrest laws with no drop prosecution policies has resulted in the prosecution of women for domestic violence charges, even in circumstances where the prosecutor admits that the woman's actions—in the overall dynamics of the relationship—were defensive.[15] Even if the prosecutor declines to prosecute, when victims are arrested the results are devastating. Children may be placed in foster care, women lose their jobs, and batterers realize that they can use mandatory arrest policies to punish and intimidate their victim partners.

In response to the problems of inappropriate arrests of women victims, several states have adopted statutes that require officers to avoid dual arrests and to arrest only "primary aggressors." Statutes that define primary aggressor as the party who is not acting in self-defense create problems because women's violence may be reactive without meeting a legal definition of self-defense. For example, Cecelia Espinoza related the story of Paula, a battered immigrant woman from Mexico who received support from Lideras Campensinas. Paula determined not to take her husband's abuse any longer and, with a baseball bat in hand, told him to leave the home. He tried to return three times and each time he left after Paula threatened him with the bat. Espinoza pointed out that under a mandatory arrest policy, Paula's actions would likely result in her arrest. Her actions were not clearly defensive because Paula was in no immediate danger, but her threats were responsive to the domestic violence. Even in jurisdictions that have adopted a broader definition of who is not a primary aggressor, arrests of victims continues to be a problem.

Increased numbers of victim arrests occur in both pro-arrest and mandatory arrest jurisdictions, but may be more prevalent in mandatory arrest jurisdictions. One small study that compared arrest outcomes in two Michigan cities may be suggestive of this difference.[16] This study compared arrest statistics in the cities of Ann Arbor with a mandatory arrest policy and Ypsilanti with a pro-arrest policy. In the mandatory arrest city of Ann Arbor, men were more likely to be arrested for domestic violence in cases in which the victim reported a history of abuse to police at the scene. Women were more likely to be arrested when the police had been called to the house before. Officers may categorize battered women as pathological or as abusers of the system when they "fail" to separate once "given the opportunity" to do so via police response. Forced to make an arrest, they may retaliate against victims. If mandatory arrest policies are more likely to create backlash against women who "stay," then that backlash will likely be felt disproportionately by low-income women. Such a backlash may be fueled by a tendency to treat women as pathological if they do not separate from their abusers, coupled with preexisting social stereotypes of deviance based on race and class.

Even when battered women are not arrested, mandatory arrest policies may increase poor women's exposure to state control. For example, some jurisdictions require that police report as suspected child abuse every domestic violence call in which children are present. Poor women of color are particularly vulnerable to this form of state control. In addition, some women fear that an investigation of the abuse charge will uncover their own criminal activities. This risk is particularly great when mandatory arrest is coupled with aggressive prosecution policies. Women become involved in criminal activities as a direct result of being battered.[17] Even if this were not the case, women involved in criminal activity are rendered particularly vulnerable to violence. For example, drug-addicted women are particularly vulnerable both to domestic violence as well as to state violence. An investigation into domestic violence may result in the victim losing her children or in her own incarceration or both.

THE RISK OF DEPORTATION.   The Illegal Immigration Reform and Immigrant Responsibility Act provides that certain immigrants who are convicted of a domestic violence crime are rendered deportable. This provision is dangerous for battered immigrant women. While the deportation provisions likely have a chilling effect on battered women who fear that a call to the police will render their partner deportable, this is not its only devastating consequence. Given the increased numbers of arrests of victims under mandatory arrest policies, some battered immigrant women have been rendered deportable as a result of their conviction for misdemeanor domestic violence. Immigrant women who are primary caretakers of children are particularly likely to plea bargain in order to avoid jail time and thereby unwittingly render themselves deportable. Maria Sanchez's story provides an illustration.[18] When her husband came home drunk, he dragged her out of their child's room, pinned her on the couch, and began beating her. Maria bit him back.

Her husband called the police, and Maria was arrested. She tried telling the police that he had been beating her again and that she was defending herself, but, unlike her husband, she didn't speak English and the police spoke no Spanish. When she went to court, Maria signed a form, printed in English, that waived her right to counsel and entered a guilty plea to misdemeanor assault. Maria had no understanding of the forms she was signing and the court's unqualified interpreter was no help. Despite the fact that Maria's husband had a prior record for domestic violence, despite the fact that she had endured years of her husband's abuse, Maria now faces deportation because of her domestic violence conviction.

D. Summary: Material Resources, Arrest Policies, and Alternatives

This application of the material resources test to arrest-encouraging policies suggests that mandatory arrest may create significant costs for some poor women of color. These costs may outweigh the beneficial aspects of the policies; however, that calculus may vary by locale. Pro-arrest policies at the state level rather than mandatory arrest policies allow *local* governments to decide whether or not to adopt a mandatory arrest policy. This may provide the flexibility needed to assess the effect of arrest policies given local conditions. However, given the current realities of inadequate services for battered women, inappropriate arrests of women, harsh anti-immigrant policies, and laws that punish poor mothers by removing their children, it is hard to imagine a community in which a mandatory arrest policy would be worth the risk to poor women of color. At the least, mandatory arrest policies should be adopted only when agreed upon by a local battered women's advocacy community that is representative of the various communities of poor women of color, including language, immigrant, and ethnic communities.

In determining the preferred policy in their locale, activists should examine the quality of relations between poor communities of color and the police, including the presence of anti-immigrant sentiment. Relations between police and communities may be measured by a number of factors, including: the adequacy/inadequacy of police resources in a given community; the frequency of police brutality, harassment, and related complaints in a given locale; the degree to which methods are in place to report such police misconduct and the efficacy of those methods; the commitment of local police leadership to both racial fairness and to responding to domestic violence calls. Local advocates must also evaluate the strength of domestic violence community services for poor women of color and the degree to which state actors—notably prosecutors and child protection service workers—understand the circumstances of poor women of color in their locale.

The decision whether or not to mandate that police arrest perpetrators of domestic violence does not exhaust the possibilities for constraining police action. As evidenced by women's satisfaction with police responses that provide them with information regarding services and their legal rights, police can provide women with critical links to material resources. We should encourage and expand this police action by requiring police to provide or locate transportation and other services for battered women. For example, Lawrence Sherman recommended "mandatory action" policies that require police to choose from a list of actions such as offering the victim transportation to a shelter, taking the suspect to a detoxification treatment center, allowing the victim to decide if an immediate arrest should be made, or mobilizing the victim's social networks to provide her with short-term protection.

The preliminary data regarding neighborhood differences in domestic violence recidivism rates suggests a focus on community based criminal interventions. Models of community policing that engage community groups in establishing local police priorities may be useful in increasing women's resources. For example, in Chicago, which has a pro-arrest rather than a mandatory arrest policy, a number of neighborhood groups involved with city community policing efforts have determined that domestic violence is a priority issue in their neighborhood.

There may be other ways to meet the twin goals of mandating that police provide protection for poor women of color while promoting women's empowerment. For example, special citizen panels could be established to monitor police performance on domestic violence calls and serve as a complaint center for battered women. Anti-domestic violence work that is linked with work against police brutality may be particularly sensitive to the degree to which police are responsive to the needs of poor women of color. For example, the Philadelphia Barrio Project, which focuses on police brutality issues in the predominantly Latina/Latino sections of the city, coordinates its work with battered women's advocates to press for adequate police response to battered women. This kind of coordinated effort and community outreach means that battered women have recourse both against police inaction as well as against police brutality. Some activists and scholars are investigating the use of restorative justice programs such as community conferencing and peacemaking. While these processes present challenges to establishing safety for battered women, they may widen the net of responsibility so as to increase material resources available for victims, thereby increasing social supports and services for victims.

CONCLUSION: THE MATERIAL RESOURCES TEST AND SHIFTING POWER FOR BATTERED WOMEN

The most obvious impact of applying the material resources test is to shift significant monies to direct aid for victims and to target more significant aid to poor women and especially poor women of color. There are many possible steps toward this goal. Because of the possible relevance of neighborhood disintegration to domestic violence recidivism, particular services should be focused on increasing the autonomy of women in those neighborhoods through resource enhancement. Current legal remedies that enhance resources for battered women could be made more effective. For example, crime victim compensation requirements that victims cooperate with the prosecution of the batterer, renders the aid useless for many women. In addition, compensation is frequently available for psychological counseling, but not for meeting the material needs of victims. Law reform that increases criminal penalties without evidence of gains for battered women should be disfavored and law that diminishes battered women's material resources should be eliminated.

The material resources test should be incorporated into federal funding criteria for domestic violence intervention projects. Federal dollars should not support universal (statewide) mandatory arrest policies, as is currently the case. Rather, funding should encourage local assessments of the impact of arrest policies on poor women of color. In addition, funding criteria should support those programs that represent broad-based coalitions that are either focused on particular neighborhoods or particular racial/ethnic groups. Such coalitions are more likely to have the local knowledge required to assess the situation for poor women of color.

Application of the material resources test may also suggest changes in the way lawyers engage in their legal representation of battered women. For example, Legal Services in Tampa, Florida formed an organization called Child-Net to respond to the material and social support needs of battered women clients. Jeanie Williamson, director of ChildNet, explained that staff attorneys were frustrated with the inability of legal remedies to give women freedom from abusive partners. ChildNet provides women with advocates, who assist them in locating community services including education, childcare, and job training. Similarly, Linda Mills has argued for the establishment of domestic violence commissions that would assist women with housing and job needs as well as provide legal remedies such as restraining orders.

Funding for domestic violence research should prioritize research that addresses the needs of poor women, and especially poor women of color. This research must escape the black/white paradigm limitations of current domestic violence research and address the particular needs of Latinas and other women of color who are frequently ignored by research.

The measure of the efficacy of any domestic violence intervention strategy must account for, as much as possible, the various forces that mediate and shape women's experiences of battering. The material resources test attempts to do this by requiring an inquiry into the likelihood that a given intervention strategy will result in increased material resources for women, and particularly for poor women of color. Material resources are critically important in battered women's survival. Without the specific attention that the material resources test provides, this importance will continue to be overlooked.

NOTES

[Please note that for a full listing of notes and references, go to Lexis Nexis.]

I am grateful for the comments of my friends and colleagues Mary Coombs, Wes Daniels, Stacey Dougan, Angela Harris, Don Jones, Marnie Mahoney, Linda Mills, Linda Osmondson,

Bernie Oxman, Rob Rosen, Frank Valdes, and Kate Waits. I am grateful for e-mail correspondence with Eve Buzawa, Jeffrey Fagan, and JoAnn Miller who helped me sort through research findings. Of course, I am solely responsible for any mistakes in this chapter.

1. Ptacek (1999), p. 25.
2. Coker (1999), pp. 42–50.
3. Sherman et al. (1992), p. 261.
4. Crenshaw (1991), pp. 1241, 1244.
5. Judith Wittner, "Reconceptualizing Agency in Domestic Violence Court," in Naples, ed. (1998), pp. 81, 89.
6. Barbara Hart, "Battered Women and the Criminal Justice System," in Buzawa and Buzawa, eds. (1996), pp. 98, 107.
7. Bowker (1983); Miller and Krull (1997), pp. 235, 249.
8. Raphael (1995), pp. 29, 30–31.
9. Sullivan and Bybee (1999), pp. 43, 48.
10. Rivera (1994), pp. 231, 255.
11. Perilla (1999), p. 125
12. Buzawa et al. (1999).
13. E-mail correspondence from Marie De Santis, attorney, director of the Women's Justice Center, Sonoma County, California (Dec. 20, 1999) (on file with author).
14. Ibid.
15. Espinoza (1999), p. 163.
16. Lyon (1999), pp. 253, 271–297.
17. Richie (1996), pp. 114–116, 120–123, 123–127.
18. Pan (2000), p. A1

SELECTED REFERENCES

Bowker, Lee. 1983. *Beating Wife-beating.* Lexington, Mass.: Lexington.

Buzawa, Eve, and Carl G. Buzawa, eds. 1996. *Do Arrests and Restraining Orders Work?* Thousand Oaks, Calif.: Sage.

Buzawa, Eve, Gerald Hotaling, Andrew Klein, and James Byrne. 1999. U.S. Department of Justice, Response to domestic violence in a pro-active court setting: Final report, executive summary. Washington D.C.: National Institute of Justice. Available at: http://www.ncjrs.org/pdffiles1/nij/grants/181428.pdf.

Coker, Donna. 1999. Enhancing autonomy for battered women: Lessons from Navajo peacemaking. *UCLA Law Review* 47: 1–111.

Crenshaw, Kimberlé. 1991. Mapping the margins: Intersectionality, identity politics, and violence against women of color. *Stanford Law Review* 43: 1241–1299.

Espinoza, Cecelia. 1999. No relief for the weary: VAWA relief denied for battered immigrants lost in the intersections. *Marquette Law Review* 83: 163–220.

Lyon, Andrea. 1999. Be careful what you wish for: An examination of arrest and prosecution patterns of domestic violence cases in two cities in Michigan. *Michigan Journal of Gender and the Law* 5: 253–298.

Miller, JoAnn, and Amy C. Krull. 1997. Controlling domestic violence: Victim resources and police intervention. In Glenda Kantor and Jana Jasinski, eds., *Out of the Darkness: Contemporary Perspectives on Family Violence.* Thousand Oaks, Calif.: Sage, 235–254.

Naples, Nancy, ed. 1998. *Community Activism and Feminist Politics: Organizing across Race, Class, and Gender.* New York: Routledge.

Pan, Philip. 2000. Victimized woman faces deportation. *Washington Post,* February 20, A1.

Ptacek, James. 1999. *Battered Women in the Courtroom: The Power of Judicial Responses.* Boston: Northeastern University Press.

Raphael, Jody. 1995. Domestic violence and welfare receipt: The unexplored barrier to employment. *Georgetown Journal on Fighting Poverty* 3: 29–34.

Richie, Beth E. 1996. *Compelled to Crime: The Gender Entrapment of Battered Black Women.* New York: Routledge.

Rivera, Jenny. 1994. Domestic violence against Latinas by Latino males: An analysis of race, national origin, and gender differentials. *Boston College Third World Law Journal* 14: 231–257.

Sherman, Lawrence, and Richard A. Berk. 1984. The specific deterrent effects of arrest for domestic violence assault. *American Sociological Review* 49: 261–272.

Sherman, Lawrence, et al. 1992. *Policing Domestic Violence: Experiments and Dilemmas.* New York: Free Press.

Sullivan, Cris, and Deborah I. Bybee. 1999. Reducing violence using community-based advocacy for women with abusive partners. *Journal of Consulting and Clinical Psychology* 67: 43–53.

CHAPTER **23**

NEIL WEBSDALE AND BYRON JOHNSON

Reducing Woman Battering

The Role of Structural Approaches

 ABSTRACT

In her discussion of law, material resources and poor women of color, Donna Coker (chapter 22) outlined the framework for the case study provided by Websdale and Johnson in this chapter. Criminal justice responses to domestic violence can not protect women from revictimization because they do not systematically address women's economic, social, and political disadvantages. Here, in this early classic research Websdale and Johnson show how a more effective way to reduce woman battering is to empower battered women by providing the underlying structural conditions for independent housing, job training and opportunities, affordable child care, and social services which allow women to break away from violent relationships. This conclusion is based on a study of poor and working-class rural women enrolled in a federally funded project, the Job Readiness Program (JRP), operating in half of Kentucky's domestic violence shelters.

Kentucky's JRPs are an example of a structural attempt to confront one of the most basic problems facing many battered women: they have no alternative but to return to their abuser upon leaving a domestic violence shelter. Major structural interventions must be cognizant of the way both poverty and patriarchy intersect to keep women in violent relationships. Contrary to the "learned helplessness" view of battered women (see Allard, chapter 13), the philosophy behind the rural Kentucky program is that, if given real opportunities to confront their victimization and poverty through job training and placement, independent housing, and learning independent living skills, battered women will demonstrate tremendous resourcefulness.

In fact, an evaluation of the JRPs between 1991 and 1994 found that 82 percent of the women experienced no revictimization up to two years after having participated in the JRP. Women who secured both housing and work significantly reduced their chances of being further victimized although receiving housing had a stronger effect in reducing violence than simply having a job. It is significant that very few of the women who secured independent housing allowed their abusers back into their homes. This finding contradicts the stereotype of the masochistic battered woman and underscores the fact that many battered women return to abusers primarily because they lack alternative housing, an acute structural problem for battered women.

Rural domestic violence in the United States provides it own unique challenges. Women live far from neighbors and sources of help; public transportation is practically nonexistent; shelter locations are just too far away. Clearly, without major structural changes, the women are isolated in their rural homes. And similar to the Weis and colleagues study of white poor and working-class women (chapter 15), the majority of survivors in the Kentucky study are white women. In both cases, rural poverty must be discussed as a racial issue. Stereotyping the poor as urban and Black fosters racism, makes invisible poor whites, and prevents poor battered women from organizing on the basis of their shared needs and interests.

Empowerment through structural supports and the provision of material resources are necessary for women to escape violent relationships and establish a more secure and safe base for themselves and their children. In the final chapter 24, Andrea Smith challenges approaches that provide individual services but disengage from broader collective social change. Analyze what you have read so far in this anthology and identify which chapters embrace parallel perspectives of individual safety, community action, and social change?

INTRODUCTION: THE NEED FOR STRUCTURAL APPROACHES TO WOMAN BATTERING

Intrafamilial violence directed against women is part of a set of structural relations and social practices that, as Sylvia Walby (1990: 20) puts it, allow men to "dominate, oppress, and exploit women." We agree with Kathleen Ferraro (1993: 175) who observes that treating woman battering as a "crime problem" diminishes the social and political significance of interpersonal violence against women. According to Ferraro, "it is vital that battering not be viewed only as a crime, but also as a manifestation of structured gender inequality."

This view is supported by a large number of empirical studies that reveal that it is mostly men who control women through violence (see Dobash and Dobash, 1979; Russell, 1990; Breines and Gordon, 1983) and women who bear the brunt of serious injuries (Dobash et al., 1992; Wilson and Daly, 1992; Dawson and Langan, 1994). Women who attack their husbands usually do so out of desperation and self-defense.

Criminal justice policies will always be of limited utility in reducing the revictimization of battered women by their abusive partners because those policies do not systematically address women's social and political disadvantage. Traditionally, violence against women in families has been seen as a misdemeanor offense, even though the injuries sustained by many women would attract felonious charges if perpetrated by a man she did not live with or know well (see Stanko, 1982; Langan and Innes, 1986). After a decade of federally funded studies on the impact of arresting batterers at domestics, researchers and policymakers still debate whether mandatory arrest is an effective intervention tool that reduces the revictimization of women (see Garner et al., 1995). Sherman (1992), for example, concludes that mandatory arrest does not reduce recidivism, and, with certain offenders (unmarried, unemployed, and African-American men), mandatory arrest actually increases recidivism. In contrast, Stark argues that none of the studies on mandatory arrest combined arrest with aggressive prosecution and incarceration (1994: 32). Abusers receive short jail terms, if any at all. Stark indicates that in jurisdictions that have combined arrest with prosecution and imprisonment (for example, Lincoln, Nebraska, Quincy, Massachusetts, and San Diego, California) violence has been reduced.

Batterers may be sent to counseling groups as an alternative to serving jail time, although the effects of these groups on reducing recidivism seem limited (see Harrell, 1991; Tifft, 1993). Dutton (1986) and Edleson and Grusznski (1988) found that batterers who participated in treatment were less likely to reoffend. However, Hamberger and Hastings find evidence of "deeply ingrained, highly treatment-resistant, and often perplexing sets of behaviors" among batterers (1988: 789). Their research is consistent with numerous other studies that suggest there is no stereotypical batterer personality upon which to base intrapersonal psychological interventions. In a similar vein, Straus argues it is doubtful if more than a small fraction of battering can be attributed to the psychopathology of the batterer (1977: 195).

Psychological explanations have tended to identify battered women as accomplices to their own victimization. They become emotionally paralyzed and unable to work their way out of abusive situations because they [are said to] suffer from learned helplessness (see Walker, 1979). Consequently, much therapy with battered women ends up reinforcing women's subordination rather than challenging their social and political disadvantage and incorporating that disadvantage into emotionally supportive strategies (see Stark and Flitcraft, 1996: 188–190). Unlike psychological approaches, we contend that a more effective way to reduce woman battering is to empower battered women (by providing independent housing and job opportunities) to break away from violent relationships, if they so choose. In suggesting such an approach, we do not mean to set up a false dichotomy between housing/work-related issues and all the personal/emotional contradictions and ambiguities of ending an intimate relationship.

In this chapter we report case study findings from a unique federally funded project in Kentucky that was designed to reduce the revictimization of battered women by providing battered women with job training, employment, independent living skills, independent housing, assistance with negotiating the welfare system, education, legal support, childcare, and a multitude of other services. This preventive "structural" intervention is known as the Kentucky Job Readiness Program (JRP). The JRP has been in operation in Kentucky for four years (1990 to 1994) and has been funded by a U.S. Department of Labor demonstration grant. By the fall of 1994, the JRPs operated in seven of the sixteen spouse abuse shelter sites in Kentucky. No other state has implemented JRPs exclusively in their spouse abuse shelter system. The uniqueness of the Kentucky JRPs makes it all the more important to report the case study findings on the revictimization rates of battered women receiving JRP interventions.

JRPs AND THE REVICTIMIZATION OF BATTERED WOMEN IN KENTUCKY: THE SIGNIFICANCE OF RURAL CULTURE IN KENTUCKY

Our research focuses on the primarily rural state of Kentucky. We are aware of the difficulties with labeling a state "primarily rural" (see, for example, Bachman, 1992: 547). According to the U.S. Census Bureau, a town or locality is considered rural if its population is under 2,500. There are a large number of small towns in Kentucky with populations of 5,000 to 10,000 people in which social life has many of the cultural qualities that sociologists call "traditional society." In these towns residents know each other fairly well; there appears to be a greater commitment to shared values and less tolerance of diversity. The economy tends to be based on farming or other extractive industries. A core of families has lived in the community for several generations, and there is less anonymity and privacy (see Bushy, 1993). In many cases, particularly in more remote rural areas, the family is both the primary means of production and socialization. There is an antipathy to state intervention, a suspicion of state representatives, and a reliance on local or county government for getting things done. The influence of religion, particularly fundamentalist Christian religion, is strong and reactionary, especially regarding the roles of women, which are typically much more traditional than those found in urban areas (Bushy, 1993: 191; Gagne, 1992: 395–398).

If we use U.S. Census criteria, then Kentucky ranks eighth out of the fifty states and the District of Columbia, with 48.2 percent of its population being rural. Of those states with a higher percentage of rural dwellers than Kentucky, only North Carolina has a higher rural population. Kentucky therefore typifies the most rural states in the country. The rurality of Kentucky is highly significant with regard to patterns of revictimization. In a yearlong survey of 510 women conducted by female interviewers in the sixteen spouse abuse shelters in Kentucky, we found that 75 percent of sheltered women were married to their abusers and another 22 percent were cohabiting with them. In other words, these women were often in long-term relationships with abusers. We have no way of knowing for sure whether sheltered women are generally representative of battered women in Kentucky. However, our extensive in-depth interviewing work with spouse abuse shelter workers (who perform outreach services, take crisis calls, and otherwise work with nonresident battered women) suggests that the sheltered population only differs significantly around the question of social class. Upper- and middle-class battered women tend to use shelters only rarely. This contrasts with Evan Stark's observations (1993: 667) based on urban research, in which he observes that "despite the ideological bias that has excluded unmarried women from population surveys of domestic violence, the vast majority of battered women (75 percent or more) are single, separated, or divorced, with separated and divorced women facing the greatest risk of severe ongoing violence, including homicide."

The significance of the rural-urban difference is profound. Stark argues that it is more difficult for battered women who have resided in an urban shelter for a couple of weeks to return to their abuser, simply because their abuser is difficult to locate. Stark paints a picture of more transient abusive relationships in urban areas, and we do not at this point take issue with his argument. Although precise data are unavailable for Kentucky, we estimate that 80 to 90 percent of battered women who leave Kentucky shelters without completing JRPs return to their abusers within six months (personal communication with Helen Kinton, president, Kentucky Domestic Violence Association, November 7, 1994). We suspect that programs such as JRPs may be potentially more beneficial in rural areas because of the social, economic, and cultural pressures for women to return to their husbands. Kinton's estimate of an 80 to 90 percent return rate for battered women is consistent with a number of studies that document just how difficult it is for battered women to leave violent relationships (see, for example, Browne, 1987: 109–130; Jones, 1994: 129–166).

WOMAN BATTERING IN KENTUCKY

Violence against women in Kentucky, like elsewhere, is a serious social problem. In 1979, Louis Harris and Associates conducted a survey sponsored by the Kentucky Commission on Women (Schulman, 1979). It was based on 1,793 telephone interviews with women who were living with husbands or male partners. In that survey one in ten Kentucky women said they had experienced some degree of physical abuse in the preceding year and 21 percent of married women reported having experienced at least one incident of spousal violence at some time. The more recent Bluegrass State Telephone Poll (1991), conducted by the *Louisville Courier-Journal* revealed that about half of Kentuckians know a woman who has been physically abused. This finding is consistent with a number of national studies.

The Centers for Disease Control (CDC) recently studied the phenomenon of homicide/suicide in Kentucky from 1985 through 1990 (Currens et al., 1991). Researchers defined a homicide/suicide as one or more homicides with the subsequent suicide of the killer. The sixty-seven homicide/suicides identified resulted in a total of eighty people being murdered, accounting for 6 percent of all Kentucky homicides during this period. Perhaps most significantly, 97 percent of the perpetrators were male, and 73 percent of the homicide victims were women. In ninety-six homicide/suicide clusters, the homicide victim and perpetrator were known to each other. In 70 percent of the cases, the perpetrator was either a current husband, boyfriend, or a former husband of the homicide victim. This gendered perpetrator-victim dyad is consistent with the aforementioned research findings indicating that it is largely women who are victimized by men.

The Kentucky Domestic Violence Association (KDVA) conducted one of the most extensive studies of marital rape (KDVA, 1989). The organization surveyed 660 battered women in spouse abuse shelters in Kentucky. Forty-five percent had been raped by their husbands or live-in partners. Of 295 women responding that their current spouse or live-in partner had forced sexual relations, 57 percent were forced to have sex after being beaten, 30 percent were forced to have oral-genital sex, and 16 percent described being penetrated by a variety of objects including bottles, plastic toys, wooden spoons, belt buckles, and, in one instance, a lead pipe.

THE EMERGENCE OF JRPs IN KENTUCKY SHELTERS

Since the late 1970s, sixteen spouse shelters have formed to provide women with refuge from violent men. Spouse abuse centers in Kentucky provide a range of services for their clients, including some or all of the following: safe shelter, nonresidential counseling, support services, clothing, legal advice, economic assistance, counseling, childcare, access to medical services, transportation, assistance in finding housing, and a range of other informal supports. The majority of women using the services of spouse abuse shelters are poor. In a statewide survey of 510 battered women in Kentucky shelters, 51 percent reported having annual incomes below $3,000 and 87 percent below $10,000 (Websdale and Johnson, 1997). With few options for independent economic survival, these sheltered women return to the shelter between seven and nine times before leaving a violent spouse. As we have noted, a large percentage return to their abusers and the communities they are a part of. Our analysis of JRP case studies will show that the rate of return for JRP graduates is much lower. Shelters in Louisville, Lexington, Newport, Hopkinsville, Elizabethtown, Mount Vernon, and Paducah offered JRP services to battered women who were interested and/or able to partake. These seven sites qualified for federal funds because of their proximity to labor markets, the grant writing initiatives taken by their staff, and the more secure funding bases at the shelter.

The innovative JRPs were designed not only to extend the baseline of shelter services but also to provide a comprehensive range of preventive interventions, including economic self-sufficiency, emotional empowerment, autonomous living skills, and practical support. This self-sufficiency was not designed to translate only into the acquisition of minimum-wage jobs but also to provide women with a substrate of skills and confidence, which, if their circumstances and individual leanings permitted, would enable them to climb the career ladder. In a nutshell, the JRPs were a structural attempt to confront the problem of battered women having no other choice but to return to violent households. The philosophy behind these structural interventions is that battered women, contrary to the astructural approach of theorists such as Lenore Walker (1979), do not suffer from learned helplessness and are not emotionally paralyzed to the point that they cannot effectively problem-solve. Rather, if given real opportunities to confront their victimization and poverty through job training, learning independent living skills, and independent housing, battered women will seize upon them and demonstrate tremendous resourcefulness under very trying conditions.

THE NATURE OF JRPs

The JRPs are multifaceted preventive programs that very pragmatically confront the structural disadvantages of battered women. Each component is designed to confront a particular structural impediment, which, if overcome, gives battered women a chance to redirect their considerable resistive powers away from mere physical and emotional survival and toward the construction of a more peaceful lifestyle, usually with their children.

JRP employment counselors usually meet with interested potential enrollees early on during their first week in shelter. Counselors may have read clients' files before making initial contact. Screening refers to the way in which JRP staff assess the appropriateness of a potential client for enrollment. Across all sites, very few interested clients are screened out by JRP personnel. JRP staff know from experience that employment skills are an essential component to the pursuit of economic independence. These skills provide not only a means of financial support, but also a much needed confidence boost for entry into a world often denied them by their violent and controlling partners.

JRPs offer a wide range of skills training and services to battered women. Programs include the provision of training services, support services, housing services, and job placement services. The unpaid, marginalized, and trivialized nature of the household labor performed by many clients diminishes their self-esteem concerning their work capabilities. The JRP, through the notion of transferable skills, attempts to invert women's self-deprecating observations about their potential employability. As Ann Oakley (1974) and Christine Delphy (1984) argue, the work of housewives is unpaid and unrecognized because they are housewives and not because of the nature of the work they do. The same work in the socialized labor market would be paid. JRPs invert this structural disadvantage by identifying the numerous skills battered women possess from their housework and present the possibility that JRP clients could be paid to use these skills. Alternatively, this baseline of skills could be refined and reoriented to the more social world of the labor market, as opposed to the isolated and personalized private sphere of housework.

Training services consist of various interventions designed to prepare battered women for the world of work and independent living. These include, but are not limited to, the following: job counseling, job training/job search, and remedial education and literacy. Job counseling is the process of assisting participants to realistically assess their abilities, needs, and potential, and providing guidance in the development of participants' vocational goals and the means to achieve those goals. Job training/job search is the process of helping participants to develop or enhance their job-seeking skills. In most cases, a job search may include a structured activity focusing on building practical skills and knowledge in order to identify and initiate employer contacts and interviews. This knowledge includes labor market information, job application/resume writing, interviewing techniques, and finding job openings. Remedial education and literacy entails instruction in reading comprehension, math computation, language arts (writing and verbal communication), and reasoning skills that enable an individual to function in the labor market. JRP support services greatly extend the baseline of spouse abuse shelter services and better prepare clients for the difficult task of economic self-sufficiency. These support services offer assistance with transportation, food/meals, personal needs, clothing, work equipment, money management, self-esteem/ motivation, independent living/life skills, daycare, and advocacy.

Battering relationships are often characterized by abusive men controlling the movements of "their" women. Solving the problem of getting around the power plays of an abusive relationship is another way in which the JRPs confront the structural disadvantage of battered women. Transportation is provided to participants so they can travel to training, shelters, job interviews, and jobs. At times, participant placement funds have been used to buy clients secondhand cars. Such provision is particularly valuable in rural areas where public transportation is very limited. JRPs also provide food for clients and their children. Other personal needs are also provided, including goods and services such as toothbrushes, shampoo, other personal hygiene supplies, pen and paper, false teeth, eyeglasses, and shower and laundry services. Clothing for women who are entering the job market is important, particularly when certain jobs require special clothing. For example, overalls may be purchased for women entering nontraditional jobs and suits may be provided for those entering clerical work.

Interventions around clothing are not just pragmatic. They symbolize a subversiveness in terms of the presentation of the self in everyday life since many battered women either did not "dress up" or were likened to whores by their abusers for doing so. Similarly, some employers require employees to own certain kinds of equipment (for example, tools for construction or carpentry work) and the JRPs were sometimes able to provide these. Money management and budgeting workshops teach some clients how to handle money. Financial training is essential, especially since many women have never been allowed by their abusers to own and control their own money. Women are given the opportunity to attend individual or group meetings to enhance their self-esteem and increase their motivation for life and work. Independent living/life skills are offered to assist the individual to learn how to cope with everyday problems. JRPs also offer assistance with locating appropriate daycare services. Such services are essential if women are to enter the world of paid employment. Finally, legal advocacy may involve hooking the client up with the appropriate legal services or making clients aware of some of their legal rights vis-à-vis issues such as emergency protective orders, child custody, and child support.

Structural subversion is also seen through providing independent housing. This housing offers physical and emotional space away from the abuser, who was used to managing his "castle" in certain ways. JRP housing services (mostly public housing) for battered women include emergency housing assistance, transitional housing placement, permanent housing placement, deposit and rent assistance, assistance with furnishings and moving, and housing assistance counseling. Emergency housing assistance refers to financial or other assistance that results in the participant securing short-term housing. This assistance is usually in the form of direct placement at an emergency shelter, referral to an emergency shelter, or a voucher for a hotel or motel room. Transitional housing placement usually takes the form of short-term housing for able-bodied persons that permits limited length of residency (usually up to twenty-four months), or housing for the mentally, emotionally, or physically disabled that includes supportive services, some degree of supervision, and subsidized rent. Transitional housing for members of these disabled groups is usually not time limited and in effect becomes permanent. JRPs also provide help with finding permanent housing where the participant has a legal right to stay for a specified amount of time by virtue of a lease or ownership. JRPs facilitate the entry into permanent housing by helping with deposits and rent assistance. Assistance with furnishings and moving is another important service. Housing assistance counseling consists of one or more meetings between the participant and a housing specialist, case manager, or other advocate to discuss housing options, housing assistance, specific housing referrals, and so on.

Having identified, celebrated, refined, and extended many of the unrecognized skills possessed by battered women, these JRP clients are often ready to consider entering the world of paid employment. JRP job placement services include job development, direct placement, post-placement follow-up, self-help support groups, and mentoring. Job development is the process of marketing a JRP participant to employers, including informing employers about what the participant can do, and soliciting and securing a job interview for that individual. In cases where the JRP staff have developed linkages with local private employers, a job may be "developed" or created for a particular participant. Direct placement is a job placement after intake, enrollment, and receipt of case management, support services, and/or housing services, but without the benefit of job training services. Postplacement follow-up services are designed to support program participants once employment is secured. Self-help support groups are meetings of JRP participants who provide positive reinforcement for each other and improve their personal comfort in learning new things, searching for jobs and housing, and attaining long-term success in the workplace. Mentoring is accomplished as an experienced person, teacher, or counselor intervenes on a battered woman's behalf. The mentor becomes a champion of the client and over a long period of time can be counted on for emotional support and career guidance.

Appendix.   Statewide Delivery of Selected JRP Services, 1992–1994

SERVICES	1992–93	1992–93	1993–94	1993–94
	Carry-over Clients N = 175	New Enrollees N = 261	Carry-over Clients N = 250	New Enrollees N = 247
Training services				
Job counseling	135	240	224	198
Job training/job search	129	226	205	168
Remedial education/literacy	27	45	37	42
Support services				
Transportation	80	163	141	157
Food/meals	69	164	137	154
Personal needs	70	167	141	157
Clothing/work equipment	84	163	149	162
Money management/budgeting	78	116	103	116
Self-esteem/motivation	127	230	205	187
Indep. living/life skills	70	135	120	102
Daycare/advocacy	59	98	92	104
Advocacy	80	122	133	129
Housing services				
Emergency housing assistance	6	86	60	53
Transitional housing placement	7	41	28	31
Permanent housing placement	65	103	131	70
Deposit/rent assistance	40	45	56	30
Assist w/ furnishings/moving	28	47	53	42
Housing assist counseling	96	168	182	145
Placement services				
Job development	106	107	135	49
Direct placement	99	77	109	51
Post-placement follow-up	131	94	156	64
Self-help support groups	64	79	101	68
Mentoring	132	162	167	123

Battered women in the JRPs avail themselves of many different kinds of services (see Appendix). It is the comprehensive nature of these services that we believe provides the impetus for battered women to make strides to independent living and self-sufficiency. Contrary to the widely held opinion that battered women suffer from what Lenore Walker (1979) calls learned helplessness, the JRP data affirm that battered women, if given the chance, draw upon all kinds of opportunities to protect themselves from revictimization. In particular, high percentages of JRP clients complete job training and job counseling. Large numbers of women also benefit from various support services. These services are an essential accompaniment to moving toward the world of employment, economic self-sufficiency, and a life free of violence. The most utilized support service was individual and group meetings to improve participants' self-esteem, thereby rendering them more effective in the workplace. It is important to reassert that this support service was not offered because clients were seen as psychologically passive and helpless. Rather, these support services were part of a structural intervention package that included confronting the fallacy that women were trapped and could not resist.

In the majority of cases the delivery of job training and support services begins before the provision of housing services and job-placement services. Often job training and support services pave the way for the difficult transition into the world of independent housing and employment. These are major changes for victimized women, who in many cases have lived in an environment that is tightly controlled by their abusers and where they have been led to believe that they are totally dependent upon [them]. As difficult as it is to find safe, affordable housing for mostly poor women with children, many women use housing services. Likewise, for women who have multiple barriers to securing employment (such as no prior work history outside the home, drug and alcohol problems that are often associated with their victimization, or limited formal educational qualifications), significant numbers not only secure jobs, but also continue to draw upon postplacement support and services. Again, we see this as evidence of resistance rather than psychological paralysis.

METHODOLOGY

As part of the official evaluation of the U.S. Department of Labor Demonstration Grant, the KDVA gathered 153 case studies on JRP clients who passed through the program between 1991 and 1994. These case studies were written by JRP staff and counselors at participating shelters and detailed the program participation and postshelter residence living situations of JRP graduates. Case studies were completed on women who had been out of shelters for at least three months and sometimes up to one year. To learn more about the workings of the JRPs and to improve the program, JRP staff constructed case studies on clients who had a variety of experiences in the program. They were specifically asked not just to write about the "success" stories where battered women overcame tremendous obstacles and found and retained high-paying jobs. Indeed, most of the JRP women did not dramatically change their economic situation by obtaining well-paying jobs.

For reasons of women's safety and security, no systematic demographic data are included in the 153 cases. The KDVA felt that to reveal that a client was, for example, a thirty-five-year-old African American from the Hopkinsville shelter with two children under six would seriously compromise that client's identity. Consequently, we do not have systematic data on the age, race, work history, income, or educational level of this sample of women. Such data gaps are to be expected when working with battered women who fear for the safety of themselves and their children. We would have obviously liked to control for these demographic variables, but such a control was not possible with this vulnerable population of women. However, we are able to offer summary demographic data on the total of 684 JRP women (see "Findings" below). Case workers took a typical cross-section of women, and we, having interviewed a number of these women ourselves, feel that the selection constitutes a representative sample of clients in terms of their age, race, educational background, marital status, number of children, and employment history.

For ethical reasons no control group of case studies was set up. The philosophy of the KDVA is inconsistent with assigning some women to the JRP group and excluding an equal number of women from such opportunities. We believe that the 153 cases out of the 684 battered women enrolled in the JRPs from 1991 to 1994 represent a typical cross-section of outcomes. Although some of the 531 remaining clients had not been out of shelter for more than three months and were therefore not eligible for inclusion in the study, the main reasons for collecting case studies of only 153 battered women were the limited resources available to the shelters and women's own reluctance to be tracked. The caseload carried by shelter case workers is tremendously high. In addition, the Department of Labor required the final evaluation within a tight time schedule that only allowed us to request twenty to twenty-five case studies from each of the seven shelter sites. Similar to other states, life in underfunded spouse abuse shelters in Kentucky is hectic, stressful, and not conducive to producing neat, clean studies with large [numerical] sizes.

Clients themselves informed the JRPs whether they wanted to be tracked. A significant number of women did not want to be tracked on leaving shelter and, when asked, told JRP staff of their reluctance. We might assume at first glance that the women willing to be tracked would also be more likely not to return to their abusers. If this were the case, then those women tracked would indeed be those more likely to report less revictimization. In reality, most women getting ready to exit shelters, whether enrolled in JRP programs or not, report that they have decided not to return. Nevertheless, most still return to abusers. In short, their agreement to be tracked by JRP staff does not mean that these women were any more likely to report lower rates of revictimization.

Even if all 684 women had been willing to be tracked, neither the KDVA nor the evaluators (ourselves) had the resources to track all 684. In addition, for various reasons clients lose contact with shelter personnel as they move on to new lives or return to their abusers. This is particularly so if clients move outside the regional area served by the shelter or even more so if women move out of state.

It might be objected that although we had requested case workers to write histories of "typical" cases, they could have offered the best possible picture of the program to ensure future funding. This possibility is unlikely for a number of reasons. First, the JRP was a demonstration grant funded by the U.S. Department of Labor for a set period of time (five years), and the staff knew this. Second, the case studies formed only a small, albeit important, qualitative part of the program. As evaluators for the 1992 to 1993 and 1993 to 1994 cycles of the grant, we conducted in-depth interviews with over 200 people involved in the program, including JRP clients, staff, and members of social service agencies who liaised with the JRP. Had the case studies been unrepresentative of the overall performance of the program, we would have easily picked up on it. Moreover, JRP staff knew in advance of our extensive evaluation and would have known that presenting more "favorable" cases would have easily been detected. Third, shelter directors, who knew of the grant's limited life, confirmed the representativeness of the 153 cases.

Our content analysis of cases focuses on the JRP services women received, whether they entered their own housing independent of their abusers, whether they resided with family members or friends independent of their abusers, whether they entered and retained jobs, and, whether they were revictimized. When battered women leave spouse abuse shelters they can be revictimized in a multitude of ways. They may be killed, raped, and assaulted, as well as subjected to a range of emotional abuse that is very difficult to quantify. In this chapter we use the term revictimization to refer to physical assaults that could result in the arrest of the perpetrator. We realize this obscures other forms of abuse that may in some ways be more damaging for some women. For example, batterers will revictimize women by failing to make support payments, or to make them on time, not returning children on time from visits with them, not turning up to take children after women have gotten children ready for a visit, and generally using the child custody issue to coerce women into compromises they might not otherwise make. Since we cannot easily track, quantify, and verify whether these forms of emotional abuse occurred, we do not focus on them in this study. In general, our definition encompasses those forms of physical and/or sexual abuse that could have resulted in criminal prosecution.

Of course, ascertaining patterns of victimization is problematic. It could be objected that battered women who enter the JRP program are less or more likely to report abuse than non-JRP battered women who pass through the shelter. JRP women often strike up deeper relationships with shelter staff and especially JRP staff. This may lead to a more candid disclosure of patterns of victimization. If this were the case, our measures of victimization might be artificially higher among JRP clients than among battered women in general, who perhaps do not develop such close relationships. However, our experience and conversations with shelter workers and JRP staff across the State of Kentucky tell us that a countereffect operates that works against JRP clients reporting abuse. Developing a close relationship with JRP staff might make it more difficult, rather than less, for JRP clients to report abuse. According to JRP staff, this under-reporting might occur because clients who often become very close to staff do not want to disappoint them by sharing later abuse. Clients may feel as though they are letting the JRP staff down by returning to their abuser. The JRP philosophy is one of nonjudgmental advocacy, and many sites report working extremely hard to let battered women know that they will support them whatever the outcome of their situation. Nevertheless, we would be remiss in not noting that we feel there are some occasions, perhaps not many, when JRP clients do not inform JRP staff of their revictimization.

Where case studies were not clear, we called JRP staff for clarification or more up-to-date information. In a dozen or so cases, we were able to verify that JRP graduates had not reported being revictimized for two or three years. We also relied upon the knowledge of legal advocates at the shelters, shelter directors at the seven sites, and other staff to fill in details. Shelter staff often knew of the outcome of a case and, for example, whether women had been revictimized, because they had seen them in court, read their names on court dockets for domestic violence court, or simply heard of ongoing abuse from other ex-shelter residents. In other words, wherever possible we took steps to go beyond the originally detailed case studies to clear up any inconsistencies or apparent anomalies.

FINDINGS

Demographic Profile of the JRP Clients

As noted above, it would have been nice to control for certain demographic characteristics of the JRP clients. Since such a control is not possible, we provide summary demographics of all 684 cases to provide readers with a broad appreciation of the demographic features of all the women who passed through the JRP from 1991 to 1994, JRP clients had the following characteristics:

- Average age was 31.85 years;
- 78.1 percent were Caucasian, 18 percent African American, 0.8 percent Asian or Pacific Islanders, 1.4 percent Hispanic, 1.1 percent American Indian or Alaskan Natives, 0.6 "other";
- 28.4 percent were married, 32.2 percent separated from their husbands, 19 percent single, and 19.7 percent divorced;
- 63.3 percent had children aged six and over;
- 40.4 percent had high school diplomas, 21.6 percent GEDs, 16 percent vocational certificates, and 2.4 percent college degrees;
- 16.3 percent were employed, 77 percent unemployed, and 6.7 percent not in the wage-earning labor force. Nearly all of the women had worked for wages at some time in their lives (96.7 percent); and
- 42.9 percent were service workers, 13 percent laborers, 12 percent marketing/sales, and 9.9 percent technical or support staff.

Statistical Analysis of JRP Service Delivery and Revictimization

Our analysis of the 153 cases indicates that all battered women who participated in the JRP took advantage of job training and services, 67.3 percent of participants secured employment (see table 23.2), and 85.6 percent of clients secured housing and lived independently of their abusers (see table 23.1). Perhaps most significantly, 82 percent of battered women experienced no revictimization.

An analysis of the 125 clients out of 153 who experienced no revictimization revealed the following:

- Ninety-eight of these clients had independent housing and jobs and were not living with family or friends.

Table 23.1. Cross-tabulations for Victimization by Housing Situation

| HOUSING SITUATION | VICTIMIZATION | | ROW TOTAL | |
	CONTINUED VICTIMIZATION	NO FURTHER VICTIMIZATION		
Living separate	9	122	131	Count
from abuser	32.14	97.60	. . .	Column %
	6.87	93.13	85.62	Row %
Living with abuser	19	3	22	Count
	67.86	2.40	. . .	Column %
	86.36	13.64	14.38	Row %
	28	125	153	Column
	18.30	81.70	100.00	Total

Note: Chi Square = 124.8; D.F. = 1; p < .001

Table 23.2. Cross-tabulations for Victimization by Employment Status

| EMPLOYMENT STATUS | VICTIMIZATION | | ROW TOTAL | |
	CONTINUED VICTIMIZATION	NO FURTHER VICTIMIZATION		
Placed in employment	8	95	103	Count
	28.57	76.00	. . .	Column %
	7.77	92.23	67.32	Row %
Not placed in	20	30	50	Count
employment	71.43	24.00	. . .	Column %
	40.00	60.00	32.68	Row %
	28	125	153	Column
	18.30	81.70	100.00	Total

Note: Chi Square = 23.39; D.F. = 1; p < .001

- Twenty-four clients acquired housing, but were not employed.
- Two had jobs and were living independently of their abusers either with family or friends.
- One had completed the JRP and had no housing independent of the abuser and no job.

Table 23.1 shows that those women who live separately from their abusers are significantly less likely to be revictimized than women who remain with their abusers. Of those women who secure independent housing, 97.6 percent report no further victimization. Conversely, of those women who return to their abuser, 86.4 percent report further victimization. These findings strongly suggest that providing independent housing arrangements to formerly battered women has a profound effect on their revictimization.

Data reported in table 23.2 indicate that women who secure employment are significantly less likely to experience further battering from their abuser. Seventy-six percent of the women who were employed as a result of the JRP

Table 23.3. Logit Coefficients for Regression for Revictimization on Independent Variables: Housing and Employment

INDEPENDENT VARIABLES	MODEL
Constant	2.24**
	(.68)
Housing	−4.05**
	(.73)
Employment	−1.26*
	(.62)
Number of observations	153

* $p < .05$ (two-tailed test)
** $p < .001$ (two-tailed test)
Note: Numbers in parentheses are standard errors. Revictimization is coded so that negative coefficients indicate a higher level of the independent variable is associated with the decreased odds of being revictimized.

report no further victimization. On the other hand, among the women not able to secure employment, 40 percent were revictimized. Although not as significant as independent housing, employment is still an important factor in whether women are victims of further violence.

Additional analysis reveals patterns related to employment, housing, and further victimization:

- Of the ninety-eight women who were able to acquire housing independent of their abuser (that is, not with friends or family) and found employment, ninety-three (95 percent) experienced no further victimization.
- Of the thirty-three women who secured independent housing but no job, twenty-nine (88 percent) experienced no further victimization.
- Only five women who indicated they were living with their abuser were able to secure and retain jobs. Three of these five were revictimized.
- Seventeen women returned to live with their abuser and could not find employment. All but one (94 percent) experienced further victimization.

To test the independent effects of housing and employment (independent variables) upon revictimization (dependent variable), we ran a logistical regression analysis. As table 23.3 indicates, independent housing and job placement both have statistically significant and independent effects on the likelihood of reduced victimization. In other words, securing independent housing and employment significantly reduce one's chances of experiencing further victimization. This result further strengthens our findings by showing these two variables (independent housing and employment) have important independent effects in the model.

The absence of revictimization associated with the acquisition of both independent housing and jobs suggests that provision of these services is a powerful mechanism for preventing the revictimization of battered women. Having housing (with no job) is more closely associated with no victimization than having a job (with no housing). This suggests that placing women in independent housing apart from their abusers and with all the support that this entails is a more powerful way of reducing or preventing their future victimization. Women who found independent housing for themselves and/or their families appear to have made a cleaner and more decisive break with their abusive pasts.

We can only speculate on why the acquisition of employment is a less powerful mechanism for reducing revictimization than the procurement of independent housing. The world of work clearly discriminates against women. Many JRP women enter low-paid jobs. For many, the ability to hold down any kind of employment is a real achievement. However, for some, the rigors of the workplace and especially the low wages, combined with the demands of single parenthood, are too much. In these cases some JRP clients clearly calculate that receiving welfare support and spending more time with their children is more beneficial to their long-term safety than remaining in paid employment. If we add to this some of the other hostilities in the workplace, such as sexual harassment, then the gendered capitalist workplace may be too threatening for some battered women at this critical juncture in their lives. A significant number of women reported experiencing sexual harassment in their new-found jobs, particularly if they entered nontraditional settings for women (for example, construction work). In addition, if abusers found out where JRP clients were working they sometimes harassed women in their workplaces. This observation is consistent with the literature on the workplace harassment of women by abusive partners or ex-partners (see, for example, Stark and Flitcraft, 1996: 128) and may go some way toward explaining why the provision of employment alone seems to have less of a preventive effect than the acquisition of independent housing.

It is significant that of the large number of women who secured housing apart from their abusers, very few allowed the abusers back into their homes. This is strong evidence that women are not masochistic and will not flock back to abusers if given half a chance. In fact, the JRP case studies are a tribute to the resistance, ingenuity, and emotional reserves of battered women (see also Stanko, 1996: 54; Stark and Flitcraft, 1996: 164). Our findings, like those of other authors, are inconsistent with the victim-blaming themes that undercut the ideology of learned helplessness.

CASE STUDY ILLUSTRATIONS OF THE STATISTICAL DATA

From our analysis of these cases and our extensive contact with the spouse abuse shelter movement in Kentucky, we know that most Kentucky women who leave violent men have some contact with those men after leaving a spouse abuse shelter. From our analysis of the case studies and from our conversations with shelter directors, it appears that battered women who have been through JRPs are better equipped to defend themselves against the controlling tactics of their abusers. This resilience seems to stem from several factors. First, JRP women tend to have closer contacts with shelter staff and are more willing to call for support. Second, they are more likely to resort to evasive tactics to resist his controlling initiatives. For example, one shelter director reported that JRP women were more likely to buy answer phones to avoid conversations with ex-abusers. The enhancement of battered women's resistance through structural supports such as the JRPs is difficult to track quantitatively, but it clearly requires more systematic research.

We now present a selection of edited excerpts from the 153 case studies to illustrate how the JRP structurally affects the lives of battered women.

Basic Needs

In all cases the JRP confronts the basic needs of clients. The provision of basic needs precedes and often prefaces entry into paid employment. For example: W.J. and her two sons had nothing but the clothes on their backs when they arrived at the shelter.

> She received clothing from the shelter clothes closet and the boys received school clothing and shoes from the Board of Education. When N.J. first came to shelter, referrals to DSS for food stamps and AFDC were made immediately. Clothing was made available to N.J. from the shelter clothes closet.

Job Training/Search/Placement

As noted above, once women's basic survival needs have been met, the JRP staff begins the process of training battered women for employment. The following cases illustrate the provision of job-training services:

> R.B. was talented at typing and practiced in the shelter. She was enthusiastic about working, saying that she loved to work and was comfortable working. R.B.'s concerns at intake included the need for training in word processing/WordPerfect to enhance her secretarial skills. She expressed great interest in computer training. R.B.'s progress was strong. She found a great job at a law firm making $7.50 per hour.

> F.J. participated in workshops such as resume writing, interviewing skills, job retention, and job search. F.J. found employment as a program aide at a residential facility for mildly to severely retarded adults. She started work in June 1991 and is still employed at this facility.

> The JRP assisted T.G. in establishing her business. She cleans residential and commercial buildings and new construction sites. The JRP paid part of her tuition for college.

> W.B. has worked in a number of nontraditional jobs such as garbage collection, truck driver, construction worker, and security guard. She decided that she

would like to stay away from these types of positions because they cause quite a bit of friction between herself and the male workers. W.B. was referred to a cleaning company and has worked there since January 1992. She is doing such a good job that the owners have offered her a partnership.

Support Services

These services are offered to assist in the process of finding and retaining work. As noted above, these services take many forms, including transportation, provision of meals, clothing, personal needs, life skills, childcare, and self-esteem building workshops.

The JRP purchased W.J. suitable shoes for work and provided transportation until she could receive her Kentucky driver's license, auto insurance, and tags. The JRP provided funds to remove this barrier to transportation by paying these costs for the client. The program also assisted her with childcare and legal advocacy.

E.E. is a forty-two-year-old woman who enrolled in the JRP while in transitional housing. Her goal originally was to save enough money to relocate out of state. E.E. attended JRP workshops and significantly upgraded her skills in computer training. Her main barrier to employment was transportation. While E.E. was in transitional housing, her van was vandalized. The insurance on the van was in her husband's name, and he refused to file her claim. We assisted E.E. as she went through the divorce process and had the insurance changed to her name. We used JRP money to make repairs on her van and to help her rent an alternate vehicle to maintain the job while the van was being repaired.

M.M. came into the shelter with two small children fleeing from an abusive, alcoholic husband. She needed affordable housing, a means of support, childcare while attending A.A. meetings, and a chance to formulate her goals for the future. M.M. only needed the funds for one semester of college to receive a degree in English. Since she had defaulted on a student loan in 1987 when she was having trouble with alcoholism, she was not eligible for any student loans or grants. Many resources for college funding were checked, but none worked out. The JRP assisted M.M. in moving to a small town where she got a job at a restaurant. . . . She will begin taking one class at a time to finish her degree while still looking for funding. Her husband has gone through treatment for alcoholism, but they have not reunited. Placement funds for M.M. were used for rent/telephone deposits, car insurance, and childcare while at A.A. M.M. still attends the JRP monthly support group meetings.

While JRPs do not offer legal advice to clients, the programs have developed an extensive system of networks with a variety of legal organizations. For example:

C.S. decided to file for a divorce and needed assistance. She was referred to Legal Aid. Legal Aid is a major linkage that is used by the shelter. Legal Aid will handle divorces at no fee for the women if they are low income.

Likewise in the arena of emotional support, although JRP staff offer invaluable help, the program has a number of linkages with professional mental health agencies that clients can be referred to. For example:

> C.P. was referred to the mental health center for her depression. Clients are referred to this agency when they need counseling on issues other than domestic violence.

Housing

The unavailability of affordable housing is a major structural problem in the United States caused by a failure to build low-income housing and the general drift toward low-income jobs (see Kozol, 1988). This lack of affordable housing is a particularly acute problem for battered women. JRP assistance with obtaining housing does not just mean finding clients safe and affordable housing. Other services must be provided to help clients through this difficult transition to living in their own home. The following examples illustrate some of these points.

> S.S. has used her new salary to get an apartment of her own, and JRP purchased beds for her children. Recently she had a phone installed and this weekend will be buying a car.

> After gaining employment, the JRP program assisted W.J. in obtaining Section 8 housing by issuing her a housing voucher for the local Housing Authority.

> Because of T.K.'s credit problems, it was difficult to find affordable housing. At one point, she was offered low-income housing, only to find that she had to deny it due to the location. The JRP helped T.K. and her son find housing in a private apartment complex. The JRP staff have assisted T.K. with rent, bus tokens, and transportation.

> T.D. did not qualify for public or Section 8 housing and was given a list of landlords by the JRP employment counselor. From that list, T.D. was able to obtain affordable housing. She was assisted with rent and utility deposits by the JRP. She was also able to get furniture from the shelter's furniture shed.

Victimization

In the following excerpts from JRP case studies, no revictimization of clients is evident. In these examples, the lack of revictimization is associated with clients having established themselves in work and independent housing apart from their abusers.

> R. was forced to walk away from a position as a customer service supervisor with a large department store chain in order to escape her abusive situation. She and her six children transferred to our spouse abuse shelter because her husband had learned of her whereabouts at the previous shelter. R. is highly motivated and able to take advantage of the opportunities available to her. She

has landed a job as a sales associate with a clothing store and took a second job. With independent housing she has remained separate from her abuser and stays in touch with JRP staff.

P.T. left her abusive husband of twelve years after two years of unsuccessful counseling. Her husband contacted her and became verbally abusive when she refused plans for reunification, erasing any hopes she may have had that he would change. P.T. continues to live independently and currently works at a local women's apparel store. She remains in contact with the JRP staff and attends evening support groups.

In cases where JRP clients are revictimized, there are usually multiple barriers, including primarily the failure to acquire independent housing and employment. For example:

S.J. came to the JRP with severe injuries from an attack by her abuser. She had a possible skull fracture and had to wear a neck brace for months. S.J. has completed treatment for a substance abuse problem and has completed the job training workshops, but has not been able to search for employment due to her severe injuries. She has returned to the abusive relationship.

There are other barriers that work against women retaining jobs. One such barrier is sexual harassment in the workplace. For example:

J.T. came into the shelter reporting severe abuse by her husband. Her husband refused to let her go to the doctor, use utilities, or eat food unless he was witnessing it. He also kept her from seeing friends and family and pulled guns on her. After gaining employment J.T. was sexually harassed at work by a coworker. She threatened to quit and was encouraged to report the incident to her supervisor and the police. She reported it to the supervisor, and the man was only reprimanded. During this time J.T. had found an apartment. However, after working two weeks, J.T. went back to her abuser.

In rare cases it is clear that the acquisition of a job and an independent living situation still cannot prevent future victimization. For example:

After completing the JRP, S.E. found full-time work in a supermarket. She found an efficiency apartment and moved from the shelter. S.E. reported that her abuser was still in jail but had sent a few of his friends to her apartment to give her a message. The two men broke into her apartment and threatened her with a gun. They also beat and raped her. S.E. did not report this latest incident to the police due to fear for her life. She has now vacated her apartment and is living with friends.

S.A. had acquired independent housing and was living with her child. She had found stable employment. Her abusive ex-husband arranged for two people (a man and a woman who had lived in a local spouse abuse shelter for a while) to murder the ex-wife. The ex-husband arranged to visit the child at the time of the murder, thus providing himself with an alibi. The two hired killers decapitated the wife. The perpetrators were paid $200 by the ex-husband. All three killers are now incarcerated on first-degree murder charges, and the child is living with a grandparent.

MAKING THEORETICAL SENSE OF THE EFFECTS OF JRPs ON REVICTIMIZATION

The battered women who form the subject of this study are working class and poor. The gendered capitalist workplace offers them, and most other women, low-paying jobs. Their ongoing brutalization is often accompanied by extreme isolation from friends and family. Many of them earn little money and often do not work for wages. They are usually heavily dependent upon their batterers for economic support. In rural areas of the state, this dependence is compounded by geographical isolation, a sociocultural milieu that dictates highly stereotypical roles for women, and a dislocation from the potentially supportive institutions of the state (see Websdale, 1995a, 1995b). We have argued that the plight of battered women in Kentucky's shelters is deeply rooted in the social disadvantage of women.

There is evidence to suggest that battering is more prevalent among working-class and poorer families. The argument has been made that men at the disadvantaged end of the class hierarchy take out their hostility and alienation on their wives. These men may have little control over their work lives, but they can at least coerce their wives into submission. Elizabeth Wilson (1983) argues that in times of economic stress and higher unemployment, men in lower classes express their frustrations through spousal abuse. The disadvantaged/marginalized men in the system of capitalist class relations have a tendency above and beyond their socialization as men in general to resort to violence. In other words, the degradation, demoralization, and alienation of class oppression confound existing gender power relations that "legitimately" posit women as the objects of male control and, in extreme cases, male violence. Wilson's position is supported by the work of Gelles (1974) and Straus and colleagues (1980), who found twice as much domestic violence in blue-collar than in white-collar families. They found that families living below the poverty line were five times more likely than families in the highest income brackets to engage in acts of domestic violence. When it comes to severe violence, Straus, Gelles, and Steinmetz (1980) found that spousal assault is twice as likely among unemployed men, compared with men who are in full-time employment. Likewise, Eisenhower (1969) reported that women who lived in families with an annual income of less than $6,000 in 1967 reported being raped three to five times more often.

As noted, the JRPs cut to the heart of both class and gender power relations for this group of batterers and their victims. If battered women are provided with both outside economic and emotional support, roughly 70 percent express a keen interest in living apart from their abuser and less than 30 percent see couples, individual, or family counseling as viable alternatives (Fleming, 1979: 178–179). This finding is supported by the JRPs, which show women to be keen to change their situation. These findings tell us that the long-term solution to battering must include major structural interventions that remain cognizant of the way in which both poverty and patriarchy intersect to keep women in violent relationships.

We suspect from our observations in Kentucky and numerous conversations with shelter workers that middle-class battered women do not use the shelter or criminal systems very often. Middle-class women have other resources and husbands may strategize more carefully before using violence as a control mechanism. These observations are borne out by other research data. For example, Baumgartner's (1985) field research in a New York suburb revealed a reluctance on the part of middle-class couples to use the legal system to solve intramarital strife.

It is not our intent to enter the debate as to whether woman battering occurs with equal frequency and/or severity in all social classes (for examples of this position for certain forms of woman battering, see Russell, 1990; Pizzey, 1974). Rather, our focus is firmly on the working-class women in Kentucky shelters who seem to benefit from the JRPs. Consequently, we argue that the JRP reduces revictimization, in part by confronting the imbalance of power between the spouses. As Kalmuss and Straus (1982) have suggested, the more dependent women are upon men, the more vulnerable they are to extreme battery. Empowering women through extending opportunities to acquire independent housing, employment, independent living skills, educational opportunities, and a range of other support services will confront this power differential.

There is another perhaps more commonsense reason why JRPs reduce the revictimization of battered women who pass through Kentucky shelters. The "routine activities" approach in criminology argues that crime rates are often affected by the opportunity to commit crime. Cohen and Felson argue that "most criminal acts require a convergence in space and time of likely offender, suitable targets, and the absence of capable guardians" (1979: 588).

Cohabiting (mostly married) heterosexual couples, the focus of this chapter, coexist in a milieu that is characterized by the convergence that Cohen and Felson refer to. The offender has the time and the confined space (the home) and absence of adequate guardianship (criminal justice intervention) that increase the likelihood of violence against women. Cohen and Felson found that crime rates were related to the proportion of female-headed households and/or the proportion of households where husbands and wives worked outside the home. Our research concurs with theirs, but takes a different turn as well. By joining the labor force, or living independently with or without children, the JRP women in our study may indeed be more exposed to what Cohen and Felson call "predatory crime." However, it is our argument that the greatest threat to the safety of these women comes from the "predator" in their own home, rather than the burglar who may burglarize her house just because she is now living alone or is out at work. As Cohen and Felson stress, the routine activity approach "specifies that household and family activities entail lower risk of criminal victimization than non-household non-family activities" (Cohen and Felson, 1979: 594).

Many researchers have shown that women have most to fear from the men they know and are in intimate relationships with (see Russell, 1990; Stanko, 1982). Our work on woman battering in Kentucky is consistent with this research. The "commonsense" logic of the routine activities approach is therefore redundant when it comes to assessing the risk of further revictimization for JRP clients. These women seem to have the most to gain in terms of personal safety by living independently of their abusers and finding paid employment.

CONCLUSIONS AND POLICY IMPLICATIONS: MOVING TOWARD MULTIFACETED PREVENTIVE APPROACHES

Much of the debate about solutions to the problem of woman battering has narrowly focused on criminal justice strategies such as mandatory arrest. Woman battering is not solely, or even primarily, a problem that is amenable to criminal justice solutions. Criminal justice solutions sometimes temporarily remove batterers from the family. In most cases he returns to that unchanged family environment and often engages in further acts of violence. Strategies such as mandatory arrest alone will not stem the tide of violence against women within families.

Our data show that the Kentucky JRPs, and especially the provision of independent housing and the acquisition of employment (with the latter contributing to a lesser, but still highly significant, degree), reduce the revictimization of battered women residing in the JRP shelters. We contend that this structural intervention is potentially more powerful than the approach of criminal justice systems, which are limited to astructural interventions such as arrest, conviction, incarceration, and/or counseling. As noted, all of these criminal justice "solutions" ignore or downplay the social generation of crime. Theoretically, we have explained the preventive impact of the JRPs largely in terms of empowering women to move beyond their violent relationships. Battered women in Kentucky often find themselves trapped in these abusive relationships, not because they suffer from learned helplessness or battered woman syndrome, but because of structural forces such as poverty, low educational qualifications, no childcare options, no safe affordable alternative housing, and little enthusiasm on the part of most judges or police to incapacitate batterers long enough to provide women with time to think through their options. In addition to our argument that the JRPs reduce revictimization because they empower women structurally, we also find that, up to a point, the routine activities approach in criminology helps explain the lowering of revictimization.

The documented evidence from the JRP case studies strongly suggests that a multifaceted community response is potentially a much more effective way of reducing or preventing the revictimization of battered women. Woman battering is a wide-ranging social problem that has at its heart the intersecting power relations of gender and class. We contend that such a problem must be comprehensively addressed by interagency cooperative efforts that strike at the disadvantageous position of women in abusive relationships. Woman battering must not be seen astructurally as a criminal justice problem, but rather structurally as an economic, public health, labor, housing, human rights, and educational issue.

Our findings suggest that much more funding should be made available for preventive programs that change the structural conditions affecting battered women's options concerning leaving violent familial relationships. The implications of our research go well beyond developing structural interventions to reduce the revictimization of battered women. If the power imbalance between men and women in abusive relationships can be effectively altered and revictimization subsequently reduced, then is it not reasonable to suggest that by moving toward equality for women in their relationships with men that we might lower the outbreak of woman battering in the first place? Put simply, if structural interventions can reduce revictimization, why shouldn't they lower initial victimization?

REFERENCES

Bachman, Ronet. 1992. Crime in nonmetropolitan America: A national accounting of trends, incidence rates, and idiosyncratic vulnerabilities. *Rural Sociology* 57(4): 546–560.

Baumgartner, M. P. 1985. Law and the middle class: Evidence from a suburban town. *Law and Human Behavior* 9(1): 3–24.

Breines, W., and L. Godon. 1983. The new scholarship on family violence. *Signs: Journal of Women in Culture and Society* 8: 490–531.

Browne, Angela. 1987. *When Battered Women Kill.* New York: Free Press.

Bushy, Angeline. 1993. Rural women: Lifestyle and health status. *Rural Nursing* 28(1): 187–197.

Cohen, Lawrence, and Marcus Felson. 1979. Social change and crime rate trends: A routine activity approach. *American Sociological Review* 44 (August): 588–608.

Currens, S., et al. 1991. Homicide followed by suicide—Kentucky, 1985–1990. *CDC Morbidity and Mortality Weekly Report* 40(38, September 27): 652–659.

Dawson, John M., and Patrick A. Langan. 1994. *Murder in Families.* U.S. Department of Justice, Bureau of Justice Statistics Special Report. Washington, D.C.: U.S. Government Printing Office.

Delphy, Christine. 1984. *Close to Home.* London: Hutchinson.

Dobash, R. Emerson, and Russell Dobash. 1979. *Violence Against Wives.* New York: Free Press.

Dobash, Russell P., R. Emerson Dobash, Margo Wilson, and Martin Daly. 1992. The myth of sexual symmetry in marital violence. *Social Problems* 39(1, February): 71–90.

Dutton, D. G. 1986. The outcome of court-mandated treatment for wife assault: A quasi-experimental evaluation. *Violence and Victims* 1(3): 163–175.

Edleson, J., and R. Grusznski. 1988. Treating men who batter: Four years of outcome data from the Domestic Abuse Project. *Journal of Social Service Research* 12: 3–22.

Eisenhower, Milton S. 1969. *To Establish Justice, To Ensure Domestic Tranquility.* Final Report of the National Commission of the Causes and Prevention of Violence. Washington, D.C.: Government Printing Office.

Ferraro, Kathleen. 1993. Cops, courts, and woman battering. In Pauline Bart and Eileen Geil Moran, eds., *Violence Against Women: The Bloody Footprints.* Newbury Park, Calif.: Sage, 165–176.

Fleming, Jennifer Baker. 1979. *Stopping Wife Abuse.* New York: Anchor Books.

Gagne, Patricia L. 1992. Appalachian women: Violence and social control. *Journal of Contemporary Ethnography* 20(4, January): 387–415.

Garner, Joel, Jeffrey Fagan, and Christopher Maxwell. 1995. Published findings from the Spouse Assault Replication Program: A critical review. *Journal of Quantitative Criminology* 11(1): 3–28.

Gelles, Richard J. 1974. *The Violent Home*. Newbury Park, Calif.: Sage.

Hamberger, L. K., and J. E. Hastings. 1988. Skills training for treatment of spouse abusers: An outcome study. *Journal of Family Violence* 3: 121–131.

Harrell, A. 1991. Evaluation of court-ordered treatment for domestic violence offenders (final report). Washington, D.C.: Urban Institute.

Jones, Ann. 1994. *Next Time She'll Be Dead: Battering and How to Stop It*. Boston, Mass.: Beacon Press.

Kalmuss, D., and M. Straus. 1982. Wife's marital dependency and wife abuse. *Journal of Marriage and Family* 44: 277–286.

Kentucky Domestic Violence Association (KDVA). 1989. Report on marital rape in Kentucky. Kentucky.

Kozol, Johnathan. 1988. *Rachel and Her Children: Homeless Families in America*. New York: Crown Publishers.

Langan, P., and C. Innes. 1986. *Preventing Domestic Violence Against Wives*. Washington, D.C.: Bureau of Justice Statistics, U.S. Department of Justice.

Louisville Courier-Journal. 1991. Home violence called common. Wednesday, October 23: A1, A6.

Oakley, Ann. 1974. *The Sociology of Housework*. Oxford: Martin Robertson.

Pizzey, Erin. 1974. *Scream Quietly or the Neighbors Will Hear*. Harmondsworth: Penguin.

Russell, Diana. 1990. *Rape in Marriage*. Bloomington: Indiana University Press.

Schulman, Mark A. 1979. *A Survey of Spousal Violence Against Women in Kentucky*. Washington, D.C.: U.S. Department of Justice, U.S. Government Printing Office.

Sherman, Lawrence. 1992. *Policing Domestic Violence: Experiments and Dilemmas*. New York: Free Press.

Stanko, Elizabeth A. 1996. Reading danger: Sexual harassment, anticipation, and self-protection. In Marianne Hester, Liz Kelly, and Jill Radford, eds., *Women, Violence, and Male Power*. Buckingham: Open University Press, 50–62.

———. 1982. Would you believe this woman? In N. H. Rafter and E. A. Stanko, eds., *Judge, Lawyer, Victim, Thief: Women, Gender Roles, and Criminal Justice*. Boston: Northeastern University Press.

Stark, Evan. 1994. Should police officers be required to arrest abusive husbands? *Health* (September): 32.

———. 1993. Mandatory arrest of batterers: A reply to its critics. *American Behavioral Scientist* 36(5): 651–680.

Stark, Evan, and Anne Flitcraft. 1996. *Women at Risk: Domestic Violence and Women's Health*. London: Sage.

Straus, Murray A. 1977. A sociological perspective on the prevention and treatment of wife beating. In Maria Roy, ed., *Battered Women*. New York: Van Nostrand, 194–238.

Straus, Murray A., Richard J. Gelles, and Suzanne K. Steinmetz. 1980. *Behind Closed Doors: Violence in the American Family*. New York: Doubleday/Anchor.

Tifft, Larry L. 1993. *Battering of Women: The Failure of Intervention and the Case for Prevention*. Boulder, Colo.: Westview Press.

Walby, Sylvia. 1990. *Theorizing Patriarchy*. Cambridge, Mass.: Basil Blackwell.

Walker, Lenore. 1979. *The Battered Woman*. New York: Harper and Row.

Websdale, Neil. 1995a. An ethnographic assessment of the policing of domestic violence in rural eastern Kentucky. *Social Justice* 22(1): 82–102.

———. 1995b. Rural woman abuse: The voices of Kentucky women. *Violence Against Women* 1(4): 309–339.

Websdale, Neil, and Byron Johnson. 1997. The policing of domestic violence in rural and urban areas: The voices of battered women in Kentucky. *Policing and Society* 6: 297–317.

Wilson, Elizabeth. 1983. *What Is to Be Done About Violence Against Women?* Harmondsworth: Penguin.

Wilson, Elizabeth, and M. Daly. 1992. Who kills whom in spouse killings? On the exceptional sex ratio of spousal homicides in the United States. *Criminology* 30(2): 189–215.

CHAPTER **24**

ANDREA SMITH

Looking to the Future

Domestic Violence, Women of Color, the State, and Social Change

———————————— ABSTRACT ————————————

In this final chapter, Andrea Smith thinks "outside the box" as she suggests strategies to end domestic violence that must deal simultaneously with the reality of structural as well as state violence, especially state violence within the criminal justice system. She brings us full circle as she argues that one cannot look to the criminal justice system for safety because state violence is intimately connected to domestic violence, in short, the state cannot be relied on to heal domestic violence. Thus, she asserts, if we truly put poor women of color at the center of our analysis, as Coker (chapter 22) and Richie (chapter 4) before her suggest, then we are forced to reconsider the current remedial violence models that rely on social service programs and criminal justice interventions.

At the same time, a currently popular alternative model, Restorative Justice, often proffered as a model to address domestic violence, has its own serious limitations because it lacks accountability to survivors' needs. Andrea Smith argues that battered women need to be part of a grassroots community organizing effort—a movement for social change—to *end* domestic violence, not simply to receive services, even culturally competent services, in marginalized communities, especially those of color.

Andrea Smith then explores alternative strategies that articulate several principles by using models from other countries and communities that do not and/or cannot depend on the police to solve domestic violence. These strategies call for interventions that address state violence and interpersonal violence simultaneously, emphasize base-building approaches which define domestic violence survivors as organizers or potential organizers rather than simply "victims" or "clients," develop community accountability strategies based not on romanticized notions of "community" but rather that ensure safety for survivors, and, finally, build transnational relationships in the fight to end violence against all women.

Women of color live in the dangerous intersections of gender and race. Within the mainstream anti-violence movement in the United States, women of color who survive sexual or domestic abuse are often told that they must pit themselves against their communities, often portrayed stereotypically as violent, to begin the healing process.[1] Communities of color, meanwhile, often advocate that women keep silent about the sexual and domestic violence in order to maintain a united front against racism. Therefore, the analysis proposed in this chapter argues for the need to adopt anti-violence strategies that are mindful of the larger structures of violence that shape the world in which we live. That is, strategies designed to combat violence within communities (sexual/domestic violence) must be linked to strategies that combat violence directed against communities, including state violence (for example, police brutality, prisons, militarism, racism, colonialism, and economic exploitation).

The traditional or mainstream remedies for addressing sexual and domestic violence here in the United States have proven inadequate for addressing the problems of gender violence in general, but particularly for addressing violence against women of color. The problem is not simply an issue of providing multicultural services to survivors of violence. Rather, the analysis and strategies around addressing gender violence have failed to address the manner in which gender violence is not simply a tool of patriarchal control but also serves as a tool of racism, economic oppression, and colonialism. That is, colonial relationships as well as race and class relations are themselves gendered and sexualized (see Incite!–Critical Resistance, chapter 8).

Within the context of colonization, racism, and class oppression, sexual and domestic violence do not affect men and women of color in the same way. However, when a woman of color suffers abuse, this abuse is not just an attack on her identity as a woman, her identity as a person of color. The issues of colonial, race, class, and gender oppression cannot be separated. Women of color do not just face quantitatively more issues when they suffer violence (for example, less supportive media attention, greater language barriers, lack of support in the judicial system), but their experience is qualitatively different from that of white women. Hence, the strategies employed to address violence against women of color must take into account their particular histories and current conditions of violence.

BEYOND THE POLITICS OF INCLUSION AND
CULTURAL COMPETENCY

As the anti-violence movement has attempted to become more "inclusive," attempts at multicultural interventions against domestic violence have unwittingly strengthened white supremacy within the anti-violence movement. That is, all too often, inclusivity has come to mean that the "domestic violence model," which developed largely with the interests of white middleclass women in mind, should simply add a multicultural component to it. Anti-violence multicultural curricula are often the same as those produced by mainstream groups with some "cultural" designs or references added to this preexisting model. Models for most domestic violence programs servicing communities of color do not dramatically differ from the mainstream models, except for "community outreach workers" or bilingual staff. Women of color are constantly called upon to provide domestic violence service providers "cultural sensitivity programs" where we are supposed to explain our cultures, sometimes in thirty minutes or less. Even with longer trainings (for example, forty one-hour meetings), only one or two of those hours are devoted to "cultural diversity." The naive assumption is that "the culture" of people of color is something simple, easy to understand, requires little or no substantive engagements with communities, and is homogeneous. Furthermore, those people who are marginalized even *within* communities of color, such as lesbian, gay, bisexual and transgendered (LGBT) or queer people, sex workers, or addicts, are often marginalized within these "cultural" representations.

Of course, many women of color in domestic violence programs have been active in expanding notions of "cultural competency" to be more politicized, less simplistic, and less dependent on the notion of culture as a static concept. However, cultural competency, no matter how reenvisioned, is limited in its ability to create a movement that truly addresses the needs of women of color because the lives and histories of women of color call on us to radically rethink all models currently developed for addressing domestic violence.

An alternative approach to "inclusion" is to place women of color at the center of the organization and analysis of domestic violence. That is, we do not assume what a domestic violence *program* should look like; we ask instead: What would it take *to end violence against women of color*? What would this movement look like? What if we do not presume that this movement would necessarily have anything we take for granted in the current domestic violence movement? And in fact, Beth E. Richie suggests we need to go beyond just centering our analysis on women of color. Rather, she suggests: What if we centered our attention on those abused women most marginalized within the category of "women of color"? This is of utmost importance because it is within this context, she argues, that we must ultimately "be accountable not to those in power, but to the powerless."[2]

BEYOND THE SHELTER SYSTEM

In "Disloyal to Feminism," Emi Koyama (2002) suggests some possible ramifications of locating women of color, particularly women of color who have been criminalized by the state, such as sex workers, at the center of our analysis and work. Koyama notes that some components of what we now see as integral to a domestic violence program would not necessarily be a strategy we might want to continue to adopt. In particular, she critiques the "shelter system" as mirroring the abusive patterns of control that women seek to leave in battering relationships and isolates women from their communities. Thus, as Isabel Gonzalez of Sista II Sista (a young women's community-based organization in Brooklyn, New York) argues, the domestic violence shelter system is often modeled on a pattern similar to the prison system: women's activities are monitored and policed, and they are cut off from their friends and families.[3] In fact, some shelters have gone so far as to conduct background searches on clients and having them arrested if they have outstanding warrants, despite the fact that these outstanding warrants are often the direct result of escaping abusive relationships. As Jael Silliman notes, many anti-violence activists in other countries do not rely on shelters as their primary strategy to address violence. Rather than assume that the absence of a shelter system signals "underdevelopment," perhaps these countries employ strategies from which we can learn.[4] (See Recommendations below.)

When we center women of color in the analysis, it becomes clear that we must develop approaches that address interpersonal, state (for example, colonization, police brutality, prisons), and structural (for example, racism, poverty) violence simultaneously. In addition, we find that by centering women of color in the analysis, we may actually build a movement that more effectively ends violence not just for women of color but for all people.

DISCUSSING POSSIBLE REMEDIES

The Need to Anchor Violence against Women in Larger Systems of Racism, Colonialism, and Inequality

The anti-violence movement has always contested the notion of home as a safe place because the majority of violence that women suffer happens at home. Furthermore, the notion that violence happens "out there," inflicted by the stranger in the dark alley, makes it difficult to recognize that the home is in fact the place of greatest danger for women. Ironically, however, the strategies that the domestic violence movement employs to address violence are actually premised on the danger coming from "out there" rather than at home. That is, reliance on the criminal justice system to address gender violence would make sense if the threat was posed by just a few crazed men whom we can lock up. But the prison system is not equipped to address a violent culture in which an overwhelming number of people batter their partners, unless we are prepared to imprison tens of millions of people.

Furthermore, state violence in the form of the criminal justice system cannot provide true safety for women, particularly women of color, when it is directly implicated in the violence women face as described previously. Unfortunately, the remedies that have been pursued by the mainstream anti-violence movement have often had the effect of strengthening rather than opposing state violence. Thus, for example, the anti-sexual/domestic violence movements have been vital in breaking the silence around violence against women and providing critically needed services to survivors of sexual and domestic violence. However, these movements have also become increasingly professionalized around providing services and, consequently, are often reluctant to address sexual and domestic violence within the larger context of institutionalized violence (Schecter, 1982; Meyers, 2001). Many state coalitions on domestic/sexual violence, by arguing that this issue is not a sexual/domestic violence issue, have refused to take stands against the anti-immigration backlash and its violent impact on immigrant women. As the immigration backlash intensifies, many immigrant women do not report abuse for fear of deportation. However, it is impossible to seriously address sexual/domestic violence within communities of color without addressing these larger structures of violence, such as militarism, attacks on immigrants' rights and Indian treaty rights, the proliferation of prisons, economic neo-colonialism, and institutional racism and homophobia. Consequently, it is critical that those interested in combating sexual/domestic violence adopt anti-violence strategies that are mindful of the larger structures of violence that govern our world.

As a case in point, increasingly, mainstream anti-violence advocates have demanded longer prison sentences for batterers and sex offenders as a front line approach to stopping violence against women.[5] However, the criminal justice system has always been brutally oppressive toward communities of color. In 1994, for instance, one out of every three African American men between the ages of twenty and twenty-nine was under some form of criminal justice supervision (Mauer, 1999). Two-thirds of men of color in California between the ages of eighteen and thirty have been arrested. Under such conditions, it is problematic for women of color to go to the state for the solution to the problems that the state has had a large part in creating. Consider these examples:

1) An undocumented woman calls the police because of domestic violence. Under current mandatory arrest laws, the police must arrest someone on domestic violence calls. Because the police cannot find the batterer, they arrest her and have her deported. (Tucson)

2) An African American homeless woman calls the police because she has been the victim of group rape. The police arrest her for prostitution. (Chicago)

3) An African American woman calls the police when her husband who is battering her accidentally sets fire to their apartment. She is arrested for setting the fire. (New York)

4) A Native woman calls the police because she is the victim of domestic violence, and she is shot to death by the police. (Albert Bay, Canada)

In fact the *New York Times* recently reported that the effects of the strengthened anti-domestic violence legislation is that battered woken kill their abusive partners less frequently; however, batterers do *not* kill their partners less frequently, and this is more true in Black than white communities (Butterfield, 2000). Thus, ironically, laws passed to protect battered women are actually protecting their batterers!

In addition, as Beth Richie (1996) notes in her study of Black women in prison and as Luana Ross (1998) describes in her study of incarcerated Native American women, women of color are generally in prison as a direct or indirect result of gender violence. For example, they both document how women of color who are involved in abusive relationships are often forced to participate in men's criminal activities. In addition, in one study, more than 40 percent of the women in prison in Arizona were there because they murdered an abusive partner (Jurik and Winn, 1990). Thus, the criminal justice system, rather than solving the problems of violence against women, often revictimizes women of color who are survivors of violence. In her study of Native American women in prison, Luana Ross (1998) discusses how the criminal justice system actually criminalizes the attempts of women of color to resist and survive violence.

Donna Coker (chapter 22) notes that if we hold "poor women of color as the standard," the ineffectiveness of mandatory arrest laws becomes clear. I would add, however, that if we use poor women as the standard, then we also see how the strategy utilizing state violence (that is, relying on the police and the criminal justice system) to curb private violence ultimately fails all women. Reliance on the criminal justice system takes away our sense of collective power to address violence ourselves. This leaves women feeling disempowered and alienated. It also promotes an individualistic approach toward ending violence such that the only way people think they can intervene in stopping violence is to call the police. Community accountability strategies require *collective action.* If we pose the question as "What can *I* do?" then the main answer will be to call the police. But if we pose the question as "What can *we* do?" then we may be surprised at the number of strategies we can devise. Ultimately, violence will end only when our communities believe that domestic violence should no longer be tolerated and we are empowered to make nonviolence a reality.

Increasingly, domestic violence advocates are recognizing the limitations of the criminal justice system, as is reflected in many of the articles in this book and especially in this section (for example, Almeida and Lockard, chapter 18; B. Smith, chapter 19; Coker, chapter 22; Websdale and Johnson, chapter 23). This recognition gave rise to the joint statement by Incite! Women of Color Against Violence and Critical Resistance on "Gender Violence and the Prison Industrial Complex: Interpersonal and State Violence against Women of Color" in chapter 8 of this book.[6] This document critiques the reliance of the anti-violence movement on state violence as the primary strategy for eradicating violence against women in general and women of color in particular. Since this statement was developed, many prominent advocates and activists have signed it, including the National Coalition Against Domestic Violence.

Restorative Justice/Peacemaking

However, in critiquing the current mainstream strategies against domestic violence, the question becomes, what strategies can end violence against women? Unfortunately, many alternatives to incarceration, promoted under the "restorative justice model," have not developed sufficient safety mechanisms for survivors of domestic/sexual violence. The umbrella term "restorative justice" describes a wide range of programs that attempt to address crime from a restorative and reconciliatory rather than a punitive framework. That is, as opposed to the U.S. criminal justice system that focuses solely on punishing the perpetrator and removing him (or her) from society through incarceration, restorative justice attempts to involve all parties (perpetrators, victims, and community members) in determining the appropriate response to a crime in an effort to restore the community to wholeness. These models have been particularly well-developed by many Native communities, especially in Canada, where the sovereign status of Native nations allows them an opportunity to develop community-based justice programs (R. Ross, 1997; Zion and Zion, 1996). In one program, for example, when a crime is reported, the working team that deals with sexual/domestic violence talks to the perpetrator and gives him the option of participating in the program. The perpetrator must first confess his guilt and then follow a healing contract, or go to jail. The perpetrator is free to decline to participate in the program and go through normal routes in the criminal justice system.

In the restorative justice model, everyone (victim, perpetrator, family, friends, community members, and the working team) is involved in developing the healing contract. Everyone is also assigned an advocate through the process. Everyone also holds the perpetrator accountable to his contract. One Tlingit man noted that this approach was often more difficult than going to jail:[7]

> First one must deal with the shock and then the dismay on your neighbors' faces. One must live with the daily humiliation, and at the same time seek forgiveness not just from victims, but from the community as a whole. . . . [A prison sentence] removes the offender from the daily accountability, and may not do anything toward rehabilitation, and for many may actually be an easier disposition than staying in the community. (R. Ross, 1997, p. 18)

These models seem to have much greater potential for dealing with "crime" effectively because, if we want perpetrators of violence to live in society peaceably, it makes sense to develop justice models in which the community is involved in holding him or her accountable. Under the current incarceration model, perpetrators are taken away from their community and are further hindered from developing ethical relationships within a community context. As Rupert Ross (1997), an advocate for restorative justice models notes: "In reality, rather than making the community a safer place, the threat of jail places the community more at risk" (p. 18).

The problem, however, with these models in addressing sexual/domestic violence is that they work only when the community unites in holding perpetrators accountable. However, in cases of sexual and domestic violence, the community often sides with the perpetrator rather than the victim. So, for example, in many Native American communities, these models are often pushed on domestic violence survivors to pressure them to "reconcile" with their families and "restore" the community without sufficient concern for their personal safety (see below).

In addition, the Aboriginal Women's Action Network (AWAN),[8] as well as Native American domestic violence advocates, have critiqued the uncritical use of "traditional" forms of governance for addressing domestic violence. AWAN argues that Native communities have been pressured to adopt "circle sentencing" because it is supposed to be an indigenous "traditional" practice.[9] However, AWAN contends that there is no such traditional practice in their communities. Moreover, they are concerned that the process of diverting cases outside a court system can be dangerous for survivors.[10] In one example, Bishop Hubert O'Connor (a white man) was found guilty of multiple cases of sexual abuse of Aboriginal women, but his punishment under the restorative justice model was to participate in a healing circle with his victims. Because his crimes were against Aboriginal women, he was able to opt for an "Aboriginal approach"—an approach, AWAN argues, that did little to provide real healing and accountability for the survivors. In addition, Goel (2000) cautions that using sentencing circles among Aboriginal Canadians without understanding the whole history on which they are based, can lead to greater problems for battered women. She argues that restorative justice principles can be used, but *not with domestic violence, until* Aboriginal (and Native American) women are returned to their original status of equals with men, a set of social relations that was systematically eroded under colonization.

M., an Ojibwe anti-violence activist, argues that there is a tendency to romanticize and homogenize "traditional" (that is, Native) alternatives to incarceration.[11] First, she notes that these traditional approaches might, in fact, be more harsh than incarceration. Many Native people presume that traditional modes of justice focused on conflict resolution. In fact, M. argues, penalties for societal infractions were not lenient; they entailed banishment, shaming, reparations, and sometimes death. M. notes that making attempts to revise tribal codes by reincorporating traditional practices is not a simple process. It is sometimes difficult to determine what these practices were or how they could be made useful today. For example, some practices, such as banishment, would not have the same impact as today. Prior to colonization, Native communities were so close-knit and interdependent that banishment was often the equivalent of a death sentence. Today, however, Native peoples can simply leave home and join the dominant society.

F., a Navajo anti-domestic violence advocate, further argues that Navajo Peacemaking, which is often heralded as a panacea for addressing "crime" within the community, has not been a positive experience for domestic violence survivors.

> We also asked the elders about what used to happen when a woman was abused. None of them could recall what had happened in the past until finally after an hour or so—a very old elder said that he seemed to remember that the woman's maternal uncle would talk to the abuser, set limits and—if it happened again—see that the abuser left the camp. He also spoke of the practice of the woman setting his saddle and other belongings outside the hogan if she did not wish for him to continue to be a part of the family any longer. Both of these practices have been lost. There WERE within Navajo culture an acknowledgment that women were abused and there WERE traditional methods of responding to violence to protect the women and children. The problem—from my vantage point is that many, many traditional practices and responses have been lost—just as many healing ceremonies have been lost. Our traditional counselor spent several months talking to senior traditional practitioners and . . . came to the conclusion that at one time there had been a ceremony for women who were abused—to help strengthen her and help her find balance. It's lost.
>
> What I see having been substituted are Western-European legal systems that do not acknowledge the value of restorative justice. But MORE importantly traditional responses have also been lost. How can you employ an appropriate cultural response if you don't know what it is? Well, I think what happens in the absence of that knowledge is you start adopting the mindset and practice of the dominant system. The blaming and shaming of Navajo women in the Peacemaking system mirrors the blaming and shaming of women within the W[estern] E[uropean system].[12]

Also of concern is that restorative justice models proposed by its advocates to address domestic violence have a tendency to locate these models almost solely within the criminal justice system, as can be seen by Brenda Smith's description of these models in chapter 19. A similar limitation exists in the important anthology, *Restorative Justice and Family Violence* (Strang and Braithwaite, 2002). Some reasons try to justify this tendency: many domestic violence advocates argue that these models only work if they are backed by the threat of incarceration should the perpetrator not act in good faith; however, the problem with such an approach is that it can actually strengthen the criminal justice system with all its inherent racism rather than challenge it. Prison abolitionist Stanley Cohen argues that alternative models are typically coopted to serve state interests, increase the net of social control, and often lose their community focus as they become professionalized (Cohen 1985, 129). Indeed, the history of prison reform indicates time and time again that minor reform programs actually strengthen the prison system and increase the number of people who fall under its purview (Rotman 1995, 152; Foucault 1977). For instance, women religious reformers in the 1800s advocated reforms for women prisoners kept in the same brutal institutions as men. These reformers imagined women prisoners not as "criminal, fallen women" deserving harsh treatment, but as "sick" or "wayward" women in need of a cure or proper retraining. They fought for the establishment of sex-segregated "reformatories" rather than prisons to provide women the guidance they needed to fulfill their domestic roles. As a result, great numbers of women suddenly found themselves in the criminal justice system receiving domesticity training (Freedman 1981; Zedner 1995). As Luana Ross points, the outgrowth of this ideology is that women often find themselves in prison longer than men until they can prove they have been "cured" (Ross 1998, 118). Simply adding restorative justice to the present criminal justice system is likely to further strengthen the criminal justice apparatus, particularly in communities of color that are deemed in need of "restoration." In addition, as I discuss later in this chapter, a continued emphasis on simply reforming the criminal justice system takes us away from considering grassroots, political organizing strategies that have the potential to address the root causes of violence.

We face a dilemma: on the one hand, the incarceration approach for addressing sexual/domestic violence promotes the repression of communities of color without really providing safety for survivors; on the other hand, restorative justice models often promote community silence and denial around issues of sexual/violence without concern for the safety of survivors of gender violence under the rhetoric of community restoration. Thus, the challenge looms: how do we develop community-based models of accountability in which the community actually holds the perpetrator accountable? Although there are no simple solutions to violence against women of color, it is clear that we will not develop effective strategies unless we stop marginalizing women of color in our analysis and strategies around both racial violence and gender violence.

RECOMMENDATIONS: STRUCTURAL CHANGE, SOCIAL CHANGE

Today, increasingly more community-based organizations are developing strategies to end domestic violence that do not primarily rely on the state. These interventions are not largely based in what are typically known as "domestic violence" programs, and hence they often do not receive sufficient attention for their innovation and creation. In addition, because these models attempt to get at the root causes of violence, they do not offer simple panaceas for addressing this problem. However, this work does suggest some possible directions that the anti-violence movement could take in eradicating violence, including sexual and domestic violence.

A simple question all anti-domestic violence advocates must ask themselves is: Is our primary goal to develop solid domestic violence programs or to end domestic violence? While we may say that our goal is the latter, most work is geared toward the former. Providing services to survivors is important, but services in and of themselves will not stop domestic violence. Thus, it becomes critical that we create more space to ponder the second goal: to end domestic violence in communities of color. If we do, some directions we might take could include a number of strategies.

Develop Interventions that Address State Violence and Interpersonal Violence Simultaneously

War escalates rates of sexual/domestic violence—both sexual assaults committed against the women with whom the United States is at war and increased domestic violence rates in aggressor countries. The connection between military violence and domestic violence was brought home with the recent murders of Teresa Nieves, Andrea Floyd, Jennifer Wright, and Marilyn Griffin, who were killed within days of each other by their military partners who had recently returned from the war in Afghanistan. Before invading Afghanistan, "there had been no deaths attributable to domestic abuse by Fort Bragg personnel in two years" ("Rash of Wife Killings at Fort Bragg Leaves the Base Wondering Why," 2002). In the same article, Jennifer Wright's mother comments, "until he came back from Afghanistan, I didn't worry about violence." In fact, the Miles Foundation reports rates of domestic violence are two to five times higher in military homes.[13] It is simply inconsistent to say it is okay to bomb civilians in Iraq, but it is not okay to beat your wife.

One group that has attempted to organize around the intersections of state and interpersonal violence includes Korean American Women in Need (KAN-WIN), described by Lisa Sun-Hee Park (see chapter 21). At the same time KAN-WIN organizes around domestic violence, it also organizes around the impact of militarism on survivors of violence. The value of this strategy is that it has enabled them to make links with activist organizations in other communities of color. For instance, it was active in supporting a conference on genocide in 1992 that was organized by Women of All Red Nations (an American Indian women's organization in Chicago).

Another important organization is Communities Against Rape and Abuse (CARA) in Seattle. CARA began monitoring incidents of police brutality in Seattle. They found, the majority of time, that those police officers involved with brutality on the job did so in poor neighborhoods of color where they were responding to domestic violence charges. As a result, CARA began organizing around the issue of prison abolition from an anti-violence perspective. At a prison abolition film festival in 2002, which CARA cosponsored with Critical Resistance, CARA outlined its philosophy in the program book:

> Any movement seeking to end violence will fail if its strategy supports and helps sustain the prison industrial complex. Prisons, policing, the death penalty, the war on terror, and the war on drugs, all increase rape, beatings, isolation, oppression, and death. As an anti-rape organization, we cannot support the funneling of resources into the criminal justice system to punish rapists and batterers, as this does not help end violence. It only supports the same system that views incarcerations as a solution to complex social problems like rape and abuse. As survivors of rape and domestic violence, we will not let the

anti-violence movement be further co-opted to support the mass criminalization of young people, the disappearance of immigrants and refugees, and the
dehumanization of poor people, people of color, and people with disabilities.
We support the anti-rape movement that builds sustainable communities on a
foundation of safety, support, self-determination, and accountability.

Also significant about CARA is the manner in which they have followed
Beth Richie's mandate to organize around the women of color who are least
acceptable to the mainstream public. In particular, they began a campaign
against "Children Requiring a Caring Kommunity" (CRACK), which pays
women (and some men) who are substance abusers to be sterilized and
focuses primarily in recruiting women from poor communities of color.[14]
CARA's organizing framework emphasizes how an organization that targets
substance abusers necessarily targets survivors of violence. Furthermore,
CARA is unique in organizing specifically around women with disabilities. In
the CRACK campaign, for instance, they address the manner in which the
success of CRACK is dependent on the notion of "crack babies" as being
"damaged goods" because they may have disabilities.

Emphasize Base-building Approaches that See Domestic Violence Survivors as Organizers or Potential Organizers Rather than Simply Clients

Long-time activist Suzanne Pharr argues that one way in which the domestic
violence movement fails to be a violence reduction movement is its focus on
providing services to "clients" rather than seeing survivors as organizers or as
potential anti-violence organizers.[15] Because they become focused on providing services, those involved in the anti-violence movement tend to be professionals who may or may not be interested in truly challenging the larger
norms and structures of society that give rise to violence. In addition, they
miss the opportunity to significantly increase the number of women involved
in the anti-violence movement on a grassroots level by refusing to see survivors as much more integral to organizing the movement's success rather
than simply serving as clients.

One organization that focuses on base-building (recruiting people who are
not currently activists to become activists) is Sista II Sista in Brooklyn, New
York.[16] This organization of young women of color addresses violence against
girls in the neighborhood committed both by the police and other members
of the community. Sista II Sista created a video project documenting police
harassment after one girl was killed and a second was allegedly sexually assaulted and killed by the police. In addition, it has recently created a community accountability program, called "Sisters Liberated Ground," to organize
its members to monitor violence in the community without relying upon the
police. One way the group increases its base of support is by recruiting young
women to attend freedom schools that provide political education from an integrated mind-body-spirit framework that then trains girls to become activists
on their own behalf.

Develop Community Accountability Strategies that Do Not Depend on a Romanticized Notion of "Community" and Ensure Safety for Survivors

Rhea V. Almeida and Judith Lockard (chapter 18) suggest a therapeutic model based on community accountability strategies which they term the "Cultural Context Model." Some promising aspects of this model are: (a) it looks at violence within the larger cultural context and engages "culture" as multiple and variable, depending on the context of the client's life; (b) it attempts to "de-individualize" the client by engaging members of the community to hold perpetrators accountable; (c) it attempts to prioritize safety for survivors and highlights sexism and gender violence as a primary site of concern (issues that are often minimized in general restorative justice models); (d) it does not seek to rely primarily on the criminal justice system; and (e) it attempts to link social service work with activist organizations. However, as Pharr's analysis suggests, the success of community accountability models is always limited as long as survivors are seen as "clients" rather than as organizers. Furthermore, community accountability models are limited in their success if they do not happen in the community itself.

One such group that has developed a model for accountability within communities is Friends Are Reaching Out (FAR Out) in Seattle, an organization that works with queer or LGBT communities of color. The premise of this model is that when people are abused they become isolated. The domestic violence movement further isolates them through the shelter system, where they cannot tell their friends where they are. In addition, the domestic violence movement does not work with the people who could most likely hold perpetrators accountable—their friends.

This model begins with encouraging people to have conversations with their friends to build connections in an ongoing relationship so that it is less likely for people to become isolated. Many times, when people begin a relationship, according to FAR Out, they put their friendships to the side. If a person ends up in an abusive relationship, she or he is more likely to become isolated, making it difficult to resume friendships. FAR Out's model is based on developing friendship groups to make regular commitments to stay in contact with each other. In addition, these groups develop processes to talk openly about relationships. One way abuse continues is that we tend to keep our sexual relationships private. By talking about them more openly, it is easier for friends to hold us accountable. In addition, if a person knows she or he is going to share her/his relationship dynamics openly, it is more likely that she or he will be accountable in the relationship.

Perpetrators listen to the people they love before they listen to court-mandated orders, contends FAR Out. In addition, given the homophobia in the criminal justice system, involving the criminal justice system is not generally workable in queer communities. What has made this model work is that it is based on preexisting friendship networks. As a result, it develops the capacity of a community to handle domestic violence.

At the same time, as previously mentioned, it is important to critically assess these community resources for their accountability to survivors of violence. Brenda Smith (chapter 19) attempts to reclaim Christian notions of "forgiveness" as a possible tool for healing communities torn apart by violence. There is value to this discussion, particularly for communities of color, that must consider how to both hold perpetrators accountable *and* develop strategies that bring healing and restore wholeness to the community at large. B. Smith also notes that forgiveness does not preclude holding perpetrators accountable. However, it is also important to remember, as I have argued elsewhere, that notions of forgiveness are often used to silence survivors to promote a façade of the loving and forgiving church. Many Christian anti-violence activists, such as Marie Fortune, have also struggled around reclaiming concepts of forgiveness. However, what Fortune notes (and what is absent from B. Smith's analysis) is that forgiveness must happen within the context of repentance (Fortune 1983; Smith 1995). That is, a perpetrator cannot be forgiven unless she or he repents. Repentance implies not simply an apology, but a complete change in one's life and accountability around violence that he or she has perpetrated.

Sometimes it is easy to underestimate the amount of intervention that is required before a perpetrator can really change his behavior. Often a perpetrator subjects herself or himself to community accountability measures, but a perpetrator can eventually tire of them. If community members are not vigilant about holding the perpetrator accountable *for years* and not assume that he is "cured," then the perpetrator can turn a community of accountability into a community of enablement. For instance, L. reports that she was involved in a community accountability strategy in which the community's strategy was to refuse any physical affection to an individual until this person learned proper boundaries. This individual was willing to be held accountable; yet, according to L., it took several years of constant vigilance on the part of the community before this person was ready to resume physical contact with the community.[17]

Expand Our Definition of Community

Given the high-level of mobility in geographically based communities, the challenge is how do we develop accountability structures when people can so easily leave communities or when these communities may not really exist. Thus, part of establishing community accountability processes may involve developing communities themselves.

In addition, it is important to expand our notion of community to include communities based on religious affiliations, employment, hobbies, athletics, and so on and attempt to develop strategies based in those communities. For instance, one man was banished from a community for committing incest; however, he simply moved out of that area. But because he was a well-known academic, the family held him accountable in the academic community by making sure that when he gave academic talks in different communities, his history of incest was exposed.

Traci C. West's (chapter 20) work is very important in this regard as it looks to church communities as possible sites for building strategies of accountability. Particularly noteworthy is T. West's attempt to locate at least some crisis intervention services within community structures (in this case, the church), rather than separately constituted agencies that often force women to leave their communities (or involve the criminal justice system). Her approach also involves communities holding social service agencies accountable to those communities.

Build Transnational Relationships in the Fight to End Violence against Women

Currently, the mainstream domestic violence model in the United States is exported to other countries as the model for addressing violence. This export is based on the notion that the United States is the enlightened country on this issue. However, in many countries where reliance on the state is not an issue or a possibility, other organizations have developed creative strategies for addressing violence that can actually inform the work done in the United States. Masum, a women's organization in Pune, India, addresses violence through accountability strategies that do not rely on the state.[18] The members of Masum actively intervene themselves in cases of domestic violence by using such nonviolent tactics as singing outside a perpetrator's house until he stops his abuse. They report they have been able to work on this issue without community backlash because Masum simultaneously provides needed community services such as micro credit, health care, education, and so on. After many years, this group has come to be seen as a needed community institution and, thus, has the power to intervene in cases of gender violence where their interventions might otherwise be resisted.

A model from Brazil is a strong "Movement of Landless People" (known as Movimento dos Trabalhadores Rurail Sem Terra or MST).[19] This movement is based in networks of families who claim territory that is privately owned but not being used. The families set up tents and fences and defend the land, which is called an "occupation." If they manage to gain control of the land, then they form a settlement in which they build houses and more permanent structures.[20] Over the past twenty years, 300,000 families have been involved in these occupations. Families rather than individuals take part in this resistance. About twenty families form a nucleus, which is coordinated by one man and one woman. The nuclei are then organized into the following sectors: (1) production/cooperation/ employment, (2) education/trading, (3) education, (4) gender, (5) communication, (6) human rights, (7) health, and (8) culture. Both men and women participate in the gender sector. This sector is responsible for ensuring women are involved in all decision-making positions and are equally represented in public life. Security teams are mixed gender. The gender team trains security to deal with domestic violence. Obviously, because the MST is not a legal organization and, thus, cannot utilize the state to address domestic violence, it must develop accountability structures from within.

All issues are discussed communally. As time progresses, participants report that domestic violence decreases because interpersonal relationships are communal and transparent. Also, because women engage in "physical" roles, such as being involved in security, women become less likely to be seen as "easy targets" for violence; and the women also think of themselves differently.

In addition, sectors and leadership roles rotate so that there is less of a fixed, hierarchical leadership. Hierarchical leadership tends to promote power differentials and hence abuse. This leadership model, thus, helps prevent the conditions of abuse from happening in the first place.

In a sense, the Kentucky Job Readiness Program (JRP), articulated by Neil Websdale and Byron Johnson (chapter 23), reflects analyses similar to the Masum (South Asian Indian) and MST (Brazilian) models: "multifaceted preventive programs" are required to address violence. The fact that funding for domestic violence programs in the United States has been primarily linked to the criminal justice system has limited our imagination with regard to strategies to combat domestic violence. Beth Richic asks the question: What if funding had been located in agencies other than criminal justice?[21] Perhaps we would be organizing around providing affordable housing for women so they can leave. Or perhaps we would be focused on ending poverty so that women would not be trapped in abusive relationships because of economics. By decentering a criminal justice approach we can enlarge the strategies we employ. One crucial difference between Masum of India, MST in Brazil, and JRP in the United States, however, is that in Masum and MST, the women in the communities are the organizers and advocates rather than the "clients." Again, thinking beyond social services—that is, thinking about real social change—could potentially increase the effectiveness of programs such as the Job Readiness Program in Kentucky.

Of course it is important not to make the mistake of simply appropriating models from other countries without assessing how the current conditions in the United States may impact what will and will not work. However, one principle that seems to come through clearly from these models is that it is a mistake to look at developing community accountability only from the point of crisis intervention. And that is why the criminal justice approach ultimately cannot stop domestic violence—because it only works at the point of crisis rather than preventing the abuse from happening. Strategies to prevent and respond to domestic violence will be more effective if they address the underlying structural and cultural conditions in the community that make abuse possible in the first place. In short, social change is demanded to end violence against all women. And if we focus our attention on preventing violence against women of color, then all women will benefit.

NOTES

1. Unless otherwise specified, material in this chapter comes from my direct experience working in the anti-violence movement for the past twenty years and from conversations with activists in the anti-violence movement.

2. Beth Richie, Plenary address, Color of Violence: Violence Against Women of Color conference, Santa Cruz, California, April 2000.

3. Ford meeting on domestic violence, Clinton, Tennessee, March 2003.

4. Ibid.

5. For a history and critique of this position, see Schneider (2000).

6. Incite! Women of Color Against Violence, www.incite-national.org, is a transnational organization of feminists of color that organize around the intersections of interpersonal and state violence. Critical Resistance: Beyond the Prison Industrial Complex organizes against the prison industrial complex. They came together in order to develop a document that could help bring together the anti-prison and the anti-violence movement in closer collaboration.

7. Tlingits are Native peoples whose tribes are located in Alaska and Canada.

8. Aboriginal and First Nation are the terms used in Canada; they are similar to the term Native American in the United States.

9. Sentencing circles involve victims, offenders, esteemed community members, and support people form both sides to determine the sentence for a crime.

10. Some people argue that now that we have laws against domestic violence, marginalized groups of women should be able to use them or not—as they see fit. That is, they should not be penalized from using the criminal justice system as a resource for trying to stop violence in their lives (e.g., see Stark, 1993).

11. Sources in this and the following example are from personal interviews or correspondence.

12. Email correspondence on CAVNET, a listserv that addresses sexual/domestic violence in Native communities.

13. Available at: members.aol.com_ht_a/milesfdn/myhomepage/.

14. The racism of the CRACK organization and its violence against women of color and their communities is discussed at www.cara-seattle.org and www.cwpe.org. For a realistic discussion of the impact of crack and other drugs on pregnant women, see "Cocaine and Pregnancy" (1997) and Rosenbaum (1997).

15. Keynote address, New Jersey Coalition against Domestic Violence annual conference, November 2002.

16. Available at www.sistaiisista.org.

17. Incite! Women of Color Against Violence and Sista II Sista Community Accountability Strategies Meeting, Brooklyn, N.Y., February 8, 2003.

18. Masum's email is masum@vsnl.com.

19. MST is available at http://www.mst.brazil.org.

20. In actuality, they do not "own" the land per se, but they can win the right to produce on the land and occupy it.

21. Over-Reliance on the Criminal Justice System meeting, Philadelphia, January 2002.

REFERENCES

(AWAN) Aboriginal Women's Action Network. Available at: www.awan.ca. Email: nacec1@look.ca. Phone: 604-255-3998. Address: 309–877 East Hastings St., Vancouver, B.C. V6A 3Y1 Canada.

Associated Press. 2002. Rash of wife killings at Fort Bragg leaves the base wondering why. *New York Times,* July 27, A7.

Butterfield, Fox. 2000. Study shows a racial divide in domestic violence cases. *New York Times,* May 18, A16.

(CARA) Communities Against Rape and Abuse. Available at: www.cara-seattle.org.

Cocaine and Pregnancy. 1997. New York: The Lindesmith Center/Open Society Institute.

Cohen, Stanley. 1985. Community control: To demystify or to reaffirm. In Herman Bianchi and Rene van Swaaningin, eds., *Abolitionism: Toward a Non-Repressive Approach Towards Crime.* Amsterdam: Free University Press, 127–132.

Donziger, Steven, ed. 1996. *The Real War on Crime: The Report of the National Criminal Justice Commission.* New York: HarperPerennial.

FAR Out. Friends Are Reaching Out. Available at: www.nwnetwork.org. Address: P.O. Box 20398, Seattle WA 98102. Phone: 206-568-7777. Email: info@nwnetwork.org.

Fortune, Marie. 1983. *Sexual Violence: The Unmentionable Sin.* New York: Pilgrim.

Foucault, Michel. 1977. *Discipline and Punish.* New York: Vintage.

Freedman, Estelle. 1981. *Their Sisters' Keepers.* Ann Arbor: University of Michigan Press.

Goel, Rashmi. 2000. No women at the center: The use of the Canadian sentencing circle in domestic violence cases. *Wisconsin Women's Law Journal* 15: 293–334.

Incite! Women of Color Against Violence. N.d. *Violence Against Women of Color.* Available at: http://www.incite-national.org/issues/violence.html. Retrieved 8/27/02.

Jurik, Nancy, and Russ Winn. 1990. Gender and homicide: A comparison of men and women who kill. *Violence and Victims* 5(4): 227–242.

Koyama, Emi. 2002. Available at: www.eminism.org.

Masum. Address: 11, Archana Apartments; Kanchangunga Arcade 163, Solapur Road, Hadapsar, PUNE 411040, Maharashtra, India. Phone: +91 20 687 5058. Email: masum@vsnl.com.

Mauer, Marc. 1999. *Race to Incarcerate.* New York: New Press/W. W. Norton.

Meyers, Nancy J. 2001. Now you see it, now you don't: The state of the battered women's movement. *Off Our Backs* 31 (November): 10.

Miles Foundation, P.O. Box 423, Newtown, Conn. 06470-0423. Email: Milesfdn@aol.com. Phone: 203-270-7861. Available at: members.aol.com/_ht_a/milesfdn/myhomepage/.

MST. Available at: http://www.mst.brazil.org.

Richie, Beth E. 1996. *Compelled to Crime: The Gender Entrapment of Battered Black Women.* New York: Routledge.

Rosenbaum, Marsha. 1997. Women: Research and policy. In Joyce H. Lowinson, Pedro Ruiz, Robert B. Millman, and John G. Langrod, eds., *Substance Abuse.* 3d ed. Baltimore: Williams and Wilkins, 654–665.

Ross, Luana. 1998. *Inventing the Savage: The Social Construction of Native American Criminality.* Austin: University of Texas Press.

Ross, Rupert. 1997. *Return to the Teachings.* London: Penguin.

Rotman, Edgardo. 1995. The failure of reform. In Norval Morris and David Rothman, eds., *The Oxford History of the Prison.* New York: Oxford University Press, 149–177.

Schechter, Susan. 1982. *Women and Male Violence: The Visions and Struggles of the Battered Women's Movement.* Boston: South End.

Schneider, Elizabeth. 2000. *Battered Women and Feminist Lawmaking.* New Haven: Yale University Press.

Sista II Sista. Available at: www.sistaiisista.org. Email: info@sistaiisista.org. Phone: 718-366-2450. Address: 89 St. Nicholas Ave, Brooklyn, N.Y. 11237.

Smith, Andrea. 1995. Born again, free from sin? Sexual violence in evangelical communities. In Carol Adams and Marie Fortune, eds., *Violence Against Women and Children: A Christian Theological Sourcebook,* 339–350.

———. 1999. Sexual Violence and American Indian Genocide. In Nantawan Lewis and Marie Fortune, eds., *Remembering Conquest: Feminist/Womanist Perspectives on Religion, Colonization, and Sexual Violence.* Binghamton: Haworth, 31–52.

Stark, Evan. 1993. Mandatory arrest of batterers: A reply to the critics. *American Behavioral Scientist* 36: 651–680.

Strang, Heather, and John Braithwaite, eds. 2002. *Restorative Justice and Family Violence*. Cambridge: Cambridge University Press.

Zedner, Lucia. 1995. Wayward sisters: The prison for women. In Norval Morris and David Rothman, eds., *The Oxford History of the Prison*. New York: Oxford University Press, 295–324.

Zion, James, and Elsie B. Zion. 1996. Hazho' Sokee'—Stay together nicely: Domestic violence under Navajo common law. In Marianne O. Nielsen and Robert A. Silverman, eds., *Native Americans, Crime, and Justice*. Boulder: Westview, 96–113.

Biographical Notes

About the Editors

Natalie J. Sokoloff, professor of sociology at John Jay College of Criminal Justice where she has taught for more than thirty years, is a member of the doctoral faculties in sociology, criminology, and women's studies at The Graduate School, City University of New York. For a decade, beginning in 1994, she also was a scholar of the Institute for Teaching and Research on Women at Towson University, part of the University of Maryland system. Formerly associated with the New York State Division for Youth in its research and evaluation program and the Mount Sinai School of Medicine in its Department of Community Medicine (New York City), she holds a B.A. from the University of Michigan (*magna cum laude*), an M.A. from Brown University (as a National Institute of Mental Health scholar), and a Ph.D. from The Graduate School, City University of New York. Professor Sokoloff is the author of *Between Money and Love: The Dialectics of Women's Home and Market Work* (Praeger, 1980), *The Hidden Aspects of Women's Work* (coeditor, Praeger, 1987), *Black Women and White Women in the Professions: Occupational Segregation by Race and Gender, 1960–1980* (Routledge, 1992). In 2003, the third edition of *The Criminal Justice System and Women: Offenders, Prisoners, Victims, and Workers* was published (coeditor, McGraw-Hill). A highly acclaimed work, the third edition is a completely new contribution (1982, Clark Boardman Ltd; 1995, McGraw-Hill). Professor Sokoloff's *Bibliography on Multicultural Domestic Violence* has been used widely by individuals, groups, and institutions and is available on the web at: www.lib.jjay. cuny.edu/research/DomesticViolence/. Professor Sokoloff has published widely in the areas of feminist theory, women and work, women and imprisonment, and domestic violence in marginalized communities.

Christina Pratt, assistant professor of social work and gender studies and director of field education at Dominican College of Blauvelt (Orangeburg, N.Y.), received her masters in social work from Columbia University. She is a doctoral candidate at The Graduate Center, City University of New York, Program in Criminal Justice. She engages in research and grant writing for prisoner reintegration, community justice experiments, and problem-solving Family Treatment Courts. She is a Fulbright Scholar (India; Pakistan), a Malone Faculty Scholar (Israel, Palestinian Authority, Jordan, Syria, and Tunisia), and served as an accredited delegate to the United Nations Fourth World Conference on the Status of Women, Beijing, China, and NGO Forum, Huairou.

About the Contributors

Margaret Abraham, professor and chair of sociology and anthropology at Hofstra University, received her doctorate in sociology from Syracuse University. Her areas of specialization are ethnicity, migration, gender, domestic violence, and the South Asian diaspora. Her book, *Speaking the Unspeakable: Marital Violence among South Asian Immigrants in the United States* (Rutgers University Press) won the 2002 Outstanding Book Award from the American Sociological Association's Section on Asia and Asian America. She works closely with *Sakhi for South Asian Women* in addressing domestic violence in the South Asian immigrant community and was honored by them for her work in 1999. Professor Abraham is a member of the advisory board for the National Evaluation of the Arrest Policies Program under the Violence Against Women Act Project of the National Institute for Law and Justice.

Sharon Angella Allard received her J.D. from the University of California, Los Angeles School of Law. She practices law in Los Angeles.

Rhea V. Almeida received her doctorate in social work from Makerere University in Kampala, Uganda, and her postgraduate training at Columbia University. She is the director of the Institute for Family Services in Somerset, New Jersey, which she founded in 1980. Dr. Almeida has written on domestic violence, Asian Indian families, mentoring, supervision, and unexamined assumptions in service delivery systems. She has published two books: *Expansions of Feminist Family Theory through Diversity* and *Transformations of Gender and Race* (both Haworth/ Harrington Park). She is currently working on *The Cultural Context Model*, a book that describes a shifting paradigm in family therapy.

Corrine Bertram, a doctoral candidate in social-personality psychology at The Graduate Center, City University of New York, is currently at work on her dissertation, which provides an analysis of conflict and community building within a feminist organization. Her interests include feminist and critical psychologies.

Michele Bograd received her doctorate in human development at the University of Chicago and is a psychologist in private practice in Massachusetts. She was one of the first voices in the field of family therapy to draw critical attention to the issues of gender, power, and domestic violence. Coeditor with Kersti Yllo of the important early volume *Feminist Perspectives on Wife*

Abuse (Sage), she is nationally recognized as a feminist psychologist, speaker, author, and teacher.

Ricardo Carrillo received his doctorate from the California School of Professional Psychology in Fresno, California. He is director of Latino Mental Health for Kaweah Delta Health Care District (Vasalia, California) and director of training and technical assistance for the National Latino Alliance on Domestic Violence (Alianza) and the National Compadres Network, and he also maintains a private practice. He is recognized as an expert witness and international consultant in the areas of family therapy, domestic violence, cross-cultural psychology, forensic psychology, and cultural competence. He has provided leadership in the areas of program development with domestic violence offenders, Latino mental health, and chemical dependency populations. With Jerry Tello, he coedited *Family Violence and Men of Color* (Springer).

Donna Coker, professor at the University of Miami School of Law, received her J.D. from Stanford Law School and her M.S.W. from the University of Arkansas at Little Rock. Professor Coker, working as a social worker, community activist, attorney, and legal scholar, has been involved in the battered women's movement since 1978. The current focus of her work is the development of domestic violence policy and law that responds to the needs of women who are marginalized on the basis of race, poverty, and immigration status. Her most recent publications include: "Transformative Justice: Anti-Subordination Processes in Cases of Domestic Violence" in Braithwaite and Strang's *Restorative Justice and Family Violence: New Ideas and Learning from the Past* (Cambridge University); "Crime Control and Feminist Law Reform in Domestic Violence Law: A Critical Review," *Buffalo Criminal Law Review* (2001); and "Enhancing Autonomy for Battered Women: Lessons from Navajo Peacemaking," *U.C.L.A. Law Review* (1999).

Critical Resistance (CR), founded in 1998, seeks to build an international movement to end the Prison Industrial Complex (PIC) by challenging the belief that caging and controlling people makes a community safe. CR believes that basic necessities such as food, shelter, and freedom are what really make communities secure. As such, the organization's work is part of global struggles against inequality and powerlessness. The success of the movement requires that it reflect communities most affected by the PIC. CR's website is available at: www.criticalresistance.org; and CR can be reached at: crnational@criticalresistance.org.

Shamita Das Dasgupta is a cofounder of *Manavi, Inc.*, an organization in the United States that focuses on violence against women in the South Asian community. She is a clinical adjunct assistant professor of law with the New York University Law School. She has published several articles in the areas of her specialization: ethnicity, gender, immigration, and violence against women. Dasgupta is the author of two books, *The Demon Slayers and Other Stories: Bengali Folktales* (1995, Interlink Books) and *A Patchwork Shawl:*

Chronicles of South Asian Women in America (1998, Rutgers University Press). Currently, she is working on two books; one on women's rituals in Bengal, and the other on domestic violence in the South Asian American context.

Ida Dupont, assistant professor of criminal justice at Pace University (New York City), completed her doctorate in the Criminal Justice Program at The Graduate Center, City University of New York in 2004. She has worked for ten years in the domestic violence field in a variety of capacities: as a counselor of battered women; facilitator of court-ordered programs for batterers; public educator on teen dating violence; advocate on behalf of battered women who are in prison for fighting back against their abusers; and now as a researcher. For the past three years, she has been doing research based on extensive interviews with battered women from low-income neighborhoods in New York City.

Michelle Fine, distinguished professor of social psychology at the Graduate Center, City University of New York (CUNY), has taught at CUNY since 1990. Her work focuses on questions of social injustice in schools, prisons, and communities by drawing from feminist psychology, critical race, and Marxist thought; spaces of possibility in which youth struggle for what could be and against what is; the relation of scholarship and activism, and questions of theory, ethics, and method in participatory research. Some of her recent publications with Lois Weis include: *Silenced Voices and Extraordinary Conversations: Re-Imagining Schools* (Teachers College); *Speed Bumps: A Student Friendly Guide to Qualitative Research* (Teachers College), *Construction Sites: Excavating Race, Class, and Gender among Urban Youth* (Teachers College), *The Unknown City: The Lives of Poor and Working Class Young Adults* (Beacon), and *Off White* (also with Linda Powell and Mun Wong; Routledge). Most recently, she has published with M. Torre, K. Boudin, and others, "Participatory Action Research: Behind Bars and Under Surveillance," in P. Camic and J. Rhodes, eds., *Qualitative Methods* (American Psychological Association) and has coedited (with C. Daiute) a special edition on youth perspectives on violence and injustice in the *Journal of Social Issues.*

Sherry L. Hamby is research associate professor in the psychology department at the University of North Carolina at Chapel Hill. She has written more than thirty articles on family violence and conducted one of the first studies of domestic violence in a reservation community. She currently serves as vice president of the board of directors of her local domestic violence and rape crisis center. She is the 1998 recipient of the Alfred M. Wellner Memorial Award from the National Register for Health Service Providers in Psychology for a project on issues relating to translating domestic violence research and interventions to groups other than middle-class whites. In addition to her work in reservation communities, other interests include the perceptions of victims, the relationship of domestic violence with other forms of intimate victimization, and the use of qualitative techniques to address some of the persistent conceptual difficulties and controversies in domestic violence.

Robert L. Hampton, president of York College, City University of New York, received his doctorate in sociology from the University of Michigan. He has taught and published extensively in the field of family violence. His research interests include partner violence, family abuse, community violence, stress and social support, institutional responses to violence, and social change. He is currently exploring the use of popular culture in the war against violence and is addressing racial, ethnic, and religious understanding of that violence in the United States. He is one of the founders of the National Institute on Domestic Violence in the African American Community. Dr. Hampton is the author of several classic pieces on Black domestic violence including *Violence in the Black Family: Correlates and Consequences* (Lexington) and (with R. J. Gelles and J. W. Harrop) "Is Violence in Black Families Increasing? A Comparison of 1975 and 1985 National Survey Rates," in *Journal of Marriage and the Family* (1989).

Beverly Horsburgh, professor at St. Thomas University School of Law (Florida), graduated from Smith College and the University of Miami School of Law. She is a member of the Law and Society Association and the Section on Domestic Violence of the American Bar Association (ABA). Locally, she is a well-known speaker on the topic of Jewish domestic violence. Her article included in this anthology has been cited in the ABA Report on Domestic Violence, the Florida Governor's Task Force on Domestic Violence, and in various law school textbooks.

Incite! Women of Color Against Violence, founded in 2000, is a national activist organization of radical feminists of color advancing a movement to end violence against women of color and their communities through direct action, critical dialogue, and grassroots organizing. Incite!'s community accountability/criminal justice taskforce specifically works at developing community accountability models for addressing violence against women that do not depend on the criminal justice system. The web site for Incite! can be found at www.incite-national.org; it can also be reached by email at incite_national @yahoo.com.

Byron Johnson is director of the Center for Research on Religion and Urban Civil Society and distinguished senior fellow in the Robert A. Fox Leadership Program, both at the University of Pennsylvania. He is also a senior scholar in the Center for Civic Innovation at the Manhattan Institute. Before coming to the University of Pennsylvania, Professor Johnson directed the Center for Crime and Justice Policy at Vanderbilt University. His research focuses on studying the role of religion and faith-based organizations in addressing urban social problems. He also conducts research on domestic violence and the potential role of fatality review as an effective coordinated community response to lethal violence.

Jyl Josephson is associate professor in the department of politics and government at Illinois State University. She is the author of *Gender, Families, and State: Child Support Policy in the United States* (Rowman & Littlefield); coeditor (with Sue Tolleson-Rinehart) of *Gender and American Politics* (M. E. Sharpe); and coeditor (with Cynthia Burack) of *Fundamental Differences: Feminists Talk Back to Social Conservatives* (Rowman & Littlefield). Two major current projects include a book that examines privacy and intimate life from the perspective of groups whose privacy claims most frequently have been disparaged and foreclosed and an ongoing research project on the development of a faith-based community organization in western Texas.

Valli Kalei Kanuha, associate professor at the University of Hawai'i at Manoa, School of Social Work, received her doctorate in social welfare from the University of Washington. Her professional interests are in the areas of violence against women; multicultural practice focused on the intersection of race, gender, and sexuality; and feminist theory. During the past thirty years she has worked as a clinician, social service administrator, organization consultant, and activist in Hawai'i and the continental United States. Her current research includes development, implementation and evaluation of a domestic violence intervention using Native Hawaiian values, traditions, and practices with Hawaiian batterers and battered women as well as an examination of community-based accountability strategies for violence against women with a particular focus on the use of indigenous methods with Native Hawaiians in contemporary contexts.

Joan Kim [Jeung] received her M.D. from the University of California, San Francisco. She practices medicine in the San Francisco area.

Kathryn Laughon is assistant professor of nursing at the University of Virginia, School of Nursing. She received her doctorate in nursing at Johns Hopkins University School of Nursing where her research topic concerned the role of substance use and mental health in explaining the increased risk of sexually transmitted diseases in battered women. Until 2004 she was director of a nursing clinic at the House of Ruth, a shelter for battered women in Baltimore. She holds a master's degree in community health nursing and a bachelor of science in nursing from the University of Virginia. Prior to beginning her doctoral studies, she was the Domestic Violence Services Coordinator for the University of Virginia Health System and a member of their Sexual Assault Nurse Examiner team. Laughon is coauthor of several research articles and book chapters on intimate partner violence.

Judith Lockard, a senior clinician and supervisor at the Institute for Family Services (in Somerset, New Jersey), a teaching and treatment facility dealing with all forms of trauma in families, is a licensed clinical social worker, a certified alcoholism counselor, a post-graduate-trained family therapist, and a domestic violence specialist. She is a member of the American Family Therapy Academy. She has maintained a private practice in Rocky Hill, New Jersey, working with families with addiction histories for more than twenty years and has trained extensively on this topic. Her most recent writing has focused on the intersection of domestic violence and the recovery process delineating some of the hazards for women's safety inherent in 12 step programs. She is currently working on a novel about family process.

Julia Marusza teaches the social foundations of education at D'Youville College in Buffalo, New York. Her research focuses on education and globalization and health education.

Amira Proweller, associate professor of social and cultural foundations in education, holds a doctorate in education from the State University of New York, Buffalo. She is the author of *Constructing Female Identities: Meaning Making in an Upper-Middle Class Youth Culture* (State University of New York Press). Her research interests are in the cultural policies of schooling, gender identity formation, youth culture, feminist theory, qualitative research methodologies, and the socialization of urban teachers. She is currently involved in a research project exploring the development of urban teacher identities in the context of an alternative certification program for the preparation of middle grades math and science educators.

Beth E. Richie, chair of African American Studies and professor in the departments of criminal justice and women's studies at University of Illinois at Chicago, holds a master's of social work from Washington University in St. Louis and a doctorate in sociology from The Graduate Center, City University of New York. Her research interests center on battered African American women and the relationship between violence against women and women's participation in crime. Professor Richie is senior research consultant with the Institute on Research and Response to Violence in the Lives of African American Women. She also serves as a consultant to various organizations, including The Social Science Research Council and the National Institute of Corrections. She is the author of the important work on *Compelled to Crime: The Gender Entrapment of Battered Black Women* (Routledge).

Rosemarie A. Roberts is a doctoral candidate in social personality psychology at The Graduate Center, City University of New York. She is a recipient of numerous awards including both National Science Foundation and American Psychological Association Minority fellowships. She teaches psychology, critical race theory, qualitative research methods, and Afro-Caribbean dance. Her dissertation focuses on the practice of critical consciousness through African-derived Black dance. Two of her publications include contributed chapters in *Speedbumps: A Student Friendly Guide to Qualitative Research* (Weis and Fine, eds., Teachers College) and *The Unknown City: Poor and Working Class Young Adults in Urban America* (Fine and Weis, eds., Beacon).

Andrea Smith, a member of the Cherokee nation, is a cofounder of Incite! Women of Color Against Violence. She is the former Women of Color caucus chair of the National Coalition Against Sexual Assault and cofounder of the Chicago chapter of Women of All Red Nations. She teaches in Native studies and women's studies at the University of Michigan and also works at Amnesty International for the research project on Sexual Assault and Native American Women.

Brenda V. Smith, associate professor at the Washington College of Law at American University, is an expert on issues affecting women in prison and has published widely in this area including: *An End to Silence: Prisoners' Handbook on Identifying and Addressing Sexual Misconduct* (2d ed., Washington College of Law); *A Vision Beyond Survival: A Resource Guide for Incarcerated Women* (National Women's Law Center); "Watching You, Watching Me," *Yale Journal of Law and Feminism* (2004); "Sexual Abuse Against Women in Prison," *American Bar Association Criminal Justice Magazine* (2001). Professor Smith's scholarly work has been informed by her experiences providing direct legal services to economically and socially marginalized women, including women in conflict with the law.

Julia Sudbury is Canada Research Chair in Social Justice, Equity, and Diversity and coordinator of the University of Toronto's Social Justice Cluster, a multidisciplinary collaboration that promotes research and pedagogy on social justice issues and provides opportunities to showcase models of activist scholarship. Dr. Sudbury's research and teaching interests include community organizing by women of color and Aboriginal women; theorizing intersections of race, class, gender, sexuality, and nation; globalization and transnationalism; women's criminalization and imprisonment; feminist and post-positivist research methodologies. Her current program of research examines the innovative strategies deployed by women of color and Aboriginal women to oppose the detrimental effects of globalization, economic restructuring, and criminalization.

Lisa Sun-Hee Park, assistant professor of ethnic studies and urban studies and planning at the University of California, San Diego, received her doctorate in sociology from Northwestern University. Her research areas include immigrant women's work, health, and family. She is coauthor (with David N. Pellow) of *The Silicon Valley of Dreams: Environmental Injustice, Immigrant Workers, and the High-tech Global Economy* (New York University Press).

Leti Volpp, associate professor at American University Law School, has published articles on gender, migration, culture, citizenship and identity in journals, including the *Columbia Law Review*, the *UCLA Law Review*, the *Harvard Civil Rights—Civil Liberties Law Review*, the *Harvard Women's Law Journal*, the *Yale Journal of Law and the Humanities,* and *Citizenship Studies*. Before entering academia she worked as a public interest lawyer, funded in part by the Skadden Foundation Fellowship. She is the recipient of a MacArthur Foundation individual research and writing grant and two Rockefeller Foundation Humanities fellowships. She is a former board member of the New York Asian Women's Center and was both a board member and staff member of the Asian Women's Shelter of San Francisco.

Neil Websdale is professor of criminal justice at Northern Arizona University and director of the National Domestic Violence Fatality Review Initiative. He has published four books, including *Rural Woman Battering and the Justice System: An Ethnography* (Sage), which won the Academy of Criminal Justice Sciences Outstanding Book Award in 1999; *Understanding Domestic Homicide* (Northeastern University Press); *Making Trouble: Cultural Constructions of Crime, Deviance, and Control* (Aldine, coedited with Jeff Ferrell); and *Policing the Poor: From Slave Plantation to Public Housing* (Northeastern University Press), winner in 2002 of both the Academy of Criminal Justice Sciences Outstanding Book Award and the Gustavus-Myers Center for the Study of Bigotry and Human Rights Award.

Lois Weis is professor of sociology of education at the University at Buffalo, State University of New York. She is the author and/or editor of numerous books and articles on the subject of social class, race, gender, and schooling. Her most recent publications (all with Michelle Fine and published by Teachers College) include *Silenced Voices and Extraordinary Conversations: Re-Imagining Schools, Speed Bumps: A Student Friendly Guide to Qualitative Research*, and *Construction Sites: Excavating Race, Class, and Gender among Urban Youth*. Also with Fine, she has published *The Unknown City: The Lives of Poor and Working Class Young Adults* (Beacon) and *Off White* (with Linda Powell and Mun Wong, Routledge); and with Maxine Seller, *Beyond Black and White: New Faces and Voices in U.S. Schools* (State University of New York Press). She sits on numerous editorial boards and is a former editor of *Educational Policy*.

Carolyn M. West, associate professor of psychology in the interdisciplinary arts and sciences program at the University of Washington, Tacoma, received her doctorate in clinical psychology from the University of Missouri, St. Louis, and completed a postdoctoral research scholarship at the University of New Hampshire's Family Research Laboratory. She is editor/contributor of *Violence in the Lives of Black Women: Battered, Black, and Blue* (Haworth). In 2000, she received the Outstanding Research Award from the University of Minnesota's Institute on Domestic Violence in the African American Community.

Traci C. West, associate professor of ethics and African American studies at Drew University Theological School, received her doctorate from Union Theological Seminary (New York City). Her teaching includes courses on violence against women for seminary and graduate students. She is the author of *Wounds of the Spirit: Black Women, Violence, and Resistance Ethics* (New York University Press) as well as articles on sexism in the church, welfare policy, and racial justice. She is an ordained minister in the New York Conference of the United Methodist Church and has previously served in parish and campus ministry.